John Henry Walsh, Robert McClure, Ellwood Harvey

The Horse, in the Stable and the Field

His Management in Health and Disease

John Henry Walsh, Robert McClure, Ellwood Harvey

The Horse, in the Stable and the Field
His Management in Health and Disease

ISBN/EAN: 9783743329935

Manufactured in Europe, USA, Canada, Australia, Japa

Cover: Foto ©ninafisch / pixelio.de

Manufactured and distributed by brebook publishing software (www.brebook.com)

John Henry Walsh, Robert McClure, Ellwood Harvey

The Horse, in the Stable and the Field

THE HORSE

IN THE STABLE AND THE FIELD;

HIS MANAGEMENT IN HEALTH AND DISEASE.

By J. H. WALSH, F.R.C.S.
("*Stonehenge.*")
AUTHOR OF "BRITISH RURAL SPORTS," ETC., ETC.

From the Last London Edition.

WITH COPIOUS NOTES AND ADDITIONS,

By ROBERT McCLURE, M.D., V.S.,
Author of "Diseases in the American Stable, Field, and Farmyard."

AND AN ESSAY ON THE AMERICAN TROTTING HORSE, AND SUGGESTIONS ON THE BREEDING AND TRAINING OF TROTTERS.

By ELLWOOD HARVEY, M.D.

ILLUSTRATED WITH OVER EIGHTY ENGRAVINGS.

PHILADELPHIA:
PORTER & COATES,
No. 822 Chestnut Street.

Entered according to Act of Congress, in the year 1869, by

PORTER & COATES,

in the Clerk's Office of the District Court of the United States, in and for the Eastern District of Pennsylvania.

MEARS & DUSENBERY, STEREOTYPERS.   SHERMAN & CO., PRINTERS.

PREFACE.

We believe it may be asserted, without fear of contradiction, that no book has yet been published, in the English or any other language, which even professes to give a complete description of the Natural History, Physiology, Pathology, and General Management of the Horse, in a form and style suited to the country gentleman of the nineteenth century. It is true, that some of these departments are adequately described in separate works; but they are generally written in technical language, suited rather to the Veterinary Student than for the use and comprehension of the ordinary reader. The writings of Percivall in England, and of Girard, Chauveau, and Colin in France, contain full and accurate details of the Anatomy and Physiology of this animal; while the Structure and Diseases of his Foot have been the subjects of various elaborate treatises by Bracy Clark, Spooner, Coleman, and Turner, in this country. But in order to reach the information which he requires, the reader has to wade through many long and wearisome chapters, wholly irrelevant to the practical subjects in which he is interested, and he therefore gives up the study in disgust as a hopeless task. So, also, in reference to the general diseases of the horse, Percivall's "Hippopathology" is a mine of information; but it is so elaborate, and so diffuse in style, that it is consequently never or rarely seen on the library shelves of the private gentleman. Stable management was well described by Stewart, of Edinburgh, five-and-twenty years ago, and his work still continues to be the best manual on this particular subject; but since it was written many great changes have been introduced into general use, and it is therefore now somewhat behind the times. For these reasons the author of this work has thought that a book, combining all the above subjects, treated in a practical manner, and in a style popularly intelligible, yet containing the most recent views of eminent authorities in veterinary knowledge, would supply a deficiency which has long been complained of by all who are interested in the proper management of the horse.

PREFACE.

In order to compress within the limits of one volume the information which has hitherto been spread over so many, it has been necessary to forego all attempts at illustration by anecdote or by records of cases; and the several chapters, therefore, will be found to contain only what is absolutely necessary for the elucidation of each subject, with the aid of numerous engravings, accurately drawn and carefully engraved after drawings by Barraud, H. Weir, Zwecker, Scott, &c., &c.

THE AUTHOR.

In bringing before the American public, this edition of a work which has long been acknowledged as the ablest authority on the subject in England, the publishers have spared neither time nor expense in adapting it in every particular to the requirements of the American Farmer and Amateur. There is not a page in the English edition but has been carefully revised, some local and purely scientific matter of no interest whatever to the American owner of a horse has been omitted, late authorities consulted, and every page brought down to the present state of knowledge on the subject. This was intrusted to the skilful hands of Dr. McClure, the well-known author of "The Diseases of the American Stable, Field, and Farmyard."

The Essay on the American Trotting Horse, by Dr. Ellwood Harvey, of Chester, Pa., a gentleman thoroughly conversant with his theme, was written at the urgent request of the publishers, and embodying, as it does, the study and research of years, it will be found a valuable addition to the work.

Our thanks are due to Gen. Welch, Chestnut Hill, Philada.; Robert Bonner, Esq., New York; C. P. Relf, Esq., Norristown, Pa.; and D. Swigert, Esq., of Spring Station, Ky.; for their kindness in permitting us to obtain correct likenesses of the noble animals whose portraits appear in these pages, and for the interest they have shown in the success of this work; and to Messrs. Scheiber & Son, and Wenderoth, Taylor & Brown, of Philada., and Mr. George G. Rockwood, of New York, for the excellent photographs they have taken of the celebrated horses they represent.

THE AMERICAN PUBLISHERS.

CONTENTS.

CHAPTER I.

EARLY HISTORY OF THE HORSE.

                                                                                                 PAGE

The Horse of Scripture—The Greek Horse—That of the Romans—The Arab of Antiquity—Egyptian, Libyan, Numidian, and Moorish Horses—The original British Horse—Ancient methods of using the Horse .   13

CHAPTER II.

GENERAL CHARACTERISTICS.

Habits—External Form as indicated by Points—Proportions—Maturity—Average Age—Periodical Moulting—Mental Development—Small Stomach 18

CHAPTER III.

THE HORSES OF THE EAST.

The Barb—The Egyptian Horse—The Horses of Dongola and Abyssinia—Other African Horses—The Modern Arab—The Persian Horse—The Turkish Horse—Other Asiatic Horses—The Australian Horse . . 30

CHAPTER IV.

THE HORSES OF THE WESTERN HEMISPHERE.

The South American Horse—The Mustang—The Indian Pony—The Canadian Horse—The Morgan Horse—The American Trotter—The Narraganset Pacer—The American Thorough-bred—The Vermont Cart-Horse—The Conestoga Draught-Horse 45

CHAPTER V.

THE THOROUGH-BRED HORSE.

Early Maturity—Object of Encouraging the Breed—Essentials in the Thorough-bred—Purity of Blood—External Formation—Height—Color—Coat, Mane, and Tail 57

CHAPTER VI.

ON THE LOCOMOTIVE ACTION IN THE VARIOUS PACES.

Natural and Acquired Paces—Distribution of Weight—Attitude assumed in Standing—Mode of Progression—The Walk—Trot—Canter—Hand-Gallop—Extended Gallop—The Amble—Racking, Pacing, and Running—The Paces of the Manege—Leaping, or Jumping 76

CHAPTER VII.

THE PRINCIPLES OF BREEDING APPLICABLE TO THE HORSE.

Theory of Generation—In-and-in Breeding—Out-Crossing, Advantages and Disadvantages of each Plan—Causes of a "Hit"—Importance of Health and Soundness in both Sire and Dam—Best Age to Breed from—Influence of Sire and Dam respectively—Choice of Sire and Dam—The kind of Horse most likely to be profitable to the Breeder—Concluding Remarks on Breeding 99

CHAPTER VIII.

THE BROOD MARE AND HER FOAL.

The Hovel and Paddock—General Management of the Brood-Mare—Treatment when in Foal—After Foaling—Early Management of the Foal—Weaning and After Treatment of the Foal 117

CHAPTER IX.

THE BREAKING OF THE COLT.

Rarey's Principles and Practice—Ordinary English Method of Breaking for the Saddle—Superiority of the Latter when properly carried out—Breaking to Harness 128

CHAPTER X.

STABLES.

Situation and Aspect—Foundations—Stalls and Loose Boxes—Hay Chamber and Granary—Materials for Floors—Doors and Windows—Drainage and Water Supply—Ventilation and Lighting—Stable Fittings—Harness Room—Coach-House—Servants' Rooms—Ground Plans of Stables—Necessity for Airing New Stables 155

CHAPTER XI.

STABLE MANAGEMENT.

Theory and Practice of Feeding and Watering—Dressing or Grooming—Clipping, Singeing, and Trimming—Use and Application of Bandages—Management of the Feet—Daily Exercise—Proper Temperature of the Stable—Remedies for Stable Vices and Bad Habits—Preparation for Work—Ordinary Sweating—The Turkish Bath—Physic—Final Preparation—Treatment after Work—Summering—Care of Saddlery and Harness 177

CHAPTER XII.

RIDING.

Mounting and Dismounting—The Seat—Management of the Reins—Modes of Starting the Horse into his Various Paces—Riding to Hounds—Outdoor Vices and Bad Habits 230

CHAPTER XIII.

CLASSIFICATION OF THE VARIOUS ORGANS, AND PHYSIOLOGY OF THE SKELETON.

Classification of the Various Organs—Structure of Bone—Of the Skeleton in General—The Artificial Skeleton—Number of Bones composing the Skeleton—General Anatomy of the Spinal Column—Of the Head and Face—Of the Thoracic Arch and Anterior Extremities—Of the Pelvic Arch and Hind Extremities—Of the Tail—Of the Fore and Hind Extremities considered as Organs of Support and Locomotion . . . 248

CHAPTER XIV.

THE TEETH. 257

CHAPTER XV.

OF THE JOINTS AND MUSCLE—THE TISSUES ENTERING INTO THEIR COMPOSITION.

The Joints—Cartilage—Fibrous Tissue—Physiology of Muscle . . . 266

CHAPTER XVI.

THE THORAX.

Contents of the Thorax—The Blood—General Plan of the Circulation—The Veins—Physiology of Respiration 272

CHAPTER XVII.

THE ABDOMINAL AND PELVIC VISCERA.

The Abdomen and its Contents—Physiology of Digestion—Structure of Glands and Physiology of Secretion—Depuration, and its Office in the Animal Economy—The Stomach—The Intestines—Liver—Spleen—Pancreas—Kidneys—Pelvis—Bladder—Organs of Generation, Male and Female 278

CHAPTER XVIII.

THE NERVES AND SPECIAL ORGANS.

The Nerves—The Organ of Smell—The Eye—The Ear—The Organ of Touch—The Foot 286

CHAPTER XIX.

THE DISEASES AND INJURIES OF BONE.

General Remarks—Splints—Ringbone and Sidebone—Ossification of the Lateral Cartilages—Bone Spavin—Exostosis of the Humerus and Scapula, or Shoulder-Joint Lameness—Fistula of the Withers, or Thiselo—Poll Evil—Caries of the Jaw—Osteo Sarcoma, or Big Head—Fractures . 297

CHAPTER XX.

INJURY AND DISEASES OF THE JOINTS, MUSCLES, AND TENDONS.

Diseases of Muscle, Tendon, and Ligament—Of Cartilage and Synovial Membrane—Inflamed Tendinous Sheaths—Inflamed Bursæ Mucosæ—Strains—Those of the Back and Loins—Of the Shoulder—Of the Knee—Of the Fetlock—Of the Coffin Joint—Of the Suspensory Ligaments—Of the Back-Sinews—Breaking Down—Strains of the Hip-Joint, Stifle, and Hock—Curb—Dislocation—Wounds of Joints 311

CHAPTER XXI.

DISEASES OF THE THORACIC ORGANS AND THEIR APPENDAGES.

General Remarks—Catarrh, or Cold—Influenza, or Distemper—Bronchitis—Chronic Cough—Laryngitis, Roaring, Whistling, etc.—Pneumonia and

CONTENTS. ix

PAGE

Congestion of the Lungs—Pleurisy—Pleurodynia—Phthisis—Broken Wind—Thick Wind—Spasm of the Diaphragm—Diseases of the Heart—Diseases of the Blood Vessels in the Chest and Nose 326

CHAPTER XXII.

DISEASES OF THE ABDOMINAL VISCERA AND THEIR APPENDAGES.

General Remarks—Diseases of the Mouth and Throat—Gastritis—Stomach Staggers—Dyspepsia—Bots—Inflammation of the Bowels—Colic—Diarrhœa and Dysentery—Strangulation and Rupture—Calculi in the Bowels—Worms—Disease of the Liver—Of the Kidneys—Of the Bladder—Of the Organs of Generation 350

CHAPTER XXIII.

DISEASES OF THE NERVOUS SYSTEM.

Phrenitis, or Mad Staggers—Epilepsy and Convulsions—Megrims—Rabies, Hydrophobia, or Madness—Tetanus, or Lock-jaw—Apoplexy and Paralysis—String Halt—Coup de Soleil, or Sun-stroke 375

CHAPTER XXIV.

DISEASES AND INJURIES OF CERTAIN SPECIAL ORGANS.

Diseases of the Ear—Inflammation of the Eye—Cataract—Amaurosis—Buck-eye—Surfeit—Hidebound—Mange—Lice—Mallenders and Sallenders—Warbles, Sitfasts, and Harvess-Galls—Grubs—Bites and Stings of Insects—Swelled Legs—Chapped Heels—Grease, or Scratches—Warts—Corns—Sandcrack—False Quarter—Quittor—Thrush—Canker—Laminitis—Seedy Toe—Contraction of the Foot—Navicular Disease—Accidents to the Legs and Feet 383

CHAPTER XXV.

CONSTITUTIONAL DISEASES.

Fevers—Anasarca—Glanders—Farcy 417

CHAPTER XXVI.

SHOEING, ... 422

CHAPTER XXVII.

OPERATIONS.

Administration of Chloroform—Methods of Confining the Horse—Bleeding—Firing—Setons and Rowels—Blistering—Castration—Docking and Nicking—Unnerving—Reduction of Hernia—Administration of Physic—Clysters—Back-Raking 432

CHAPTER XXVIII.

THE PRINCIPAL MEDICINES, AND THE DOSES IN WHICH THEY CAN SAFELY BE ADMINISTERED.

                      PAGE

Alteratives—Anodynes—Antiseptics—Anti-Zumins—Aperients—Astringents—Blisters—Caustics, or Cauteries—Clysters, or Injections—Detergents—Diuretics—Embrocations, or Liniments—Febrifuges—Lotions, or Washes—Physic Balls and Drenches—Stimulants—Stomachics—Tonics—Traumatics—Vermifuges, or Worm Medicines 448

CHAPTER XXIX.

LIST OF IMPORTED HORSES. 461

ESSAY ON THE AMERICAN TROTTING HORSE, AND SUGGESTIONS ON THE BREEDING AND TRAINING OF TROTTERS 467

PEDIGREES OF CELEBRATED TROTTING HORSES 507–523

LIST OF ILLUSTRATIONS.

FULL PAGE ENGRAVINGS.

FLORA TEMPLE AND HER COLT. From a photograph from life, by SCHREIBER & SON.
MAMBRINO PILOT. From a painting from life, by E. TROYE.
LEXINGTON. From a drawing from life, by E. TROYE.
ETHAN ALLEN. From a photograph from life, by SCHREIBER & SON.
DEXTER. From a photograph from life, by SCHREIBER & SON.
HAMBLETONIAN (RYSDYK'S). From a painting from life, by GLOVER.
SKELETON OF THE HORSE.
DISEASES OF THE HORSE.
SECTION OF THE ABDOMEN AND PELVIS, WITH THE INTESTINES AND LIVER REMOVED—
    LONGITUDINAL SECTION OF THE THORAX, ETC.

	PAGE
POINTS OF THE HORSE	20
OBLIQUE SHOULDER	22
UPRIGHT SHOULDER	22
PROPORTIONS OF THE VARIOUS POINTS	27
THE GODOLPHIN ARABIAN	31
CHABAN, AN ARABIAN STALLION	35
THE CANADIAN HORSE	47
CONESTOGA DRAUGHT-HORSE	56
FISHERMAN—AN ENGLISH THOROUGH-BRED	62
SAUNTERER—AN ENGLISH THOROUGH-BRED	64
STARTING FOR THE WALK	80
RECEIVED INTERPRETATION OF THE WALK	81
EXCEPTIONAL MODE OF STARTING	82
ACTION IN THE TRUE TROT	88
THE CANTER	90
RECEIVED INTERPRETATION OF THE GALLOP	91
CORRECT VIEW OF THE GALLOP	94
MARE AND FOAL	125
RAREY'S LEG-STRAP, NO. 1	131
RAREY'S LEG-STRAP, NO. 2	132
CRUISER WITH THE LEG-STRAP AND SURCINGLE ON	132
CRUISER IN THE POWER OF HIS MASTER	133
THE HORSE BOUNDING ON HIS HIND LEGS	134
THE HORSE ON HIS KNEES, ABOUT TO FALL ON HIS SIDE	135

LIST OF ILLUSTRATIONS.

	PAGE
THE HORSE TAMED	138
RAREY'S HALTER OR BRIDLE FOR COLTS	142
DOOR FOR LOOSE BOX	161
VENTILATING WINDOWS	162
SECTION OF CATCH-PIT	163
IRON-SURFACE GUTTER	165
VENTILATING SHAFT	167
HEAD OF SHAFT	167
THE HANGING BAIL	168
IRON-FITTINGS FOR STALLS AND LOOSE BOX	172
GROUND-PLAN OF A RACING OR HUNTING STABLE	175
GROUND PLAN OF A STABLE FOR FOUR OR FIVE HORSES	176
BAR-MUZZLE FOR CRIB-BITERS	203
REMEDY FOR TEARING THE CLOTHES	205
GROUND-PLAN OF A TURKISH BATH FOR HORSES	214
THE HUNTER TURNED OUT TO GRASS	226
READY	230
PROFILE VIEW OF THE BONES OF THE HEAD AND FACE	254
SECTION OF INCISOR	257
THREE-YEAR OLD MOUTH	259
MOUTH OF THE COLT AT FOUR-AND-A-HALF YEARS	260
UPPER NIPPERS AND TUSHES AT FIVE YEARS OLD	261
LOWER NIPPERS AND TUSHES AT FIVE YEARS OLD	262
LOWER NIPPERS AND TUSHES OF A SIX-YEAR OLD HORSE	262
UPPER NIPPERS IN THE EIGHT-YEAR OLD HORSE	263
LOWER NIPPERS AND LEFT TUSH OF A VERY OLD HORSE, THE RIGHT HAVING FALLEN OUT	264
SECTIONAL PLAN OF THORAX AND ITS CONTENTS (THROUGH THE GIRTH-PLACE)	272
GENERAL PLAN OF THE CIRCULATION	275
SECTION OF THE PARTS ENTERING INTO THE COMPOSITION OF THE FOOT AND THE FETLOCK AND PASTERN-JOINTS	291
THE HOOF	292
FRONT VIEW OF THE FOOT, WITH THE HOOF REMOVED	292
THE UNDER SURFACE OF THE FOOT	292
VIEW OF VESSELS OF THE FOOT, INJECTED	294
VIEW OF THE ARTERIES OF THE FROG AND SOLE. INJECTED	295
GROUP OF BOTS ATTACHED TO THE STOMACH	356
SECTION OF THE FOOT IN CONFIRMED LAMINITIS	405
A SOUND FORE FOOT PREPARED FOR THE SHOE	426
SHOEING	428
SETON NEEDLES, ONE-QUARTER SIZE	439
CLAMS LINED WITH VULCANIZED INDIA-RUBBER	442
THE ECRASEUR	443
DOCKING-KNIFE	444
FLORA TEMPLE TROTTING	489

THE HORSE.

CHAPTER I.

EARLY HISTORY OF THE HORSE.

The Horse of Scripture—The Greek Horse—That of the Romans —The Arab of Antiquity—Egyptian, Libyan, Numidian, and Moorish Horses—The original British Horse—Ancient methods of using the Horse.

THE HORSE OF SCRIPTURE.

HE EARLIEST RECORD of the Horse which we possess is in the Old Testament, where we first find him inferentially mentioned in the thirty-sixth chapter of Genesis, as existing in the wilderness of Idumea about the beginning of the sixteenth century before Christ. Many commentators, however, render the word which is translated "mules" in our version, as "waters," and thus a doubt is thrown upon the correctness of the inference which is thence drawn. Moreover, in the thirty-second chapter of Genesis, camels, goats, sheep, cattle and asses are all severally alluded to, but no horses; so that it is highly probable that in the time of Jacob, whose departure from Laban is there narrated, horses were unknown to the Israelites. It was not until after their arrival in Egypt that the horse is clearly alluded to. Jacob, on his deathbed, leaves us no room to doubt his knowledge of the horse, and of its being domesticated, for he speaks of the "horse and his rider" in the same sentence. We need, therefore, go no further for a proof of the early existence of this animal in Egypt, and may assume that there were large numbers of them there, for Pharaoh is recorded to have taken "six hundred chosen chariots, and all the horses," to pursue the Israelites to the Red Sea. It is generally supposed from the omission of all mention of horses while the Israelites were in Arabia, that this country, which has since become so celebrated for them, was at that time entirely without them. The proof, however, is entirely of a negative character, though I confess that it is as strong as any of that nature can well be. Indeed,

six hundred years later, Arabia could not have been remarkable in any way for her horses, for Solomon, while he resorted to her for silver and gold, mounted his cavalry from Egypt. Yet the latter country could scarcely be the native land of the Horse, not possessing the extensive plains which are peculiarly suited to his existence in a wild state, and it is considered probable that he was introduced from the central regions of Africa, which are undoubtedly the native plains of the Quagga, the Zebra, and some other congeners of the Horse; but where, curiously enough, he is not now found in a wild state. Thence he would naturally find his way into Egypt, and through Arabia to Persia, Tartary and Greece, ultimately reaching Great Britain; but in what century he was introduced there we are quite at a loss to conjecture.

THE GREEK HORSE.

OF THE PRECISE FORM of the Horse of Scripture we have no account, beyond the glowing language of Job, which will apply to almost any variety possessing the average spirit of the species. The horse of the Greeks is far better known, being handed down to us in the writings of Xenophon, and preserved in the marble friezes of the Parthenon, which are now removed to our own National Museum. The above Greek writer, in giving his advice on the purchase of a horse, says, "On examining the feet, it is befitting first to look to the horny portion of the hoofs, for those horses which have the horn thick are far superior in their feet to those which have it thin. Nor will it be well, if one fail next to observe whether the hoofs be upright both before and behind, or low and flat to the ground; for high hoofs keep the frog at a distance from the earth, while the flat tread with equal pressure on the soft and hard parts of the foot, as is the case with bandy-legged men. And Simon justly observes that well-footed horses can be known by the sound of their tramp, for the hollow hoof rings like a cymbal when it strikes the solid earth. But having begun from below, let us ascend to the other parts of the body. It is needful then, that the parts above the hoof and below the fetlocks be not too erect like those of the goat, for legs of this kind being stiff and inflexible, are apt to jar the rider, and are more liable to inflammation. The bones must not, however, be too low and springy, for in that case, the fetlocks are liable to be abraded and wounded, if the horse be gallopped over clods or stones. The bones of the shanks should be thick, for these are the columns which support the body, but they should not have the veins and flesh thick likewise; for if they have, when the horse shall be gallopped in difficult ground, they will necessarily be filled with blood, and will become varicose, so that the shanks will be thickened, and the skin be distended and relaxed from the bone; and when this is the case, it often follows that the back sinew gives way and renders the horse lame. But if the horse, when in action, bend his knees flexibly at a walk, you may judge that he will have his legs flexible when in full canter; for all horses as they increase in years increase in the flexibility of the knee. And flexible goers are esteemed highly, and with justice, for such horses are much less liable to blunder or to stumble than those which have rigid, unbending joints. But if the arms below the shoulder-blades be thick and muscular, they appear stronger and handsomer, as is the case also with a man. The breast also should be broad, as well for beauty as for strength, and because it causes a handsomer action of the fore-legs, which do not then interfere, but are carried wide apart. And again, the neck ought not to be set on like that of a boar, horizontally from the chest, but like that of a game-cock, should be upright towards the crest, and slack towards the flexure; and the head, being long, should have a small and narrow jaw-bone, so that the neck shall be in front of the rider, and that the eye shall look down on what is before the feet. A horse thus made will be the least likely to run violently away, even if he be very high-spirited, for horses do not attempt to run away by bringing in, but by thrusting out, their heads and necks. It is also very necessary to observe whether the mouth be fine or hard on both sides, or on one or the other. For horses which have not both jaws equally sensitive, are likely to be hard-mouthed on one side or the other. And it is better that a horse should have prominent than hollow eyes, for such a one will see to a greater distance. And widely-opened nostrils are far better for respiration than narrow, and they give the horse a fiercer aspect; for when one stallion is enraged against another, or if he become angry while being ridden, he expands his nostrils to their full width. And the loftier the crest, and smaller the ears, the more horse-like and handsome is the head rendered; while lofty withers give the rider a surer seat and produce a firmer adhesion between the body and shoulder. A double loin is also softer to sit upon, and pleasanter to look at, than if it be single; and a deep side, rounded toward the belly, renders the horse easier to sit, and stronger, and more easy to keep in condition. The shorter and broader the loin, the more easily will the horse raise his forequarters and collect his hind-quarters under him in going. These points, moreover, cause the belly to appear the smaller; which, if it be large, at once injures the appearance of the animal, and renders him weaker and less manageable. The quarters should be broad and fleshy, in order to correspond with the sides and chest; and, should they be entirely firm and solid, they would be the lighter in the gallop, and the horse would be the speedier. But if he should have his buttocks separated under the tail by a broad line, he will bring his hind legs under him with a wider space between them, and, so doing, he will have a prouder and stronger gait and action, and will in all respects be the better on them."

Here we have described, in most exact terms, a cobby but spirited and corky horse, with a light and somewhat peculiar carriage of the head and neck, just as we see represented in the Elgin marbles.

THE ROMAN HORSE.

OF THE ROMAN HORSE we know far less than of that of the Greeks; but the fact of its inferiority to those of the surrounding nations is established, for no sooner were they brought into collision with the cavalry of Macedonia and Epirus than they succumbed. This could only be owing to the quadruped, for the Roman foot-soldier was still unmatched. Cæsar depended for his cavalry upon Gallic horses, which were able to ride down the Roman horses of his rival Pompey without the slightest difficulty. So also Crassus was unable to make head in Asia against the Parthian horse; and from his day until British horses were transported to Oriental soil, the superiority of Asiatic horses remained undisputed.

THE ARAB OF ANTIQUITY.

THE ARAB OF THE PRESENT DAY is said by his countrymen to be the same in form, in courage, and in endurance, with the horse which existed in Arabia before the time of Christ. I have shown that there is every reason to believe that the Israelites who dwelt in Arabia had no horses in the time of Jacob, and therefore it is scarcely likely that this variety could have arrived at its present state of excellence much before the commencement of the Christian era. But beyond the traditional accounts which are preserved in the various tribes, there is no means of arriving at the truth, and they are to be regarded with considerable suspicion. Buffon comes to the conclusion, nevertheless, that Arabia is the birthplace of this animal, and his opinions are followed by a host of subsequent writers; but I have already given the reasons for the contrary conclusion. The dry nature of the country, and the scantiness of herbage, show that in a wild state the horse could hardly exist there, and that it is only by the care and superintendence of man that the Arabian horse has become so famous.

EGYPTIAN, LIBYAN, NUMIDIAN, AND MOORISH HORSES.

THE EGYPTIAN HORSE is handed down to us on some of the sculptures found in the ruins of Nineveh; the carvings of which are in a high state of preservation, and are very elaborate and spirited. Even the superficial veins are carefully rendered; and hence we may place some reliance upon the fidelity of the portraiture. In all these bas-reliefs the animal is represented with a large and coarse head, a high crest, and a heavy, lumbering body, not very dissimilar to the Flemish horse of the nineteenth century.

OF THE LIBYAN, NUMIDIAN, AND MOORISH horses, which are alluded to by classic writers, we know little beyond the cursory description of Ælian, who says that they were slenderly made, and carried no flesh.

THE ORIGINAL BRITISH HORSE.

THE NATURE OF THE ORIGINAL STOCK which formed the foundation of the modern European horse is extremely doubtful. In Great Britain horses' bones are found in caves which are of extreme antiquity, but they do not define with any certainty the form of the original British horse, nor can we, with certainty, arrive at the exact era at which the animals to which they belonged lived and died. It is, however, an ascertained fact that when the Romans invaded Great Britain they found the people in possession of horses, and using them for their chariots as well as for the purposes of riding. After the irruption of the Goths, and the commencement of the dark ages, we have no reliable history to guide us, and we are left to grope in the dark from the fourth century, when Vegetius wrote on the veterinary art, until the time of the Stuarts, when attention was first paid to the improvement of the breed of horses in this country.

ANCIENT METHODS OF USING THE HORSE.

THE MODE OF USING the horse adopted by the ancients was at first by harnessing him to a rude chariot, without springs. In course of time, the grooms who took care of him found that they could manage him while on his back without the aid of the saddle and bridle, which are comparatively modern inventions. Hence, we see the horse represented in the Elgin marbles as ridden without either the one or the other; and there is also abundant written testimony in support of this mode of equitation being practised by the early Greeks. This ingenious people, however, invented the snaffle-bridle, and both rode and drove with its aid, after the establishment of the Olympian games, in which chariot races formed an essential feature. The curb-bit was invented by the Romans, or, at all events, was first used by them; but both that people and the Greeks were ignorant of the use of the stirrup, and either vaulted on their horses, or used the back of a slave as a stepping-stone, or sometimes had recourse to a short ladder for the purpose. The earliest period when it can be proved that the stirrup was in use was in the time of the Norman invasion of this country. The incidents of this event in history were recorded on the Bayeux tapestry by the wife of William the Conqueror, and on this the stirrup was depicted, according to the authority of Berenger, as a part of the trappings of the horse. Shoeing was not practised by either the Greeks or Romans, and only in cases of lameness was the foot defended by a sandal, which, however, was sometimes tipped with iron.

UNTIL SOME TIME AFTER THE INSTALLATION OF THE OLYMPIAN GAMES the use of the horse was confined to war and the chase These games were held every four years, and are supposed to have commenced about 774 years before Christ, and as it was not until the twenty-third Olympiad that the horse was introduced in the arena, the birth of horse-racing may be fixed at about the year 680 B.C. At first the horses were ridden, and the distance was about four miles, but in the twenty-fifth Olympiad the chariot was introduced, and after this time became the prevailing instrument of testing the speed and powers of the Grecian horse. Here, also, the distance was about four miles, but as a pillar was to be rounded several times, the race depended quite as much on the skill of the charioteer as on the qualities of his horses.

CHAPTER II.

GENERAL CHARACTERISTICS.

Habits—External Form as indicated by Points—Proportions—Maturity—Average Age—Periodical Moulting—Mental Development—Small Stomach.

HABITS.

THE HABITS of the horse in a wild or free state, are similar to those of most of the gregarious and graminivorous animals. That is to say, he places his safety in flight; but when compelled to make a stand against any of the larger carnivora, he fights strongly with his heels and teeth. In all countries he feeds upon grass (green, or dried as hay), straw, or grain; in addition to which articles may be placed camel's milk, which is used occasionally in the deserts of Arabia, when the usual supply of food is altogether deficient. In a free state, where the horse has to travel far for his food, he becomes inured to fatigue, and is able to make long journeys, without the training which the domesticated animal requires. Thus the South American and Californian horses, immediately after being taken with the lasso, are able to carry their riders for sixty or seventy miles on end at a fast pace, suffering, of course, from the unaccustomed pressure of the saddle, but not otherwise the worse for their exertions. The walk and gallop are the only natural paces of the wild horse; the trot and canter being acquired, though to some extent exhibited by the domesticated horse before breaking, and evidently the result of the tendency which is always displayed to hand down from one generation to another habits which are not natural to the species.

EXTERNAL FORM, AS INDICATED BY POINTS.

THE ANATOMY of this animal will form the subject of a special division of this book, but the external form may now be discussed with propriety. By horsemen in general this is considered under certain subdivisions, which are called "points," and which are severally represented by figures in the outline on the following page.

THE RELATIVE PROPORTIONS of, and exact shape desirable in, each of these points, vary considerably in the several breeds. Thus, when speed and activity are essential, an oblique shoulder-blade is a *sine quâ non;* while for heavy harness it can scarcely be too upright, enabling the pressure of the collar to be more easily borne, and allowing the animal to exert his strength at right angles to its long axis. Many men are good judges of hunters and hacks, but are almost wholly ignorant of the qualities desirable in a coach or cart-horse. There are some elements, however, which are wanted in any horse, such as big hocks and knees, flat legs with large sinews, open jaws and full nostrils. It will, therefore, be necessary to describe the points of each breed; but I shall here give those which are always to be attended to as being of importance in any kind, whether used for racing or hunting, for the road or for agricultural purposes.

TAKING FIRST THE HEAD :—It should be known that the volume of brain contained within it determines the courage and other mental qualities of the individual. Now as, *cæteris paribus*, size is power, so without a wide forehead (which part marks the seat of the brain) you cannot expect a full development of those faculties known as courage, tractability, good temper, &c. The size of the muzzle is partly regarded as an element of beauty, and partly as a sign of high breeding. Hence, in the cart-horse, a coarse jaw and thick muzzle are not regarded. A large and patent nostril cannot be dispensed with in horses intended for fast work, and should be desired even in the cart horse, for in drawing heavy loads on a hot day, his breathing may be rendered almost as laborious as that of the highly-tasked racehorse or hunter. So also with the jaw, if there is not ample width between the two sides for the development and play of the larynx and windpipe, the wind is sure to be affected, and, in addition, the head cannot be nicely bent on the neck. A defect in this last point is the usual cause of that straight and inelegant setting on of the head which is so common, and which the practised horseman avoids, as alike unsightly and prejudicial to the wind and the mouth; for a horse

THE HORSE.

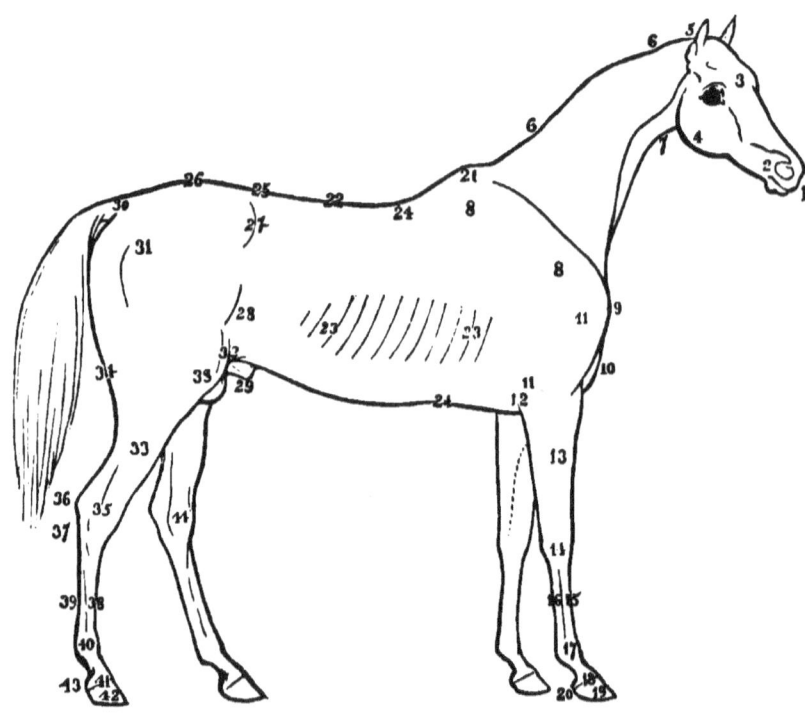

POINTS OF THE HORSE.

HEAD.
1. Muzzle.
2. Nostril.
3. Forehead.
4. Jaw.
5. Poll.

NECK.
6. 6. Crest.
7. Thrapple or windpipe.

FORE-QUARTER.
8. 8. Shoulder-blade.
9. Point of shoulder.
10. Bosom or breast.
11. 11. True-arm.
12. Elbow.
13. Forearm (arm).
14. Knee.
15. Cannon-bone.
16. Back sinew.
17. Fetlock or pastern-joint.
18. Coronet.
19. Hoof or foot.
20. Heel.

BODY OR MIDDLEPIECE.
21. Withers.
22. Back.
23. 23. Ribs (forming together the barrel or chest).
24. 24. The circumference of the chest at this point, called the girth
25. The loins.
26. The croup.
27. The hip.
28. The flank.
29. The sheath.
30. The root of the dock or tail.

THE HIND-QUARTER.
31. The hip-joint, round, or whirl-bone.
32. The stifle-joint.
33. 33. Lower thigh or gaskin.
34. The quarters.
35. The hock.
36. The point of the hock.
37. The curb place.
38. The cannon-bone.
39. The back sinew.
40. Pastern or fetlock-joint.
41. Coronet.
42. Foot or hoof.
43. Heel.
44. Spavin-place.

which *cannot* give way to the pressure of the bit is sure to become dull in his mouth, and therefore unpleasant to ride or drive. The eye is to be examined with a twofold purpose, firstly, as an index of the temper, the nature of which is marked by the expression of this organ ; and secondly, in reference to its present state of soundness, and the probability of its continuing healthy. A full and clear eye, with soft, gazelle-like expression, is scarcely ever associated with a bad temper, and will most frequently continue sound, if the management of the horse to which it belongs is proper in itself. The ear should be of medium size, not too small, nor too large, nor should it be lopped, though many good lop-eared horses have been known, and some very superior breeds, like that of the celebrated Melbourne, are notorious for this defect.

THE NECK should be of moderate length, all beyond a certain dimension being waste, and even a moderate-sized head at the end of an extremely long lever being too much for the muscles to support. It should come out full and muscular, with a sweep between the withers and the bosom, and should gradually diminish till it runs into the head, with an elegant bend just behind the ear. A very narrow throat suddenly bent at the upper part, marked as the thropple, is apt to be connected with roaring, and on that account is objected to by horsemen.

IN THE FORE-QUARTERS, there are several points to be attentively examined, and among these, the shoulder is regarded as of most consequence, when the horse under consideration is intended for the saddle. It is evident that, unless there is length of the blade, and also of the true arm, there cannot be a full surface for the attachment and play of the muscles, nor can there be the same amount of spring to take off the jar which follows each footfall. The straighter the angle formed by the long axis of each of these bones, the less spring there will be. So, also, if the angle is not sufficient, the muscles of the shoulder-blade will not thrust forward the true arm, nor will the latter be sufficiently clothed with muscles (without being loaded) to act on the fore-arm, commonly known by the horseman as the arm. Hence it is found, that with an upright shoulder, not only is the stride in all the paces short and the action stumpy, but there is not that elastic movement which enables the horse to carry his body along rapidly and evenly, without rising alternately behind and before, and thereby jarring himself or his rider. On the other hand, the upright shoulder, loaded with a thick mass of muscles, is useful in the cart-horse, and to a certain extent also, in the carriage-horse, in both of which the pressure of the collar requires a steady and comparatively motionless surface to bear it. The difference between the two extremes of oblique and upright shoulders is well illustrated in the accompanying woodcut, in which it will be seen that in the former the angle between the blade (*a*) and the true arm (*b*) is very considerable, while in the latter it is much less. Hence it results, that when the muscles of the blade bring the axis of the arm into nearly the same line with its own axis, the forearm (*c*) in the oblique shoulder will be thrust forward and raised to a greater degree than in the upright formation, as is shown in the engraving in the parts represented by dotted lines (*d e*). It follows, there-

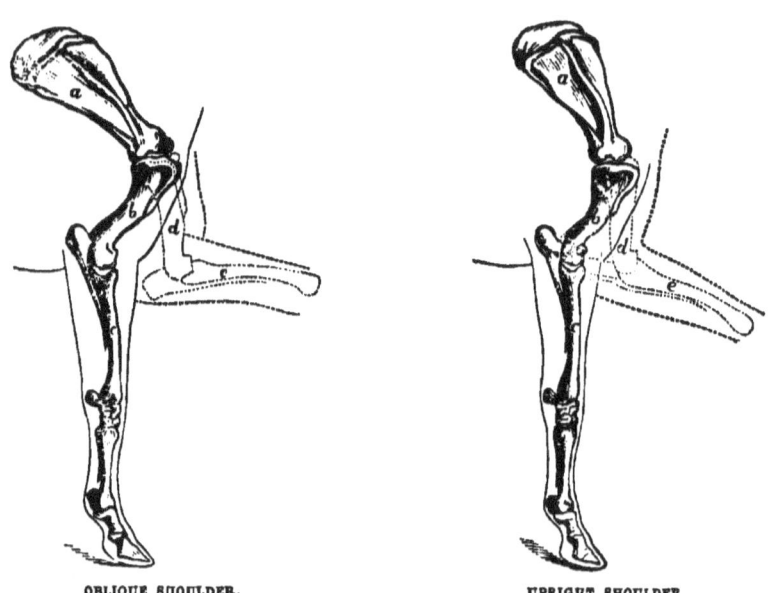

OBLIQUE SHOULDER.   UPRIGHT SHOULDER.

fore, that horses intended to have high, and at the same time forward action, should have oblique shoulders, for without them they will almost to a certainty either have very mean and low action, or, if they do bend their knees, they will put their feet down again nearly on the same place as they took them from, which peculiarity we so often see displayed in the cart breed, or those nearly allied to it. This is one of the most important uses of the obliquity of the shoulder-blade as it seems to me, and one which has not been generally admitted by writers on this branch of the subject, though all are ready to admit that in some way or other this formation is essential to good action. Another reason for the obliquity of the shoulder in the riding-horse, is that without it the saddle is not kept back in its proper place, and the horseman's weight being thus thrown too forward, the action of the forequarter is impeded. Mere obliquity, however, is not sufficient for this purpose; for, without a proper development of muscle, the blade itself will not keep the saddle in its place. If, therefore, there is a hollow just behind the top of the blade, even if this is slanting enough, you must expect the saddle to slip forward, and should, in all doubtful cases, be careful to put one on before concluding a purchase. The point of the shoulder should be well developed, but not showing any rough protuberances, which are equally objectionable with a flat or ill-developed point. The length of the true arm is mainly dependent upon that of the blade; but sometimes, when this is oblique enough, the true arm is short and upright, and the elbow stands under, or only a little behind, the shoulder point. This is a very faulty conformation, and is seldom attended with good action. The chief defect in the elbow is seen when it turns inwards, and rubs so closely against the ribs that the finger can hardly be insinuated between them and it. Here the elbow is said to be tied or confined, and the horse is very apt to turn his toes out; while the opposite formation is indicated by turned-in, or "pigeon" toes, and turned-out elbows, frequently accompanying long-standing rheumatism of the shoulders. It does sometimes happen, however, that the toes are turned in or out without affecting the elbow, but this is an exception to the rule. A long and muscular fore-arm is a sure accompaniment of strong and sweeping action, and should be carefully prized; in other respects there is little to be noted here. Next comes the knee, which should be broad, and when looked at from the front should be much wider than the limb above and below. It should taper off backwards to a comparatively thin edge, and should have a good development of the pisiform bone, which projects backwards at its upper part. The leg, immediately below the knee, should be as large as any other part, and not "tied in" there, which indicates a weakness of this part. A bending of the knee backwards is called a "calf-knee," and is not objected to in carthorses, in which it is by no means uncommon; but it is very apt to lead to strains of this joint in the racehorse or hunter. A knee naturally bending somewhat forward is much preferred by good judges, though, when it is the result of over-work, it is almost equally to be avoided with the calf-knee. Flat, and at the same time large, cannon-bones, without gumminess, are of great importance, and if attended with a full-sized suspensory ligament, and with strong, clean, and free back sinews, the leg is to be considered faultless. The fetlock-joint should be of good size and clean, whilst the pasterns should form an angle with the ground, of between forty-five and sixty degrees. Lastly, the foot should be well formed; but the construction of this part being hereafter more fully described, I shall omit its consideration here.

IN THE MIDDLEPIECE the withers come first under notice. It is usual to desire them high and thin, but they are very commonly too much developed, and if the bony processes stand up like the edge of a razor, without muscle on them, they are to be regarded as objectionable rather than otherwise. The inexperienced horseman is apt to consider the existence of high withers as a sure sign that the saddle will be carried well back, but there are some horses whose withers are the greatest annoyance to the rider, for having upright and short shoulder-blades, together with high withers, the saddle rides forward upon the latter, and chafes them in spite of all the padding which can be introduced. In looking at this point, I believe the purchaser should almost entirely disregard it, excepting to take care that it is not too high for the formation and position of the shoulder-blades. If these are long, and therefore slanting, and especially if in addition to a proper position of the bones they are furnished with plenty of muscle, the withers may be disregarded, and the action may be expected to be good even if they are so low as to show no rise between the neck and the back.

The volume of the chest is the measure not only of the capacity of the lungs, but of that of the large organs of digestion. Hence, unless there is a middlepiece of proper size, the wind is seldom good, and the stamina of the individual will scarcely ever be sufficient to bear hard work. But there is a limit to the development of this part in those breeds which are required to move with much velocity, where weight is a great object; and if the body of the racehorse or hunter was as heavy as that of the drayhorse, the speed would be greatly reduced, and the legs would give way during the first severe gallop. So also, a wide chest interferes with the free and rapid action of the shoulders and arms as they glide on the ribs; and an open bosom is almost always fatal to high speed. In the racehorse and hunter, therefore, capacity of chest must be obtained by depth rather than width; while in the cart-horse, a wide chest and a frame roomy in all directions is desired, so as to give good wind, and, at the same time, enable the animal to keep up his flesh while working eight or nine hours per day. For light, quick draught, a formation intermediate between the two is the proper one; the large frame of the cart-horse being too heavy for the legs to bear at a fast pace, and leading to their rapid destruction in trotting over our modern hard roads. The capacity of the lungs is marked by the size of the chest at the girth; but the stamina will depend upon the depth of the back ribs, which should be especially attended to.

A SHORT BACK, with plenty of ground covered nevertheless, is the desideratum of every practised horseman. Unless the measurement from the shoulder point to the back of the quarters is somewhat greater than the height at the withers, the action is confined, especially in the gallop, for the hind legs cannot be brought sufficiently forward on account of the interference of the fore-quarter; and, indeed, from the want of play in the back, they are generally too much crippled in that respect. A horse "short above and long below" is the perfection of shape in this particular.

MAMBRINO PILOT.

Copyright Secured.

From a Drawing from Life by E. Troye.

but he is not very commonly met with. Where length below is seen, there is generally too much space between the last rib and the hip, while, on the other hand, coupled with a short back, we too often see the legs all "jumped up together," and the action short and stumpy. Next to these points in the middlepiece it is important to pay attention to the upper line of the back, which should bend down a little behind the withers, and then swell out very gently to the junction with the loins, which can hardly be too wide and muscular. The inexperienced eye will often be deceived by the hips, for if these are narrow the muscles rise above them, and make the loin and back look stronger than they really are, the contrary being the case where the hips are wide and ragged. This latter formation, though not so elegant as the level hip, is prized by the man who wishes to be carried well to hounds, and he will jump at a horse which would be passed over with contempt by the tyro as " a great raw-boned brute." A slightly-arched loin is essential to the power of carrying weight; a much-arched, or " hog" back, is almost sure to give uneasy action from its want of elasticity.

IN EXAMINING THE HIND-QUARTER, so much depends upon the breed, and the purposes to which the animal is to be put, that only a few general remarks can be given. Thus, for high speed, there should be plenty of length in the two bones which unite at the stifle-joint, without which the stride must be more or less limited in extent. The exact position of the hip-joint not being easily detected, the tyro has some difficulty in estimating the length from it to the stifle-joint, but he can readily measure the length from the root of the tail, either with his eye or with a tape, if he cannot depend upon his organ of sight. In a flat outline this will come to twenty-four inches in a horse of fifteen hands three inches, but measured round the surface it will be two inches more. Again, the lower thigh, or gaskin, should be of about the same length; but if measured from the stifle to the point of the hock, it will be fully twenty-eight inches in a well-made horse of high breeding. These measurements, however, will be much greater in proportion than those of the cart-horse, who requires strength before all things, and whose stride is of no consequence whatever. In him, the length of the upper, or true thigh is generally as great as that of the thoroughbred, but the lower thigh, is much shorter, and the horse stands with a much straighter hind leg, and consequently with his hocks making a very slight angle. Muscular quarters and gaskins are desirable in all breeds; for without strong propellers, no kind of work to which the horse is put can be duly performed. The judge of a horse generally likes to look at the quarters behind, so as to get a good view of their volume, and unless they come close together, and leave no hollow below the anus, he suspects that there is a want of constitution, and rejects the animal on that account. But not only are muscles of full size required, but there must be strong joints to bear the strain which these exert, and one of the most important of all the points of the horse is the hock. This should be of good size, but clean and flat, without any gumminess or thoroughpins, and with a good clean point standing clear of the rest of the joint; the "curby place" and the situation of spavin should be free from enlargement; but to detect these diseases a considerable amount of practice is required. Lastly, the hocks should be well let down, which depends upon the length of the thigh, and insures a short cannon-bone. The pasterns and feet should be formed in correspondence with those of the fore extremity, to which I have already alluded.

Such are the recognised points to be desired in the horse; but in spite of the general opinion of good judges being in favor of them, as I have described, no one can predicate with certainty that a horse possessing them all in perfection will have a corresponding degree of action out of doors. No one who has bought many horses will be content with an inspection in the stable, even if the light is as good as that of the open air, for he well knows that there is often a vast difference between the estimate of the value of a horse which he forms indoors and out. Much of this depends upon the temper of the individual, for if he is dull and heavy he will not "make a good show," though still he may be capable of being sufficiently excited by hounds, and many such horses are invaluable hunters. Independently, however, of this element, it will be sometimes found that the frame which looks nearly perfectly symmetrical while at rest, becomes awkward and comparatively unsightly while in motion; and the horse which is expected to move well will often be sent back to his stall with "That will do, thank you," after a single run.

PROPORTIONS OF THE VARIOUS POINTS.

THE PROPORTIONS of the component parts of the horse, as I have already remarked, vary a good deal in the different breeds. The following, however, may be taken as the most perfect; but they refer especially to the racer, hunter, and hack, as well as to the lighter and more blood-like harness horses, and must not be strictly applied to the draught-horse in any of his varieties:—

This scale is drawn in inches, and, in the outline, the horse is supposed to be fifteen hands three inches, or sixty-three inches high. The measurements are the average of those carefully taken from six horses considered to be of perfect symmetry. Two of these were celebrated stallions, two thoroughbred hunters, and two chargers of great value.

PROPORTIONS OF VARIOUS POINTS.

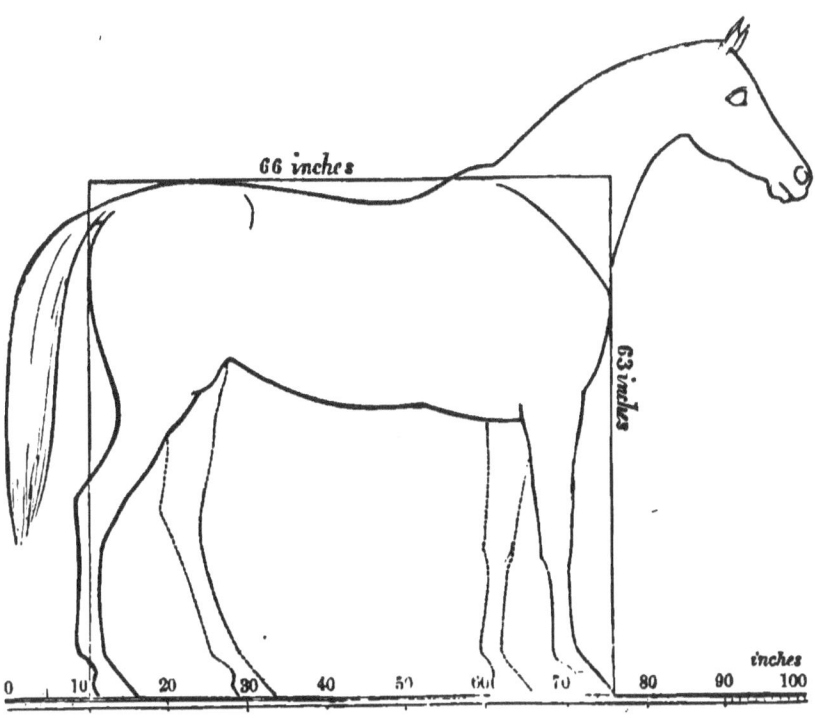

	Inches.		Inches
Height at withers and croup	63	From the withers to the hip	22
Length from shoulder-point to quarter	66	From the stifle to the point of the hock, in the attitude shown in the plan	28
From the lowest part of chest to the ground	36	From the root of tail to stifle-joint	26
From the elbow-point to the ground	39	From the point of the hock to the ground	22¼
From the withers to the pole, just behind the ears, *in a straight line*	30	Length of arm from the elbow to the pisiform-bone	19¼
The same measured along the crest	32	From the pisiform-bone to the ground	19¼
Length of head	22		
Width across the forehead	9¼		

Girth varies from 76 to 79.
Circumference of fore cannon-bone. 7¼, 8, 8, 8¼, and 9 inches.
Circumference of arm just below the elbow, 16¼ to 18 inches.

On comparing these measurements with those of Eclipse, as recorded by St. Bel, it will appear that there is some considerable variation from those of that celebrated horse, which he is said to have measured during life, and to have also checked his dimensions after death. Thus, though Eclipse was very low before, and yet was sixty-six inches high, his head was twenty-two inches long, being the same as the average length of the six horses given by myself, though they are three inches lower at the withers, and at least five inches lower at the croup. Again, though thus shown to be particularly short, it must have been of extraordinary width; for, according to the same authority, it measured one foot across *below* the eyes; but, as Mr. Percivall remarks, this must be a mistake for *above* the eyes. Indeed, I cannot help thinking, in accordance with the opinions of the above distinguished English veterinarian, that in other respects "there appears some discordance in his admeasurements" of Eclipse. Nevertheless, it may safely be assumed, according to Mr. Percivall's summing up, that "he was a big horse in every sense of the word; he was tall in stature, lengthy and capacious in body, and large in his limbs. For a big horse his head was small, and partook of the Arabian character. His neck was unusually long. His shoulder was strong, sufficiently oblique, and though not remarkable for, not deficient in, depth. His chest was circular. He rose very little in his withers, being higher behind than before. His back was lengthy, and over the loins roached. His quarters were straight, square, and extended. His limbs were lengthy and broad, and his joints large, in particular his arms and thighs were long and muscular, and his knees and hocks broad and well formed."

The scale which I have given likewise differs in many particulars, though only slightly, from that which is usually found in treatises on the horse; but I have preferred trusting to Nature herself rather than to the observations of previous writers, which may be consulted by the reader at any time.

MATURITY.

THE HORSE COMPLETES HIS DENTITION at five years old, when he may be said to be mature. At eight or nine years the lower teeth lose their marks, or black concavities, after which there is no reliable evidence of age, which can, however, be tolerably accurately guessed at from the length of the front teeth or nippers, and from the general appearance of the horse, especially about the eyes, as will be hereafter shown.

MARES ARE VERY COMMONLY ALLOWED TO BREED in their third year, being put to the horse as two year olds. They often, however, come "in season" as yearlings, and many would then breed if allowed to be covered. It is found by experience that the foal robs the dam of some part of the nourishment which is destined by nature to develop the maternal frame, and hence the young mare is injured in size and substance if she breeds before she has come very near to maturity.

AVERAGE AGE.

THE AVERAGE AGE of the horse, when allowed to live without the risk of accidents and disease which he incurs in his usual work, is about twenty-five years. Instances of greater longevity are recorded on good authority, and there is reason to believe that occasionally he has reached to thirty-five or even forty years, but these are rare exceptions, and there are few which live beyond the twenty-eighth year, while a large proportion die before the twenty-fifth. Stallions are over-fed and under-exercised in proportion, so that it is no wonder they become diseased, and seldom die from old age; but brood-mares are not so mismanaged, and it is found that they become quite worn out soon after their twentieth year; and even if allowed to live they waste away and die by degrees, generally somewhere between their twenty-third and twenty-eighth year.

PERIODICAL MOULTING.

THE HORSE SHEDS HIS COAT once a year in all countries, and in our climate a second half-moult is performed in the autumn, when the summer short coat is partially shed. This second change consists, however, chiefly in a growth of the already existing hairs, which become coarser and longer, especially about the legs and under-parts of the body. At the same time the coat loses its gloss, and the color is less rich, blacks becoming rusty brown, and bays more yellow or sandy-colored than before. The hair of the mane and tail is constantly in a state of growth, and is not shed periodically.

MENTAL DEVELOPMENT.

IN MENTAL DEVELOPMENT the horse ranks below the dog, but he is capable of a considerable degree of education, though in countries where he is kept constantly confined he does not appear to great advantage in this respect. That he may be made to understand what is said to him is clear enough from the mode of managing farm-horses, which are all taught to obey the voice. I have on one occasion seen a circus-horse walk, trot, and gallop at the word of command, and change his paces on the instant; but this feat I have never known performed by any other exhibitor, nor do I think it would easily be imitated. It requires a high order of intellect to distinguish between the three paces and change them on the instant, and if I had not myself witnessed the performance on two several occasions I should scarcely have credited it. The brain of this animal does not require much rest by sleep, and four or five hours in quiet are sufficient to keep him in health if he is not very hard worked. He readily sleeps standing, and some individuals never lie down; but this habit of sleeping standing should not be encouraged, as it greatly distresses the legs, and tends to produce fever of the feet, or some other mischief in the lower extremities.

SMALL STOMACH.

ONE OF THE GREATEST PECULIARITIES in the structure of the horse is the small size of his stomach, which is also of a very simple nature. He is likewise without a gall bladder, showing that the digestion must be continuous and not interrupted by distinct intervals, as in the ruminants and carnivora. Nature has thus framed this animal, in order that he may be at all times able to exert his utmost speed, which he could not do with the mass of provender in his stomach which is carried by the cow or sheep. The same provision is shown in the udder of the mare, which is not larger than that of the goat or sheep.

All these several characteristics of the horse will be more minutely considered under the different heads to which they each belong; but they are here grouped together to give a better general idea of the animal which is under examination.

CHAPTER III.

THE HORSES OF THE EAST.

The Barb—The Egyptian Horse—The Horses of Dongola and Abyssinia—Other African Horses—The Modern Arab—The Persian Horse—The Turkish Horse—Other Asiatic Horses—The Australian Horse.

FOR THE FOLLOWING DESCRIPTIONS of Oriental varieties of the horse I am indebted to the accounts of travellers, having only seen one or two of them, and those only as single specimens, with the exception of the Arab.

THE BARB.

THIS KIND is named after the country in which it is found, which is rather an extensive one, comprehending the states of Tunis, Tripoli, Algiers, Fez, and Morocco, all lying on the northern coast of Africa to the west of Egypt. Vegetation is very luxurious in the valleys watered by the streams which descend from the Atlas Mountains in their course to the Mediterranean, and grass is abundant in the early spring and autumn, but in the summer season the great heat burns it all up; and therefore the horse is dependent upon the care of man for fodder during a great part of the year. Berenger describes the true Barb as follows:—

"The fore-hand is long, slender, and badly furnished with mane; but the neck rises distinctly and boldly out of the withers; the head is small and lean; ears, of good size, and well placed; shoulders, light, obliquely sloping, and broad; withers, thin and high; loins, straight and short; flanks and ribs, round, and well developed; haunches, strong; croup, somewhat too long; quarters, muscular and full; legs, clean, and the tendons clearly marked and separate from the bone; pasterns, somewhat too long and slanting; feet, sound and of good shape. In size they are lower than the Arabs, seldom measuring more than fourteen and a half hands, and they have not as much spirit, speed, or endurance, although in external things they are perhaps superior to him."

The GODOLPHIN ARABIAN, of which the annexed cut is a representation, is said to have been imported into France from Barbary, and is supposed to have been presented by the Emperor of Morocco to Louis XIV. as a fine Barb; but he was thought so little of in Paris that he was set to draw a cart about the streets, from which ignoble occupation he was rescued by Mr. Coke, and brought over to England. This gentleman gave him to a Mr. Williams, who kept the St. James' Coffee-house, and by him he was presented to the Earl of Godolphin for stud purposes. It

was, however, only by chance that his value was discovered; for being used as teazer to Hobgoblin, he was merely put to Roxana on the refusal of that horse to cover her, the produce being Lath, one of the best horses of the day. The Godolphin Arabian was of a brown bay color, and is said to have been about fifteen hands in height. He is supposed to have been foaled about the year 1724, and died in 1753. A remarkable feature in this horse is the height of his crest, and he is also invariably represented with round and drooping quarters. Several portraits of him are in existence, but all render these points in the same manner. I am not aware that there are any reliable grounds for considering this celebrated horse as a Barb rather than an Arab, and according to the usual description of the former, his size is against the hypothesis. Still, as he is generally so considered, I have added his description to that of the Barb, leaving my readers to draw their own conclusions.

THE EGYPTIAN HORSE.

IN THE FIRST CHAPTER I have shown that there is a strong reason for believing that the horse was introduced to Arabia through Egypt, and that the latter country again derived its supply from the central regions of Africa, which probably also furnished the Barbary States. The modern Egyptian horse is a very second-rate animal, and, according to Burckhardt, "is ugly, of coarse shape, and looking more like a cart-horse than a racer." He says, "Their legs and knees, and short and thick necks, are frequent defects among them. The head is sometimes fine; but I never saw good legs in an Egyptian horse. They are not able to bear any great fatigue, but when well fed their action occasionally is more brilliant than that of the Arabian; their impetuosity, however, renders them peculiarly desirable for heavy cavalry, and it is upon this quality alone that their celebrity has ever been founded."

There are said to be some fine breeds in the interior of the country; but, as a rule, the Egyptian horse stands very low in the estimation of travellers. Of late years more attention has been paid to his breeding by the Viceroy and his subordinates, and it is said that some considerable improvement has taken place.

THE HORSES OF DONGOLA AND ABYSSINIA.

THE DONGOLA BREED has been celebrated by that trustworthy authority, Mr. Bruce, as of the highest symmetry, size, and strength. He also praises highly their temper and docility, but seems to know nothing of their actual performances. Other writers, however, find fault with their want of substance, and pronounce them to be deficient in stoutness.

THE ABYSSINIAN HORSE is generally described as of good size and power, but I know of no reliable authority on which to depend in reference to particular points.

OTHER AFRICAN HORSES.

BESIDES THE ABOVE DISTINCT BREEDS of African horses there are several others which are not clearly made out, but to which individual travellers have alluded as, in their opinion, decided varieties of the animal. Thus Mr. Tully speaks of the Bornou horse as superior both to the Barb and Arab, but his statement is not verified by travellers of later date. The South African horse, used by the Kafirs in the recent wars with the Boors of the Cape of Good Hope, is a most wiry and useful animal; but there is no doubt that he has been greatly altered from the original form of the native horse by crosses with the English and Arabian breeds, which have been obtained by theft. In the early days of this settlement the native horse was very small, seldom reaching to fourteen hands, and though hardy and capable of standing a good deal of work, yet plain and unsightly in appearance. The colonists have so improved this original stock that they can now furnish several thousand horses annually for exportation, averaging fifteen hands in height, and of very superior form and action. They show a great deal of Arabian blood, but many of them bear a strong resemblance to the thorough-bred English horse, several of which breed have been at various times introduced into the colony.

THE MODERN ARAB.

THE CONTROVERSY relating to the value of this breed in the stud has raged with such vehemence that it is difficult to obtain an unprejudiced opinion upon it. One thing, however, is quite clear, namely, that to it in a great measure we owe the pre-eminence of our English thorough-bred. But how long it would take to bring a modern Arab, even of the highest caste, to the state of perfection in which we find our own West Australians and Stockwells it would be difficult to say. This subject, however, will be better discussed in treating of the English breed itself.

ALI BEY, who has investigated the subject with great acuteness, and who has had opportunities beyond the reach of ordinary writers, describes six distinct breeds of Arabs. "The first," he says, "named the 'Dgelfe,' is found in Arabia Felix. They are rare at Damascus, but pretty common in the neighborhood of Anaze. They are remarkable for speed and fire, yet mild as lambs; they support hunger and thirst for a long time, are of lofty stature, narrow in the chest, but deep in the girth, and with long ears. A colt of this breed at two years old will cost in his own country two thousand Turkish piastres.

"The second breed, called 'Seclaoni,' comes from the eastern part of the Desert, resembles the 'Dgelfe' of Anaze in appearance, but is not quite so highly valued.

"Next comes the 'Mefki,' handsome, though not so swift as the two former breeds, and more resembling the Andalusian in figure. They are very common about Damascus.

"Then the Sabi resembles the Mefki; and the fifth breed, called Fridi, is very common, but it is necessary to try them well, for they are often vicious, and do not possess the excellent qualities of the other breeds.

"Sixth, comes the Nejdi, from the neighborhood of Bussorah, and if they do not surpass, they at least equal, the 'Dgelfe of

Anaze, and Seclaoni.' Horses of this breed are little known at Damascus, and connoisseurs assert that they are incomparable; thus their value is arbitrary, and always exceeds two thousand piastres."

The first and last of these breeds are those which are most sought after by East Indian sportsmen; and Colonel Bower, who is one of their strongest admirers, tells us that he once possessed a three-year-old colt which stood fifteen hands and an inch at that age. He describes him as having "the stereotyped assortment of Eastern beauties: could stick his nose in a tumbler, and looked the gentleman all over; remarkably muscular, and as stately in his bearing as an autocrat, but his clean flat wiry legs, measuring eight inches round the shank below the knee, had nothing English in their composition. This was a pure Anaze Arab, but his career in the field was cut short by his casting himself in his stall, and dislocating his hip." It will be seen that no mention is here made of the breed which has been so long familiar to those who read our modern histories of the horse as that called "Kochlani" or "Kailhan," descended from the stud of Mahomet, who is supposed by many historians to have laid the foundation of the Arabian pedigrees. There is a tradition that the Prophet, being desirous of selecting mares for his stud, had a number of them which had been used as chargers kept for two days without water. At the end of that time, when mad with thirst, they were set at liberty, and at the moment when they were close to the coveted water, his trumpets sounded a war charge, which had such an effect upon five of them that they abandoned the water, and gallopped to the spot where they expected to meet with the still greater excitement of war. These five were therefore selected to form the foundation of his stud, and from them it is supposed that the race called "Kochlani" are descended. There is a slight similarity between this name and that of the second in the list enumerated by Ali Bey, and perhaps his "Seclaoni" may be identical with the "Kochlani" of previous writers. It is asserted by Oriental travellers that pedigrees exist which can be traced five hundred years back, and in the highest breeds there is no doubt that at present great care is taken, and many ceremonies performed at the covering of the mare. After the birth of the foal, a certificate is always duly made out by the local authority, and this must be done within seven days of its being dropped.

ARABIA is, in great measure, made up of rocky mountains and sandy deserts; but in Arabia Felix there are numerous valleys of remarkable fertility; though it is chiefly on the limited oasis surrounding each well or spring of water that the Arab horses are dependent for their food. It is found even in this country that a very luxuriant herbage does not suit the horse, whose frame becomes coarse and heavy if he is reared upon the succulent grasses of rich meadows, and therefore it is probable that much of the wiryness of leg and lightness of frame in the Arab is due to the sandy soil in which the grasses of these oases take their roots. Besides this, the dry air may have something to do with the development of muscle and tendon, while the soft sands of the desert render it unnecessary to protect the feet with iron shoes, and thus they are enabled to grow into the form which nature has designed for them as the most suitable to bear the superincumbent weight.

"CHABAN," AN ARABIAN STALLION.

PURE ARABS are considerably smaller than our modern thorough-breds, seldom exceeding 14 hands 2 inches in height. The head is remarkable for the width across the forehead, which is also full and square, while the muzzle is finer, the face more hollowed out, and the jaws more fully developed in their proportions than in any other breed with which we are acquainted. The eye is full and soft, yet sparkling with animation on the slightest excitement; the ear is small; the neck arched; the shoulders oblique, but muscular; the withers moderately high and thin; the chest rather light in girth, but the back ribs deep in proportion, and the hips.

though narrow, well united to the back by a rounded mass of powerful muscles. The croup is high, and the tail set on with a considerable arch. The bones of the legs are large in proportion to the size, and the tendons full and free, the suspensory ligaments being particularly strong and clean. The hocks are large and free both from curbs and spavins; and, lastly, the feet, though small, are sound, and capable of bearing an amount of battering which few well-bred English horses can sustain. The prefixed engraving of "Chaban," an Arabian stallion, shows most of these points extremely well, and the general characteristics of the breed are particularly well indicated by the artist, who took the sketch from a celebrated Arabian of high caste in the stud of the King of Wurtemburg.

FROM THE FULL DEVELOPMENT of the brain in this breed it might be expected à *priori*, that the amount of intelligence and courage possessed by them would be far above the average; and such is the result. of experience. Most of them are extremely docile, and in their native plains, where they pass their lives in constant communion with their masters, they are possessed of fine tempers; but if they are highly fed, and at the same time deprived of exercise and cruelly treated, their nervous system is so sensitive that they rebel, and when they fight they persevere to the death. A vicious Arabian is, therefore, a very unmanageable brute, and difficult to cure of his bad propensities. Good treatment, however, has its effect upon him, and when he once shows his forgiveness he may be depended on by the individual that he takes into his good graces. This trait has been well exemplified in the savage Arabian lately tamed by Mr. Rarey, and in a still more marked manner in former years in the case of Chillaby, who was, if possible, more savage than Cruiser, and yet was so completely tamed by Hughes, the celebrated circus-horse trainer, that he was able to exhibit him as a trained horse, and was never once disappointed by him. This is, I believe, more than Mr. Rarey can say of the above well-known savage horse, which was one of the first he operated on in this country.

THE FOOD of this kind of horse is of a very dry though nourishing nature, and neither when at liberty nor when tied up can he get much water, the prevalent opinion being that an unlimited supply of this fluid injures his shape, and interferes with his wind. It is said that the Arab horse is only fed twice a-day; but I conclude that this only refers to his allowance of corn, and that in the intervals he is permitted to pick up what little dry herbage the soil affords. Wonderful stories are told of the distances which young colts are compelled to go when first mounted, but I confess that I look with great suspicion upon these travellers' tales. About five or six pounds of barley or beans, or a mixture of the two, constitute the daily allowance of corn, which is about the weight of half a peck of good oats, and would be considered poor feed by our English horses, unless the proportion of beans is very large.

THE COLORS of the Arabian horses are mostly bay, chestnut, and gray, but occasionally black. The skin itself of the gray horses is of a deep slate color, and the manes and tails are darker than the rest of the body.

THE SPEED of the Arabs, which have recently been brought over to this country, is undoubtedly not nearly equal to that of our thorough-bred horses for courses of moderate length, that is, not exceeding two miles; and there is no reason to believe that at longer distances there would be an essential difference in the result. In the Goodwood Cup an allowance is made them of a stone, yet no Arab has ever had a chance of winning, and as far as this test goes they are proved to be inferior to the French and American horses. In India a difference of weight, varying from 1 stone to 1 stone 7 pounds, is made in favor of Arabs as against imported English horses, " in order to bring the two together" in racing parlance, yet even then few Arabs can compete with the second-rate horses which are imported from this country. Colonel Bower tells us that " in India the weights range from 7½ stone to 10 stone, and no uncommon timing for Arabs is 2 minutes and 54 seconds the mile and a half; 3 minutes and 52 seconds the 2 miles—it has been done in 3 minutes and 48 seconds, and the Arab that did it was once my property, and his name was the Child of the Islands. He was a daisy-cutter, and yet I have ridden him over the roughest ground, and never detected him in a trip. A pleasanter, safer hack could not be, and a fleeter Arab the world never saw. He stood 14 hands 2 inches, bay with black points, wiry limbs, very muscular all over, and measured 7¾ inches round a fore leg of the finest bone and flattest sinew." This time is as good as that of the average of our Derbys, but the test is a very fallacious one, and unless the time is taken over the same course, and that in the same running condition, no comparison can possibly be drawn.

Captain Shakspear, in his recently published work on the " Wild Sports of India," gives the following most minute description of the Arab, as he is now met with in India. As it differs in some particulars from the accounts of other observers, I extract it entire. The price of a good Arab, he says, varies from 150*l*. to 200*l*., and there is plenty of choice in the Bombay and Bengal markets.

" The points of the highest caste Arab horse, as compared with the English thorough-bred, are as follow : the head is more beautifully formed, and more intelligent; the forehead broader; the muzzle finer; the eye more prominent, more sleepy-looking in repose, more brilliant when the animal is excited. The ear is more beautifully pricked, and of exquisite shape and sensitiveness. On the back of the trained hunter, the rider scarcely requires to keep his eye on anything but the ears of his horse, which give indications of everything that his ever-watchful eye catches sight of. The nostril is not always so open in a state of rest, and indeed often looks thick and closed; but in excitement, and when the lungs are in full play from the animal being at speed, it expands greatly, and the membrane shows scarlet and as if on fire. The game-cock throttle—that most exquisite formation of the throat and jaws of the blood-horse—is not so commonly seen in the Arab as in the thorough-bred English racehorse; nor is the head quite so lean. The jaws, for the size of the head, are perhaps more apart, giving more room for the expansion of the windpipe. The point where the head is put on to the neck is quite as delicate as in the English horse. This junction has much more to do with the mouth of the horse than most people are aware of, and on it depends the pleasure or otherwise of the rider. The bones, from the eye down towards the lower part of the head, should not be too concave, or of a deer's form; for this in the Arab as in the English horse denotes a violent temper, though it is very beautiful to look at. Proceeding to the neck, we notice that the Arab stallion has rarely the crest that an English stallion has. He has a strong, light, and muscular neck, a little short, perhaps, compared to the other, and thick. In the pure breeds, the neck runs into the shoulders very gradually; and generally, if the horse has a pretty good crest, comes down rather perpendicularly into the shoulders; but often, if he is a little ewe-necked, which is not uncommon with the Arab, it runs in too straight, and low down in the shoulders. The Arab, however, rarely carries his head, when he is being ridden, so high in proportion as the English. He is not so well topped, which I attribute to the different way he is reared, and to his not being broken in regularly, like the English horse, before he is put to work. His shoulders are not so flat and thin, and he is thicker through in these parts generally for his size than the English thorough-bred horse. His girth does not show so deep, that is, he does not look so deep over the heart; but between the knees and behind the saddle, where the English horse very often falls off, the Arab is barrel-ribbed; and this gives him his wonderful endurance and his great constitutional points. This also prevents him from getting knocked up in severe training or under short allowance of food, and in long marches. His chest is quite broad enough and deep enough for either strength or bottom. The scapula, or shoulder-blade, is both in length and backward inclination, compared to the humerus, or upper bone of the arm, quite as fine in the high-caste Arab as in the English horse; while both bones are generally better furnished with muscles, better developed, and feel firmer to the hand. But some of the very fastest Arabs have their fore legs very much under them; indeed, so much that no judge would buy an English horse so made. Yet, whether it be that this form admits of the joints between these bones becoming more opened, when the horse extends himself, or whatever be the cause, it is a fact that blood-horses thus made are almost always fast horses. The upper part of their shoulder-blade seems to run back under the front part of the saddle, when they are going their best. This formation is most common in the lower-sized Arab, and apparently makes up to him for his deficiency in height. The very finest-actioned Arabs have had this peculiarity of form. They are rather apt to become chafed at the elbow-points by the girths, and almost require to have saddles made on purpose for them. The elbow-point, that essential bone, which for the sake of leverage should be prominent, is fine in the Arab, and generally plays clear of the body. The fore-arm is strong and muscular, and is pretty long; the knee square, with a good speedy cut for the size of the animal, equal to the English horse; while below the knee the Arab shines very conspicuously, having a degree of power there, both in the suspensory ligaments and flexor tendons, far superior, in proportion to his size, to the English horse. These are distinct and away from the shank-bone; they give a very deep leg, and act mechanically to great advantage. The bone looks small, but then it is very dense, the hollow which contains the marrow being very small, and the material solid, more like ivory than bone, heavy, and close-grained. The flexor tendons are nearly as large and as thick as the canna bone. The pasterns and their joints are quite in keeping with the bones above them, and are not so long, straight, and weak as those of the English horse. The feet are generally in the same proportion: but the Arabs themselves appear to be very careless in their treatment of them. The body or centre piece of the Arab horse has rarely too great length. This is a very uncommon fault in the pure breed; and there is no breed of horses that are more even in this respect than the Arab. Behind this, we come to a great peculiarity in the breed—his croup. I might say an Arab horse is known by it: he is so much more beautifully made in his hind quarters, and in the way his tail is put on, than most other breeds. His loins are good; he is well coupled; his quarters are powerful, and his tail carried high; and this even in castes that have very little more than a high-bred stallion to recommend them. The straight-dropped hind leg is always a recommendation, and almost all racing Arabs have it; and this, when extended, brings the hind foot under the stirrup, and the propellers being of this shape give a vast stride, without fear of overreach. The thighs and hocks are good; the latter very rarely know either kind of spavin or curbs. The points and processes are pre-eminently well adapted for the attachment of the muscles; while the flexor tendons of the hind legs generally correspond with those of the fore. The hocks are not so much let down, nor the hind legs so greyhound-like, as in the thorough-bred English horse. In stride, too, he is somewhat different, inasmuch as it is a rounder way of going, and is not so extended or so near the ground, but is more like a bound. However, there are exceptions; and I have bred pure Arabs whose stride, for their size, was very extended, and quite like that of English racehorses."

THE MARE is commonly supposed to be more highly prized by the Arabs than the stallion; but this idea is said to be unfounded by the celebrated Abd el Kader, in a highly interesting letter to General Daumas, which is published in the fifth number of *Baily's Magazine of Sports*. He remarks :

"It is true that the foal proceeds from the sire and from the dam, but the experience of ages has proved that the essential parts of the body—such as the bones, the tendons, the nerves, and the veins—proceed always from the sire. This is beyond all doubt. The meanest Arab knows now that any malady specially belonging to the bones, under which the sire may be suffering at the time of covering, will be perpetuated in his produce, such as splints, bone and blood spavins, the shape of the bones, and all diseases of the vertebral column. The dam may give to her produce color, and a certain amount of resemblance in form, the foal naturally partaking of some of the qualities of the animal which had so long borne it; but it is an incontestable fact, that it is the sire who gives strength to the bones, substance to the tendons, vigor to the nerves, rapidity of pace, in short, all the principal qualities. He also communicates what may be called moral qualities, and if he be unquestionably of high blood the foal is preserved from vice. Our fathers have said, *El aônd pôr ma audouche hiela*—'A horse of noble race has no vices.' An Arab will lend his stud horse gratuitously; he never accepts payment for his services. To hire out a stud horse for money is, in the eyes of an Arab, an unworthy action, and is contrary to the generosity for which he is renowned, and although the law allows it, I have never known an instance of it. But though the Arab lends his stud horse gratuitously, he does not do so to the first comer, nor for any mare. No; the suppliant is often obliged to make use of the intercession of persons of great interest, or even of his wives, if he would not see his request refused. On the other hand, the Arabs are very difficult in their choice of a stud horse, and if they cannot find one of pure blood, they prefer leaving their mares unproductive rather than put them to a common horse. To procure a good sire they do not hesitate to travel any distance. The preceding has already intimated to you my conclusion, that the sire has more to do with the foal than the dam. And my conclusion is identical with the universal opinion of the Arabs. They say, *El hôr ilebal el fahal*—'The foal follows the sire.'"

In corroboration of this opinion, he describes the Arab horses as distinguished under the following heads :—" *El Horr, El Hadjim, El Mekueref,* and *El Berdoune. El Horr* is that in which sire and dam are both of noble race; that takes the lead. *El Hadjim* is that in which the sire is noble and the dam of common race; it is considered less than *El Horr,* its name *Hadjim,* 'defective,' being derived from the word '*Hurdjiss,*' which signifies faulty. *El Mekueref* is that in which the dam is high bred and the sire is half bred; although this approaches the *Hadjim,* it is of much less value. The name of this class is derived from '*haraf*,' mixed. *El Hadjim* is superior in quality on the same principle that a man whose father is white and whose mother is a negress is superior to him whose mother is white and whose father is a negro. *El Berdoune* is that class in which both sire and dam are badly bred. This animal is a stranger to our country. The value of a horse is in its breeding."

THE PERSIAN HORSE.

SIR JOHN MALCOLM and Sir Robert Ker Porter, both of whom resided many years in Persia, are the chief authorities on this subject. The former says :—" A variety of horses are produced in Persia. The inhabitants of the districts which border on the Gulf still preserve here those races of animals which their ancestors brought from the opposite shore of Arabia. In Fars and Irak they have a mixed breed from the Arabian, which though stronger is still a small horse compared with either the Toorkoman or Khorassan breed, which are most prized by the soldiers of Persia. Both these latter races have also a great proportion of Arabian blood." Sir Robert thus alludes to them :—" The Persian horses never exceed fourteen or fourteen and a half hands high; yet certainly on the whole they are taller than Arabs. Those of the Desert and country about Hillah seem very small, but are full of bone, and of good speed. General custom feeds and waters them only at sunrise and sunset, when they are cleaned. Their usual provender is barley and chopped straw, which, if the animals are picketed, is put into a nosebag and hung from their heads; but if stabled, it is thrown into a lozenge-shaped hole, left in the thickness of the mud wall for that purpose, but much higher up than the line of our mangers, and then the animal eats at his leisure. Hay is a kind of food not known here. The bedding of the horse consists of his dung. After being exposed to the drying influence of the sun during the day, it becomes pulverized, and in that state is nightly spread under him. Little of it touches his body, that being covered by his clothing, a large *nummud* from the head to the tail, and bound firmly round his body by a very long surcingle. But this apparel is only for cold weather; in the warmer season the night-clothes are of a lighter substance, and during the heat of the day the animal is kept entirely under shade. At night he is tied in the court-yard. The horses' heads are attached to the place of security by double ropes from their halters, and the heels of their hinder legs are confined by cords of twisted hair, fastened to iron rings and pegs driven into the earth. The same custom prevailed in the time of Xenophon, and for the same reason, to secure them from being able to attack and maim each other, the whole stud generally consisting of stallions. Their keepers, however, always sleep in their rugs amongst them to prevent accidents, and sometimes notwithstanding all their care they manage to break loose, and then the combat ensues. A general neighing, screaming, kicking, and snorting soon raise the groom, and the scene for a while is terrible. Indeed no one can conceive the sudden uproar of such a moment who has not been in Eastern countries to hear it, and then all who have must bear me witness that the noise is tremendous. They seize, bite, and kick each other with the most determined fury, and frequently cannot be separated before their heads and haunches stream with blood."

THE TURKISH HORSE.

THIS VARIETY seems to be merely the Arab developed by higher food into a larger size and more massive proportions. The horses of Constantinople are often sixteen hands in height, with very elegant proportions and a crupper more highly developed than that of the Arab. They are said to be extremely docile, and the two specimens which I have seen imported into this country certainly bore out this character, both of them, though stallions, being as quiet as any English geldings. They had very high crests and arched necks; and this is said to be one of the characteristics of the breed. In the records of the turf in this country, many of the most celebrated sires are mentioned as Turks; but though imported from Turkey, it is very probable that some of these were genuine Arabs.

OTHER ASIATIC HORSES.

THE HORSES OF TOORKISTAN are described by Sir R. K. Porter as scanty in barrel, long in the leg, with ewe necks and large heads. When crossed with those of Persia, they, however, are said by him to produce a most magnificent animal, all elegance and elasticity, and of a stronger form and somewhat larger size than the best

Arabians. Sir Alexander Burns attributes to them, on the other hand, a very high crest, and large and bony though somewhat long bodies. He says, also, that in Bokhara there is a breed of Kuzzak horses, sturdy and small, with shaggy coats and very long manes and tails, much and deservedly admired.

THE TARTAR HORSES are small and narrow, with long necks, weak legs, large heads, and light middles. Nevertheless they are described as fast and untiring, and of the most hardy nature, so that they can support themselves on a quantity and quality of food upon which even our donkeys would starve.

IN VARIOUS PARTS OF TARTARY horses are found in a wild state, and present a rough inelegant form not unlike that of our New Forest ponies. In them the characteristics of the domesticated Tartar horse already described are exhibited in a marked manner, and there is every reason to believe that the two breeds are identical, and that the ranks of the latter are recruited from the enormous herds of wild horses which are found in countless thousands on the edges of the vast deserts of the country. They are generally of a red color, with a black stripe along the back, and manes and tails of the latter color, but almost always reddish at the roots of the dock and edges of the mane. The Tartars eat the flesh both of the wild and domesticated horse, and are said to cook the meat under their saddles. They also manufacture a drink called *koumiss* from the milk obtained from the mare, which is fermented and distilled into an intoxicating beverage.

IN SO VAST A COUNTRY AS INDIA, it might be expected that numerous breeds of horses would be found, varying almost as much as the climates and soils of Bengal and Cabool. In the immediate neighborhood of the three presidencies imported and country-bred Arab, as well as Persian and Turkooman horses, are common enough, as also are importations from the Cape of Good Hope, Australia, and Van Dieman's Land. English horses are not nearly so numerous, the expense and risk of the voyage deterring most people from the speculation, the doubtful nature of which may be estimated from the fact that the insurance is twenty-four to twenty-five per cent., and this only insures the landing of the animal alive; for if it is so wasted and worn as to die an hour afterwards, the policy is of no value to the insured. Williamson, in his *Wild Sports of the East*, describes the native Bengal breeds in the following terms:—" They have generally Roman noses, and sharp, narrow foreheads, much white in their eyes, ill-shaped ears, square heads, thin necks, narrow chests, shallow girths, lank bellies, cat hams, goose rumps, and switch tails! Some occasionally may be found in every respect well shaped. They are hardy and fleet, but incapable of carrying great weights. Their vice is proverbial; yet until they arrive at four or five years they are often very docile and gentle; after that period they, for the most part, are given to rearing, kicking, biting, and a thousand equally disagreeable habits." Other writers have defined the several breeds found throughout the southern parts of India, and named them also, as *Toorky*, *Cozakee*, *Tazsee*, &c.; but I understand from good authority that there are really no such breeds in existence now, and probably they were only called into being by the active imaginations of inventive writers. Large breeding studs were kept by some of the native princes, but these were mainly dependent upon imported Arabs and Persians, and could claim no peculiar strain as their own. The same mixture of blood prevails in the present day, with the exception of the horses in the northern provinces.

THE BIRMAN HORSE is very small, being seldom higher than thirteen hands, and it is said that some specimens are less than eleven. The same remark applies also to those of CHINA, SIAM, and JAVA.

THE AUSTRALIAN HORSE.

THE IRISHMAN'S FIFTH QUARTER OF THE WORLD is now abundantly supplied with horses of the first class, in size, speed, and stoutness, though little more than half a century ago the animal was altogether unknown there. At first, from the proximity of India and the Cape of Good Hope, the horses of these colonies, and those of inferior value only, were imported into the new settlement; but about the year 1835 great efforts were made by several enterprising settlers, both in the Island of Van Dieman and also on the continent of Australia, and several horses of good breeding were imported from this country, especially by Mr. Wilmore in the former island. It was soon found that the climate is admirably suited to this animal, and there are now colonial-bred horses, adapted for the turf and the road, as well as for agricultural purposes, superior in soundness and probably in stoutness, even if they are deficient in face, as compared with the British thoroughbred. As far as I know, no Australian horse has been imported into England, so that we have no means of comparing the two on terms advantageous to the mother country; nor possibly can we altogether depend upon the glowing accounts which are furnished us of the appearance and performances of our Antipodean rivals. Still I am inclined to believe that as the soil and climate are admitted to improve the appearance of the imported horses, as indeed they do all our domestic animals, and as disease of all kinds is extremely rare, so it will be found that in all good qualities the Australian horse is at least on a par with our own. Their breeders are so spirited and determined that neither money nor trouble is spared in procuring the best blood, an evidence of which is afforded by the fact that at the recent sale of Lord Londesborough's stud, the large sum of 3120 guineas (about $15,000) was invested for

Australia. This, probably, is the heaviest price yet paid at one sale by any colonial breeder, but numerous smaller speculations have been going on for the last twenty years. Hence, whatever position is attained by our friends over the water, they will entirely owe to the parent country; and I strongly suspect that before long we shall have to go to them to procure sound horses of high breeding for our own studs.

CHAPTER IV.

THE HORSES OF THE WESTERN HEMISPHERE.

The South American Horse—The Mustang—The Indian Pony—The Canadian Horse—The Morgan Horse—The American Trotter—The Narraganset Pacer—The American Thoroughbred—The Vermont Cart-Horse—The Conestoga Draught-Horse.

THE SOUTH AMERICAN HORSE.

FOR SOME TIME AFTER THE DISCOVERY OF AMERICA, at the conclusion of the fifteenth century, the horse was entirely unknown in that hemisphere, but according to Azara a few specimens were introduced there by the Spaniards in the year 1535, and in the year 1537 several were shipped to Paraguay. From these have been bred the countless herds which have since spread over the whole southern part of the western world, and passing the Isthmus of Panama have wandered into North America. In both these divisions the horse runs wild, wherever there are plains suitable to him, and not yet brought under cultivation; but it is in the south that the wild horse is to be found in the greatest numbers, on the extensive plains which stretch almost unbroken from the shores of La Plata to Patagonia. Here herds numbering some thousands in each are to be met with, each under the guidance of a master stallion, who enforces entire submission to his will as long as he has the power to do so. Here the native Gaucho has only to throw his *lasso*, and he can at any time supply himself with a horse which will carry him for miles at a hand gallop, when he changes him for another, and is thus always mounted at a cheap and easy rate. In this way Captain Head rode all across the continent from one shore to the other, nearly using up one horse in the course of fifty or sixty miles, and then looking out for another before the first was so spent as to be unable to assist him in making the exchange. These wild horses greatly resemble their Spanish ancestors in make and shape. They are said to be possessed of a fair amount of speed, but not above the average of foreign breeds. They are, however, from their roving habits, in excellent wind, and it is said that a Gaucho has been known to ride one fresh caught nearly a hundred miles without drawing bit.

THE MUSTANG, OR WILD HORSE OF NORTH AMERICA.

LIKE THE WILD HORSES OF SOUTH AMERICA, those of Mexico and California are in all probability descended from Spanish blood, and indeed it is impossible now to discover, with anything like certainty, the source of the Indian Ponies, large herds of which run wild in the northern and north-western parts of this extensive continent. So little do the Americans now know or care about these wild horses, that the late Mr. Herbert, who has treated of the American Horse in two vols. quarto, omits all mention of them, excepting the most cursory allusion to the Mustang as the origin of the Indian Pony, in common with the Canadian horse. I shall, therefore, not weary my readers with extracts from Mr. Catlin's somewhat fanciful writings, but at once proceed to allude to the modern domesticated breeds of horses met with in the United States and Canada.

ACCORDING TO MR. HERBERT, who seems to have taken great pains to arrive at the truth, "with the one solitary exception of the Norman horse in Canada, no special breeds have ever taken root as such, or been bred, or even attempted to be bred, in them purity, in any part of America. In Canada East the Norman horse, imported by the early settlers, was bred for many generations entirely unmixed; and, as the general agricultural horse of the province, exists, yet so stunted in size by the cold climate and the rough usage to which he has been subjected for centuries, but in no wise degenerated, for he possesses all the honesty, courage, endurance, hardihood, soundness of constitution, and characteristic excellence of feet and legs of his progenitor." Besides this native Canadian there are also, among the more active kinds, the Morgan horse, the American trotter, the Narraganset pacer, and the thorough-bred descended from English imported horses, with scarcely any admixture of native blood; and of the agricultural varieties, the Vermont and Conestoga draught-horses, in addition to several others not so easily made out.

THE INDIAN PONY.

THE INDIAN PONY, which seldom or never exceeds thirteen hands in height, is remarkable for activity and strength, as compared with its size, appearing, like its Scotch congener, to be almost overwhelmed with its rider, whose feet nearly touch the ground, yet moving under its load with freedom. It has a high crest, and a flowing mane and tail, with a proud carriage of the head of a very pleasing character. The body is strongly built, and the legs and feet are made of the most lasting materials. Large herds of these ponies run wild in the prairies of the north-west, and many are brought into Canada for the use of the inhabitants.

THE CANADIAN HORSE.

THE CANADIAN HORSE.

THE CANADIAN HORSE is generally about fourteen to fifteen hands high, and is a remarkably hardy animal, capable of travelling very long distances, but in his pure condition not above the average in speed. When crossed, however, with a thorough-bred horse, he combines the speed of the latter with his own endurance and iron constitution and legs, and in this way a great many of the best American trotters are bred. Mr. Herbert says, " His crest is lofty, and his demeanor proud and courageous; his breast is full and broad; his shoulders strong, though somewhat straight, and a little inclined to be heavy; his back broad, and his croup round, fleshy, and muscular; his ribs are not, however, so much arched, nor are they so well closed up, as his general shape and build would lead one to expect; his legs and feet are admirable—the bone large and flat, and the sinews big and nervous as steel springs; his feet seem almost unconscious of disease; his fetlocks are shaggy; his mane voluminous and massive, not seldom, if untrained, falling on both sides of his neck, and his tail abundant, both having a peculiar crimpled wave, if I may so express myself, the like of which I never saw in any horse which had not some strain of his blood." I give a sketch on the preceding page of one of these horses, showing the shape and action peculiar to them. It is said by good judges to be an excellent likeness.

THE MORGAN HORSE.

THE MORGAN HORSE has recently been paraded in America as a distinct strain, kept pure in its own district for more than half a century, and descended from a single horse, in the possession of Mr. Justin Morgan, a schoolmaster in Vermont. In the present day the "Morgans" are so much sought after that in the year 1856 the Agricultural Society of Vermont offered a prize for the best essay on the subject, which was awarded to Mr. Linsley, an inhabitant of the same state. According to this authority, the founder of the family, or strain, was got by a horse called "True Briton," which was said to have been stolen, and whose pedigree is therefore doubtful. Mr. Linsley endeavors to prove, however, that he was a son of the English thorough-bred horse Traveller, which he assumes to be identical with the son of Partner, known as Morton's Old Traveller, giving as his authority a pedigree inserted in the Albany "Cultivator" of 1846. The same authority is also adduced to prove that the dam of True Briton and also of Justin Morgan's horse were of nearly pure English blood, and that the latter was descended from the famous "Cub" mare; but the facts adduced seem of the most doubtful nature, and I believe that the Morgan horse would in this country be considered as undoubtedly half-bred.

Mr. Linsley describes the founder of the Morgan strain in the following terms:—He "was about fourteen hands high, and weighed about nine hundred and fifty pounds. His color was dark bay, with black legs, mane, and tail. He had no white hair upon him. His mane and tail were coarse and heavy, but not so massive as has been sometimes described; the hair of both was straight, and not inclined to curl. His head was good, not extremely small, but lean and bony, the face straight, forehead broad, ears small, and very fine, but set rather wide apart. His eyes were medium size, very dark, and prominent, and showed no white round the edge of the lid" (Qy. iris?). "His nostrils were very large, the muzzle small, and the lips close and firm. His back and legs were perhaps his most noticeable points. The former was very short, the shoulder-blades and thigh-bones being very long and oblique, and the loins exceedingly broad and muscular. His body was rather long, round, and deep, close ribbed up; chest deep and wide, with the breast-bone projecting a good deal in front. His legs were short, close jointed, thin, but very wide, hard and free from meat, with muscles that were remarkably large for a horse of his size, and this superabundance of muscle manifested itself at every step. His hair was short, and at almost all seasons soft and glossy. He had a little long hair about the fetlocks, and for two or three inches above the fetlock on the back side of the legs; the rest of his limbs were entirely free from it. His feet were small, but well shaped, and he was in every respect perfectly sound and free from blemish. He was a very fast walker. In trotting his gait was slow and smooth, and his step short and nervous; he was not what in these days would be called fast, and we think it doubtful whether he could trot a mile much, if any, within four minutes, though it is claimed by many that he could trot it in three. Although he raised his feet but little, he never stumbled. His proud, bold, and fearless style of movement, and his vigorous untiring action, have perhaps never been surpassed."

He describes him as being fast for short distances, by which he explains that he means a quarter of a mile, which he says was the usual distance run in those days. From this celebrated horse are descended, more or less remotely, "Black Hawk," "Ethan Allen," "American Eagle," and a host of horses celebrated for gameness, and many of them for fast-trotting powers. But those who dispute the claims of Mr. Justin Morgan's horse to be considered the founder of the family, assert that before his time a similar horse prevailed in this district which was made up of crosses between the Canadian horse and the English thorough-bred. I shall, however, leave this much-vexed question for the Americans to settle among themselves, contenting myself with a description of the modern Morgan horse as he is recognised throughout the states of America. He is generally, though not universally, admitted to be very stout and enduring, with good action, especially in the trot, and great hardness of constitution. He shows very little evidence of pure blood; indeed it may be said that the reverse is the case, as he invariably possesses a thick and long mane and tail, with a considerable curl in both, signs which may be truly said are fatal to his claims. In height he seldom exceeds fifteen hands. His frame is corky, but not remarkably well put together, there being generally a deficiency in the coupling of the back and loins. The forehead is very light, and carried high, somewhat in the fashion of the Canadians, but not so heavy in the crest and junction of the neck to the shoulder, though the setting of the head is equally thick. On the whole, the Morgan horse may be described as extremely useful, but deficient in what we call "quality," in proportion to the absence of thorough blood.

THE AMERICAN TROTTER.

THE TRUE MODERN TROTTING HORSE is a most remarkable instance of what may be done by keeping an animal to one kind of work for generations, and selecting the specimens best fitted for it to breed from. In this country a thorough-bred horse, or even one of nearly pure blood, could not be found at any price to trot a mile in three minutes, yet in America there are plenty, of blood almost entirely derived from the English turf horse, which will perform the distance in two minutes and forty seconds, and some in considerably less time. In America private and public trotting matches in harness have been for many years the chief amusement of the town population, and, until very recently, when flat racing or running, as it is called there, has been more developed, a fast trotter fetched a higher price than any other description of horse. Trotting matches are, in fact, *the* national sport, just as racing is that of our own country. Latterly, however, the amusement has been somewhat on the decline, the aristocratic classes holding themselves aloof, and patronizing the turf in preference. Still there is no diminution in the pace of their trotters, and, on the contrary, the celebrated Flora Temple has recently made the best time on record, having, on the 15th of October, 1859, when fourteen years old, done a third mile heat in two minutes, nineteen and three-quarter seconds, and having, in June, 1861, performed three separate mile heats in the wonderfully short time of seven minutes, six and a half seconds.*

Mr. Herbert, in his quarto work on "The Horse of America," clearly shows the reason why our transatlantic cousins excel us in their trotters, and why they take to this species of amusement in preference to others. After enumerating several which do not appear to us quite so cogent as to him, he more pertinently says, "Another reason, inferior in practical truth to the others adduced, but physically superior, is this,—that before American trotters could be generally used in Great Britain, the whole system of British road-making must be altered, which is not likely to occur. On an ordinary English macadamized turnpike, which is exactly the same as the hardest central part of the New York Third Avenue, without any soft track alongside of it, an American trotter would pound his shoes off in an hour's trot, and his feet off in a week's driving; and this is doubtless, whatever may be said of the objections heretofore offered, one which must operate for ever against the general use of trotters after the American fashion,

---

* Since the above was written the renowned "Dexter" has eclipsed all previous records, having trotted three separate mile heats in 6m. 5s., and a mile in the unprecedented time of 2m. 17¼s.—EDITOR.

unless they be trained and kept exclusively for sporting purposes. This, however, is no more, but even less likely to occur than the total alteration of the whole system of English road-making, and the entire change of the tastes and habits of the English people: since the point which renders the trotting horse so popular here would then be wanting, namely, his equal adaptability to ordinary road driving and purposes of general utility, and to occasional matching and turf amusements of a peculiar though inferior description." This is the true cause of the "decline and fall" of trotting horses in England, for in the early part of the nineteenth century there were ten good performers on the trot for one now. The pace is not a natural one, and in its highest perfection, especially, it must be developed by constant practice. But this is forbidden on our modern roads, which, as Mr. Herbert truly remarks, would ruin the legs and feet of any horse ridden or driven at such a pace as to do a mile in two minutes and thirty seconds. I fully believe that the horses of America have sounder legs and feet than those of our own country, partly from being kept cooler in their stables, partly from their being less stimulated by inordinate quantities of oats and beans, but chiefly from their ancestors having been less injured by hard roads than those of our own. If this is the case we must have in every succeeding generation more and more difficulty in getting sound roadsters, and such, I believe, is really the fact.

BY MANY people it is supposed that the American trotter is a distinct breed or strain of horses, and that we can in this country easily obtain plenty of horses able to do their mile "within the thirties," by importing individuals and breeding from them. This hypothesis, however, appears to be unfounded according to the evidence of Mr. Herbert, as recorded in his " magnum opus," and that of other writers in the New York sporting press. The former gentleman, who is "well up" on this subject, says:—"And first we shall find that the time trotter in America is neither an original animal of a peculiar and distinct breed, nor even an animal of very long existence since his first creation. Secondly, we shall find that in an almost incredibly short space of time, owing to the great demand for and universal popularity of the animal, united to a perfectly devised, and now ubiquitously understood, system of breaking, training, and driving him so as to develop all his qualities to the utmost, the trotting horse of high speed, good endurance, showy style of going, and fine figure, has become from a rarity a creature of every-day occurrence, to be met with by dozens in the eastern and middle states, and scarcely any longer regarded as a trotter, unless he can do his mile in somewhere about two minutes and a half. Thirdly, it will appear that the trotting horse is, in no possible sense, a distinct race, breed, or family of the horse;

and that his qualities as a trotter cannot be ascribed or traced to his origin from, or connection with, any one blood more than another. It is true, and it is to be regretted, that of trotting horses the pedigrees have been so little alluded to, and probably from the nature of circumstances are so seldom attainable, that few, indeed, can be directly traced to any distance in blood. Enough *is* known, however, to show that some horses of first-rate powers have come from the Canadian or Norman-French stock; some from the ordinary undistinguished country horse of the southernmost of the midland states; some from the Vermont family; some from the Indian pony; and lastly, some mainly, if not entirely, from the thorough-bred. To no one of these families can any superiority be attributed as producing trotters of great speed. All have shown their specimens by means of which to claim their share in the production. Only it may be affirmed, generally, that while some very famous trotting horses have been nearly, if not entirely, thorough-bred, the low, lazy, lounging, daisy-cutting gait and action of the full-blooded horse of Oriental blood is not generally compatible with great trotting action or speed. Still it is true that the best time-trotters have not the round, high-stepped action which is prized in carriage-horses, or parade-horses for show, and which probably originated and existed to the greatest extent in the Flemish or the Hanoverian horse of the coldest of all imaginable strains of blood; and that they have in a great measure the long reaching stride, the quick gather, and the comparatively low step of the thorough-bred."

THE NARRAGANSET PACER.

It is supposed that this beautiful variety of the American horse, which is now nearly or quite extinct, is descended from the Spanish horse. There are several traditions afloat in support of this and other theories, but by general consent it is admitted that the above theory as to his origin is the true one. According to this, he was introduced into New England by Governor Robinson, from Andalusia, and for many years the breed was kept up for the supply of Cuba, the voyage being much shorter than that from the mother country, Spain. These horses were of good size and natural pacers, the action being on alternate sides, but remarkably easy, which is more than can always be said of the modern rackers or pacers. As the roads improved, however, in the West India islands, carriages were introduced, and then, the demand ceasing almost entirely, the breed was neglected, and is now unknown in its pure form.

THE AMERICAN THOROUGH-BRED.

Until the English Thorough-bred Horse is described, it is scarcely possible to enter fully into the pedigree of the American, descended as the latter is from stock imported from the mother country. But, taking the fact for granted, I may proceed to allude to the progress which has been made in the United States, from the date of the first importation. It appears that shortly prior to the year 1750, a Mr. Ogle, the Governor of Maryland, was in possession of Spark, presented to him by Lord Baltimore. About the same time he also imported Queen Mab, by Musgrove's gray Arab; and, soon afterwards, Colonel Tasker obtained Selima, daughter of the Godolphin Arabian; while Colonel Colville's Miss Colville, known in the English Stud Book as Wilkes' Old Hautboy mare, Colonel Taylor's Jenny Cameron, and Routh's Crab, were severally introduced into the colony. In 1747, Monkey, by the Lonsdale bay Arab, though in his twenty-second year, crossed the Atlantic, and got some good stock, followed during the next year by Jolly Roger, by Roundhead, out of a Partner mare. About 1764, Fearnought, a son of Regulus and Silvertail, and therefore of the very highest English blood, went to America, and within a few years of that date Morton's Traveller, by Partner, out of a mare by the Bloody Buttocks Arabian, which completes the list of the importations prior to the War of Independence. It must be observed, that, before the year 1829, no Turf Register existed in America, and hence there is not the same guarantee for the fidelity of a pedigree as in England, where there are authentic records which reach to a much earlier period. Moreover, the war upset the homes of so many families, that multitudes of documents were lost; but, nevertheless, I believe sufficient has been preserved to prove the authenticity of the pedigrees belonging to the horses which I have enumerated, and whose progeny can be traced down to the present day, their blood being mingled with that of numerous importations of a more recent date. The love of racing was very soon implanted in the colonists of Maryland and Virginia, from whom it spread to North and South Carolina, and in these southern states the sport has been kept up to the present day with great spirit. Tennessee was inoculated with the virus of the racing mania soon after its first settlement, as also may be said of Kentucky, both states having possessed some very celebrated horses at various times. New York joined in at a much later period than the southern states, no organized racing-club existing there until after the commencement of the present century; although there were small racecourses at Newmarket and Jamaica before the Revolution. But the energy of the true Yankee sent the New Yorkites ahead, and they soon became worthy rivals of the southern statesmen. From 1815 to 1845, the great stables of the North and South were carried on under a most honorable rivalry; but at the second of these dates, it so happened that a vast number of the most energetic supporters of the turf in the northern states withdrew from the arena, and, as they disappeared, none filled the gaps, except a few professed trainers and jockeys, who carried racing on entirely as a business, and regardless of that honorable spirit which had previously distinguished it. Trotting also came into fashion, and the fanatics preached a crusade against both, which took double effect upon the sport, already tottering to its fall. It may indeed be said, that from 1845 to 1855, racing in America was confined entirely to the south; but about 1855 or 1856 a new jockey-club was established in New York, and its members laid out a new racecourse on Long Island; but still the second effort was not equal to the first, and New Orleans has taken the wind altogether out of the Long Island sails, by the spirited attempt which has been made by Mr. Ten Broeck to match his stud against the first English horses on their own ground. That he has failed in carrying off the Derby with Umpire is no proof of the general inferiority of American horses to those of England, any more than his other great successes are enough to insure a conviction of the opposite condition in any unprejudiced mind. Umpire might have been an exceptional horse, and granting to him the high form which he was last year (1859) assured to possess, it would prove nothing *quoad* the general form of the horses of his country. Still it cannot be denied that they are much nearer to our own than was believed to be the case before Mr. Ten Broeck came among us; but how near they are is yet a vexed question, which will take some time to settle.

THE AMERICAN THOROUGH-BRED HORSE is said to be much stouter than the modern English strains; and without doubt Mr. Ten Broeck's Prioress can stay better than most English horses, though she is not considered by the Americans themselves to be quite up to the best staying form which they possess. This subject, however, will be better considered after the performances of the English horse are carefully examined. It must be remembered that, with the exception of the horses recently brought over to this country, we have no means of comparison beyond the time test, which is not a reliable one; firstly, because we have no time-races here; and, secondly, because none of our long distances are run from end to end. As far as I have had an opportunity of seeing, and with the single exception of Charleston, all Mr. Ten Broeck's horses have been extremely narrow, the crack Umpire in particular being "like two deal boards nailed together," as the "men of stable mind" say here. His hips are the narrowest 1 ever saw in a horse supposed to be of first class, and those of Prioress are not much more developed. The celebrated horse, Lexington, who is out of the same mare as Umpire, is also reported to have been very narrow in the hips, so that probably this pecu-

Copyright Secured.

LEXINGTON.

From a Drawing from Life by E. Troye.

larity runs throughout that strain of blood, but whether derived from Alice Carneal or from Boston (who got both Lexington and Lecompte, the latter the sire of Umpire) I cannot say. Nevertheless, unless the time-test is utterly fallacious, both Lexington and Lecompte must have been stout, for they have each done four miles, under seven stone two, in seven minutes twenty-six seconds, with a start similar to that adopted in England. Lexington, with the same kind of start, has performed the same task in seven minutes twenty-three and a half seconds, and with a running start against time, in the extraordinarily short time of seven minutes nineteen and three-quarter seconds.*

THE VERMONT CART-HORSE.

A DISTINCT BREED of draught-horses under this name is described by Mr. Herbert as existing in Vermont and the adjacent country, though now, he says, less marked than it was prior to the introduction of railroads. I cannot, however, find any other authority for it, nor do I quite agree with the above writer in thinking the breed, if he rightly describes it, as identical with the Cleveland Bay. He says, "These are the very models of what draught-horses should be; combining immense power with great quickness, a very respectable turn of speed, fine show, and good action. These animals have almost invariably lofty crests, thin withers, and well set on heads; and although they are emphatically draught-horses, they have none of that shagginess of mane, tail, and fetlocks, which indicates a descent from the black horse of Lincolnshire, and none of that peculiar curliness or waviness which marks the existence of Canadian or Norman blood for many generations, and which is discoverable in the manes and tails of very many of the horses which claim to be *pure* Morgans. The peculiar characteristic, however, of these horses, is the shortness of their backs, the roundness of their barrels, and the closeness of their ribbing up. One would say that they are ponies until he comes to stand beside them, when he is astonished to find that they are oftener over than under sixteen hands in height."

THE CONESTOGA DRAUGHT-HORSE.

THE LAST on the list of American horses is that known under the above name, which was given to it from being produced in the valley of Conestoga, within the state of Pennsylvania. It is a very large muscular horse, often reaching to seventeen hands and upwards, and closely resembling the heaviest breeds of German and

---

* In a race against time (October 17th, 1867), Kentucky, the famous son of Lexington, then four years old, ran 4 miles in 7 min. 31¾ sec. The first two miles were run in 3 min. 36 sec., the first three in 5 min. 29 sec. Kentucky carried a weight of 120 lbs.

CONESTOGA DRAUGHT-HORSE.

Flemish cart-horses. The early settlers of this part of the United States were mostly Germans, and they either brought over with them some of the horses of their country, or else they have since selected from those within their reach the animals most resembling in appearance their old favorites when in their fatherland. There is, however, no record of the origin of the breed, and all that can be done is to describe it as it now exists.

THE ACCOMPANYING sketch embodies the general appearance of these horses, and by comparing it with the London dray-horse, it will be seen that it differs only slightly, having the same heavy outline of form, united with similar comparatively light limbs, but not burdened with the mountains of flesh and heavy crests which have been produced in England for purposes of show. In Pennsylvania, these horses are chiefly used for wagons, and some few of them, when of inferior shape, for the canal traffic. They are good honest workers, and are quicker and lighter in their action than might be expected from their weight. Indeed, some of them are still used for heavy carriages; but even in Pennsylvania, for quick work, they are generally replaced by the Vermont horse, or some nondescript of mixed blood, with which America is completely overrun.

In color they follow the Flemish horses, except that black is rare among them, but like the Flemish they are free from chestnut, and the larger proportion of them are bay, brown, or iron grays.

CHAPTER V.

THE THOROUGH-BRED HORSE.

Early Maturity—Object of Encouraging the Breed—Essentials in the Thorough-bred—Purity of Blood—External Formation—Height—Color—Coat, Mane, and Tail.

EARLY MATURITY.

IT IS AN UNDENIABLE fact, as I believe, that preternaturally early maturity is incompatible with lasting qualities of any kind; but, though the same rule generally holds good throughout nature, there are some exceptions. Thus, the oak is more lasting than the larch, and the elephant outlives the horse, but the goose and the duck, which arrive at maturity in the same number of months, do not live through a corresponding series of years. The forcing process in gardening is always productive of tenderness, whether the produce be the cucumber or the sea-kale, and this tenderness is only another name for imperfect formation to resist decay. In the days of Eclipse and Childers they were permitted to attain their full growth without forcing, and, not being wanted till five years old, their ligaments, tendons, and bones had plenty of time to be consolidated before they were submitted to the strains and jerks of the extended gallop. There is also reason to believe that they were not nearly so much or so soon stimulated by large feeds of oats, as is now invariably the custom, but that they were allowed to remain at grass, with the shelter of a hovel, during the first three or four years of their lives. All this is now changed; the foal is filled with corn as soon as he will eat it, and at the end of the first year he is furnished as much as the old-fashioned three-year-old. One chief difficulty of the trainer now is to keep his horse sound, and, unfortunately, as disease is in most cases hereditary, and too many unsound stallions are bred from, the difficulty is yearly on the increase. Without doubt roaring is far more common than it used to be, and the possession of enlarged joints, and back sinews, is the rule instead of the exception. During the last ten years, the Derby has five times been won by an unsound animal, which the trainer was almost immediately afterwards obliged to put out of work, either from diseased feet or a break-down, and yet few breeders think of refusing to use such horses as these. Nevertheless, good legs and feet, and a hearty constitution, are no small recommendations, and Mr. Merry may thank them for winning him the great prize of the year 1860, with Thormanby, a son of that wonderful mare Alice Hawthorne. Thormanby, however, is not an instance of a colt having been reserved till he was arrived at his growth, for there are few horses which have been more used, having run fourteen times as a two-year-old; but his naturally excellent legs and feet, and the fine down on which he is trained, have enabled him to pull through unscathed. Now the reliance which was placed by his backers on these good qualities, proves that he is an exception to the rule; for if they were at all common, they would be of comparatively little advantage. The truth really is, that the average racehorse of modern times is of such forced growth, that he is unable to bear the wear and tear of training as he used to do, and hence a much larger percentage of unsound animals is to be met with. He is bred mainly for speed, superadded to which is as much stoutness and soundness of constitution as can be procured among the most speedy horses at the service of the breeder. By a perseverance in this method of selection, he has undoubtedly become more speedy, and less lasting in proportion to his speed, that is to say, he cannot be extended for as long a *time* as he used to bear with impunity. But that he cannot cover as much ground in a given time as formerly is, I think, an error,—for there is every reason to believe that any distance may now be run in as short a time at least, as either in the middle of the last century or the beginning of this.

OBJECT OF ENCOURAGING THE BREED OF HORSES.

THE GREAT OBJECT of encouraging the breed of racehorses is, however, lost sight of, if suitable crosses for hunting, cavalry, and hack-mares cannot be obtained from their ranks. In these three kinds, soundness of the feet and legs is all important, together with a capacity to bear a continuation of severe work. These qualities are highly developed in the Arab, and until lately were met with in his descendants on the English turf. Even now a horse with a stain in his pedigree will not bear the amount of training which a thorough-bred will sustain, his health and spirits soon giving way if forced to go through the work which the racehorse requires to make him "fit." But the legs and feet of the latter are the drawbacks to his use, and the trainer of the present day will generally be sadly taxed to make them last through a dry summer. Our modern roads are also much harder since the introduction of macadamization, and thus, in proportion to our greater demands, is the absence of the material to meet them. A hack that is not pretty well bred is now neglected, except for high weights, because his paces are not soft and pleasant, and he does not satisfy the eye. But how many of the fashionable sort will bear constant use on the road without becoming lame? And how many sound horses are there to be met with out of a hundred, taken at random from the ranks of any kind tolerably well bred? Every horse proprietor will tell you, scarcely five per cent.; and some will even go so far as to say, that a sound horse is utterly unknown. In considering the principles and practice of breeding, I shall again refer to this subject; but I wish now to impress upon my readers that while the racehorse of 1860 is as fast as ever, as stout as ever, and as good looking as ever, he is made of more perishable materials in proportion as he comes to maturity at an earlier period. Any of our modern two-year-olds would probably give two stone, and a beating to Eclipse at the same age, but if afterwards they were put to half-bred mares for the purpose of getting hacks, chargers, or hunters, the stock of Eclipse or Childers would be much more valuable than any which we have at present. We are sadly in want of sound and well bred stallions for general purposes, and if the government of the country does not soon interfere, and adopt some means of furnishing these islands with them, we shall be beaten on our own ground, and shall have to import sound useful horses from Belgium, France, Hungary, or Prussia, whichever country can best spare them. The old-fashioned and sound thorough-bred horse has been the means of improving the above three breeds; and even now we possess horses which are perfect in every other respect but soundness, being excellent hacks, hunters, and light carriage-horses, and often all in one. This last kind is the perfection of the horse; and if many such could be produced it would be a great advantage, because most people would like a horse which could "make himself generally useful," if such an animal could be obtained. Without high-breeding, however, this is impossible; and yet with most of our purest strains, though it is attainable for a time, the condition in which it exists does not last long, in consequence of the effect of the hard road upon their soft legs or contracted feet. Consequently, as I have already remarked, there is a necessity for government interference to produce such a breed of thorough-bred horses, by careful selection, as shall give us the above three kinds of horses useful in civil life, from which may be culled a plentiful supply of cavalry horses, whenever wanted; for the very same qualities are demanded in all, and what will suit the one will be equally advantageous to the other.

But even though the thorough-bred horse is well fitted to compete with others in all cases where speed is the chief point of trial—

as in flat-racing, steeple-chasing, hunting, &c.,—yet he is not so well qualified for some kinds of harness-work, or for road-work of any kind, as the horse expressly bred for these purposes. There is no doubt that thorough-bred horses *might* be selected and bred expressly for this kind of work, and would excel all others, because originally their limbs and constitutions were at least as sound as, or perhaps even sounder than, any other class of horses; but while they are selected and bred solely for speed, without much reference to these other qualities, it is useless to expect much improvement; but on the contrary, they may be expected to become yearly more and more soft and yielding. For many purposes the Eastern horse is wholly unfit—as, for instance, for heavy and dead pulls; here his high courage, light weight, and hasty temper are adverse to the performance of the task, and he is far excelled by the old English, or modern improved cart-horse. No thorough-bred horse would try again and again at a dead pull like many of our best breeds of cart-horses; and therefore he is little calculated for work which requires this slow struggling kind of exertion. The pull of the Eastern horse, or his descendant, is a snatch; and though it may to a certain extent be modified by use, yet it can never be brought up to the standard of the English cart-horse, even if the weight of carcase and size and strength of limb of the former could be sufficiently increased.

ESSENTIALS IN THE THOROUGH-BRED.

SUCH THEN ARE THE GENERAL QUALITIES of the thorough-bred horse and the purposes to which he can be beneficially applied. It remains now to consider the formation and *specific* characteristics best adapted to the turf, which is his chief arena; and also to the hunting-field, which now absorbs a very large number of his breed. Finally, it will be necessary to consider him as a means of improving other breeds, such as the cavalry-charger, hack and harness horse, but these subjects will fall under the respective heads here mentioned.

PURITY OF BLOOD.

IN THE FIRST PLACE PURITY OF BLOOD must be considered as a *sine quâ non*, for without it a horse cannot be considered thoroughbred, and therefore we have only to ascertain the exact meaning of the term "blood." It is not to be supposed that there is any real difference between the blood of the thorough-bred horse, and that of the half-bred animal; no one could discriminate between the two by any known means; the term "blood" is here synonymous with *breed*, and by purity of blood is meant purity in the breeding of the individual animal under consideration; that is to say, that the horse which is entirely bred from one source is pure from any mixture with any other, and may be a pure Suffolk

Punch, or a pure Clydesdale, or a pure thorough-bred horse. But all these terms are comparative, since there is no such animal as a perfectly purely bred horse of any breed, whether cart-horse, hack, or racehorse; all have been produced from an admixture with other kinds, and though *now* kept as pure as possible, yet they were originally compounded from varying elements; and thus the racehorse of 1700, was obtained from a mixture of Turks, Arabs, and Barbs. Even the best and purest thorough-breds are stained with some slight cross with the old English or Spanish horse, as I have heretofore shown, and therefore it is only by comparison that the word pure is applicable to them or any others. But since the thorough-bred horse, as he is called, has long been bred for the race-course, and selections have been made with that view alone, it is reasonable to suppose that this breed is the best for that purpose, and that a stain of any other is a deviation from the clearest stream into one more muddy, and therefore impure; the consequence is, that the animal bred from the impure source fails in some of the essential characteristics of the pure breed, and is in so far useless for this particular object. Now, in practice this is found to be the case, for in every instance it has resulted that the horse bred with the slightest deviation from the sources indicated by the stud-book, is unable to compete in lasting power with those which are entirely of pure blood. Hence it is established as a rule, that for racing purposes every horse must be thorough-bred; that is, as I have already explained, descended from a sire and dam whose names are met with in the stud-book.

EXTERNAL FORMATION.

NEXT COMES THE EXTERNAL SHAPE or conformation of the racehorse, which is a subject very much studied by those who have the selection and management of them. Experienced trainers, and those who have watched the performances of the celebrities of the turf for successive years, will tell you that "the horse can run in all forms," and so no doubt he *can* as an exception, but the rule nevertheless is, that there is a standard which should be regarded as the best suited for the race-course, and this will vary somewhat according to the performance which is required of each individual. There is no doubt that the most skilful selection is not always attended with success, and the statistics of the turf do not lead us to believe that £1000 invested under the advice of John Scott or John Day, in the purchase of a yearling, will always bring a remuneration. Indeed, the contrary has so often been the case, that high-priced yearlings are generally regarded with suspicion, when they make their first appearance on the course. The winner of the Derby of 1860 went a-begging, and was at last bought for a very moderate price. So also with Butterfly, the winner of the Oaks, no store was set upon her until she came to be tried; and even on the morning of the race she was not generally thought good enough to win. The celebrated Blink Bonny was a mean-looking mare, and would not have fetched £50 at Tattersall's, from her appearance

FISHERMAN.

alone, and that wonderful animal Fisherman was never liked till he proved his powers. Still, it cannot be denied that a good judge will select the ten best horses out of twenty, or perhaps out of a hundred; but he will possibly leave the very best out of his list. The theoretical rule is simple enough, but it requires great experience, and a good eye to carry it out in practice. It is simply this, that, *cæteris paribus*, the horse which is formed in the mould most like that of the greatest number of good racehorses, will run the best. Thus, supposing it is found that out of fifty good horses, forty-nine have neat heads, light necks, deep chests, oblique shoulders, long racing hind-quarters, strong hocks, &c., the presumption will be that a horse resembling those forty-nine in shape, will also resemble them in speed and endurance. On the other hand, it is admitted on the turf, that high-breeding is of more consequence than external shape, and that of two horses, one perfect in shape, but of an inferior strain of blood, and the other of the most winning blood, but not so well formed in shape, the latter will be the most likely to perform to the satisfaction of his owner on the racecourse. On this principle the proverb has been framed and handed down to us, that " an ounce of blood is worth a pound of bone," and with the above explanation such is really the case. But in spite of all this recognised superiority of blood, it is indisputable that for the highest degree of success there must be not only high purity of blood, and that of the most winning strains, but there must also be a frame of the most useful character, if not always of the most elegant form. Many of our very best horses have been plain, and even coarse-looking—as, for instance, most of the Melbournes, and especially that very fast horse, Sir Tatton Sykes ; but in spite of their plainness, all their points are good and useful, and the deficiency is in elegance, not in real utility. On the other hand, there are some strains which unite elegance with utility, such as the fast and stout Venisons, which are remarkable for their beautiful frames and neat Arabian heads. But there must always be a distinction made between what is really useful and what is only agreeable to the eye. There are some characteristics which, over and above their mechanical advantages, indicate high-breeding, and as such are regarded with especial favor by purchasers. For these a term has of late years been invented, the meaning of which is well understood, but somewhat difficult to define. Thus, we hear it often remarked, that a particular horse is deficient in "quality," or that he has it in perfection; and in proportion to the one or the other of these conditions is he meant to be praised or condemned. . It is not simply a word synonymous with "breeding." for a horse may show high breeding, and yet be deficient in "quality," but if with a look which convinces you that he has a pure pedigree, he conjoins a perfect symmetry in all his parts, and in the shapes displayed by the thorough-bred, he then comes up to the description which stamps a horse in these days with the highest seal of approbation, for " he has plenty of quality."

But what is the recognised form of the racehorse? I must here explain to the tyro that the word "form" is used with two different significations by racing men, and like the word "box" is very puzzling to foreigners. In the common acceptation it is synonymous with "shape," and merely means the mechanical development of the individual. But in the language of the turf, when we say that a horse is "in form," we intend to convey to our hearers that he is in high condition and fit to run. So again, the word is used in still another sense, for we speak of a horse's "form" when we wish to allude to his powers on the turf, as compared with other well-known animals. Thus, if it is supposed that two three-year-olds, carrying the same weight, would run a mile-and-a-half, and come in abreast, it is said, that "the form" of the one is equal to that of the other. It is necessary, therefore, in order to make a description intelligible, when using the term in its mechanical signification, to add the adjective, external, although, at first sight, it may appear to be an instance of tautology, for it might be alleged that internal forms can only be ascertained by dissection. With this explanation, I must now proceed to discuss what are generally considered to be the best shapes, for the purpose of combining speed with stoutness, remembering that we are examining the thoroughbred horse, and are not alluding to any other. As an instance of a very opposite conformation to that of Fisherman at page 62, I insert here a portrait of Saunterer, both after careful paintings by

SAUNTERER.

Mr. Barraud. These are generally admitted to have been the two best horses of their time, yet it is scarcely possible to imagine a greater difference to exist in first-class animals, than is displayed by them. Fisherman, short and strong, looks more like a hunter than a racehorse; while Saunterer, long and elegant, appears incapable of carrying more than ten stone. The student will do well to study these animals carefully, but it must not be omitted that the portrait of Fisherman was taken after he was thrown out of training.

THE BODY or trunk is the grand centre of all the muscular pullies and bony levers, which are used to move the horse, and it must, therefore, first come under consideration, although, as a matter of convenience, the horseman generally commences with the head. It is quite true that it in turn receives its orders from the brain, as will be hereafter explained, in treating of the nervous system, but as a mere machine it may be regarded independently of that organ altogether. It must, however, be viewed in three different aspects, inasmuch as it has three different offices to perform. These are, first, to carry its load, and propel it by means of the levers connected with it. Secondly, to afford room for the heart and lungs to perform their functions in its "chest," without interfering with the play of the shoulders; and, thirdly, to lodge an efficient apparatus of nutrition. The first of these divisions comprehends THE BACK, LOINS, AND CROUP; the second is THE CHEST; and the third may be considered under the head of THE BACK-RIBS, FLANK, AND BELLY.

THE BACK, LOINS, AND CROUP of the race-horse, as indeed of all horses but those used exclusively for draught, are generally described as necessarily moulded more or less in the form of an arch. Every architect is aware that this formation is best adapted to carry weight. A straight-backed greyhound is by some experienced coursers, preferred to one which has a slight arch in that part; but in this animal there is no weight to be carried beyond that of his own carcase, and, therefore, even granting the superiority in him of a straight loin (which I do not), there is no analogy between the two animals. Nor do I believe altogether in the received theory which attaches importance to the arched loin, *because of its greater capacity for bearing weight from its mechanical form.* Practically I concede, as an admitted fact, that a horse with this construction of frame will carry weight better than one which has a hollow loin; but, on examining the skeleton of each, it will be seen that in neither are the bodies of the vertebræ in this part of the spine arranged so as to form an arch, or if there is one, it has its concavity, not its convexity upwards, which certainly will not conduce to its weight-bearing powers. The fact really is, that in the arched loin the spinous processes are unusually long, and are raised into a crest like the high withers. By this development of bone an extra space is afforded, for both the lodgment and attachment of muscles, and herein is the secret of the extra power. Between the pelvis and the bodies of the vertebræ a true arch is formed, and according to the slope or fall of the quarters will it be useful in carrying weight; but this is quite irrespective of the loin, which may be arched or flat in conjunction with either formation. It is, however, most common to find an arched loin united with an inclined pelvis, and when the two are found together, the horse possessing this formation may be considered so far as "up to weight." Sometimes we see the pelvis inclined, but the tail set on high, and the loin hollow, and then we may surely predicate that there will be a want of power in these parts, and that the seven stone of Lord Redesdale will be quite sufficient for the animal to carry. With this objectionable shape, there is a hollow on each side of the croup, which is very characteristic of the defect, and which is carefully eschewed by the experienced horseman. If the spine between the two supports afforded by the fore and hind extremities were really an arch, length would but little affect it, for we know that an arch of ninety feet span, is no stronger than one of a hundred feet, if both are properly constructed; but being nearly a straight line, with its component parts kept in their proper places, by a series of levers and pullies, length tells most unfavorably; and "a short back, with plenty of length below," is the height of the horseman's ambition to possess.

Mr. Percivall has fallen into a strange error in estimating the advantages of a long back, as may be readily seen on an examination of the following passage:—" Regarding the dorsal portion of the spine, with its superimposed burthen, as a pole or lever, supported in front by the fore limbs, and behind by the back limbs, after the manner of a barrel of beer, or a sedan between its bearers; it is manifest, that the greater its length, the greater must be the leverage, and consequent reduction of the weight of the burthen. On this principle, the legs of the long-backed horse are actually sustaining less load than those of the short-backed horse, even though their riders or burthens may be of equivalent weights, from the circumstance of their operating at a greater distance from the load." The fallacy of this argument is apparent to every person who has the slightest knowledge of mechanical powers; but as my readers may not at all be in a position to estimate its value, I shall just make a few observations upon it, as I have heard it adduced on several occasions, to support the advantage of a long back. Now we will suppose a weight of 500 pounds on a plank, supported upon four props, two being five feet from the other two, and the pairs one foot apart, resembling, in fact, the relative position of the feet of a horse. Let the whole be arranged on a weighing machine, so that only the four legs touch its table, and take the weight. Then remove the two pairs of legs to a distance of six feet, and again take the weight. According to Mr. Percivall it ought to be less than before, but, tested by actual experiment, there will not be the hundredth part of a grain variation, even if the instrument is sufficiently delicate to register that weight. A. and B. carry a weight between them, suspended to a pole, and they find it more convenient to have that pole tolerably long, because they can shift the weight from one to the other more easily than with a shorter one, but they carry the same weight in either case. A. can raise it by means of his long lever more easily than with a short one, but he can only effect this by making use of B.'s hand as a fulcrum, and for the moment throwing the weight off himself upon it, while B. returns the compliment in his turn, and both are relieved. For the mere purpose of carrying weight, therefore, a short back is to be preferred; but there is a limitation put to this by the necessity for length of limb to give pace, and if the legs are too long for the back, the action of the fore-quarter is impeded by the hind, and *vice versâ*. Hence, in all horses, a reasonable length is preferred, and this will vary according to the occasion for weight-carrying power. In the thorough-bred horse, pace is essential, and his back must consequently be of sufficient length to allow the free use of such limbs as will give stride enough to develop it. We shall hereafter find, that the cart-horse may have a much shorter back, even though he has no weight to carry, but he requires strong couplings of the hind and fore-quarter for the former to act upon, in dragging heavy weights, and as in him pace, beyond the walk, is never required, a short back may be allowed to be a great advantage, without any attendant evil.

The most important elements of strength in the back and loins are the depth and breadth of its muscles, for they, and not the bones, as I have shown, are the real mechanical means by which not only weight is carried but propelled. Now to lodge these muscles, there must be high spinous processes, wide hips, and such a formation of the ribs as to give width at their upper parts. Generally speaking the two last coincide, but sometimes the hips stand out in a very "ragged" or prominent position, while the ribs are flat. This formation, however, comes next to the most approved combination, and is far better than the narrow hips and flat sides which we now see in too many of our thorough-bred horses. In connection with this division of the body may be taken the croup, the upper outline of which is formed by the prolongation of the spine towards the root of the tail; but the essential parts are made up by the pelvis. It is very generally assumed that in order to develop high speed, the pelvis must be long, and this I believe to be perfectly true; but the length need not be in a perfectly horizontal direction, and is I think much better if developed at an inclination of about twenty-five degrees, that is to say, with a considerable fall. With this formation there may be the same length for the attachment of muscles, and the same leverage in their action on the thigh, for the situation of the hip joint (or round bone) is not altered in relation to them, though it is lower and more forward in reference to the spine. Hence the muscles which draw the thigh forward have more power, and also act much more quickly, giving that rapid thrust of the hind legs forward which is essential to good and strong action. With the perfectly horizontal croup you may have a long sweeping stroke which tells over such a course as Newmarket, but you very rarely meet with a quick coupling and uncoupling, unless the pelvis is set on the sacrum or continuation of the spine, at a considerable angle, so as to give the quarters more or less droop. Most of our best horses have exhibited this formation, while a great number of very handsome, but utterly useless brutes, might be enumerated which possess the high croup of the Arab in an exaggerated condition, of which Mr. Gratwick's Ethiopian is a good example. If the portraits of the Godolphin Barb are at all to be depended on, we are indebted to him for the introduction of this useful, though not particularly elegant shape, and I believe that it is in this direction, and in point of size, that he has been so useful in the stud. The eye is captivated by the animal, which, as the dealers say, "has both ends up;" and experience teaches every horseman, who will profit by it, that both the stargazer and the high-crouped horse are to be avoided. In selecting the thorough-bred horse, then, choose such as have a deep and wide back and loin, avoiding either the "roach back," which causes that part to be inflexible, and the hollow one, which tends to give way too much under weight, but regarding as most desirable such a width of ribs and hips, and depth of spinous processes as shall give sufficient lodgment for muscles, and looking also for a proper length of spine, not too short for stride, nor too long for strength. Lastly, let the pelvis be attached at such an angle as to give a slight droop to the quarters, whether the tail be set on in correspondence with it or not, for the dock does not always come out of the pelvis in the same position viewed in relation to that part alone

Some of the above opinions are in opposition to those of Mr. Percivall, who objects to a great width of hip in the race-horse, and also asserts that he cannot be too lengthy and straight in his quarters. He says, "Although the race-horse may prove disadvantageously broad across his hips, I believe he will never be found either too *lengthy* or too *straight* in his quarters; by which I mean the length and elevation of an imaginary line carried from either hip to the point of his quarter, or of another carried from the summit of his rump to the root of his hock. Such straight formation of quarter implies small degree of inclination in the position of the pelvis, the effect of which is extension of the angles between the pelvis and the femoral bones, and corresponding increase of the distances between the pelvis and the stifles in front, and between the pelvis and hocks behind; thereby augmenting the dimensions of the muscles running between these salient points, and at the same time furnishing them with, under the circumstances, the greatest advantages in their action. Length and straightness in the quarters must therefore be regarded as characteristic attributes of the race-horse." Of the probability of meeting with too great a width of hip in the race-horse I am extremely doubtful, and until I see it I shall continue sceptical. The Melbournes, which have this part wider than in any other strain, are certainly not to be despised, and, in spite of Mr. Percivall, I must, on the contrary, continue to admire them, whenever they are to be found; my chief regret is, that wide hips are so scarce among the descendants of that horse.

THE SECOND DIVISION OF THE BODY, OR THE CHEST, in the thorough-bred horse, must afford sufficient room for the heart and lungs, but it must not be too wide, or it will interfere with the free play of the shoulder-blade as it glides on the side. An open bosom is regarded as a sure sign of want of pace by every racing man of experience, and I know of no single exception. One of the finest two-year olds I ever saw in every other respect was Lord Standbroke's Rose de Florence; but I could have laid any reasonable odds that she would be deficient in pace, because she was made as wide as a cart-horse between the forelegs, and so she proved to be on trial. A horse of fifteen hands three, or sixteen hands when in stud condition should measure at least seventy-four inches, and should be wide through the part where the rider's knees come on the saddle; but below this the ribs should rapidly shelve inwards, and in this way allow the shoulder points to come closer together, and the elbows to act without being "tied." The anatomy of this part is treated of elsewhere, and I am now regarding it simply in proportion to the rest of the body. Anatomically, and considered *per se*, a round or barrel-like chest is the best, because it admits of more free expansion and contraction, but when either high speed or smooth action is required, this formation is objectionable for the reasons I have given above, and in all cases it is to be avoided in the thorough-bred horse, while in some other breeds it must be looked for with great anxiety. It has been proved that good wind may be obtained from a chest possessing great depth without much width, and in some cases with a very narrow bosom, as in the celebrated Crucifix (dam of Priam); and as the opposite proportions are incompatible with speed, they must on that account be altogether rejected. THE WITHERS are generally thin, and sometimes raised quite into a razor-like form, which, however, is a defect, as it is attended with no advantages to counterbalance the difficulty which it presents in the way of the saddler, who is constantly being called on to prevent his tree hurting the horse's back. A moderate development of the spinous processes is required to give attachment to the muscles which support the neck and move the shoulder, but the excessive height which we sometimes see is not of the slightest avail for this purpose

THE NEXT AND LAST COMPONENT PARTS of the body are THE BACK-RIBS, FLANK, AND BELLY. Here we have chiefly to consider the proper lodgment of the organs of nutrition; but there is also the junction of the fore and hind quarters to come under review. For both these purposes the back-ribs should be long, or, as such a formation is generally called, " deep," so as not only to give protection to the contents of the belly, but to afford a strong attachment to the muscles which connect the chest to the hips. The space, also, between the latter and the last rib should not be large, or there will be an element of weakness; but if too limited, the action in the gallop will be confined, and the hind legs will not be brought sufficiently forward. About the breadth of the hand is the proper allowance to make for this space in a horse of average size and make, and either more or less than this may be considered a defect. To obtain this formation, the ribs themselves must be set wide apart, and not huddled up together, as you sometimes see, leaving a great space between the last and the hip. When the back-ribs are long, the lower outline of the belly swells considerably below the level of the girth-place, and a very elegant shape is developed, as well as one generally united with a hardy constitution. Sometimes, it is true, the two are not combined, and now and then we meet with a very good feeder and robust animal with shallow back ribs; but the rule may be considered to be as I have stated it, and the purchaser will do well to attend to it in making his selection, when he knows nothing of the character of the individual. For fast road-work, where the failure of the legs is generally the limit to the amount of work, a very heavy carcase is an objection, as it increases the weight upon them; and an overtopped harness-horse—that is, one with a body too big for his legs—is a most worthless brute; but in the thorough-bred there is seldom this formation, and the tendency is, on the other hand, to be too light in the flank, rather than too deep. A light-carcased or herring-gutted horse when "set" for the race-course or the fast hunting country looks cut in two, and his performances generally correspond with his appearance.

PROJECTING FORWARD with a beautiful sweep, the neck comes out of the chest in this kind of horse with a most elegant outline. Of a greater length than in any other, it is also proportionally thin; but both these dimensions may easily be exaggerated, a very long and thin neck being objectionable, and rarely corresponding with good wind. The lines resemble greatly those of the neck of the gamecock; and when there is a decided angle about three or four inches from the jaw, the horse is said to be " cock-throppled," and it is then generally supposed that he is more than usually liable to become a roarer or a whistler. The curve of this part a good deal depends upon the breaking and subsequent riding, different hands producing a great variation in the carriage; but if the bones are so formed and connected together that the natural curve has its concavity upwards, it is almost impossible to produce a proper bend in the other direction, though still much may be accomplished by perseverance. A "ewe neck," as this is called, is very objectionable on this account; but it is very often combined with speed, fine action, and great gameness. More depends upon the junction between the head and neck, than upon the latter in itself, for by long-continued perseverance, it may be made so supple as to bend at the rider's will; but if the jaws are too narrow to allow the head to bend upon the neck, no means that can be applied will make any impression, and the result is that the mouth is spoiled, and frequently the temper also. A large and free windpipe, that is, one of sufficient diameter for the passage of air, and not tied down by any bands of fascia, will be necessary for good wind; and this point should specially be examined.

IN THE HEAD is contained the organ of intelligence, which is also the chief seat of that nervous energy which animates the whole body. Here also are the eyes, and the external apertures of the breathing apparatus; so that the form of this part of the body is of great importance. Size is power, and, *cæteris paribus*, a large brain is to be regarded as a most valuable adjunct. Hence the head should be wide above the eyes, as well as between the ears, and somewhat full or projecting in the forehead also, in order to give lodgment to a brain of good volume. It is the great development of this organ in the thorough-bred and his Eastern relations, that gives the extraordinary stoutness and fire for which they are so remarkable; and therefore a horse of this breed deficient in volume of brain will be found in these respects no better than his low-bred rivals. In every other part, the weight should be reduced to the minimum necessary for carrying on the functions peculiar to it, save only the eye, a very small one being generally found to be prone to disease. The thorough-bred horse has a beautifully full and gazelle-like eye; but in this organ many half-bred animals are quite equal to him—the eye of the cart-horse, however, showing the opposite extreme. A very prominent or unnaturally convex eye, called a " buck eye," is not to be regarded as desirable, being an evidence of shortness of sight, and therefore not to be confounded with the full and *soft* expression indicative of good manners, high courage when roused, and soundness. Next to the eyes in importance are the nostrils, which should be open, and when the horse has galloped should stand out stiffly, showing the red lining membrane, and admitting the air freely. Of course, even the smallest nostrils are of larger area than the windpipe;

but there is generally a coincidence between their size and that of the internal passages higher up, and on that account a patent nostril is to be looked for with some anxiety. I have known some horses with small nostrils possess excellent wind, because in them the internal conformation was of full size, and if, as I before remarked, the area of the two nostrils together is always much greater than that of the windpipe, they cannot *in themselves* offer any impediment to breathing. Without a trial, however, as the internal passages cannot be measured, the size of the nostrils must be accepted as the best guide to that of the more essential parts, and practically this is sufficient for general purposes, only inferior to an actual trial. The ears should be moderately long, thin, and not inclined to "lop." The muzzle should be fine; but in those very pointed jaws, which their owners regard with so much pride, as "small enough to drink out of a quart pot," the nostrils are seldom large enough, and hence they are to be regarded with great suspicion, beautiful as they undoubtedly are. A slight concavity in the front line, descending from the forehead to the front of the muzzle, is regarded as a mark of breeding, and, if not too marked, deservedly so; but a very deep concavity is often attended with a vicious temper. Lastly, a lean and *wide* lower jaw should not be omitted as a grand desideratum; the former point is merely a sign of breeding, but the latter is (as I before remarked in describing the neck) essential to the proper bending of the one part on the other. The experienced horseman always passes his fingers between the angles, and if there is not plenty of room, he knows that the head cannot be well carried, and he is inclined to suspect that the larynx will be impeded in its functions, and that, consequently, respiration will be affected either by roaring, whistling, or some or other of the many forms of "making a noise." With all these dimensions, which may, comparatively, readily be described, there should be combined a cheerful and airy expression of countenance, without any appearance of vice. The thorough-bred horse is not often too sluggish, and it is not in that direction that we should look for infirmities of temper; nor is it easy to describe the marks or signs by which vice of any kind can be at once recognised from the mere expression. Still the horseman will do well to study the countenance of this as well as other breeds of horses, and he will find, in course of time, that no little assistance will be derived from it.

THE SHOULDER-BLADE is, like the head, peculiarly formed in the Eastern horse, having greater obliquity in its position, and a superior length and breadth, as compared with all others. For the reasons which may be alleged for the desirability of these characteristics, I must refer to pages 21–22, where I have already given them. Suffice it to observe, that an obliquely-placed and *broad* blade, well clothed with muscles, is the desirable formation of this part, added to a well-developed "point," as the prominence at the joint between the blade and true arm-bone is called by the horseman. If this is too level and smooth, the muscles which are attached to it have not sufficient leverage; while if it is very ragged and prominent, it is a mark of diseased or excessive growth of bone, and is generally attended with a stiffness of the part. Indeed, in examining a shoulder blade, freedom of action is to be regarded much more than its exact position when at rest; for if you have the desired effect, it matters not (except for breeding purposes) whether it is exceptional or not; and, as a matter of course, it is better to have a freely-playing shoulder which when at rest is too upright than a perfectly formed one confined to its place, as we sometimes see it. The oblique shoulder-blade is specially required in all horses which come down upon their fore legs after a spring, whether this is in the gallop, or the leap, or the trot, for the use of it is by its elasticity to break the jar which is thereby occasioned. The upright form is stronger, as the weight is placed more directly over the column which bears it, but it allows of less elasticity under the sudden shock given by the impetus of the body as it approaches the earth, and for this reason is only suited to the slow work of the cart-horse, or heavy machiner. In conjunction with the oblique, and therefore long blade, is always found a long true arm, which is sometimes so extended backward as to place the elbow absolutely in the way of the girths, and then perhaps may be considered as too long, especially as it throws the weight of the fore-quarter much in front of the fore legs, and tends to make the horse possessing it somewhat unsafe, unless his action is particularly free. This part also should be well clothed with muscles.

THE FORE ARM OR ARM, as it is generally called, is not remarkable for any great peculiarities, but it is somewhat larger in proportion to the cannon bone than in other breeds.

THE KNEE is broad and deep, from before backwards, and the leg below the knee is peculiarly free from that contraction or "tying in" which in the cart-horse and allied breeds is so objectionable, being an element of weakness when the joint is exposed to the strains incidental to fast work of any kind. So also a bending backwards of the joint called the "calf-knee," common in the cart-horse, is condemned in the race-horse for the same reason.

THE BONE OF THE LEG both in the fore and hind-quarter is small, but of compact substance, while the suspensory ligament and back sinew are so large, and stand out so freely, as to appear to form quite one-half of the leg. The fetlock joints are clean and of good size, the pasterns long and elastic, and the feet though small as compared with other breeds, yet large enough for the weight they have to carry, their horny covering being also tough and compact.

IN THE HIND-QUARTER the Eastern horse and his descendants excel all others in symmetry and in the length of the various parts composing it. Comparing the cart-horse with the subject of the present investigation, one is struck with the greatly increased length of the thighs of the latter, approaching almost to the proportions of the greyhound. In the cart-horse, when walking, the stifle joint can hardly be seen, while in the race-horse it is brought out prominently at every step. This gives the stride necessary for pace, and the fast strain of blood known as that of Selim, and his brothers Castrel and Rubens, possesses this peculiarity in a marked manner, though from the high position of the stifle in them, and their straight hocks, many people lose sight of this peculiarity. With regard to the hocks of a race-horse, they should be of full size, clean, and as a matter of course, free from curbs or spavins. They are also generally considered to require very long points, that is to say, the projecting lever to which the ham-string is attached should be long. From an examination of many race-horses I am satisfied that for speed this may be over-done, for though power is gained by it, quickness is sacrificed; and a very long point to the hock is apt to give long, dull, and dwelling action, entirely opposite to quick pace, though perhaps telling over a long flat. All are agreed that the gaskin or lower thigh must be muscular, and both for beauty and effect this is a most important point. In other respects, the hind-quarter of the thorough-bred should resemble that of any other variety of the species.

THE WHOLE of these points should be in proportion to one another; that is to say, the formation of the horse should be "true." He should not have long well-developed hind-quarters, with an upright, weak, or confined fore-quarter. Nor will the converse serve, for however well formed the shoulder may be, the horse will not go well unless he has a similar formation in the propellers. It is of great importance, therefore, that the race-horse should have all his various points in true relative development; and that there shall not be the hind-quarter of a long racing-like horse, with the thick confined shoulder which would suit a stride less reaching in its nature. A remarkable instance of the advantages of such a formation is exhibited in Saunterer, whose frame is not characterized by power or any other special perfection, but being perfectly true in his formation he was one of the best, if not the very best, horse of his year, as he proved by his various achievements. At page 64 will be found an engraving of him, copied from one of the best portraits I ever saw, by Mr. H. Barraud, which should be carefully examined.

HEIGHT.

IN HEIGHT the race-horse varies from fifteen hands to sixteen and a half, or even seventeen hands; but the general height of our best horses is about fifteen hands three inches. Few first-class performers have exceeded the height of Surplice, who is sixteen hands one inch, as is also another Derby winner, Wild Dayrell. Sir Tatton Sykes was fifteen and a half hands; and between his height and that of Surplice may be ranged every great winner for the last ten or twelve years. This average, therefore, may fairly be laid down as the best height for the race-horse, though it cannot be denied that for some small and confined courses—as, for instance, that of Chester, a smaller horse of little more than fifteen hands height has a better chance, as being more capable of turning round the constantly recurring angles or bends.

COLOR.

THE COLOR of the thorough-bred horse is now generally bay, brown, or chestnut, one or other of which will occur in ninety-nine cases out of a hundred. Gray is not common, but sometimes appears, as in the recent case of Chanticleer and many of his stock. Black also occasionally makes its appearance, but not more frequently than gray. Roans, duns, sorrels, &c., are now quite exploded, and the above five colors may be said to complete the list of those seen on the race-course. Sometimes these colors are mixed with a good deal of white, in the shape of blazes on the face, or white legs and feet; or even all these marks may occur, and the horse may have little more than his body of a brown, bay, or chestnut. Most people, however, prefer a self color, with as little white as possible; and nothing but the great success of a horse's stock would induce breeders to resort to him if they were largely endowed with white. Gray hairs mixed in the coat, as in the Venison's, are rather approved of than otherwise; but they do not amount to a roan, in which the gray hairs are equal, or even more than that, to those of the other color mixed with them.

COAT, MANE, AND TAIL.

THE TEXTURE of the coat and skin is a great proof of high breeding, and in the absence of the pedigree would be highly regarded; but when that is satisfactory it is of no use descending to the examination of an inferior proof; and, therefore, except as a *sign of health*, the skin is seldom considered. In all thorough-bred horses, however, it is thinner, and the hair more silky than in common breeds; and the veins are more apparent under the skin, partly from its thinness, but also from their extra size and number of branches. This network of veins is of importance in allowing the circulation to be carried on during high exertions, when, if the blood could not accumulate in them, it would often choke the deep vessels of the heart and lungs; but by collecting on the surface great relief is afforded, and the horse is able to maintain such a high and long-continued speed as would be impracticable without their help. Hence, these points are not useful as a mere mark of breed, but as essential to the very purpose for which that breed was established.

THE MANE AND TAIL should be silky and not curly, though a slight wave is often seen. A decided curl is almost universally a mark of degradation, and shows a stain in the pedigree as clearly as any sign can do. Here, however, as in other cases, the clear tracing of that all-powerful proof of breeding will upset all reasoning founded upon inferior data. The setting on of the tail is often regarded as of great importance, but it is chiefly with reference to appearances; for the horse is not dependent for action or power upon this appendage. Nor is strength of dock of any certain value as a sign, for I have known some very stout horses with flaccid and loosely pendent tails; but still it may be accepted as a general rule, that when the muscles of the tail are weak, those of the rest of the body are likely to be so also.

CHAPTER VI.

ON THE LOCOMOTIVE ACTION IN THE VARIOUS PACES.

Natural and Acquired Paces—Distribution of Weight—Attitude assumed in Standing—Mode of Progression—The Walk—Trot—Canter—Hand-Gallop—Extended Gallop—The Amble—Racking, Pacing, and Running—The Paces of the Manege—Leaping.

NATURAL AND ACQUIRED PACES.

IN A STATE OF NATURE it is probable that the horse only possesses two paces, namely, the walk and the gallop; but when he is the produce of a domesticated sire and dam, even before he is handled, he will generally show a slight tendency to trot, and sometimes to amble, rack, or pace, if any of his progenitors have been remarkable for these artificial modes of progression. In this country, however, it may be assumed that the horse, without being taught, walks, trots, and gallops, more or less perfectly, according to his formation and temperament.

DISTRIBUTION OF WEIGHT.

EXCEPT IN THE GALLOP AND CANTER, in the fast trot, and in leaping, the weight of the horse is borne by two or more of the legs, and we shall find that in consequence of the projection forwards of the head and neck, the larger moiety is sustained by the fore leg (or legs) than by the hind. This can easily be demonstrated in the act of standing; but the same rule which applies to that position will also serve for any other.

It is important to the horsemaster to ascertain the circumstances which will change these proportions, because he finds practically that, in road work, the fore legs wear out faster than the hind, and consequently any means by which the weight on them can be reduced will be a gain to him in a pecuniary point of view. M. Baucher placed a horse with his fore and hind legs on separate weighing machines, and found that a hack mare when left to assume her own attitude, weighed on the fore scales 210 kilogrammes, while her hind quarters drew only 174, the total weight of the animal being 384 kilogrammes, each of which is equal to 2lbs. 2ozs. 4drs. 16grs. avoirdupois. By depressing the head so as to bring the nose to a level with the chest, eight additional kilogrammes were added to the front scales, while the raising of that part to the height of the withers transferred ten kilogrammes to the hindermost scales. Again, by raising and drawing back the head, in a similar way to the action of the bearing rein, eight kilogrammes were transferred from the fore to the hind scales, and this should not be forgotten in discussing the merits and demerits of that much-abused instrument of torture. M. Baucher then mounted the mare, when it was found that his weight, which was sixty-four kilogrammes, was placed in the proportion of forty-one kilogrammes on the fore quarters to twenty-three on the hind. A considerable change was of course produced by leaning backward, and by using the reins in the manner of the bearing rein, the former transferring ten kilogrammes from the fore to the hind quarters, and the latter act adding eight more.

EVERY PRACTISED horseman knows that his horse's fore legs will suffer in proportion to the weight which is thrown on them, while their relief is an additional source of strain to the hind legs. The spavined, and more especially the curby-hocked horse, relieves these parts by using his fore legs to carry more than their proper proportion of weight, while the animal affected with any painful disease of the fore limbs carries almost all the weight of his body on his hind legs, which are advanced under him in the most peculiar manner. The value of artificially changing the natural carriage of the horse, so as to make his hind legs come forward and carry more than their own share of weight, is chiefly felt in chargers, hacks, and harness horses, while, on the contrary, it is injurious to the hunter and the race-horse, whose hind quarters bear the greatest strain.

THE ATTITUDE ASSUMED IN STANDING.

STANDING may be considered under two heads, the first comprising the attitude naturally assumed by the horse when inclined to rest himself, and the second that forced upon him by education, for the sake either of appearances, or to keep him ready to start at a moment's notice, as in the cavalry horse. When standing free or naturally the horse always rests one leg, and that generally a hind one, changing from one to the other as each becomes tired in its turn. In the forced attitude all four are on the ground, and each supports its share of the superincumbent weight. In either case the different joints are kept from bending, by the almost involuntary combined action of the flexor and extensor muscles, which will keep him standing even in sleep, in which respect he differs from the human subject. The oblique position of the pasterns affords a considerable aid, but without the semi-involuntary support afforded by the muscles, the stifle and hock joints behind, and the shoulder and elbow before, would inevitably give way.

MODE OF PROGRESSION.

IN MOVING FORWARD, whatever the pace may be, the hind quarters are the main propellers, and thrust the body forward on the fore legs, which serve as imperfect segments of wheels, each in its turn making a revolution forwards and backwards through a segment of a circle, like a pendulum. This forward motion is either effected by one hind leg at a time, as in the walk, trot, amble, and rack, or by the two, nearly if not quite synchronously, as in the canter, gallop, and leap. In any case, the hind legs (or leg) must be drawn forwards under the body, or the body thrust backwards upon them, when a contraction of various muscles tends to straighten them, and as they are fixed upon the ground, which acts as a fulcrum, the body must give way, and thus passes forward with a speed and force proportionate to the muscular power exerted. In the various paces this mechanical action is differently effected in detail, but the principle is the same in all those contained in each class to which I have alluded. In the first, the weight is borne by the hind and fore quarters between them, while propulsion is effected by one side of the former; but in the second, it is taken at intervals by the fore and hind limbs, the latter propelling it with great force, and the former serving as props to it when it comes to the ground from the air, and also causing it to rebound for another interval of time.

THE WALK.

THERE ARE TWO questions involved in this pace which have led to discussions without end. *Firstly*, there is that connected with the order of sequence in which the feet are moved. *Secondly*, that relating to the part of the foot which first touches the ground. Of each of these, therefore, I must enter into a particular description.

IN EXAMINING THE ORDER OF SEQUENCE in which the feet are taken off the ground, it appears to me that a very simple matter has been converted into a complicated one. No one with a grain of observation can dispute that all the four legs in this pace move separately, and not, as in the trot and amble, by twos of opposite or the same sides. Solleysell, however, says that "in a walk the horse lifts the near fore leg and far hind leg *together*," and Percivall, in quoting this passage, calls him "this true observer of Nature;" but, nevertheless, the latter author goes on to disprove the correctness of the very passage he has just quoted, though he does not seem very clear upon the subject. His description is as follows:—" At the mandate of the will to move forward, the fore leg is first put in motion, the order of succession in the walk appearing to be this:—supposing the right or off fore leg to move first, that is no sooner carried off the ground than the left or near hind foot is raised, the former being placed upon the ground prior to the latter. The two remaining feet move in respect to each other, in the same order of time, the left or near fore after the off hind, the right or off hind after the near fore; it being observable that as each hind foot follows in the line of movement of its corresponding fore foot, the latter would very often get struck by the former, did it not quit its place immediately prior to the other being placed upon, partly or entirely, the same ground." Can anything be more confused than this jumble of words, which is solely so because it is desired to make the horse begin with a fore foot in preference to a hind one. Any one who examines the action of the feet of one side only will have no difficulty in perceiving that the hind foot is raised from the ground and moved forward for half its stride before the fore foot is disturbed, the same order being observed on the other side in succession. Hence, if the horse is started from the standing position with all the feet on the ground, it follows that he *must* begin with a hind foot, because with whichever of the sides he starts he lifts the hind foot half a pace before the fore foot, as is admitted by Percivall himself, for he says, "the latter (fore foot) would often get struck by the former (hind foot) did it not quit its place immediately prior to the other being placed upon, partly or entirely, the same ground." It is very difficult to convey a correct idea of this fact by illustration, because the eye has become accustomed to the erroneous view which is conventionally received by artists. However, with the assistance of Mr. Zwecker, who has himself studied the subject carefully, I am enabled to present the following engraving, which, though apparently awkward and ungraceful, is literally correct. Here the near hind foot (1) is just

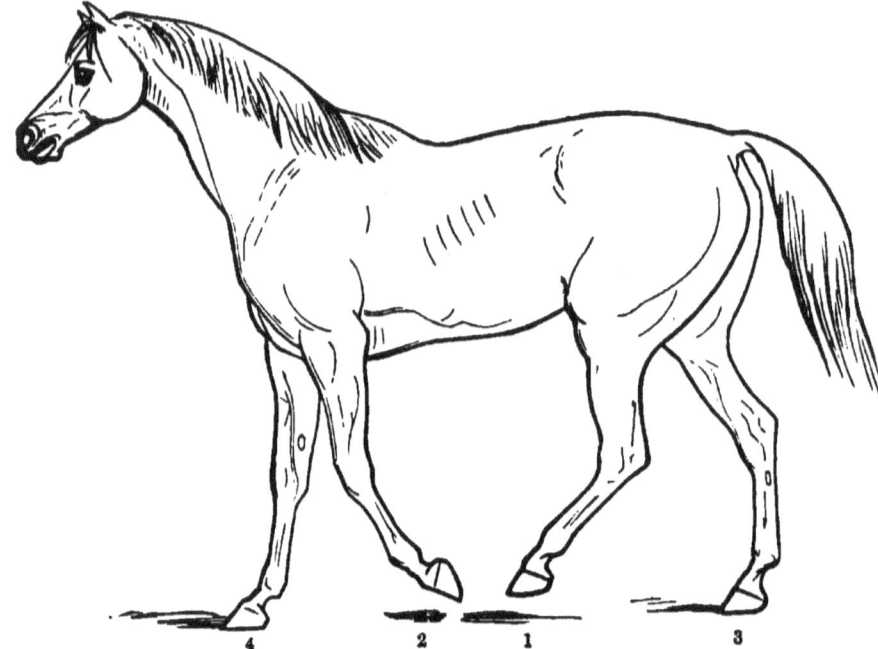

STARTING FOR THE WALK.

about to be placed on the ground, on the spot which the near fore foot (2) has just left. The off hind foot (3) will follow next in succession, and lastly the off fore foot (4) will complete the cadence. But if each fore foot leaves the ground just as the corresponding hind foot is finishing its stride, it follows as a matter of necessity, if the action is carried on throughout in the same way, that in starting from a point of rest the hind foot of one side or other is the one to begin the walk. Next follows the fore foot on the same side, then the opposite hind foot, and lastly the fore foot of the opposite side. The order of progression, be it observed, is the same, whether the description commences with the hind or fore foot, and the argument is after all of little consequence; but the truth is really, as was observed by Borelli, that the hind foot is the first to move when the horse starts into a walk from a state of rest in which all four feet are placed as in ordinary standing. There may be positions in grazing where the fore foot advances first; but then the pace cannot be considered as the customary walk.

IN THE ACCOMPANYING OUTLINE the horse is represented in the manner usually accepted by artists, with the near fore foot (2) in the air, and apparently leading off. But if, as I have endeavored to show, the hind foot must of necessity start first, although this

THE WALK.

RECEIVED INTERPRETATION OF THE WALK.

engraving affords to the eye of the observer the most graceful and striking position which is taken up in the walk, yet it is not the one with which the horse commences that pace. Here the near hind foot (1) has already been brought forward and placed on the ground, on or near the spot occupied by the fore foot, which is in the air; the off hind foot (3) is just about to leave the ground, having expended its share of progressive force, and the weight of the body is borne by the off fore foot and the near hind one. Whenever a fore foot starts first (which, as I have already remarked, may occasionally occur, as, for instance, in grazing, or when the weight is unnaturally thrown upon the fore quarters), the attitude is most constrained, and the proper sequence, or cadence, if the animal is forced into a quicker pace, is not fallen into without a most grotesque degree of rolling, which conveys to the eye a full idea of the forced nature of the pace. Mr. Zwecker has endeavored to fix this upon paper in the annexed engraving, but though I fully admit that the drawing is correct, I confess that I am not satisfied with the result of his labors. However, it may serve to convey to my readers the fact which I wish to impress

F

upon the mind, viz., that a walk in which either fore leg commences the cadence is unnatural, or, at all events, exceptional.

I HAVE THUS ENDEAVORED TO SHOW (and it may, I think, be considered as the most simple mode of describing the pace) that, as a rule, when the horse is starting from a state of rest into a walk he commences with one of the hind feet, the particular one chosen being that which at the time bears the least weight of the body upon it. Next follows the fore foot of the same side, then the opposite hind foot, and lastly the fore foot also of the opposite side.

EXCEPTIONAL MODE OF STARTING.

WHEN ONCE IT IS SHOWN that the hind foot almost touches the heel of the foot which precedes it, before the latter is raised, of which a moment's observation will satisfy any careful observer, the order of sequence becomes clear enough, and, as I set out with observing, a subject which is generally made extremely complicated becomes as simple as possible. In nine hundred and ninety-nine cases out of a thousand the horse starts on the walk with a hind foot, and the only exception is when he is, from circumstances, at the time in an unnatural attitude.

THE SECOND QUESTION in dispute to which I have alluded is that involving the part of the foot which first touches the ground in this pace. In this country veterinary writers have generally considered that in the sound foot the toe first reaches the ground, and undoubtedly Mr. Percivall is no exception, for he says at page 143 of his Lectures, " To the eye of the observer there is the slightest perceptible difference between the toe and heels coming to the ground in favor of the former, a difference that need not disturb the horseman's good old rule, that *a horse in his walk should place his foot fairly and flatly down.*" This theory has, as far as I know, never been admitted by practised horsemen, and in the year 1855, in describing the perfect hack, at page 526 of "British Rural Sports," I wrote as follows : " The walk should be safe and pleasant, the fore foot well lifted and deposited on its heel." The first veterinary surgeon, however, who combated the opinions of his brethren, was Mr. Lupton (a disciple of Mr. Gamgee), who early in the year 1858, inserted in the *Edinburgh Veterinary Review* the following " Physiological Reflections on the Position assumed by the Fore Foot of the Horse in the varied Movements of the Limb":—

" 1. The foot of a living horse in a state of rest remains firmly on the ground, that is the toe and the heel are on the ground at one and the same time; but if during this position the extensor muscles were to contract, then the toe would be raised from the ground; and if, on the other hand, the flexor muscles were to contract, then the heel would be raised from the ground. Now, during progression, the first movement which takes place is the contraction of the flexor muscles, by which (together with the muscles of the arm) the foot is raised, the toe being the last part of that organ raised from the ground. The foot is now in a position to be sent forward, which is brought about by the contraction of the extensor muscles; the foot is then thrown out as far as the flexor muscles will admit, and when at the greatest allowable point of tension, the heel is brought in apposition with the ground. The flexors now in their turn contract, the heel is first raised from the ground, and lastly the toe, which brings me back to the point I started from.

" 2. Viewing the leg of a horse as a piece of mechanism (allowing the leg to be even in a state of anchylosis), and comparing it to the spoke of a wheel, during the revolutions of which the posterior part of the inferior extremity, or, in other words, that part which is attached to the tier, comes in contact with the ground first; if in the place of the spoke the above-mentioned leg of the horse were there placed, the heel in that case would come in contact with the ground first, and the toe last.

" 3. As to the anatomy of the foot.

"The foot is composed of the os pedis, os naviculare, and a small portion superiorly of the os corona. Between the alæ of the os pedis we have the frog and the fibrous frog, in fact, a beautiful elastic cushion; and postero-laterally the lateral cartilages, readily yielding on the application of pressure. Seeing this arrangement, I naturally seek to find the cause of its existence, and I suggest that it is there in order, by coming in contact with the ground, first to break the concussive effect, likely, if being hard and unyielding as the formation at the toe, to be productive of much cost to the animal frame.

"4. The progress of action is from the heel to the toe. For example, man, during progression, puts his heel to the ground first; the ox also places his heels similarly on the ground first, and dogs bring their pads in contact with the ground first; does it not, then, seem undeniable, when reasoning by analogy, that the horse similarly brings his heels to the ground first?

"During progression, the body moves forward; during which movement the toe, as evident to every observer, leaves the ground last, that is, when the flexors are contracting. If such be the case, then, for the toe to come in contact with the ground first, as some affirm, and the heel last, is a retrograde and impossible movement.

"Three principal impressions are made on the foot during progression, namely:

"1. On the heel, when great expansion and yielding takes place, owing to the pressure on the frog, which is forced upwards, causing the ultimate expansion of the walls of the hoof, &c.

"2. On the middle part of the foot, when the bones bear the weight of the body. The flexors and extensors being, for the instant, in a state of quietude, *i. e.* neither of them are extending or contracting.

"3. On the toe, when the animal gives a push, by which an impetus is given to send the body forwards.

"The foot comes on the ground nearly flat, I admit, but the heel is for an instant on the ground before the toe.

"I humbly assert, in conclusion, that the progress of action is from the heel to the toe, and not from the toe to the heel."

It appears to me that argument is here thrown away, for as it is admitted by both sides that the toe and heel are each in certain cases placed on the ground first, it is manifest that either *may* be in all. Observation, therefore, and not theoretical argument, must determine under what circumstances the foot is deposited with its toe on the ground, and *vice versâ*. Mr. Spooner, and nearly the whole of the London school, say that the toe touches first in all cases but in the disease known as laminitis; Mr. Lupton, Mr. Gamgee, and the Edinburgh new school, assert, on the contrary, that, as a rule, the heel touches the ground a shade the first. Their assertions reach to all paces; but here I think a mistake is committed, for I am confident that in trotting, the toe touches the ground slightly before the heel in a large proportion of cases. In the walk I am quite satisfied that Mr. Lupton and his followers are right, and that the heel is presented to the ground in all good walkers, but so slightly first as to escape the notice of careless observers. If the toe is not raised it is apt to tip the inequalities of the ground, and we have that disagreeable sensation of insecurity in the walk which a bad hack invariably gives. Many horses go very close to the ground, but if the extensors turn the toe well up in bringing the leg forward, however closely to the ground it is carried, it is safely deposited on it. On the contrary, a high action, with the heel raised, is never safe, either on the walk or the trot. It is quite contrary to the experience of horsemen out of the veterinary profession to assert that either toe-action or heel-action is invariably met with in sound horses, and I believe the facts to be as I have stated them. That in laminitis the toe is raised in an exaggerated form no one will deny, but the extent is far greater than any one supposes to exist in a healthy foot. I have possessed one or two horses which, though perfectly sound, would wear out the heels of their shoes before their toes, and one of them was a high-stepping mare with remarkably good feet. Now the friction in all cases after the foot is put down must be greater on the toe than the heel, because it scrapes the ground, more or less, as it leaves it. When, therefore, the heel is worn out first, it proves that this part touches the ground first, though the converse does not hold good, for the reason which I have given.

Having discussed these two questions, I come now to examine what is done in each movement of the legs, independently of the order of their going, and of the above toe and heel controversy, and shall proceed to consider in what the good walk differs from the bad.

WRITERS ON THE HORSE divide each movement of the leg into three acts, consisting of the lift, the swing, and the grounding. In the first act, the foot is raised; in the second, it is thrust forward; and in the third, it is firmly but lightly deposited on the ground. But these may severally be well performed, and yet the horse be a bad walker, because his body is not well balanced on the legs in contact with the ground while the other or others are moving. A good walker should take short quick steps, *with his hind legs well under him*, and then he will be able to plant his fore feet firmly but lightly on the ground in succession. If his stride is too long, his hind legs cannot be always well under him, because they must be wide apart when both are on the ground; and the body cannot then be balanced securely, because there is too long an interval elapsing while the one hind leg is passing the other. Hence, in such a horse, there is a waddling movement from side to side, so often seen in the thorough-bred horse, whose full tail shows it very manifestly, but whose rider feels the inconvenience much more clearly than it is seen by the uninterested looker-on. The clever hack, on the contrary, moves forward without his body deviating a hair's breadth from the line in which it is progressing, neither undulating to the right and left nor up and down. The rider of a first-rate hack should be able to carry a full glass of wine in his hand for any distance without spilling a drop; and if the action on the walk is not smooth enough for this, it cannot be considered as approaching to perfection. Many horses step short and quick, and yet do not walk well, because their shoulders have not liberty enough to thrust their arms forward during the act of swinging the leg; and hence the pace is slow, for the foot is put down very near to the spot from which it was lifted. In choosing a good walker, therefore, see that his feet are lifted smartly, that they are well thrust forward, and placed firmly but lightly on the ground. Look at him well from behind, and observe whether he hits himself on the fetlock joints as one foot passes the other; and at the same time examine whether, as he lifts his fore feet, he turns them out, or "dishes," which is a very serious fault, in consequence of the loss of time which it occasions. In most horses the hind foot oversteps the place from which the corresponding fore foot has been removed; but in a good hack this should not exceed an inch, or the pace will not be smooth and smart, as I have already observed. Very few walkers actually touch one foot with the other, as in the trot, nor do they overreach with violence so as to injure their heels; the only objection, therefore, is to the length of stride, which I have shown to produce an uneasy effect upon the rider. But whenever the horse appears to move as if his fore feet are in the way of the hind, he will rarely, even with the best tuition, become a pleasant and safe hack.

THE RATE OF WALKING is very seldom quite five miles an hour, though horses are to be found which will accomplish the distance in that time, or even less. Many will do a mile in twelve minutes and a half; but to get beyond this is a very difficult task. Indeed, there are few horses which in their walk will bear pressing to the utmost speed of which they are capable, without breaking. It may, I think, be assumed, that the average pace of good walkers is about four miles and a half to four miles and three-quarters per hour.

THE TROT.

THIS PACE may be described under three heads, namely, the jog trot, the true trot, and the flying trot. In all three the diagonal limbs move exactly together, but in the first the time during which each foot is on the ground is much greater than that in which it is in the air. In the second the contrary is the case; while, in the third, the horse is carried completely off his legs for a considerable space of time, between the several bounds which are made by the two feet of opposite sides as they touch the ground in succession. The jog trot seems to come naturally to the horse when he is first mounted; and, as long as he is fresh and fiery, the colt will maintain this pace, unless he is permitted to exceed it. He will prefer it to the walk for a long time; and it is only by good hands, combined with patience, that a spirited colt can be made to walk; for he can generally jog quite as slowly, and often much more so. Farmers are very apt to accustom their young horses to the jog trot, because they find by experience that it does not injure their legs or feet; but to a rider unaccustomed to this pace it is by no means an easy one. In the true trot, as exemplified below, the feet are on the ground a comparatively short space of time, the body being carried so rapidly forward that they are moved off almost as soon as they are deposited on it. By examining this outline, it will be seen that the position of the fore and hind limbs of the two opposite sides exactly corresponds, and this will be the case, whatever may be the period of the action in which the observation is made. As in the walk, each step may be divided into three acts; but I see no advantage in thus attempting to separate or analyze what must be considered in its totality, if it is to be regarded with any advantage to the observer. In the flying trot, which is well shown in the portrait of Flora Temple, at page 489, all the legs are for a very short period of time off the ground, as is there delineated, but still there is always an exact correspondence between the position of the fore and hind legs of opposite sides. The chief difference between these three varieties of the trot consists in the rapidity of the propulsion which is going on. This in the first is very slight; and the more elastic the fetlock joints, the better and softer is this pace. The feet are raised, and the legs are rounded or bent; but the body is not thrust forward nor are the shoulders moved in the same direction to any appreciable extent. The consequence is, that the feet are deposited again very close to the spot from which they are taken, and the pace is as slow as the walk. In the true trot, if it is well performed, the hind legs must be moved as rapidly as, and with more force than, the fore legs, because they have more work to do in propelling the body, the latter having only to sustain it during the operation. Good judges, therefore, regard the hind action as of even more importance than that of the knees and shoulders; for if the former do not drive the body well forward, good pace cannot be obtained, nor will it be easy and rhythmical. In this kind of trot elastic fetlocks are fatal to speed, as they prevent the instantaneous effect upon the body of the muscular contractions of the hind limbs, and cause the action to be dwelling and slow. Very fast trotters are, therefore, rough in their " feel" to the rider, and are not suited

ACTION IN THE TRUE TROT.

for the purposes of pleasure. Indeed, no one would mount one of them from choice; but when they possess good mouths, they are pleasant enough to drive. In examining trotting action, regard should be paid to the plane through which each limb passes, for if this is not parallel with that of the median line of the body the action is not true and smooth, and there is great risk of one limb cutting the other. This is best seen by watching the trot from behind as well as before, which gives an opportunity of investigating the movements of both pairs of limbs. Every horse should be so made that, when he stands, his fore canna bones should be quite parallel; but in order to be so, as they stand closer together than his elbows, they must form a slight angle with the arm at the knee; and hence, as this part is bent, there is always a slight tendency to turn out the foot, the exaggerated form of which is called "dishing." The observer will, therefore, do well to ascertain the extent to which this should be carried, or he will be apt to condemn a perfect goer as a "disher," from finding that he turns out his toes in bending the knee, though only in the trifling degree ordained by nature. If, in bending by the hand the fore foot to the elbow, the inner heel of the shoe is in contact with the outside of the arm, there will not be too much turning out of the foot, and the purchaser need not be afraid of this defect existing in the horse he is examining. Provided the fetlocks and canna-bones are not actually touched or "hit" in trotting, the fore-legs cannot be moved too closely together; but if they pass very near to one another in a fat dealer's horse, it may be suspected that when he is reduced in flesh to a proper working condition, boots will be necessary. A practised eye is required to judge of this correctly, and, if there is any doubt, one had better be consulted.

The Norfolk trotter of the present day has very perfect action, intermediate between the pointed and flying trot of the American horse, and the round high knee-action of the London park-horse. Even he, however, is not nearly so pleasant to ride as the thorough-bred, when the latter can trot at all; but many of this breed have been so long accustomed to the gallop, that their trot is a most imperfect pace. When they do perform it properly, it gives a most delightful feel, and no rider for pleasure, if money is at his command, should "throw his leg" over any but a thorough-bred, or one nearly pure in blood.

THE CANTER.

THE CANTER is a thoroughly artificial pace, at first extremely tiring to the horse, and generally only to be produced in him by the restraint of a powerful bit, which compels him to throw a great part of his weight on his haunches. It is very difficult to describe or define this pace, either in a pen-and-ink sketch or by the aid of the painter. Indeed it is often quite a matter of opinion to decide whether a horse is cantering or galloping. Many writers, and among them Mr. Blaine, have attempted to draw a distinction, by confining the canter to the pace which is executed without the feet ever leaving the ground altogether; but this definition is not generally admitted and followed, and many a horse whose canter would be readily allowed by all horsemen to be true, may be seen to leave the ground entirely for a certain interval of time, however small it may be. There is so great a variety in the modes adopted by different horses for performing the canter, that no single description will suffice, nor indeed is it easy, as I before observed, to define any one of them. Sometimes the carriage is extremely elegant, the hind legs well under the body, and all moving like clockwork, with the head bent on the neck, and the mouth playing lightly on the bit. When such a pace is performed with the right leg leading, the canter is exactly adapted for the female seat, in which the right shoulder is of necessity slightly advanced, and it is therefore the object of the breaker to obtain it. But it is only in those horses which combine a free use of their limbs with fine temper and good mouths, that such a pace can be developed, and if any one of these qualities is deficient it is useless to attempt to teach them. On the other hand, the pony or galloway will often canter without throwing any extra weight on his hind legs, with a loose rein and extended neck. This kind of pace may be detected by the ear on a turnpike road, by the quick pat-ter-ring sound which is evolved. It is extremely easy to the horseman, but is not so well adapted to female equestrianism, as it jerks the body in an ungraceful manner. The true canter, as adapted for ladies, is indicated below, though

THE CANTER.

it is so difficult to represent, that it is not so clearly done as might be wished. When the off leg leads off, the near one has to bear more than its share of work, and hence, unless a change is occasionally made, the fetlock joint of that leg is almost sure to suffer. Ladies should therefore either trot for a part of their daily rides, or teach themselves and their horses to change the lead from that with the off leg to that with the near.

THE HAND GALLOP.

BETWEEN THE CANTER and the true gallop there intervenes a pace which may be easily confounded with either, unless Mr. Blaine's definition of the canter is accepted, when the hand gallop can easily be distinguished from it. This pace is merely a slow and measured gallop, in which for a very short period all the legs leave the ground, but in which the propulsion is steadily given, and not with those snatches or jerks which are necessary to develop the high speed of the extended gallop. The body also is not nearer the ground than in the act of standing, and this may be considered as one of the best distinctions between the hand gallop and the extended stride of the faster pace. The French writers distinguish between the two by asserting that in the hand gallop there are three beats, while in the flying gallop two only are performed; but in practice there is no such variation.

THE EXTENDED GALLOP.

ACCORDING TO MOST OBSERVERS, this pace is a succession of leaps, smoothly and rhythmically performed, but Mr. Percivall has shown that there is a considerable difference between the two actions. He says in his lectures,—" In galloping a horse, in hunt-

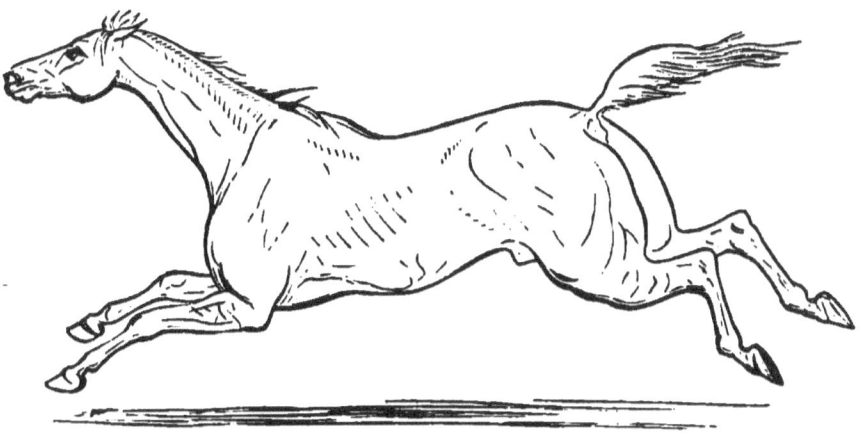

RECEIVED INTERPRETATION OF THE GALLOP.

ing, for example, the rider needs no person to tell him of the moment when his horse is taking a leap, however trifling it may be; his own sensations inform him of every *grip* or furrow his horse leaps in his course, and should he have occasion to make a succession of such jumps, the rider's sensations in his saddle are of a very different—very uneasy—kind, compared to such as he experiences during the act of galloping. This arises from two causes: from the spring or movement of the body necessary to produce the leap being more forcible or sudden than that required for the gallop, and from the latter being created and continued rather by the successive action of the two hind feet at one moment, and of that of the two fore feet at the next moment, than from the synchronous efforts of either biped, as happens in the leap. The two great propellers of the animal machine—the hind feet—are in the leap required to act *simultaneously*, to make one grand propulsory effort; not so in the gallop, that being a movement requiring maintaining, not by synchronous exhausting efforts of the hind feet, but in swift succession, first by one, then by the other; and the same as regards the office performed by the fore limbs, which latter probably amounts to little more in effect than the sustentation of the fore parts of the body. The vault into the air required for the leap is only to be effected by extraordinary subitaneous effort, but the stride of the gallop, requiring frequent repetition, does not exact this effort—amounts, in fact, to no more than a sort of lift from the ground, multiplied into a reiteration of forcible bearings forward, maintaining, increasing, or diminishing the momentum of speed, effectuated by throwing the hind feet as far forward underneath the body as possible, plunging them one after the other with inappreciable rapidity into the earth, and thus by two strenuous thrusts against the ground, one in aid of the other, working the animal machine in its fleet—almost flying—course. In the gallop as in the trot, no sooner is a certain momentum acquired, than by each successive propulsion of the hind feet the body is sprung or lifted off the ground, flying as it appears in the air, and the greater the speed, the more this volitation becomes apparent. Hence the appellation given to the pace, manifestly the utmost speed, of FLYING GALLOP. Even this, however, according to my judgment, is an action different from leaping. When a horse leaps or jumps in his gallop,—which he will do sometimes when he is beany and has but just emerged out of his stable,—he is said to buck, because his action then resembles that of the deer, in whom the gallop might with a great deal more propriety be called a succession of leaps: even the deer, however, cannot continue this bucking action after being driven into his speed, or in a state of fatigue, showing that in him it is to be regarded rather as a gambol than as his proper working onward action. And that the hind and fore feet in pairs are not grounded synchronously, I think admits of a demonstration in two ways: first, by the position they assume one in advance of the other in the gallop; secondly, by the clatter the steps of a horse in the gallop are known to make upon hard or resonant ground, and which may be heard either by a spectator or by the rider himself. Whence we probably derive the phrase, a rattling gallop."

But while I agree with Mr. Percivall that there is a difference between the act of leaping and galloping, as performed by the horse, I do not quite see that it is an abuse of terms to describe the gallop as a "succession of leaps"—that they are not precisely similar to those made in overcoming an obstacle does not necessarily make them other than leaps. The word leap is not defined in our dictionaries so as to confine its meaning beyond that appertaining to its synonym, spring, and probably even Mr. Percivall would not deny that in the gallop, the horse, as well as the deer, makes a succession of springs. The dispute is founded, as is so often the case, upon a want of agreement as to the meaning of a word, and not on a difference of opinion as the essence of the act itself. Blaine, Percivall, and every careful observer of the horse in action, well know that in the act of galloping the horse leaves the print of his hind feet one in advance of the other, while in leaping he generally, in fact almost invariably, makes them opposite one another. There is a contradiction apparent in Percivall's remarks about the deer's gallop, which in one place he observes "might with a great deal more propriety be called a succession of leaps," while in the next sentence he says that this "bucking action" in the deer "is to be regarded rather as a gambol than as his proper working onward action." The deer's gallop very closely resembles that of the horse, but as he is a stronger and higher leaper, especially in proportion to his size, he can continue those bounds with the hind legs opposite each other much longer and with more advantage than the horse, who seldom makes more than two or three in succession.

To REPRESENT THE GALLOP pictorially in a perfectly correct manner is almost impossible. At all events it has never yet been accomplished, the ordinary and received interpretation being altogether erroneous. When carefully watched, the horse in full gallop will be seen to extend himself very much, but not nearly to the length which is assigned to him by artists. To give the idea of high speed the hind legs are thrust backward and the fore legs forward in a most unnatural position, which if it could be assumed in reality would inevitably lead to a fall, and most probably to a broken back. It is somewhat difficult to obtain a good view of a horse at his best pace, without watching him through a race-glass at a distance of a quarter of a mile at least, for if the eye is nearer to him than this the passage of the body by it is so quick that no analysis can be made of the position of the several parts. But at the above distance it may be readily seen that the horse never assumes the attitude in which he is generally represented, of which an example is given at the beginning of this article. When the hind legs are thrust backwards, the fore feet are raised and more or less curled up under the knees, as it is manifest must be the case to enable them to be brought forward without raising the body from the ground. In the next act, as the hind feet are brought under the body the fore legs are thrust straight before it; and so whichever period is chosen for the representation, the complete extension so generally adopted must be inaccurate. It may be said that this is meant to represent the moment when all the feet are in the air, and theoretically it is possible that there may be a time when all the feet are extended; because, as in the fast gallop the stride is twenty-four feet long, while the horse only measures sixteen from foot to foot, it follows that he must pass through eight feet without touching the ground, and during that time, as of necessity his legs must move faster than his body, the fore legs *may* change their position from the curled up one described above to the extended one represented by all painters as proper to the gallop. Observation alone can therefore settle this question; but, as I before remarked, a race-glass at a distance of a quarter of a mile enables a careful observer to satisfy himself that our received ideas of the extended gallop are incorrect. Nevertheless, if a proper interpretation is given, the eye at once rebels, and on ex-

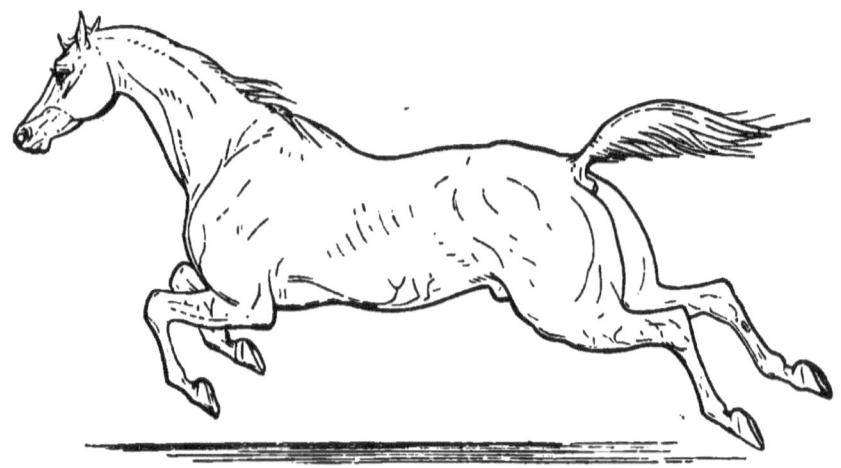

CORRECT VIEW OF THE GALLOP.

amination of such a figure as we here give, founded on perfectly correct principles, the mind refuses its assent to the idea of great pace, which is that which is desired to be given. These facts are well known to artists, and some of them, including the celebrated Leech, have tried the experiment of drawing the galloping horse properly; but their entire want of success shows the impossibility of the performance.

As IN THE CANTER so in the gallop a lead is always made of one leg before the other, and as one tires the other changes place with it. A good, true, and strong galloper will seldom require this relief, but a weak one, especially if not completely broken, will effect the change continually. Sometimes this causes the loss of a race, for it cannot be done without interfering with the action, and consequently with the pace. A good horseman prefers that his horse should not confine himself to one lead, but he does not like him to change after he has once started, for the above reason. The right leg in front is more easy even to the male rider than the left, but not materially so, and except for female equestrianism no horse should be taught to lead invariably with the right leg either in the gallop or canter. In the change the truth or harmony of action is often disturbed, and the horse jerks himself and his rider in a disagreeable manner, which is another reason why the change of legs should not be encouraged.

THERE IS A GREAT VARIATION in the length of the stride, and in the rounding or bending upwards of the foot under the knee. Sometimes even in a fast gallop the distance between the prints of the same feet will be no more than sixteen feet, while in others it will measure twenty-four, twenty-five, or even twenty-six feet. The first is too short for any race-horse; but a moderately short stride enables the horse to get off with a quicker start, and to ascend and descend hills better than a very long one. Where, however, a distance of level ground is to be covered a long stride tells, and a horse possessing it has a great advantage over one whose gallop is short, however quick and smart it may be. For this long stride there must be length of limbs, especially of the two bones meeting at the stifle joint; and this is the perfection of the form of the race-horse, as I have already described at page 73.

THE AMBLE.

LIKE THE TROT, this pace is performed by two legs alternately moving in exact correspondence with each other. Instead, however, of these being of opposite sides, they are of the same side, and one lateral half of the body is moved forward while the weight of the whole is supported on the other. The pace is altogether unnatural to the wild horse, but in some domestic breeds it has become naturalized, and the foal will in them display the amble long before it is taught anything by the hand of man. In the cameleopard the amble is the only kind of progression, whether the animal goes slowly or fast; and in dogs, especially in pointers, greyhounds, and Newfoundlands, this pace is occasionally displayed. Formerly an ambling palfrey was in great request for ladies' use, but in the present day the pace is not regarded with favor by any of the inhabitants of the British Isles.

RACKING, OR PACING, AND RUNNING.

IN THIS COUNTRY no other paces are recognised than the five which I have already described, but in America a fast kind of amble is distinguished by the name of racking, or pacing. It is performed by two legs of the same side acting synchronously as in the amble, but they are moved with much more rapidity, and the result is a speed greater than that of the fastest trot, by several seconds in the mile. This will be apparent on consulting the record of the best performances of the American horses, at pp. 504–6, where Pocahontas, a pacer, is set down as doing a mile in 2 minutes 17½ seconds, while their fastest mile trot on record occupied 2 minutes 19¾ seconds. Running is an indescribable kind of trot, in which the limbs do not move regularly together, but each seems to act independently as in the walk. The consequence is that it is impossible for the rider of a running horse to rise in his stirrups, but the action being very easy there is no occasion for this relief. It is not capable of being performed at a slow rate, and it is generally produced among horses which are ridden without a saddle, and in which as a consequence the riders do not relieve themselves and their horses by rising in it.

THE PACES OF THE MANEGE.

IN THE MILITARY SCHOOLS OF RIDING a variety of paces are taught even in the present day, but the old riding masters adopted many more, which are now discontinued. Some of them are intended to enable the soldier to use his sword or spear with double advantage, as the volte and semi-volte, but the majority of those still retained are for the purpose of carrying out the combined evolutions necessary to cavalry. The "passage," for instance, is a side movement, that enables a number of horses to be changed from close to open order, which would be a difficult task to perform with horses not taught to perform it. Backing is likewise necessary for similar purposes; but this should always be taught to every horse, whether used by the military or by civilians. A minute description, however, of the several paces of the manege would occupy too much space here, and is only useful to the cavalry soldier, who will learn their nature much better from practical instruction by the riding-master of his regiment.

LEAPING, OR JUMPING.

THE DESCRIPTION of this act given by Mr. Percivall is most unsatisfactory. He says, "The leap is either a sudden spring into the air, in which the feet quit the ground simultaneously, or else it is an act compounded of an imperfect rear and kick in quick or slow succession, according to the manner in which it is performed. The leap can hardly be regarded as an act of progression; commonly it being in a forward direction, undoubtedly progress is made by it, but it is possible for it to amount to no more than a jump or a bound off, and upon the same ground, as is the case when a horse is said to 'buck' in his leaping, that is, to come down upon or near to the spot from which he arose." Now in this sentence, short as it is, I maintain that several misstatements are made; as I shall proceed to show. To begin with the latter part. If a horse is properly said to "buck" in his leaping, it is evident that the two cannot be synonymous, or there would be no occasion for the distinction, and therefore if "bucking" means jumping up and coming down on the same ground, which is the general acceptation of the term, leaping cannot mean the same, which it is said sometimes to do by Mr. Percivall in the quotation which I have adduced. When a horse simply "bucks" in his play he does not leap forward, but springs into the air, and even then he generally makes some progression. When he "bucks" in his leaps, he must progress, because he begins on one side of the obstacle to be overcome, and finishes on the other. It is not meant that he then acts exactly as he does in play, or when viciously trying to dislodge his rider, but that his action resembles to a considerable extent this true bucking, in which little or no progression is made. I therefore hold that Percivall's exception is not founded in truth; and that the act of leaping necessarily implies progression, for without it the perpendicular spring into the air is properly distinguished by the term bucking, as admitted by Percivall himself. Then, turning back to the first sentence, I think every careful observer will admit that in the leap, whatever may be its kind, the feet do not quit the ground simultaneously. Manifestly in the standing or slow leap the fore feet rise first, unless the horse "bucks," when all rise almost but not quite at the same moment. A careful examination of the mechanism of the horse will show that this must be the case, because, as the fore legs are straight to the last, there is no spring in them, and if they were not first raised by the action of the loins and haunches, as in rearing, they would remain on the ground until they were dragged by the hind quarters turning a somerset over them. In the human body, as the legs are ordinarily kept straight, they must be bent before a spring can be taken, for even the angular ankle joint requires a bent knee to enable it to act upon the toes. In the horse the fore leg resembles that of man in this respect, but the hind leg in the standing position is bent at the stifle and hock, and is then exactly like a man's when he is prepared to take a standing jump. As a consequence of this the fore quarter of the horse when he is standing must be raised by the hind, since it has no angles to give a spring with, and if so it must leave the ground first, as I have already shown. The flying leap may readily be seen to be accomplished by the fore feet leaving the ground first, and no one I believe disputes this, so that it is unnecessary to discuss it.

It may, therefore, I think, be asserted with truth that the leap is always made by the horse raising his fore quarter, and then suddenly and powerfully straightening his hind limbs; with the ground as a fulcrum he propels his whole body forwards, and more or less upwards, according to the height of the obstacle to be overcome. In descending from the height to which the whole body has been raised, there is a considerable variation in the relative periods of time at which the fore and hind feet touch the ground. Sometimes the fore feet come down almost perpendicularly, and so far before the hind that they have to bear the whole force of the united momentum and gravity before the hind ones reach the ground, and then a very slight mistake will occasion a fall. At others they come down "all fours," that is, all the feet touching the ground at the same moment, occasioning a great shock both to horse and rider, and also a considerable loss of time in getting away again into the stride. In the best style the horse touches ground with his fore feet first, but being well extended they are in a position to do no more than act as a spring to break the shock, and the hind legs coming down immediately afterwards bear nearly the whole force of momentum and gravity, which the fore legs are unable to do safely, as I have already shown.

Mr. Percivall is also in error as to the width of ground which horses have been known to clear; for he gives twenty-two feet as an extraordinary effort in a steeplechase, whereas such a distance is covered by any hurdle-jumper in ordinary practice, as I have twenty times proved by careful measurement. I have myself seen thirty-two and thirty-three feet cleared by steeplechasers, and it is well known that Proceed and Chandler covered respectively thirty-seven and thirty-nine feet in two separate steeplechases. So a jump six feet in height is a very great performance, being eight inches higher than the withers of a horse of sixteen hands. Something more than this has however been done, and I myself once saw a horse clear a stone wall two or three inches above six feet high, with the slightest possible touch of one stone with a hind foot, but sufficient to dislodge it. Very few horses, however, can be relied on to cover more than twenty-five feet in width, and four feet, or four feet six inches in height, and an average hunter will not often do so much, especially if at all tired by a long run, or if without the excitement attendant on the chase.

CHAPTER VII.

THE PRINCIPLES OF BREEDING APPLICABLE TO THE HORSE.

Theory of Generation—In-and-in Breeding—Out-Crossing, Advantages and Disadvantages of each Plan—Causes of a "Hit"—Importance of Health and Soundness in both Sire and Dam—Best Age to Breed from—Influence of Sire and Dam respectively—Choice of Sire and Dam—The Kind of Horse most likely to be Profitable to the Breeder—Concluding Remarks on Breeding.

THEORY OF GENERATION.

THE IMPORTANCE of understanding the principles upon which the breeding of the horse should be conducted is so great that every one who superintends a stud, however small, should study them carefully. To do this with advantage, he must investigate the changes which take place after the union between the sexes, and must endeavor to ascertain the influence which the sire and dam respectively exert upon their offspring.

In the year 1855, while engaged in preparing the article on the breeding of the horse in "British Rural Sports," I carefully drew up the following epitome of the laws which govern the generation of the mammalia. Since then, the subject has constantly been before me; but, in spite of the numerous investigations carried on by other observers, I have seen no reason to modify, in any material degree, what I then wrote; and I shall, therefore, to prevent confusion, insert it entire, what slight additions may be necessary being included within parentheses.

1. THE UNION of the sexes is, in all the higher animals, necessary for reproduction; the male and female each taking their respective share.

2. THE OFFICE OF THE MALE is to secrete the *semen* in the *testes*, and emit it into the *uterus* of the female (in or near which organ), it comes in contact with the *ovum* of the female—which remains sterile without it.

3. THE FEMALE forms the *ovum* in the *ovary*, and at regular times, varying in different animals, this descends into the *uterus*, for the purpose of fructification, on receiving the stimulus and addition of the *sperm-cell* of the semen.

4. THE SEMEN consists of two portions—the *spermatozoa*, which have an automatic power of moving from place to place, by which quality it is believed that the semen is carried to the ovum; and the *sperm-cells*, which are intended to co-operate with the *germ-cell* of the ovum in forming the embryo.

5. THE OVUM consists of the *germ-cell*, intended to form part

of the embryo,—and of the *yolk*, which nourishes both, until the vessels of the mother take upon themselves the task; or, in oviparous animals, till hatching takes place, and external food is to be obtained. The ovum is carried down by the contractile power of the fallopian tubes from the ovary to the uterus, and hence it does not require automatic particles like the semen.

6. THE EMBRYO, or young animal, is the result of the contact of the *semen* with the *ovum*, immediately after which the *sperm-cell* of the former is absorbed into the *germ-cell* of the latter. Upon this a tendency to increase or "grow" is established and supported at first, by the nutriment contained in the yolk of the ovum, until the embryo has attached itself to the walls of the uterus, from which it afterwards absorbs its nourishment by the intervention of the *placenta*.

7. AS THE MALE AND FEMALE each furnish their quota to the formation of the embryo, it is reasonable to expect that each shall be represented in it, which is found to be the case in nature; but as the food of the embryo entirely depends upon the mother, it may be expected that the health of the offspring and its constitutional powers will be more in accordance with her state than with that of the father; yet since the sire furnishes one-half of the original germ, it is not surprising that in external and general character there is retained a *fac-simile*, to a certain extent, of him.

8. THE OVUM OF MAMMALIA differs from that of birds chiefly in the greater size of the yolk of the latter, because in them this body is intended to support the growth of the embryo from the time of the full formation of the egg until the period of hatching. On the other hand, in *mammalia* the placenta conveys nourishment from the internal surface of the uterus to the embryo during the whole time which elapses between the entrance of the ovum into the uterus and its birth. This period embraces nearly the whole of the interval between conception and birth, and is called *utero-gestation*.

9. IN ALL THE MAMMALIA THERE IS A PERIODICAL "HEAT," marked by certain discharges in the female, and sometimes by other remarkable symptoms in the male (as in the rutting of the deer). In the former it is accompanied in all healthy subjects by the descent of an ovum or ova into the uterus; and in both there is a strong desire for sexual intercourse, which never takes place at other times in them (with the single exception of the genus Dimana).

10. THE SEMEN retains its fructifying power for some days, if it is contained within the walls of the uterus or vagina, but soon ceases to be fruitful if kept in any other vessel. Hence, although the latter part of the time of heat is the best for the union of the sexes, because then the ovum is ready for the contact with the semen,

yet if the semen reaches the uterus first, it will still cause a fruitful impregnation, because it remains there (or in the fallopian tubes) uninjured until the descent of the ovum.

11. THE INFLUENCE OF THE MALE upon the embryo is partly dependent upon the fact, that he furnishes a portion of its substance in the shape of the sperm-cell, but also in great measure upon the effect exerted upon the nervous system of the mother by him. Hence, the preponderance of one or other of the parents will, in great measure, depend upon the greater or less strength of nervous system in each. No general law is known by which this can be measured, nor is anything known of the laws which regulate the temperament, bodily or mental power, color or conformation, of the resulting offspring.

12. ACQUIRED QUALITIES are transmitted, whether they belong to the sire or dam, and also both bodily and mental. As bad qualities are quite as easily transmitted as good ones, if not more so, it is necessary to take care that in selecting a male to improve the stock he is free from bad points, as well as furnished with good ones. It is known by experience that the good or bad points of the progenitors of the sire or dam are almost as likely to appear again in the offspring as those of the immediate parents in whom they are dormant. Hence, in breeding, the rule is, that like produces like, or *the likeness of some ancestor.*

13. THE PURER OR LESS MIXED the breed the more likely it is to be transmitted unaltered to the offspring. Hence, whichever parent is of the purest blood will be generally more represented in the offspring; but as the male is usually more carefully selected and of purer blood than the female, it generally follows that he exerts more influence than she does; the reverse being the case when she is of more unmixed blood than the sire.

14. BREEDING "IN-AND-IN" is injurious to mankind, and has always been forbidden by the Divine law, as well as by most human lawgivers. On the other hand, it prevails extensively in a state of nature with all gregarious animals (such as the horse), among whom the strongest male retains his daughters and granddaughters until deprived of his harem by younger and stronger rivals. Hence, in those of our domestic animals which are naturally gregarious, it is reasonable to conclude that breeding "in-and-in" is not prejudicial, because it is in conformity with their natural instincts, if not carried farther by art than nature teaches by her example. Now, in nature, we find about two consecutive crosses of the same blood is the usual extent to which it is carried, as the life of the animal is the limit; and it is a remarkable fact, that in practice, a conclusion has been arrived at which exactly coincides with these natural laws. "Once in and once out" is the rule for breeding given by Mr. Smith in his work on the breeding for the

turf; but twice in will be found to be more in accordance with the practice of our most successful (early) breeders.

15. THE INFLUENCE OF THE FIRST IMPREGNATION seems to extend to the subsequent ones; this has been proved by several experiments, and is especially marked in the equine genus. In the series of examples preserved in the museum of the College of Surgeons, the markings of the male quagga, when united with the ordinary mare, are continued clearly for three generations beyond the one in which the quagga was the actual sire; and they are so clear as to leave the question settled without a doubt.

16. WHEN SOME OF THE ELEMENTS of which an individual sire is composed are in a cordance with others making up those of the dam, they coalesce in such a kindred way as to make what is called "a hit." On the other hand, when they are too incongruous, an animal is the result wholly unfitted for the task he is intended to perform.

THESE PRINCIPLES, together with the observations following upon them, have been quoted verbatim, at great length, by the late Mr. Herbert, in his elaborate quarto work on "The Horse of America," with the very flattering testimony that he had done so "not for the purpose of avoiding trouble, or sparing time, but because he conceives the principles laid down to be correct throughout, the reasoning logical and cogent, the examples well taken, and the deductions such as can scarcely be denied." In support of this opinion, he adduces several instances in which a "hit" has occurred in America by carrying out the last axiom in the preceding list. Thus he says, at page 260 of his second volume, "I think myself that it is made clear by recent events, and that such is shown to be the case by the tables of racing stock given at the close of the first volume, that, previous to the last quarter of a century, the American turfman was probably breeding in too much of the old Virginia and South Carolina ante-revolutionary stock, and that the American racehorse has been improved by the recent cross of modern English blood. It is also worthy of remark, that every one of the four most successful of modern English stallions in this country which have most decidedly hit with our old stock—Leviathan, Sarpedon, Priam, and Glencoe—all trace back to several crosses of Herod blood; Glencoe and Priam not less than three or four several times each to crosses of Partner blood, and directly several times over to the Godolphin Barb, or Arabian, which are the very strains from which our Virginian stock derives its peculiar excellence It is farther worthy of remark, that two stallions have decidedly *hit* with the imported English mare Reel, as proved by her progeny, Lecompte and Prioress, respectively to Boston and Sovereign. Now Reel, through Glencoe, Catton, Gohanna, and Smolensko, has herself no less than seven distinct strains of Herod blood. Boston, as every one knows, traces directly through Timoleon, Sir Archy, Diomed, Florizel, to Herod. Sovereign, also, through Emilius, his sire, has Herod on both lines as his paternal and maternal g.g.g. sire; and Tartar, the sire of Herod, a third time, in one remove yet farther back. Now this would go to justify Stonehenge's opinion that the recurrence to the same original old strains of blood, when such strains have been sufficiently intermixed and rendered new by other more recent crosses, is not injurious, but of great advantage; and that, on the whole, it is better, *cæteris paribus*, to do such than to try experiments with extreme out-crosses."

IN-AND-IN BREEDING.

WHEN ANY NEW BREED of animals is first introduced into this country, in-and-in breeding (by which is to be understood the pairing of relations within the degree of second cousins twice or more in succession) can scarcely be avoided; and hence, when first the value of the Arab was generally recognised, the breeder of the racehorse of those days could not well avoid having recourse to the plan. Thus we find, in the early pages of the Stud-book, constant instances of very close in-breeding, often carried to such an extent as to become incestuous. The result was our modern thorough-bred; but it does not follow that because the plan answered in producing that celebrated kind of animal, it will be equally successful in keeping up the breed in its original perfection. In "British Rural Sports," I have given a series of examples of success resulting from each plan, which I shall not now repeat, merely remarking that the opinion which I formed from an attentive examination of them remains unchanged. This opinion was expressed in the following words:—

"If the whole of the pedigrees to which I have drawn attention are attentively examined, the breeder can have no hesitation in coming to the conclusion, that in-breeding, carried out once or twice, is not only not a bad practice, but is likely to be attended with good results. Let him ask what horses have been the most remarkable of late years as stallions, and, with very few exceptions, he will find they were considerably in-bred. It has been remarked, that the Touchstone and Defence blood almost always hits with the Selim; but it is forgotten that the one was already crossed with that horse, and the other with his brother Rubens. On the other hand, the Whisker blood in the Colonel has not succeeded so well, it being made up of much crossed and more distinctly related particles, and therefore not hitting with the Selim and Castrel blood, like his cousins, Touchstone and Defence. It has, however, partially succeeded when in-bred to the Waxy and Buzzard blood, as in Chatham and Fugleman, who both reunite these three strains. The same applies to Coronation, who unites the Whalebone blood in Sir Hercules with that of Rubens in Ruby; but as Waxy and Buzzard, the respective ancestors of all these horses, were both grandsons of Herod, and great-grandsons of Snap, it only strengthens the argument in favor of in-breeding. This conclusion is in accordance with the 14th and 15th axioms, which embody the state of our present knowledge of the theory of generation; and if they are examined, they will be seen to bear upon the present subject, so as to lead one to advise the carrying out of the practice of in-and-in breeding to the same extent as has been found so successful in the instances which I have given. Purity of blood is intimately connected with the practice, because the nearer it is to one standard, the more unmixed it is, and by consequence the more fully it is represented in the produce. Hence, it is doubly needful to take care that this pure blood is of a good kind; because if bad, it will perpetuate its bad qualities just as closely as it would the good, or perhaps still more so."

I have nothing to add to these remarks; and if I were to adduce the few instances in their support which can have occurred since 1855-6, when they were written, I should add little to the mass of evidence which I have already collected. An appeal to the past can only be answered in the way which I have recorded; for the evidence of repeated success in resorting to the practice of in-breeding is too strong to be gainsaid. We will now consider whether the effects of an out-cross are of superior or equal value.

OUT-CROSSING.

BETWEEN IN-AND-IN BREEDING, which I have defined as the pairing of animals within the relationship of second cousins, and the opposite extreme of uniting those which are not at all allied in blood, there are many degrees; but as, in the thorough-bred horse, there are scarcely two in the Stud-book which cannot be traced back to the same stock in one or more lines, we do not generally understand "a cross" to demand absolute distinctness of blood. For instance, Teddington is generally considered as the result of as marked a cross as we ever met with in the modern Stud-book. For five generations, the same name never appears in the pedigree tables of his sire and dam; but in the sixth, we find the name of Sir Peter occur three times on the side of his sire, and twice on that of his dam, besides six other lines of Herod blood on the part of the sire, and eight on that of the dam. Here, therefore, there was a return to the original lines of blood, which had been in-bred twice each, after five successive departures from them as far as could be effected in this particular kind of horse. The last are called "crosses," though not being exactly the reverse of in-breeding, for the reason, as I before remarked, that an absolute freedom from relationship is not to be found, or, if so, extremely rarely

Breeders very often fancy that they put two animals together which are without any corresponding lines or strains of blood in their composition; whereas, in point of fact, the relationship exists only four or five degrees off. The horse and mare are, perhaps, fourth or fifth cousins, often second or third; but, in examining the Stud-book, the blood of the sire, grandsire, and great-grandsire is apt to be forgotten, because it is not given, the name only being mentioned In the book to which I have already alluded, I have inserted a long series of pedigree tables, drawn out to the sixth generation, with a reference also to the earlier pedigrees; by which, at one glance, the breeder may see how constantly, in going back, the same names occur in every table. Eclipse, Herod, and Conductor, the three contemporary descendants of the Darley Arab, the Byerly Turk, and the Godolphin Barb, or one of their immediate descendants, will be seen in the fifth, sixth, and seventh remove of all our thorough-bred horses, and often the names of all three will be found repeated four, five, or six times apiece; yet the horse itself whose pedigree is being examined, as in the instance of Teddington, is considered to be the produce of a cross, and is not, therefore said to be in-bred.

ADVANTAGES AND DISADVANTAGES OF EACH PLAN.

HAVING THUS EXPLAINED the meaning of the two terms, and having, in "British Rural Sports," collected a series of examples of success in crossing nearly equal in number to those adduced in which in-breeding had been resorted to advantageously, I shall now proceed to say a few words upon the probable advantages to be derived from each plan. In the first place, it may be laid down that nearly an equal number of good horses have lately been bred by adopting either mode of proceeding; but no first-rate horse has appeared whose parents were incestuously allied. In the second place, it may be gathered from experiments with horses and other domestic animals, that very close in-breeding, continued for any length of time, is apt to develop the weak points in the constitutions of the breed in which it is adopted. The cautious breeder, therefore will do well to avoid running this risk, and will strive to obtain what he wants without having recourse to the practice, though, at the same time, he will make up his mind that it is unwise to sacrifice a single point with this view. Experience tells us that it is useless to expect to develop a new property or quality in the next generation, by putting a female entirely deprived of it to a male which possesses it even in a marked degree. Some instances of success will attend the adoption of this course, but as a rule it cannot be relied on in the majority of instances. Thus, a slow, stout mare, *containing no lines of fast blood* in her pedigree, will not be likely to breed a fast colt, though put to a flying stallion, whose blood is not stout in a considerable proportion of his ancestry. Two or three consecutive crosses with the same or similar blood will almost of a surety effect the object; but the first will rarely do so. Again, we know, if we put two animals together, equally in-bred or equally crossed, the produce is, on the whole, as likely to resemble the one parent as the other, though there may be a difference of opinion as to particular points. But, if not thus equally composed of similar elements, the more in-bred parent will be represented in a greater proportion than the crossed one; and hence it follows, that if it is desired to keep up the qualities of the horse or mare in his or her descendant, the mate must be selected, if possible, less in-bred than he or she is. West Australian himself and his stock are excellent examples of this theory. His sire, Melbourne, was the result of a series of crosses; while his dam, Mowerina, was in-bred to Whalebone and Whisker, own brothers; and her sire and dam were second cousins. The result has been, that both in "The West" and in his stock the Whalebone element has been universally manifested, and not the slightest trace of Melbourne has ever appeared, as far as my knowledge of his stock allows me to judge. This is in perfect accordance with the 13th anxiom in the epitome of the laws which govern the breeding of our domestic animals. (See page 101.)

CAUSES OF A "HIT."

A "HIT," in breeding, is understood to mean an instance of success; but though it often occurs, the reason for it is not always very clear. My own belief is that it generally results, as I have laid down in the 16th axiom, from the reunion of lines which have been often kept separate for several generations. Thus, it is a fact (so patent that every writer on the breeding of the horse, of late years, has admitted its truth), that the Touchstone and Sultan blood have almost invariably hit. The reason, granting the premises which I lay down, is plain enough—each goes back to Selim, the former through the dam of his sire, Camel, and the latter being son of that horse. Many other examples of a similar nature might be adduced, though not observed so extensively as in the case of Touchstone, because few horses have been put to so many mares as he has. I do not mean to assert that no hit can occur without such a reunion of previously separated lines, but I believe that, under other circumstances, it will rarely be found to show itself; and if, as I before observed, there is a relationship between all thorough-bred horses, either remote or near, there must be this reunion to some extent. This, however, is not what I mean; the return must be to a line only removed two, three, or four generations, in order to be at all marked; and if more than these intervals exist, the hit cannot be said to depend upon the reunion, since this must occur in all cases; and what is common to all cannot be instanced as a particular cause of any subsequent result.

THE FACT REALLY IS, as proved by thousands of examples, that by putting *A* and *B* together, the produce is not necessarily made up of half of each. Both parents have qualities belonging to the several members of a long line of ancestors, and their son (or daughter) may possibly be made up of as many as seven proportions of one parent, and one proportion of the other. It generally happens, that if there is any considerable degree of consanguinity, or even a great resemblance in form, to some of the ancestry on each side, the produce will draw together those elements, and will be made up of the characteristics peculiar to them in a very large proportion. This accounts for the preponderance of the Touchstone form in the West Australian stock; while the same horse is overpowered in Orlando and his stock, by the greater infusion of Selim blood in the dam Vulture, who is removed exactly in the same degree as Touchstone from Selim and his brother Castrel; and the two latter, therefore, have more influence on the stock than the former. Here, then, we have two remarkable instances, which each show a hit from the reunion of strains after two out-crosses; while, at the same time, they severally display an example of two lines overpowering one in the stock of the same horse. It may be argued, that in each case it is the blood of the dam which has overpowered that of the sire,—West Australian being by Melbourne, out of a daughter of Touchstone; while Orlando is by Touchstone, out of a mare descended from two lines of Selim and his brother Castrel. Now, I am myself a great believer in the influence of the dam over her progeny, and therefore I should be ready to accept this argument, were it not that, under ordinary circumstances, both Melbourne and Touchstone have been sure to reproduce their likenesses in their several sons and daughters. Every racing man who has been on the turf while the Melbournes and Touchstones were in their glory, was able, in almost all instances, to say at the first glance, "That is a Melbourne or a Touchstone colt or filly." But, in the cases of Orlando and West Australian, the resemblance to their respective sires was not apparent; and, as I before observed, it is still less visible in their stock. In the language of the stud, this is called "going back" to a particular strain; and it is so constantly observable, that there is no necessity for dwelling further upon it.

IMPORTANCE OF HEALTH AND SOUNDNESS IN BOTH SIRE AND DAM.

OUR PRESENT BREED OF HORSES is undoubtedly less healthy than that of our ancestors; and this tendency to unsoundness is not marked in any particular department of the animal economy, but the defect shows itself wherever the strain is the greatest from the nature of the work which the animal has to perform. Thus, the racehorse becomes a roarer, or his legs and feet give way. The hunter fails chiefly in his wind or his hocks, because he is not used much on hard ground, and therefore his fore legs are not severely tried, as in the case with the racer, who often has to extend himself over a course rendered almost as hard as a turnpike-road by the heat of a July or August sun. The harness-horse often becomes a roarer, from the heavy weights that he has to draw, especially if his windpipe is impeded by his head being confined by the bearing-rein. The hack, again, suffers chiefly in his legs, from our hard Macadamised roads; while the cart-horse becomes unsound in his hocks or his feet, the former parts being strained by his severe pulls, and the latter being battered and bruised against the ground, from having to bear the enormous weight of his carcass. But it is among our well-bred horses that unsoundness is the most frequent; and in them, I believe, it may be traced to the constant breeding from sires and dams which have been thrown out of training, in consequence of a break-down, or "making a noise," or from some other form of disease It is quite true, that roaring is not necessarily transmitted from father to son; and it is also manifest that there are several causes which produce it, some of which are purely accidental, and are not likely to be handed down to the next generation. The same remarks apply to the eyes; but, in the main, it may be concluded that disease is hereditary, and that a sound horse is far more likely to get healthy stock than an unsound one. In the mare, probably, health is still more essential; but if the breeder regards his future success, whether he is establishing a stud of racehorses, or of those devoted to any kind of slower work, he will carefully eschew every kind of unsoundness, and especially those which are of a constitutional character. If a horse gets blind in an attack of influenza, or if, without any previous indications of inflammation, he breaks down from an accidental cause, the defect may be passed over, perhaps; but, on the contrary, when the blindness comes on in the form of ordinary cataract, or the break-down is only the final giving-way in a leg which has been long amiss, I should strongly advise an avoidance of the horse which has displayed either the one or the other. I believe that a government inspection of all horses and mares used for breeding purposes would be a great national good; and I look forward to its establishment, at no distant time, as the only probable means of insuring greater soundness in our breeds of horses. I would not have the liberty of the subject interfered with. Let every man breed what he likes, but I would not let him foist the produce on the public as sound, when they are almost sure to go amiss as soon as they are worked. Ships must now all be registered at Lloyd's, in the classes to which they are entitled by their condition; and horses, as well as mares, should be registered in the same way, according to the opinion which the government inspector may form as to their health and the probability of getting or producing sound and useful foals. The purchaser would call for the registration-mark, when he asked for the pedigree of the horse he was about to buy; and if it was not a favorable one, he would, of course, be placed upon his guard. If this plan could be carried out in practice, as well as it looks on paper, much good might be done, I am assured; but we all know that inspectors are but mortals, and that they are liable to be biassed in more ways than one. Still, I believe that the evil is becoming so glaring, that something must soon be done; and I see no other mode so likely as this to be advantageous to the interests of the purchaser and user of the horse.

BEST AGE TO BREED FROM.

THE GENERAL OPINION throughout England is, that one or other of the parents should be of mature age; and that if a very young mare is chosen, the horse should not be less than eight, ten, or twelve years old. If both are very young or very old, the produce is generally small and weakly; but by adopting the plan above-mentioned, the services of young and old may be fully utilized. A great many of our very best performers on the turf have been got by old stallions; as, for instance, Whisker, son of Waxy, in his twenty-second year; Emilius, son of Orville, in his twentieth; Voltigeur and Newminster, whose sires were respectively twenty-one and seventeen; Blink Bonny, who was got by Melbourne, in his twentieth year; and Wild Dayrell, by Ion, when seventeen years old. To these may be added, Gemma di Vergy, Lifeboat, and Gunboat, three celebrated sons of Sir Hercules, and all got by him after he was twenty years old—the last named when he was twenty-five years of age. So, also, many were out of old mares; including Priam, whose dam was twenty when she dropped him; Crucifix, the daughter of Octaviana, when twenty-two years old; Lottery, out of Mandane, in her twentieth year; and Brutandorf, produced by the same mare when she was twenty-two. From these instances, the breeder may conclude that age is no bar to success, if matched with youth on the other side; but the instances of success in breeding from two aged parents are rare indeed. It is next to be ascertained what is the earliest age at which this animal can be relied on for breeding; and here, again, example is better than theory. The most remarkable instance of moderate success in adopting this plan is in that of The Ugly Buck, whose dam, Monstrosity, was put to Venison when only a two-year-old. The horse, also, was not more than seven, and the dam of Monstrosity bred her in her fourth year. But though Ugly Buck promised well as a two-year-old, he failed in his subsequent career, and his example is not, therefore, to be considered as at all conclusive. Still, his is a most extraordinary instance, and as such it should not be lost sight of. There are many cases in which the first produce of a mare has been her best; such as, in former times, Mark Anthony, Conductor, Shuttle Pope, Filho da Puta, Sultan, Pericles, Oiseau, Doctor Syntax, Manfred, and Pantaloon. Nevertheless, these may be considered to be exceptions, and a large majority of the brood mares in the Stud-book are credited with their most successful produce subsequently to their first. The rule generally adopted is to wait till the mare is three years old before breeding from her, and then to put her to a horse of at least full maturity—that is to say, seven or eight years old.

THE INFLUENCE OF THE SIRE AND DAM RESPECTIVELY.

I HAVE ALREADY, at page 40, alluded to this question as relating to the breeding of the Arab horse in his native country, and have there shown that the opinions held by Abd-el-Kader, in modern days, do not coincide with those which have long been supposed to be general in Arabia. In the passage which I have there quoted, this celebrated chief attempts to define the exact part which each parent takes in producing the foal, but he goes still farther in subsequent answers to the questions asked by General Daumas, in relation to the value put by the Arabs on their stallions and mares respectively. To these Abd-el-Kader replies as follows: "It is true that Arabs prefer mares to horses, but only for the following reasons: the first is that they look at the profit which may arise from a mare as very considerable. Some Arabs have realized as much as 20,000 dollars from the produce of one mare. They have a proverb that 'the fountain-head of riches is a mare that produces a mare.' This is corroborated by the prophet Mahomet, who says, 'Let mares be preferred, their bellies are a treasure, their backs the seat of honor.' The greatest blessing is an intelligent wife or a mare that produces plenty of foals." These words are thus explained by commentators: Their bellies are a treasure because the mare by her produce increases the riches of her master; and their backs are the seat of honor, because the pace of a mare is easier than that of a horse; and there be those that say it is sufficiently so as in time to render a horseman effeminate. The second reason is that a mare does not neigh in war, that she bears hunger, thirst, and heat better than a horse, and that therefore she is more useful to people whose riches consist in camels and sheep. Now all the world knows that our camels and sheep thrive only in the desert, where the soil is so arid that Arabs drinking chiefly milk find water seldom oftener than every eight or ten days, in consequence of the distance between the pasturages, which are only to be found in the neighborhood of wells. The mare is like the serpent, their powers increase in hot weather and in arid countries. Serpents which live in cold or watery countries have little venom or courage, so that their bite is seldom mortal, whereas those that live in hot countries are more irritable, and the virulence of their poison is increased. Whilst the horse can less easily bear the heat of the sun, the mare, doubtless from constitutional causes, finds her energies increase with the greatest heat. The third reason is that the mare requires less care and less nourishment. The owner can lead and turn her out to graze with the sheep and camels, and he is not obliged to have a person constantly watching her; whereas a horse cannot do without being highly fed, and he cannot be turned out without an attendant for obvious reasons. These are the true reasons of an Arab's preference for mares. It does not arise from the foal inheriting the qualities of the dam rather than those of the sire; it does not proceed from its being better at all times and under all circumstances to ride a mare rather than a horse; but it is based upon material interests, and on the necessities enforced by the description of life which Arabs lead. It must, however, be admitted that a horse is more noble than a mare. He is stronger, more courageous, and faster. That a horse is stronger than a mare is thus proved. If both were struck by the same mortal wound a mare would fall at once, but a horse would seldom drop until he had carried his rider into safety. I saw a mare struck by a ball on the leg; the bone was broken; unable to bear the pain she fell immediately. A horse was hit in the same manner; the broken limb hung only by the skin; he continued his course, supporting himself on his sound leg, until he bore his rider from the battle-field and then fell. The Arabs prefer mares to horses for the reasons I have given, and those reasons are sufficient to show why amongst us the value attached to the possession of a mare is greater than that they attach to the possession of a horse, even though the breeding of each were the same; for whilst on the one hand the foal takes more after the sire than the dam, on the other the proprietor of a horse cannot gain in many years as much as the proprietor of a mare can gain in one year if she throw a foal. However, when a horse has displayed any extraordinary qualities, it often happens that he will not be parted with, probably producing to his master in the way of booty or otherwise as much as the most valuable mare. I saw amongst the Annazas, a tribe extending from Bagdad to Syria, horses so beyond all price that it was almost impossible to purchase them, and certainly impossible to pay ready money for them. These animals, of a fabulous value, are sold only to the highest personages, or to rich merchants who pay for them by thirty or forty instalments, or by a perpetual rent settled on the vendor or his decendants. The birth of a horse can never be considered a misfortune by an Arab, however much he may prefer a mare for the material advantages which they procure. Mares almost always produce, and it is on that account principally that they are preferred. I repeat it—the birth of an animal that guarantees its master against humiliation can never be considered a misfortune. A poet says: 'My brothers reproach me with my debts, yet I never contracted one but for an honorable purpose. In giving the bread of heaven to all, in purchasing a horse of noble race, and buying a slave to attend upon me."—*Bailey's Magazine of Sports, June*, 1860.

MY OWN BELIEF in this matter, founded upon observations made during a long series of years on the horse as well as the dog, is that no rule can be laid down with any certainty. Much depends upon the comparative physical power and strength of constitution in each parent, even more perhaps than the composition of the blood. There have been many instances of two brothers being used in the stud, both among horses and greyhounds, in which one has almost invariably got his stock resembling himself in all particulars, not even excluding color, while the descendants of the other have rarely been recognisable as his. Thus among horses the Touchstones have been mostly brown or dark bay, and as a lot have shown a high form as racehorses, while the Launcelots have been of all colors, and have been below mediocrity on the turf. Several examples of the same nature may be quoted from among greyhounds, such as Ranter, Gipsey Prince, and Gipsey Royal, three brothers whose stock were as different as possible, but the fact is so generally recognised that it is not necessary to dwell upon it. Now surely this difference in the power of transmitting the likeness of the sire, when the blood is exactly the same as it is observed to extend over large numbers, can only depend upon a variation in individual power. Not only does this apply to the males, but the females also show the same difference. Some mares have gone on producing foals which afterwards turned out first-class whatever horse they were put to, as, for instance, Phryne (dam of winners by Pantaloon, Melbourne, and The Flying Dutchman), Barbelle, who produced Van Tromp by Lanercost, De Witt by The Provost, and The Flying Dutchman by Bay Middleton. Alice Hawthorne, successively as well as successfully put to Birdcatcher, Melbourne, Touchstone, Windhound, Melbourne or Windhound, and Sweetmeat; and lastly, Ellerdale, dam of Ellington and Ellermere, and Gildermire by Flying Dutchman, Summerside by West Australian, and Wardersmarke by Birdcatcher. On appealing to the greyhound, also, we see some remarkable instances within the last few years, of which Mr. Jardine's Ladylike and Mr. Randell's Riot may be considered as very strong cases in point.

The latter bitch also may be instanced as having been extremely successful in the stud, while her own brother, Ranter, in the same kennel, was a total failure. There must consequently be something more than mere breeding to produce a successful result, and this I am inclined to think resides in the strength of the constitution possessed by the individual.

BUT EVEN SUPPOSING the horse or mare displays this constitutional power, there is something which controls it, as we have seen in the two cases already instanced of Orlando and West Australian. In the former horse the influence of the sire, great as it usually has been shown to be, was compelled to succumb to the combination of the three lines traceable to Selim and his brother Castrel, while in the other this same horse Touchstone prevailed (still, however, on the side of the dam) apparently only because there was a combination of two very recently separated lines of Waxy blood through his sons Whalebone and Whisker. The second of these examples is the more worthy of note, because in tracing back the lines of the sire and dam, the name of Trumpeter from whom Melbourne is lineally descended is met with three times in the pedigree of the former, and four times in that of the latter. Here then but for the nearness of the two lines of Waxy I should have expected the produce to follow the Trumpator strain through Melbourne, but as I have already observed, beyond the third remove this influence is very much weakened. We may therefore come to the conclusion that it is not always superior strength of constitution, nor the greater purity or antiquity of the blood which determines the influence to be expected by either parent, but that sometimes the one and sometimes the other is the cause. And as the former cannot well be determined, the latter is the foundation for the plans of the breeder, who will on the whole do well to follow the maxims first laid down by that celebrated breeder of horses and cattle, the second Earl Spencer, whose opinions were in conformity with the 13th axiom for breeders which I have inserted at page 101.

CHOICE OF SIRE AND DAM.

THE NECESSITY FOR HEALTH in each parent has already been insisted on, but beyond this point, which is generally admitted, there are several others to be attended to. Thus, since the preponderance of either over the form and temper of the progeny will, in all probability, fall to that one which has the superior purity of blood, it follows that if the breeder wishes to alter in any important particular the qualities possessed by his mare, he must select a horse which is either better bred or some of whose lines will coalesce with those of the dam's, which it is desired to perpetuate. Thus, supposing a mare to be made up of four lines, two of which

are decidedly bad, and one which is so good as to attract the notice
of her owner, then let him look around and select some horse in
whose pedigree is to be found a similar strain, taking care that the
relationship is not so close as to lead to disappointment on the score
of the bad effects attributable to in-breeding. But there are many
brood mares not in the Stud-book, whose pedigrees are not ascertainable, and in their case this rule will not apply. Here a different
plan must be pursued, and a horse must be chosen whose shape,
action, or temper coincides with the particular quality which it is
desired to perpetuate. I am strongly inclined to believe that it is
comparatively of little use to look about for sires who possess those
qualities in which the dam is deficient. Such a course of proceeding has so constantly ended in disappointment, within my own
knowledge, that I believe I am justified in condemning it. A stallion (whether horse or greyhound, the same is observable) is known
to have been very fast, or very stout, as the case may be, and having obtained the one character or the other, breeders have supposed
that they have only to send mares deficient in either quality, and
they would insure its development in the produce. If the mare or
bitch happens to possess among her ancestry stout or fast lines of
blood, the produce will display the one or the other, if she is put to
a horse possessing them; but, on the contrary, if the lines of the
dam are all fast, or all stout, no first cross with a sire possessing
the opposite qualities will be likely to have any effect, though no
doubt there are some few exceptions to this, as to all other rules.
The instances in support of this position are so numerous within
my own knowledge, that I should scarcely be able to make a beginning, and every one draws upon his own experience, or who
will examine the "*Stud Book*" and the "*Coursing Calendar*," will
find examples without end throughout every volume of each. It
would be invidious to select any stallion now in this country, but
among those which have been well tried here in the stud, and are
here no longer, may be mentioned the Flying Dutchman. This
horse was well known to have been himself not only fast, but stout,
and, as a consequence, even those breeders who are aware of the
necessity for regarding both of these qualities were induced to
breed from him, expecting that the result would be to give them
similar stock in the next generation. The contrary, however, was
the case. In many cases speed was developed, but in almost every
instance, without an exception, that speed was not allied with staying power. The unlooked-for result has been attributed to his
sire, Bay Middleton, whose stock have been notoriously flashy; but
if the pedigree of Barbelle, his dam, is carefully examined, a still
stronger reason may be assigned. If her lines are traced back five
generations, it will be seen that out of her thirty-two progenitors
in that remove fourteen are descended from Herod or his sire,

Copyright Secured.

ETHAN ALLEN.

Photographed from Life by SCHREIBER & SON.

Tartar, and these in addition to the already overflowing quantum of the same .blood in Bay Middleton himself. Now I am a great admirer of the blood of Herod, and I believe him to be one of the chief foundations of the high form of our modern horses; but its peculiar characteristic is speed, not stoutness, and it requires a combination with the stouter blood of Eclipse, or some other horse of that strain, to make the possessor capable of staying a distance. With these fast lines the produce of Barbelle has always been fast, but it can scarcely occasion surprise that her stoutest son, Van Tromp, should be by Lanercost, nor that Orlando, with his double lines of Selim and Castrel blood, should get a mere half-miler like Zuyder Zee. The Flying Dutchman was, no doubt, a grand performer himself, but his may be regarded as a somewhat exceptional case, and this opinion is supported by the failure of his own brother (Vanderdecken) on the turf, although cast in a mould which would lead one to expect a still greater success.

IN PAYING ATTENTION TO THE PERFORMANCES of the ancestry of both sire and dam, regard must also be had to their size, as this element is considered of much importance. Neither a large nor a small sire or dam will perpetuate the likeness of himself or herself unless descended from a breed which is either the one or the other. It only leads to disappointment to breed from a tall stallion or mare if either is only accidentally so, and not belonging to a breed generally possessing the same characteristics. Many a small mare or bitch has surprised her owner by producing him animals much larger than herself, but on tracing her pedigree it will almost always be found to contain the names of animals of above the average size. Moderately small mares are generally of a stronger constitution than very large ones, and on that account they will often answer the purposes of the stud better than larger animals, *provided they are of a sort usually cast in the mould which is desired.* This should never be lost sight of by the breeder, and where, as in breeding thorough-breds, the pedigree can be traced far enough for this purpose, there is no excuse for neglecting the circumstance.

THE ABOVE PRECAUTIONS are sufficient in all those cases where the pedigree is attainable, but there are many brood mares, as I before remarked, in which nothing is known of their antecedents. Here, the breeder can only act upon the general rule that "like produces like," and cannot take advantage of the addition which I have made to the 12th axiom, at page 101, of the words, "*or the likeness of some ancestor.*" In such cases, for the reason which I have given, disappointment will constantly attend upon the first experiments, and until the mare has produced her first foal, and he has gone on to his third or fourth year, the value of the dam can hardly be ascertained. Breeding is always, more or less, a lottery but when it is carried on with dams of unknown parentage, it is ten times more so than it need be. Were I to commence the establishment of a breeding stud, whether of cart or carriage horses, hacks or hunters, I would never introduce a single mare whose dam and grand-dam as well as the sire and grand-sire would not be produceable as good specimens of their respective kinds. Beyond the second remove there would always be some difficulty in going with the lower-bred mares, but I would certainly go as far as this in all cases. If the sire and dam, grand-sire and grand-dam, were, on the whole, of desirable form and performances, I would choose the produce as a brood mare, but not otherwise; and though, of course, I should be obliged to pass over some important defects in individuals, I would not do so if they were common to all, or nearly all, of the four. In this way I should expect to do more than by simply choosing "a great roomy mare" without knowing her pedigree, in the belief that she would be sure to reproduce her likeness.

THE KIND OF HORSE MOST PROFITABLE FOR THE BREEDER TO CHOOSE.

WHEN A PERSON makes up his mind to bestow his attention on the breeding of horses as a speculation, it behooves him to consider what kind is best suited to the nature of his land and the length of his purse, as well as to his own knowledge of horses. Unless he has plenty of fine upland grass and a command of money, it is quite useless for him to think of the race-horse; nor will he do well, without these concomitants, to dabble in hunters. Cart-horses, now-a-days, pay well when there is work for them to do up to their third or fourth year; and carriage-horses are likewise a good speculation, when the land is suitable to their development. No one, however, should turn his attention to the breeding of hacks on a large scale, since they will almost inevitably cost more than they will fetch at five years old. The farmer who keeps one or two "nag" mares is the only person who can be said to rear hacks without loss; and he only does so, because he begins to use them for his own slow work as soon as they are three years old. Even in his case, however, I much doubt whether the same food which has been given the colts would not have been turned to greater profit if given to horned cattle; and the only thing which can be said in favor of the former is, that they eat coarse grass which the latter will refuse. To make the breeding of the horse turn out profitably, the hack and inferior kind of harness-horse ought to be the culls from a lot of colts intended for the hunting-field, and then, the one with the other, they may be made to pay.

CONCLUDING REMARKS ON BREEDING.

THE ANGRY DISCUSSIONS which have taken place in the year 1860, between Lord Redesdale and Admiral Rous, indicate plainly what is the general opinion on the subject of the diminution in the stoutness of our horses. Breeders, therefore, should turn their attention to this point, and should be doubly careful to avoid weedy or diseased sires and dams. It cannot be denied that our modern thorough-breds possess size and speed; but they certainly do not shine in staying powers, as I have already more than once remarked. But there are some strains particularly free from this defect, and these I have endeavored to point out. It should not, moreover, be forgotten that though the thorough-bred horse will bear more work, especially at high speed, than any other kind, yet he can only do this if well fed and warmly housed. Being a native of a warm and dry climate, he requires to be protected from the weather; and the young stock must be well reared in all respects, or they will never pay. If, therefore, the breeder is not determined to put up warm hovels in every paddock, and if he is stingy of his corn, he had far better let his stud of mares be composed of lower bred animals. If a thorough-bred horse and a donkey are both fed upon the lowest quantity and quality of food which will keep the latter in condition, the donkey would beat its high-bred antagonist over a distance of ground—that is to say, supposing the experiment to be continued long enough to produce a permanent effect upon the two animals. A cart-horse colt, or one of any kind of low blood, will do well enough if reared, till he is put to work, upon grass and hay; but a race-horse or hunter, of high breeding, would show a badly-developed frame, and be comparatively worthless for his particular kind of work, if he were not allowed his corn from the time that he is weaned.

CHAPTER VIII.

THE BROOD MARE AND HER FOAL.

The Hovel and Paddock—General Management of the Brood-Mare—Treatment when in Foal—After Foaling—Early Management of the Foal—Weaning.

HAVING ALREADY ALLUDED to the principles which should guide the breeder in the choice of his mares, I need not further allude to them beyond the remark that, independently of those which I have indicated, he must take care that they are each possessed of a frame suitable to carry a foal, and of a constitution hardy enough to sustain the drain upon the system caused by the young animal, both before and after birth. If the pelvis and back ribs are not large and deep, the *fœtus* will not have room to be developed and brought into the world; and unless the mare is a good feeder, and is also furnished with an udder which will give sufficient milk, she will not afford enough nourishment to her foal, which will, therefore, be weakly and badly developed in its proportions. The shape may be easily detected beforehand, but the constitution and milking properties cannot so well be predicated, though the experienced eye and hand of the stud-groom will enable him to give a tolerably correct guess.

HOVEL AND PADDOCK.

IF THE BREEDER is about to undertake the production of a number of horses of any kind, he must establish a regular stud-farm, which for all horses should be on sound upland, with a subsoil of chalk or gravel. The presence of fine white clovers is in itself almost sufficient to show that the soil will be suitable to the horse; but, if possible, there should be an absolute practical knowledge that the situation *has* agreed with the animal, before any heavy investment is made. If the surface fall is good, draining may not be necessary, but in most cases the herbage will be greatly improved by the introduction of tiles. Low, marshy situations may serve during the autumn months to freshen up a stall horse, but they are utterly unfit for the rearing of young stock, and should be carefully avoided. If the stud is highly bred, and the feeding is to be good, the colts will be very mischievous, and unless care is taken to make the fences safe, they will break bounds, or injure themselves in the attempt. Deep ditches are very unsafe, for the mare as well as her foal are very apt to get cast in them, with a serious or fatal injury as the result. Posts and rails answer well enough, where timber is plentiful, but, in the long run, they are expensive from the necessity for constant repairs. Banks with thorn hedges on the top are the very best of all means for enclosing the paddocks, and are even better than stone walls, which, however, are excellent for the purpose if they have the soil raised against their bases, without which the foal is liable to slip up against their surface, and thus sometimes blemish his knees. There is a great difference of opinion as to the size necessary for the paddocks, and the number of mares which should be allowed in each. In some well conducted stud-farms, as, for instance, in that belonging to the Rawcliffe Company, near York, the enclosures are very large, and a dozen, or even as many as eighteen, mares and their foals are turned out together as soon as the weather permits, and the spring grass grows high enough. In others, as at the Hampton Court and Middle Park establishments, the paddocks are each only calculated to take three or four mares and their foals; and the yearlings, also, are never allowed to exceed four in any one paddock. Mr. Martin, the clever and experienced manager of the first-named stud, is of opinion that colts should have room enough to gallop, and thus early accustom their joints and sinews to bear the strains which they must, sometime or other, be subjected to. On the other hand, the argument is held that in a small paddock the foal gallops quite as much as in the larger one, and puts his joints to the strain in stopping himself at the corners, whilst there is less injury from other accidental causes, such as kicks and the jamming of a lot together in a narrow gateway. On the whole I am inclined to believe that the latter plan is the best, for experience shows that a well-fed foal will gallop daily, for hours together, even in a two acre paddock.

AT FOALING TIME each mare must have a separate hovel or loose-box, but as, practically, it is found that she always gives some few hours' notice of her approaching parturition, it is the custom to bring her into the close neighborhood of the house of the stud-groom at night, so that he may be at hand to render her assistance, if necessary. Any loose-box answers for that purpose, if it does not open to a warm stable, which would render it too hot for an animal which has been for months exposed to the open air. But after foaling the mare will also require a hovel to herself for six weeks or two months, when the foal will be strong enough to take care of itself in running among other mares. Indeed, at all times, the mares should at night be in separate hovels, even when during the day they run in the same paddock with two or three others. This hovel should be about twelve to fifteen feet long, and not less than ten feet wide. The height may easily be too great, because in the early spring the weather is often so severe that the mare cannot impart sufficient heat to a very large volume of air. From eight to nine feet will therefore be ample, the former being well suited to the larger area which I have given above, and the latter to the smaller. It is a very common plan, when economy is much studied, to build four hovels back to back, at the angles formed by four small runs, by which a saving in the internal walls is effected. This, however, necessitates a northerly or easterly aspect for two out of the four, either of which is objectionable. Two hovels may readily be placed side by side in the most desirable situation, and these may be made to open into separate runs. The walls should be built of brick or stone, whichever is locally the cheaper material, or where gorse is abundant they may be formed from it, being the cheapest of all.

In some counties what is called "wattle and dab" is very generally employed for outbuildings of this kind, and when they are roofed with thatch, which carries the water well off the sides, it answers very well. It is composed of common wood quarterings, with the uprights connected together by transverse bars like the rounds of a ladder, about eight inches apart. When the whole framework is put together thus, some soil, which should be clay or loam, is well worked together with straw and water into a tenacious mixture, which is forked over each transverse bar in succession, and the whole smoothed down till it assumes a regular and even surface. Cottages and outbuildings are put up in this way in Devonshire and Dorsetshire at very little expense, straw costing the farmer little or nothing, either for the walls or the roof, and the wood being also the produce of his own land. The labor, therefore, is the only part which costs money, and that is not paid for at a very high rate, where wages rarely exceed nine shillings a week. When gorse is used, it is adopted in the following way:—The door-posts and uprights are first fixed, and should be either of oak—which is best—or of good sound Memel fir; they should be about six inches by four, and should be fixed six feet apart, with three feet sunk in the ground. After thus fixing the framework, and putting on the wall-plate and rafters, the whole internal surface is made good by nailing split poles of larch, or other timber, closely together across the uprights, taking especial care to round off the ends when they appear at the door-posts. Thus the whole of the interior is tolerably smooth, and no accident can happen from the foal getting his leg into any crevice between the poles, if care is taken to nail them securely, and to leave no space between them. When this internal framework is finished, the gorse is applied outside, as follows: It is first cut into small branches, leaving a foot-stalk to each, about twelve or fifteen inches in length: these branches are arranged in layers between the uprights, the stalks pointing upwards and inwards, and the prickly ends downwards and outwards. When, by a succession of layers of these brushy stalks, a height of eighteen inches has been raised, a stout and tough pole, about the size of an ordinary broom-stick, and six feet long, is laid upon the middle of the gorse, and so as to confine it against the split poles and between the uprights. The workmen kneel upon this pole, and by its means compress the gorse into the smallest possible compass, and while thus pressed down, and against the internal framework, it is confined to the latter by five or six loops of strong copper wire. When this is properly done, the gorse is so firmly confined, and withal so closely packed, that neither wind nor rain can penetrate, nor can all the mischief-loving powers of the foal withdraw a single stalk. After fixing the first layer, a second is built up in the same way, and when neatly done the exterior is as level as a brick wall; but if there are any very prominent branches they may be sheared off with the common shears, or taken off with the ordinary hedging bill-hook. When it is desired to make the exterior look very smooth, a hay-trusser's knife is used; but the natural ends, though not so level, are a much better defence, and last longer than the cut gorse. In the interior the stalks sometimes project, and if so they must be smoothly trimmed off. The roof should be covered in with some material, which is cool in summer and warm in winter, and for this purpose, therefore, nothing is so bad as slate, or so good as thatch. Objections are sometimes made to the latter material that it harbors vermin, but if the mares are well fed, I must doubt their ever becoming lousy, unless these parasites are introduced by some animal from without. In any case, tiles are preferable to slates, and on the average they are also cheaper. Pantiles are not easily made proof against the wind, but plane-tiles, when properly pointed, are quite air-tight, and are far warmer in cold weather than slates, while they are also cooler in summer. The door should be at least four feet or four feet six inches wide, and seven feet to seven feet six inches high, with all the angles to the sides and top of the frame rounded off to prevent accident from striking the hip or head. The door, of oak or elm, should be cut in half across the middle, so as to allow the lower half to be shut, while the upper, being open, admits a free supply of air. A small window should be inserted in the wall, for light and ventilation when the door is closed. When straw is abundant it is usual to leave the floor in its natural state, the litter absorbing all that falls from the mare and foal, and being changed often enough to keep the place dry. In case, however, this cannot be done, the flooring should be similar to that for ordinary stables, that is to say, laid with bricks or pebbles, clinkers being much too expensive for such a purpose. Where chalk is abundant, it forms an excellent floor, if a drain is cut all round the building, and the soil being taken out to the depth of nearly a foot, the chalk is filled in to a little above the level of the natural surface, and is then well rammed down, a drain and trap being inserted in the middle.

The last point which requires consideration is the kind of manger which is best adapted to the use of the mare and her foal, if the latter is to be fed in the way proper to thorough-bred stock. In any case, a wooden manger of the ordinary kind should be fixed, with a staple for the rack-chain to fasten her up. A hay rack should be so arranged that it can be filled from the outside without difficulty; which is easily managed by building a little wooden excrescence on to one of the outer walls, leaving a hole in the latter for the mare to feed herself through. A wooden lid, covered with zinc, lifts up and permits the introduction of the fodder without the necessity for carrying a fork into the hovel, which will sometimes injure the mare or her foal. Well-bred young animals of this species are so mischievous that when shut up they will jump into any place which can possibly hold them, and many a broken leg or back has ensued from an open hay-rack, placed near the ground, attracting the gambols of a foal. A few wooden bars nailed across the opening effectually prevents this, while the addition of a low manger in another corner provides for the feeding of the foal with kibbled oats, if such should be the plan adopted, and the fourth is occupied by a water-tank. External to the hovel the only provision necessary is a yard, which may be omitted if the paddock is always dry from the land being well drained. Unless this is the case, however, the yard should always be provided, as there are many days throughout the year when the weather is fine enough over head to allow of the foal being turned out of doors with advantage, if it can be protected from the wet grass or wetter soil. A yard is, therefore, truly valuable in the absence of a dry soil, and it should be paved with bricks, stones, or pebbles, well covered with a layer of litter, to prevent slips and strains.

GENERAL MANAGEMENT OF THE BROOD MARE.

WHEN IT HAS BEEN DECIDED to breed from a mare, if she is not already thrown out of work, it will often be necessary to cool her down, by turning her out to grass and taking away her corn, before she will become stinted. Thorough-bred mares are not, as a rule, allowed to take the horse while in work; but sometimes they are so constantly "in use," that no other means will enable the trainer to go on with his work of preparation. There is a wonderful difference in this respect: some animals are rarely "in use," once or twice a year being the outside; while others are so every nine days throughout the spring,—the average, perhaps, being in that state at about intervals of two or three months from the time of shedding their coats till the beginning of autumn. Again, some are not upset in their work by this natural process; while others refuse to feed, lose condition, and cannot be depended on for half their usual exertions. Either extreme requires a change of feeding; for, on the one hand, the cool temperament is excited by the freedom of a run at grass, and on the other, the warmer one is benefited by losing the heating qualities of her corn. At all events, it is found, in practice, that though the majority of maiden mares will become stinted while at work, yet that a large number require a run at grass before they will become in foal. As I before remarked, thorough-bred mares are generally entirely devoted to the stud from the time that they are put to the horse; but there are many others of lower breeding which their owners desire to work on for some months afterwards. It is often apparent that the legs of a hack or harness-mare are wearing out, and her owner decides upon having a foal from her, but wishes to avoid the expense of keep from the spring, when he puts her to the horse, till the next

January or February, varying, of course, with the time of foaling. All mares are the better for slow work up to within two months of foaling; but they should not be ridden or driven so fast as to occasion exhaustion. Cart-mares are generally used to within a few days of their time, taking care to keep them at light work and to avoid straining them. With these precautions, if the legs keep tolerably sound, a mare may be made to earn her keep for nine months out of the eleven which are the duration of her pregnancy.

THE TIME of sending the mare to the horse will vary with the purposes for which her produce is intended. If for racing, it is desired that she shall foal as soon as possible after the first of January; and as she carries her foal about eleven months, the first time of her being "in use" after the first of February is the period chosen for her. All other horses take their age from the first of May; and as this is the time when the young grass begins to be forward enough for the use of the mare, the breeder is not anxious to get his half-bred foals dropped much before that time. As, however, mares are very uncertain animals, he will do well to take advantage of the first opportunity after March, as by putting off the visit to the horse, he may be disappointed altogether, or the foal may be dropped so late, that winter sets in before it has acquired strength to bear it. These remarks apply to maiden mares only; those which have dropped a foal are generally put to the horse nine or ten days afterwards, when almost every mare is in season. For this reason, valuable thorough-bred mares are often sent to foal at the place where the sire stands who is intended to be used next time. The travelling to him so soon after foaling would be injurious to both the dam and her foal, and hence the precaution I have named is adopted. The mare then remains to be tried at intervals of nine days, and when she is stinted, the foal is strong enough to bear any length of journey with impunity. Mares and their foals commonly travel by road twenty miles, or even more, for this purpose; but they do not often exceed that distance, and about fifteen miles a day is quite as much as a nine days' old foal can compass without injury, and that done very quietly, the mare being led at a slow pace all the way.

TREATMENT WHEN IN FOAL.

WHEN THE MARE IS IN FOAL, if not intended to be kept at work, she should be turned out in good pasture; but it should not be so rich and succulent as to disagree with her stomach, or make her unwieldy from fat. The former mistake is a constant cause of miscarriage, the bowels becoming relaxed from the improper nature of the food. On the other hand, if it is not sufficiently good, the mare will become thin, and will starve her foal in its growth. Mares that have been corned highly all their lives should have a feed or two daily, after they are six months gone, and especially if the autumnal grasses are not rich and plentiful. Most half-bred animals, however, do very well till about Christmas; after which, hay and corn, with a few carrots, should be liberally given them, still allowing them to pick up what grass they can find in their paddocks. Excessive fat is a state of disease, and interferes with the due nutrition of the *fœtus*, while it is very dangerous at foaling-time, when it not only interferes with the process, but also tends to produce fever. Supposing the mare to be at work, she should have some kind of green food—lucerne being the best, and vetches, perhaps, the worst for the purpose, the latter being too heating, especially to the organs contained within the pelvis. Any of the grasses or clovers answer well; and, after they are done, carrots form an excellent *succedaneum*, given sliced in a bran mash every night. By adopting these articles of food, the mare is kept free from inflammation, and yet the foal is well nourished, which are the two essential points to be considered.

EXCITEMENT OF EVERY KIND is a fertile source of "slipping" the foal; and everything which is at all likely to have that effect should be carefully avoided. The smell of blood is said to have a very prejudicial influence in this way; and there is no doubt that one mare miscarrying will in some mode affect others in proximity to her. Possibly the same cause may act on all; but it seems to be generally concluded that the act is really contagious, either from what is called sympathy, or in some other as inexplicable way. If a mare has "slipped" a foal in a previous pregnancy, double care should be taken, as she will be far more likely to do so again than another which has hitherto escaped the accident. It occurs most frequently about the fourth or fifth month, therefore extra care should be taken at that time. The suspected individual should be kept quiet by herself; but it is better to allow her the run of a small retired paddock, than to confine her to her hovel, where, for want of exercise, she will become restless and anxious. Purging physic should not be given, unless it is absolutely necessary; and if the bowels are so confined as to require some stimulus of this kind, and bran mashes and other changes in the food fail to produce any effect, choice should be made of the mildest aperient which is likely to answer the purpose. With regard to the management of the mare in parturition, I shall leave its consideration to my colleague, who will, doubtless, be of the same opinion as myself, that, if assistance is demanded, it is safer to have recourse at once to a properly educated veterinary surgeon. Stud grooms who have had much experience will sometimes be able to aid Nature with advantage; but, in the long run, they will probably do more harm than good, if they attempt any serious interference.

TREATMENT AFTER FOALING.

IN A HEALTHY STATE the mare very soon recovers the efforts which she has made in bringing forth the foal; and, in fine weather, she may be allowed to enter her paddock on the second day afterwards, which is generally soon enough to suit the strength of the foal, though occasionally the young animal is very active within six hours after it comes into the world. For a couple of months, or perhaps less in some cases, the mare and foal are better kept in a paddock by themselves; but in a large stud this is difficult when the foals come very quickly; and then several mares of quiet temperament are put together, still keeping separate those which are shy or vicious. Until the mare can get plenty of grass, she should have carrots, bran mashes, and a feed or two of oats, which at first are better given in the shape of gruel—the water with which this is made having the chill taken off. Rye-grass is cultivated and cut for the mares daily by those who have early foals; but, though it is better than hay, it is not equal to good upland clover-grass. Lucerne is excellent, but it cannot be grown so early as rye. I have already described, at page 123, the proper time for again putting the mare to the horse, so that I need not enter into that subject here. During the remainder of the time of suckling, no special treatment is required, except to see that the mare is well fed and protected from the weather. At weaning-time, she sometimes requires a dose or two of cooling medicine; but generally she is so nearly dry, that no interference is required.

MARE AND FOAL.

EARLY TREATMENT OF THE FOAL.

IF THE YOUNG ANIMAL is well formed and healthy, it will require no attention beyond that which I have specified as necessary for the dam. There are, however, several accidents to which it is liable; such as rupture either at the navel or flank, inversion of the feet, &c.; all of which will be treated of in their proper places. About the time of the mare being "in use," the foal is generally purged a good deal, and a warm drench will often be required. At the end of a month, or sometimes earlier, the foal will eat bruised oats; and highly-bred young stock are generally allowed, from this time, first a single quartern, and then by degrees two quarterns of oats. Half-breds, and even cart-horses, would be the better for this stimulus to development; but if it is begun, it should be continued; and, unless the foal shows such promise that it is expected to turn out extraordinarily well, the extra expense will not be reimbursed.

The half-peck of oats cannot be put down as costing less than six pounds a year; and thus, at five years of age, the colt will have cost thirty pounds more than if he had been fed on hay and grass alone. Now, between a race-horse reared on corn, and another confined to hay and grass, the difference in value would be a thousand per cent.; and in first-class hunters, though not so great as this, it would be very considerable. But among inferior horses, on the average, it would scarcely reach the sum I have named as the prime cost of the oats; and, therefore, though in the depth of winter a quartern or half a peck is generally given with a little bran, yet, when there is good grass, this is neither necessary nor is it economical. Shelter from the weather should, however, be afforded to colts of all classes during the winter season; and unless they have this, they soon grow out of form and lose flesh, however well they may be fed. It is now fully recognised that warmth and protection from the rain encourage the growth of all our domestic animals; but in none are they more influential than in the one which I am now discussing. A colt neglected in its first winter never recovers its proper shape, nor does it grow into the size and strength of body and limbs which naturally appertain to its breed. Independently, therefore, of the cruelty in exposing the young animal to a climate for which it is not fitted, the plan does not pay; and on the latter account, if not on the former, even the most heartless, who consider their own interests, will make suitable provision for protecting their young horse-stock from the inclemency of our winter climate.

THE FOAL SHOULD BE HANDLED from the very first week of its existence; but there is no occasion to use it roughly in accustoming it to the pressure of the hand on all parts of its body and limbs. If this process is very gradually commenced, no resistance will at any time be offered, and the foal will allow its feet to be picked up, and its head and ears to be rubbed, without taking offence. Grooms are sometimes in the habit of showing off their powers in this way, by taking the foal up in their arms; but this can do no good, and may possibly lead to injury of the walls of the abdomen. About the fourth or fifth month, and before weaning is commenced, a light head-collar should be put on; and after the foal is accustomed to its pressure, by repeatedly handling the part on successive days, a leading-rein should be buckled on, and the young thing enticed to follow the groom without any absolute coercion. At the same time, it must be made to feel that resistance is useless; and if it begins to pull, it must on no account be allowed to get away, the groom yielding as long as the foal pulls straight back, but coercing it gently with a side strain. A carefully handled foal will rarely give any trouble in this way; but there is an astonishing variation in the power which different men have over the animal creation. Some will again control without using the slightest violence, while others will be always fighting with their charge, and after all will not be able to do nearly as much with them as their more quiet and clever rivals. The latter class should never be allowed to have anything to do with young horses; and though there may be occasional exceptions which require severe measures, yet if once a man is found resorting to violence with a foal which he has had the management of from the first, he should, in my opinion, be removed from his post; or, at all events, he should be carefully watched, and a repetition of the offence ought to be considered as a notice to quit. Long before the coming among us of Mr. Rarey, this was recognised amongst the most extensive breeders of horses in this country; and though cruelty was not unknown among them, any more than it is now, it was fully recognised as not only an unnecessary but an unsatisfactory means of mastering the horse.

THE WEANING AND AFTER TREATMENT OF THE FOAL.

THE USUAL AGE FOR WEANING the foal is about the end of the sixth month, that time being selected because the dam is generally about "half gone" with her next foal, and cannot bear the double drain upon her system. Nor does the foal benefit much by the milk after this age, the teeth and stomach being quite strong enough to crop and digest the succulent grasses that are to be had from August to October, those being the months during which the several breeds attain the middle of their first year. If the autumn is a dry one, and grass is scanty, a few steamed turnips or carrots may be mixed with bran, and given to the foal night and morning; but, as a rule, unless it is to be highly forced into its growth for the purpose of early racing, it will require only the grass which it can pick up when it is turned out. Three or four foals are generally placed together in the same paddock for company, and in this way they miss their dams far less than if confined by themselves. Care should be taken that nothing is left within their reach which can do injury, every fence and gate being carefully examined to see that no projecting bolt, nail, or rail is likely to lay hold of their bodies or limbs as they gallop about in their play. Foals of all ages are mischievous animals, and the better fed they are the more inclined they seem to lay hold of anything which attracts their notice.

BESIDES THE SHELTER OF A HOVEL, which I have already insisted on, the foal requires throughout its first winter good feeding proportioned to its breeding and the purposes for which it is intended. Racing colts are allowed three or four feeds of bruised oats, with steamed carrots or turnips, and sometimes steamed hay; but the general plan is to give as much as they will eat of the best upland hay, in its natural state, after they have finished their allowance of corn. Young stock intended to be sold as hunters and first-class carriage-horses are always allowed half a peck of bruised oats, and a few carrots and turnips will not be thrown away upon them. Hacks, and inferior young stock of all kinds, get through the winter upon hay and barley-straw, part being sometimes cut into chaff, and mixed with a quartern of bran, daily; and if they are very low in flesh, a few oats being added. During severe frosts the straw-yard is the best place for the foal, on account of the hardness of the ground in the fields, and here he will easily keep himself warm and dry, and he can be attended to according to his wants. Let the breeder, however, constantly bear in mind that a check given to the growth in the first winter is never afterwards entirely recovered, and that if the colt which has experienced it turns out well he would have been still better without it.

CHAPTER IX.

THE BREAKING OF THE COLT.

Mr. Rarey's Principles and Practice—Ordinary Method of Breaking for the Saddle—Superiority of the Latter when properly carried out—Breaking to Harness.

THE YEAR 1858 will ever be memorable in the annals of the English stable for the success of Mr. Rarey and his partner, Mr. Goodenough, in extracting 25,000*l*. from the pockets of English horsemen by the promise of a new method of breaking and training the animal which they all loved so well, but so often found not quite obedient to their wills. The plans by which obedience was to be insured were kept a profound secret, but to prove Mr. Rarey's power, the French coaching stallion, Stafford, the English thorough-bred, Cruiser, and a gray colt in the possession of Mr. Anderson, of Piccadilly, all notoriously vicious, were privately subdued, and afterwards exhibited in public. Subscribers were invited to pay ten guineas each, with the engagement that as soon as five hundred names were put down, the American would teach them in classes, each subscriber binding himself, under a heavy penalty, to keep the secret. The result was that eleven hundred ladies and gentlemen paid their money, and kept their promise so well that until the appearance of a small shilling volume, published by Messrs. Routledge & Co., which detailed the whole process, in the very words given to the American public some years before by Mr.

Rarey, no one but the subscribers had any certain knowledge of the secret, although it subsequently appeared that it had oozed out, and had been propounded in several directions as a rival scheme of much older date. However, it is not now my intention to attempt the discovery of the inventor of the system generally known as Rarey's, my sole object being to ascertain its real worth in breaking young stock, and in remedying or curing the vices to which older horses are occasionally subject. It will be seen hereafter that though I think the plan of great service in some cases, I doubt its utility as an aid to the breaker; but, having cost the country far more than 25,000*l.*, and having received the approval of hundreds of experienced horsemen, it would ill become me to pass the subject over without giving reasons for the conclusions to which I have arrived. I was not one of the original subscribers, but I have seen Mr. Rarey exhibit his extraordinary powers over the horse more than a dozen times, so that I am in a position to form an opinion upon the whole process as compared with our ordinary English methods, with which I have also long been practically acquainted.

IN HIS PUBLIC DEMONSTRATIONS Mr. Rarey always commenced by some introductory remarks on the natural history of the horse, in which there was nothing to impress the auditor with any great respect for his powers. At the end of this act, which was evidently intended to kill time, we were put in possession of the three fundamental principles of the new theory of the proper management of the horse, namely:—

First, " That he is so constituted by nature that he will not offer resistance to any demand made of him which he fully comprehends, if made in a way consistent with the laws of his nature."

Secondly, " That he has no consciousness of his strength beyond his experience, and can be handled according to our will without force."

Thirdly, " That we can, in compliance with the laws of his nature, by which he examines all things new to him, take any object, however frightful, around, over, or on him, that does not inflict pain, without causing him to fear."

No one will, I believe, dispute the first two of these principles, which have certainly nothing very novel in them. The third, when promulgated, was more opposed to our experience, and a demonstration of its truth was naturally enough required before it was accepted. To comply with this demand horse after horse was submitted to an exhausting and painful proof, which I shall presently describe, and then certainly anything which did not inflict pain was borne without apparently producing fear. This, therefore, was proving the letter of the third principle; but was the spirit of it established? The words just quoted, if they mean anything, signify that is only necessary to allow a horse to examine the drum and he will show no fear of it. But is this the real fact? I trow not. Before a high-couraged horse will allow a drum to be beaten on his back he must either submit to a long course of training under the old system, or he must go through the royal road of Mr. Rarey, of which nothing whatever is said in the three principles alluded to. Take an ordinary hunter after he is exhausted by a long run, and he will bear the noise of a drum, or any other alarming agent, to which he would, when fresh and active, show the greatest objection. Why, then, should we be astonished that a shorter method of exhausting the nervous energy should have the same effect, even if it is shown in a still more remarkable manner, as we shall presently see it is? As far, therefore, as Mr. Rarey's principles are concerned I have little to say against them, except that if the third is meant to apply to the exhibition of the drum beaten on the backs of his several subjects, it is not very ingenuous in the language which is used.

BEFORE MR. RAREY CAME TO ENGLAND he had, as I have already remarked, published in America a little pamphlet which described his several plans for driving a colt from pasture;—driving into a stable and haltering, and the kind of halter used, &c. It also contained an account of an experiment with a robe, showing that the horse, as soon as he discovers by his senses that an object has no power or will to hurt him, goes up to it, and soon becomes regardless of its presence. All these remarks, however, have no interest for my readers, as they are of no utility whatever, and the sole remaining contents of the pages which were published by Messrs. Routledge, and received with so much interest in this country, were the directions for throwing the horse, and afterwards handling, or "gentling" him, as the American operator calls the stroking the limbs, which he always puts into practice after the horse is down. If this little book had been published a few months earlier it would have entirely destroyed the pecuniary prospects of the partners, but coming late as it did, it prevented the payment of any more ten guinea subscriptions, and reduced the charge for the sight of the process to guinea and half-guinea tickets for seats at the Alhambra. I shall, therefore, proceed to describe the casting process, as witnessed by myself, and then examine into its nature and effect upon the horse, whether in breaking or taming him.

THE APPARATUS which is required is, first of all, an ordinary snaffle or straight bit in the mouth, without which nothing could be done with any vicious horse; and if any animal is to be "Rareyfied," the preliminary operation is to get this into the mouth. Stafford was brought to Mr. Rarey with the aid of guide-ropes, which were fastened to his head and held by grooms on each side

In him, therefore, this first essential point was accomplished. Cruiser also had a halter, strengthened with iron, and in him also there was a means of laying hold of the head, which was eagerly seized by the operator. The plan adopted in his case was to fix an iron staple to the door-post, and then running through this a strong leather strap, to which a spring hook was attached, the opportunity was seized when the horse came open-mouthed to the door, and he was securely laid hold of and drawn up to the staple, so as to compel him to allow the introduction of a bit. The gray colt at Mr. Anderson's was bitted; but the zebra was loose in his cage, and I do not at all know how the gag in which he was exhibited was forced into his mouth, but I believe it was effected by a rope thrown round his neck and drawn up to the bars of his cage.

THE SECOND PART of the apparatus is the leg-strap for the near fore leg, being very similar to a stirrup-leather, which, with the addition of a strong loop, can be made to answer the same purpose very well. Before applying this strap, which at once makes the horse harmless for offence, he must be rendered approachable, which, in ordinary animals, is effected merely with the aid of the bridle. In Stafford, however, as I before remarked, guide-ropes were used; and in the case of Cruiser, he was enticed up to a wagon loaded with hay, under which was Mr. Rarey, and through the wheel of which this leg-strap was quietly and cau-

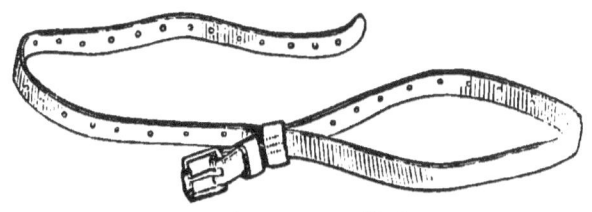

RAREY'S LEG STRAP. No. 1.

tiously buckled on his leg. As soon as this is done the horse is innocent of all mischief except with his teeth, for he cannot kick on three legs, and even his mouth may be kept away from the operator by drawing on the off rein. To bring him speedily to submit to the power of the operator, the other leg must also be confined, which is effected by first buckling on a surcingle, as represented in the last engraving, and then catching the off fetlock in the running noose of leg-strap No. 2, which is made in the annexed form. Provided with this second strap in his pocket, and having already applied the leg-strap No. 1, and the surcingle as shown

132   THE HORSE.

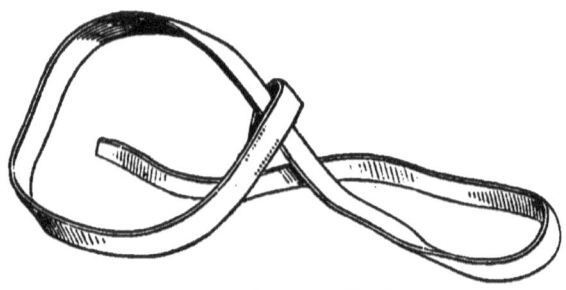

MR. RAREY'S STRAP. No. 2.

above, the subject under manipulation is either induced to drop his off foot into the noose, or it is slipped round his ankle, while the off rein is held by the other hand to keep the teeth off the operator. As soon as this loop is firmly drawn round the leg, the

CRUISER WITH THE LEG STRAP AND SURCINGLE ON.

other end is slipped through the surcingle under the belly, and entire control of the horse is only a work of time. The arrangement of these straps is well shown in the engraving, where Cruiser is sketched ready for the final struggle. Up to this time, almost

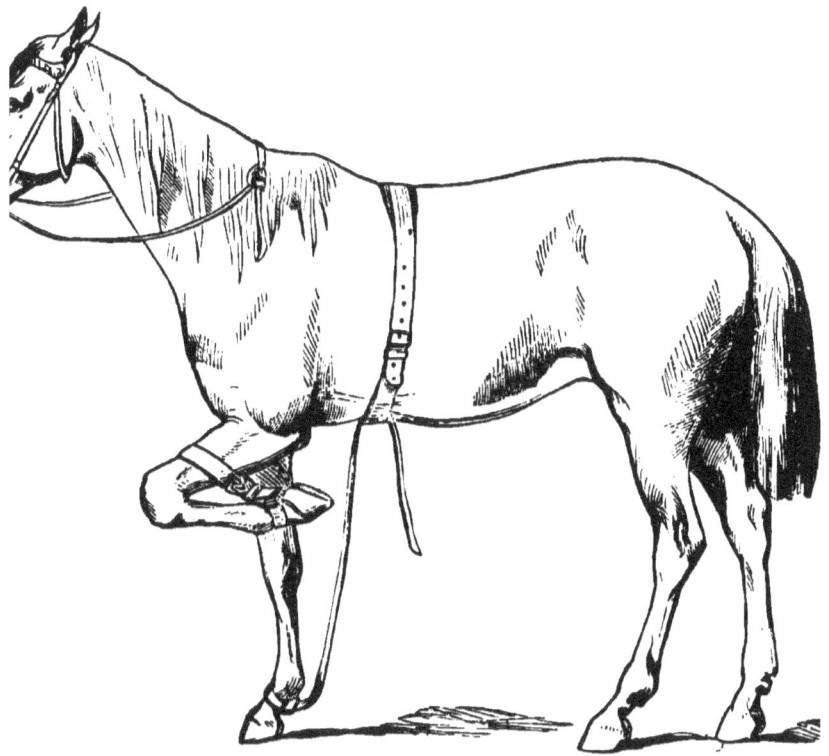

CRUISER IN THE POWER OF HIS MASTER.

every horse will be tolerably quiet and unresisting, some squealing when any approach is made to their elbows to tighten the surcingle, and others when the strap No. 2 is slipped through it. Few however, plunge much; and if they are made to hop on three legs, they are able to go on for so long a time, without producing the necessary amount of fatigue, that the operator would be tired before his pupil. It is at this stage—that is to say, with the use of the leg-strap No. 1—that the predecessors of Mr. Rarey stopped, and they consequently failed to gain the absolute control which he has invariably obtained with the slight, but really important, additions which he has made, and which he uses in the ingenious manner which I shall now describe. It may be observed that, with a violent horse, it is always better to let him feel his want of power for doing mischief with the near fore leg strapped up, and the slight degree of fatigue which a few minutes' hopping will produce, be-

12

fore the second strap is called into play, especially if the operator has not acquired great skill in the use of the apparatus. When this is done, and the second strap is applied, and slipped through the surcingle, as shown at page 133, taking care to put a stout glove on the right hand, the left rein is taken in the left hand, and gently jerked—using, if necessary, the usual slight stimulus with the tongue, to make the horse move, which he can only do by

THE HORSE BOUNDING ON HIS HIND LEGS.

raising the off fore leg off the ground in the action known as hopping. The moment this begins, the right hand firmly draws the off leg up to the surcingle, and keeps it there, when the horse must either bound into the air on his hind legs, or he must go down on the ground, supported from falling on his side in the attitude of kneeling. To avoid mischief, therefore, the loose box or yard where the operation is carried on should be thickly bedded with straw; for no knee-caps are stout enough to protect the joints from injury on hard ground; nor, if they escape being bruised, will the shock to the body on falling be at all safe. Even straw can hardly be relied on, if the floor beneath is of brick, stone, pebbles, or hard natural soil; for it is apt to give way during the struggles of the horse, and allow the knees to reach it without the intended protection. When, therefore, there is no tanned riding-school, or other similar surface, at command, a good solid bed of manure (which is always to be had wherever horses are) should be spread a foot thick at least, and over this clean straw may be laid. To return to the subject of the operation, whom we left with the alternative of bounding in the air on his hind legs, or falling on his knees in the annexed attitude, the chief art in managing this part of the process is to keep firm hold of the strap attached to the off leg close to the surcingle; the hand being protected by the glove, can easily prevent it from slipping through during the struggles of the horse, and at the same time serves as a *point d'appui* for the operator, so that he can follow the movements of the bounding animal in whatever direction he may progress. The operator must on no account attempt to stand away from his patient, nor must he advance before the girth-place; but keeping close to this, he is in

THE HORSE ON HIS KNEES, ABOUT TO FALL ON HIS SIDE.

no danger, provided he has the sense and the ability to give way if the horse should throw himself down towards his side. The rein, being still held in the left hand, prevents the horse falling away from the operator, and is also used by him as a means of guiding the animal, if he happens to progress in a direction which is not desired. Nothing else is to be attempted till the horse has quite exhausted all his energies, which those possessed of high courage will soon do; but low-bred animals are very apt to turn sulky, and, refusing to plunge, remain on their knees, in spite of every kind of stimulus which can be given them short of severe punishment with the whip, which is to be avoided, as opposed to the principles on which the whole process is founded. By taking time with these brutes, they may always be made to tire themselves, for the kneeling position is very irksome to them, and the most stubborn will give a plunge now and then to relieve themselves, though they will not follow up one with another as speedily as a thorough-bred. Sooner or later (the time varying from ten minutes to two or three hours), the tail begins to tremble, the flanks heave, and a profuse perspiration breaks out, which are signs that the horse of himself desires the recumbent position, and will lie down of his own accord, if not pulled over by the right hand of the operator. Mr. Rarey, in his public exhibitions, has never, so far as I am aware, waited for this to take place, but, perhaps to prevent wearying his audience, has always pulled his patient over on his side as soon as he could accomplish the feat. In many cases, this impatience has led to a partial failure; the horse, not being tired out, has refused to submit, and it has only been after repeating the process once or twice that complete control has been obtained. Those gentlemen, therefore, who wish to try the experiment for themselves, will do well to avoid any risk of a repetition, which they may not be able to manage with the dexterity of the great American tamer. Let them wait till the horse is thoroughly tired, and then only interfere to such an extent as to keep him leaning towards their side, by laying hold of the right rein instead of the left, as shown in the engraving at page 134; and drawing the head away from themselves. Mr. Rarey generally used the right hand for this purpose, when he wished to throw his patient before he was exhausted, because he could in that way employ more force; and, at the same time, his dexterity was such, that, if a bound was made, he was always ready to hold the strap attached to the off foot before the horse could get fairly on his hind legs. In whichever way the task is accomplished, the effect is apparently the same—the horse lies extended on his side, panting and sweating, in the most exhausted condition; but, of course, showing more of these symptoms of distress the longer he has been kept resisting the restraints put upon him. Now comes the test of the practical ability of the operator; for whereas before he had only plain directions to carry out, he has at this stage to judge how far his efforts are successful. If he takes off the straps too soon, the patient is patient no longer, but rises rapidly, and perhaps rewards him by planting a severe blow on his ribs. It is here that Mr. Rarey displayed his great skill to perfection. Apparently by intuition, he knew when his pupil was mastered; but, as he was always ready to explain, it was really by two symptoms that he judged whether he had gained the mastery or not. One of these was the expression of the eye, which it would be difficult to describe, and which experience alone could adequately convey to those who wish to understand it; but the other, being readily tested, is within the reach of every one. This consists in the entire flaccidity of the muscles of the neck and limbs; and until this is ascertained to have been obtained, the straps should not be entirely removed. Mr. Rarey's plan of proceeding at this stage was the following. A second or two after the horse went down, he let him raise his head, and then dragged it down again to the ground by the mane. On repeating this once, twice, or thrice, the animal would give in as far as that part was concerned; and being rewarded with a pat of the hand, the head remained still on the ground, and that part was "gentled." Next removing the leg straps, the fore legs were separately gently rubbed downwards; and on being lifted, and let fall, as if dead, they also were passed as in a similar satisfactory state. The operator then going round by the back, proceeded to gentle the hind limbs; and though, in vicious horses, he sometimes had narrow escapes of being kicked, yet by his great activity and clever mode of seizing his opportunity, he always succeeded in keeping out of harm's way. Finally, the operator passed in front of the legs, and performed all the usual "clap-traps" of putting his head between them, knocking the hind and fore shoes together, standing on the body, &c. While in this state, the horse lies in the attitude and with the expression which is very well represented in the accompanying sketch, and there he will gladly lie as long as he is permitted to do so. But he is not to be allowed to recruit his powers; and as soon as he had gone through the tricks which I have described, Mr. Rarey made him rise, and then showed that the power which he had gained was not lost as soon as the animal stood on his legs again. Calling for a saddle, it was in every case shown to the horse, and put first on his head, then on his neck, and finally in its proper place. The animal then always submitted to be mounted, and even allowed the dangerous plan recommended and adopted by Mr. Rarey, of standing close to the hind-quarter while putting the foot in the stirrup, to be carried out without kicking, which before the "Rareyfication" most of the vicious brutes operated on in public would probably have done.

BY THIS PLAN, it is indisputable that any active man, of good

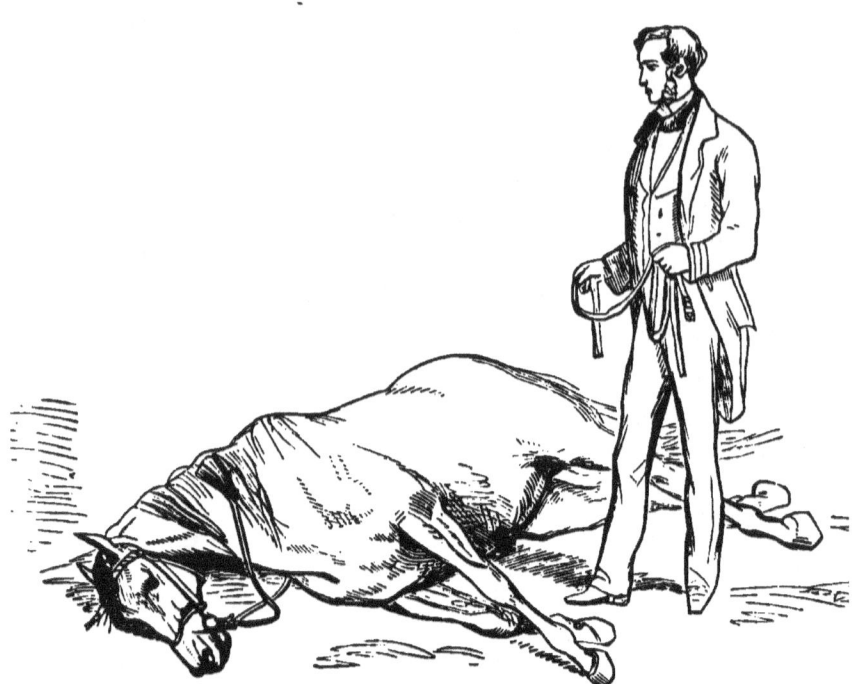

THE HORSE TAMED.

temper, but possessed of firmness and courage, and accustomed to deal with horses, may gain such a control over even the most vicious, that he can do what he likes with them in-doors. No one who has examined into the matter can doubt Mr. Rarey's power, nor can he refuse him the merit of improving upon the old system of controlling the horse, by the addition of the second leg strap, which adds so much to the power of the human arm, that the most violent and muscular horse has no chance whatever. The secret lies in two essential features; first, that the horse must never be coerced or resisted unless the man is certain of success in controlling him; and, secondly, that when the former is thoroughly convinced of his powerless condition, and his muscles are tired out, the latter interferes and relieves him of his trammels, "gentles" him, gives him kind words, and at length encourages him to rise. The effect is marvellous—the most vicious brute, who would previously tear any man to pieces, after he is thus first coerced, and then "gentled" and relieved, appears to grow fond of his master, and follows him about like a dog. Clearly, therefore, Mr. Rarey may be considered as having been eminently successful in propounding a system of horse-*taming;* but it by no means follows that his process is equally, or even at all, useful in horse-*breaking.*

THERE ARE OTHER QUESTIONS, also, which remain to be considered in relation to the method which I have described. First, is it permanent *quoad* the individual who has carried it out? Secondly, does the vicious horse who has been subdued and "gentled" by one man, show the same absence of vice towards others? And thirdly, is he injured in any way by the operation? On the first of these points there appears to be strong evidence that, if the operator gives occasionally a very slight reminder of his powers, the effect of one, two, or three lessons, repeated at short intervals, will continue for at least a year or two. There are numerous instances which have come to my knowledge of horses resuming their vicious habits within two or three months of receiving such a lesson from Mr. Rarey, that they would allow him to do what he liked with them; but in the case of the savage Cruiser, there is reason to believe that he never once rebelled against his master from the time that he first gave in. In his case, however, the operation was repeated hundreds of times; and therefore it does not go so far as I have stated to be the rule, but others might be adduced which keep strictly within it; and there are also private individuals who have practised on horses which have never been exhibited in public who have kept up their control unimpaired. The evidence in favor of the lasting nature of the controlling power, when exercised by the operator himself, is too strong to be gainsaid: and the first question may, I think, be safely answered in the affirmative. But in reference to the second, the evidence is all the other way; and on putting Cruiser into the witness-box he would tell us that he has several times turned against his groom, and put his life in danger. Still, it must be remembered that, prior to his treatment by "Rareyfication," no man dared enter his box; and on comparing his two states, before and afterwards, it may be truly said, that though not absolutely cured of his vicious propensities, he is comparatively so. Probably the same conclusion may be arrived at in those cases which are related of relapses from virtue to vice; but, at all events, such instances are numerous enough, and attested in a manner so respectable, that every possessor of a coerced horse should be always on his guard. The last question is somewhat difficult to answer, because the injury, if real, is not apparent. The chief means of testing the effect is on the powers of race-horses, several of which have felt Mr. Rarey's straps, and been controlled by his master hand. Now, I believe there is no instance of a horse which has gone through the operation doing any good subsequently on the turf. All have shown either a want of speed or heart; and whatever has been the cause of this, they have run behind those animals whose form was considered by good judges to have been previously inferior to them Thus, Mr. Merry's Miss Finch, when she first appeared, beat several fields of first class two-year-olds; and it was generally believed, when she afterwards was beaten, that it was only because her temper was so bad. Yet when this defect was so far remedied by the process I am considering, that Mr. M. Dawson could ride her constantly as a hack without much inconvenience, she never recovered her racing powers, and neither in private (as I have been informed), nor in public, certainly, did she ever exhibit any approach to her former speed.

ON THE WHOLE, THEREFORE, it may fairly be concluded that Mr. Rarey's plans are well adapted for the control of vicious horses, supposing they are not subsequently wanted for the turf, in which case the utility of the process is very questionable. As, however, all our horses are not vicious, and as by the casting and gentling nothing more is effected than a general control, it remains to be considered how far this is useful in breaking colts for general purposes. My own belief is that it acts by producing in the horse a compound feeling of fear and gratitude, the former being the result of his fruitless efforts to get rid of the controlling hand of man, and the latter being established from finding that hand relieve him of his straps and then caress and "gentle" him. If, therefore, any horse, even without vice, is required to exhibit to his master or mistress any relations more intimate than those which are usually practised in this country, great advantage will result from the establishment of this fear and gratitude. With the exception, however, of cavalry and circus horses, we generally content ourselves with that amount of intercourse which is acquired in the saddle, and we do not want our hacks to exhibit tricks, nor do we require them to follow us about at liberty like our dogs. It has been attempted to show that this particular plan gets rid of a great deal of cruelty to the horse, but this is altogether unfounded, for long before the great American trainer made his appearance, writers on the horse had denounced its use, and though many cruelly severe breakers and grooms existed, as they still exist, yet they were exceptions to the general rule. Cavalry horses, especially when on service, are required to submit to the control of the men in many ways which are never in demand for hacking or hunting, and the mere power of compelling the horse to lie down and remain on the ground is worth a great deal of trouble to acquire. As far as they are concerned, I think the use of Mr. Rarey's straps most valuable; and it must be remembered that this was all that the Canadian military authorities certified in their recommendations which Mr. Rarey brought with him across the Atlantic. The clever management of his partner, Mr. Goodenough, and the profound secrecy maintained for so long, carried the public away far beyond this, and, as in the fable of the fox who had lost his tail, all those who had spent their ten guineas were anxious to place their friends in the same predicament. This is the only way in which I can account for the extraordinary conclusions to which so many practised horsemen arrived in 1858. Since that time, it is true, the fashion has subsided, and a more temperate view has been taken, the general opinion of good judges being, I believe, pretty much in accordance with those which I have always held publicly and privately, and which I have here endeavored to convey to my readers.

BEFORE PROCEEDING TO INQUIRE into the merits of Mr. Rarey's plan as compared with our own mode of breaking, it will be well to describe what the latter is, and then ascertain which is the best mode of carrying out our object. No horseman in this country would dream of using the animal he intends to ride or drive without the control of a bit, and although he may aid this powerful instrument with his voice, his leg, his whip, or his spur, yet it always has been, and still is, the chief agent in the management of the horse. Again, no colt is to be considered as broken until his rider or driver has altered his paces, and given him such an action in the walk, trot, canter, and gallop, or in some two or three of these paces, that he has become pleasant and safe. Now the plans which I have just described do not effect either of these objects, indeed their tendency is rather to interfere with the making of a good mouth, for the bit will sometimes cut the angles of the lips, and in this way tend to make it afterwards dull. I do not mean to assert that this is necessarily carried far enough by Mr. Rarey to make his plan objectionable on that account, but merely that if anything is done towards breaking a colt, it is injurious rather than beneficial, with the single exception of the establishment of a mental control, which, as I shall presently show, is not wanted in more than one or two per thousand of our horses.

THE ORDINARY ENGLISH METHOD OF BREAKING FOR THE SADDLE.

IN THIS COUNTRY the breaker of the hack is not only supposed to produce in his pupil what is called a good " mouth," but also to teach him the use of his legs, so as to give a pleasant feel to his rider in the walk, trot, and gallop, and in the canter, where specially required. The racehorse is only "mouthed" and "backed," his subsequent education being confided to the trainer; and the hunter, in addition to these developments, is taught to get over the various fences which he is likely to meet with, in a clever manner. Each class must, therefore, go through the same preliminary process, which consists in producing a good mouth, and in making the colt bear his rider patiently in the saddle. To effect these objects when the colt is running at large he must be caught and haltered, and I shall now proceed to show how the matter is effected *ab initio*. In doing this it will be necessary to examine into the best apparatus for carrying it out.

THE HALTER, which in this country is generally first used, is the ordinary one, made of hemp-webbing, for the head, with a running eye in the back of the nose-piece, in which runs a stout rope attached to the head. Thorough-bred colts are always made to carry a light leather head-stall from the end of their first year, and so, indeed, are all well-bred yearlings of any value. The large mass of colts run unhaltered till they are to be broken, which is generally commenced when they are three-year-olds. Ponies and small hacks are then often taken into use, the latter being quietly ridden by the breeder for his own purposes till they are four or five years old, when they are sold. Mr. Rarey recommends for all

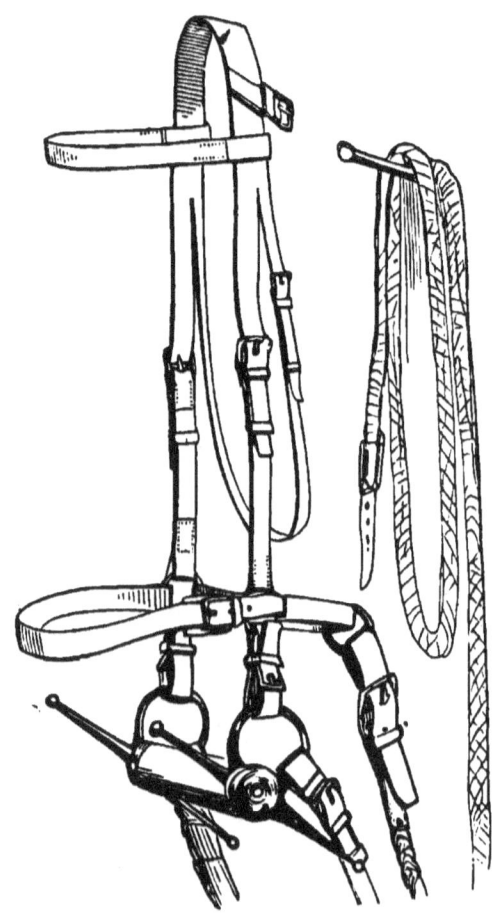

MR. RAREY'S HALTER OR BRIDLE FOR COLTS.

purposes a leathern halter, made like an ordinary head-stall, but rather lighter. This is at once put on the colt, and by buckling a leading-strap to the nose-band, either before or behind, anything may be done which is required, short of mounting. Two small billets and buckles attach any bit which may be selected to the rings which connect the cheek pieces to the nose-band, and thus the halter is converted into a very useful breaking bridle. It wants, however, the stiff padded nose-band of the cavesson, but this is only required with very violent and determined colts. The above engraving represents Mr. Rarey's halter-bridle, with his ordinary breaking bit.

THE BIT which is usually employed in England for colts is a heavy smooth snaffle, with a tongue-piece and keys depending from its central link. For racing colts a very excellent bit has lately been extensively introduced, consisting in a mere smooth ring of iron, with a loop on the upper part for attachment to the head-stall, in the same way as in Mr. Rarey's bridle. In front of this loop the ring is introduced into the mouth, and the back of the circle takes the leading rein, which is thus allowed to slip on either side, and keep a secure hold of the jaw, however much the colt may pull at it. I have a dislike to the snaffle for colts, because I have found it constantly pressing on one corner of the mouth more than the other, the animal putting his head on one side, and leaning upon that half of the mouthpiece, so as to relieve each side of the jaw alternately, instead of allowing the two divisions of the snaffle to bear equally on the angles of the mouth. I much prefer a bit made with an unjointed mouthpiece, curved in a segment of a circle, with the usual tongue-piece and keys attached to the middle by a roller. This curved mouthpiece should have smooth rings turned upon it, which will prevent the horse from rubbing his lips from side to side, and tend to form a very pleasant and delicate mouth. I have known it used with great success in breaking hundreds of colts, and I have myself found its advantages in a great number of horses, young as well as old. These, together with a martingale, buckling on to the bit, are all that are required for making the mouth.

IN ADDITION to the apparatus for this part of the colt's education, arrangements must also be made for accustoming him to bear the weight of the rider, and for attaching the bit to some part of the body. In commencing the breaking it is customary to put on merely a roller with a leathern surcingle over it, kept in its place by a crupper, which, for facility of putting on, should have a buckle on one side. In front of the surcingle, on each side, two buckles are stitched, serving to attach the reins either high up, or even crossed over the withers, or low down, or sometimes both high and low. Until within the last thirty or forty years, what is called a dumb jockey was always attached to the roller, but this is generally now dispensed with, though with the elastic reins introduced by Mr. Blackwell I think it may be made very useful. Lastly, to the crupper long hanging straps are attached, so as to accustom the young animal to the pressure of the coat or habit. Provided with this apparatus, and with a long leading rein of webbing, the breaker is prepared to subdue the wildest colt.

THE FIRST THING TO BE DONE is to get a halter or headstall on, which is only to be effected either in a stable or similar enclosed place, or among a herd of other horses, when the colt is so closely packed in that he cannot move. Every one must have seen the Welsh and Irish drovers rush into the middle of a herd, and seizing an unbroken colt round the neck, hold him till a halter is slipped over his head. The same plan greatly facilitates the haltering of any colt; but a couple of steady horses are quite enough to keep a colt steady in any building or small yard. The breaker arranges so as to have one on each side, and then going up between them, he has the colt held for him while he very slowly and quietly insinuates his hand, with the head of the halter in it, over the neck, just behind the ears. With a little dexterity, this is soon done, and then the nose-band being slipped into its place, a good hold can be secured. Every horseman must, however, agree with Mr. Rarey, that the rope halter with a running noose is most improper, and that a leathern headstall should always be chosen. It is quite true, that a single turn of the cord of the halter into a half-hitch prevents all mischief, and this is done by good breakers; but the headstall or cavesson should be put on as soon as possible, and the former may be worn constantly till the breaking is complete. With the leading-rein attached to the nose-band, the breaker can now restrain the colt from getting away; and, by kind words and gentle treatment, the young animal soon becomes accustomed to his presence, and will allow him to approach and handle him all over. When this is borne easily, he may be led out about the fields, and green lanes if there are any; but while he continues to resent the approach of moving objects by violent bounds, nothing should be put in his mouth out-of-doors. If he is very wild and ungovernable, he may be made to trot gently round and round in a circle on some soft ground, the breaker at first following him up, but soon being enabled to "longe" him while standing in the centre. After a day or two, the breaking-bit already described may be slipped into his mouth, and attached in the way shown in the engraving at page 142. It should, however, only be allowed to hang there without reins at first, and it may either be kept on while the colt is being led about, or for an hour or two daily while in the stable. In this way the jaw and lips become accustomed to the pressure of the bit, and lose the painful sensation which it at first occasions. If, on the other hand, the reins are at once buckled on, and are then strained tightly back to the surcingle, or dumb-jockey, the delicate mucous membrane becomes sore, and even ulcerated, and the foundation is laid for that dull, unyielding mouth which is so objectionable on every account.

IT SHOULD NEVER BE FORGOTTEN, that the mouth is the foundation upon which all the subsequent proceedings are to be conducted. A horse may naturally have fine action, and he may be so framed that, if he were properly bitted, he would be a delightful hack or hunter; but if his mouth is spoiled in breaking, his fine action is thrown away, because it cannot be regulated and controlled by such a trifling exercise of strength in the hand and arm as is consistent with riding for pleasure. Many a pulling brute has won a steeplechase, or shown to advantage in the hunting-field, with a professional " up," which would not be ridden for ten minutes by an amateur who could afford to make his own selection. Hence, the first thing which the breaker has to set about is the formation of a good mouth; and this is exactly what Mr. Rarey's plans fail to provide, and, indeed, it is what they interfere with in a great degree, as I have observed at page 143. Well, then, let us examine into the received mode of obtaining a good mouth in England. M. Baucher has carried the European principles of producing it to a very high degree, and it will be necessary to allude to his plans also; but, on the whole, I cannot but think them superfluous for ordinary purposes, and should be perfectly content with a horse broken in the best English methods, which now combine the "supplings" of the great French breaker with the old dead pressure adopted in the methods of our ancestors. The difference between the two is mainly this, that we in England content ourselves with confining the head by the reins in a position which, while it does not compel the horse to lean upon his bit, yet makes him try to avoid its pressure by bending his neck, and thus rendering its muscles supple. M. Baucher, on the contrary, prefers that the whole of this suppling shall be performed by the pressure of the breaker's hand; and, doubtless, his is the best plan, if the man employed is competent to the task, and the time thus devoted can be afforded. It takes a fortnight or three weeks to "make" a horse's mouth, so far as to fit him to bear the hands of his rider, in either way; but as less than two hours a day during that time will not suffice, and as in the one case the horse supples himself, while in the other a man must effect the change, M. Baucher's method costs twenty-eight hours of skilled labor, in addition to subsequent breaking, and it is therefore very expensive. The course of proceedings which good English breakers now adopt is as follows. The bit having been allowed for some days to remain in the mouth without reins, as already described, the breaker next proceeds to attach a rein to it in the ordinary way, and to buckle this loosely to the surcingle or dumb-jockey, whichever he may employ. Mr. Blackwell's india-rubber reins are thought very highly of by some for this purpose; but, as far as I have tried them, I prefer plain leather, because I object to *constant* pressure, however slight, upon the mouth. A drop of water falling constantly and regularly upon a stone will wear it away sooner than the same quantity dashed at once upon it; and, in the same manner, permanent gentle pressure upon the mouth is more irksome than a more severe occasional pull. The great art consists in shortening the reins so gradually, that the pressure can always be avoided by bending the neck, and this the horse soon learns to do; and thus, at one and the same time, he gains control over his muscles, and inures his jaws and lips to the bit. It is generally necessary, while the "bitting" is going on, whether in the stable or at exercise, to fix the head down by a martingale, buckled to each side of the bit; for without this the horse, in his struggles to get rid of his restraints, will often toss his head so high as to do himself a serious injury. If the mouthing is conducted in the stable, the horse is either put into a loose-box (which is the best plan), or he is turned round in his stall, and kept in that position by buckling the ordinary pillar reins to each side of the bit. At first, the reins should hardly confine the head at all beyond the position in which it is naturally carried when the horse is excited; but each day a hole or two may be taken up, until such pressure is made, that the horse has a tendency to relieve his neck and shoulders by advancing his fore legs and rounding his neck. The best plan is to put on the breaking tackle for an hour in the stable, then loose the reins for a quarter of an hour; after which the colt may be led out for his regular daily exercise, and may be "longed" with the reins buckled more or less tightly, according to the experience of the breaker and the condition of the mouth. In most cases, the process is hurried far too much; the breaker contracts to do all that is required for a given sum, varying from one guinea to three, and it is his object to spend as little time over each of his pupils as will serve to make them barely rideable. This is objectionable in principle, though it is very difficult to know how to improve upon it without running the risk of extortion; but when a colt is to be broken for the use of the owner, or any of his family, he will do well to see that plenty of time is devoted to the formation of the mouth, and this I have already said should extend to a fortnight. If the breeder has a lot of colts which are to be placed in the breaker's hands, the latter can, with the assistance of a few lads, go on with a dozen at the same time, and in that way too great an outlay of money is avoided; but if there is only one in his hands, he can hardly do justice to his employer at the ordinary rate. Hitherto I have only alluded to longeing, without describing it or alluding to the object with which it is adopted. I must now, however, say something more about it, because in this stage it becomes an important element of success. It may be remembered, that I have laid down a fortnight as the least interval which should elapse from the commencement of breaking before the colt is fit to be backed with *safety* to the breaker or his assistant. Not that he may not be ridden in much less time than this, but that if he is, it will be at the expense of his mouth. Longeing is a means of at once giving exercise in a short space of time, and also of accustoming the colt to use his limbs while some degree of pressure is made on the mouth by the bit, without giving himself pain from moving the head. Now, the act of keeping this part still necessitates an even and smooth style of going, and so all things work together to produce the pleasant feel which is given to the rider by a perfect hack. A good mouth may be acquired in the stable, but it is soon spoiled out-of-doors, either by longeing in a hurried manner, or by the bad hands of the rider, whether breaker or subsequent user. To keep it, great care is required at every stage of breaking; and none but a man possessed of head, temper, seat, and hands can finish a colt as he should be turned out. Longeing, therefore, I hold to be a most important part of the art of breaking; and its absence from Mr. Rarey's principles and practice shows that he has taken the dull pulling mouth of the American horse as his model, and not the beautifully yielding, yet steady one of the English hack. In the United States, where Mr. Rarey acquired his extraordinary powers, riding is little practised; and those horses which are used have leathern mouths, and are ridden with three legs, rather than with a pair of legs and a pair of hands, as with us. We need not, therefore, be surprised that he has altogether overlooked the importance of acquiring a fine mouth, and has regarded the mere control over the horse, in some way or other, no matter how, as the sole object to be desired in breaking. At length, when the breaker is satisfied that the colt has gained the power over his limbs at all paces, which he will have gradually given him in his daily longes, by increasing the tightness of the reins and accelerating the pace, (taking care to change the directions of the circles,) he thinks it time to give his pupil the finishing lessons, which can only be done in the saddle. Before mounting, however, he is enabled to teach the colt the meaning of each pressure of the rein, which at first is utterly unintelligible By taking both in each hand, and pressing backwards, he causes him to back; and by drawing them forward, to proceed in that direction. The right hand moved to the right, makes the colt move his head, and afterwards his body, towards that side, and *vice versâ* with the left hand. In this way, all is prepared for the mounting, which should be first attempted when the colt is somewhat tired after a long and steady longe. The breaker should, during the last week's daily exercise, put on a saddle instead of a roller and surcingle, keeping it in its place by *loose* girths and a crupper. Every day he should bear occasionally upon the stirrups, smacking them against the saddle, and thus accustoming the colt to noises, and also to pressure on his back. When all is ready, he has only to put his foot in the stirrup, standing with his back to the shoulder, and then, after partially rising two or three times, and coming down again, he finally plants himself firmly in the saddle. Most careful breakers have a roll of cloth buckled firmly in front of their saddles; and with this precaution, even if the colt bucks or kicks, it is almost impossible for him to dislodge them. When thus mounted, the breaker should be in no hurry, but let the colt get accustomed to the intruder. Let him wait till the pupil has somewhat recovered from the shock, and then only let him urge him forward at as slow a pace as he likes. If all has been conducted well throughout the preliminary stages, and the colt is good-tempered, he will walk away quietly enough, and generally no trouble will be given for a day or two; when, probably, there will be some slight fight, which may be either in causing the pupil to go where he does not want to go, or in making him face some object which frightens him. At first, neither whip nor spur should be used, for the object of neither is understood; and if the colt will not readily move forward, he should be led or driven by an assistant, and not whipped or spurred by his rider. In process of time, however, he is made gradually to understand these signs by the tact of the breaker; and then if he offends, he must be punished accordingly, but it must always be remembered that the fault must be met immediately, or not at all.

THE AMUSING AND EXPERIENCED author of "The Horse and his Rider" has drawn attention to the misconception of the differences in character between a wild horse and a tame one, which is entertained in this country. He says: "It is generally conceived that in the difficulty of sticking on to the back of a horse there exist three degrees of comparison, namely:

"1. That it is rather difficult to ride a horse that has been broken in.

"2. That it is exceedingly difficult to ride a tame one that has *not* been broken in.

"3. That it must be almost impossible to mount and ride a wild horse just caught, that has never been broken in.

"We will, however, humbly venture to assert that, in certain instances, the three steps of this little ladder might be reversed.

"1. In a state of nature the horse is such a zealous advocate of our popular principle of 'self-government,' he is so desirous to maintain his 'independence,' that although he will allow almost any quadruped, even wolves and lions, to approach within a certain distance, yet the moment he sees a man, though on horseback, he instinctively turns his tail towards him, and, when followed, gallops away.

"If, consequently, by the triumph of reason over instinct, he be caught, saddled, and if all of a sudden, to his vast astonishment, he finds sitting astride his back, with a cigar in his mouth, the very human being he has always been avoiding, his first and almost only feeling is that of *fear*, and, accordingly, if he be retained by the bridle, instantaneously, by a series of jumps on all four legs, he makes impromptu his first hurried, untaught, unpractised effort to dislocate a rider. But if, instead of being as it were invited to perform these unsophisticated antics, he be allowed, or rather by whip and severe spurs, be propelled to do what he most ardently desires, namely, run away, his power of resistance is over, and his subjection inevitable. For at the top of his speed, just as when swimming, a horse can neither rear, kick, nor plunge, and accordingly at his best pace he proceeds on his sure road to ruin, until not only all his wind is pumped out of him, but after that, until twisted hide-thong and sharp iron have converted his terror of man into an ardent desire to be obedient to his will. In fact, like a small nation that has unsuccessfully been contending against a great one, he wishes to put an end to the horrors of war, and to sue for the blessings of peace.

"2. If a domestic horse that has never been broken in be suddenly saddled and mounted, the rider has greater difficulties to encounter than those just described; for the animal is not only gifted by nature with all the propensities of the wild horse to reject man, but, from being better fed, he has greater strength to indulge in them; besides which he enjoys the immense advantage of being in a civilized, or, in plainer terms, an enclosed country. Accordingly, instead of being forced to run away, his rider is particularly afraid lest he should do so, simply because he knows that the remedy which would cure the wild horse would probably kill him. In fact, the difference to the rider between an open and an enclosed field of battle is exactly that which a naval officer feels in scudding in a gale of wind out of sight of land, and in being caught among sand-banks and rocks in a narrow channel.

"3. Of all descriptions of horses, wild and tame, by far the most difficult to ride is that young British thorough-bred colt of two or three years old that has been regularly 'broken in' *by himself*, without giving the slightest warning, to jump away sideways, spin round, and at the same moment kick off his rider. This feat is a beautiful and well arranged combination of nature and of art. Like the pugilistic champion of England—Tom Sayers—he is a professional performer, gifted with so much strength and activity, and skilful in so many quick, artful tricks and dodges, that any country practitioner that comes to deal with him is no sooner up than down, to rise from his mother earth with a vague, bewildered, incoherent idea as to what had befallen him, or 'how he got there.'

"If a horse of this description and a wild one in his own country were to be mounted there simultaneously, each by an equally good rider, both the quadrupeds, probably at the same moment, would be seen to run away; the Briton forever, to gain his liberty; the other quadruped, just as surely, to lose it!"

Nothing can better convey to the reader the difficulties which the English horse-breaker has to contend with, than this extract from the pages of Sir F. B. Head, who has had ample opportunities of judging both the varieties of the species which he describes. It shows the necessity for the cautious proceedings which I have endeavored to describe as the proper mode of breaking our young horses, and which I am satisfied will enable the breaker to perform his task in a way which will be satisfactory to his employer. It may, however, be worth while to examine into the methods adopted in the French school, as first introduced by M. Baucher.

HIS "METHOD OF HORSEMANSHIP" was published nearly twenty years ago, and has been generally received on the continent, where the principles of the *manége* have always been more highly prized than in this country. The author tells us, as his first principle, "that all the resistances of young horses spring from a physical cause, and that this cause only becomes a moral one by the awkwardness, ignorance, and brutality of the rider. In fact, besides the natural stiffness peculiar to all horses, each of them has a peculiar conformation, the greater or less perfection of which constitutes the degree of harmony that exists between the forces and the weight. The want of this harmony occasions the ungracefulness of their paces, the difficulty of their movements—in a word, all the obstacles to a good education." To remove these defects, M. Baucher adopts certain methods of suppling the neck, in which he considers the chief obstacle to perfect action resides. Without going into the long details of the various supplings, it will be sufficient to describe the general division of the work which the author considers necessary. This, he thinks, must extend to two months, divided into one hundred and twenty lessons of half an hour each, two being given each day. During the first series of eight lessons, the breaker will devote twenty minutes to the stationary exercise for the flexions of the jaw and neck, which can hardly be efficiently described without the illustrations given in the book itself. During the remaining ten minutes, he will make the horse go forward at a walk, without trying to animate him; applying himself all the time to keeping the horse's head in a perpendicular position. In the second series, comprising ten days, the first fifteen minutes will be occupied in stationary supplings and backings, followed by an equal time devoted to moving straight ahead in the walk and trot. The rider, while taking care to keep the head in good place, will commence a slight opposition of hand and legs, in order to give regularity to the paces. The third series, making up twelve days, will combine the previous supplings with *pirouettes;* while the fourth and fifth series, making up the whole time, will go on to develop the various elementary paces of the *manége.* Now, in all this, it appears to me that we have only our best English modes of breaking carried out to excess; and I am yet to learn that any great novelty has been introduced by this standard authority of the French school.

SUPERIORITY OF THE ORDINARY METHOD.

IT WILL READILY BE GATHERED from what I have already written that for breaking the average colt I greatly prefer the methods which have been in use for many years in this country. Mr. Rarey is entitled to every credit for introducing a novel mode of controlling a vicious horse, which is also of service in training cavalry and circus horses. Beyond these departments, however, his plans effect no good as far as my judgment goes, and instead of improving the mouth they have a tendency to injure it. I have shown that time and patience are grand elements of success in horse-breaking, and that it is a disadvantage to hasten the process, which is all that Mr. Rarey pretends to effect. We do not want to manage our horses without reins, but on the contrary to guide them and stop them with the slightest possible touch consistent with the equilibrium to be maintained in the saddle. Hence the first object is the formation of a good mouth, and as this requires a considerable time to develop, there are ample opportunities for gradually accustoming the colt to the presence and control of his master while it is being produced. If several breakers were to be pitted against each other as to which should first ride a high-spirited unbroken colt, undoubtedly Mr. Rarey would come off victorious; but, on the other hand, I would back against any horse broken by his method, another which had been submitted to a good breaker on the old English plan, if the palm was to be given to that one which should prove to have the most perfect mouth and action.

BREAKING TO HARNESS.

THE EARLY PROCEEDINGS in breaking a colt to harness are exactly the same as for the saddle, and indeed it is well in all cases to make him handy to ride before he is put into the break. We may therefore assume that this has been done, or at all events that a good mouth has been made, and the colt handled and accustomed to bear the hip-straps hanging loosely over his sides prior to putting him in harness.

THERE IS SOME DIFFERENCE OF OPINION among breakers as to the best plan of conducting this operation. Some contend that for every kind of harness the horse ought to be put in with another, who will compel him to move or stop at the will of the driver. Others assert that on the contrary, every young horse should be put in first by himself, and then if he refuse to move he can be allowed to wait till he is tired of inactivity, which practically he soon is. My own opinion is founded upon more than twenty years' experience with all sorts of horses, and I am persuaded that by far the safest and best method is to put every horse into double harness first. Many farmers break their colts in by putting them to plough between two other horses, but the pull at this work is too dead for well-bred colts, and many jibbers are produced in this way. Every high-couraged horse has a tendency to jump forward on the first impulse to do so, and feeling the restraint of the collar he is irritated to increase his pull, whereby his shoulders are galled, causing him to dislike his work from the pain which he suffers. It is quite possible to break in a colt of average good temper for single harness without putting him first into double, but the plan is always attended with danger to both horse and driver, and I should strongly caution my readers against it. Even after two or three lessons in the double break, which have been quietly submitted to, the colt often turns restive when put in by himself, but still by that time he knows what he has to do, and is not made sulky by being punished without cause.

THE APPARATUS necessary for breaking to harness consists of, 1st, a set of strong double and single harness, made in the ordinary way, except that the crupper for the colt should buckle on one side; 2dly, a double break of the ordinary construction; but it is a safe plan to have the whole space between the fore carriage and the splinter-bar made up with iron rods so close together that if a horse kicks he cannot get his legs hung over the bar; 3dly, a single break, to be hereafter described.

BEFORE THE COLT is put to draw he should be accustomed to the pressure of the harness, and as a matter of course in any case he must have this put on him. Every groom ought to know how to do this, but at the same time in a colt he should be cautioned to proceed slowly and quietly, so as not to frighten him. Mr. Rarey's plan of showing the horse everything which is to be put on him is a very good one, and taking advantage of it, before the collar is slipped over the head a little time may be allowed for the future wearer of it to smell it and examine it with his eyes also. Many breakers, to avoid the danger of alarming their pupils by putting the collar over their heads, have this part made to open at the withers, where a buckle secures it after it has been slipped up under the neck. But collars made in this way are not so firm as when constructed in the ordinary mode, and are more liable to punish the shoulders, so that what is gained in one way is lost in the other. A quiet and handy man can always slip a collar over a horse's head if he will take time, and especially if he has previously handled the animal and made him accustomed to his presence. As soon as this part of the harness is in its place the pad and crupper must be gently put on the back, and then quietly raising the tail with every hair gathered and firmly grasped in the left hand the right slips the crupper under it, and as soon as this is done the left drops the tail and assists the right to buckle the two parts together. In the previous breaking the colt has been accustomed to the crupper, so that there is no occasion for extra care in this part now. The pad is then drawn forward to its place, the bellyband buckled, and the rest of the harness being put on in the ordinary way, the colt is allowed to feel it for a few minutes, and should then be led out in a yard or other convenient place for an hour. The general practice is after this to put him to at once, but it is far better if the colt is at all shy to take off the harness and postpone the commencement of actual breaking till the next day.

THE ACTUAL PUTTING TO is managed differently in double and single harness, but as I have endeavored to show that the former should always precede the latter, I shall commence by describing it. In breaking to double harness a steady old horse should be provided, usually called a break-horse. All that is wanted is an animal of good courage and free from vice, who will draw steadily off on the slightest notice, and will stop firmly when required. Some old horses which have had a great deal of practice in the break will assist their masters in a wonderful manner. If a colt kicks over the pole they will press against the intruding leg and cause him so much pain that he remains quiet till he is relieved. Indeed, it matters not what the attempt is, they defeat it by some counter manœuvre, but these horses are rare and fortunately are by no means essential to success. Before attaching the colt the break-horse should be put to, and it is usual to place him on the near side. Then, having the break conveniently situated for starting, the colt is brought out with a halter on and the cord knotted to his tracebearer, so as to give a good hold in case he plunges or kicks. The pole-piece is then loosely buckled up, after which the inside trace is slipped over the roller bolt, and then the breaksman pushing the quarters forcibly inwards the outside trace is carefully adjusted and the pole-piece buckled up to its proper length. Quickly but quietly and without fuss the reins are crossed and buckled, and the ends being taken by the breaker he mounts to the box, gives the word to the break-horse to move, and the break is quietly started without any notice to the colt, or effort on his part. In the great majority of instances no resistance is made, and all goes on smoothly for some time. The break should be driven slowly for three or four miles, and then the breaksman who assists the breaker going to the side of the colt pulls him round by the halter as the breaker drives the break-horse in a wide circle for turning. In returning the horses should be stopped and started again several times, and if the colt is pretty handy the turning may be repeated once or twice, but more than an hour's drive should not be attempted for fear of galling the shoulders, to prevent which the inside of the collar should be well oiled on all occasions just before starting. When taking the young horse out the process of putting to should be exactly reversed. A repetition of this lesson, and constant turning into narrow lanes and crowded streets, together with uphill and downhill work, will soon make the young horse handy in double harness, though for town work a considerable time must elapse before he can be depended on in a crush, especially without a steady companion. No horse should be depended upon until he has been roused either by accidental circumstances, or, if these do not present themselves, by an application of the whip, for it often happens that a colt will go quietly enough while his temper is unruffled, but when it is once upset he shows fight until he is conquered or himself gains the victory. Now it is far better that this should occur while in the hands of the breaker than after he is sent home as thoroughly perfect in harness.

WHEN THE COLT has had five or six lessons in double harness, and has been made to show the nature of his temper in the way I have just described, he may safely be put in the shafts, but not till then. The single-break is a stoutly-built two-wheeled vehicle, with strong and straight ash shafts. It should be so high as to preclude the possibility of the horse kicking over the drawing-bar; and though occasionally it will happen that a clever animal will kick very high indeed, yet there are few that will get over a bar three feet from the ground. A kicking-strap and safety-rein should always be used, for fear of accidents; and a breaker of experience generally uses the driving-rein in the cheek and the safety-rein in the lower bar; both being held in the same way as for four horses. No bearing-rein should be employed; and the tugs should be made open above, so as to drop the shafts into them. With these precautions, there is no difficulty in putting a colt into single harness; but, if at all stubborn, he may not be easily made to start, having no break horse to take him off. Usually, however, when five or six lessons in double harness have been given, the colt walks off quietly enough; but, after one or two lessons, he discovers that what is to be done must be done by him unassisted, and he is then very apt to give himself airs, if his temper is at all inclined to be bad. Kicking may be kept under by the kicking-strap; running away may be restrained by the bit; but jibbing in single harness is very difficult to get over. If necessary, an outrigger may be applied to the break, and a second horse put on; but it is better to exercise the patience by quietly sitting still, when, after a short time, the jibber generally moves on of his own accord. Beyond these expedients, nothing more is required than time and practice.

CHAPTER X.

STABLES.

Situation and Aspect—Foundations—Stalls versus *Loose Boxes— Hay Chamber and Granary—Doors and Windows—Drainage and Water Supply—Ventilation and Lighting—Stable Fittings— Harness Room — Coach-House — Servants' Rooms — Ground Plans of Stables—Necessity for Airing New Stables.*

SITUATION AND ASPECT.

THE TWO MOST IMPORTANT POINTS to be regarded in the choice of a situation, are, first, the power of excluding damp; and, secondly, the best means of keeping up a tolerably even temperature in winter and summer. It is seldom that the stables are fixed without regard to the convenience of the inmates of the house itself, the corner most out of sight being the one usually selected as good enough for them. It should not, however, be forgotten, that the horse is a native of a *dry* country, and cannot be kept in health in a damp situation either in-doors or out. Nothing, except starvation, tells injuriously so soon upon the horse as damp when exposed to it—he loses all life and spirit; work soon tires him; his coat stares; he will scarcely look at his food, and he becomes rapidly emaciated, severe disease, often in the shape of some prevailing epidemic, showing itself after a short time, and generally soon ending in death. Grease and cracked heels, swelled legs, hide bound, inflamed eyes, and coughs and colds, are the evils which attend damp, when exhibited only in a slight degree; but these are sufficient to interfere with the use of the horse, and, irrespective of other reasons, as domestic comfort is greatly dependent on the carriage being always at command, the stables should not be sacrificed, as they too often are, to a fancy for keeping them out of sight.

IN CHOOSING THE SITUATION, therefore, a spot should be looked out which will be high enough to allow of perfect drainage at all seasons of the year. No periodically overflowing brook should ever be allowed to discharge its contents into the foundations, for even if the floor of the stable itself is kept above the water, yet the soil underneath will be saturated, and acting like a sponge, will allow the damp to creep up the walls incessantly. Sometimes, in order to keep the stables well out of sight, a hollow is chosen, and the floor is then excavated below the level of the surrounding surface. The consequence is, that even in a summer-storm, the rain-fall of the surrounding land finds its way—either into the stable, or around it; and the effect is equally injurious in either. Concrete under the floor, and courses of slate at the bottom of the walls, will do something to meet the evil; but it is better to avoid it altogether by choosing a site at least two or three feet out of the way of all flood-water, and with a good fall into a sewer or adjacent running stream.

AS TO THE ASPECT, there is some difference of opinion whether it should be northerly or southerly, all being adverse to a direction either due east or west; the former being too cold, and the latter too hot. As far as I know, all writers on the subject have preferred a southerly aspect, until the recent appearance of Mr. Miles' "General Remarks on Stables," in which valuable work an opinion is expressed that "the prevailing desire to have the front of the stable due south is a mistake." The reasons for coming to this conclusion are grounded upon the fact, which is undeniable, that a more even temperature can be maintained if the situation is sufficiently sheltered from the stroke of the wind. No doubt, a southerly aspect allows the sun to enter with great power in the summer; but my experience does not lead me to believe that flies are less likely to get in through a door or window open to the north, than through similar openings looking south. Mr. Miles even objects to the heat of a winter's sun, which, he says, in the middle of the day makes the stable almost as hot as in the summer; the heat being often suddenly succeeded by a degree of cold approaching the freezing point. Here, again, I certainly cannot follow him, and I should hail with pleasure any beams of the sun which show themselves between November and March, either in the stable or kennel. Animal life is always benefited by the direct rays of the sun, although, when the heat produced by them is intense, the mischief done is so great as to counteract the advantage. Still, in the winters of this country, such a thing is not, in my opinion, to be dreamt of, as a properly ventilated stable becoming too hot, and I look upon Mr. Miles' conclusions as being considerably strained when he is arguing in favor of a northerly aspect. I do not mean to assert that, on the whole, he is wrong, but that his arguments are based upon certain assumed facts which I hesitate to accept. It should not be forgotten that his own stable, which is undoubtedly a pet one, was accidentally built to face the north; and, therefore, while, on the one hand, his experience of the advantages of this aspect should be accepted with all respect; on the other, it may be conceded that he naturally has a tendency to overlook the disadvantages because they are inevitable.

FOUNDATIONS.

IN MOST CASES stables are not built of more than the basement story, with a loft over, which is generally, almost entirely, constructed in the roof; the walls, therefore, are not high, and do not require deep foundations, even if they are built on clay, which is more liable to cause cracks, &c., than any other species of soil of a uniform character. It is a very common plan, on this account, to lay the foundations of any kind of coarse and stony material; but if this is done, a course of broken slates should be laid in cement a little above the level of the ground; or, instead of this, a course or two of hard bricks should be laid in the same material, so as to prevent the damp from striking up the walls by capillary attraction. A neglect of this precaution has, in several instances within my own knowledge, kept stables damp in spite of attention to drainage and a resort to all sorts of expedients which could be carried out subsequent to the building of the walls.

STALLS AND LOOSE BOXES.

WITH REGARD TO THE NUMBER of stalls or loose boxes which should be grouped together in one apartment, there is little difference of opinion now-a-days among practical men, that more than from four to six horses should not be allowed to stand together. The former number is the better; but sometimes there may be circumstances which will excuse the latter being adopted; as, for instance, when this number are kept, and the space occupied by a partition-wall is an object. Even then, however, a boarded partition may be introduced, and as it will not occupy an additional room, there is no objection on that account. When a larger number of horses are stabled together, there is great difficulty in keeping up an even temperature, unless, as in the case of omnibus and cab horses, the same number are nearly always absent at work. In private stables, however, all or nearly all the horses are often out at once, and then in a large space the temperature is reduced so much, that when they return, two or three at a time, followed by others, and compel the doors to be constantly opened and shut, there is, first of all, danger of chilling each as he comes in, and if he escapes this, of producing that injurious effect when the next horse comes home. Practically it is found that the long row of stalls does not conduce to the health of the horses, and although it may please the eye of the master to look down a long line of valuable animals, this arrangement is by no means to be recommended. Either two stalls with a loose box at one or both sides, or, perhaps, as I said before, even four stalls with a similar arrangement of loose boxes, should be the aim of the builder of a stable for general private work, and in this, as well as in all other cases, appearances should be sacrificed to utility.

OF LATE YEARS there has been a great demand for loose boxes, and every private horse-keeper who could afford the extra space, has adopted the plan, at all events for a large proportion of his stud. For hunters and race-horses, when they are doing severe work, there can be no doubt that the quiet and liberty allowed in a box are far preferable to the restraint of a stall, where the horse is constantly liable to be disturbed by the ingress and egress of men and horses. In the stall, also, there must be a slope (though not necessarily a great one), from before backwards, so as to provide for surface drainage; and this compels the horse who is tied to the manger to stand with his hind feet lower than his fore, which is a tiresome position if continued for any length of time, and which therefore induces so many to stand back to the full length of their reins. But the horse is a social animal, and does not like solitary confinement any more than the dog; indeed, some which will do well when placed in a stall, will even refuse their food, and actually lose condition, if removed to a loose box, out of sight of companions. If therefore the quiet and comparative liberty of a loose box can be combined with the society of the stall, the only objections to each are got rid of, and the best kind of accommodation for the horse is provided, though even in a loose box it is not always desirable to leave the inmate loose.

IN LARGE STABLES intended for business purposes, such as for omnibus, cab, and wagon horses, loose boxes are out of the question, on account of the area which they require, extra width being necessary for the horse to turn round in, inasmuch as he cannot in them put his head over the travis, as he always does while turning in a stall. A full-sized animal must have his box at least 10 feet wide by 12 long, which gives an area of 120 superficial feet, instead of 80 or 85, the area required for a six-foot stall, including the gangway. Indeed, the above dimensions are scarcely large enough for a box, a roomy one being from 15 to 18 feet long by at least ten feet wide. Again, the consumption of straw in a box is much greater than in a stall, the droppings of the horse not being deposited in any one place, as in the latter, but scattered all over the surface, and spoiling the litter whereon they may happen to lie. For these reasons loose boxes are not introduced into any

HAY CHAMBER AND GRANARY.

stables but those for race-horses, hunters, and in a certain proportion for hacks and carriage horses. In every large establishment a small number must be set aside for the sick and lame, but I am now solely discussing their merits as applied to horses doing work.

IN EVERY STABLE conducted economically, whether in town or country, a space should be allotted for storing hay, straw, and corn. Hay and straw are either sold by the ton or by the load, which is two cwt. less, and on that account the loft should always hold at least a ton of hay, and the same quantity of straw, because if a smaller bulk is purchased, it cannot be obtained at the regular market price. Now a ton of hay cut into trusses will nearly occupy the space over an ordinary loose box, supposing that the walls of the loft are not carried up far above the floor, and every additional yard in height of wall allows stowage for another ton. Straw occupies more space by nearly one-half, and it may be calculated that a loft formed entirely in a tiled roof of the usual pitch, must have an area equal to two roomy loose boxes, or two stalls and a box, to stow away a ton of hay and a ton of straw, and even then there will be little space for any other purpose. To find room for a corn-bruiser and chaff-cutter, as well as for a stock of oats, a granary with an area at least as large as a loose box should be arranged, and with these conveniences a stable may be said to be complete—that is to say, with dry and airy stowage-room, *somewhere*, amounting altogether to about 2000 cubical feet. If the number of horses kept is larger than three or four, the hay-chamber need not generally be increased to any great extent, because the hay and corn are purchased by the ton or load; but it is often a great convenience to have accommodations for two or three months' provender, and therefore it is always well to be provided with space enough for that purpose, if it can be so arranged.

WITH THESE CALCULATIONS TO GUIDE HIM, the builder has next to consider where he shall fix the stowage-room which I have said will be necessary. Formerly a loft was almost always provided over the stable, in which the provender was kept; but in those days, when high racks were in vogue, a trap-door was left over them to keep them supplied, and the consequence was, that, in the first place, the horses were continually annoyed with the dust falling through, and, in the second, the hay was injured by the vapor from the stable reaching it through the same opening. On these accounts a great outcry was raised against placing the loft in this situation; and stable-architects insisted upon a hay *chamber*, as it was called, being built on the ground-floor, or at all events in some other situation than that usually allotted to it. There was great sense in this precaution, and for a time credit was due to the promoters of the improvement; but on the subsequent introduction of low racks (*which the grooms did not object to when they had to bring their hay in through the stable door*), and the simultaneous dismissal of the openings over them to the loft, the objections to the old situation of the latter were done away with; and the objections of the grooms having been removed, no opposition could be offered by them, and thus it has come to pass that in most of our best stables low racks are established without openings over them, and with the hay and straw stowed in a loft overhead, perfectly protected from injury from the stable emanations, by means of a sound floor and a good ceiling beneath it. The fodder so placed does good instead of harm, inasmuch as being a bad conductor of heat it tends to keep the stable cool in summer and warm in winter. Arrangements are easily made for throwing it down through a shaft in some convenient spot, clear of the horses; and as it can more readily be filled from the cart or wagon through the window than a chamber on the ground, labor is economised also. On the whole therefore it may be laid down that if low racks are adopted, which I shall hereafter show are the best on every account, the loft should be placed over the stable, while even if high ones are preferred, it may be fixed in the same situation, provided no openings which will allow the passage of dust and steam are left above them.

THE CONSTRUCTION of the hay chamber should be such as will provide for getting the hay and straw into it; for the daily supply of these articles out of it into the stable can always be easily managed without mechanical assistance. Mr. Miles, in the work which I have already quoted, suggests the introduction of a spout leading down from the loft to the manger, so as to convey the corn and chaff into it; but I have a great objection to any plan which allows of a direct communication from the one to the other, and as neither corn nor chaff is a bulky article, it is easy for the groom to carry them in his sieve. Moreover, each feed of corn should be sifted and examined for stones, which cannot so well be done in the bulk. I should therefore strongly advise the planner of a stable to avoid all such premiums upon laziness, and to keep the ceiling of his stable perfectly intact, except for the purpose of carrying off the obnoxious gases which are the product of respiration.

THE GRANARY, however, will require several fittings; and, in the first place, it should be so constructed as to be mice-proof. If the walls are soundly built, no mice can gnaw through them, but even if they are of soft materials, a lining of Roman cement will exclude mice altogether. This article also keeps the corn dry, and forms an excellent floor, as well as lining for the walls. If the granary is on the ground, instead of using boards, which harbor vermin of all kinds, lay a course of bricks edgeways upon concrete, and then upon the former have an inch of Roman cement carefully laid, and take care to allow time for it to harden. When this is done, corn may be stored without fear of loss by mice, and all that is necessary is to turn it over every fortnight if at all new, or once a month if dry. Few grooms are to be trusted with an unlimited supply of oats, as they will almost all waste them in some way or other. It is better therefore to shut off a part of the granary with open lattice or wire-work, admitting a free current of air, but not allowing anything large enough to contain corn to pass. At stated intervals the allowance of corn may be taken out and kept in the other part of the granary till wanted. Here also should be fixed a corn-bruiser and chaff-cutter, and also a bin for oats, beans, and chaff.

MATERIALS FOR FLOORS, DOORS, AND WINDOWS.

AN ATTEMPT has recently been made to revive the old plan of laying an open or perforated wooden floor so as to allow the urine to pass through, and thus keep the litter dry. Mr. Haycock, in his "Gentleman's Stable Manual," is a strong advocate for this plan, but I cannot say that I am impressed with his arguments in its favor. That it may save the litter to some extent is clear enough, but it only does so at the expense of cleanliness, for as the wood absorbs a great deal of the urine in its descent, ammonia is constantly being given off, and the stable is never sweet. For this reason these floors were abandoned in the early part of the present century, when they were extensively tried, and I should much regret their general re-introduction. It may be laid down that no material should be used for stable floors which absorbs the urine, but to select one which in itself is liable to decomposition is doubly wrong.

THE DOORS of stables are generally made of yellow, or, as it is called in the midland districts, red deal. Sometimes elm is used, but it is very liable to cast or warp. Unless the proprietor is very particular about appearances, what is called a "ledge door" is considered sufficient, the rails being of inch-and-half stuff, and the boards which are only nailed on, from three-quarters of an inch to one inch thick. The ordinary thumb-latch is very apt to catch in the skin of the horse as he passes through, causing often a severe wound, and on that account a sunk catch is preferred which drops into a recess made for it in the door-frame, but this is not

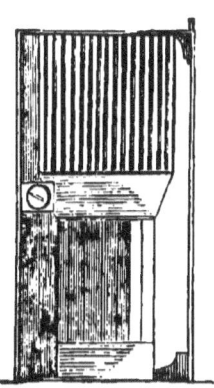

DOOR FOR LOOSE BOX.

14 * L

adapted for a "ledge door," a frame at least two inches in thickness being necessary to allow of the lock being let in. For loose boxes a door may be made with the upper half of open iron work as in the annexed engraving, but these are expensive and can only be adopted when money is not considered. In a door of this construction the hinges are so arranged that with a rounded edge to the frame there is no sharp projection, and even when wide open the hip of the horse passing through cannot possibly be injured. No door should be less than three feet six inches wide and seven feet high, and the outer door is better if made three feet nine or even four feet in the clear.

ALL STABLE WINDOWS should be of iron, and if they are cast with iron bars six inches apart from centre to centre, no horse will break the glass.' Every other bar may be made to project so as to form the framework for the glass, and in this way serve a double purpose. In building new stables I should always prefer to place the windows close to the ceiling and above the mangers, so as to give the horse the fresh air where he wants it. If they are made to open in a valvular form, as represented below, on the same principle as has long been adopted in church windows, and as I have for years recommended for lighting and ventilating kennels, there is no down draught, and every advantage is obtained from the fresh air without the disadvantage which ensues when it blows down upon the back or loins. In the engraving (*a*) represents the window perfectly closed, in the state admitting light but no air; (*b*) shows the same window opened as far as the framework will allow, intermediate degrees being regulated by the ratched rod (*c*), which is fixed to the upper edge of the frame, and catches on the top rail of the sash. Iron frames of this shape may be obtained by order order of any iron-founder, or they may be made of wood. The glass must be guarded with bars either fixed to the sashes themselves or to the framework. It will be seen in the figure (*b*) that I have indicated with an arrow the direction which the air inevitably takes as it enters the stable. Of course these windows may be fixed in any wall other than that at the head of the horse, but I prefer the latter as being the nearest to the nostrils where the air is wanted for the purpose of respiration.

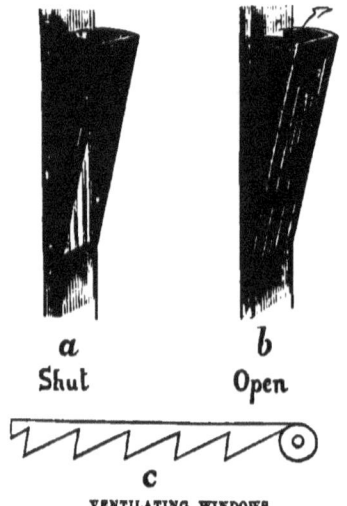

a Shut   *b* Open
c
VENTILATING WINDOWS.

The size should be about two feet square. The additional cost is very trifling when it is considered that no other openings need be provided for the admission of air.

DRAINAGE AND WATER SUPPLY.

NEXT IN IMPORTANCE to the choice of the situation and aspect, is the method to be adopted in draining the stable. The former cannot well be altered, but the latter may, and therefore I have placed it second. To ensure the perfect performance of the office of cleansing the stable, the first thing to be done is to provide a means of receiving the liquid which constantly must fall upon the flooring, consisting partly of the urine of the horses, and partly of the water used in keeping them clean. Several plans are adopted for this purpose, some of which are founded upon true principles of economy, while others are wasteful in the extreme. In towns and cities provided with sewers and water pipes, liquid manure is seldom worth the cost of removing it, and hence in them there is no choice, and the whole of the liquids flowing through the drains must pass off into the common sewers. Even here, however, a catch pit should be provided somewhere outside the stable, without which the traps will either become clogged if made gas-tight, or they will admit the foul emanations from the common sewer if they are so arranged as to allow of the free flow of drainage from the stable into them. Such a pit as that represented below will

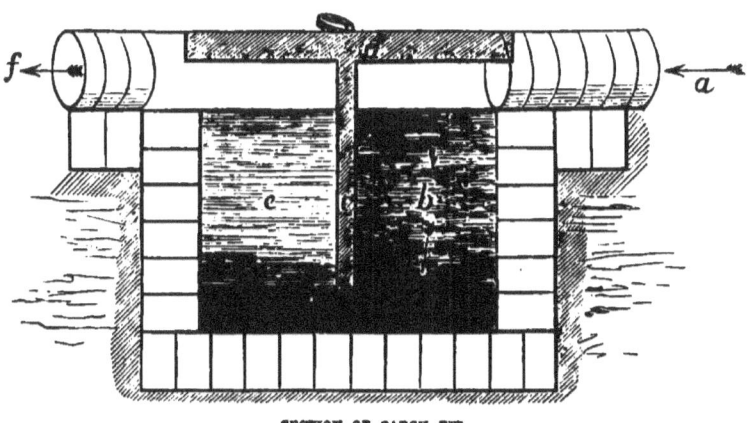

SECTION OF CATCH PIT.

serve all the purposes required, and if it is regularly cleaned out once a week by the groom there will never be an overflow, while in no case can any gas pass through it from the sewers. It is merely a square pit lined with brick or stone and cemented. The size must depend on the number of horses, but if made on the calculation of one cubical foot per horse up to four horses, and half an additional foot for each horse beyond this number it will fulfil all the conditions required. The principle on which it acts is as follows: The liquid drainage enters from the stable at (*a*), and falls into the inner half of the pit, marked (*b*), which is separated from the other half by an iron partition (*c*). This is fixed above in a stone or iron lid (*d*), which, being fitted in a frame at the top of the pit, effectually closes it except when taken up by the groom for the purpose of removing the solid contents at (*b*). The sides of the iron partition (*c*) should run in grooves cut in the cement lining the pit, which it should pretty accurately fit, but only so as to keep all solid matter from passing through. A space of from two to four inches according to the size of the pit is left beneath the iron partition and the bottom or floor, and through this the liquid passes, filling the outer half (*e*) and overflowing through the pipe (*f*) as fast as it has run in at (*a*), the same level being always maintained in the two halves of the pit. With this simple apparatus properly constructed all internal stench traps may be done away with, and the iron surface-drains which I shall presently describe alone introduced.

THE FIRST THING in all stables is to provide for the *rapid* removal of any fluid which falls upon the litter, whether it be urine or water used in washing legs or floor. Without this damp arises and the health of the inmates suffers in proportion. Foul gas, such as is given off from decomposing matters in sewers, is no doubt prejudicial, but damp is still more so; and while I would be careful to guard against the former I would still more cautiously attend to the exclusion of the latter. Hence it is that I would exclude all internal traps; and every one who has watched the proceedings of his own stablemen will have seen how constantly, if they know their business, they are obliged to clean out the stench traps if they are furnished with them, or on the contrary how slowly these articles allow the fluids to pass off if they are not thus attended to. Even the old-fashioned simple plan of making the stalls to fall rapidly to an open gutter, and carrying this straight behind the horses through an opening in the wall to the manure-hole, will answer better than neglected stench traps; and as it is always wise to count upon the occasional carelessness of the men, it is expedient to arrange on this basis if it is practicable, which I know by experience it is, by the adoption of the catch-pit I have described. In the country such a pit may be interposed between a liquid manure tank and the stable, or it may simply be placed outside, taking care that the drain (*f*) has some safety valve to allow of the escape of any gas which is generated beyond it either in the liquid manure cistern or in the drain which carries away its contents, whatever they may be. No trap will prevent the passage of gas if the pressure is greater than that of the atmosphere, and in many cases decomposing animal matter at a high temperature evolves gas under one considerably greater. The best stench trap will then be offensive, but a bad one choked with solid matter will be doubly so. By thus doing away with all internal traps, and simply using wrought iron gutters of the annexed form, which are

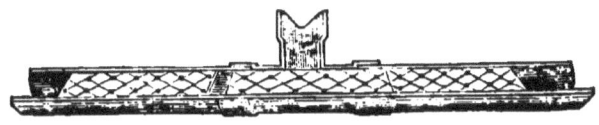

IRON SURFACE GUTTER.

provided with moveable covers, that allow of their being regularly cleaned out with a common besom, such perfect drainage may be attained that the stable neither smells badly nor feels at all damp. It will be seen that *angular* joints are forged so as to connect the stall drains with those at the backs of the horses, and in this way there is no difficulty whatever in keeping the litter perfectly dry excepting just at the spot where the urine or water first falls. If the drain at the backs of the horses is a very long one it must be sunk beneath the surface and carried on by means of glazed earthenware or iron pipes, with grated openings behind each horse (not trapped), but the iron gutters above described are quite sufficient to provide for three or four horses.

WATER-PIPES, where there is no pump, must be laid in the ground so as to be out of the reach of frost, and should be furnished with a good-sized cistern in or near the saddle-room, where it can be kept from freezing. The system of laying on water pipes to the mangers, by which they may be readily filled, is a good one, but it costs money and is by no means necessary. If the iron surface drains which I have described are used no flushing is required, a besom easily cleaning them out, but pipe drains are certainly the better for a good flushing now and then. Hard pump water is not so good for drinking as soft or river water, but in many situations nothing else can be obtained. When soft water is within reach it may easily be conducted into a cistern in the saddle-room, where its temperature will be always nearly that of the stable.

VENTILATION AND LIGHTING.

I HAVE ALREADY entered to some extent upon the best form of windows for stabling, and have shown how far they may be applied to the purpose of supplying air from without. Sometimes, however, there are already in the building windows of the ordinary construction; and in that case it will be necessary to introduce ventilators, of some shape or other, to admit the external air. In all cases, some provision should be made for preventing any draught falling upon the horses, and for regulating the amount of air. The common round tube, with a bend at a right angle downwards on the outside of the wall, is the cheapest form in which this can be done; but it is very apt to be rendered totally inefficient by being stuffed with hay in cold weather, and left in this state ever afterwards. Several patents have been lately taken out for getting a down-draught by the side of the up-draught tube; of which Mr. Moir's four-sectioned plan is, perhaps, the best. In this a large tube of iron is made to descend from the apex of the roof to the stable ceiling; and being divided into four tubes by iron plates, which rise above the top, the wind always descends through one or two of these tubes whenever there is the slightest air moving. Unfortunately, however, it happens that when it is most wanted it is totally inactive—namely, in the hot calm days of summer. Ventilation is always easy enough when there is a wind blowing; and, indeed, the difficulty then is to moderate it; but it is when there is no air moving that stables become so hot and close. I have known these down-current tubes tried in all sorts of places, including stables, kennels, work-rooms, cigar-divans, &c.; but I have always found that, without the power of moderating the down-draught by closing-valves placed at the bottom of the tubes, they are not only useless in calm weather, but highly dangerous in a wind. Now, horses have not the sense to close valves, when a wind rises in the night, and grooms are absent from 8 o'clock P. M. till 6 A. M., during which time a whole stableful of horses may be chilled to an alarming extent. Hence, if adopted, I should never venture to leave these ventilators open during the night, and this would take away from their efficiency sufficiently to forbid their use. I greatly prefer the valvular window which I have described at page 162, for the introduction of air, and a plain ventilating shaft, such as I shall presently allude to, for carrying off the foul air. Failing the window from any cause, nothing is better than a latticed ventilator, which should be fixed in the head wall, or in either of the side walls, near the head.

HAVING THUS PROVIDED for the admission of fresh atmospheric air, the next thing to do is to carry it off, when it has been used for the purposes of respiration. As I before remarked, it is not safe to depend upon the wind for this purpose; and the only remaining agent is the diminution in its specific gravity when air is warmed by respiration. By taking advantage of this principle, the foul air is carried off from the upper parts of the stable if a shaft is fixed there for its passage. Sometimes a small shaft is introduced over the head of each horse; but in practice it is found that one large shaft, about a foot square, will purify a stable containing four or five horses. It is better to fix this about the middle of the stable, as regards its length, but near the heads of the

VENTILATING SHAFT.

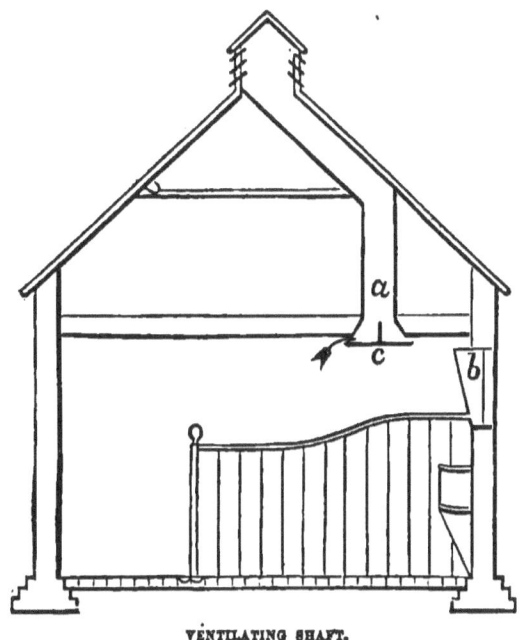

VENTILATING SHAFT.

horses, as shown in the above section of a stalled stable. The tube may be made of wood—and, indeed, this material is better than iron, because it does not condense the steam as it ascends nearly so much as metal, and there is less dropping of water from it. The upper end of this shaft should be guarded from down-draughts, either by a cowl which will turn with the wind, or by a covered ventilator of galvanized iron fixed on the ridge of the roof, the price of which will depend on the size. At the bottom, a sheet of iron, considerably larger than the shaft, should be fixed about three inches below the mouth, so as to prevent any down-draught striking the horses; and also to catch any drip from the condensation of the steam of the stable, as it comes in contact with the

HEAD OF SHAFT.

interior of the shaft. This, however, will be almost entirely avoided by making the shaft of wood, as I have already mentioned. Loose boxes must be ventilated separately, if they are not open to the stable; but if they are, the same shaft will take off their foul air as is used for the stalls, provided there are not more than four or five horses in the same space. A shaft about six inches in diameter is amply large enough for one box; and this, with the ventilating window or the separate ventilator I have described, will keep any box in a healthy condition, if its drainage is properly attended to. There is a very common notion that no ascending shaft will remove the carbonic-acid gas, which is one of the results of respiration, because its specific gravity is so great that it lies close to the floor. This, however, is a fallacy in practice, though perfectly correct in theory, because all gases have a tendency to mix rapidly together; and hence, although the weight of pure carbonic acid gas is so great that it may be poured from one glass into another, yet, as it is given gradually off by the lungs, it does not remain separate, but mixes with the bulk of air in the stable, and is carried off with it. For this reason, there is not the slightest necessity to admit the fresh air near the bottom of the stable, as is sometimes contended for. If it is attempted, nothing can prevent a draught falling upon the bodies of the horses when they are lying down, and they inevitably catch cold. If the upper regions are kept pure, the whole air soon mixes; and thus, when the openings are fixed near the ceiling, as I have described, all the good which is wanted from them is obtained without any risk of draught.

STABLE FITTINGS.

THE HANGING BAIL.

THERE ARE TWO MODES OF SEPARATING stalls from each other; that most commonly adopted in private stables being the travis, whilst in cavalry and cab stables the hanging bail is used for the sake of economy of money and space. The latter being considerably cheaper than the former, I shall describe it first. All that is necessary is a strong pole of ash, oak, or elm, which is fixed about three feet from the ground between the horses, one end being attached to the manger by a strong iron hook and eye, and the other being either suspended from the ceiling by a chain or attached to a post, reaching from the ground to the ceiling in such a way that, if the horse gets fixed under or over it, he can readily be relieved by striking upwards the ring (*a*), which liberates the hook (*b*) and allows the ball (*c*) to fall to the ground.

A better plan is to use a plank of elm instead of a pole for the bail, and the difference of cost is not very great. I have myself adopted this plan with advantage in a two-stalled stable, which is too narrow for a travis, the whole width for two horses being barely ten feet. Here, of course, two stalls would be unsafe, for no horse can be accommodated properly with less than five feet six inches from inside to inside of stall-posts, and this would require eleven feet six inches, being eighteen inches more than I had to do with. I find that a plank of elm, one inch and a half in thickness and eighteen inches deep, will protect a horse very effectually from the kicks of his neighbor; and as I happen to have had an inveterate kicker in one of the stalls for six months, without injury to her fellow, the trial has been a pretty severe one. The hangings at each end are just the same as for bails, a chain, in my stable, descending from the ceiling, and no tail-post being used on account of the propensities of the mare in question. She would have demolished any fixed post behind her in a single night; but the hanging plank of elm not being a fixture, gave way to her blows, and she soon left it alone. If the horse is tied up with one rein only, he can bite his neighbor with great facility over the bail, but two reins are just as efficient with hanging bails as with a travis, and these should never be neglected.

THE LENGTH OF THE TRAVIS should never be less than six feet six inches, and if the stable is fourteen feet deep, which it ought at least to be, the travis may be seven feet long with advantage. Beyond this length it should not extend except in very roomy stables, as there is danger of straining the back in turning out of a narrow gangway into the stall. No travis should be less than seven feet in height at the head, and four feet six, or five feet at the tail-post. If lower than this, the horses can bite each other over the head, or kick over the tail, and so become hung, from which latter accident serious mischief may ensue. The tail-post is generally made only to reach high enough to take the ring for the pillar reins, but it is far firmer if carried to the ceiling. When the stable is to be built from the ground, the tail-posts may be made to economize wood in the flooring-joists above, as they diminish their length by one-half. A moderately stout beam, say eight inches by four, is carried from end to end, and into this the posts are framed, while the joists, running in the direction of the stalls, are only seven feet long each, for which a very small scantling will suffice, even if heavy weights of hay and straw are placed in the loft. This is a great consideration, as the floor of the loft requiring to be made strong, the joists, when fourteen or fifteen feet long, should be at least ten inches deep. If wooden posts are sunk into the ground, which they must be if short, they soon decay, whereas, when they reach the ceiling, as I have advised, they may be dowelled into a stone rising above the floor, and thus escape destruction. Charring the part buried is the usual expedient adopted to prevent decay, but though it acts beneficially to some extent, it does not long put off the decomposition of the woody matter by the damp of the floor.

A GANGWAY BAIL is sometimes used in stables, when valuable horses are kept in stalls, such as hunters and race-horses. It is merely a strong piece of oak which is dropped into a mortice in the stall-post at one end, and into another made in the wall opposite; so that, if either of the horses gets loose, he cannot reach his neighbors. It also serves to prevent two horses from hanging back and kicking at each other, which vicious animals will sometimes do.

THE MANGERS AND RACKS are now almost invariably made of the form, as shown on p. 172, whether of wood or iron;* the addition of a separate cavity for water, bran mashes, or gruel, being a modern invention. With the single exception of Mr. Miles, I am not aware of any recent authority on the subject who has written in favor of the old high rack, and after about fifteen years' experience of each in my own stables, I can confidently recommend the low position for its manifold advantages both to the horse and his master. The above-named writer gives as the reasons for his preference of the high rack, "that besides the chance there is of a horse getting his feet into a low rack, when he is either frolicsome or alarmed, it is open to the objection that he is constantly hanging his head over his food, and breathing on it while he is feeding, which renders the undermost portion of it moist and warm, and makes him reluctant to consume the whole." Now the first of these objections may be tenable, for, no doubt, a horse can get his feet into a low rack, but so he can into his manger, and as this *must* be placed low, no farther harm is done in the one case than in the other. Moreover, the rack being placed in the corner is not so likely to receive the feet as the manger in the middle. But, in either case, if the bottom is strong enough to bear the weight, which it ought to be, no mischief is done, and the horse gets down again when he likes. The second objection I contend to be wholly without foundation, and I do this after carefully trying the experiment for a month, with the same four horses, tended by the same men, and doing the same kind of work. It so happened that in the year 1845 I required two additional stalls; and at that time having high racks in my own three-stalled stable, I hired one of two stalls close adjoining. In this I placed two of the three horses for a month, and carefully weighed the hay which

---

* *i. e.* In England. In this country the high racks are generally preferred.—EDITOR.

was consumed by them during that period, at the same time weighing that eaten by the other three horses in the three-stalled stable. At the end of the month I changed the two horses for two of those in the three-stalled stable, and again weighed the hay consumed by each. The result was, in round numbers, a saving of ten pounds of hay per week per horse, and this was done without any further limitation than the judgment of the head groom, who, moreover, was prejudiced in favor of high racks. I immediately introduced low racks into my own stables, and have used them since with the greatest satisfaction and advantage. Such is the result of my own experience, and I find that all those of my acquaintance who have tried the low racks, are strongly impressed with their advantages, nor have I ever known an accident result from them. The only place where they are dangerous is in the loose box of the brood mare with her foal, where the latter may damage itself by getting into the manger, but against this risk I have cautioned the breeder at page 122. In those stables where a long wooden manger is fixed, the alteration of a part to form the low rack is easily accomplished, and the saving in hay will soon pay for the trifling outlay.

WITH REGARD TO THE MATERIAL of which the racks and mangers should be made, I am not quite so settled in my convictions. Wood is undoubtedly the cheapest, and it has the advantage in its favor that the horse, in laying hold of the cap with his teeth, when he is being dressed, which most high-couraged horses do, wears them out much less rapidly than with the iron manger. This objection is met by making the cap so wide that the horse's jaw will not embrace it, and with this modification I have nothing to allege against the metal but its price,—while it has the advantage that mice cannot gnaw through it, and that it does not become decomposed by remaining constantly damp, which is the case with wood. The iron is generally lined with enamel, but as I believe that its oxide is absolutely advantageous to the health of the horse when taken into the stomach with his food, I do not care whether this additional expense is incurred or not. The enamel always looks and is clean, which is in its favor, but, as I said before, this is its only real advantage. With these preliminary observations, I shall describe each, so that in fitting up a stable the proprietor may take his choice.

(1.) WOODEN MANGERS may be economically made in part of elm or deal, and in part of oak, which latter wood should always be used for the capping, on account of the wear occasioned by the teeth, and for the bottoms, to prevent decay. The top of the cap should be from 3 ft. 3 in. to 3 ft. 6 in. from the ground, and the manger itself should be 13 inches wide at the top and 9 inches at the bottom; depth 11 inches. The caps should be 4 inches deep and 3 inches wide, and these should be firmly wedged into the wall or travis at each end. The bottoms may be of inch oak, and the backs, ends, and fronts, of inch elm, or, if deal is used, they should be a little stouter. Supposing low racks to be introduced also of wood, they should be 2 feet wide, and should project 5 inches beyond the manger, making them 18 inches deep inside. An oak post must be dropped into the floor at the junction of the two, so as to give strength at this part, and the two caps may be strongly nailed or bolted to the top of this. The rack is generally made from 2 ft. to 2 ft. 3 in. deep outside, which leaves a space below sufficient to insure the free passage of seeds and dust.

(2.) IRON MANGERS are made of the same dimensions as the above, but in general the capping of the rack is continuous with that of the manger, as shown in the engraving on this page. Both are five inches wide, to prevent the horse laying hold of the iron and thus wearing down his teeth. A water-tank occupies one end of the space at the head of the stall, the manger the middle, and the rack the other end,—the two former being generally enamelled inside. The addition of the tank is in favor of iron as a material; for water remaining in wood soon rots it, and hence even if wooden mangers are preferred, the tank, if adopted, must be of iron.

THE ONLY REMAINING FITTING yet to be described is the enamelled tile, which is now very generally introduced in first-class stables at the heads of the stall above the mangers. I cannot say that I see any great advantage in them, as a coat of sound Roman cement will be as impervious to all kinds of diseased secretions as the best enamel,—that is to say, when each is washed. Nevertheless, I have shown these tiles in the annexed engraving of a couple

IRON FITTINGS FOR STALLS AND LOOSE BOX.

of stalls and a loose box, which is taken from the pattern plan exhibited at the St. Pancras Iron works. Here all the iron fittings which I have already described are introduced, and my reader may judge for himself of their appearance, which is certainly, in my opinion, extremely neat and well adapted to the requirements of the horse. The stalls show the iron manger, rack, and trough, as described at page 170. The floor is laid with blue paviors, cut to fit the wrought-iron gutters alluded to at page 165. The loose box is lined with inch deal, and the partition from the stalls is of open iron-work. This also shows the corner manger-rack and trough suitable for a loose box. The only objection that I know to these very complete fittings is on the score of expense.

I HAVE ALREADY SAID that I object to corn and chaff-shoots arranged so as to open into the manger, on account of the dust which they bring down. If the corn and chaff are kept upstairs, a shoot may be arranged so as to deliver them at or near the gangway, the particular spot chosen depending on circumstances which will vary with almost every stable. A granary, or corn-room, on the ground floor, does not admit of a shoot.

THE WALLS of a stable should be lined, whenever they come in contact with the horse, with inch elm or deal. Without this, in cold weather, the brick or stone, whether plastered or not, is too cold, and if a delicate horse lies down with his loins against it, he will probably be attacked with rheumatism, or perhaps with inflammation of the kidneys. Usually, also, as I have already observed at page 172, the head wall above the manger is lined either with boards or enamelled plates, which have lately been introduced as being cleaner than boards, as they undoubtedly are. They are either of enamelled iron, nailed on to boarding, or of vitrified plates set in cement, the latter being cheaper and having nearly the same appearance.

HARNESS-ROOM.

EVERY HARNESS-ROOM should be provided either with a stove or open fireplace, in order to dry the saddles, harness, and clothing, when they come in wet. If, also, it can be so arranged that a supply of hot water can be obtained, by fitting a boiler to the back of the fire, the groom will be always provided with what he must occasionally obtain from some source or other. No establishment can be considered complete which does not provide plenty of hot water when wanted; and if it is heated in the saddle-room, so much the better.

WHEN THE SADDLES AND HARNESS are cleaned, they must be put away till wanted; and here they must be protected from injury, either in the shape of scratches, damp, or dust. Harness and saddle brackets are made either of wood or iron; the former being the cheaper, but the surface they present being necessarily larger, they do not allow the stuffing to dry so well as iron brackets, which are made to turn up and form a hook below, on which bridles may be hung. This is a capital plan where space is scanty, but otherwise it is not to be recommended. Where a long cupboard can be separated off by hanging doors, either of glass or panel, the harness and saddlery can be kept in very nice order; and even a curtain of cloth or canvas will serve a similar purpose, when drawn across in front of them. In addition to the brackets, bridle hooks, either single or double, must be attached to the walls, to hang the bridles, stirrup leathers, &c., to. Masters who are particular about their stable arrangements have many other fittings, such as wheels for whip-lashes to hang over, &c. &c.; but those which I have enumerated are the essentials for a harness-room intended for use rather than show. A double hook suspended from the ceiling, where it can be used to hang dirty harness on while washing it, is extremely useful; but any groom who understands his business will suggest something of the kind, according to circumstances.

COACH HOUSE.

IN THE COACH HOUSE mere standing room is all that is necessary to provide if the harness-room stove is made to answer the double purpose of airing both, which should always be managed. Open carriages may be kept in tolerably good order without any stove, but the lining of close carriages soon becomes mouldy unless heat in some form or other be applied.

SERVANTS' ROOMS.

LITTLE NEED BE HERE SAID of the servants' rooms, but I certainly agree with Mr. Miles in his objection to placing them *over* the horses. Quiet is essential to the sleep of these animals, and if grooms are to be walking over head at all hours their sleep must necessarily be disturbed. It is always well to have a groom's room within hearing of his horses, so that if any of them get cast, or are taken ill, he may be able at once to go to their assistance, but this can readily be done without placing any lodging rooms over the stalls or boxes.

GROUND PLANS OF STABLES.

IN DECIDING ON THE BEST ground plan for stabling a great deal must always depend upon the kind and number of horses to be placed in it. In the following plans I shall consider the two extremes afforded by those for racehorses or hunters on the one hand, and on the other by the hack or harness stable for two or three horses where space is a great object. As a general rule racehorses and hunters require a loose box each, because they are often greatly distressed, and must then have entire rest and quiet to enable them to recover themselves. They are also a great many hours together in the stable, and being called upon for great exertions when out they ought to have plenty of air when indoors

The best proportions for their boxes are sixteen to eighteen feet long by twelve feet wide and nine or ten high, but these are perhaps a little above the average. Nevertheless I have given these in the annexed plan of a

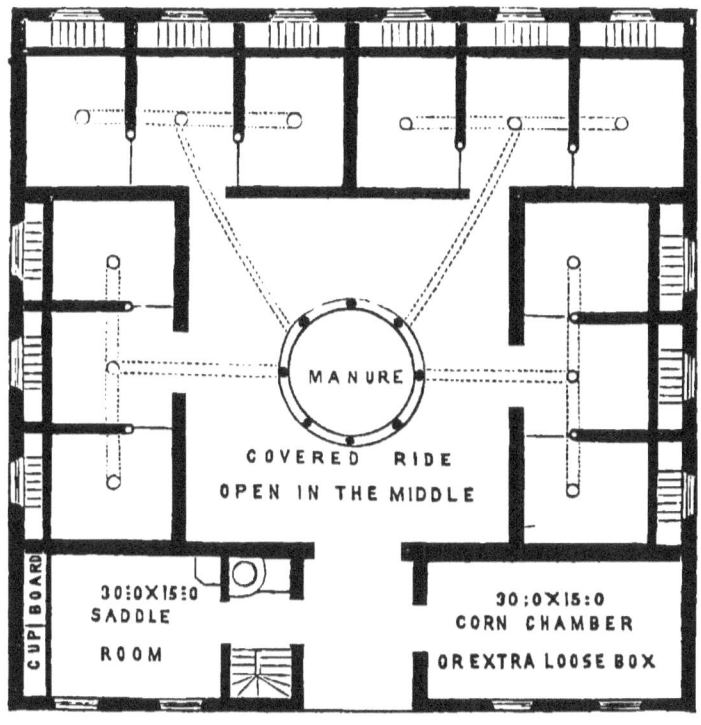

RACING OR HUNTING STABLE.

It is divided into four separate stables thirty-six feet long and eighteen wide, in which three or even four loose boxes may be separated by partitions nine feet high with open iron tops, as shown at page 172, or one or more may be divided by travises into six stalls each six feet wide. I have already alluded to the fittings for each, and therefore I need say nothing more here beyond alluding to the plan itself.*

---

* The plan on the ensuing page, of a stable belonging to Mr. Samuel R. Phillips, of Philadelphia, was selected after a careful examination, as being unusually well arranged for four or five horses. It has now accommodations for five horses, but it could be made very convenient for four by taking out the partition between the fourth and fifth stalls, thus making three stalls and a loose box.—EDITOR.

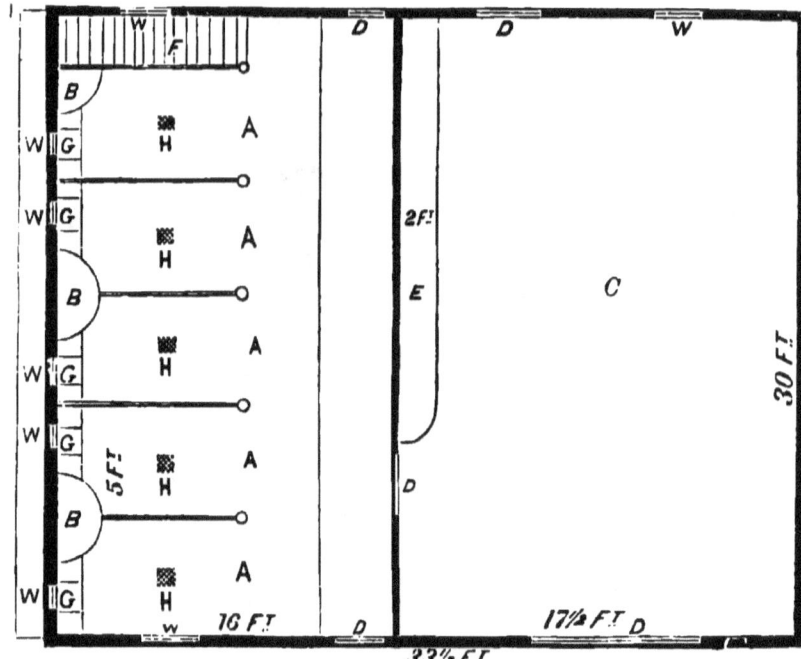

PLAN OF STABLE FOR FOUR OR FIVE HORSES.

A Stalls.
B Hay-Rack.
C Carriage House.
D Doors.
E Closet for harness, with glass doors.
F Stairs to the Hay Loft, &c.
G Manger.
H Stench Trap.
W Windows.

NECESSITY FOR AIRING NEW STABLES.

To PUT HORSES INTO NEW STABLES without airing them is to give them cold or rheumatism. Indeed those which have been merely uninhabited for some months are not fit for horses that are accustomed to be kept warm and dry, without taking the following precautions. If the walls are very new some open stoves should be kept burning for at least a week, not with the windows and doors shut, as is often done, but with a good current of air blowing through the whole building. In the absence of regular stoves loose bricks may be built up so as to allow a good draught of air through the coals or wood burnt in them, and thus to give out as much heat as is wanted. For stables that have merely been closed for a month or two a fire kindled on the floor and kept burning for a few hours will suffice, but when the horses are first brought in, their beds should previously be made up ready for them, and then the doors, windows and other ventilators should all be shut till the stable becomes thoroughly warmed by the natural heat of their bodies, which it soon is. When this is accomplished, if the weather is warm, the ventilators should be opened as usual, and the windows also if necessary; but it is better to err on the safe side, and not to do this till the groom is perfectly satisfied that his charge are all comfortably warm.

CHAPTER XI.

STABLE MANAGEMENT.

Theory and Practice of Feeding and Watering—Dressing or Grooming—Clipping, Singeing, and Trimming—Use and Application of Bandages—Management of the Feet—Daily Exercise—Proper Temperature—Remedies for Stable Vices and Bad Habits—Preparation for Work—Ordinary Sweating—The Turkish Bath—Physic—Final Preparation—Treatment after Work—Summering—Care of Saddlery and Harness.

IN THE FOLLOWING PAGES, my attention will be specially directed to the management of private stables; and therefore the race-horse, the omnibus and cab horse, and the poster, will not pass under review. Those who are engaged in their superintendence make it their business to ascertain what is best to be done; and, whether they do or not, each of them fancies that he knows better than any one else how to effect his object.

THE THEORY AND PRACTICE OF FEEDING AND DRINK.

IN ADAPTING the quantity and quality of horse-keep to the wants of each horse, regard must be paid *first* of all to the small size of this animal's stomach, which affects all alike; *secondly*, to the work for which he is designed; and *thirdly*, to the peculiar constitution of each individual. From the first of these causes the horse must never be allowed to fast for any long period if it can possibly be avoided, it being found from experience that at the end of four hours his stomach is empty, and the whole frame becomes exhausted, while the appetite is frequently so impaired if he is kept fasting for a longer period that when food is presented to him it will not be taken. Previously to the introduction of railroads harness-horses were often required to do long distances in the day, and it was found that if the whole journey must be performed without stopping to bait, it exhausted the horse less to increase the pace up to nine or ten miles an hour than to dawdle over the ground on an empty stomach. If two horses are driven or ridden fifty or sixty miles under similar conditions as to the weight they have to draw or carry, and the one is taken at the rate of six miles an hour, which will keep him fasting from eight and a half to ten hours according to the distance, while the other is travelled fast enough to do it in six or seven hours, the latter will be less exhausted than the former, though even he would be all the better for a feed in the middle of the journey, the time devoted to this act being easily picked up by the increased energy which would be given by the corn. No horseman of experience is ignorant of these facts, and after a long day the hunting man who knows what he is about will always be seen on the look out for a feed of corn or a pint of oatmeal for his hunter, before he attends to his own wants. The human stomach will bear hunger far better than that of the horse, and if the rider feels his appetite pretty keen, he may be satisfied that the animal which carries him is still more in want of food. The *kind of work* which the horse is intended for affects not only the quantity of food required, but also its quality. Thus very fast work, as in racing and hunting, strains the muscular system as well as the heart and lungs to the utmost, and therefore the food which is best fitted for the development of the former to the highest degree consists of those kinds which present the elements contained in the muscular tissue in the *largest proportions consistent with the due performance of the digestive powers*. These are found in oats and beans, but nature herself teaches every animal instinctively to keep within such limits as are safe, and hence it is found that though every horse will greedily devour a peck or a peck and a half of corn daily, yet he will not go beyond this quantity even though it is not sufficient for his wants, and in spite of his being deprived of every other kind of food. The demands of his muscular system are supplied by the corn, but there are certain saline matters in hay which are not found in the former, and being necessary for the performance of several important functions the stomach receives its warning through the appetite and no more corn is received into it. On the other hand, the hardworked horse fed on hay alone craves for corn, and will greedily devour almost any quantity put in his manger until he upsets his digestive powers, when the appetite for it ceases. It is found by experience that a certain proportion of hay and corn is best adapted to each horse according to the work he has to do, and his own particular constitution, so that in laying down rules for feeding it is necessary first of all to ascertain what demands will be likely to be made upon the system. Few owners of carriage-horses would like to see them driven to the door with their muscles showing the lines between them as they ought to do in a race-horse when fit to run. Such a state of high training as will put the latter in condition would be impracticable for the former without wearing his legs out, and not only destroying his rounded and level appearance but taking away the air of high spirit and life which tends so much to gratify the eye. Hence the feeding suited to give the one nothing but muscle is not fitted for the other, who must have more hay and less oats, as well as less work. So also in deciding upon the proportion, if any, of oats and beans, regard must be had to the amount of work which is demanded, for there can be no doubt that while admitting the good effects of beans in large quantities upon the severely tried cab or omnibus horse, they are injurious to the carriage-horse, whose blood soon becomes heated under their constant use. *Lastly*, the peculiar constitution of each horse must be studied before it can be known whether the average quantity and quality of food which will suit the majority of horses doing the same kind of work, will be enough or too much for him. Some washy animals pass their food through them so quickly that they do not absorb from it one-half of the nutritive elements contained in it. These must be fed largely if they are kept at work, and those articles of food must be selected for them which have a tendency rather to confine the bowels than to relax them. Independently of this extreme case it never can with certainty be pronounced beforehand what amount of food will keep an untried horse in condition, but in a large stable an average can easily be struck, and it is this quantity alone which can be estimated here. The blood of a horse fed on highly nitrogenized food does not differ on analysis from that of another which has been kept on the opposite kind of diet. Physiological research, however, tells us that muscle is chiefly composed of fibrine, and that every time a bundle of its fibres contracts a certain expenditure of this material is made, calling for a corresponding supply from the blood, which cannot be afforded unless the food contains it. Hence the badly fed horse if worked soon loses his flesh, and not only becomes free from fat, but also presents a contracted condition of all his muscles. And thus science is confirmed by every-day experience, and the fact is generally admitted that to increase the muscular powers of a horse he must have a sufficient supply of nitrogenized food. As I have remarked above, the nutrition of muscle requires fibrine—but in addition the brain and nerves must be supplied with fatty matter, phosphorus, and albumen. The bones demand gelatine and earthy salts, and the maintenance of heat cannot be effected without carbon in some shape or other. But it is chiefly with nitrogenized food that we have to deal in considering the present question, there being plenty of the other substances I have mentioned in all the varieties of food which are not largely composed of fibrine. It may therefore be taken for granted that the hardly worked horse requires oats or beans, or both mixed together in varying proportions, together with such an amount of hay as will supply him with the starch, gum, sugar, fat, and saline matters which his system requires, while on the other hand the idle animal does not use his muscular system to any extent, and therefore does not require much or any oats or beans.

SALT is the only kind of seasoning which has stood the test of experience in this country, and even it is by no means generally employed. Some grooms give an ounce of common salt in the water daily, others give it by sprinkling it on the hay, while a third set leave a lump of rock salt constantly in the manger for the horse to lick. The last is the only really safe and useful mode of using this article, and I am persuaded that all horses will thrive better if they are allowed a lump of rock salt constantly within their reach. The quantity which is thus taken is by no means large, for rock salt does not easily dissolve by the mere contact of the moist tongue. A lump weighing two or three pounds is placed in the manger, and it will generally be found that a pound will last nearly a month, but there is a great variation in the quantity consumed by different horses.

THE WATER which is given to the horse will materially affect his condition if it is not suitable to him in quality or quantity, or if he is allowed to take it when heated by work. Thirst is most distressing to this animal, and if he has not his water regularly when his stomach demands it, he will not only refuse his solid food, but he will drink inordinately when he has the opportunity, causing colic or founder to supervene. For this reason it has lately been the fashion to provide iron tanks on a level with the manger, which are intended to be kept constantly full, and indeed some are arranged with cisterns and ball-cocks for that purpose. But those who contend for this constant supply have overlooked the fact that every horse when he first comes into the stable is unfit to be allowed to " take his fill" of water, and yet he will be sure to do so if the water tank is open to him. Undoubtedly for horses which are never heated by work the tank is perfectly safe, because as they never become thirsty, since they prevent the full development of the appetite by drinking small quantities as it arises, so they are never induced to do themselves an injury by imbibing large quantities of water at any time. On the other hand, working horses are kept out of the stable without water for five or six hours on the average, and when they come in they are not only very thirsty, but they are generally in a state in which a full draught of fluid will seriously injure them. For this reason I think the tank unsuited to the ordinary private stable, though of course it is easy to prevent mischief by taking care either to have a cover over it, which is kept down till the horse is cool, or to let off the water for a similar period. The question is one involving a choice of evils incidental to carelessness, and it is doubtful whether in the long run the horse is more likely to be injured by being allowed to fill himself with water at the time I have

Copyright Secured.

Photographed from Life by Rockwood.

alluded to, or by being deprived of his proper allowance of it at regular intervals. Nothing is more easy for the master to detect, when he visits his stable (as he should do at uncertain hours), than a state of thirst. Few horses are allowed as much corn as they will eat, and the rattling of the sieve or bin will make every occupant of a stall place himself in an attitude of expectation. But if the lifting of a bucket produces the same eager look, and especially at any hour but the usual time of watering, it may at once be concluded that the horse is not regularly and sufficiently supplied with fluid, and it will generally be found that his condition suffers accordingly. It is astonishing how little water will suffice if it is given at regular intervals, and it is the neglect of this periodical supply which produces the craving that leads to dangerous repletion. If it is decided to adopt the tank, provision should also be made for emptying it readily, without calling upon the groom to bale it out with a teacup, which I have actually seen done in one particular stable, the owner of which prided himself on the perfection of his arrangements. If the water only came into contact with the iron, no great harm would ensue, because the oxyde formed by the union of the oxygen in the water with the metal itself, in the shape of common rust, is by no means prejudicial to health. But no iron manger containing water will long remain free from decomposing vegetable matter, unless it is regularly scrubbed out daily, because the horse, as he holds his head over it during his feeding, drops particles of hay, corn, &c., into the water, and this being raised in temperature to that of the stable, soon dissolves the starch and other ingredients which are prone to decomposition. The consequence is that the sides of the tank become foul, being covered with a thick slime, which not only renders the water nauseous to the horse, but also makes it prejudicial to his health. For this reason a waste-pipe and stopcock are absolutely essential, for by their aid alone can the groom be expected to do his duty.

THE QUANTITY OF WATER which will be imbibed by horses varies even more than that of their solid food, yet ignorant grooms are too apt to give all alike. The most strenuous advocate for the continuous supply would doubtless make an exception at those times when horses are just about to be severely galloped, as in hunting or racing; and on the other hand, almost all grooms who know their business allow their charge to fill themselves at night, and also give them a liberal allowance when they have done their work and are dressed and cooled down after it. I have found in my own stable, in measuring the actual quantity of water drunk by the horses, that even among those which are doing the same amount of work and eating similar food both in quantity and quality, the water will vary from two buckets a day to nearly five.

If salt is given, it will produce considerable thirst at first, but after a time this effect ceases, and I have not found it in the long run make much difference. Green food will also make less alteration in the desire for water than might be expected, which may be accounted for by the fact that it increases the secretions of urine and perspiration, and also acts gently on the bowels; so that, though more fluid is taken into the system with the green food, yet a proportionably large quantity passes off. It is, however, necessary to be cautious in the allowance of water to horses which have just begun to eat grass, for if given in the usual quantity on a stomach full of green food, it will very probably bring on an attack of colic. As a rule, no horse should go to any moderately fast work with more than half a bucket of water in him, and that should have been swallowed at least an hour. This subject, however, will be better considered under the next head.

THE QUALITY OF WATER best suited to the horse is one moderately soft, but it should not be rain water collected in tanks, which soon becomes full of decomposing vegetable matter. I have known the health of a whole stable full of horses seriously injured by using rain water, as was proved by the fact that its filtration through charcoal, gravel, and sand soon restored the animals to a fair state of health, without any alteration in their solid food or work. On the other hand, very hard water disagrees almost to an equal extent, often producing the state of the skin known as "hide-bound," and sometimes affecting the bowels in the form of serious diarrhœa. But in course of time most sound horses become accustomed to hard water, and then a change to that which is soft must be carefully avoided whenever work is to be demanded of them. Thus in sending hunters or harness-horses used in fast work from home, when they have been accustomed to either kind of water, it often happens that their health is upset, and this is quite as likely to occur when the change is from hard to soft, as from soft to hard water. Trainers of valuable race-horses are so aware of this fact, that irrespective of the risk of poisoning, which they thereby avoid, they take water with them, knowing the injurious effects likely to be produced by a sudden change.

THE PROPER TEMPERATURE OF THE WATER given in the stable is a matter of serious importance, and the effect of a bucketful of cold water to a horse just come in from his work is very serious. Even in a state of rest cold water will often produce cramp or colic, so that careful grooms never give it by any chance without warming it, either by the addition of a little hot water, called "chilling" it, or by letting it stand for some hours in the stable or saddle-room. If the former method is adopted, it should not be made to feel actually warm, for in that state it nauseates a delicate feeder, but it should merely have the chill taken off, so that in dipping the hand into it, no sensation of cold is produced.

DRESSING, OR GROOMING.

BY THE TERM DRESSING is generally understood the purification of the skin, which the horse requires. He is never in the highest health unless the pores are kept free from the scurf which forms on them whenever he sweats, and the object of the strapping which he receives at the hands of his groom is to get rid of this mechanical obstruction, as well as to brace the nerves of the surface by the friction of the brush or whisp. This dressing must be renewed daily, even if the horse has not been sweated, and each time that he comes in from work it is necessary to repeat it. The former operation is or should be conducted in the same manner every day, but the latter will vary according to the state of the animal when he comes in, that is to say, depending upon whether he has been sweated and is cool again, or if he is still wet, or has been in the rain with or without exercise enough to warm him, or lastly, if he has been ridden or driven through dirty roads or over a deep country. Each of these conditions will therefore require a separate consideration.

THE USUAL MORNING'S DRESSING is commenced either as soon as the horse has done his early feed, or on coming in from exercise, if such is allowed or enjoyed. The utility of grooming after work cannot be denied, for it would be absurd to contend that a horse coming in wet and dirty should be left in that state till the next day; but it is perhaps necessary to explain to the idle groom that it is not a mere polishing of the surface of the coat which is wanted, but a deep steady pressure of the brush into the roots of the hair, so as to remove all the scurf which collects around them and clogs the pores, through which the sweat ought to be allowed to exude freely. Practically it is found that an hour's good strapping daily, not only gives a polish to the coat, but it causes the secretion of a fine oil, which has a tendency to throw off water, and thus may save the horse exposed to the rain from catching cold. Moreover, it certainly stimulates the nerves so as to enable them to bear exposure to the weather, which would otherwise tell injuriously on an animal which is covered up with thick clothing in-doors, and stripped of everything, even of the long coat which nature gives him, when he is submitted to the "pelting of the pitiless storm." When the horse is turned out to grass, he is washed by every shower of rain, and though his coat continues to look dirty on the surface, yet the skin itself is braced by the winds and cleansed by the waters of heaven. Not so, however, in-doors. Here his clothing keeps his coat short, and keeps up a continual state of insensible perspiration, the watery particles of which pass off through the woollen rug or serge, leaving the salts and animal matters behind, as is apparent on examining the internal surface of any clothing which has been worn for any length of time without washing, when it will be found to be lined with scurf, and matted with oily animal matters. There are many drugs which will give a gloss to the skin, but they will diminish instead of increasing its capability to bear exposure, and hence their use is altogether forbidden by those who know their injurious effects. The horse which is little used requires dressing to take the place of exercise, and if he has plenty of good strapping, his coat will look like satin; but the hunter and the hack or harness-horse, exposed to all weathers, must be carefully groomed and receive plenty of elbow grease, or his coat will look hollow and stand out like "the quills of the fretful porcupine," whenever he is allowed to stand for a few minutes in a cool wind.

THE FIRST THING WHICH THE GROOM does in commencing his morning's task is to turn the horse round in his stall, and fold the quarter piece back upon itself, so as to expose the whole of the fore quarters. Then, taking his brush in the hand nearest the head, whichever side he begins with, he works away at the head and face till he has thoroughly cleansed those parts, carefully clearing out the dust and dirt from the roots of the ears, where it is very apt to lodge, and continually cleaning his brush with the curry-comb held in the other hand. Next proceeding to the neck, he works at that part in the same way, turning the mane over to the other side, and then going to the shoulders, bosom, and legs, and finishing off with a whisp of hay slightly damp, instead of the brush. Having thoroughly worked at this half of the body, the horse is turned round in his stall, and the hind quarters and flank treated in the same way, the clothing being removed entirely while this is going on. In the spring and autumn, when the coat is being shed, the brush should never be used, and the whisp alone should be depended on. Nothing spoils the look of the new coat so surely as the brush, except perhaps the currycomb; but this latter should not, under any circumstances, touch the skin of a horse when it is in proper order, and it is scarcely necessary to forbid its use when the coat is being shed, at which time it would be positively cruel, as well as injurious to the appearance. The brush and whisp having effectually cleansed the skin, and given the hair itself a certain amount of polish, the finishing stroke is put to the dressing by means of the linen rubber, with the addition, in well-managed stables, of the leather. Either or both of these in succession are steadily passed over the surface in the direction of the hair of each part, and then the quarter piece or rug, as the case may be, is replaced, taking care to throw it lightly in front of its proper place, and then to draw it steadily backwards, so as not to disturb the proper position of a hair. The roller is smoothly put on, being first laid on the back double, and then the off side is turned over into its place, when the straps being laid hold of under the belly, it is properly tightened and the quarter piece smoothed beneath it. This completes the dressing of the body, but there are several minor points still to be attended to. A clean sponge is squeezed out, and with it the nostrils, eyes, and anus are sponged clean, and, if necessary, the mane is damped so as to enable the groom to comb and brush it smoothly down on its right side. The tail also is carefully combed out, beginning at the lower end, if it is a full one, and not touching the top until the bottom is smoothly arranged. Lastly, the legs and feet are attended to, the stopping, or whatever may be in the latter, being picked out, the legs washed if stained, and then carefully rubbed dry. Many grooms, when they have white legs to keep clean, begin the dressing by washing them, and then putting on flannel bandages, they leave them on till they have done the body, when they are taken off and the legs rubbed with the leather and linen rubber, till they are quite dry, finishing with plenty of hand rubbing if they are at all inclined to fill. All this being done, the litter is put straight, and the horse is ready to have his second feed. A good deal of muscular exertion, and laid out in the right way, is necessary for the due performance of the groom's daily task. There is no royal road to make a horse's coat, when in work, really look well, and not less than an hour's hard strapping will suffice for this daily. White and light gray horses will take up even more time than this, as with all the care that can be exercised the thighs and legs will occasionally become stained by lying in the dung dropped during the night. Soap and water laid on warm, and well rubbed, will get rid of a great deal of the brown color left, and if it is not suffered to increase by successive layers, it may be removed with comparative ease. The slight tinge which remains may be got rid of by the aid of washerwoman's blue, a bag of which is to be dipped into clean water and the skin washed with this after the soap has been got rid of. A little experience is required to ascertain the exact amount of blue, but one or two experiments will soon teach an intelligent groom.

WHENEVER A HORSE IS WANTED to go out, he must again be whisped over before his saddle or his harness is put on. The groom strips the whole of the clothes off, turns him round in the stall, and carefully clears all the dust away from the ears and head with the rubber; then, proceeding regularly backwards, the whole body is smoothed over, and the saddle and bridle or harness put on. Lastly, the feet are picked, and an oil-brush is rubbed over the outside of the hoofs, to give them a neat appearance, when the pillar reins are buckled to the bit on each side, and the horse is left till he is wanted.

DRESSING AFTER WORK depends upon the state in which the horse is returned to the stable, when he may be cool and clean, or in a profuse sweat still going on, or with his sweat dried in, or completely smothered with dirt, or wet from rain, but chilled rather than too hot; or lastly, when exhausted from a severe run or other hard work.

WHEN THE HORSE RETURNS COOL AND CLEAN, the groom throws his rug lightly over his quarters, and, taking a bucket and a brush he proceeds to pick and wash out the feet, standing on the near side, with his back to the horse's head, so that he can use his left hand to hold the feet, and his right for the brush. If the legs are quite clean, there is no necessity for washing them at all; but most grooms do so as a matter of course, and if they are properly dried afterwards, there is no objection to the plan. Hunters, and valuable horses of all kinds, are immediately protected by flannel bandages; but in ordinary stables the legs are merely partially dried with a rubber, and are left in that state till the horse is dressed over. If the work has been continued for more than four or five hours without feeding, it will be well to put on flannel bandages, and let the horse have a feed of corn; but, otherwise, it is better to finish the dressing first. The cloth being removed, a whisp of hay is taken in the hand, and first the head and neck, and then the body, is dressed over; finishing off with the rubber, as previously described. The clothing is then put on, the legs thoroughly dried, the litter put straight, and the task is finished.

WHEN BROUGHT IN STILL SWEATING PROFUSELY, if the weather is warm, the horse must be led about in the shade, *with the saddle on*, till he is nearly or quite dry; for if he is put into the stable before he is cool, he will break out again as badly as ever, and if the saddle is removed the back will become sore. A hemp halter is cooler and more handy than a head-collar, and it is usually employed out of doors for all purposes connected with cleaning. In the winter, this exposure to the air out of doors is not necessary; and, indeed, it would often be dangerous, the stable being generally cool enough to stop all tendency to sweat, even with a light rug on. At this season, therefore, after the legs are washed and the bandages put on, which they should be whenever the horse is in a sweat, the dressing may be conducted in the usual way, in the expectation, which will seldom be disappointed, that at the end of half an hour's strapping, the skin will have become quite cool, and will look all the better for the profuse cleansing which it has received by means of the watery fluid given off by it. A scraper will be necessary, which may be either of wood or iron; and with this all the superfluous moisture is at once scraped from the surface, which greatly facilitates the process of drying. Two men ought then to set to work, each taking a side, and working first at the head, and then gradually backwards. In this way, no part is allowed to chill, and the moisture is removed as rapidly as possible. In the use of the whisp, the rubbing need not always be hard; and it should be chiefly against the direction of the hair till it is nearly dry, when the proper direction is again taken. There is a good deal of art in drying a sweating horse, and nothing but experience and practical teaching will give it. As a general rule, it takes two men nearly three-quarters of an hour to thoroughly dress a horse coming in profusely sweating, supposing the weather to be only moderately warm. In very hot weather, such an attempt would be quite fruitless, and the only resource is to wait patiently till the effects of exercise are abated sufficiently to allow of the ordinary clothing being worn. Experience soon tells the groom how soon he can venture to begin, and no rule can possibly be laid down which will supply the place of this valuable power. Even when the horse is taken in, he must not at first be clothed, but he must be dressed without anything on him; and in summer he must often be left for some time afterwards in a naked state. When there is a good open yard shaded from the sun, the dressing should be done out of doors; and when this can be managed, it may be commenced much sooner than in the stable, unless this is a very cool one. Slight muscular action, either by walking, or in some other shape, is necessary to prevent congestion of blood in the internal organs; but it matters not whether it is effected by simply leading the horse about, or by stirring him up, as is always the case in dressing even the dullest animal. In other respects, there is no difference from the plan last described.

WHEN THE SWEAT IS COMPLETELY DRIED IN, the hair is full of powdery matter, which must be thoroughly brushed out, before the skin will look well or the horse be properly dressed. To do this, nothing more is required than the use of the brush previously to the whisping over; but a good deal of time must be spent in getting rid of all the foreign matters left behind on the evaporation of the watery particles of the sweat. There is an amount of grease in it which makes the powder stick to the hair, and nothing but hard labor will get it away. For this reason, many grooms adopt the plan of washing their horses all over with soap and water, when they come home in this state; and although I prefer dry rubbing, I would rather have water used than let the skin remain full of dry sweat. A common water brush is generally used, or, if the coat is thin, a sponge will be far better. No time must be lost in the operation; and unless two men can be spared, the rug must be thrown on as soon as the water is scraped off with the scraper, and the skin is just partially dried. In this state he may be left for a few minutes; attention, in the meantime, being paid to the thorough drying of the head and neck, which cannot well be clothed advantageously. These parts soon dry; for in washing them there is no occasion to wet the mane, which may be turned over to the other side while each is being cleaned, and the ordinary coat of the head and neck holds very little water. After they are made comfortable, the cloth is turned partly back over the loins, and the shoulders, ribs, and bosom are dried with the whisp and rubber; after which the whole is stripped off, and the hind quarters thoroughly dried.

A HORSE SMOTHERED IN DIRT is by careless grooms too often left to dry with it all on; and then it is brushed out, or, if idleness reigns triumphant, a besom is taken in hand for the purpose. Where the particles of mud are few and far between, and are already dry or nearly so, there is no objection to their being removed by friction alone; but if they are wet and (as they generally are) in large masses, water must be used to get rid of them; and the whole of the legs, belly, flank, and tail will often require a good slushing with a brush and water before the dirt is removed— the tail being placed in the bucket itself, if it is a long one, and thoroughly cleansed in that way. A scraper is then employed to get rid of the water, the legs are superficially rubbed and then bandaged, the clothing is thrown on, and the dressing may be commenced as usual.

IN CASE THE SKIN IS WET FROM RAIN, whether the work has been fast or not, it is seldom necessary to provide against a continuance of the moisture, for the chill of the rain will generally prevent any tendency to break out in a sweat. The horse is, therefore, at once taken into the stable, and, if very wet, he is scraped; after which he is rubbed over, and his clothing put on while his legs are being attended to, by washing, bandaging, &c. The dressing is then conducted as in the case of the horse coming in sweating in cool weather.

AN EXHAUSTED HORSE demands all the resources of the groom's art, without which he will suffer in more ways than one. An extreme case seldom occurs, except in hunters, who require the greatest care to bring them round after a severe run. On coming into the stable, if their powers have been taxed to the utmost, and their ears are cold and drooping, the first thing to be done is to get these warm by friction; an assistant, in the meantime, preparing some gruel, while another puts some warm flannel bandages on the legs. It is wonderful what a restorative is found in the friction of the ears, after a few minutes of which, a moderately tired horse will look quite a different animal, evidently enjoying the process, and dropping his head to the hands of the groom with the most perfect air of enjoyment. Where, however, there is only one groom for the whole task, the bandages should be put on first—that is to say, as soon as the clothing is thrown on; then the gruel should be given, and as soon as this is swallowed the ears should be warmed by friction. No attempt at dressing should be made till the gruel is taken and the ears are warm; and if they cannot be restored to their proper temperature, a warm cordial of ale and spices should at once be given. Usually, however, there is no occasion for this; and, after getting the stomach attended to, the skin of the body begins to recover its natural temperature, and the extremities become warm again. In the course of an hour, the dressing may generally be effected; but no time should be lost in it, and the skin must not on any account be chilled. After it is done, a feed of oats and a few split beans may be given, if the appetite seems inclined to return; but sometimes, when the exhaustion is excessive, no solid food can be taken with safety till the next day; and gruel, with cordials, must be resorted to as the only kind of support which the stomach will bear.

CLIPPING, SINGEING, AND TRIMMING.

THE COAT OF THE HORSE is changed twice a year, the long hair of winter coming off in April and May, or sometimes earlier, when the stables are warm, and there is no exposure to severe cold. A slight sweat hastens this shedding, as every horseman knows by experience, and even in harness the hairs are cast in the face of the driver to his great annoyance on a windy day. Clipped horses are longer than others in shedding their coats, and present a most disagreeable mottled appearance, which makes the state still more noticeable. The long hair on the legs is about a month later in coming off, and indeed it will not fall till midsummer, unless some more violent means than are used in ordinary dressing are adopted. With some breeds and individuals the winter coat is not very much longer and coarser than that of the summer; but all, save blind horses, show more or less difference in favor of the summer coat. Curiously enough, horses which are totally deprived of sight, have almost invariably a good winter's coat, often better than that which they show at other seasons; but why this is so no one has ever been able to explain, though I have never known the fact disputed. About the middle of October, or early in November, the summer coat is thrown off; but some of the hair appears to remain as a sort of undercoat, among which the long, coarse hairs of winter make their appearance. These continue growing for six weeks or two months if they are clipped or singed, and even after Christmas, if the weather is cold and the skin is much exposed, there will be an evident increase in length of some of the hair. In accordance with the growth of this on the body is that of the hair on the legs, which become feathered all the way down below the knees in the forelegs, and half way down the backs of the canna bones in the hind legs. Low-bred horses have more hair on these parts than thorough-breds; but even these latter, if they are not stabled tolerably warmly, exhibit a great deal of hair on their legs. Those who can see no possibility of improving on nature come to the conclusion that this long hair is a defence against the cold, which ought not to be removed, and they argue that clipping and singeing are on that account to be rejected altogether. But these gentlemen forget that the horse in his native plains has always a short coat, and that the winds and rains, which cause him here to throw out an extra protection, are not natural to him. Moreover, if the animal is left to follow his own impulses, even when turned out in this country, he will be all the better for his long coat, for while it has the great advantage of protecting him from the cold, it is not wetted by sweat, because he does not voluntarily gallop long and fast enough to produce that secretion. The natural protection is therefore undoubtedly good for the horse when left in a state of nature; but when man steps in and requires the use of the horse for such work as will sweat him severely, he discovers that a long coat produces such great exhaustion, both during work and after it, that it entirely forbids the employment of the horse for hunting, or any fast work. I have myself many times found it impossible to extend a horse for any distance on account of his long coat, which distressed him so much as to make him blow directly, whereas on removing it with the clipping scissors he could gallop as lightly as a race-horse, and be able to go as fast and as far again as before. When this happens in the course of the week following the previous failure, the only change made being in the coat, there can be no mistake made, and a constant repetition of the same result leaves no room for dispute as to the beneficial effects of removing the hair. But, say the opponents of the plan, "All this may be true, yet it is unsafe to expose the clipped horse after he has been warmed, or indeed at any time." Experience tells a very different tale, and informs us that so far from making the horse more liable to cold, clipping and singeing render him far less so. Suppose one of ourselves to be exposed to a cold wind, should we rather have on a thin dry coat or a thick wet one? Assuredly the former, and undoubtedly the wearer of it would be less liable to cold than he who has the wet one on. So with the horse. As long as his winter coat can be kept dry he is protected by it, and the slow worker, who is not made to pull such heavy weight as to sweat him, will be all the better for its protection, but the moment the pace is sufficiently accelerated to warm the skin the sweat pours forth, and is kept up in-doors by the matted mass of moist hair with which the horse is covered. In former days I have had horses wet for weeks together, from the impossibility of getting them dry in the intervals of their work. They would break out afresh when apparently cool, and by no possible means could they be thoroughly dried. This, of course, wasted their flesh to a frightful extent, but on clipping them it was soon put on again, showing the great advantage of the plan. A chronic cough almost always accompanies this state of constant sweat, and it will be lucky for the owner of a horse so treated if it does not become acute and put an end to the miserable existence of the poor ill-treated brute. The case is not always fairly put, as, for instance, by Stewart, in his *Stable Economy*, at page 120, where he says, " A long coat takes up a deal of moisture, and is difficult to dry; but whether wet or dry it affords some defence to the skin, which is laid bare to every breath of air when deprived of its natural covering. Every one must know from himself whether wet clothing and a wet skin, or no clothing and a wet skin, is the most disagreeable and dangerous. It is true that clipping saves the groom a great deal of labor. He can dry the horse in half the time, and with less than half of the exertion which a long coat requires; but it makes his attention and activity more necessary, for the horse is almost sure to catch cold, if not dried immediately. When well clothed with hair he is in less danger, and not so much dependent on the care of his groom." Now, I maintain that this passage is full of fallacies and misstatements. The comparison is not between wet clothing and a wet skin, and *no clothing* and a wet skin; but, as I have before observed, between a wet long coat and a dry short one. The clipping removes the tendency to sweat, or if this secretion is poured out it ceases directly the exercise which produced it is stopped. But taking Mr. Stewart on his own terms, who has not experienced the relief which is afforded by taking off wet gloves and exposing the naked hands to the same amount of wind and cold? This is exactly the case as he puts it, and tells directly against his argument; but it is scarcely worth while to discuss the subject at any length, for I know no horseman of experience in the present day who does not advocate the use of the scissors or the lamp, whenever the winter coat is much longer than that of summer. That horses are occasionally to be met with which show little or no change in the autumn I know full well; but these are the exceptions to the rule, being few and far between. The vast majority would have their hair from one to two inches long if left in its natural state, and they would then be wholly unfit for the uses to which they were put. We may therefore consider that it is admitted to be the best plan to shorten the coat in the autumn, and all I have to do is to discuss the best modes of effecting the purpose, with a view to decide whether clipping or singeing is to be preferred.

CLIPPING is seldom performed by any but the professed artist, inasmuch as it requires great practice to make the shortened coat look even and smooth. When a horse is well clipped his skin should look as level and almost as glossy as if he had on his ordinary summer coat; but inferior performers are apt to leave ridges in various directions, marking each cut of the scissors. It should not be done till the new hair has attained nearly its full length, for it cannot be repeated at short intervals like singeing. If it is attempted too soon the new coat grows unequally, and the skin in a fortnight's time looks rough and ragged. A comb and two or three pairs of variously curved scissors are all that are required, with the exception of a singeing lamp, which must be used at last to remove any loose hairs which may have escaped the blades of the scissors. Two men generally work together, so as to get the operation over in from sixteen to twenty hours, which time it will take to clip an averaged-sized horse properly. These men were formerly in great demand at the clipping season, and it was extraordinary how little rest sufficed for them, but now the use of the gas singeing-lamp has nearly superseded that of the scissors, and clippers are not so much sought after. While the process is going on, the horse ought to be clothed as far as possible, careful men removing only as much of the quarter piece as is sufficient to expose the part they are working at and no more. As soon as the whole body is gone over as well as the legs, the singeing-lamp is lightly passed over the surface, which will leave the hair burned to such an extent as to require either washing or a sweat, which latter is generally adopted, in the belief that it has a tendency to prevent cold. My own opinion is that this is a fallacy, and that soap and water used quickly and rapidly, followed up by a good strapping and the use of plenty of warm clothing, is far less likely to chill the horse than the exhaustion consequent upon a sweat. I have tried the plan repeatedly, and known it tried by others still more frequently, but I have never heard of any ill effects resulting. Very often a sweat is exceedingly inconvenient, either from the difficulty in getting ground, as happens in towns, or from the infirm state of the legs. But soap and water can always be obtained, and if carefully used there is not the slightest danger attending them. Of course, after the removal of a long coat the skin requires an extra protection in-doors in the shape of a double allowance of clothing, and it will be necessary to avoid standing still out of doors, though, as I before remarked, on the whole the risk of taking cold by horses worked hard enough to sweat them is less if they are clipped than if they have their long coats on.

SINGEING requires less practice than clipping, but it cannot be done without some little experience of its difficulties, and a novice generally burns the skin as well as the hair. To keep a horse's coat in good order it must be singed several times in the course of the autumn, beginning as soon as the new growth has attained a length of half an inch beyond what is usual. The singeing-lamp is then passed lightly over the whole body, and soap and water being used, as I have described under the head of clipping, or a sweat given if that plan is preferred, the coat is left for a fortnight or three weeks till it has grown another half-inch, when the process is repeated, and again a third, and even a fourth time if necessary. On account of these repeated applications of the lamp, the professed singer is not so often employed as the clipper, especially as the former's work is not so difficult to perform as that of the latter.

The lamp now in common use is attached to a wide copper comb made like a rake in principle, and so arranged that the teeth raise the hair and draw the ends into the flame. Where gas is procurable the comb is attached to the gas-pipe by a flexible tube, and the lamp consists merely in a number of holes perforated along the edge of the comb, so that a series of jets of gas are lighted, and burn so strongly, that the coat is completely removed as near the skin as the teeth of the comb raise it. If gas cannot be obtained, a wide wick of cotton is inserted in a flat holder, and the ends protruding to the level of the teeth, while a reservoir filled with naphtha supplies them with that inflammable fluid, a constant flame is maintained, but not nearly equal in strength to that from gas. As the coat is not allowed to grow so long before it is singed, so the clothing need not be much increased after its removal, and, indeed, in well regulated stables there is little or no change required. Singeing is performed in less than one quarter the time of clipping, and a shilling's worth of naphtha is enough for one horse, unless his coat is unusually long.

SHAVING was introduced some years ago to a limited extent, but it requires so long a confinement of the horse after it is performed, that it was soon abandoned. The hair is lathered and cut off with the razor as closely as from the human chin, and unless this is done exactly at the right time, the growth subsequently is too short or too long. Instances have been known in which horses have remained naked until the next spring, and were thereby rendered perfectly useless, as they were chilled directly their clothing was removed. The only advantage in shaving over clipping is to be found in the reduced labor required; a good razor, or rather set of razors, soon going over the surface. But the invention of singeing did away with this superiority, and the shaving of horses is therefore one of the fashions of a day which have now disappeared.

TRIMMING. The jaws, nostrils, ears, legs, mane and tail, are all more or less subjected to the care of the groom, who removes superfluous hairs from each or all by various means, as follows:—

The *jaws*, *nostrils*, and *ears* are singed, the last named not being touched inside, as the internal hairs are clearly a protection of the delicate lining membrane of the ear from the cold and wet. The long bristles of the nostrils may either be cut off, pulled out, or singed off, but the first plan is the easiest and the most humane. There are, also, some bristles about the eyes which are generally removed, but it is very doubtful whether many an eye would not be saved from a blow in the dark if they were left untouched. Fashion, however, dictates their removal, and her orders must generally be complied with. The hair which grows an inch or more in length beneath the jaw, being of the same nature as the rest of the coat, can only be singed off with advantage, and it should be done as fast as it grows, especially if the singeing is not universal, or there will be a different color presented in these parts. Nothing gives a horse such a low-bred appearance as a goat-like beard, and the trimming of this part alone will completely alter the character of the animal where the hair has been at all long. The legs are trimmed partly by singeing, and partly either by clipping or pulling out the hairs. Great dexterity is required to manage this performance in a workmanlike manner, so as to avoid the stale and poster-like appearance which is presented by a leg clipped all over (without a corresponding clipping of the body), and at the same time to remove all, or nearly all, the superfluous hair. In the summer, a clipped leg is totally inadmissible, and even from the legs of a badly-bred horse the hair may be pulled by gradually working at it for a little time every day with the fingers, armed with powdered resin. This prevents the hair slipping through them, and by its aid such a firm hold may be obtained that, as I said before, perseverance will enable the groom to clear the legs entirely, with the exception, generally, of a strong lock of hair behind the pastern. When this is very obstinate, it is allowable to use the scissors to clear away the hair below the horny growth which is found there, but there should always be left a slight fringe round this, so as to avoid the sharp and stiff outline presented by the clipped leg. In the winter, the arms and backs of the knees, as well as the bosom and the insides of the quarters, will generally want singeing, whether the body is submitted to the lamp or not; but in the summer, even if any long hairs are left there, they are easily removed by the hand armed with resin. Unless general clipping or singeing is practised, the front surfaces of the legs do not require trimming at any season of the year.

The mane is not now usually cut, but formerly it was a very common practice to "hog" it, that is, to cut it to a sharp-pointed ridge, sticking straight upwards from the crest, and giving that part the appearance of extraordinary height. Sometimes, however, the mane is very thick, and then for the sake of appearances it is necessary to thin it, which is done by twisting a small lock at a time round the comb, and pulling it out; this gives some little pain, but apparently not much, and evidently not more than the trimming of the legs, and not so much as in pulling out the feelers or bristles growing from the nostrils. A small lock of the mane is generally cut just behind the ears where the head of the bridle rests, as it would otherwise lie beneath that part in an untidy manner.

In trimming the tail various methods are adopted, when it is cut square; for if the hairs are allowed to grow to the full length, no interference is necessary beyond an occasional clipping of their points to prevent them from breaking or splitting. A square tail, however, whether long or short, demands the careful use of the scissors or knife, without which the horse to which it belongs is sadly disfigured. Two modes are practised,—in the first the tail is carefully combed out, and then allowing it to fall in its natural position, it is gathered up in the hand just above the part to be cut off, and here a sharp knife is drawn across it backwards and forwards without notching it, till it passes clean through. The tail is then released, and any loose hairs projecting are removed with the scissors. The second mode is not so easy, but when well carried out is more satisfactory to the eye, inasmuch as it is capable of giving a sharper and more defined edge to the square tail. As in the first method, the tail is carefully combed out; it is then held by an assistant's hand, placed beneath the root of the dock, as nearly as may be in the position which it assumes in the animal out of doors. While thus poised the operator takes a pair of sharp scissors, and holding the blades horizontally open, he insinuates one of them through the middle of the tail at the place to be cut, passing it straight backwards, and cutting the hair quite level from the central line to the outside on his own left. Then reversing the blades, and keeping to the same level, he cuts towards the right, and if he has a good eye and can use his hands in accordance with its dictates, he will have presented a very prettily squared tail. On the other hand, if these organs are defective, or if he wants experience, he will have notched the end of the tail in a most unsightly manner. If the groom wishes to try his hand in this operation, he should get hold of a long tail, and begin far below the point where the squared end is intended finally to be. This will afford him five or six experimental cuts, and if he cannot satisfy himself, as he nears the proper length, that he will be likely to succeed, he can still call in the aid of a more skilful operator before it is too late. The hair of the tail grows so slowly, that two or three months are required to remove the disfigurement which is sometimes caused in this way, and consequently it behooves the groom to be doubly careful, for his own sake as well as his master's.

To make the mane lie smoothly on its proper side, which it sometimes obstinately refuses to do, it must be plaited in small locks, and the ends loaded with lead, if it cannot be made to lie down without. An experienced groom, however, will generally succeed in so managing the plaits that they lie close to the neck, which is all that can be effected by the aid of lead, but sometimes the hair is so obstinate that nothing else will effect the object in view.

USE AND APPLICATION OF BANDAGES.

BANDAGES are applied to the legs of the horse for three different purposes. First, to give support to the blood-vessels and synovial capsules; secondly, as a vehicle for applying cold lotions; and thirdly, for drying and warming them.

For the mere purpose of support either linen or flannel bandages may be put on, according to the weather, and the tendency to inflammation. The legs of seasoned old horses are seldom so prone to become hot as those of young ones, and excepting in very warm weather, flannel bandages seem to suit them better than linen. On the contrary, if flannel is applied to the legs of a colt, even if they are not inclined to inflame, they will become hot and uncomfortable, and he will learn to tear them off, in which some horses become perfect adepts. Whichever kind of bandage is put on, it should be previously tightly rolled with the strings inwards, then taking it in the right hand, and unwrapping about six inches, they are laid against the canna bone on the side nearest to the groom, so that the folds shall have a tendency to unroll *from* him and not *to* him. While the left hand keeps the end from slipping, the right passes the roll of bandage closely round the leg till it meets the left, when the latter, still pressing the end against the leg, lays hold of the roll, and allows the right to be brought back to meet it on the other side. After which the coils are repeated till the whole bandage is run out and the leg encased, one row being slightly above or below the level of the next, as may be required. The great art consists in avoiding unequal pressure, and yet giving sufficient to accomplish the purpose for which bandaging is designed. From the projection backwards of the pastern-joints it is impossible to make the folds lie perfectly smooth, and there must be loose parts, which however are covered over by the next turn. No written description, however, will suffice to teach this little operation, and the young groom should watch a good bandager, and imitate him as exactly as he can. The strings at the end serve to tie the bandage on, and these also must neither be so tight as to cut the leg, nor so loose as to allow the bandage to fall down.

When cold lotions are to be applied by means of bandages, linen is the proper material, as flannel is too bad a conductor of heat, by evaporation, for the purpose. The whole bandage, after being rolled up rather tightly, should be dipped in cold water, or in the lotion which may be recommended, and then while quite wet it is to be applied in the way which I have just described. The following lotion is useful for the purpose :—

>   Take of Tincture of Arnica a wine-glassful.
>   " Nitre ½ oz.
>   " Sal Ammoniac 1 oz.
>   " Water half a bucketful.

Mix and use by dipping the bandages in before applying them, and by wetting them with this solution afterwards by means of a sponge.

If the groom is careful, he may remove inflammation of the legs better by means of dipping them in cold water, or the above lotion may be applied with a sponge every half-hour, holding each leg over the bucket, than with the aid of bandages. A cold douche by means of a forcing garden engine is also extremely beneficial to the legs, but it must be used out of doors, as it will wet the litter and the walls of the stall if the water is splashed over them within doors.

FOR DRYING AND WARMING THE LEGS when the horse is being dressed, flannel is the only proper material for bandages. Its mode of application is not of much consequence, provided the bandages are put on rather loosely, for tight pressure has a tendency to prevent the return of natural heat, which is so much desired. After wetting the legs the bandages should be applied somewhat more tightly, so as to absorb the moisture as much as possible.

MANAGEMENT OF THE FEET.

IN THE STABLED HORSE THE FEET require constant care, for they are not only artificially shod, but they are allowed to stand on a material which is a much worse conductor of heat than the surface of the earth, by nature designed to bear them. Hence, if neglected, they either become hard and brittle, or they are allowed to be constantly wet, and then the soft covering of the frog is decomposed, and emits a disagreeably smelling discharge, which soon wastes it away, leaving no other protection to the sensible organ beneath, and constituting what is called an ordinary thrush. Again, it is found by experience, that not only must the shoes be renewed as they wear out, but even if no work is done, and consequently they are not reduced in size, they no longer fit at the expiration of about three weeks, and they must then be removed, to allow of a portion of the sole and crust being cut away before they are again put on. The groom must therefore attend to the following points :—*First*, to prevent the feet from becoming too dry; *secondly*, to take measures against their becoming thrushy from wet; *thirdly*, to see that the shoes are removed at the end of every three weeks, or more frequently if necessary; and *fourthly*, to examine carefully every day that they are securely nailed on without any of the clenches having started up from the surface, so as to endanger the other leg.

DRYNESS OF THE FEET is prevented by the use of what is called stopping, which is composed either of cow-dung alone, or cow-dung and clay mixed, or of cow-dung and pitch. The first is by far the most powerful application, but it moistens the sole too much if employed every night, and then produces the opposite evil in the shape of thrush. A mixture of equal parts of cow-dung and clay may be used every night with advantage, and this I believe to be the best of all stoppings. It should be kept in a strong box of wood, about a foot long and eight inches wide, with a handle across the top, and it should be applied the last thing at night to the soles of the fore feet only, by means of a thin piece of wood, a foot long and a couple of inches wide, with which the space within the shoe is completely stuffed. If the feet are obstinately dry, in spite of repeated stoppings with cow-dung alone, which will rarely be the case, a table-spoonful of salt may be added to the cow-dung, and this will never fail. For most horses stopping with cow-dung alone once a week is sufficient, but the groom can judge for himself, by their appearance, of the number of stoppings required. If three parts of cow-dung and one of clay are used, the feet may be stopped twice a week, or, perhaps, every other night, and if equal parts of each are adopted as the composition, almost any feet will bear being stopped every other night, with the exception of flat or pumiced soles, which should never be stopped at all. On the night before shoeing, every horse, even if he has flat soles, will be the better for having his feet stopped, the application softening the horn so as to allow the smith to use his knife to slice it without breaking it into crumbling fragments. Several patents have been taken out for felt pads, to be soaked in water, and then inserted in the hollow of the shoe, but they do not answer nearly so well as cow-dung stopping, which has far more emollient qualities than mere water. I believe nothing has yet been discovered which has qualities at all equal to this old-fashioned natural remedy.

THRUSHES are prevented by keeping the frogs free from ragged layers of the elastic substance of which they are partly composed, and at the same time by maintaining a dry state of the litter on which the horse stands. I am not now considering the management of the horse at grass, where thrushes are generally produced when the weather is very wet, or when the pasture is of too marshy a character, but the frogs of the stabled horse, which ought never to be allowed to be so moist as to become decomposed. Some ulcerated conditions of the frog which are still considered to come under the general denomination "thrush," are due to severe internal disease of the bones of the foot, and are not caused by moisture at all. Still these are rare exceptions, and the ordinary thrush of the stable may be considered as invariably caused in the latter way. Cases are also occasionally to be met with, in which, from general grossness of the system, the sensible frog throws off part of its horny covering, and secretes a foul matter instead. The management of these diseased conditions comes within the province of the veterinarian, and I shall therefore not enter upon its consideration; but the prevention of the mere decomposition of the external surface by moisture is a part of the duties of the groom, and so is the application of the proper remedies for it, as soon as the nature of the case is clearly made out. Here antiseptic astringents, which are quite out of place in inflammatory thrush, are the only useful applications, and by their means alone can the decomposition be stopped. Of these Sir W. Burnett's solution of chloride of zinc is the best, but in mild cases, Condy's fluid, which is the permanganate of potass, will answer well, and is not so poisonous in its nature if carelessly left about. Friar's Balsam, with as much of the sulphate of zinc dissolved in it as it will take up, is the old-fashioned grooms' remedy for thrush, and a very good one it is if carefully insinuated into the cleft of the frog on a piece of tow wetted with it. The grand principle, however, is to prevent thrush rather than to cure it, but when horses are bought, or come home from grass with it, the curative method must be carried out.

THE REMOVAL OF THE SHOES at regular intervals, whether they are worn out or not, is a most important part of the duties of the groom. On examining the shape of the foot it will be seen that the diameter of the circle in contact with the shoe is greater than that of the coronet, and hence as the shoe is forced away from its original position by the growth of the horn it confines the walls to the extent of the difference between the diameter of the foot at its old position and that of the part which it now occupies. For if two lines from the surface of the coronet on each side were continued through the outside surface of the crust to the new seat of the shoe, they would be far from parallel, and yet the shoe nails must have been carried on in perfect parallel lines on account of the unyielding nature of iron. For this reason a shoe, when it has not been removed at the end of a month, will be found to lie within the heel of one side or the other, by which to some extent contraction is prevented, but at the expense of the heel, into which the corresponding part of the shoe has entered. This is a frequent cause of corns, and horses which have once been subject to that disease should have their shoes removed once a fortnight.

ONE OF THE MOST ANNOYING ACCIDENTS to the horseman is the loss of a shoe, whether it happens in the hunting field or on the road. Some horses can scarcely be prevented by any care of their grooms from pulling off a shoe in hunting when they get into deep ground, but on the road there is no such excuse, and the frequent loss of a shoe by the hack or harness-horse is sufficient to condemn the groom of carelessness in this particular. Every morning when the feet are picked out it is easy to look the shoes over and feel if they are tight. The clenches also ought to be examined, and if they are not raised at all it may safely be predicated that the day's journey will be completed without the shoe being lost. A raised clench may severely cut a horse on the inside of the other leg, and in those who are predisposed to "speedy cut" it may cause severe injury, and perhaps occasion a fall of the most dangerous character.

DAILY EXERCISE.

WITHOUT REGULAR EXERCISE no horse can long be kept in health, and I believe that as far as this point is concerned even those which are hard-worked would be the better for half an hour's airing every morning as soon as they have been fed and before they are dressed. But those masters who are particular about the mouths of the animals they ride or drive, find that the hands of their grooms are generally so heavy that they spoil the delicate "feel" on which the comfort and pleasure of riding and driving so much depends. Hence in such cases the poor horse is condemned to confinement in his stable, not only on the day when he is to be ridden or driven, but on those also when he is to be idle. The health of the body is sacrificed to the maintenance of that delicate condition of the mouth which is so highly prized by good horsemen and accomplished whips, and I confess that I plead guilty to having for a long series of years acted on this principle. A fair share of health may be maintained without exercise if the work is never interrupted for more than a single day, and at the same time there being only one pair of hands to interfere with the mouth, its delicacy is not impaired, that is to say if they are not as bad as those of the groom. Sometimes a large and smooth snaffle is allowed as an exercise bridle, in the hope that it cannot injure the mouth, but even this will do mischief if the weight of the rider is thrown upon it, as is too often the case. Leaving out of the question this objection to the adoption of exercise, there can be no doubt that a daily walk out of doors for half an hour or an hour, especially if it can be managed on turf, will be of the greatest service to the horse's health.

PROPER TEMPERATURE OF THE STABLE.

THERE IS SCARCELY ANY POINT upon which there is so much difference of opinion, as in relation to the temperature of stables.

PROPER TEMPERATURE OF STABLE.

Some contend for an amount of heat which would raise Fahrenheit's thermometer to 65° or 70°, while others would never have their stables, if they could help it, above 45°. So much depends upon the kind of horse in them, and the work he has to do, that is to say, whether he is much exposed to the cold or not, that no rule can be laid down which is applicable to all stables, but I believe it may be asserted that none should be above 60°, or below 50°, if it can be avoided. There are days in the summer season, when the air out of doors in the shade stands at 90° or 95°, and, of course, in such weather, it is impossible, even with the doors and windows wide open, to keep the stable at a lower degree, or even within several points of those above stated. So also, with a thermometer scarcely above zero, it will be difficult to keep the air wholesome, and yet to prevent its temperature falling lower than 45°, which, at such seasons, feels very warm to those who come in from the external air. But, with these exceptions, I think the rule which I have laid down is a good one. The warmer the stable, the better the coat looks, till it is exposed to the weather, and even if it is so, it will take no injury if the horse is kept moving, but if not, it soon becomes chilled, and not only does the general health suffer, but the appearance also. There is, however, another, and very serious objection to hot stables, consisting in their ill-effect upon the legs and feet, which inflame much more readily in a warm atmosphere than in a cool one. I have often known horses stand severe rattling for months together, while standing in a stable which was so cold as to make their coats as rough as badgers, but when removed to warmer quarters, they have at once gone "all to pieces," their legs or feet becoming inflamed from missing the refrigerating effect of cool air after their daily work. The body may easily be kept warm enough by extra clothing, and, if necessary, a hood and breastplate may be worn all day and all night, but not even wet bandages will cool the legs if they are surrounded by hot air. On the whole, therefore, for the private gentleman's stable, including those for hunters, hacks, and carriage horses, I should advise a regular temperature to be preserved as near 55° of Fahrenheit as possible. In coming in from the external air this will appear very warm to the sensations, but it is far below the high state of heat at which many of our stables were kept, until within the last few years. I have often known 70° to 75° of Fahrenheit insisted on as the lowest which would suffice to get a hunter into condition, but practice proves the reverse, and that with plenty of clothing he will do in a cool stable of the temperature I have recommended, far better than in one possessing a higher range. The celebrated "Nimrod" (Mr. Apperley) was a great advocate for a hot stable, which he thought ought never to be reduced much below 70° or 75°; but his opinions, valuable as they undoubtedly are in the main, cannot be looked upon as in all points to be relied on.

REMEDIES FOR STABLE VICES AND BAD HABITS.

CRIB-BITING is a diseased condition of the stomach, for which there has never yet been a cure discovered, except on the principle of restraint. It may, therefore, be considered under the present head. In crib-biting the teeth are applied to some fixed object—generally the manger, so as to afford a fulcrum for the muscles of the neck to act from, and by preventing this, or by contriving so that the contraction of the muscles of the neck shall give pain, the vicious habit is got rid of for the time. The most common method is to buckle a leather strap so tightly round the neck, just behind the jaw, that when the horse attempts to crib, he tightens the muscles of that part, and these being pressed against the strap, occasion such pain that the act is not completely carried out, and even if it is on the first occasion, the attempt is not repeated. The strap is buckled sufficiently tight to do this, without much impeding the act of swallowing, or the flow of blood from the head, through the jugular veins to the body; but in confirmed cribbers no ordinary pressure will suffice, and then the head often becomes affected from the impediment which is caused to the return of the blood from the brain to the heart. To remedy this defect Mr. Cook, Saddler, of Long Acre, two or three years ago, invented a neck strap, containing a number of prongs, which pass through holes in a spring guard, and unless this is strongly pressed, they do not touch the skin. It is applied by throat straps to an ordinary head collar, and in slight cases it is found to answer most perfectly, but when the vice has become confirmed, and the desire to indulge in it is very strong, the pain occasioned by the prongs is endured, and no effect at all is produced. It is not therefore of much use, as the common strap does no injury in those cases where Mr. Cook's is effectual, and the latter will not avail when the plain strap is forbidden, on account of the extreme pressure required. I cannot, therefore, recommend any plan but such as will totally prevent the prehension of the manger, and this is accomplished by one of two ways. In the first of these, the manger itself is either concealed, or the corn and hay are placed on the ground, in a space slightly separated from the rest of the stall by a row of bricks, or other similar bodies, which cannot be laid hold of. To the concealed manger and rack there is the objection, that while the horse is feeding, he can go on cribbing without interruption, and as this is the time chiefly chosen for the act, success is only partly achieved. Placing the food on the ground is entirely successful in stopping the habit, but it leads to some waste of provender, as the horse is apt to tread upon it, after which he will refuse to eat it. By far the best preventive, in my opinion, is the bar muzzle, consisting in an iron frame work, covering the lips and nose, and suspended from the head by a leather head collar, so that the lips can reach the

BAR MUZZLE FOR CRIB-BITERS.

corn or hay, but the teeth are too wide to pass through the bars and seize the manger. This mechanical contrivance is entirely harmless, and perfectly effectual, the sole objection to it being the fact that it proclaims the wearer to every one who looks into the stable as a cribber. This may be a valid reason for rejecting its use for dealers' horses, but in a gentleman's stable, utility and humanity ought to have precedence of such a feeble argument. When the bar muzzle is adopted, it should always be kept on, excepting, of course, when the bridle replaces it for work or exercise, or while the head is being dressed.

KICKING THE WALL OR STALL POST is sometimes a very annoying trick, and though not always done in a vicious manner, it is objectionable, because the kicker is liable to lame himself, or one of his neighbors. In mares it is often of a sexual nature, and in them it is much more common than in geldings,—the extent to which it is carried by them being generally greatest at the beginning and end of their being "in use." At such times some mares go almost mad, if they have an irritating neighbor, who keeps smelling them, and I once had one who kicked herself to pieces in a paroxysm of this kind, which nothing but tying up the fore-leg could restrain. There are several remedies in common use, but none can be relied on in all cases. Foremost among these is the use of gorse, nailed to the stall-post, which will almost invariably quiet a low-bred animal, especially if a gelding, but high-bred mares will sometimes kick at it all the more, for the punishment they receive. A padded leather strap, buckled round the canna bone, with a common sinker attached to it, or, instead of this, a few links of heavy chain, will generally keep the horse from kicking, because in making the attempt he gives his coronet and pastern a heavy blow. If, however, this plan is unsuccessful, it is liable to cause lameness, from the inflammation produced by the blows, and, therefore, the effect must be carefully watched. Few horses kick out with both legs, and a pair of hobbles buckled round the hind fetlocks will, in a vast majority of cases, put an end to the trick as long as they are worn, without any risk, or producing any serious annoyance, save only what is inseparably connected with the prohibition of the indulgence in the desire to kick. A narrow strap buckled round the part just above the hock, so as to confine the ham string, will have the desired effect, by giving intense pain when any attempt to strike out is made, but is a most annoying infliction to the horse, and generally prevents his lying down, from the necessity which there is for bending the hock, in reaching the ground. I should, therefore, give the preference to the bunch of gorse, or if that is not readily procurable, to the sinker of wood or iron suspended to a strap round the leg.

IN SCRATCHING THE EAR with the hind foot, the horse is very apt to get his leg over the collar rein, if the sinker is not heavy enough to keep the rein tightly strained between the head collar and the ring in the manger. Impatient animals, also, which are continually pawing at their litter, will sometimes get one of their fore feet over it, but this is not so serious an accident. To prevent the mischief occasioned in either case by the struggles to get free, especially when the hind leg is thus caught, the rings for the collar reins are sometimes made to draw down with a spring-catch, which releases them when pulled in that direction, but in no other. When, however, the sinker is properly weighted, it is almost impossible for such an accident to occur; and this simple invention has now become obsolete.

TEARING THE CLOTHES OFF is by no means an unusual stable habit, and it is one very difficult to cure. There are two effectual preventives, however: one of which consists in the regular employment of a rough horsehair cloth, made like that for hops, outside the rug, and which is so disagreeable to the teeth, that no horse will attempt to tear it; the other is carried out by means of a pole of ash, about three-quarters of an inch in diameter, with an iron eye attached to each end. One of these is fastened, by means of a short leathern strap and buckle, to the side of the roller-pad,

STABLE VICES.

while the other has a strap or chain about a foot long, which attaches it to the head collar. The pole should reach about fifteen inches beyond the point of the shoulder, and it should be fixed on the side which is generally uppermost when the horse lies down, so as not to be under him in that position. It is a very simple and cheap apparatus, and any village blacksmith can make and apply it. The following engraving will illustrate my meaning better than the most detailed description without it.

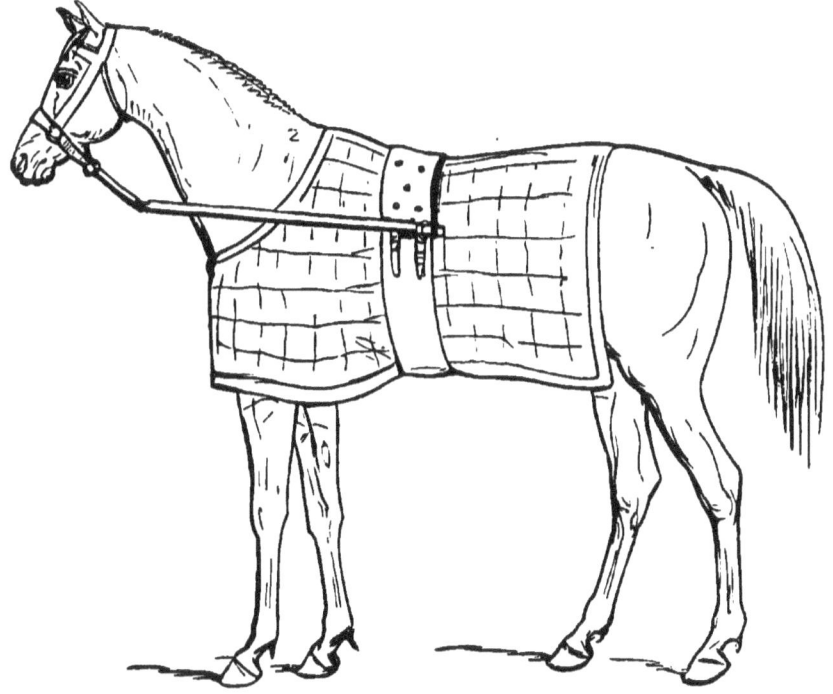

REMEDY FOR TEARING THE CLOTHES.

WEAVING is a mark of an irritable nervous system, beyond which it is harmless, but quite incurable. It consists in a perpetual moving of the head from one side of the manger to the other, with an action like that of a wild beast in his den. The constant friction soon wears out the collar-reins when there are two, and on that account a single rein may be adopted in this particular instance with advantage.

EATING THE LITTER is a peculiar appetite, which chiefly occurs either in those horses which are kept short of hay on account of their tendency to fatten, or when the animal possessing it has been stabled for a very long time together and requires a change. In the former case nothing but the muzzle will be of the slightest service, but in the latter a run at grass, or soiling indoors for a month or two, will remedy the disorder of the stomach. Rock salt in the manger will sometimes have the desired effect, producing a degree of thirst which will make dry litter distasteful.

KICKING AND BITING savagely are marks of actual vice, and scarcely come within the limits of the present section. Still the groom must know how to guard against them in the best way, so as to save himself from danger without unnecessarily punishing the horse. There are some animals which cannot be effectually restrained without severity, but on the average, kindness and firmness united will overcome any horse. Sometimes it is necessary to put on the muzzle while the dressing is going on, but this is chiefly because the skin is so irritable that the brush or whisp excite sensations which lead to the use of the teeth or hind legs to prevent their recurrence. In such cases as these Mr. Rarey's method of subduing a savage horse is extremely valuable.

PREPARATION FOR WORK.

I HAVE ALREADY OBSERVED that these pages are not intended to serve as a guide for the trainer of the race-horse, and that they chiefly apply to the management of the hunter, hack, and carriage-horse belonging to the private gentleman. The description of the mode of preparation for work will therefore include the mode of fitting the hunter for his duties, and of getting the hack and carriage-horse into condition, from the state in which they are usually first brought into the stable, either from grass or the dealer's hands.

IN THE PRESENT DAY, THE HUNTER is prepared almost as carefully as the race-horse or steeple-chaser, when he is intended for any of the grass countries. Nothing short of a regular preparation will enable a horse to go through a fast thing in Northamptonshire or Leicestershire, and no man in his senses would ride a horse there in the front rank, unless he was thoroughly fit. The stud-groom, therefore, requires for his purpose a training-ground where he can give his horses their sweats, without which it would be impossible to get them into condition. A very large space is not necessary, but a very small one will not suffice, the constant turning incidental to a limited gallop producing a great strain upon the joints. If possible a gallop measuring at least a mile and a half or two miles in circumference should be obtained, and with this length, including a moderate rise in its extent so as to open the horse's pipes well at the finish of the sweat, it is the groom's fault if his charge is not brought out thoroughly fit when the hunting season commences. Of course, when making this assertion, I am calculating that he has been allowed sufficient time, which will depend greatly upon the state in which he finds his horses in August. If they have been at grass, it is almost impossible to get them ready by the middle of November, but a well summered horse soiled in a loose-box with a proper allowance of corn, may be thoroughly prepared by that time if he is set to work by the middle of August. This will allow of two clear preparations, with an intervening week for cooling physic. Should the horse be up from grass, another month or six weeks at least will be required, which must be employed in giving him nothing but walking exercise, with a dose of physic at the beginning, and repeated at the end of three weeks or a month. Horses at grass in the summer are seldom allowed any corn, and the change from grass to the more stimulating food of the stable must be made gradually, or some of the important organs will assuredly fail. Hence the necessity for extra time, and the addition which I have made to the calculated period for conditioning a hunter summered indoors, is barely sufficient for this purpose, when he is full of grass or of the fattening food which is given to make him up for the dealers. In either case great care and some experience are necessary in altering the entire management of the animal, so as to give him corn and exercise enough to prepare his frame gradually for the strains which it will have to bear in the hunting field, without producing inflammation. With all the objections which I hold to physic, I must confess that here I think it to be indispensable; and invariably, as soon as a raw horse is settled in the stable, I should get him thoroughly cleaned out before I began to give him hay and corn. I have always found it advantageous just to allow a couple of days to elapse before giving the physic, which will serve to fill the large bowels with the new kind of food. A mash should then be administered at night, and repeated if necessary till it has had the desired effect in softening the dung, when the physic may be given. Two or three days will elapse before it has set sufficiently to allow of walking exercise; but as soon as this can be ordered with safety, the horse should be walked out twice a day for an hour and a half each time, or two hours in the morning and one in the evening, whichever may be preferred. The division of the exercise into two periods is far better than keeping the green horse out for so long a time as three hours, which will make him weary; whereas, the shorter period will not tire any horse, and a mid-day rest will restore his whole frame, and enable him to go out again in the evening as cheerfully as ever. I need scarcely observe that the shoes should be attended to, and the feet put in proper order, for three hours' walking exercise in ill-fitting shoes will do great harm, especially to feet that are not accustomed to their pressure. By persevering with steady slow work, and feeding on a moderate allowance of hay and corn, the latter not exceeding two feeds at first and three at the end of the month, the horse will be ready by the middle of August to have a second dose of physic, after which he may commence in earnest his *first real preparation*. This also is chiefly confined to slow work, but if the horse is gross he may have in the course of the four or five weeks to which it extends, one or two sweats of moderate length and speed. Great caution must always be exercised by the groom at this time ; on no account should any fast work be given, unless he is satisfied that his horse is in perfect health and in good spirits. Every increase in the food and work should be carefully watched, and its effects noted, so as to guide him in deciding whether he can venture to take another step. It must be remembered that hitherto the feeds of corn have been only three quarterns of oats daily, and the exercise has not extended beyond a walk; but during the next few weeks the former must be doubled, or nearly so, and the latter must go on into a daily slow trot of two or three miles on turf, with an occasional steady gallop in place of this, and, as I have before remarked, one or two sweats if the system is overloaded with fat. But unless the hunter is very fleshy, nothing more than slow trots and canters will be required until after the next dose of physic. The increase in the quantity of corn will seldom tend to put on fat, and as the amount of hay should be small, not exceeding 10lbs. a day, unless the horse is gross in his nature, he will have put on muscle, and lost some of the internal fat which is so prejudicial to condition.

THE OBJECT OF THE SWEATING PROCESS is to remove superfluous fatty matters, which act prejudicially in a twofold manner. In the first place the fat itself is so much dead weight to carry, and on the calculation that seven pounds are equal to a distance in an average length of race, it may readily be understood that the huge quantity of adipose tissue, which is carried by a fat horse, will, by its weight alone, retard any attempt at high speed. But, not only is fat to be objected to on this score ; for it is also known by experience, that its pressure on the important internal organs, when it is deposited around them, interferes with the proper performance of their several functions. . The muscles of the limbs, when they are marbled with fat, as we see them in the slaughtered ox and sheep, are unable to contract vigorously, but when a similar condition occurs in the muscular tissue of which the heart is composed, violent exertions are interdicted, or, if they are attempted, they are attended with dangerous and often fatal results. Again, it is ascertained that sweating has a local, as well as a general effect, and that, by producing a copious discharge of fluid from the skin covering any particular part, there will be a removal of any superfluous fat which may be lodged beneath it, before the rest of the body is perceptibly acted on. Hence, when the groom thinks that his horse is loaded with fat about the heart, he puts on extra "sweaters" over that part, or on the contrary, if his object is to unload the ridge of dense adipose membrane, which constitutes a high crest, he puts on two or three extra hoods, and sweats chiefly in that region of the body. The local effect of these partial sweats is, perhaps, a good deal overrated, but undoubtedly there is some foundation for the general belief. The use of clothing for sweating is not nearly so frequent as it used to be, even in racing stables, and horses are not now drawn so fine, by a great deal, as they were twenty or thirty years ago. At that time runners in the Derby, or in any other great race, when they were saddled, looked like living skeletons, and to an eye unaccustomed to the hard lines presented by their limbs, the beauty of their forms was entirely gone. Now a different system prevails; the object is not to reduce the horse as much as he will bear, but to bring him out as big as he can be, consistently with good wind. The celebrated trainer, John Scott, has shown what can be done in this way, and his example is now generally followed. So also with hunters, although they are often required to do more, perhaps, than any other variety of the horse, and in the grass countries are made as fit as if they were going to run in a steeplechase, yet they are brought to covert looking big and full of muscle, without any pretensions to be considered as drawn fine. Still the sweat, either in clothes or without them, must be occasionally carried out, or the internal organs will continue loaded with fat, as is natural to them when they have been for some time in a state of rest, coupled with high feeding. The use and amount of sweaters must be proportioned to the constitutional peculiarities of the individual; in one horse a slow gallop will produce a perfect lather on the skin, while in another treated in all respects in the same way, there shall be hardly a hair turned. So also the effect of apparently the same degree of sweating on different horses is very variable, producing a great relief in one case, and scarcely any in another. The groom must not attempt to carry out any fixed rule, but must watch the effect of each day's work, and increase or diminish the amount next day according to circumstances.

AS I BEFORE REMARKED, a sweat may be with clothes or without, the object in each case being not so much to do a certain amount of work, but to get rid of a fixed quantity of superfluous fat and humors. On the other hand, a gallop has quite the opposite end in view, being intended to brace the muscles, heart, blood-vessels and lungs, by stimulating them to act in an extraordinary degree, but without any view to reduce the weight of the body or any part of it. In a sweat, therefore, the pace is slow and long continued; no exertion is made to render it smart, or to develop action in any shape, the whole attention of the groom being devoted to the single object which is connected with the removal of fat. It is usual, therefore, to send the horse along at a slow, steady, hand-gallop for four miles, or in very gross animals for five or six, the last half mile only being done at anything like a fast pace, and even then the horse should not be extended to the utmost, on account of the great extra weight he has to carry, if he has two or three sweating blankets on. It is quite necessary to bear in mind this special object of the sweat, inasmuch as it has lately become the fashion to sweat without either clothing or exercise, by means of the Turkish bath. The opponents of this practice contend that it can never supersede the old plan, because, though it will get rid of superfluities, it will not develop muscle; but they forget that it is not used for the latter purpose, but is solely confined to the one object, which by the employment of sweating blankets out of doors is accompanied with considerable risk. The Turkish bath is, in fact, a means to one end only, and must not be employed for any other. No horse could have his muscles and heart, his wind and limbs, made more wiry and enduring than before by any number of baths; but he may be put into a condition which shall fit him for being so, without the risk to the legs and feet which a number of sweats in heavy clothing will always cause. No wonder, therefore, that trainers eagerly resort to the use of the bath, especially as every year their horses seem to be getting more and more liable to break down. It is quite true that the old fashioned sweat combines muscular exercise with the process of unloading the system, but in so doing, the time of the groom is the only thing saved, and no one would take that into the calculation, as being worthy of consideration. In the new mode, when he is too gross, the horse is sweated on one day, and on the next he may be galloped, if necessary, the bath producing so little fatigue, that he may have any amount of exercise directly after it, to which he is accustomed. Newmarket trainers are not very easily induced to adopt a novelty, but many of them have made up their minds as to the advantages of the bath, and several of those who are to be regarded as the highest authorities, have erected one on their premises. In resorting to the bath at first the attempt was made to save doubtful legs only, but the good effect was soon found to extend beyond this, and in almost all cases where there would be any necessity for sweats and clothing, the Turkish bath is adopted instead, by those who have the means at their disposal. I shall, therefore, describe each of these plans in detail.

ORDINARY SWEATING.

WHEN THE OLD FASHIONED SWEAT is intended to be given, and it is not proposed to reduce any part in particular, it is usual to put on an old rug next the skin, or, in large stables, a sheet kept expressly for the purpose, and hence called a "sweater;" then an old hood and breast-cloth, next a second quarter-piece is put on, and even a third in some cases, and lastly, a complete set of clothing over all, the saddle, as usual, completing the arrangement. If any special part is to be reduced, as, for instance, the brisket or bosom, an extra cloth is folded like a shawl, and the ends being crossed over the withers, it is kept in its place under the breast-cloth, by the pressure of the saddle; or a rug may be folded and placed round the chest, without extending to the loins, in case the heart is supposed to be oppressed with fat. All these points of detail will call upon the groom for an exercise of ingenuity and tact, and if he possesses these qualities, he will have no difficulty in placing his sweaters where they will be required. When they are all securely fixed the horse is ridden out, and after walking for a short time to empty himself, he is started off to go his sweat, which is generally four miles, doing three quarters of the distance at a slow pace, and then being set going a little faster, and at last brought out to his top-speed, if in full training, or nearly so if in his second preparation. By his top-speed, however, is not to be understood the very outside pace which can be got out of the horse, but only such a speed as is short of that by so much as will preserve his stride in full vigor, and prevent that over-pacing which leads to the rupture of muscular or tendinous structure. In his first preparation he should seldom be extended, and it is better to increase the distance rather than to accelerate the speed beyond the steady gallop; but few horses refuse to sweat at a slow pace in this stage of training.

As soon as he has finished the distance, the trainer examines his state, and either directs him to be walked or trotted on to the rubbing place, which should be a box set apart for the purpose, either on the training-ground or at the usual stables; or if the ground is at a distance from any available stable, the shelter of a haystack or high hedge should be sought for. The full benefit of the sweat is not obtained unless the fluid is scraped off before it has had time to be re-absorbed, which is the result, if it is allowed to remain on the skin after this has ceased to give out any fluid. Its vessels in that case, instead of perspiring, adopt the opposite extreme, and appropriate the sweat by their own power of absorption; thus doing away with the chief benefit which was expected and desired from the sweat itself. When the hand of the groom, applied to the shoulder of the horse under his breast-cloth, tells him that the sweat is coming kindly, the horse may have a couple of rugs heaped upon him, and be suffered to give out fluid for a very few minutes only; but if it does not break out at once, three or four must be put on him, and he must wait a quarter of an hour or twenty minutes before he is fit to scrape. If he sweats freely, the groom in charge of his head may rub his ears and wipe his eyes, so as to refresh him slightly; but if there is any difficulty in bringing on the sweat this will only retard the process, and he may be allowed to stand quite quietly, and without any attempt to refresh him by the above little attentions, or by rubbing his legs, or wiping his thighs or bosom. As soon as the groom is satisfied, the hood is taken off, and the head and neck rapidly scraped, together with the bosom, from which the breast-cloth is removed, and the rugs and quarter-piece turned back so as to expose the whole neck and the points of the shoulders. One or two strappers may be employed in scraping and afterwards drying this part, besides the one holding the bridle; but if the horse is quiet enough, this may be removed, and the head dressed all the more effectually. A very few minutes suffice for drying this half of the horse, when the bridle should be readjusted, and the quarter-piece and sweaters wholly turned off over the croup; upon this the strappers again set to work with their scrapers and rubbers, they soon get rid of every particle of sweat, and have the coat perfectly dry and smooth. Much depends upon the stage of training; in the early part, the sweat is profuse, thick, and soapy, and takes more time to dry; while in the latter stages, when the horse is getting fit, it is watery and scanty, the horse will scarcely scrape, and dries without the slightest trouble. This is a good sign of condition, and the necessity for a repetition of the sweat may generally be gathered by the appearance of the fluid, which, when thick and lathery, shows that there is much gross fat in the system requiring removal; but, nevertheless, it also shows that great care must be taken in the process, lest mischief should be done, by calling upon nature too rapidly while the animal is in this fat state, and liable to inflammation of all kinds. After rubbing all the coat dry, and smoothing it down with the leather rubber, the usual clothing should be put on, and the horse allowed his exercise, which he may have as usual, care being taken that he does not catch cold if the weather is severe. The reason why the horse is taken out again is, that if he were left in the warm stable he would break out into a second sweat, and if he were placed in a cool one he would surely take cold. Walking exercise, therefore, with a short canter, is adopted as a means of avoiding both of these injurious conditions; but he should not continue it longer than to put him into a cool state, and restore his nerves and blood-vessels to their usual condition. The length of ground and pace for sweating vary with the age, condition, and purpose for which the horse is trained, the *maximum* length being six miles, and the *minimum* two to three, with a speed varying with every individual case, and depending upon the age, breed, and action of the horse, as well as his constitution and legs, and the state of preparation in which he is. Sweats are given at periods varying from once a week to once a fortnight after the first preparation, but seldom so often during that time. When sweats are given without clothing, they are in other respects just the same as described above, and the strappers are required in a similar way to dry the horse at once; but the quantity of sweat is not nearly so great, and two good hands will generally suffice for the purpose. In almost all cases, even where clothing is not used, it is heaped on when the horse is taken into the stable, in order to encourage the flow of perspiration.

THE TURKISH BATH.

THE TURKISH BATH when employed for horses, requires two boxes to be prepared, contiguous to each other, and, if economy is an object, to the saddle-room also, in order that one fire shall serve for all. The annexed plan has been carried out on this principle, the fire-place A being placed in the saddle-room, and heating it, as well as a boiler for hot water. It is sunk eighteen inches beneath the floor of the saddle-room, so as to allow of the commencement of the flue at B entering the bath-room, with its bottom two feet from the floor of that apartment, and to pass beneath the final exit of the flue, as it leaves to enter the chimney at F. The flue is supported on arches, clear of the wall, from B to C rising two inches in the foot, so that when it reaches the corner C, its bottom is four feet from the ground. It is built exactly like the usual flue of a hot-house, with dampers, and all the arrangements peculiar to that apparatus. From C to D it may be either on arches, or supported on slate built into the wall, as the heat is from this point not sufficient to crack that material. At D the bottom is about six feet high, and when it reaches the entrance B, it will give plenty of head room for a horse to pass beneath. On this side it is built in the wall, but still on arches so as to expose as large a radiating surface as possible, and serves to heat the other box H to the temperature required to prepare the horse for his sweat. Finally, it passes along the upper part of the fourth wall, in which also it is built in the same manner, and makes its exit over the part where it entered, at F. Here the flues are so arranged by dampers, that the current of warm air may either be directed along the flue B C D E F, or it may be turned off into the chimney F, entirely or partially. Ventilators must be introduced freely in the walls, so as to give plenty of fresh air when it is required, or to shut it off completely, to raise the temperature to the proper degree before the horse is admitted. One or two valves, in addition to the door I, all capable of being opened and closed at will, must also be fixed in the wall, between the boxes G and H, and by their means, added to the heat given off by the flue in it, this preparatory-box may be heated to 80° or 90° of Fahrenheit, so as

214   THE HORSE.

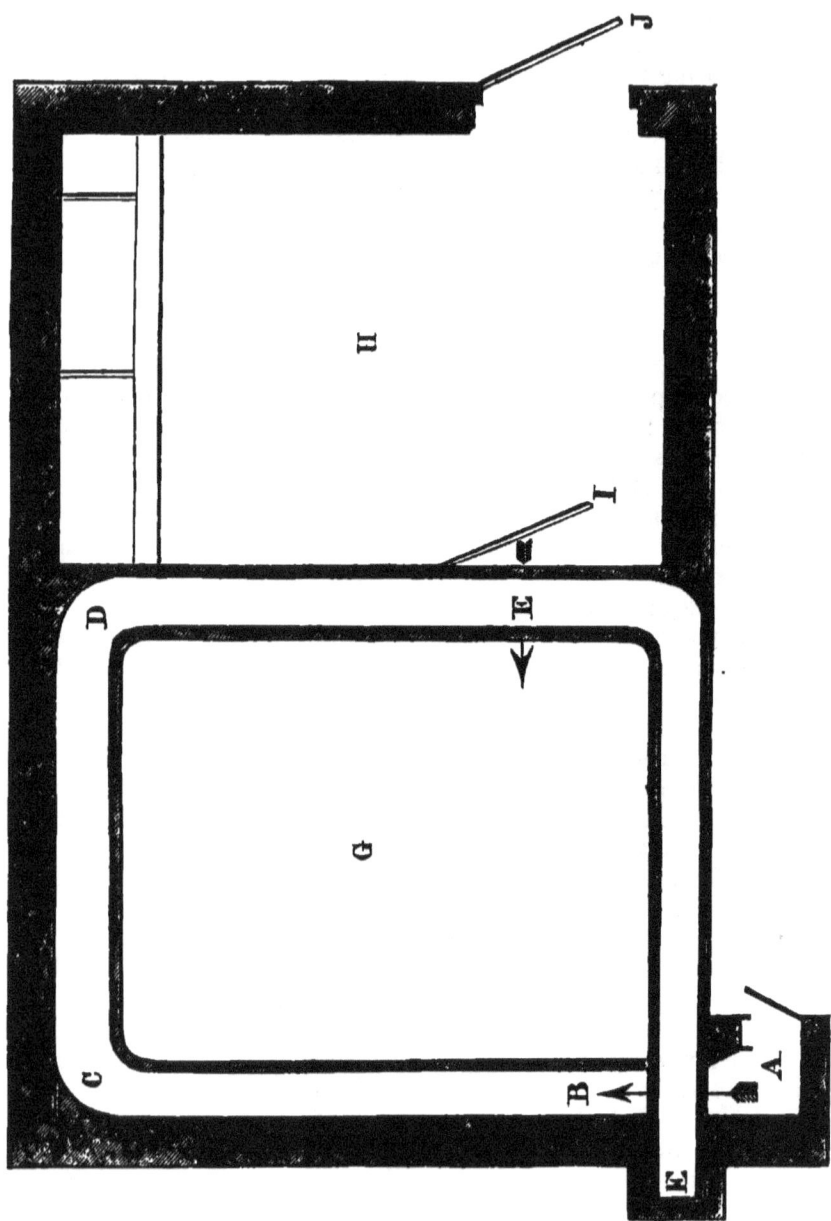

to bring on a gentle action of the skin, before the horse is introduced to the actual sweating-box—G. The preparatory-box, H, may be fitted up like a common loose box, and may be used as such, whenever the bath is not required, but the latter should have no manger or any other projecting body of metal, for when the heat is raised to 160°, the contact with the teeth and tongue is by no means pleasant. Tan forms the best material for the floor, or, if this cannot readily be obtained, sawdust will answer nearly as well, if the wetted parts are changed after each bath. A brick floor feels too warm to the feet, and when the bath is given very hot, it may injure them, if uncovered by some non-conductor of heat, so that it is better to avoid all risk, by using tan or sawdust. With this apparatus in working order, and the fire lighted in the stove A, the box H is heated to 80° or 90° of Fahrenheit, by robbing G of its warm air through the open door I, and the valves in the wall between the two to which I have already alluded. As soon as this is prepared, the horse is brought into it with his clothing on, and allowed to remain for a short time, which may be twenty minutes, half an hour, or an hour, according to the state of his skin, and the warmth of the box. As soon as he is settled in it, the clothes may all be removed, and here he may remain, with a whisp of hay in the rack, to amuse him, and chilled water in the tank, till his skin shows evident symptoms of breaking out, and the bath is prepared, that is, until the latter is raised to a temperature of 140° at the least. To effect this the door I and the adjacent valves may have been closed, if necessary; for a small box once raised to 80° or 90°, will keep its temperature with the horse in it for the time which is required. The groom must be careful not on any account to take his charge into the bath till his skin is beginning to sweat, for if he does, the blood may be driven too forcibly to the brain, without the relief which is afforded by the natural discharge from the skin, and dangerous mischief may be produced. On being taken into the bath G, a bucket of chilled water is placed within reach, and he is tied up with his head in the corner nearest the entrance door, which must be left open, so as to allow him plenty of fresh air. In about a quarter of an hour the sweat begins to pour out in large volumes, and this should be encouraged by friction with the hand, which may be guarded with horsehair gloves. As it becomes very profuse, a scraper may be applied occasionally, but two grooms, each with horsehair gloves on, will be able to remove it by keeping up continuous, deep, and steady pressure upon the skin, so as at once to squeeze out the watery particles from the hair, and to remove any scurf and other tenacious matters which accumulate there. According to the amount of reduction which is required to be made in the fatty deposits, and to the action of the skin, will be the time required to be devoted to this operation, but in general it is completed in half an hour. Some horses, however, have been kept sweating for a full hour, as I am informed, without apparent injury, and have afterwards gone out to exercise as full of life as ever. Indeed, it is said that the effect is usually to increase the spirits and liveliness of all the horses submitted to it. During the operation of the bath, the preparatory room should have had its doors and windows thrown freely open, and it should be left in this state when the horse returns to it, some grooms liking to have a strong draught through it while the horse is being cooled. In this process there is a considerable variation in the practices adopted in those stables where this novel kind of sweating is introduced. Some grooms wash the horse all over with cold water; others dash the water over the whole body the moment he comes from the bath, while a third set content themselves with the free admission of a current of cold air to the skin. Time must determine which of these plans is the best, but I am told on excellent authority, that they have all been tried with advantage. The fact is that when the skin is sweating freely under the stimulus of heat, and before its vessels are beginning to flag in their action, cold in any shape may be applied, so long as it is not continued long enough to reduce the pulse below its natural standard. Again, there are some grooms, who, after they have applied cold water, return the horse to the bath for a few minutes, the air in it being reduced to about 100° of Fahrenheit, and on bringing him out, take him at once to his box or stall, when he is dressed as usual, till he is perfectly dry, after which he is clothed and fed.

AS MAY NATURALLY BE EXPECTED, "the stable mind" is very much agitated by this innovation on established usages. On the one hand, it is argued by the thick-and-thin supporters of the bath, that, with the aid of walking exercise alone, and without a single gallop, a horse may be got into perfect condition, either for the race-course or the hunting-field. I have been told by a gentleman whose authority is fairly to be relied on, that he has ridden a stableful of horses thus prepared, in the front ranks of the crack countries, and that he never was so well carried in his life. None of them were galloped, except by himself; and until the season (1860–1) began, not one of them had been taken off a walk, as far as he knew, and he said he had the greatest confidence in his groom. On the other hand, the opponents of the bath hold that it only removes fat and fluids of all kinds, and that fast work must be given to the same extent as without it, the additional sweat produced by the former exhausting the horse very materially, to the prejudice of his condition. As far as my own opinion goes, I am inclined to believe that the truth lies between these opposite extremes; and that though a horse may be made light and airy by means of the bath and walking exercise alone, his muscles cannot be braced and rendered bigger, as they are by actual fast work. Incredible as it may appear, I have been told on very high authority, that a horse sweated twice, or even three times in the week, will do as much work, and as fast too, as if he had not gone through the process. If the bath has removed all fat and humor, he will not sweat in his gallops; and if any of either is left, it will do him no harm to get rid of it. Indeed, after all, the difference from the old plan of sweating in the stable without exercise is not very great in principle; and that was always found to be of service when the legs or feet were unsound. Under that plan, the horse was heavily clothed, and being just gently trotted, was taken back to his box, loaded with more clothes until he sweated freely, and was thus relieved of his fat without being galloped.

PHYSIC.

IN MY PREVIOUS REMARKS I have alluded to physic as necessary for the purpose of getting rid of the food which the horse may have been taking, before he comes into the stable, without injury, but the effects of which are somewhat in opposition to the condition required for hard work. In addition to this object, however, physic is given with several other purposes in view; but these may be said to bring it within the province of the veterinarian rather than of the groom. Thus, in the horse recently brought up from grass, it will often be necessary to expel worms; and though the experienced groom may be able to do this without risk, yet it is scarcely safe to recommend the young hand to attempt the task. At all events, if he does, he must be guided by the directions given in another part of this book; and I shall merely direct my attention to the effects of physic—firstly, in getting rid of injurious food; secondly, in cooling the stomach and general system, and thus enabling the latter to bear the increased stimulus afforded by extra food; and thirdly, to get rid of internal fat and humors in conjunction with sweating.

TO THE EFFECTS OF PHYSIC IN GETTING RID OF INJURIOUS FOOD, I have already alluded; but I may here mention two or three circumstances which will serve to modify the dose, or to forbid it altogether. Curiously enough, when a horse comes in from grass, his bowels being in the usual loose state which accompanies that kind of feeding, he will generally require more aloes than when fed upon dry food. The reason of this seeming paradox is simple enough: his bowels have become accustomed to the stimulus presented by grass to their lining membrane, and are not easily roused to action by aloes, which is only a vegetable, still more stimulating, it is true, but simply in degree. A man accustomed to drink, will not be so much affected by swallowing a pint of brandy, even if he is already half drunk, as a perfectly sober man would be, if he had not previously been inured by long usage to its effects. The groom must not, therefore, fancy that a physic-ball of three drachms, or even sometimes four drachms, will be sure to act on a horse of average size and constitution, just up from grass; for he will find from four and a half to five and a half drachms more likely to serve his purpose. Unless he knows the constitution of the animal, he had better content himself with the former; but generally this quantity will not have much appreciable effect beyond a very gentle clearing out of the bowels. No mash is necessary, because the grass has already prepared the bowels quite sufficiently. Of course, if the horse is already too low in flesh, no physic should be given at this time.

THE COOLING POWERS OF PHYSIC are those which render it particularly valuable in aiding the preparation of the horse for fast work. If at any time the legs become hot, a dose will carry off the plethoric condition which shows itself in this way, and the rest which must be given after it will assist in relieving them. At this time, a mash should always precede the physic; and a second on the following night will often be necessary before the dose can safely be given. The same effect would be produced by permanently taking away some of the corn; but this would put an end to the preparation altogether, and it is to avoid this alternative that the physic is given. The old plan was in all cases to give a course of three doses, at intervals of nine days, to every horse when first taken into work; but if plenty of walking exercise is used, and the corn is gradually increased, with an ounce of nitre in the mash every Saturday night, this routine is quite unnecessary, and a couple of doses at the intervals I have fixed will suffice. Very gross, lusty horses will, perhaps, require one, or even two additional doses; and, on the contrary, light herring-gutted animals will do without any. The art of the groom consists in fixing upon the proper *quantum*, beyond or below which he ought not to go.

THE THIRD OBJECT OF PHYSIC is that which is superseded by the use of the Turkish bath, with much less injury to the system. Both act by removing superfluous fluids from the body, through the agency of the blood-vessels, absorbents, and secreting organs; all of which must co-operate in either case. The fluids lie stored up in the meshes of the cellular membrane, either in the shape of oily or watery matters. To remove them, the blood in circulation must first be called upon to part with some of its corresponding materials, which it does either through the mucous membrane of the bowels, when physic is given, or by means of the skin, when sweating is adopted. This sudden drain from the blood is then made up from the store which has been previously taken from it, and laid by in case of such an emergency; and thus, though the external means employed are very different, the real effect is the same. Both drain the blood of large quantities of water, containing certain soluble matters; and this sudden call upon the vital fluid compels its vessels to fall back upon the stored-up materials which are lodged around the heart and other internal organs, and which it is the grand object of the training-groom to remove.

BUT THE EFFECTS OF PHYSIC are not always so simple and innocent as those to which I have alluded. A strong horse is sometimes over-purged by a very mild dose, and a weak one will occasionally die from this cause. Hence, this agent should not be idly used; and not only is it actually dangerous to life in some few cases, but it weakens the tone of the stomach in many more. Still, in the majority of horses, a well-mixed physic-ball, carefully given, and followed by proper management, will freshen the digestive organs rather than weaken them, and may be regarded as a most valuable addition to the resources of the groom.

FINAL PREPARATION.

TO GET A HUNTER THOROUGHLY FIT, he must not only have gone through the preparatory work which I have described, but he must undergo a further winding up, according to the old-established rule on the subject, and irrespective of the vexed questions connected with the Turkish bath, which may be considered to be yet in abeyance. Having had a gentle dose of physic at the end of his first preparation, he is proceeded with as follows:— Every day he is walked out for three or four hours, either at one or two periods of the day. If he is thorough-bred, he will bear some brisk gallops and one or two sweats, with or without clothing, every week; but half-breeds do not stand much fast work, and are better confined to walking and trotting exercise, with an occasional spirt of half a mile. These low-bred animals cannot bear any liberties to be taken with their systems; and I am told that with them the Turkish bath is far more effectual than with the horse of pure Eastern blood. I can easily imagine this, as I know how badly the former class bear reduction, and yet how important it is to clear their wind. The feeding should be confined to oats and hay, with a bran-mash on Saturday night. About five quarterns of oats will, on the average, suffice; but no rule can be laid down, nor can it be positively asserted that no beans should be given. In some cases the appetite is so bad, that without them enough corn will not be taken; and this is especially true with reference to those old horses which have been accustomed to beans for many years. When the feet and legs, as well as the wind, are all sound, beans may be allowed without fear; but when there is a screw loose in any of these departments, they produce inflammation there, and should be carefully avoided. Ten pounds of hay may also be laid down as the average quantity of this article suited to the hunter; but here, also, no absolute rule can be carried out. Some horses would "drop in two," as the grooms say, if only allowed ten pounds of hay daily; while others would look quite lusty with that quantity. A handful of chaff with each feed of corn is all that should be given of this article, as more than this is apt to fill the horse out in the middle of the day. Towards the end of this period, which may extend to five or six weeks, the horse gradually gets into high condition, and at any time, on a day's notice, he may be ready for the hunting-field. All that is required is to give him no hay on that morning, but to feed him twice on his usual allowance of corn, with a few go-downs of water only each time. The hunter does not require to be "set" overnight, like the race-horse, and he may advantageously be given his usual weight of hay at the bedding him up the night before; but if he has any tendency to eat his litter, it is prudent at all times, but more especially then, to put a muzzle on him late at night, when he has eaten his hay.

HACKS AND HARNESS-HORSES demand nearly as much time and care to prepare them for their work, especially in relation to the amount of corn which is allowed them. They seldom want so much as five quarterns daily; but whatever quantity they may require, it should not be given them until they are gradually accustomed to its use. So also with regard to the hammering of their feet and legs on the road, it will be found that these demand seasoning as much as their wind and muscles. If this is not attended to, the best formed legs and feet will become inflamed, and a valuable horse may be lamed, when, with proper care, he might be made to do his work with ease. Our own bodies, when untrained to bear the blows of the fist, show the marks of the glove clearly enough; but in the course of time, when the skin has gradually become inured to the stimulus, even the terrible right hand of Tom Sayers would fail to leave its mark upon the ribs of a well-trained opponent. This difference in the result of the application of physical force arises partly from the tendency to inflammation being subdued by temperate living and abundant exercise, and partly from the nerves and vessels of the skin becoming habituated to the blows which they receive. So also with the hack and harness-horse; when first they are brought into the stable, their vessels are full of gross humors, and their feet and legs have long been accustomed only to the soft and elastic turf upon which they have been reared. They are, therefore, prone to inflammation in every way; and until their systems have been hardened by plenty of exercise, and their legs and feet have been gradually inured to our hard roads, they should be kept from every kind of fast work.

TREATMENT AFTER WORK.

AFTER WORK the horse requires to be treated according to its nature and the extent to which it has been carried. Thus the hunter may demand remedies for exhaustion, blows on the legs, thorns in the legs, overreaches, cuts, &c.; but the hack and carriage-horse will only need the ordinary grooming, which has been described at page 183; that is to say, provided the feet are not in pain from ill-fitting shoes.

EXHAUSTION is sometimes so great that before any food can be taken a cordial must be given, in the shape either of a warm ball, or a quart of warm spiced ale. Generally, however, some gruel will suffice, when aided by a warm box and the other comforts which are afforded by the groom, including dressing, clothing, bandaging, &c.

BLOWS on the legs are reduced by hot fomentations, continued for half an hour at a time, and repeated at intervals of one, two, or three hours, in proportion to the severity of the mischief. Cold applications are too apt to relieve the skin and cellular membrane beneath it at the expense of the joints, and I have never seen them of much service. Nothing, I believe, is so valuable in all blows received in the hunting-field as hot fomentation, but it should be thoroughly carried out, and not done by halves, as it too often is by careless grooms. It no doubt has a tendency to increase the swelling for a time, but in doing this the blood is drawn to the surface, and internal mischief is often prevented. I have had young horses come home with their knees and shins terribly bruised over timber and stone walls, but though the fomentation with hot water has enlarged the knees to a frightful size, there has been no lameness on the next day; and the swelling has gradually disappeared, leaving the joints as free as ever at the expiration of forty-eight hours. On the other hand, I have tried cold wet bandages for similar injuries, but I have invariably found that they gave present relief to a slight extent, but left the limbs stiff and rheumatic often for the next two or three weeks. The addition of a little tincture of arnica to the water for fomentation is a great improvement when it is at hand, and I should always advise the hunting groom to keep a stock of it by him during the season. A wineglassful is enough for half a bucket of hot water.

THORNS are most troublesome to the groom, and it is often a question of great doubt whether to persevere in the endeavor to remove them, or to leave them alone until they manifest themselves by the inflammation they produce. When the hunter comes home, his legs should be carefully examined while they are wet (that is to say, if his exhausted condition does not forbid the loss of time); and if the hand clearly detects any projection, search should at once be made with a view to the removal of the foreign body. Usually, however, the thorn has buried itself, and it is only when it has produced some considerable degree of inflammation that attention is drawn to the spot. When lameness is shown in any of the limbs on coming home from hunting, the groom always is inclined to suspect a thorn as the cause of mischief, and I have known the penknife used in half-a-dozen different places to cut down upon what was supposed to be a buried thorn, which was never discovered, for the plain reason that no such matter was present in the leg.

OVERREACHES must be dried up as quickly as possible, and should not be treated like common wounds, for the reason that the horny substance of the foot, when it becomes softened and decomposed by the matter flowing from a wound near it, acts like a poison upon the ulcerated surface. It is better, therefore, to apply a little friar's balsam, or some other astringent, such as sugar of lead, rather than to use wet bandages or bran poultices, which I have sometimes known to be applied.

SIMPLE AS WELL AS CONTUSED CUTS are far better treated in the horse with hot fomentations than by any attempt to heal them at once. Unless they are very extensive or deep, the only point in which they are to be regarded is with reference to the blemish which they may leave. Sometimes the edges gape so wide, that a stitch or two must be inserted, but in such a case it is better to intrust the operation to a competent veterinary surgeon.

SUMMERING.

UNTIL MR. APPERLY first drew attention to this subject, forty years ago, at which period those horses which were not required to work through the summer, were invariably turned out to grass; hunters, as a regular rule, were stripped of their clothing in April, and sent to grass on or about the first of May, that is, as soon as the first young blades showed themselves, this kind of food being supposed to be particularly advantageous to them, from its cooling powers.

The sudden change from a warm stable to the cold nights often met with in May frequently produced inflammation of the lungs or bowels, and this alone was sufficient to cause the plan to be looked on with great suspicion as soon as it was shown that it was by no means absolutely necessary. But not only was this danger incurred; for even if the hunter remained in good health during the summer, yet when he came up in August he was so fat and unwieldy from eating the succulent grasses of that season, that he was quite unfit to be ridden, and had to go through a series of severe sweats, which he was ill able to bear. Considering the slow pace at which hunting was carried on in the eighteenth century, a horse recently up from grass, if he had been allowed corn while out of doors, as was generally done, was able to go through a run, though it might be at the expense of the coat tails worn by his rider, which were liberally lathered with soapy sweat. But in the present day, when the hunter requires to be as fit as a race-horse, he must have the same amount of preparation; and we all know what sort of chance a horse would have of winning a race in November if he is eating nothing but grass in August. Indeed, a fast run in Leicestershire is even more trying to condition than an ordinary race, because, though the pace is not quite so good, it is more true, and lasts four or five times as long. Hence the old plan has been almost universally given up, and the hunter is summered in a loose box, where he is generally "soiled" on vetches, lucerne, and clover. Moreover, it is found by practical experience, that far more good may be done in renovating the legs in-doors than out at this season of the year. In the winter, cold, starvation, and soft ground all combine to restore the legs to a cool and healthy state; and a run from October to May will do far more good than the same time passed in a loose box. But during the summer the ground is hard, the sun shines fully upon the legs, so as to inflame them if they have any tendency that way, and the grasses are so succulent that the body becomes heavy and the blood full of gross humors, both of which last conditions tell with double force upon the legs and feet. Again, the flies which are so tormenting to horses in June, July, and August, cause them often to gallop about in the most frantic manner, and thus not only is another obstacle presented to their improvement, but it very often causes these parts to become worse than in the season. But some will say that much of this risk may be avoided by turning the hunter out into the marshes, where the soil is always cool, soft, and moist. This is quite true; nevertheless, the gain to the legs is at the expense of the general system, which is so completely upset by moist grasses, that instead of eight or nine weeks it will require as many months to eradicate their ill effects. As far as the hunter is concerned, there can be no question in my mind that a loose box is the proper place for him during the summer; and that he should be allowed a yard to run into if it can possibly be so arranged admits of little doubt, but if this is inconvenient, the Nimrodian plan of confining him in the ordinary loose box is to be accepted in its entirety. The hack or harness horse does not receive so much injury from a summer's run as the hunter, but if he requires rest for his legs, it is far better to turn him out in the winter season than during the opposite division of the year. Nevertheless, as there are still some advocates of the summer's run at grass, I shall give directions for it, as well as for the soiling in the stable, as advised by "Nimrod."

Soiling is conducted as follows :—At the conclusion of the hunting season the horse is gradually cooled down, either by removing his clothing in the stable, and letting him first stand there naked for two or three weeks, or by putting him with it on into a moderately warm loose box, and after he has been there a day or two taking it away by degrees. At the same time he is deprived of his corn, and fed upon hay only; but this change also must not be too sudden, demanding a month for its complete carrying out, which will bring the time on to the beginning or middle of the month of May. A large airy loose box should then be provided, the floor being covered with six inches of tan or sand, and the door being so arranged that in warm weather it may be left open, a chain being drawn across from post to post. Here the horse is left for a few days till he is thoroughly accustomed to his new berth, and his coat is full of dust and scurf, when he may have a dose of physic, and while under its effects his legs may be blistered, or dressed with iodine ointment, or some of the many applications which are used for the purpose of producing absorption of the morbid deposits which have been thrown out during the winter.

AFTER THE PHYSIC IS SET, green food of some kind may be commenced, consisting of Italian rye grass, young vetches, or lucerne, or, if these cannot be obtained, of ordinary meadow grass. At first an equal quantity of hay must be allowed for old hunters, or the change from dry food to green will produce too great an effect on the bowels. Young and hearty horses will, however, be none the worse for this; and, indeed, when they are turned out, all have to bear the change in its fullest extent. I am not fond of vetches for soiling horses, as they either purge them when they are young, or heat them too much when their seed-pods are fully developed. For working horses the latter condition is especially suited, as they have the effect of beans, and when green food is wanted merely to renovate the stomach without depending on its soiling properties, I see no objection to them. But for hunters when soiled heating food is to be avoided, and on that account I cannot see the advantage of vetches to this kind of horse. As there is no galloping over hard ground the shoes may be removed altogether, and even tips may be dispensed with. The feet should be pared out nicely, the blacksmith removing all broken fragments of horn, and inspecting them afterwards at least once a month. Now is the time to attend to any early symptoms of sand crack, seedy toe, &c., prompt measures at this season often leading to a prevention of these annoying evils. If the horse is not more than ten or twelve years old, his corn may be stopped altogether while he is eating green food in June and July, but a favorite old hunter should be indulged with a couple of quarterns daily, or he will probably lose flesh to a great extent. The young horse is always prone to inflammation, which a cooling treatment will remove, but the old one is more seasoned, and he will get more harm from being lowered in his general system than the benefit to his legs will repay. By the month of August all these plans will have co-operated to produce the desired effect; the legs are cool and fine, and the lumps and bumps incidental to the hunting-field have entirely disappeared. If they have been very extensive, two or three doses of physic should have been given, but in general one dose as ordered at the beginning of the soiling, and another at the end, when the commencement of training takes its turn, will be sufficient. I have now brought the horse to the middle of the month of August, at which time the preparation for work, described at page 206, *et sequitur*, must be commenced in earnest.

TURNING OUT TO GRASS, OR PASTURING, demands some little attention, which however horses seldom receive. Excepting in the height of summer it is a very dangerous practice to turn a previously warmly clothed and stabled animal into the fields without gradually accustoming him to the change of climate. The average temperature of our spring nights is not more than 40° of Fahrenheit, and frequently this degree of cold is united with a keen wind and sharp rain. Even if a hovel is provided, the horse is almost sure to get wet before he betakes himself to its protection, and its door being necessarily open the wind can enter freely It is therefore found that at all other seasons but the summer quarter two or three weeks at least must be devoted to the hardening of the skin to bear the climate out of doors. This is done by first of all removing the clothes by degrees, avoiding all attempts at dressing, so as to allow the scurf to accumulate and protect the skin, and then changing the warm stable for a cooler box, which may be closed at first, and day by day left more and more open to the weather by admitting the air through its various apertures. If the horse is of a delicate constitution, and the weather is cold and wet, the turning out should be delayed till there should be a change for the better, or if it is decided on at all risks the precaution should be taken for the first two or three nights to bring him under some dry shelter, avoiding, of course, a warm stable, as doubly injurious.

WHEN UNSOUNDNESS OF THE FEET OR LEGS is the inducement to turn out, and the time at which it is desirable to do this is the summer season, the choice should fall upon a marsh. Hard ground will increase the mischief, and, between July and September, although it may be soft just at one particular time, it cannot be expected to remain so long. In any case some precaution should be taken against the horse galloping about on his first being let loose, which, from the joy he experiences at getting his liberty, he almost invariably does. To prevent this, the legs should be blistered a few days before, so as to seize the opportunity when they are swollen, stiff, and sore, and when, as a natural consequence, a gallop would be so extremely painful as to be altogether out of the question. A cradle must be kept on to prevent blemishes, but this is no more objectionable out of doors than in. In almost every case this application would be necessary for the diseased condition of the extremities, whether the horse was turned out or not; but it is better to seize the opportunity while the legs are still stiff and sore. Fetters or hobbles may be put on the forelegs with the same object, if the feet only are the seat of mischief; but to inflamed joints or back sinews they are not so well suited, from the pressure they produce on the former, and the strains which they cause to the latter. After a few days' liberty,

THE HUNTER TURNED OUT TO GRASS.

the tendency to gallop will be lost, and as the legs gradually recover their elasticity the horse is not so prone to overdo himself in his exercise, and will generally remain content with a moderate pace; or, if the legs are very unsound, the blister may be repeated.

THE RENOVATION OF THE HEALTH, when this has been broken down by disease or hard work, is best effected on good sound uplands. The herbage on salt marshes will sometimes agree with the horse even better than ordinary meadow grass, but this forms the exception to the rule, and is not to be relied on in general. In selecting a run in such a case care should be taken that the herbage is of the desired nature, the best proof of which is that it has agreed with horses in previous seasons. Experienced judges can generally pronounce upon the probability of the desired result after inspecting the situation, but on the whole their opinion, however well founded, is not so much to be relied on as the fact that horses have actually become fresh while turned out there.

THE FORE FEET should always be protected by "tips," which are merely short shoes reaching only two-thirds of the way to the heels, which are then left uncovered. The object is to avoid the risk of breaking away the toes, which is incurred whenever the foot is battered on hard ground, as it often is when it is stamped continually, as horses are very apt to do, on the bare surface which is kept dry beneath a sheltering tree. Here the flies are very apt to collect around the horses, and to get rid of their annoyance the legs are constantly in motion. If the full shoe is left on, the hind toe is very apt to catch its heel in deep ground, and tear it wholly or partially off; and, moreover, it is too often neglected, and either the heels press into the sole, producing corns, or they confine the frog, and lead to disease of that important organ. Tips may safely be left on without removal for two or three months, whereas shoes require attending to every three or four weeks. The hind shoes are always taken off, partly because the hind feet are not so liable to be broken at the toes, but chiefly because they would be dangerous to other animals if they were left on from the severe damage which is done by a kick with an armed heel.

HORSES WHOSE JUGULAR VEINS have become obliterated from adhesive inflammation following bleeding, are unfit to be turned out in consequence of the difficulty which is presented to the return of the blood from the head by its low position in grazing. So also those which have recently suffered from staggers should not be sent out to grass, for fear of the position causing a return of the disease.

CARE OF SADDLERY AND HARNESS.

THE MANAGEMENT OF SADDLERY must have a treble object. *First*, the groom should take care that he does nothing which shall injure the horse. *Secondly*, he must have a due regard to his master's comfort in using it. And, *thirdly*, he must please the eye. I must therefore show how each of these purposes can best be effected.

TO AVOID INJURING THE HORSE the groom should begin when he first comes in from work, *and before he removes the saddle or collar*. It is ascertained by experience that if these are taken off when the skin beneath them is hot and sweating, inflammation will almost surely follow, while by leaving them loosely in their places for a short time no injurious effect is perceived. If a groom who is master of his business is watched when his horses come in, he will be seen to loosen their girths and lift the saddles from their backs for a second, replacing them loosely, and leaving them there while he takes off the bridles and makes his arrangements for dressing. In harness-horses everything but the collars may be taken off, and after turning them to remove the harness and traces, they may be replaced and left as near to the shoulder as the position of the horse with his head in the manger will allow. This rule should be invariably followed whenever horses come into the stable after having done any amount of work. If they have merely gone out for a short airing, and the skin beneath the saddle or collar is not even damp, there is no occasion for the precaution, and the saddle or collar may at once be removed. The next thing to be done to the saddlery in reference to the horse's comfort is to dry the lining carefully before it is again used. Even the lining of harness-pads should be attended to, and in the winter this cannot be done without placing each before the fire. After the serge lining is dry, it is an excellent plan to beat the stuffing with a stick, so as to remove the powdery particles left by the sweat, which soon clog up the interstices and form a matted cake with the woollen materials used if they are allowed to remain.

IN ATTENDING TO THE COMFORT OF THE MASTER the groom must take care to keep all the leather which comes in contact with the hands or legs perfectly supple, yet so clean that no stain is left behind. Nothing is more annoying than to get off the saddle for the purpose of paying a morning call, and find the insides of a light pair of trousers stained all the way down. This is perfectly inexcusable, and its occurrence marks the ignorance and carelessness of a servant in the most unmistakeable manner. The same remark applies to the reins, which never ought to soil a pair of white gloves. Whenever blacking is applied to harness it is impossible altogether to prevent the tendency to leave a stain, but if it is carefully put on, and well brushed, as long as it is kept dry it may be lightly handled with impunity. If buckles are to be altered, the gloves must suffer, and for this reason, when gentlemen drive their own horses, they generally prefer brown driving reins, which may be treated in the same way as riding reins, and kept clean accordingly. The following directions for cleaning saddles and riding bridles, and also for brown driving reins, or any other parts of the harness made of undyed leather, will serve the purpose extremely well. As long as the leather remains dry and clean it needs no attention, but when it is wetted, either by rain, or by the water necessary for cleaning it from road dust, it becomes hard and stiff, and must be softened with some kind of oily matter. Neat's-foot oil is that usually employed, but for saddles it is rather of too greasy a nature, being apt to leave a mark on the trousers if it has been liberally applied. The best application is deer's suet, which should be gently warmed and rubbed in before the leather is quite dry again, after being wetted; that is to say, while it remains limp, for if it is held to the fire long enough, all wet leather becomes hard and stiff. A very little oil or suet will suffice, if it is used as soon as the leather is nearly dry, after each wetting, but when leather has been left for days in a dry place after being thoroughly wet, it becomes so stiff that nothing but a good soaking with oil will restore its pliability, and even with this it remains stiff to a certain extent, unless it is very slightly damped, in conjunction with the use of the oil. Vegetable oils, with the single exception of castor oil, are too much inclined to become hard to suit leather, and none but the latter should ever be employed. Its nauseous smell is an objection to it, but otherwise it will answer the purpose almost as well as neat's-foot. Horse-fat, if used carefully, and in very small quantities, is a capital application, but one liberal dressing with it spoils the look of leather, giving it a sodden appearance, which it never recovers.

TO MAKE SADDLERY AND HARNESS LOOK WELL to the eye, several receipts, and directions for using them, are necessary; including the following, for avoiding injury from chemical decomposition:—

(1.) Do not allow brass or plated furniture to be within reach of the air of the stable; for the ammonia given off from the urine will tarnish them. Gas, also, is prejudicial; and if it is burned in the harness-room, it should be contained within a glass chamber, which has a ventilating shaft, so as to carry off the products of combustion into the external air. Gas stoves are particularly prejudicial; and, indeed, so are all stoves which allow the fumes given off by the coals to pass into the room.

(2.) As soon as possible after the harness is taken off, if the weather is fine, take a leather, kept specially for the purpose, and wipe off the dust; sponging with a damp sponge those parts which are soiled with sweat. If the traces, belly-band, &c., are splashed with mud, wash them at once; on no account soaking them in water, or using more of it than is necessary. Dry them, as far as possible, with the leathers. If the black dye with which the leather is stained has come off to any serious extent, a little of a solution of green copperas may be used, but this is not often necessary. Unbuckle the bits from the bridle, put them in clean water for a short time, then take them out, and remove every particle of dirt from them. Dry with the leather, and rub a very little neat's-foot oil on them. Before they are used again, they must be polished with the dry leather, aided by a little silver sand, if they have become at all rusty. The curb-chain will always want rubbing loosely in the hand with a little silver sand, finishing with the leather.

BLACK HARNESS must be kept constantly polished by hand-brushing it with some composition specially prepared for the pur-

20

pose. This must be of a greasy or waxy nature, to prevent the rain from dissolving it, and washing it off upon the coat of the horse. One or other of the following compositions will answer the purpose:

RECIPES FOR HARNESS BLACKING.

No. 1.

Spirit of Turpentine	1 pt.
Beeswax	4 oz.
Prussian Blue	1 oz.
Lamp Black	½ oz.

Slice the wax very thin, put it in a jar and pour on the turpentine. Let it stand twenty-four hours, then grind the other ingredients together on a stone or marble slab, and mix carefully up. It must be kept in a covered tin box.

No. 2.

Take the above composition and add the following, which improves the polish:—

Spirit Varnish	1 pt.
Gum Benzoin	2 oz.
Soft Soap	1 oz.

Melt together in a water bath, and when thoroughly incorporated mix all together on a stone and cover up directly.

CHAPTER XII.

RIDING.

Mounting and Dismounting—The Seat—Management of the Reins—Modes of Starting the Horse into his Various Paces—Riding to Hounds—Out-door Vices and Bad Habits.

MOUNTING AND DISMOUNTING.

THE CELEBRATED RAREY has recently given us a new light upon the subject, which is quite at variance with those directions which have hitherto been considered to be the correct ones in this country. Thus, Captain Richardson, in his valuable work on Horsemanship, advises as follows:—" Stand opposite the near fore-foot of the horse, place the left hand

"READY."

on the neck near to the withers, having the back of the hand to the horse's head, and the reins lying in front of the hand. Take up the reins with the right hand, put the little finger of the left hand between them, and draw them through until you feel the mouth of the horse; turn the remainder of the reins along the inside of the left hand, let it fall over the fore-finger on the off-side, and place the thumb upon the reins. Twist a lock of the mane round the thumb or fore-finger, and close the hand firmly upon the reins. Take the stirrup in the right hand, and place the left toe in it as far as the ball; let the knee press against the flap of the saddle, to prevent the point of the toe from irritating the side of the horse; seize the cantle of the saddle with the right hand, and springing up from the right toe, throw the right leg clear over the horse, coming gently into the saddle by staying the weight of the body with the right hand resting on the right side of the pommel of the saddle; put the right toe in the stirrup." Now this is in the main applicable to a man of five feet ten inches or six feet, but to a shorter individual attempting to mount a horse of fifteen hands three inches, it is an impossibility, simply because he cannot reach the cantle from the same position which enables him to hold the stirrup in the left hand. The Captain is also wrong, in my opinion, in directing that the body should be raised into the saddle directly from the ground, with one movement. This will always bring the rider down into the saddle with a very awkward jerk; and the proper direction is to raise the body straight up till both feet are on a level with the stirrup-iron, and *then* with the left leg held against the flap of the saddle by the left hand on the pommel, the right leg is easily thrown over the cantle, and the body may be kept in the first position until the horse is quiet, if he is plunging or rearing. A short man can generally place his foot in the stirrup while held in his hand, but it should be known that all cannot do this, because I have seen young riders much vexed at finding that they could not possibly do what is directed. Most of our writers on horsemanship are of the military school, and endeavor to cut every one's cloth by their own coats. They are able to do certain things easily, and so are their men, because they are mostly of the height already specified, but as sportsmen and civil equestrians are of all heights, I shall endeavor to accommodate my remarks to all heights and classes. In all cases the rider should stand at the shoulder, though with a short man it is much easier to mount a tall horse from the hind-quarter, but the danger of kicking is very great; and even in mounting with "a leg," in the jockey style, I have known the thigh very nearly broken by a kick. If the hand *can* steady the stirrup it should do so, but if the person is too short, the foot can be placed in the stirrup without its aid; then taking the reins between the fingers, much as directed in the passage already quoted, and grasping a lock of the mane with the finger and thumb, the body is raised till the right foot is brought to a level with the left, when the right hand seizes the cantle, and with the left grasping the pommel, the body is steadied for a short time, which, in the ordinary mount, is almost imperceptible, but in a fidgety horse is sometimes of considerable length. The leg is now thrown gently over the saddle, and as it reaches the cantle the hand is withdrawn, after which the body sinks into the saddle in an easy and graceful manner. The right foot is then placed in the stirrup, with or without the aid of the right hand holding it.

SUCH IS THE ENGLISH METHOD. Mr. Rarey, in opposition to this plan, advises that the right hand and arm shall be thrown over the saddle, the horseman standing with his back to the quarters, and thus incurring the chance of being severely kicked.

THE SEAT.

THE POSITION OF THE rider in the saddle, called "the seat," admits of several variations according to the purpose to which he is devoted, but it is mainly influenced by the length of the stirrups. In the military style these are so long that the weight of the body is conveyed to the saddle by the inside of the thighs, or "fork" alone, while in that adopted in the East this part scarcely touches the saddle, and the breech and feet distribute the weight between them. Colonel Greenwood, who is the only military writer on horsemanship that can be taken as a guide for the road, tells us—"There is one direction which I think applies to all seats. Turn the thigh from the hip, so as to bring the hollow to the saddle; this places the foot straight to the front, with the heel out and the toe in. Trotting without stirrups on the thigh only, with the heel down and the toe up, shoulders back, a snaffle rein in each hand like a rough-rider, is the best possible position for sitting." Now the latter part of this is quite true, but the former is not quite consistent with my own experience, for if the short stirrups of the Eastern horseman are adopted, the hollow of the thigh cannot be brought to the saddle, yet this style he admits is "admirable in its way." Dismissing then the military seat for which Colonel Greenwood's directions may suffice, I may assert that, in the ordinary English style, there are four points necessary to be considered; namely, (1) the position of the weight, which will be mainly influenced by (2) the position of the knees well forward on the flap, (3) the proper length of the stirrup-leathers, and (4) the carriage of the body. If the weight is not laid upon the middle of the saddle, which is the axis of the "see-saw" motion made in the gallop, it has to be raised at every stride, and thus additional labor is thrown on the horse. With long stirrups in the military style this is of necessity done; but, with short stirrups, the knees are often placed on the flaps behind the leathers, and then the breech remains close to the cantle and sometimes almost overlapping it. To get the length of leather adapted to most men, though there are occasionally exceptions, the rider should sit well on his fork, and then the stirrups should be taken up or let down till they just touch the ankle bone. For road riding this enables the hollow of the thigh to touch the saddle, because the ball of the foot being on the stirrup, the heel is down an inch and a half below it; whilst, in the hunting-field, as the stirrup is worn "home," the knee is carried higher and more forward on the saddle, and the weight is distributed between it, the breech, and the foot. With regard to the carriage of the body, all the directions in the world will not make it easy, and without the supervision of a master, or a friend, to point out defects, no one can be sure that he is sitting in a good, much less an elegant style. It is not possible even to know that the shoulders are square, or that the body is not carried on one side, defects which I have known persisted in for years without the slightest consciousness of them on the part of the rider, who would gladly have rectified them if he had known of their existence. One rule may, however, be given, namely, that no effort should be made to move in any direction, and that, on the contrary, every endeavor should be directed to keep the body and legs as still as the action of the horse will allow, bearing in mind that the opposite extreme of stiffness is almost equally bad.

MANAGEMENT OF THE REINS.

THERE ARE THREE DISTINCT MODES of holding and managing the reins. In the first, adopted by the military school, the left hand does all, without any assistance from the right, which is occupied with the sword, lance, or carbine. In the second, the left hand holds the reins, aided occasionally by the right; and in the third, or "two-handed method," the reins are permanently held one in each hand. The first of these is only needed in the *manège*, and I therefore shall not allude to it; while the last requires no description, further than to mention that it is the mode adopted by the colt-breaker, and that it gives far more control over the mouth than either of the others. As single and double reins are differently placed in the hand, a description of each will be necessary.

THE SINGLE REIN is held by placing all the fingers but the first between the two leathers, and then, making both turn over that one, they are firmly held by pressing the thumb against it. This gives a firm grasp, and at the same time allows of either being pulled tighter than the other by turning the wrist. To shorten the grasp, the right hand has only to lay hold of the loose part of the rein, and then the left, sliding forwards towards the neck, can close wherever it may be desired. In order to be sure that the elbow is held against the side, the thumb should always point towards the horse's ears; and the nearer the little finger can be carried to the pommel of the saddle the better. In using the single rein, the management of the mouth, *if a good one*, is easy enough; nevertheless, there are various directions for the purpose adopted in different schools, which are dependent upon altogether conflicting principles. Every tyro knows that the horse turns to the left by pulling the left rein, and to the right by pulling the opposite one; and the problem to be solved is to do this by one hand only. Now, this with the single rein is easily effected by raising the thumb towards the right shoulder, when the right rein is to be pulled, or by drawing the little finger towards the fork for the left; in both cases by a turn of the wrist, without lifting the whole hand. But over and above this action on the mouth, and in many cases independent of it, is a movement which, in trained horses, is capable of much greater delicacy, and which depends upon the sensibility of the skin of the neck for its due performance. It is effected by turning the whole hand to the right or left, *without any wrist action*, so as to press the right rein against the neck, in order to cause a turn to the left, and the left rein against the neck for the opposite purpose; at the same time rather slackening the reins, so as not to bear upon the mouth by so doing. In this way a horse may be turned with a much greater degree of nicety and smoothness than by acting on the corner of his mouth. But highly-broken horses, such as the military troop-horses, are often too much used to their bits to answer to this slight and delicate manipulation; and therefore it is eschewed by Captain Richardson, as well as by Colonel Greenwood, but, strangely enough, for opposite reasons, and each attempting to substitute a very different process for it. I am well aware that some horses can never be taught it, but must always have a bearing made on the mouth before they will turn; yet, when it can be inculcated, it makes the animal so tractable and agreeable to ride, that it is a highly desirable accomplishment; and I cannot, therefore, join in condemning its use, but should rejoice if it could in all cases be fully developed.

THE DOUBLE REIN is usually held by those who ride for pleasure in this country as follows:—Begin by taking up the snaffle-rein, and place the fore and middle fingers between its two portions; then lay hold of the curb-rein, and either hook it loosely on to the little finger, if not immediately wanted, or draw it up to the requisite degree of tightness and turn it over the fore finger, when it will lie upon the snaffle-rein, and, together with it, will be gripped by the thumb. By adopting this plan, the curb-rein is always at the command of the right hand; and it may be shortened or let out in a moment, which is of constant occurrence in every day's ride. The hand is held as with the single rein, with the thumb pointing to the horse's ears; in turning, however, there is much less power of bearing on either side of the bit by raising the thumb or lowering the little finger, because the distance between the snaffle-reins is only half what it was, and therefore the mode of turning by pressure upon the neck is doubly desirable; and hence its general adoption in those cases where double-reined bridles are used, as in the field and on the road. Sometimes, to obviate this objection, the snaffle-reins are placed as in the single-reined bridle, outside the little finger, and then the curb is hooked over the ring-finger, between the snaffle-reins, so as to allow of the full manipulation of the mouth by the hand, without bearing upon the neck. But the objection to this is, that the curb cannot be shortened without releasing the snaffle; and therefore the horse must either be ridden on the curb alone while this process is being effected, or his head must be loosed altogether; whereas, in the other mode, his mouth is still under the control of the snaffle all the time that the curb is being let out or taken in.

THE ATTAINMENT OF "GOOD HANDS," by which is to be understood a light and delicate handling of the reins, is, or ought to be, the aim of every rider. The most delicate mouth in the world is soon spoilt by bearing heavily on it, as is too often done by grooms, and, indeed, by the average run of our horsemen. So also in hunting, if the horse is not allowed his head in making his effort, he will be almost sure to fail in exactly doing what he meant, and will hit timber, if he is put at that class of fence, or will drop his hind legs into the ditch, if there is one. Bad riders use the reins as a means of balancing themselves in the saddle, and this is especially done in the hunting-field, where they would be utterly unable to maintain their seats without the aid thus afforded to the proper grip and balance. Every one in learning to ride ought to be taught to go through all the paces, and to jump the bar without any reins in his hand; and when he finds he is able to do without them, he will learn to use them only in the way for which they are intended.

MODES OF STARTING THE HORSE INTO HIS VARIOUS PACES.

TO MAKE A HORSE start off in a quick walk, when he is not inclined to do so, either from being too fresh or too raw, is by no means an easy task. I have often ridden one for several days in succession, before I could make him settle down to a fair walk, and even then the slightest excitement would upset all my apparent previous progress. This is especially true of those horses possessed of such elastic joints, that they could "jog" at a rate much slower than they could walk. Here restraint by the bridle is out of the question, and any excitement by the voice or heel increases the jog into a full trot, without passing through any intermediate stage. The difficulty consists in the fact that for a perfect walk the head must be at liberty, and when this is allowed to a generous horse, he is inclined to go off at a rate faster than suffices for the pace in question. The only plan, therefore, is to ride such horses quietly, till they are leg weary, whatever the number of hours may be required, and then it is possible to loose their heads without their taking advantage of the liberty to go off "at score." Indeed, in the walk, the head should never be much confined, and yet the rider should not entirely leave it uncontrolled; the finest possible touch is enough, so that on any trip the hand is at once informed of it by the drop of the head, when, by a sudden jerk of the bridle, not too forcible, it rouses the horse, and prevents his falling. It is not that he is kept up by pulling the rein, but that he is roused by it and made to exert himself, for many horses seem regardless of falls, and would be down twenty times a day if they were not stimulated by the heel and bit. Confinement of the head in the walk is absolutely injurious, and more frequently causes a fall than saves one. A good walker will go on nodding his head to each step, more or less as it is a long or a short one; and if this nodding is prevented by the heavy hand of the rider, the fore-foot is not properly stretched forward, the step is crippled, and very often the toe strikes the ground; when, if the head were at liberty, it would clear it well. In horses which are apt to stumble in the walk, I have generally found that a loose rein, with the curb held ready for a check, is the safest plan; and then the horse soon finds that he is punished the moment he stumbles, and in a very short time he learns to recover himself almost before he is reminded. I do not like the spur or the whip so well, because the use of either makes the horse spring forward, and often blunder again in his hurry to avoid this kind of punishment. The check of the curb, on the other hand, makes him recover himself without extra progress, or rather by partially stopping him, and thus he is better able to avoid his fall. The body is allowed to yield slightly to the motions of the horse, but not to waddle from side to side, as is sometimes seen. Some horses do not stir the rider at all, while others throw him about and fatigue him greatly; and this may generally be foretold when the tail sways much from side to side in the walk, which is caused by the over-long stride of the horse, a very desirable accomplishment in the race-horse or hunter, but not in the hack.

THE JOG TROT is a pace that there is seldom any difficulty in effecting, and on the contrary, as I have just observed, the rider is often engaged for hours or days in breaking the young horse of it.

THE REGULAR TROT is generally easy to produce, but sometimes when the canter has been much adopted, it is not so readily effected. The best plan is as follows:—Take hold of both the reins of the snaffle, and bear firmly, but steadily, upon the mouth, lean slightly forwards in the saddle, press the legs against the horse's sides, and use the peculiar click of the tongue, which serves as an encouragement to the horse on all occasions. If properly trained, he will now fall at once into the trot, but if he breaks into a canter or gallop, he must be checked and restrained into a walk, or a "jog-trot." Where the horse has been much used to canter, and can go at that pace as slowly as he walks, there is often great difficulty in making him trot, for no restraint, short of a total halt, will prevent the canter. In such cases, laying hold of an ear will often succeed, by making the animal drop his head, which movement interferes with the canter, and generally leads to a trot. The rising in the stirrups is generally practised in civil life, as being far less fatiguing to both horse and rider; but in the military schools the opposite style is inculcated, because among a troop of horse it has a very bad effect if a number of men are bobbing up and down, out of all time. If it were possible for all to rise together, perhaps the offence against military precision might be pardoned; but as horses will not all step together, so men cannot all rise at the same moment, and the consequence is that they are doomed to bump upon the sheep-skins in a very tiresome manner, fatiguing alike to man and horse. This rising in the saddle of itself, encourages horses which have been accustomed to it to trot in preference to any other pace, and they understand the faintest indication of it as a sign that this particular pace is to be commenced, and trot accordingly. The civilian's mode of riding the trot is as follows:—At the precise moment when the hind and fore legs are making their effort to throw the horse forward in progression, the body of the rider is thrown forcibly into the air, in some horses to so great an extent as to make a young rider feel as if he never should come down again. After reaching the utmost height, however, the body falls, and reaches the saddle just in time to catch the next effort, and so on as long as the trot lasts. In this way, the horse absolutely carries no weight at all during half his time, and the action and reaction are of such a nature that the trot is accelerated rather than retarded by the weight. No horse can fairly trot above twelve miles or thirteen miles an hour without this rising, though he may run or pace in the American style, so that it is not only to save the rider's bones but also to ease the horse that this practice has been introduced, and holds its ground in spite of the want of military sanction. It is here as with the seat; utility is sacrificed to appearances; and whenever the long and weak seat of the barrack-yard is supplanted by the firm seat of the civilian, I shall expect to see the rising in the trot abandoned, but certainly not till then. The military length is not now what it was thirty years ago; and perhaps some time or other soldiers may adopt the rise, but I am afraid not until they have produced many thousands more sore backs than they need have done if they had never practised it. In the trot, the foot should bear strongly on the stirrup, with the heel well down, and the ball of the foot pressing on the foot-piece of the stirrup, so that the elasticity of the ankle takes off the jar, and prevents the double rise, which in some rough horses is very apt to be produced. The knees should always be maintained exactly in the same place, without that shifting motion which is so common with bad riders, and the legs should be held perpendicularly from the knee downwards. The chest should be well forward, and the waist in, the rise nearly upright, but slightly forward, and as easily as can be effected without effort on the part of the rider, and rather restraining than adding to the throw of the horse.

GOOD HANDS and a quiet seat only, with the aid of a curb bit properly adapted to the mouth, are required to develop the canter, by restraining the gallop; but to make a horse start off at once, with a lead of either leg as desired, is altogether another matter. To do this, the canter with either leg leading must first be completely taught, so that there is no difficulty in making the horse display that particular pace at any time. Then just at the moment before starting, pull the rein, and press the heel on the side opposite to the leg which it is desired the horse should lead. The reason of this is obvious enough; every horse in starting to canter (and many even in the canter itself) turns himself slightly across his line of progress, in order to enable him to lead with that leg which he thereby advances. Thus supposing a horse is going to lead off with the off-foreleg, he turns his head to the left and his croup to the right, and then easily gets his off-leg before and his near-leg behind into the line which is being taken. Now, to compel him to repeat this action, it is only necessary to turn him in the same way, by pulling his head to the left, and by touching him with the left heel, after which he is made to canter by exciting him with the voice or whip, whilst at the same moment he is restrained by the curb. When once this lead is commenced, the hold on the curb and pressure on the legs may be quite equal; but if, while the canter is maintained, it is desired to change the leading leg, the horse must be collected and roused by the bit and voice, and then reversing the pull of the reins and the leg-pressure, from that previously practised, so as to turn the horse in the opposite way to that in which he was started, he will generally be compelled to change his lead, which is called "changing his leg." The seat in this space is a very easy one, the knees taking a very gentle hold of the saddle, the feet not bearing strongly upon the stirrups, and the body tolerably upright in the saddle. The hands must not be too low, but should keep a very gentle but constant pressure upon the bit, and should, if there is the slightest tendency to drop the canter, rouse the mouth by a very slight reminder, and also stimulate the spirits by the voice or whip.

THE GALLOP being generally, though not always, his fastest pace, the horse may be forced into it readily enough by the stimulus of the voice, whip, or spurs. Sometimes very fast trotters cannot gallop so fast as they can trot, but these are rare exceptions, and need not be considered in any other light. It is therefore useless to describe the mode of starting this pace; but some allusion may advantageously be made to the best method of riding it. There are two seats adopted, the ordinary one being to sit down into the saddle and keep as close to it as possible, but another being also practised called standing in the stirrups. The former is the usual seat, and it is only in racing or in the very fast gallop at other times that the latter is adopted. In sitting down the feet may be either resting on the ball of the toe, as in the other paces, or with the stirrup " home" to the boot, as is common in all field-riding. The body is thrown easily and slightly back, the knees take firm hold, the rider being careful not to grip the horse so tight as to distress him, which fault I have known very muscular men often commit. The hands should be low, with sufficient pull at the mouth to restrain, but not to annoy him and make him "fight;" and if he is inclined to get his head down too much, or the reverse, they must be raised or lowered accordingly. When the standing in the stirrups is to be practised, the weight is thrown upon them, steadying it with the knees and thighs, which should keep firm hold of the saddle. The seat of the body is carried well back, while at the same time the loin is slightly arched; but by this combined action the weight is not hanging over the shoulder of the horse, as it would be, and often is, when the breech is raised from the saddle and brought almost over the pommel, with the eyes of the rider looking down his horse's forehead, or very nearly so. If a jockey of more than seven or eight stone, with a good seat, is watched, it will be seen that his leg does not descend straight from the knee, but that it is slightly thrown back from that line, and consequently that his centre of gravity is behind it, so that he can, by stiffening the joint, carry his body as far behind it as his stirrup is, without ceasing to stand in it. Very light jockeys adopt a somewhat different seat, riding with longer stirrups and throwing their weight greatly on the muscles of the thigh, while they raise the breech entirely from the saddle, but only for a comparatively small distance. This gives them a strong hold of their horses, without which, being so small, they could not ride them. Standing in the stirrups cannot long be maintained without fatigue to the rider, and it is only adopted in racing or in short gallops over bad ground, as in hunting, when there is a deep piece of fallow, or a steep hill, or any other kind of ground calculated to tire the horse.

RIDING TO HOUNDS.

THE KIND OF SEAT generally adopted in riding to hounds has been already described, and I need not therefore allude to it again. I may, however, remind the tyro that the less he depends upon balance, and the stronger hold he can get of the saddle with his knees and calves, the more likely he will be to avoid a fall without his horse coming down also. If this accident happens, a loose seat sometimes befriends the rider by causing him to be thrown out of the way of the horse, but in the long run the man who has a strong grip of his saddle will fare the best. Good hands and judgment are equally necessary, and the combination of these three qualities makes up the finished performer across country, always supposing the presence of nerve in addition.

THERE ARE CERTAIN RULES adopted in all hunting countries, which must be stringently carried out in order to insure the safety of the hounds and horsemen, and avoid those disputes which would otherwise constantly occur between riders jealous of each other's prowess. These may be summed up in the following plain directions:—

WHEN NEAR THE HOUNDS keep to the right or left of them, and not directly behind, where you are always in danger of riding over some of the tail hounds. So also when the pack are crossing a thick fence, when there is often only one gap weak enough to allow of their getting over, avoid its proximity, and take a place at least a dozen yards off.

INDEPENDENTLY of hounds, every rider should take a line of his own, or if he is unable to do this and must follow a leader, let him keep such a distance behind that if a fall takes place he can avoid jumping upon him. In a large field of horsemen, every one cannot possibly take a different line, nor is it easy to keep always at a safe distance; but at big places there is generally some hesitation, and a proper interval can be maintained. No one should attempt to pass his neighbor either on the right or left of the line he has chosen, when near a fence; but of course this is not to deprive him of his chance of taking the lead in the middle of a large enclosure, when a little racing can do no harm. By the adoption of this rule, jostling and crowding at a weak place are avoided, which without it would be sure to lead to serious accidents.

USE YOUR JUDGMENT in saving your horse in deep ground, making up for the apparent loss by putting him along whenever a sound headland or good turf can be obtained. It is not going straight over sound land that distresses a horse, but the making use of him over deep ground, and at the wrong time Many men seem to know no difference between sound turf and rotten or wet arable, and will kick their horses along over high ridge-and-furrow in a wet clay district, at a pace which no horse can bear for more than a mile or two in such a country. A workman would look out for headlands or footpaths, &c.; and would, by a slight *détour*, gain upon those who disdained to leave the line even for a few yards. Wet and sticky ridge-and-furrow tires a horse dreadfully, and the consequence is, that if he is pushed over it he speedily loses his powers and wind, and falls in a very ugly way at the first fence he comes to of a size above the average. Hence, every man who aspires to go well to hounds must learn to be a "judge of pace," and should endeavor to make out the signs of distress, and the best way of avoiding it. So much depends upon condition and breeding, that it is very difficult for a man with a strange horse to know what liberties he may take with him. Some well-bred ones will be blown, yet if nursed they will come again and again, while the dunghill-animal will give up when once he has lost his wind, and is gone for that day at least. In ascending steep banks, a careful and active horseman will dismount and lead his horse up, and by so doing often gains a mile or two upon his less humane and cautious antagonist. In ascending hills it is often expedient to make a zigzag; but in descending you can never go too straight, as the opposite course often leads to a dangerous slip on the side, with a crushed knee or ankle as a consequence. Few horses fall forwards, and they always manage to save themselves by slipping down on their haunches. This is a point of great importance, and should always be strictly attended to.

THERE ARE TWO GENERAL DIRECTIONS, which will serve for almost all descriptions of fence. These are, that if a height is to be overcome, the horse should be taken slowly up to it, in a collected manner, with his haunches well under him. On the other hand, width requires impetus, and the pace should be forced during the last few strides up to a very high rate. Under the former head may be classed timber (in all the varieties of gates, single posts and rails, stiles, and palings), walls, strong pleached fences, and banks. To the latter belong water in all shapes, double posts-and-rails, bullfinches, and those fences with a ditch on both sides, as well as those which have a wide one on the landing side. In addition to these there are the actual standing leap, seldom practised in the present day, the creeping style, the "on and off" leap, and the "drop," which is a variety of the standing leap.

IN COLLECTING THE HORSE, and properly putting him at his fence, there is a great art, and nothing but practice will give it in perfection. Double-posts-and-rails require a great deal of collecting and rousing, and the horse must go pretty fast at them, as also must he at all wide jumps, including water in all its forms. One essential is, that the horse shall have confidence in his rider; for if he thinks he *may* turn to the right or left he will most probably do so, unless he is very fond of jumping. Nervous men communicate their feelings to their horses, and though it may be difficult to explain how it is done, there is no doubt of the fact. It is remarkable how soon horses find out what kind of man they carry, and how they alter under different hands. This is partly owing to a mismanagement of the mouth, but in great measure also to the trepidation of the rider. Unless, therefore, he has full confidence in his own courage, he need never expect his horse to go steadily and straight at his fences. The collecting is much easier than the management of the bit at the leap itself, for there are two opposite things to be done, and the delicate point is to hit the moment of change from one to the other to a nicety. The first is to "catch hold of the horse's head," as it is called—that is, to bear more or less upon the mouth, pull the horse on his haunches and rouse him, either by voice, heel, or whip. This lasts till the moment of the effort made to rise over the obstacle, when the head should be released, so that the horse may have all his bodily powers at his command. If the head is confined the haunches do not act fully, because in making the spring the head is protruded, and pain is given by the bit if it is still held fast; and hence, to avoid the pain, the extension does not take place, the leap is not made with sufficient spring or power, and the horse alights too near the ditch, if there is one, or possibly in it. But in releasing the head judgment is required, for if the rein is too loose the horse is apt to alight in such a position that he is "all abroad," and without great help he will often fall; hence, most good performers, though they do not absolutely confine the head, yet they keep a very gentle and delicate hold of the mouth, and not only thus prevent the horse over-extending himself, but are also prepared to assist him if he is inclined to fall. This is the finished style of riding, and is only in the power of a man with a good seat as well as good hands. Both are wanted, because without the former it is impossible to avoid "riding the bridle"—that is, holding on by it as well as by the saddle; and without good hands that delicate management of the bridle which I have attempted to describe is impracticable. What is called "lifting" the horse is sometimes attempted with the bit, but I do not recognise its utility. When a horse is likely to touch the top bar of a gate, or in any way to use too small an effort, a stroke of the whip down the shoulder is the best lift. Rousing and collecting are quite distinct from lifting, which I believe to be a myth altogether. In creeping, good hands and quietness in the saddle are the chief elements of success, and without them both, no one is likely to do much in this particular style; hence it is that so few men can "creep" well, even though they have horses accustomed to it under other hands. When the horse has been thoroughly taught to creep, his head may almost be left without control, merely guiding him quietly to the gap, and then letting him take his own way; but where the horse has to be made to creep, a rein should be taken in each hand, and the head guided as if with a silken thread, to the right or left, or wherever the animal is required to go. These remarks will perhaps be useful to all who have no experienced friend ready to afford a practical demonstration of the same fundamental points. One actual lesson in the field is worth all the reading in the world; but, in default of this, the preceding observations will serve to assist the young aspirant for honors in riding to hounds.

OUT-DOOR VICES AND BAD HABITS.

OUT-DOOR VICES depend upon the temper of the individual, and include shying, rearing, kicking, lying down, plunging or bucking, shouldering, and running away. Bad habits arise from a defective formation of the body, and are confined to stumbling and cutting.

SHYING generally arises from timidity, but sometimes it is united with cunning, which induces the animal to assume a fear of some object for the sole purpose of finding an excuse for turning round. The usual cause of shying is doubtless the presence of some object to which the colt has not been accustomed, and if he has buck eyes, which render him short-sighted, it will be difficult to convince him of the innocent nature of the novel object. There are endless peculiarities in shying horses, some being dreadfully alarmed by one kind of object, which to others is not at all formidable. When a horse finds that he gains his object by turning round, he will often repeat the turning without cause, pretending to be alarmed, and looking out for excuses for it. This is not at all uncommon, and with timid riders leads to a discontinuance of the ride, by which the horse gains his end for the time, and repeats the trick on the first occasion. In genuine shying from fear the eyes are generally more or less defective; but sometimes this is not the cause, which is founded upon a general irritability of the nervous system. Thus, there are many horses which never shy at meeting tilted wagons, or other similarly alarming objects, but which almost drop with fear on a small bird flying out of a hedge, or any other startling sound. These last are also worse, because they give no notice to the rider, whereas the ordinary shyer almost always shows by his ears that he is prepared to turn round.

THE BEST PLAN OF TREATMENT which can be adopted, is to

take as little notice as possible of the shying, and to be especially careful not to show any fear of its recurrence when a wagon appears in the distance. When the horse begins to show alarm, but not till then, the rider should speak encouragingly to him, and, if necessary, with a severe tone, which may even be supported by the use of the whip or spurs, if his onward progress cannot be otherwise maintained. The principle which should be carried out is to adopt such measures as will get the horse to pass the object at which he shies somehow or other, and this should be effected with as little violence as possible, always commending in an encouraging tone as soon as the purpose is gained. Nothing has so great a tendency to keep up the habit as the plan so common among ignorant grooms, of chastising the shyer after he has passed the object of his alarm. If he can be persuaded to go quietly up to it and examine it with his muzzle as well as with his eyes, great good will be effected; but this can seldom be done with moving wagons, and heaps or stones are generally only alarming from defect of vision, so that each time they assume a new phase to the active imagination of the timid animal.

REARING is seldom met with excepting among raw colts, or if it is continued to a later period it is generally incurable. When existing in an aggravated form it is a most dangerous vice, as a fall backwards over the rider has often led to fatal consequences.

THE USUAL REMEDY for it in the colt is the ordinary running martingale, which will keep down the rearer who is merely indulging in his playful fancies. When, however, the vice has become confirmed, nothing short of severe punishment will be of any service, and the horsebreaker generally resorts to the plan of knocking the horse down as he rises by a blow between the ears with a loaded crop. This stuns the horse for a time, and alarms him so much that he is often cured by one act of the kind; but it is attended with some danger of injuring the horse, and the rider does not always escape. Another plan adopted by active breakers is to wait till the horse is just on the balance, and then slipping off to the left, it is easy to pull him over backwards; but this also is often followed by severe injury to the horse when the ground is hard. I have almost invariably found that bad rearers have very supple necks, which increases the difficulty of keeping them down by any kind of martingale, and probably this will account for the habit having become inveterate. A stiff-necked horse can scarcely rise high if his head is confined even by the running martingale; but when the side-straps are tightly buckled to the bit, he is effectually restrained, whereas with a loose neck the head can be so bent in to the brisket that no obstacle is offered. In such cases I have known a cavesson with the noseband lined with sharp prickers, and the martingale buckled to it; a most effectual prevention, as the slightest pull opens it, presses the prickers into the nose and gives acute pain. Whenever the rider finds a horse inclined to rise, he should at once lean forward, and after ineffectually trying the martingale to keep the horse down, he must loose his head, or he will be almost sure to bring him backwards and cause a severe fall.

For KICKERS, except when the habit is merely a mode of letting off superfluous spirits, severity is the only remedy, and a strong application of the whip down the shoulder the best means of using it. At the same time the snaffle-reins ought to be firmly held, and by their means the head kept up, for there is always a tendency to lower this part in the act of kicking; the gag snaffle is very effectual for this purpose.

LYING DOWN is rare in the present day, being chiefly confined to under-bred horses and Welsh ponies, which are gradually going out of use. The spur is the only means likely to keep a stubborn brute up; but in some cases its application is followed by the animal throwing himself down suddenly, instead of gradually.

PLUNGING may be described as a series of bounds into the air, which when they are made up and down in the same place, or nearly so, are called "bucking," from their resemblance to the playful antics of the deer. A bucking horse is very difficult to sit, but by sawing the mouth with a twisted snaffle it may generally be stopped at once.

BY SHOULDERING is understood the attempt to crush the leg of the rider against a wall, which some ill-tempered horses are fond of doing. It is easily avoided by pulling the horse's head round *to* the wall, instead of from it.

RUNNING AWAY is too well known to need description. In some horses it is a species of temporary madness, and scarcely any bit, however severe, will stop them. When there is room and scope enough, the *remedy* is simple, but, unfortunately, runaway horses generally choose a crowded thoroughfare to indulge their fancies in. A gallop to a stand-still, with the free use of the spur or whip at the latter part of it, will sometimes prevent a recurrence of this vicious act; but where the tendency is very strong it will have little effect. Punishing bits only make some high-couraged horses worse, but the majority of runaways would be dangerous with a plain snaffle only, and yet there are some which will go quietly enough in it, while the adoption of a curb will rouse their tempers at once. Of course they can only be ridden with great care and judgment, and must never be roused unnecessarily. Fortunately the mouths of horses are now made so much more carefully than in former times, and their management is so much better understood, that we seldom hear of or see an accident from this cause, either in the saddle or in harness. The most essential part

21 *

of the treatment of a runaway is the proper selection of a bit, which should be sufficient to control him without exciting opposition from the pain it gives.

STUMBLING arises from a variety of causes, and the nature of any particular case should be thoroughly investigated before any remedy for it is attempted. Sometimes it is merely dependent upon low or "daisy cutting" action, and then it is possible that it may not be attended with danger. I have known many horses which would stumble at least every half-mile, but yet they would travel for years with sound knees, the other leg being always ready to catch the weight. In other cases a stumble would only occur at rare intervals, but if the trip was made it was rarely recovered, and a fall was almost sure to follow. Again, it happens with some horses that when they are fresh out of the stable, their action is high and safe, but after a few miles the extensors of the leg tire, and they are constantly making a mistake. Inexperienced judges are very apt to examine the action of the fore legs alone, while that of the hind quarter is of quite as much importance to safety, and is more so as regards the ease of the rider. Lameness is a frequent source of a fall, from the tendency to put the foot too soon to the ground in order to take the weight off the other. And lastly, upright pasterns will produce stumbling, when the shoulders are so formed that the foot is put down too near the centre of gravity.

THE BEST PLANS FOR REMEDYING these several conditions are as follows. If the cause is weakness of the extensors no care can be of much service, all that can be done being to be on the look out for a trip, and then to take the weight off the fore quarter as much as possible by sitting well back, at the same time using such an amount of sudden pressure on the bit as to cause the horse to exert himself, without any attempt to keep up the head by mechanical force, which is an impossibility. When laziness is the cause, the stimulus of the spur or whip will suffice, and it often happens that a horse is safe enough at his top pace while a slower one is full of danger. In lameness of course the remedy is to wait till the foot or feet are sound again.

CUTTING depends either upon the legs being set on too near together, or on their joints not acting in a proper hinge-like manner. Many horses cut when in low condition, but are quite free from the defect when in flesh, and in such cases it is only necessary to let them wear a boot until they have had time enough to become fresh. Wherever horses "go close" care should be taken that the shoes do not project beyond the hoof, and the clenches of the nails should be carefully watched, the groom seeing that they are filed down by the smith if they stand up at all above the level of the horn. Cutting may take place either on the prominent part of the fetlock-joint, or midway between it and the knee, or just below the latter, which is called "speedy cutting," and is very apt to cause a fall. A boot should be fitted to the leg in either case, and worn till the part is thoroughly healed and all swelling has disappeared, when if any likely method of treatment has been adopted the horse may be tried without it, but no journey should be undertaken without one in the pocket in case it may be needed. A peculiar method of shoeing, called a feather-edged shoe, will often prevent this bad habit as long as it is adopted.

THE ANATOMY OF THE HORSE

CHAPTER XIII.

CLASSIFICATION OF THE VARIOUS ORGANS, AND PHYSIOLOGY OF THE SKELETON.

Classification of the various Organs—Structure of Bone—Of the Skeleton in General—The Artificial Skeleton—Number of Bones composing the Skeleton—General Anatomy of the Spinal Column—Of the Head and Face—Of the Hyoid Arch—Of the Thoracic Arch and Anterior Extremities—Of the Pelvic Arch and Hind Extremities—Of the Tail—Of the Fore and Hind Extremities considered as Organs of Support and Locomotion.

CLASSIFICATION OF THE VARIOUS ORGANS.

THE BODY OF THE HORSE, like all the vertebrate animals, may be considered as made up of several distinct apparatuses or systems. Of these, the *first* is a machine composed of the bony SKELETON, or framework, the various parts of which are united by JOINTS, and moved by MUSCLES. *Secondly*, there are contained within the thorax the organs which supply the whole body with the means of nutrition in the form of blood, and purify this fluid. *Thirdly*, in the abdomen are presented to view the important organs which assimilate the food to the condition of the blood; while in the adjoining cavity, the pelvis, are the urinary and generative apparatuses. *Fourthly*, the nervous system may be considered, as comprising the grand centre of the mental faculties, and, also, as presiding over and controlling the whole of the functions performed by the several organs; and *fifthly*, certain special organs, as, for example, those of sense, and, likewise, the foot will complete the circle.

OF THE STRUCTURE OF BONE.

THE BONES are composed of a tissue peculiar to them, enveloped by a membrane, the *periosteum*. They contain a semi-fluid of a

STRUCTURE OF BONE. 249

fatty nature, the *marrow*, and are pierced in various directions by *blood-vessels* and *nerves*.

THE PROPER TISSUE of the bones is made up of two distinct substances, either of which may be removed by artificial means, leaving the other entire. If, for instance, a bone is submitted to the heat of a furnace, it retains its shape and rigidity, but becomes much whiter in color, and is rendered extremely brittle. In fact, the mineral salts entering into its composition are left, but the animal matter binding them together is completely decomposed and carried off in a gaseous form. On the other hand, by immersing a bone for two or three weeks in diluted hydrochloric acid, the earthy salts are dissolved, while the animal matter is untouched. Here the bone retains its original shape, but it is soft and flexible; and instead of presenting its usual opaque yellowish-white color, it is semi-transparent, and resembles the ordinary gelatine of the shops. According to Berzilius, bone is chemically composed of the following constituents—namely, cartilage, reducible to gelatine by boiling; blood-vessels; phosphate of lime; carbonate of lime; fluate of lime; phosphate of magnesia; soda and chloride of sodium.

Considered mechanically, the bones form the framework of the animal machine. In the limbs they are hollow cylinders, admirably fitted by their shape and texture to resist violence and support weight. In the trunk and head they are flattened and arched, to protect the contents of the cavities they form, and to provide an extensive surface for the attachment of muscles. In certain situations their exterior is raised into projections called *processes*, which serve as levers for the muscles to act upon; in others they are grooved into smooth surfaces for the easy gliding of tendons, when these are stretched between the fleshy part of a muscle and one of its attachments. Lastly, they sometimes present a large hollow for the lodgment of the belly of a muscle, as in the case of the scapula.

When microscopically examined, bone is seen to be made up of a dense and homogeneous substance (basis substance), in which are numberless minute cells (corpuscles of Purkinje). The basis substance is partially fibrous and slightly lamellated, the layers being concentric in long bones and parallel in flat; it is traversed in all directions (more especially in the long axis, where there is one) by canals (Haversian canals), which frequently branch and inosculate, giving passage to vessels and nerves. In certain situations the lamellæ separate, and leave between them spaces of various sizes, called *cancelli*. Besides entering into the composition of the basis substance, the lamellæ are collected concentrically round the Haversian canals, the boundaries of which they form, generally to the extent of ten to fifteen layers. Both the compact and spongy tissues are, therefore, composed of the same elementary structure, the former being especially intended to afford resistance to violence with as little weight as is consistent with its office, for which reason it is hollowed into a tube; while the latter is enlarged as much as possible without unnecessarily adding to its weight, the problem being solved by its development in a cellular form.

The Periosteum is a dense fibrous membrane which covers every part of the surface of the bones, excepting their extremities when they enter into the composition of a joint, its place being then occupied by cartilage. When this membrane covers the bones of the skull it is called *pericranium*, and when it invests the cartilages of the ribs it receives the name *perichondrium*. It is full of bloodvessels, especially in the young, and they freely communicate with those of the surrounding soft parts. Hence it is extremely liable to inflammation, either caused by injury to itself or to the parts which cover it.

The marrow, or medullary substance, is contained in the cavities formed within the bones, being of a yellow color and oily nature in the shafts of the long bones; and more or less red, from the admixture with blood, in the flat and irregular bones, and in the heads of the long bones. It is contained within the areolar meshes of a membrane, which lines these cavities, answering to the periosteum, which has been already described. This medullary membrane is of excessive tenuity, and is composed of blood-vessels ramifying in fine cellular tissues. The use of marrow in the animal economy is not very clearly demonstrated.

In the embryo, all the bones originally exist in the state of cartilage, being soft and flexible. By degrees vascular canals are developed within its substance, by the union of its cells in rows. These concentrate towards some one or more points, which in a long bone are one in the centre of the shaft and one at each extremity. Starting from this point (*punctum ossificationis*), fibres run out, embracing clusters of cells, and sending branches between the individuals composing each group. In this manner the network, characteristic of bone, is formed, the cells uniting to form the permanent areolæ and Haversian canals. At first the contents of the cells are transparent, then granular, and finally opaque, from the pressure of amorphous mineral matter. The several ossified portions are quite distinct for a long time in the young animal, and may readily be separated by boiling or maceration.

OF THE SKELETON IN GENERAL.

THE NAME SKELETON has been given from the Greek word σκέλλω (*to dry*), it being the only part of the body which will bear desiccation without change of form. In the *vertebrata* it is an internal bony framework, but in the *crustacea* it invests the soft parts, and forms an insensible covering to them, while at the same time it serves the purpose of locomotion. In both these divisions of the animal kingdom the skeleton forms a series of arches or rings, capable of moving on each other, but so firmly attached as to secure protection to the important organs contained within them. In the horse, as in all the higher mammalia, these rings or arches are double—one set, the superior, being continuous throughout the whole length of the animal from the head to the root of the tail, and containing the nervous system; while the other lying below, but closely connected to them, is interrupted in certain localities, being found to exist chiefly in three regions:—1st, where it forms the jaws and bone of the tongue; 2d, where, by means of the ribs and sternum, it constitutes the thorax and its appendages, the anterior extremities; and, thirdly, where, in the shape of the pelvic arch, it protects the organs of generation, and, through the posterior extremities prolonged from it, assists in locomotion. The superior of these arches, from containing the brain, and its prolongation, the spinal cord, is called the neural arch. The inferior is termed the hæmal arch ($αἷμα$, *blood*), because it protects the heart and its large blood-vessels as the latter pass from the thorax towards the head and posterior extremities. In all the vertebrata the neural arch consists of one continuous cavity, defended from end to end by bony plates, strongly joined together; and in some of the lower forms (lizards) the hæmal arch is nearly as complete, these animals having cervical ribs; while the dugong and some others are furnished with ribs in their tails. Consequently, it is fair to consider the whole skeleton in the superior forms of the animal kingdom as composed of two series of arched plates, firmly united together, but still allowing more or less motion, and serving to protect the centres of the nervous and sanguineous systems, from which they have received their names.

THE ARTIFICIAL SKELETON.

THE BONES of the Horse, as of the other mammalia, may be preserved with their natural ligamentous attachments connecting them in a dry state, in which condition the skeleton is called a natural one. It is usual, however, to macerate them so long that all the soft parts readily separate, leaving the bones without any of the ligaments or cartilages which are firmly fixed to them during life. They are then put together by wires, &c., the cartilages being represented by leather and cork. In this way it often happens that the proportions are not exactly preserved, and, on reference to an articulated skeleton in any museum, the inexperienced eye may be greatly misled. Thus it is very common to represent the thorax in the artificial skeleton as much shallower than it is in nature, where its lower margin is on the average about midway between the top of the withers and the ground. Again, in the fresh state, the intervertebral fibro-cartilage is in some parts of the spine of considerable thickness; and if the proper substance is not artificially supplied, the skeleton will be too short, or if too thick a material is added it will be too long. In the engraving of the skeleton occupying the opposite page, which is drawn from the skeleton in the Museum of the Veterinary College of London, the spine is correctly represented, but the thorax is too shallow, and the scapula, together with the whole fore extremity, is placed too far forward.

NUMBER OF BONES COMPOSING THE SKELETON.

THE SKELETON is composed of two hundred and forty-seven separate bones, which are united by joints to form the spine, thorax, pelvis, tail, and fore and hind extremities. The spine is finished anteriorly by the head, which is divided into the cranium and face, and contains the teeth. Suspended from the head is the os hyoides, which completes the number of bones. Thus:—

THE SPINE consists of 7 cervical, 18 dorsal, and 6 lumbar vertebræ—Total 31
THE THORAX is made up of the dorsal vertebræ, with 18 ribs on each side, and the sternum in the middle—Total . . 37
THE PELVIS comprises 2 ossa innominata (or ilium, ischium, and pubes), and 1 sacrum—Total 3
THE TAIL contains on the average 17 bones 17
THE FORE EXTREMITY is made up on each side of the scapula, humerus, os brachii, and 8 carpal bones, 3 metacarpal, os suffraginis, os coronæ, os pedis, os naviculare, 2 ossa sesamoidea—Total on both sides 40
THE HIND EXTREMITY has the femur, patella, tibia, fibula, 6 tarsal bones, 3 metatarsals, os suffraginis, os coronæ, os pedis, os naviculare, 2 ossa sesamoidea—Total 38
BONES OF THE CRANIUM 10
BONES OF THE FACE AND LOWER JAW 18
TEETH 40
BONES OF THE INTERNAL EAR, 4 in each organ 8
OS HYOIDES, OR BONE OF THE TONGUE, made up of five sections 5

Grand total 247

GENERAL ANATOMY OF THE SPINAL COLUMN.

THE VERTEBRAL OR SPINAL COLUMN is the first rudiment of internal skeleton seen in the lower vertebrate animals, and this constitutes the type of that great division of the animal kingdom. In the horse, also, it is the portion of the skeleton first developed in the embryo, and forms the centre around which all the other parts are framed. At its first appearance it is a cartilaginous cylinder, surrounding and protecting the primitive trace of the nervous system; but as the embryo increases in growth, points of ossification are developed corresponding to each vertebra, the whole tube being finally divided into distinct pieces called *vertebræ*, to which the bones of the head are a prolongation, corresponding in their nature, though differing outwardly in form.

The vertebræ are divisible into true and false, the former reaching from the head to the pelvis, and the latter extending thence backward, being respectively called the sacrum and coccyx.

The true vertebræ comprise the 7 cervical, 18 dorsal, and 6 lumbar vertebræ. Each consists of a body, from which two laminæ or plates project upwards, terminating in a spinous process. In addition to these are two lateral projections (transverse processes), which serve the purpose of firmly connecting the vertebræ together by means of the muscles attached to them, and also to the ribs and extremities below. Lastly, each vertebra has two small surfaces before and the same number behind (articular surfaces), which form distinct joints between them.

Between the body, the laminæ, and the spinous process, is an opening, more or less triangular in shape, in which lie the spinal cord and its investments. The edges of this opening are attached to those before and behind by ligamentous tissues (*ligamenta subflava*), which, opposite each intervertebral space, are pierced by openings on each side to give exit to the vertebral nerves passing out to the exterior of the body and to the extremities. Opposite to these openings the bone is notched above and below, and these *intervertebral notches* complete the parts common to the whole series. Thus the vertebral or spinal column serves as a firmly secured but flexible tube for the lodgment of the spinal cord, while at the same time it gives passage to its nerves. By this formation it is far less liable to injury, and also more useful as an aid to locomotion, than if it were made of one solid piece of bone, which, from its length, would be readily broken.

OF THE HEAD AND FACE, AND OF THE HYOID ARCH.

MODERN ANATOMISTS, following out the idea first suggested by Maclise and Owen, consider the head as made up of six vertebræ; the posterior one, or that nearest to the neck, being the occipital bone, the next two being made up of the temporal bone, and the ultimate vertebræ consisting of the sphenoid and æthmoid bones. This is a somewhat fanciful hypothesis, when worked out in detail; but it is obvious that the several bones of the skull subserve the same purposes as the vertebræ, and resemble those parts of the skeleton in forming a series of irregular arches to protect the brain, the division into separate pieces being far more secure than if the whole were in one.

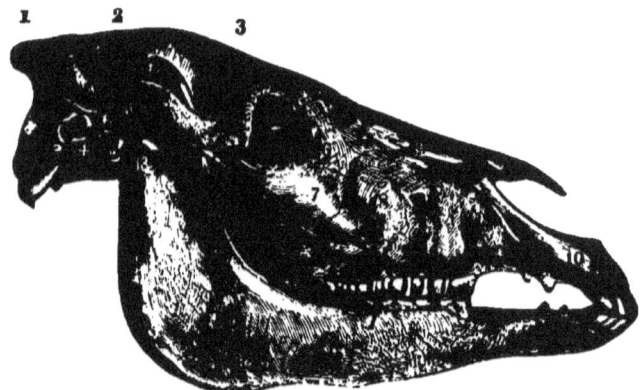

FIG. 1.—PROFILE VIEW OF THE HEAD AND FACE.

1. Occiput.
2. Parietal bone.
3. Frontal bone.
4. Petrous portion of temporal bone.
5. Zygomatic arch
6. Lachrymal bone.
7. Malar bone.
8. Posterior maxillary bone.
9—11. Nasal bone.
10. Anterior maxillary bone.
11. Temporal fossa.
12, 13. Lower jaw.

THE BONES OF THE FACE, including the lower jaw and os hyoides, depend from the neural arch or brain-case much in the same way as the ribs and pelvic bones posterior to them are attached to the vertebræ, and though they enclose organs of less vital importance, yet they are perfectly analogous to these parts in their types and in the offices which they perform.

OF THE THORACIC ARCH AND ANTERIOR EXTREMITIES.

LYING IN THE HORSE AT SOME DISTANCE POSTERIORLY to the three first segments of the hæmal arch (the bones of the face, lower jaw, and os hyoides), and separated from them by the neck, where there is a hiatus, the thoracic arch and anterior extremities depend from the vertebræ corresponding to them. In many of the higher vertebrates the fore extremity is firmly united by a joint to the thorax, and may be considered with it; but in the horse it is only attached by muscles, the thorax being slung between the upper edges of the blade-bones by means of two broad sheets of muscular fibres. Hence the collar-bone is entirely absent in this animal; and thus, while he is free from dislocations and fractures of that bone, to which he would be constantly subject if it were present, he is rendered more liable to strains and rheumatic inflammations of the muscular sling, by which freedom of action is impaired.

THE SKELETON.

IN THE ARTICULATED SKELETON it is usual to consider the thorax as made up by the eighteen dorsal vertebræ superiorly, the eighteen ribs and their cartilages on each side, and the sternum with its cartilages below. But the cavity of the thorax, as bounded by the diaphragm posteriorly, is not nearly so large as would be supposed from a consideration of the dry skeleton, for though the diaphragm is attached to the twelve posterior ribs near their cartilages, yet its surface is so convex towards the thoracic cavity, that a very large space within the bony thorax is really occupied by the abdominal organs.

THE PELVIC ARCH AND HIND EXTREMITIES.

BEHIND THE THORAX occurs a second interval corresponding to the loins, where the hæmal arch is deficient; but at the pelvis the circle is completed by the bones of the ischium, ilium, and pubes, united to the sacrum above, and having the hind extremities firmly articulated to them at the hip joints. The pelvis constitutes not only a firm and solid case for the protection of the large blood-vessels, and of the urinary and genital organs, but it is also intimately connected with locomotion, to which the posterior extremities largely contribute.

THE TAIL.

THIS ORGAN appears to be intended chiefly to protect the body from insects; but it also serves to some extent as an aid in balancing the body when rapidly moving in any new direction. It is made up of from fifteen to eighteen bones.

THE FORE AND HIND EXTREMITIES CONSIDERED AS ORGANS OF SUPPORT AND LOCOMOTION.

REGARDING THE LIMBS AS MEANS OF SUPPORT, it must be remembered that the fore limbs are nearer the centre of gravity, and, therefore, sustain more weight than the hind. The fore quarter is suspended between the bases of the two shoulder-blades, chiefly by the serrati magni, and in such a way as to require no special muscular contraction. The four parts of which the limb itself is composed being bent at various angles, are prevented from giving way by the muscular actions of the extensors of the humerus and ulna, the carpus (or knee) having little tendency to yield, and the pastern being supported by the flexor muscles and suspensory ligament. The hinder limbs, though sustaining less weight, are not so favorably circumstanced for this purpose, the angles between their several parts being generally more acute. But if these are attentively regarded, there is not so much difference as is generally supposed. Thus, the first joint, the ilio-femoral, forms a less acute angle than its analogue, the shoulder joint. Again, though the stifle joint is considerably bent, it is not more so than the elbow joint, which will be clear on comparing the two in the skeleton given at page 252. The chief disadvantage sustained by the hind limbs as means of support will be found in the hock, as compared with the knee, the latter being nearly straight, while the former is much bent; but as it has a long lever to assist it (the os calcis), and as this is kept in position by the powerful hamstring muscles, each of which serves its purpose far more completely than the flexor of the carpus inserted in the os pisiforme, it may readily be understood that the hind limb is not greatly at a disadvantage in supporting the weight of the body.

As AGENTS OF LOCOMOTION, the offices of the fore and hind limbs are widely different. Each has been already described as consisting of four sections, bent at angles on each other. In the fore limb these angles are framed to serve as springs, so that when the feet touch the ground, they are enabled to adapt themselves so as to avoid altering the line of progression of the body. In those animals which have small and short fore legs, as the kangaroo and hare, the most rapid locomotion ever consists in a series of curves; whereas, in the horse at full speed, the body progresses in one straight line, owing to this elastic structure of the anterior limbs. So, also, in descending from an extraordinary leap, the springy action of the fore limbs of the horse is so powerful that he can get off again without dwelling, whereas the kangaroo and hare must depend almost entirely upon their hind legs, and consequently stop for a second after their descent. On the other hand, the angular formation of the hind limbs is intended to enable the animal to drive its whole body forward, by first flexing all the joints, and thus drawing the feet under the belly; and then suddenly extending them with the feet fixed in the ground, the weight is necessarily propelled. Or if the feet are not fixed they are lashed out backwards, developing the action so well known as "kicking." The difference between the powers displayed by the two limbs, in straightening their component parts, is well displayed in comparing kicking with the striking out of the fore foot, which is common enough among vicious horses. It is true that the latter will sometimes cause a severe blow; but it could very rarely break a limb, which is the least amount of mischief to be apprehended from the full force of a lash out with the hinder limb.

CHAPTER XIV.

THE TEETH.

THE TEETH are developed within their appropriate cavities or sockets, which are found exactly corresponding with their number in the upper and lower jaws, being narrower in the lower than in the upper. Before birth they are nearly all in a state of incomplete growth, covered and concealed by the gums, but soon afterwards they rise through it in pairs, the first set, or milk teeth, being in course of time superseded by the permanent teeth as in all the mammalia. The following is the formula of the complete dentition of the horse:—

Incisors $\frac{6}{6}$, canine $\frac{2}{2}$, molars $\frac{12}{13}$.

EACH TOOTH is developed within its corresponding cavity in the jaw, and is made up of three distinct substances—cement, enamel, and dentine. The *cement* of the horse's tooth (sometimes called crusta petrosa) closely corresponds in texture with his bone, and, like it, is traversed by vascular canals. The *enamel* is the hardest constituent of the tooth, and consists of earthy matter arranged in the animal matrix, but contained in canals, so as to give the striated appearance which it presents on splitting it open. *Dentine* has an organized animal basis, presenting extremely minute tubes and cells, and containing earthly particles, which are partly blended with the animal matter in its interspaces, and partly contained in a granular state within its cells. These three substances are shown in the annexed section of an incisor tooth, see Fig. 2, which is of the natural size.

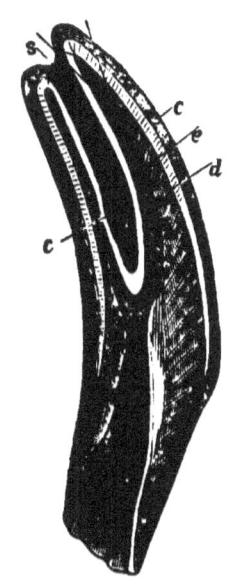

FIG. 2.—SECTION OF INCISOR.

c. Cement on external surface.
c. Cement reflected within the cavity.
e. Enamel also reflected.
d. Dentine.
s. Tartar, colored black by decomposition of food, contained within the cavity.

IN THE MOLAR teeth the arrangement of these three substances is the same, except that the cement and enamel dip down into two or more cavities instead of one, and are also reflected in a sinuous manner upon the sides. This inequality in the hardness of the component parts of these teeth causes them to wear away with different degrees of rapidity, and thus leaves a rough surface, which materially aids in grinding down the hard grain which forms a large portion of the animal's food. In the upper jaw, the table presented by each molar tooth is much larger than those of the corresponding lower teeth, and therefore it is easy to distinguish the one from the other.

THE TEMPORARY OR MILK INCISORS differ in shape a good deal from the permanent set The milk teeth are altogether much smaller, but especially in the neck, which is constricted in them, whilst in the permanent set, which go on growing as they wear out, the diameter is nearly the same throughout. The former are also whiter in color, and have grooves or indentations on their outer surfaces, running towards the gum. Lastly, the mark on the table is much slighter than in the permanent teeth. The temporary molars are not distinguishable from the permanent teeth of that class.

AS A CONSEQUENCE OF THIS ARRANGEMENT OF PARTS, the teeth, as they wear down, present a different appearance according to the extent to which their attrition has reached. On this fact is founded a means of arriving at a knowledge of the age of the horse after he has shed his milk teeth, which as a rule he does in pairs at certain fixed periods. In order, therefore, to be able to estimate the age of the horse from his teeth, it is necessary to ascertain, as nearly as may be, the exact time at which he puts up each pair of his milk or sucking teeth, and afterwards the periods at which they are replaced by the permanent teeth. Finally, it becomes the province of the veterinarian to lay down rules for ascertaining the age from the degree of attrition which the permanent teeth have undergone. For these several purposes, the horse's mouth must be studied from the earliest period of his life up to old age.

In horseman's language the incisors are called *nippers*, the canine teeth *tushes*, and the molars *grinders*.

BY THE END OF THE FIRST YEAR the colt has cut his twelve nippers and sixteen grinders, which usually pierce the gums at the following months. Before birth, the eight anterior grinders have generally shown themselves, followed about a weeek after foaling by the two central nippers. At the end of the first month another grinder makes its appearance all round, and in the middle of the second the next nipper shows itself. By the end of the second month the central nippers have attained their full size, and the second are about half-grown, requiring another month to overtake their fellows. Between the sixth and ninth months the corner nippers are cut, and towards the end of the first year reach their full size. This first set of nippers consists of teeth considerably smaller in size than the permanent teeth and somewhat different in shape. They are more rounded in front, and hollow towards the mouth, the outer edge being at first much higher than the inner. As they wear down, these two edges soon become level, but the corner nippers maintain this appearance for a long time. At six months the central nippers are almost level, with the black "mark" in their middle wide and faint; and about the ninth month the next nipper on each side above and below is also worn down almost to a level surface.

DURING THE SECOND YEAR the following changes take place:— In the first month, and sometimes towards the end of the first year, a fourth grinder is cut all round, which commences the set of permanent teeth, the three first molars only being shed. At a year and a half, the mark in the central nippers is much worn out, and has become very faint; the second is also worn flat, but is not so faint; and the corner nippers are flat, but present the mark clearly enough. In colts which have been reared on corn and much hay, the wearing down proceeds more rapidly than in those fed upon grass alone.

THE THIRD YEAR is occupied by the commencement of the second dentition, which is effected in the same order in which the

FIG. 3.—THREE-YEAR-OLD MOUTH.

B. Anterior maxillary bone.
1. 1. Central permanent nippers, nearly full-grown.
2. 2. Milk teeth worn down.
3. 3. Corner milk teeth, still showing central mark.
4. 4. Tushes concealed within the jaw.

milk teeth made their appearance. Both sets are contained within the jaw at birth, the permanent teeth being small and only partially developed, and lying deeper than the milk teeth. As the mouth grows, it becomes too large for its first set of teeth; and the roots of these being pressed upon by the growth of the permanent set, their fangs are absorbed, and allow the new teeth to show themselves, either in the places of the former, or by their sides, in which case they are known by the name of *wolf's teeth*. This change proceeds in the same order as the cutting of the milk teeth, commencing with the first grinder, which is shed and replaced by a permanent tooth early in the third year, a fifth grinder (permanent) making its appearance about the same time. Towards the end of this year the sixth grinder shows itself, but grows very slowly, and the central nippers above and below fall out, and are replaced by permanent ones, which, as before remarked, are considerably larger in size and somewhat different in form.

AT THREE YEARS the mouth presents the appearance shown on the preceding page, the development of the permanent teeth varying a good deal in different individuals. At three years and four or six months, the next nipper all round falls out, and is replaced by the permanent tooth. The corner nippers are much worn, and the mark in them is nearly obliterated. About this time also the second grinder is shed.

AT FOUR YEARS OF AGE, the mouth should differ from that

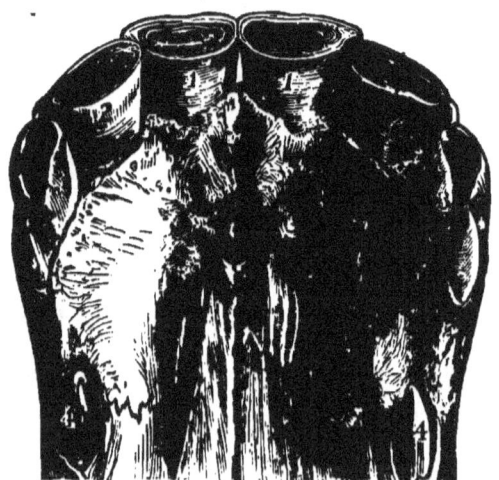

FIG. 4.—MOUTH OF THE COLT AT FOUR AND A HALF YEARS.

A. Anterior maxillary bone.
1. 1. Central nippers, considerably worn down.
2. 2. The next pair, fully developed, with their edges slightly worn.
3. 3. Corner permanent nippers, in a state of growth, with the edges of the cavity sharp, and the mark very plain.
4. 4. The tushes showing themselves through the gum, but not full-grown.

represented in fig. 3 in the following particulars:—The central nippers begin to lose their sharp edges, and have grown considerably in substance. The next nipper all round has grown nearly to its full size, but not quite, and its edges are still sharp, with the mark deep and very plain. The corner milk nippers still remain, unless they have been knocked out for purposes of fraud, which is sometimes done to hasten the growth of the permanent teeth, and give the horse the appearance of being four or five months older than he is.

BETWEEN FOUR AND A HALF AND FIVE YEARS, the corner nippers are shed, and the tush protrudes through the gum. These changes are shown at fig. 4.

AT FIVE YEARS, the mouth is complete in the number of its teeth; and from this date it becomes necessary to study their aspect in both jaws. Fig. 5 shows the upper teeth at this age, by comparing which with fig. 4 the slight growth in the half-year

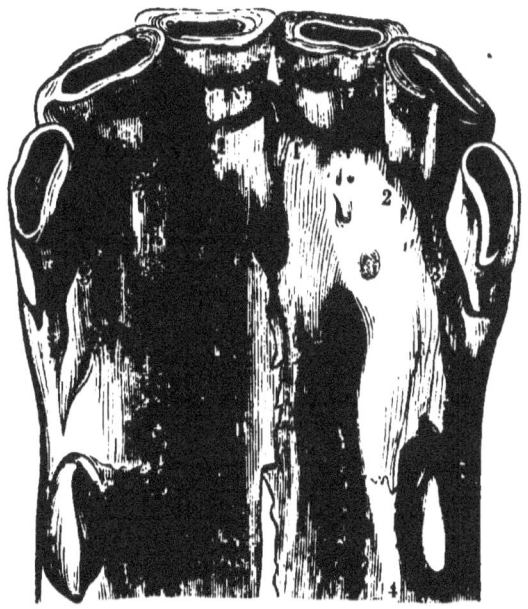

FIG. 5.—UPPER NIPPERS AND TUSHES AT FIVE YEARS OLD.

1. 1. Central nippers, with the mark still unobliterated.
2. 2. Next nippers, with the mark still plainer.
3. 3. Corner nippers, with the edges very slightly worn.
4. 4. Tushes, well developed, and still showing the groove on the outside plainly.

may be traced. In the lower teeth of the same mouth, the edges of the central cavities are much more worn away, the central nipper having only a small black speck in the middle of a smooth surface, while the next is much worn, and the corner teeth, though showing the mark very plainly, bear evidence of having been used. The tush is much grown, with its outer surface regularly convex, and its inner concave, the edges being sharp and well defined. The

FIG. 6.—LOWER NIPPERS AND TUSHES AT FIVE YEARS OLD.

1. 1. Central nippers, with their marks almost entirely worn out.
2. 2. Next nippers, showing marks partially worn.
3. 3. Corner nippers, with the mark plainly seen, but the edges partially worn.
4. 4. Tushes, with the grooves inside almost obliterated.

sixth molar is at its full growth, and the third is shed to make room for the permanent tooth in its place. These two last-named teeth should always be examined in cases where there is any doubt about the age. After five years, no further shedding occurs in any of the teeth.

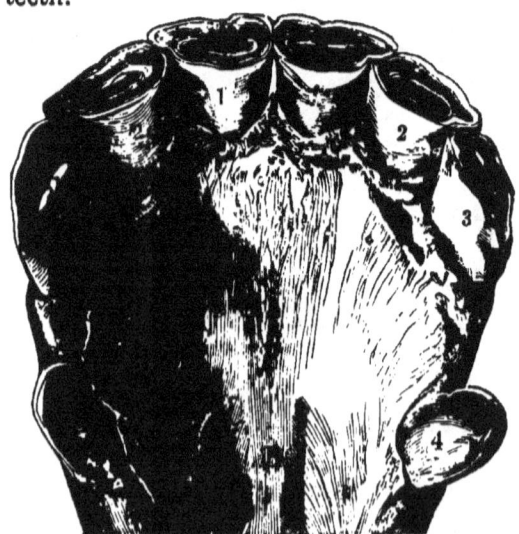

FIG. 7.—THE LOWER NIPPERS AND TUSHES OF A SIX-YEAR-OLD HORSE.

B. The lower jaw.
1. 1. The central nippers, with the marks worn out.
2. 2. The next nippers, with the marks disappearing.
3. 3. The corner nippers, showing the mark plainly enough, but with the edges of the cavity considerably worn.
4. 4. The tushes, standing up three-quarters of an inch, with their points only slightly blunted.

THE six-year-old mouth is the last upon which any great reliance can be placed, if it is desired to ascertain the age of the horse to a nicety; but by attentively studying both jaws, a near approximation to the truth may be arrived at. It is ascertained that the nippers of the upper jaw take about two years longer to wear out than those of the lower; so that until the horse is eight years old, his age may be ascertained by referring to them, nearly as well as by the lower nippers at six. But as different horses wear out their teeth with varying rapidity, it is found that this test cannot be implicitly relied on; and in crib-biters or wind-suckers the upper teeth wear out wonderfully soon. Fig. 7 is taken from the lower jaw of a six-year-old horse, showing the marks of the central nippers almost obliterated, but still presenting concentric circles, of discolored brown tartar in the middle; next to which is the cement, then the enamel, and the dentine, with a thin layer of enamel outside. Up to this age, the nippers stand nearly perpendicular to each other, the two sets presenting a slight convexity when viewed together, as seen in figure on p. 254. Afterwards the nippers gradually extend themselves in a straight line from each jaw, and, in the very old horse, form an acute angle between them.

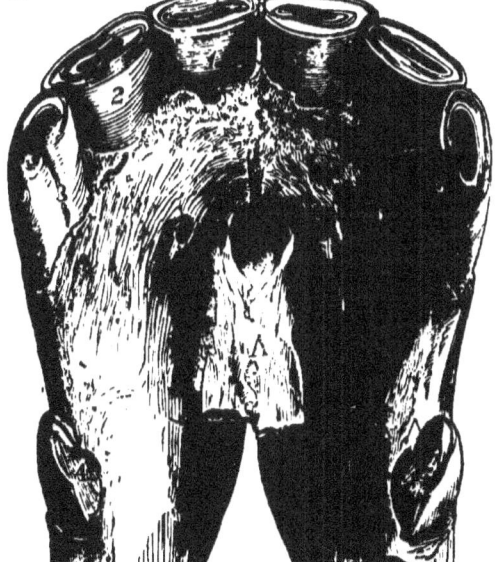

FIG. 8.—UPPER NIPPERS IN THE EIGHT-YEAR-OLD HORSE.

A. Anterior maxillary bone.
1. 1. Central nippers, worn to a plane surface.
2. 2. Next pair, still showing a slight remnant of the cavity.
3. 3. Corner nippers, showing the mark plainly enough.
4. 4. Tushes, more worn down than in the lower jaw of the six-year-old mouth.

AT ABOUT THE EIGHTH YEAR, the upper nippers present the

same appearance as already described in the lower nippers at six years old. Both tushes are considerably worn away at their points, and the upper ones more so than the lower.

AT NINE YEARS OF AGE the upper middle nippers are worn down completely. The next pair have a slight mark left, but their surfaces are quite level, and the corner nippers have only a black stain, without any central depression.

FIG. 9.—LOWER NIPPERS AND LEFT TUSH OF A VERY OLD HORSE, THE RIGHT HAVING FALLEN OUT.

AFTER NINE YEARS the age of the horse can only be guessed at from his teeth, which gradually grow in length, and are more in a line with the jaw. The section of each nipper presented to the eye becomes more and more triangular instead of being oval, as seen in figs. 7 and 8; but after about the twelfth year the triangular section disappears, and the tooth becomes nearly round. In accordance with the increase of length is the color of the tooth altered, being of a dirty yellow in very old horses, with occasional streaks of brown and black. The tushes wear down to a very small size, and very often one or both drop out.

ALLUSION HAS ALREADY BEEN MADE to the practice of removing the milk nippers for the purpose of inducing a more rapid growth of the next set, which, however, is not materially affected by the operation; but dishonest dealers have recourse to another deception, called *bishoping*, by which an aged horse may be passed off upon an inexperienced person for a six-year old. The plan adopted is to cut off all the nippers with a saw to the proper length, and then with a cutting instrument the operator scoops out an oval cavity in the corner nippers, which is afterwards burnt with a hot iron until it is quite black. It is extremely easy to detect the imposition by carefully comparing the corner nippers with the next, when it will be seen that there is no gradation from the centre to the corner nippers, but that the four middle ones are exactly alike, while the corners present a large black cavity, *without a distinct white edge to it*, the dentine being generally encroached upon without any regularity in the concentric rings. Moreover, on comparing the lower with the upper nippers, unless the operator has performed on the latter also, they will be found to be considerably more worn than the lower, the reverse of which ought naturally to be the case. Occasionally a clever operator will burn all the teeth to a properly regulated depth, and then a practised eye alone will detect the imposition. In the present day there is not so great a demand for six-year-old horses as was formerly the case, and purchasers are contented with a nine or ten-year-old mouth if the legs and constitution are fresh. Hence bishoping is seldom attempted excepting with horses beyond the age of eleven or twelve; and the mere use of the burning-iron without cutting off the teeth will seldom answer the purposes of the "coper." Formerly it was very common to see mouths with the corner nippers burnt to show a "good mark," and nothing else done to them; but, for the reasons given above, the plan is now almost entirely abandoned.

IRREGULARITIES in the growth of teeth are by no means uncommon in the horse, often caused by the practice of punching out the milk teeth to hasten the growth of the permanent set. Instead of having this effect, however, the teeth are induced to take a wrong direction, and not meeting their fellows they do not wear down as they naturally should. In punching out the corner nipper it is very often broken off, and the fang is allowed to remain in the socket. The consequence is that the picking up of the food does not hasten the removal of the fang of the milk tooth, and instead of accelerating the growth of the permanent tooth in the natural position, it retards it and sometimes drives it to seek a passage through the gums behind its proper socket. Here, not meeting the corresponding nipper of the upper jaw, it grows like a tush, and has sometimes been mistaken for a second tooth of that kind. Some horses are naturally formed with "pig jaws"—that is to say, with the upper longer than the lower—and in these cases the whole set of teeth grow to a great length, and interfere with the prehension of the food.

CHAPTER XV.

OF THE JOINTS AND MUSCLE,—THE TISSUES ENTERING INTO THEIR COMPOSITION.

Joints—Cartilage—Fibrous Tissue—Physiology of Muscle.

THE JOINTS.

THE JOINTS are all formed between two or more separate bones, having a soft and elastic substance interposed, whose structure varies with the amount of motion. Where this is extensive, as in the joints of the limbs, the adjacent surfaces are covered with a peculiar kind of cartilage arranged in a thin and very smooth layer upon them. In addition to this protection against friction and vibration, the bones are firmly bound together by strong bands of white fibrous inelastic tissue under the general name of ligaments, each bundle receiving a distinct appellation. In those situations where the motion is limited, a mixture of cartilage and fibrous tissue is inserted between the ends of the bones and attached to both, as in the vertebræ, ischio-pubic symphysis, &c.; while in order to reduce the vibration and friction in certain important joints fibro-cartilages are introduced, with both surfaces free, and in contact only with the usual layer of cartilage, as in the stifle and jaw. A lubricating fluid (called synovia) is required to reduce the amount of friction; and to produce it, as well as to keep it within proper limits, a membrane (synovial) is developed. This is attached to each bone in a peculiar manner, to be presently described. Lastly, an elastic fibrous tissue (yellow) is met with in certain situations, the most remarkable being the great ligament of the neck.

CARTILAGE.

TRUE CARTILAGE (which is familiarly known to all when it shows the large white masses in a breast of veal, as dressed for the table) is a homogeneous, white, semi-transparent substance, possessing a certain amount of elasticity, and easily cut with a knife. In the early embryo it exists as the sole foundation of the skeleton, bone being afterwards deposited in its meshes and finally substituted for it. This is called temporary cartilage. In after life it invests those parts of the bones which enter into the composition of the joints (articular cartilage, which is what we are considering just now), and also forms the costal cartilages, the ensiform and cariniform cartilages, and those of the larynx, trachea, and nose. *Reticular* or *membraniform* cartilage, differing slightly from true cartilage, is met with in the Eustachian tube, the external ear, and the epiglottis.

STRUCTURE.—On putting a slice of true cartilage under the microscope, it is seen to consist of a number of minute cells disseminated through a vitreous substance. The cells are oval, oblong, or polyhedral in shape, and more or less flattened by packing. The membrane forming the cell-wall is usually blended with the matrix, but sometimes consists of concentric layers. White fibres usually enclose the mass of cells, and even dip sometimes into those cells more superficially placed. The cells or corpuscles are contained in hollow cavities, called lacunæ. Sometimes they do not entirely fill up the lacunæ, so that a vacant space is left. The corpuscles are usually dispersed in groups, varying in size and form, through the matrix; the groups towards the surface of the cartilage are generally flattened conformably with the surface. *In articular cartilage*, the matrix in a thin section appears dim and presents a granular aspect, the cells and nuclei of which are small. The parent-cells enclose two or three younger cells. The groups they form are flattened near the surface, and lie parallel with it. In the internal part of this cartilage the cells assume a linear direction, and point towards the surface. Near its attached surface cartilage blends with the bone, the cells and nuclei of which become surrounded by little granular bodies, which seem to be the rudimentary deposit of bone. *In costal cartilage* the cells are very large; they contain two or more nuclei, which are clear and transparent, and some contain a few oil globules. The cells, internally situated, form oblong groups, disposed in lines radiating to the circumference. We observe a great quantity of intercellular tissue, in the form of white fibrous structure, the fibres of which are parallel and straight.

PERICHONDRIUM ($\pi\varepsilon\rho\grave{\iota}$, *around*, and $\chi\acute{o}\nu\delta\rho\upsilon\varsigma$, *cartilage*), is a white fibrous substance, which covers the external surface of all cartilages, except those of the joints. In this membrane the bloodvessels which supply the cartilage with blood, ramify. It is analogous to the periosteum which covers the external surface of bones.

NERVES.—No nerves have been traced into any of the cartilages; they are destitute of sensation while free from inflammation.

BLOOD-VESSELS.—Cartilage is non-vascular; it receives its nourishment from the bone and perichondrium by imbibition. The law of endosmose coming into operation when the tissue is thick, as in the costal cartilages, canals are formed through which the vessels pass to supply the parts which are too far removed from the perichondrium. In articular cartilages no vessels enter. When cartilage is removed by mechanical means, or by absorption, it is not regenerated, and when fractured, as in the ribs, there is no reunion by cartilage, but by fibrous, or most frequently by osseous deposition.

CHEMICAL COMPOSITION.—True cartilage contains three-fifths of its weight of water. It is ascertained that the cells and the intermediate substance are composed of different materials. The membranes of the cartilage cells are not resolved by boiling, and offer a lengthened resistance to alkalies and acids. The contents of the cells coagulate in water and dilute acids, and are dissolved by alkalies. The intermediate substance consists of chondrin, which differs from gelatine in not being precipitated by the mineral acids.

FIBROUS TISSUE.

FIBROUS TISSUE exists very generally throughout the body, being composed of fibres of extreme minuteness. It is found under three forms, as *white fibrous tissue, yellow fibrous* tissue, and *red fibrous* tissue.

WHITE FIBROUS TISSUE is composed of cylindrical fibres of exceeding minuteness, transparent and undulating. They are collected first into small fasciculi and then into larger bundles, which, according to their arrangement, compose thin layers or membranes, ligamentous bands or tendons. *The membraneous form* is seen in the periosteum and perichondrium, the fasciæ covering various organs, the membrane of the brain, &c.—*Ligaments* are glistening and inelastic bands composed of fasciculi of fibrous tissue generally ranged side by side, sometimes interwoven with each other. These fasciculi are held together by separate fibres, or by areolar tissue. They are of all forms, from the round band to the expanded membrane known as a capsular ligament.—*Tendons* are constructed like ligaments, but usually in larger and more rounded bundles. Sometimes they are spread out in the form of aponeuroses.

YELLOW FIBROUS TISSUE is also known as elastic tissue, from its most prominent physical characteristic, in which it differs from white fibrous tissue. It is so elastic that it may be drawn out to double its natural length, without losing its power of returning to its original dimensions. Its fibres are transparent, brittle, flat or polyhedral in shape, colorless when single, but yellowish when aggregated in masses. When this tissue is cut or torn, the fibres become curved at their extremities in a peculiar manner. It is met with in the ligamenta subflava of the vertebræ, the ligamentum colli, the chordæ vocales, and membranes of the larynx and trachea, and the middle coat of the arteries.

RED FIBROUS TISSUE, also called contractile tissue from its possessing the power of contracting under certain stimulants, is intermediate between yellow fibrous tissue and muscular fibre. Its fibres are cylindrical, transparent, of a reddish color, and collected in bundles. It has no connection with the joints, but is met with in the iris, around certain excretory ducts, and in the coats of the veins.

FIBROUS TISSUE—PHYSIOLOGY OF MUSCLE.

Chemical Composition.—The flexibility of fibrous tissue is owing to the presence of water in it, of which it contains about two-thirds of its weight. A tendon or ligament will readily dry and become brittle. Acetic acid causes it to swell up, and here the acid discloses the existence of nuclei and elastic fibres. It is chiefly composed of gelatine, which is extracted by boiling.

Blood-vessels.—White fibrous tissue contains few blood-vessels. They usually follow the course of the fasciculi; in ligaments they run in a longitudinal direction, sending off communicating branches across the fasciculi, and eventually forming an open network. The periosteum is much more vascular, but the vessels do not strictly belong to the membrane, as the ramifications found in it are chiefly intended for supplying blood to the bone which it covers.

Nerves.—Small tendons contain no nerves, and large ones only small filaments. In the periosteum, nerves are abundant; they exist there chiefly for supplying the bones with sensibility. The pain caused in rheumatism, which is an intensely painful disease, is a proof of the sensibility of white fibrous tissue.

PHYSIOLOGY OF MUSCLE.

WITH trifling exceptions the whole of the movements of the body and limbs are performed by the agency of that peculiar substance, known in our butchers' shops as "flesh," and recognised by anatomists as muscular tissue. This constitutes the chief bulk of the soft parts external to the three great cavities (the cranial, thoracic, and abdominal), and in the half-starved subject of the knacker or highly-trained race-horse, in which the fat has almost entirely disappeared, the ordinary observer will detect nothing but muscles (with their tendons) and bones beneath the skin covering the limbs. On the trunk they are spread out into layers varying in thickness, sometimes interrupted by flat tendons, so as to form, at the same time, a protection to the organs within, easily capable of extension or contraction, and a means of moving the several parts upon each other.

TENDONS resemble ligamenti in being composed of white fibrous tissue, described at page 268. They serve to connect muscle with bone, and are useful as affording an agent for this purpose of much less compass than muscle itself, and also of a structure not so easily injured by external violence. Thus they are generally met with around the joints, the muscular substance chiefly occupying the space between them. There are three varieties of tendon—1. *Funicular*, consisting of cord-like bands; 2. *Fascicular*, including bands of a flatter and more expanded nature; and 3. *Aponeurotic*, which are membranous, and are chiefly met with around the abdomen. The fibres are firmly attached to the bones, which generally present rough surfaces for this purpose, and are also closely incorporated with the periosteum. This union is so strong, that it very rarely gives way; and when extreme violence is used, either the bone itself breaks, or the tendon snaps in its middle. Tendons are non-elastic.

To THE NAKED EYE, an ordinary muscle appears to be composed of a number of small bundles of fibres, arranged in parallel lines, and connected by a fine membrane. These bundles may still further be separated into what seem at first to be elementary fibres; but when placed in the microscope, they are found to be themselves made up of finer fibres united into fasciculi by delicate filaments. These ultimate fibrillæ are polyhedral in section, according to the observations of Mr. Bowman, so as to pack closely together, and are variable in size in different classes and genera of animals. They also differ in appearance, one class presenting stripes while the other is without them. The former includes all the muscles whose movements are under the control of the will as well as those of the heart, and some of the fibres of the œsophagus, while the latter is composed of the muscles investing the stomach, intestines, bladder, &c., which are comprehended under the general term involuntary.

THE SARCOLEMMA is the name given by Mr. Bowman to the areolar tissue investing each fibre, sometimes also called *myolemma*. It is very delicate and transparent, but tough and elastic; in general it has no appearance of any specific structure, but sometimes it presents an aspect as if there was an interweaving of filaments

WHEN A FIBRILLA of striated muscle is examined under the microsc pe of a high magnifying power, it is seen to present a beaⁿ . appearance as if made up of a linear aggregation of dis-tⁱ . cells, alternately light and dark When the fibrilla is axed, each cell is longer than it is broad; but, during the .... .ⁿf ᵗhe muscle, it assumes the opposite dimensions, the increase ... ..ⁿᵢ .ⁿr being always in ⁿⁿoportion to th diminution of tⁱ the contraction takes ⁿlaceᴍᵗ.ⁿsubstance becomes ...er than before, but the bⁱⁱlk ...mains the same, the mass merely gaining in thickness. wha it has lost in length. The application of certain stimulating aⁿents will produce the contraction for a certain period afte. life iⁿ destroyed, varying according to the vitality of the anⁱⁿ l (ⁱⁱⁱ .mented upon and the nature of the indivⁱ l muⁿ Thⁱⁱs called *irritability* in the striated ...usⁱ whicⁱ .bit pow ful contractions, alternating with re-lⁱⁱxⁱⁱtic -w in the ...voluntary muscles a more steady, permᵤᵗⁱⁱ ... lerate contraction is met with, to which the name of *tⁱ* ... as .ⁿⁱⁱ .ⁱⁱ ⁱ.

PURE ⁱUSⁱUIⁱR ⁱ ⁱRE appears to be identical in composition

with the fibrine of the blood, being made up of about seventy-seven parts water, fifteen and a half parts fibrine, and seven and a half parts of fixed salts. The whole of the flesh of the body is largely supplied with blood, and it is found by experiment, on the one hand, that if this is cut off contraction ceases very speedily after; and on the other, that in proportion to the amount of muscular action will be the demand for fresh supplies of blood. None of the striated muscles, except of the heart and the muscles of respiration, can go on acting without intervals of rest, during which, repairs in their structure are effected. If, therefore, the voluntary muscles are to be brought into the highest state of vigor and development of size, they must be regularly exercised and rested at proper intervals. During the former condition blood is attracted to them, and at the same time that fluid itself is rendered more fit for the purposes of nutrition; while, during the latter period, the increased flow of blood continuing allows for a complete reparation of the tissues. Thus we find the muscles of the well-trained racehorse full and firm to the touch; but if sufficient intervals of rest are not allowed between his gallops, they will present a very different feel, being flabby and wasted, and indicating that he has been "overmarked."

THE VOLUNTARY muscles assume various shapes, according to their positions and offices. Sometimes they are merely long strips of muscular tissue, with a very short tendon at each end, as in the levator humeri, and are then called *fusiform*. At others their fibres radiate as in the latissimus dorsi, which is thence called a *radiating* muscle. A third set are called *penniform*, from their fibres being attached to one side of a tendon, or *bipenniform*, when they are fixed to both sides like the full tail or wing feather of a bird. A muscle with two masses of its tissue connected in the middle by a tendon is called *digastric*.

IN DESCRIBING EACH MUSCLE, it is usual to speak of it as having an *origin* from one bone, or set of bones, and an *insertion* another, the former term being generally assigned fixed division of the This is, however, mere of convenience, and is entirely arbitrary.

BURSÆ MUCOSÆ, which are shut sacs, varying in size from that of a pea to a moderate pear, and lined with synovial membrane, are placed on all the prominent points of bone over which tendons glide. Thus there is a large one at the point of the hock, and another on the elbow, both of which inflame and become filled with synovia, constituting the states known as capped hock and elbow. A third situation is just above the sesamoid bones, where the swelling from inflammation bears the name of windgall. Where, as in the legs, the tendons have to glide to a great extent, they are invested with SYNOVIAL SHEATHS, which are bound down by white fibrous tissue at the points where the strain is the greatest. In the LIMBS the muscles are bound up into masses by strong but thin layers of intercrossed white fibrous tissue, which receives the name of FASCIA. In the horse this is very firmly attached to the surface of the muscles beneath, and greatly interferes with the clean dissection of them.

CHAPTER XVI.

THE THORAX.

Contents of the Thorax—The Blood—General Plan of the Circulation—The Veins—Physiology of Respiration.

CONTENTS OF THE THORAX.

THE THORAX, OR CHEST, is that cavity formed by the bodies of the dorsal vertebræ superiorly; by the ribs and their cartilages with the connecting muscles laterally; by the sternum inferiorly; by the diaphragm posteriorly, and by the inner margins of the first ribs and body of the first dorsal vertebra anteriorly. It contains the central parts of the important organs of circulation and respiration, and gives passage to the œsophagus, as it connects the pharynx with the stomach. As these lie within it, they are allowed to play freely in performing their functions, by being enveloped by smooth serous membranes, called the *pleura* and the *pericardium*, the latter being also protected by a fibrous layer. A section of the thorax, as shown in the plan, fig 10 will give some idea of the relative situation of those organs and their investments, as well as of the shape of the cavity itself in this direction. The heart is shown at A, lying between the two bags of the pleura, in the space called the *mediastinum*. The lungs are shown at B B, covered by a fine serous membrane (H H), *pleura pulmonalis*, except at their roots,

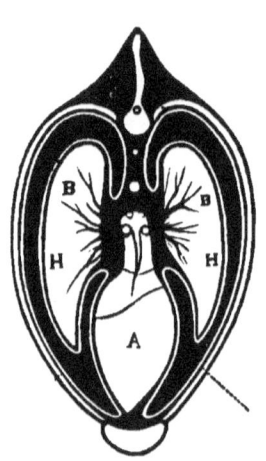

FIG. 10.—SECTIONAL PLAN OF THORAX AND ITS CONTENTS (THROUGHOUT ITS GIRTH-PLACE).
A. Heart.
B. B. Lungs.
C. E. D. F. Walls of the thorax.
G. G. Pleura costalis.
H. H. Pleura pulmonalis.

where the air-tubes and blood-vessels pass into their substance. This portion of the pleura is continuous with the serous membrane lining the ribs (G G, *pleura costalis*), which thus allows them to expand and contract freely, by allowing one surface to glide against the other. Thus, the pleura on each side covering the lungs, and reflected thence to the inside of the ribs, and the thoracic side of the diaphragm, forms a shut sac or bag, which in the natural state contains only sufficient serum to lubricate its walls; but in disease this is often increased to an enormous extent, ending in dropsy of the chest, or in a collection of pus when the membrane is greatly inflamed.

As the walls of the thorax expand by the action of the muscles which move the ribs, as well as by the contraction of the diaphragm, rendering its thoracic surface less convex, the cavity is enlarged and air is drawn in through the trachea, constituting the act of inspiration. On the other hand the contraction of the walls, and the forcing upwards against the diaphragm of the stomach and liver, by the action of the abdominal muscles, reduces the size of the thorax, forces out the air, and induces expiration. The repetition of these two actions is known by the general term respiration.

Before proceeding to describe the heart and lungs, it will be necessary to examine the blood, for transmitting which fluid to all parts of the body the heart and its vessels are formed; while, for its proper aeration, the lungs, windpipe, and larynx, are intended by nature.

THE BLOOD.

THE BLOOD, supplied from the food by the digestive process hereafter to be described, furnishes all the tissues of the body with a constantly renewed stream of the materials which they severally require, whether for their nutrition or for the functions of secretion and excretion performed by the various organs devoted to these purposes. It is necessary, therefore, that this fluid should be composed of elementary matters capable of combining to form the materials required, or of those substances ready prepared. Thus, the muscles demand for their proper action fibrine and oxygen, both of which are largely combined in arterial blood, while the nervous system cannot respond to the calls of its grand centre without having a due supply of fatty matter, also, in combination with the oxygen obtained by respiration, which, however, is not only intended to afford this gas, but also to remove the carbon that would otherwise accumulate to a prejudicial extent. For these several purposes the blood must be supplied with liquid elements by absorption from the digestive organs, and with its oxygen, by imbibition through the delicate membrane lining the lungs on which it is spread as it passes through the system of blood-vessels specially set apart for that purpose. When it is considered that the stomach, bowels, liver, pancreas, and spleen, are all occupied almost solely in supplying the fluid with its grosser materials, and that the heart, lungs, kidneys, and skin, are constantly engaged in circulating it, supplying it with oxygen, and purifying it from noxious salts and gases, its importance in the animal economy may be estimated as it deserves.

As IT CIRCULATES in, or immediately after it is drawn from, its appropriate vessels, the blood consists of an opaque, thickish fluid, composed of water, fibrine, albumen, and various salts, and called *Liquor sanguinis*, colored red, by having suspended in it a quantity of *corpuscles* of a peculiar nature, some being without any color. When drawn from an artery or vein, and allowed to remain at rest for a few minutes, a coagulation takes place, by which the blood is separated into the clot (coagulum) and the serum. The former is composed of fibrine, having entangled in its meshes the corpuscles; and the latter is the liquor sanguinis, without its fibrine. The blood corpuscles of the horse measure about the five-hundredth part of a line in diameter, being considerably larger than those of man, whose diameter is only the four-hundred-and-thirtieth part of a line; those of the ass being still smaller, though only slightly so. As in all of the mammalia but the camels, these bodies are circular flattened discs, and are of the same size (nearly) in all animals of the same species, whatever may be the age or sex. According to Messrs. Prevost and Dumas, the blood of the horse contains less solid matter than that of man, in the proportion of 9.20 to 12.92 in 1000 parts. The temperature is also lower by about two degrees of the centigrade thermometer, the pulse slower in the proportion of 56 to 72, and the respirations 16 per minute against 18 in our own species. The shade of color in the red corpuscles depends upon the proportion of carbonic acid and oxygen combined with them. If the former preponderates, a deep purple-red is developed, known as that of venous blood; while a liberal supply of oxygen develops the bright scarlet peculiar to arterial blood. The saline matters dissolved in the liquor sanguinis consist of the chlorides of sodium and potassium (which comprise more than one-half of the whole salts), the tribasic-phosphate of soda, the phosphates of magnesia and lime, sulphate of soda, and a little of the phosphate and oxyde of iron.

GENERAL PLAN OF THE CIRCULATION.

THE BLOOD IS CIRCULATED through the body, for the purposes of nutrition and secretion, by means of one forcing-pump, and through the lungs, for its proper aeration, by another; the two being united to form the heart. This organ is therefore a compound machine, though the two pumps are joined together, so as to appear to the casual observer to be one single organ. In common language, the heart of the mammalia is said to have two sides, each of which is a forcing-pump; but the blood, before it passes from one side to the other, has to circulate through one or other of the sets of vessels found in the general organs of the body, and in the lungs, as the case may be. This is shown at fig. 11, where the blood, commencing with the capillaries on the general surface at (A), passes through the veins which finally end in the vena cava (B), and enters the right auricle (C). From this it is pumped into (D) the right ventricle, which, contracting in its turn, forces it on into the pulmonary artery (E), spreading out upon the lining membrane of the lungs, to form the capillaries of that organ at F, from which it is returned to the left auricle (G) through the pulmonary veins. From the left auricle it is driven on to the left ventricle; and this, by its powerful contractions, forces the blood through the aorta (I), and the arteries of the whole body, to the capillaries (A), from which the description commenced. But though this organ is thus made up of two pumps, yet they are united into one organ, and the two auricles and two ventricles each contract at the same moment, causing only a double sound to be heard, instead of a quadruple one, when the ear is applied to the chest. In the diagram it will be seen that one-half of the cavities and vessels is shaded, indicating that it contains dark blood, while the other contains blood of a bright red color. But though we commonly call the one venous, and the other arterial, the distinction only applies to the general circulation; for that of the lungs is exactly the reverse, the pulmonary artery (E) containing dark blood, and the pulmonary veins bringing it back to the heart after it is purified, and has again received oxygen sufficient to develop the scarlet color again. Between the auricles and ventricles, and again at the openings of the latter cavities into their respective arteries, valves of a form peculiar to each are placed, so

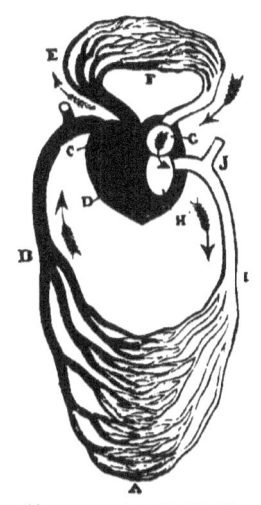

FIG. 11.—PLAN OF THE CIRCULATION.

A. Capillaries on the general surface.
B. Vena cava
C. Right auricle.
D. Right ventricle.
E. Pulmonary artery.
F. Capillaries of the lungs, uniting to form the pulmonary veins, which enter
G. The left auricle.
H. The left ventricle.
I. The aorta posterior, dividing into smaller arteries, and united with the capillaries at A.
J. The trunk of the aorta anterior.

as to allow of the free passage onwards of the blood, but not of its return by regurgitation. If they become diseased, the action of the heart is impeded, and the circulation of the blood is more or less seriously interfered with. So, also, if the muscular fibres, of which the walls of the auricles and in much thicker layers of the ventricles, are composed, become weak by want of proper exercise, or from the deposit of fat in their interspaces, a corresponding degree of mischief is effected in the passage of the blood. The force with which the left ventricle contracts may be estimated from the fact, that if a pipe is inserted in the carotid artery of a horse, and held perpendicularly, the blood will rise in it to a height of ten feet; and the rapidity of his circulation is such, that a saline substance will pass from the veins of the upper part of the body to those of the lower in little more than twenty seconds. Now, as this transmission can only take place through the current that returns to the heart, and passes thence through the lungs and back again, afterwards being forced into the lower vessels through the aorta, it follows that every particle of this fluid passes completely through the whole circulation in the above short period of time.

THE VEINS.

THE VEINS generally correspond with the arteries, the blood of which they return to the heart. Thus, there is a large vein which conveys all the blood from the anterior half of the body supplied by the anterior aorta, and this is called *vena cava anterior*. In a similar manner the *posterior vena cava* is made up of veins which accompany the several arteries that are found throughout the body, with one remarkable exception connected with the secretion of bile.

ALTHOUGH, IN GENERAL, the veins and arteries correspond in their ramifications, yet there is a large class of superficial veins which are not accompanied by any of the latter vessels. In horses which for many generations have been accustomed to fast work, these superficial veins are strongly developed, and are particularly plain in the Arab and his descendants. As a consequence of this, and of the fact that many of the arteries are accompanied by two veins, the whole number of veins is much greater than that of the arteries, and the internal area of the former may be considered to be nearly double that of the latter. In their walls the veins are much thinner than the arteries, though, like them, they have three coats, the serous and cellular being very similar in structure, but the fibrous is very much thinner and devoid of muscular fibres. A feature peculiar to the veins is the existence of valves, which are sometimes single, at others double, and occasionally arranged in threes and fours around the interior of the large veins. They vary in numbers, and are altogether absent in the pulmonary veins, in the venæ cavæ, and the vena portæ.

PHYSIOLOGY OF RESPIRATION.

THE ESSENCE of the act of breathing consists in the absorption of oxygen from the air, and the excretion of carbonic acid from the blood which is circulated through it. In a state of rest this interchange must go on with regularity, for carbonic acid is constantly developed by the decay of the tissues, arising from the peculiar necessities of the muscular and nervous tissues, and by the conversion of the carbon of the food which appears to be required for the development of heat. But when the muscles of the whole body are called into play with unusual rapidity and force, the development of carbonic acid is largely augmented, and thus, not only is there a necessity for extra means of excreting the carbonic acid, but there is also a demand for more oxygen to unite with the carbon, which is the result of the disintegration of the muscular fibres employed. Hence the acts of respiration are more complete and rapid during exercise than in a state of rest, and while much more carbonic acid is given off, a greater volume of oxygen is absorbed from the air which is inspired.

IT IS FOUND BY EXPERIMENT that if venous blood is exposed to the action of oxygen, through a thin membrane such as bladder, it absorbs a portion of that gas, and changes its color from dark red to a bright scarlet. This is in accordance with the recognised laws of endosmose and exosmose; and as the blood circulates in very fine streams within the vessels of the lungs, whose walls are much thinner than an ordinary bladder, it may readily be understood that it is placed in more favorable circumstances for this interchange of gases than when tied up in a large mass within a comparatively thick membrane. On examining the structure of the lungs, they are found to be made up of a pair of cellular sacs, communicating with the trachea, which admits air into them; and these sacs are furnished with a fine network of capillary vessels distributed on their walls, and on those of the numerous cellular partitions of which they are composed. Thus the blood, as it enters the lungs in a venous state, is submitted under very favorable circumstances to the agency of atmospheric air; it readily absorbs the oxygen while it gives off large volumes of carbonic acid gas, the result of the combination of previously absorbed oxygen with the carbon given off by the various organs of the body already alluded to.

THE EXACT CHEMICAL CHANGES which have taken place in the atmospheric air exhaled from the lungs and in the blood itself are believed to be as follows: 1. A certain portion of oxygen has disappeared from the air. 2. It has received a considerable volume of carbonic acid. 3. It has absorbed fresh nitrogen. 4. It has parted with some of the nitrogen of which it was previously made up. The last two changes cannot readily be demonstrated, but are inferred from the fact that, under varying conditions of the body, the nitrogen in the exhaled air may be either above or below the proper proportional. Besides these, the air also receives a considerable quantity of moisture, and some organic matters, which in certain cases are largely increased. The changes in the blood are not so fully known; but it is now the general opinion of physiologists that the formation of carbonic acid does not take place in the lungs, but that the blood arrives there surcharged with it already made, and not with carbon, as was formerly believed. The action chiefly consists in the excretion of this carbonic acid, and in the absorption of oxygen, which is stored up for the several purposes for which it is required in the course of its circulation through the body. Magnus demonstrated by experiment that arterial and venous blood contain very different quantities of carbonic acid, oxygen, and nitrogen in a free state, for on obtaining, by means of the air-pump, a volume of the gas contained in each kind of blood, and analyzing them, he found them to be made up as follows:—

	Arterial.	Venous.
Carbonic acid	62·3	71·6
Oxygen	23·2	15 3
Nitrogen	14·5	13·1

It appears, therefore, that in passing through the capillaries, the gas in the arterial blood loses about eight per cent. of oxygen, and receives about nine per cent. of carbonic acid, which action is reversed as it passes through the lungs.

CHAPTER XVII.

THE ABDOMINAL AND PELVIC VISCERA.

The Abdomen and its Contents—Physiology of Digestion—Absorption—Structure of Glands and Physiology of Secretion—Depuration and its Office in the Animal Economy—The Stomach—The Intestines—Liver—Spleen—Pancreas—Kidney—Pelvis—Bladder—Organs of Generation, Male and Female.

THE ABDOMEN AND ITS CONTENTS.

LYING IMMEDIATELY BEHIND THE THORAX, from which they are separated only by the diaphragm, are the important organs of digestion, and the space in which they are closely packed is called the abdomen. This part is capable of being distended downwards and sideways to an enormous extent, or of contracting till the lower walls approach very closely to the upper. The anterior boundary, as before remarked, is the diaphragm, the plane of which moves considerably in active respiration, causing the flanks, or posterolateral walls of the abdomen, to rise and fall, in a corresponding manner, and thus to indicate the extent of distress in an exhausted animal, or any peculiarity of breathing, as in "broken wind," or in the several inflammatory conditions of the lungs. Posteriorly, the boundary is an open one, being the anterior boundary of the pelvis, and corresponding with the brim of that cavity. Superiorly are the crura of the diaphragm, the lumbar vertebræ, and psoas and iliacus muscles; and laterally, as well as inferiorly, the abdominal muscles, and cartilages of the false ribs. Although the abdominal muscles are capable of great dilatation, yet in the natural condition they maintain a gentle curve only from their pelvic to their costal attachments, and hence the depth and width of the back-ribs and pelvis are the measure of the ordinary capacity of the abdomen. Shallow and narrow back-ribs give a small abdominal cavity, and generally speaking, a correspondingly weak condition of the digestive organs; for though this rule is not invariable, yet it is one which may be held as a sufficient guide for practical purposes. Instances do occur of stout and hearty horses possessed of contracted middle pieces, but they are so rare as to be merely objects of curiosity. The small space which is devoted to the organs of digestion in the horse whose back ribs are shallow will be readily understood by reference to the annexed section, in which the enormous mass of intestines and the liver have been removed, leaving only the stomach and spleen. When the walls of the abdomen are distended laterally and downwards, as they always are in horses at grass, the capacity of the abdomen is at least doubled.

THE CONTENTS OF THE ABDOMEN are the stomach, the liver, the pancreas, the spleen, the small and large intestines, the mesenteric glands and chyliferous ducts, and the kidneys, together with their vessels and nerves. Some of these organs are fixed close to the spine, as the kidneys and pancreas; but the others glide upon each other as they are alternately empty or full, and to facilitate this motion they are (like the lungs) invested with a serous coat, *the peritoneum.* They may be divided into the hollow organs, which form one continuous tube (the alimentary), and the solid viscera, which, with the exception of the spleen, are all of a glandular structure, though differing in their minute anatomy. The alimentary canal consists throughout of three distinct layers: the external serous coat (*peritoneal*), the middle or *muscular coat*, and the internal *mucous* coat, which are united by cellular membrane, sometimes regarded as forming two distinct additional coats.

PHYSIOLOGY OF DIGESTION.

BEFORE PROCEEDING TO EXAMINE into the anatomy of the abdominal organs, it may be well to investigate the nature of the processes which are carried out by them. To do this, the food must be traced from its prehension by the lips and teeth to its expulsion from the anus. Thus, commencing with the mouth, we find it there ground into a coarse pulp, and mixed with the saliva, which acts as a kind of *ferment* in converting the starchy matters, which form so large a proportion of the horse's food, into sugar, and, with the aid of the gastric juice, into the proteine compounds necessary for the formation of flesh. Perfect mastication and insalivation are therefore highly important processes to healthy digestion. When it reaches the stomach, the food undergoes still further changes by the agency of the gastric juice and of maceration; but this organ being small in the horse, it cannot remain there long enough to be converted into perfect *chyme* (the result of the first process of digestion), but is passed on into the duodenum for that purpose. Here it is further elaborated, and receives the bile and pancreatic juice, which are poured out through their ducts opening on the internal surface of this intestine. The nutricious parts of the food are now gradually converted into *chyle;* and as it passes into the jejunum and ilium, it is there absorbed by the lymphatics (here called *lacteals*), whose mouths open upon the villi thickly lining this part of the canal. These unite into one duct (the *thoracic*), and the chyle is by it carried into the veins through an opening at the junction of the left vena cava anterior, with the allary vein. From the small intestines, the food, minus its nutritive portions, is passed on into the large intestines, and finally reaches the rectum and anus, in the form known as fæces. The peculiar offices performed by the bile and pancreatic fluid will be described under the sections treating of each of those organs.

THE ABSORPTION OF FLUID from the interior of the alimentary canal is effected in two different modes—first, by the lacteals, which take up the chyle through their open mouths; secondly, by the veins, which absorb it through their walls by the process known as endosmose. In the former case the chyle is at once carried to the heart; but in the latter, it passes through the liver, and becomes purified and chemically altered in that organ. The lacteals pass through the mesenteric glands, which lie between the layers of the mesentery.

STRUCTURE OF GLANDS AND PHYSIOLOGY OF SECRETION.

A GLAND may be defined to be an organ whose office it is to separate from the blood some peculiar substance, which is poured out through an excretory duct, whose internal surface is continuous with the mucous membrane, or skin. A simple gland is, in fact, nothing more than a pouch of mucous membrane; and a collection of these pouches constitutes a compound one, which, if the groups of which it is composed are loosely bound together like grapes, as in the salivary glands, is called *conglomerate;* while, if they are united into a solid mass, such as the liver, the term *conglobate* is applied.

BY SECRETION is understood the process of separation of various matters from the blood; the term being also applied to the products of the process, such as saliva, bile, &c , which are commonly known as secretions. These are all removed from the blood for one or two purposes—first, in order to be employed for some ulterior object in the various processes going on in the body, either for its own preservation, or that of others; or, secondly, as being injurious to its welfare, and therefore to be discarded. The term secretion is sometimes confined to the former, while the latter action receives the distinguishing term *excretion :* but as in many cases the fluid which is removed as being injurious to the system is also used for beneficial purposes the distinction is not capable of being strictly maintained. The nature of the process is essentially the same in all cases, being carried out by the development of simple cells, each possessing its own independent vitality. These cells select certain ingredients from the blood, and then set them free by the rupture of their walls; and being situated on the free surface of the lining membrane of the gland, which is continuous with the mucous membrane or skin, the secreted fluid gradually reaches the one or the other. It is impossible, at present, to ascertain the precise means by which each gland is made up of cells having special powers of selection; but that the fact is so, is capable of demonstration. Thus, the cells of the liver select the elements of bile; those of the salivary glands, saliva; and so on. But, as we shall hereafter find, there are minute points of difference in the arrangement of these cells in the different glands. It is now ascertained that the elements of the various secretions exist in the blood; and therefore the office of the glands is confined to the selection and separation of their products, and they have little or nothing to do with their conversion.

DEPURATION, AND ITS OFFICE IN THE ANIMAL ECONOMY.

THE WHOLE OF THE VARIOUS SECRETIONS which go on in the body are necessary for the due preservation of its health; but the most important of the class alluded to above as *excretions*, must be removed from the blood or death will speedily ensue. Thus, if saliva and gastric juice, as well as the other secretions aiding digestion, are not mixed with the food, the nutrition of the body will be imperfectly carried on, and its health will suffer. But if the element of bile and urine are retained in the blood, not only is the system upset, but absolute death is produced in severe cases. Hence it follows, that attention to the state of the organs of depuration, or excretion, is of more importance even to those of secretion, using these terms in the sense explained in the last paragraph. The chief organs of depuration are the lungs, which remove carbon from the blood; the liver, which secretes the bile; the kidneys which get rid of the urea; and the skin, which relieves it of its superfluous watery and some small proportion of its solid particles. Experiment shows that the retention of carbon, or urea, in the blood is speedily followed by death; while the non-secretion of bile, if entire, poisons the system; and in milder cases, its absence from the alimentary canal interferes with the due elaboration of the chyle.

THE STOMACH.

THE STOMACH is situated on the left side of the abdominal cavity, immediately behind the diaphragm. It resembles in shape the bag of the Scotch bag-pipes, having two openings, two curvatures (a lesser and a greater), two surfaces, and two sacs, which are generally divided by a constriction. Its volume varies with its contents, but in the horse of average size it will not contain more than three gallons, while the stomach of man, whose weight is only one-eighth that of the horse, holds three quarts.

THE INTESTINES.

THE INTESTINES, large and small, constitute a hollow tube, very variable in diameter, and measuring from eighty to ninety feet in length in an average-sized horse. They extend from the stomach to the anus; and though nature has only divided them into two portions, the small and large, yet anatomists have subdivided each of these into three more, namely, duodenum, jejunum, and ileum —cœcum, colon, and rectum.

THE SMALL INTESTINES are about seventy feet long, and vary from an inch to an inch and a half in diameter, except at their commencement, where there is a considerable dilatation, forming a sort of ventriculus or lesser stomach. They are gathered up into folds, in consequence of the mesentery, which attaches them to the superior walls of the abdomen, being of very limited extent as compared with their length; and thus they may be described as presenting two curves, a lesser mesenteric curvature, and an outer or free one covered by the peritoneum. The outer layer of the muscular coat consists only of a few and scattered fibres, while the inner one is circular in its arrangement, and though thin as compared with the stomach, yet it is easily distinguished. The mucous coat is gathered into a few longitudinal folds when empty, which are very marked at its commencement; but there are no valvular appendages as in the human intestines. It is everywhere studded with *villi* or little projections, like the pile of velvet, through the open mouths of which the chyle is taken up, and beneath it are numerous glands named after their discoverers.

THE LARGE INTESTINES, as their name implies, are of much greater diameter than the small; but they are not above one-third of their length. Instead of being convoluted, they are puckered into pouches by a peculiar arrangement of the longitudinal muscular fibres, which are collected into bundles or cords, and being shorter than the intestine, gather it up into cells. The mucous membrane also has very few villi, which become more and more rare towards the rectum.

THE LIVER.

THIS IMPORTANT ORGAN is in close contact with the right side of the diaphragm. It is of an irregular figure thick in the middle and thin at the edges; divided into three lobes; convex on its anterior surface, where it is adapted to the concave aspect of the diaphragm; concave posteriorly. The color is that which is so well known, and peculiar to itself. It is everywhere invested by the peritoneum, excepting the spaces occupied by the large veins as they enter and pass out, and the coronary ligament which suspends it, as well as the three other folds of peritoneum, which have also received particular names.

THE FUNCTION of the liver is doubtless chiefly of a depuratory nature, but the soapy nature of the bile seems to be destined to aid in dissolving the fatty materials which are contained in the food, and to stimulate the intestines to perform their duties.

THE SPLEEN.

THE SPLEEN can scarcely be considered as a gland, inasmuch as it has no excretory duct, but it contains within its substance a number of little bodies, called Malpighian corpuscles, which most probably perform the same office as the absorbent glands. Its weight as compared with the whole body is about the same as in man, whose spleen weighs six ounces, while that of the horse rarely exceeds three pounds. It is attached by the lesser omentum (a fold of the peritoneum) to the stomach, and occupies the left side of that organ. It is covered by a serous coat continuous with the peritoneum, and its internal structure is spongy, and made up of cells which contain a large quantity of blood.

THE FUNCTION of the spleen is not positively ascertained, but it is believed to perform the office of a reservoir for the blood required by the stomach, with which it is closely connected by a set of vessels (vasa brevia), and also to effect some change in the blood itself.

THE PANCREAS.

The pancreas is an elongated gland resembling in structure the salivary glands, placed close to the spine, above the stomach. It has two excretory ducts, which carry the pancreatic fluid secreted by it into the duodenum through a valvular opening common to it and the hepatic duct. The use of the pancreatic fluid appears to be similar to that of the saliva.

THE KIDNEYS.

The kidneys are two oval organs situated beneath the psoas muscles, and only retained in their position by the fatty cellular membrane which envelops them, and by the upward pressure of the other abdominal viscera below them. The right kidney is completely within the ribs, but the left scarcely advances at all beyond the eighteenth rib: each averages about forty ounces in weight, but there is a considerable variation in size and form. Unlike the corresponding organ in the cow, the horse's kidney is not split up into lobules, though there is some little irregularity of outline and surface.

THE PELVIS.

The cavity of the body known as the pelvis is situated behind the abdomen, with which it communicates freely, each being lined by a continuation of the peritoneum. A ridge of bone (the brim of the pelvis) is the line of demarcation anteriorly. The sacrum and os coccygis bound it superiorly, the anus posteriorly, and the ossa innominata inferiorly and laterally. It contains the bladder and rectum in both sexes, and in each the organs of generation peculiar to it.

THE BLADDER.

The bladder is a musculo-membranous bag destined to contain the urine as it is gradually received from the ureters, which bring it down from the kidneys. It lies in the middle of the pelvis, occupying also more or less of the abdomen according to its condition in point of repletion or emptiness. It is of an oval shape, with its posterior extremity somewhat more pointed than the other, and called its neck. At this point it gives origin to the urethra, a canal for carrying off the urine. It receives the two ureters at its superior surface, about an inch in front of the neck, where they pierce the several coats in an oblique direction forming a complete valve which prevents the return of the urine, and so invisible that the presence of two openings is scarcely ever suspected by the ordinary observer. Only about one-third of the bladder is covered by the peritoneum, the remainder being made up solely of the muscular and mucous coats which compose all the hollow viscera. It is retained in its place by the cellular membrane which connects it with the lower walls of the pelvis, posteriorly by the urethra, and by the folds of the peritoneum which are continued from it to the sides of the pelvis, and are called the broad ligaments of the bladder.

THE ORGANS OF GENERATION, MALE AND FEMALE.

THE MALE ORGANS OF GENERATION consist of the testes and their ducts the vasa deferentia, the latter conveying the semen to the urethra or to the vesiculæ seminales, which are oval bags connected with the upper surface of the neck of the bladder. Here the seminal fluid is stored up for use, and when wanted is conveyed into the vagina by means of the external organ or penis. The anatomy of the testicles is that which mainly concerns the horsemaster, as they are generally removed by operation. They are contained within the scrotum, which is externally composed of skin wrinkled in the foal, but subsequently distended by the size and weight of its contents. Beneath this is a layer of a pale yellowish fibrous membrane called the dartos, which envelops the testes and forms a separation between them. A thin coat of cellular membrane alone separates this from the double serous membrane, the tunica vaginalis, which almost entirely envelops each testis just as the pleura does the lung. In the early stages of fœtal life the testes are contained within the abdomen above the peritoneum, but being attached to the scrotum by a thin muscle (the cremaster) they are gradually dragged downwards through the inguinal canal and each brings a double layer of peritoneum, which continues its connection through life, so that fluid injected into the cavity of the tunica vaginalis will flow into the peritoneum. Hence inguinal hernia in the horse becomes scrotal in a very short space of time, and rarely remains confined to the former position. The testicles with their appendages, the vesiculæ seminales, form the semen by the usual process of secretion. They are of about the size of a duck's egg, and besides their attachment by the reflexions of the tunica vaginalis to the scrotum, they have also the spermatic cord which suspends them to the inguinal canal through which it passes. This cord it is which is divided in castration, and it is well to ascertain its component parts. They are, 1st. The artery which supplies the testicles with blood, and is of considerable size and tortuous in its course. 2d. The artery of the cord, small and unimportant. 3d. The veins which accompany these arteries. 4th. The nerves and absorbents, the division of the former giving great pain and causing a slight shock to the system. 5th. The vas deferens or duct carrying the semen to the urethra, and possessing walls of such thickness that it feels like whipcord under the finger. These several parts are connected together by cellular membrane and covered by the two layers of reflected peritoneum, namely, the tunica vaginalis and tunica vaginalis reflexa, by the thin layer of cremaster muscle, as well as by a fourth investment, a continuation of the superficial fascia of the abdomen. All these parts must be divided before the canal is reached, for operating in castration.

THE FEMALE ORGANS OF GENERATION are essentially the ovaries, the uterus and its appendages forming the bed in which the embryo is nurtured to maturity. The ovaries are two small oval bodies, about the size of large walnuts, situated behind the kidneys, and having the fimbriated extremities of the fallopian tubes hanging loosely adjacent to them. These tubes, one on each side, terminate in the uterus, which is of a remarkable shape in the mare. It consists of a body and two horns. The body has a mouth, or *os*, which opens into the end of the vagina, while, in itself, it is oblong, and in the unimpregnated state it is entirely contained within the pelvis. Anteriorly it divides into two horns (cornua), which diverge towards the loins, turning upwards, and lying under the wings of the ossa ilii (see fig. facing p. 251). They terminate in rounded extremities. Each cornu receives the fallopian tube of its own side, the opening being so small as scarcely to admit a silver probe. The vagina lies between the bladder and rectum, and is about eighteen inches in length; it is lined with mucous membrane, and surrounded with muscular fibres, which form the sphincter vaginæ.

CHAPTER XVIII.

THE NERVES AND SPECIAL ORGANS.

The Nerves—The Organ of Smell—The Eye—The Ear— The Organ of Touch—The Foot.

THE NERVES.

THE NERVOUS SYSTEM may be compared to the fuel that heats the water of the steam-engine, and converts that apparently most simple and innocent fluid into the powerful agent which is capable of developing almost any amount of force. This fuel, however, is itself inactive until it is endowed with life by the agency of fire; and, in the same way, the nervous system of the animal being must be provided with the living principle, of whose nature we can only judge by its effects when present, and by the cessation of all action when absent. There are many processes which are carried on in the animal as in the vegetable without the necessity for any direct stimulus from a nervous centre, such as the growth of each separate tissue throughout the body, which takes place in the former, just as it does in the latter, by a species of cell-development and metamorphosis independent of nervous energy; but though this growth is thus accomplished, yet it would soon be starved out for want of pabulum, were it not for the supply of food to the stomach, which requires the mandate of the nervous system for its performance, and so on with every corresponding action of the body.

THE NERVOUS SYSTEM is made up of two distinct substances, one grey in color, and granular in structure, which is the seat of all nervous power; the other white and fibrous, which is the telegraph wire by which this power is communicated. Sometimes the grey matter envelops the white, and at others it is enclosed within it, but in every case each has its peculiar office, as above mentioned. Each collection of grey matter is called a ganglion, whatever its shape may be; but the white fibres may be either in the form of commissures for connecting the ganglia together, or they may be agents for communicating with other organs, and are then called nerves.

THE ORGAN OF SMELL.

THE NOSE of the horse, like all the solipedes, is endowed with a sensibility far greater than that of man; but in this respect he is not equal to many other animals, such as the dog and cat kinds, and the sole use which he makes of this sense is in the selection of his food.

THE EYE.

THE ORGAN OF SIGHT may be considered as consisting first of all of an optical instrument very similar to the camera obscura, now so commonly used in photography, and secondly of the parts which are employed to move, adjust, and protect it from injury.

THE EYE itself consists of three transparent humors, which answer the purpose of the lens of the camera, by collecting the rays of light upon the back of the eye. These are the aqueous in front, the crystalline lens in the middle, and the vitreous humor behind. The first is a perfectly transparent and limpid fluid, secreted by the lining of the chamber in which it lies, and capable of being rapidly renewed in case of a puncture letting it out. The lens, on the contrary, has the consistence of very hard jelly, and is arranged in concentric layers, like the coats of an onion. It is merely a double convex lens, precisely like that of the camera in its action, and is the chief agent in producing the impression of an object upon the sensitive part of the eye. Behind it is the vitreous humor, composed, like the aqueous, of a limpid fluid, but instead of being unconfined except by the walls of the chamber in which it lies, it is bound up in a network of transparent cells, which give it the consistency and appearance of a delicate jelly. Upon the perfect transparency and proper shape of these humors depends the sight of the animal; but in addition to the risk of blindness from any defect in these parts, if the investing coats or membranes are inflamed or disorganized, their functions are not performed, and the sight is either impaired or destroyed. Thus the rays of light may be fairly collected, so as to throw the impression of every object within the sphere of vision upon the back of the eye, and yet the horse may be blind, because the retina or expansion of the optic nerve is disorganized by disease. When inflammation attacks the coats of the eye, it generally extends to the investments of the humors, and to the substance of the lens itself, producing cataract or opacity of that part, but it is possible to have the sight impaired from a mere defect of shape in the anterior coat, so as to make the surface too convex and thus alter the focus of the sight. This is the "buck-eye," which leads to shying, and is perfectly incurable. The membranes are, *first*, the cornea, a perfectly transparent coat, placed in front of the eye, and inserted, like a watch glass, in the schlerotic coat covering the posterior four-fifths of the globe. The latter is a white fibrous membrane, strong and inelastic, so as to afford protection to the parts within it from external violence. This forms the white of the eye, which, however, is only occasionally visible in the horse. Beneath the schlerotic is the choroid coat, consisting of a network of blood vessels, and lined with a black pigment, which again has on its internal surface, at the part opposite the pupil, a greenish-white iridiscent lining, called tapetum lucidum, or luminous carpet. Lastly, within the whole of this surface is spread a beautiful expansion of the optic nerve, called the retina, which receives the impressions derived from the rays of light, forming a distinct figure upon it exactly similar to the objects which are presented to it, except in point of size, and in being inverted. Beyond these parts, there is a provision made for moderating the rays of light according to their intensity. This is effected by means of an opaque septum, pierced with an oval hole—the former being called the iris, and the latter the pupil. The substance of the iris itself is composed of contractile tissue, which has the power of expanding or contracting the pupil in obedience to the impression produced upon the retina, and thus, if the eye is examined in a strong light, the pupil will appear large when shaded by the hand, but contracts immediately on exposing the eye. The horse's iris is brown, varying somewhat in shade in different individuals, and at the upper part of the pupil it presents one or two little floating appendages, which serve to moderate the sun's rays. Sometimes the brown color is absent, and the iris is either partially or entirely white, in which case it is called a "wall eye;" but though this is considered unsightly, it does not interfere with vision. The iris is stretched across the chamber of the aqueous humor, and is thus enabled to act freely. There are many other delicate structures worthy of being examined, but want of space must prevent any further allusion to them.

THE APPENDAGES of the eye are 1st. The conjunctiva or membrane protecting the exposed surface of the eye. 2d. The eyelids. 3d. The membrana nictitans or haw. 4th. The muscles of the eye. 5th. The lacrymal apparatus. *The conjunctiva* covers the whole front of the eye, being thin, and perfectly transparent in a healthy state, but on the occurrence of inflammation speedily becoming red and puffy. It is reflected from this face to the inside of the eyelids, and the whole membrane is extremely liable to inflammation from any external irritation. The *eyelids* have nothing very remarkable about them, being merely cartilaginous shutters covered with fine skin, and lined with conjunctiva, and raised and lowered by muscles peculiar to them. The *membrana nictitans* or haw is a cartilage lying just within the inner corner of the eye, but capable of being thrust outwards so as to partially cover it when the muscles retract the eye, and for want of space drive it forward. This happens whenever the eye is irritated either by an insect, or by the dust or hayseeds which are so often deposited upon the conjunctiva, and which, causing the eye to be drawn back, displace the fat deposited in the back of the orbit, and this again pushes forward the haw. For this reason, in all irritable states of the eye, the haw is prominent, but it by no means follows that its removal will diminish the irritation; on the contrary, the usual effect is to increase it, and the operation is not only useless, but injurious. The *muscles* move the eye in all directions, and have the peculiar property of keeping the long diameter of the pupil always nearly in a line parallel with the horizon. Practically they are not of any great importance. The *lacrymal apparatus* consists of the lacrymal gland, situated beneath the outer wall of the orbit, and secreting the tears, which are intended to wash the conjunctiva clear of any foreign body. The secretion is thrown out upon its surface through a number of small ducts, and, traversing from the outer angle to the inner, is conducted through two small openings in the lids to the lacrymal sac, and from that by the nasal duct to the nose.

THE EAR.

THIS ORGAN is divided into the external ear for collecting the waves of sound, and conveying them inwards, and the internal ear which is situated within the petrous part of the temporal bone.

The latter is a very complicated and delicate organ; but its formation does not differ in any essential features from that of the other vertebrate animals, nor are the diseases attacking it in the horse of any particular importance, so that its description will be omitted.

THE ORGAN OF TOUCH.

THE SENSE OF TOUCH is necessary for the proper appreciation of the mechanical form and nature of the objects placed in apposition to the body, and of their temperature. It is seated generally in the terminations of the nerves of sensation on the skin; but there are certain parts specially endowed with these nerves, which in the horse are the lips and the four extremities.

EVERY PART OF THE SKIN is sensible to impressions from external objects, but the sense of touch, such as we possess in the fingers, can only be said to reside in the lips, and partially in the feet. All these parts are profusely supplied with nerves of sensation, and the horse may often be observed to use them in examining external objects, especially his lips, which are the most delicate of his organs of touch. Mr. Rarey has lately drawn special attention to this subject; but it has long been known to those who are familiar with the habits of the horse. The feet are also largely supplied with nerves, though not to the same extent as the human fingers, and being covered with horny matter, the sensibility of the surface is greatly reduced; still there can be no doubt that the horse uses them occasionally in making out the nature of objects presented to him, and this is especially the case with the fore feet, though it will sometimes happen that the hind extremities are used for the same purpose, as for instance, in ascertaining the nature of a hard body before kicking at it.

THE FOOT.

IT IS NECESSARY TO EXAMINE the structure of the foot most carefully, not as an object of curiosity connected with the sense of touch, but on account of the numberless diseases and accidents to which it is subject. No part of the horse is so liable to the effects of hard work and mismanagement as this, and there is consequently none which more requires our care both in health and disease.

THE PARTS, entering into the composition of the foot, will be better understood by a reference to the annexed section of the phalanges or fingers terminating the metacarpal or metatarsal bones, as the case may be, with their investments. It will be seen that there is very little space between the pedal bone and the crust, which, together with the sole, forms a horny case or natural shoe, for the sensible and delicate investments of the bone. So small is this space, that when inflammation takes place

THE FOOT.

FIG. 12—SECTION OF THE PARTS ENTERING INTO THE COMPOSITION OF THE FOOT AND THE PETLOCK AND PASTERN JOINTS.

A. Os suffraginis.
B. Os coronæ.
C. Os pedis.
D. Os naviculare.
E. E. The perforans and perforatus tendons.
G. Inferior sesamoideal ligament.
H. Cleft of frog.
I. Side of frog cleft.
J. Sole.
K. Crust.
L. Coronary substance.

there is no room for any swelling (the invariable accompaniment of that disease), and intense pain is occasioned, as well as rapid disorganization of the structure itself. The horny case is attached to the foot by a delicate membrane, which lies in folds upon the pedal bone, and it can be torn away by violence, or when putrefaction has commenced, with great ease. These parts are separately displayed. The several parts which we shall have to examine, commencing from without, are—1. The horny case or hoof; 2. The parts which secrete it; 3. The arteries which supply it with blood; and 4. The pedal bone and cartilages, as well as the navicular bone, which it encases.

THE HOOF consists of three distinct parts, which, though in the recent state they are inseparably united, may be readily separated after maceration for a few days. These are the external wall or crust, the sole or slightly concave surface forming the bottom or floor of the case, and the triangular central portion of this called the frog. The *crust* reaches from the edge of the hairy skin to the ground, and averages about three inches and a half in depth.

The front is the toe, the back the heel, and the intermediate part the quarter on each side. It is said by Bracy Clark to be a segment of a cylinder, but it is really narrower at the top than at

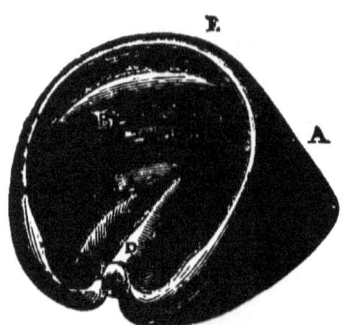

FIG. 13.—THE HOOF.
A. Outer surface of crust.
B. Inner surface of crust.
C. Upper surface of sole.
D. Part corresponding with the cleft of the frog.
E. Coronary band.

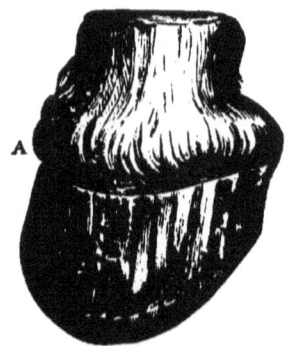

FIG. 14.—FRONT VIEW OF THE FOOT, WITH THE HOOF REMOVED.
A. Coronary substance.
B. Laminæ.

the bottom, and it should rather be described as a section of a truncated cone. When examined from the side, the anterior surface should form an angle of about forty-five degrees with the line of the sole, and the upper edge or coronary band should join the sole, so as to leave a moderate substance at the heel; for if too great the foot does not expand, and is liable to disease from that cause; or if too thin and narrow, the foot is weak and gives way downwards, ending in a convexity of the sole instead of the reverse. The front of the crust is rather more than half an inch in thickness, and in a strong foot of average size gradually diminishing to the quarters, at the back of which it is generally barely a quarter of an inch thick, especially at the inner of the two. This proportion is however confined to the fore foot, for in the hind there is little difference between the toe and quarters in point of thickness. The superior border, or coronary band, is marked by its whitish color. On its external surface it resembles the crust below; but internally it differs in being smoothly excavated,

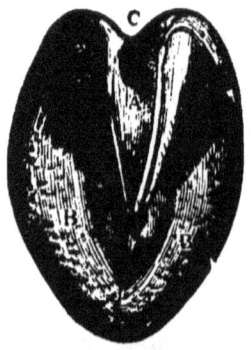

FIG. 15.—THE UNDER SURFACE OF THE FOOT.
A. Cleft of frog.
B. B. Sole.
C. Cleft between heels.

whilst the crust exhibits perpendicular striæ, corresponding with the laminæ; but this is not well shown in Fig. 13. In examining the cut of the sole, Fig. 15, it will be seen that the crust is bent inwards towards the frog at the heel on each side; there are the bars, which in the natural foot appear as sharpened prominences, extending from the heels into the centre of the foot, between the sole and the frog, and which are useful as buttresses, supporting the crust from being crushed inwards by the superincumbent weight. The *sole* is the plate at the bottom of the foot, which should be slightly concave downwards, and is fixed to the inner edge of the crust, and the outer sides of the bars, and not to their lower surfaces. Its usual thickness is about one-sixth of an inch, but it will vary greatly in different horses, and it is thicker where it runs back between the bars and the crust. It is secreted in plates, which can readily be separated with a knife in that direction. The *frog* is the prominent, triangular, and elastic substance, which fills up the space between the heels posteriorly, the bars on each side, and the sole in front. In the middle is a longitudinal fissure, called the cleft, the sides of which should form an angle of about forty-five degrees. In front of this cleft is a solid wedge of the elastic horny substance, constituting the frog, which lies immediately beneath the navicular bone and has received the name of the *cushion*. Posteriorly it is spread out into a thin band on each side which covers the bulbs of the heels, and passes round the upper part of the wall constituting *the coronary frog-band* of Bracy Clark, which is continuous with the coronary substance. The structure of the horn which forms these three divisions, varies a good deal. In the crust it is fibrous, somewhat resembling whalebone in this respect, but not quite so hard; these bristly fibres are united by a gelatinous substance, but they are arranged so as to lie in straight lines descending from the coronary circle to the ground. The wall may, therefore, be considered as composed of hairs agglutinated together, and each secreted by one of the villi, which are so thickly spread over the surface of the coronary circle. The sole is also fibrous, but not nearly so much so as the wall; and the fibres are not arranged in so parallel a manner, taking rather an oblique direction from behind forwards, and being more easily separated into scales. The frog differs from both, in possessing finer fibres and in smaller quantity, in comparison with the gelatine, which formation renders it more soft and elastic and also more prone to decomposition. The horny matter is sometimes colored a grayish brown, sometimes white, and sometimes marbled by a mixture of the two colors.

THE HOOF is developed by secretion, which has its seat in the coronary substance and laminæ. It consists in a pouring out on their surface of a plasma, in which rounded cells develop themselves, in correspondence with the villi from which the secretion is poured out. These cells are arranged in layers, corresponding with the secretory surface. In the crust this growth takes place from the superior border to the inferior, but in the sole and frog, from the internal surface to the external. This growth is constant through the life of the animal, and it would give the hoof an excessive development if it were not either for the wear of the soil in the unshod horse, or of the action of the smith's knife in the shod one; but the increase of the wall being solely from above downwards, it does not require any reduction on its external surface. The *coronary substance*, sometimes called the coronary ligament, is a fibro-cartilaginous band intervening between the skin of the leg and the hoof, covered with cuticle externally, and with villi, which form a secretory surface on the edge towards the hoof. It is most liberally supplied with blood, as we shall presently see, and is attached to the upper part of the coffin bone and extensor tendon by cellular tissue. It gradually becomes thinner as it descends upon the pedal bone, and ends in puckers or folds, which are continuous with those of the laminæ, and are not even separable from them by maceration. The *laminæ* thus continuing upon the pedal bone, consist of about five hundred parallel folds or plaits, plentifully supplied with blood, and forming a secretory surface, which aids the coronary substance to form the horn. They lie upon an elastic substratum of fibrous periosteum, which is of great service in taking off the jar from the foot in its battering upon hard roads, for it appears that the weight of the body is suspended *from* these plates, and not carried *upon* the sole. The laminæ are continuous at the toe with the sensible

FIG. 16.—VIEW OF VESSELS OF THE FOOT, INJECTED.
1. Plantar vein.
2. Plantar artery.
3. Branches to the coronary substance and laminæ.
4. Posterior division of plantar artery.
5. Perpendicular branch.
6. Anastomosis with opposite plantar artery.

sole, which is a vascular membrane covering the floor of the pedal bone, and secreting the horny sole. In the centre of the posterior part of this is the sensible frog, which is of nearly the same shape as the horny frog, and is still more liberally supplied with blood than the sensible sole.

THE ARTERIES supplying these vascular structures with blood, and the veins taking it back, are of great importance, and doubly so because it is in these vessels that an operation is often performed in inflammation of the foot, calculated to afford relief by a local abstraction of blood. Commencing with the large metacarpal artery, which is the continuation of the radial below the knee, we find it descending by the side of the tendo-perforatus under the posterior-annular ligament. Immediately above the fetlock joint it splits into three branches; the middle one passing to the deep parts of the leg, and the two others, forming the plantar arteries, descend on each side the postero-lateral parts of the coronary substance. Here they divide into two leading portions, the anterior running round to meet its fellow of the opposite side, and giving off with it a complete fringe of vessels, which

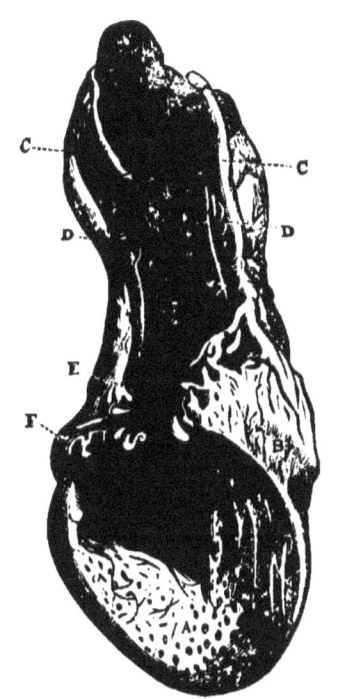

FIG. 17.—VIEW OF THE ARTERIES OF THE FROG AND SOLE, INJECTED.

A. Lower porous surface of pedal bone.
B. Lateral surface of pedal bone.
C. C. The plantar veins.
D. D. The plantar arteries.
E. Lateral cartilage contracted by drying.
F. Veins of the frog, injected.

are displayed in the accompanying representation of an injected preparation of the foot. The branches uniting in front of the foot and encircling the coronary ligament are called the superior coronary circle. The posterior division of the plantar artery gives off, opposite the pastern joint, the artery of the frog, which descends obliquely inwards through the substance of the sensible frog, and divides into two branches within it, after which it supplies the whole of that substance with numerous vessels, and then goes on to the sole, to which it gives off a number of radiating branches. After giving off the artery of the frog, the plantar artery ends posteriorly in the lateral laminal branch which passes through the foramen in the ala of the os pedis, and supplies the laminæ Thus the whole of these structures are full of blood-vessels, for not only are the arteries above described ramifying thus extensively upon them, but the blood is returned by corresponding veins.

BESIDES THE PEDAL AND NAVICULAR BONES, there are also two cartilaginous plates at the back of each ala of the pedal bone, which are of considerable importance. These have been called by the late Professor Coleman the lateral and inferior cartilages, whilst others have given them the name of the true and false. The *lateral cartilages* extend backwards and outwards from the posterior and upper borders of the coffin or pedal bone. They are united in front with the expanded terminations of the extensor tendon, and by cellular membrane with the lower end of the os coronæ. Posteriorly they wind upwards around the ala of the pedal bone, to which they are firmly fixed, forming the foundation for the heel. But in addition to these lateral or true cartilages, there are also two others, of a fibro-cartilaginous nature, which commence from the sides of the former and proceed forwards towards the heels of the pedal bone, and spread inwards upon the surface of the tendo-perforans. They are scarcely worthy of being described as distinct cartilages, and appear more like ordinary condensed cellular membrane.

It will thus be seen that the foot of the horse is a most complicated structure, which is liable to derangement whenever the hoof or horny case is interfered with, and this may occur either from mismanagement in shoeing, causing mechanical injury, or from inflammation of the secreting surface, which will end in the formation of imperfect horn, or from punctures or other wounds of the foot. Perhaps in no organ does an injury so soon produce a return at compound interest, for the inevitable first result is a malformation of the hoof, and this again only adds to the original mischief. Hence it is that in the foot, more than in any other part even, prevention is better than cure, for in many of its diseases it happens that a cure cannot be obtained without rest; and yet it is also the fact that the secretion of horn will not go on perfectly without the stimulus of necessity afforded by exercise. The position of the leg is such that its veins have a hard task to perform at all times in returning the blood from the feet, but when the horse is not exercised at all they become doubly sluggish, and congestion in them is almost sure to occur.

1. Caries of the lower jaw.
2. Fistula of the parotid duct.
3. Bony excrescence or Exostosis of the lower jaw.
4. Swelling by pressure of the bridle.
5. Poll-evil.
6. Inflamed parotid gland.
7. Inflamed jugular vein.
8. Fungus tumor, produced by pressure of the collar
9. Fistula in the withers.
10. Saddle-gall.
11. Tumor of the elbow.
12. Induration of the knee.
13. Clap of the back sinews.
14. Malanders.
15. Splint.
16. Ring-bone.
17. A Tread upon the coronet.
18. Quittor.
19. Sandcrack.
20. Contracted or Ring foot of a foundered horse.
21. Capped hock.
22. Malanders.
23. Spavin.
24. Curb.
25. Swelled sinews.
26. Thick leg.
27. Grease.
28. A crack in front of the foot, called cow-crack
29. Quarter-crack.
30. Ventral hernia.
31. Rat-tail.

DISEASES OF THE HORSE.

THE

DISEASES OF THE HORSE,

AND

THE ACCIDENTS TO WHICH HE IS LIABLE, WITH THEIR TREATMENT.

CHAPTER XIX.

THE DISEASES AND INJURIES OF BONE.

General Remarks—Splints—Ringbone and Sidebone—Ossification of the Lateral Cartilages—Bone Spavin—Exostosis of the Humerus and Scapula—Fistula of the Withers—Poll Evil—Caries of the Jaw—Osteo Sarcoma—Fractures.

GENERAL REMARKS.

THE DISEASES OF BONE are not commonly attended by any constitutional disturbance, and neither require an examination of general symptoms, nor the adoption of any but local treatment, beyond that attention to the health which is always necessary. They may all be included under the heads of,—1st. Exostosis, or increased growth of bone. 2d. Caries, or ulceration. 3d. Anchylosis, or unnatural union of two bones, in consequence of exostosis, or caries, or both. 4th. Fractures, or disunion by external force. Malignant diseases of the bone also occur very rarely in the horse, so that it will be scarcely necessary to occupy any space with their description, especially as they are perfectly incurable.

EXOSTOSIS is the result of increased action in the nutrition of the part, and is much more prevalent in young horses than in old. Indeed, after six or seven years of age it is very rarely met with, and never attacks the bones at that age for the first time. It may be recognised by a hard swelling of the part, which in recent cases is painful on pressure; but sometimes its site cannot be reached with the finger, and the disease can then only be detected by its effects. A blow upon any of the bones, when unprotected by anything but skin, will produce inflammation followed by exostosis but the most ordinary cause is the over-stimulus of hard work. Heavy horses are more prone to exostosis than light ones, partly from the weight of their bodies and their high lumbering action jarring their limbs in a greater degree, but also from the more spongy and open texture of their bones, which admit of the pressure of large blood-vessels within them, and are thus more liable to congestion, and consequent morbid secretion. Exostosis is shown in the form of splints, ring and sidebone, and ossified lateral cartilages, as well as in the growths which occur occasionally in other parts of the body which have received no distinguishing name. The vitality of the new growth in exostosis is less than that of healthy bone, and as a consequence, when excessive inflammation is set up in the part, it will often die and be separated by absorption.

CARIES (ulceration) occurs as a consequence of inflammation, and in the horse either results from external injury, as in poll evil and fistulous withers, or from mismanagement, as in navicular disease, which latter affection will be considered under the diseases of the foot. It is always attended with pain, and in severe cases with the formation of sufficient matter to require an outlet, but in very restricted ulcerations, such as occur in navicular disease, the pus passes into the joint, and is reabsorbed with the synovia.

ANCHYLOSIS, when it is the result of caries in the two adjacent surfaces of a joint, produces union between them, but in the horse it is generally of a secondary kind, the result of bony growths (exostosis), thrown out from the surfaces of the two bones near the joint, which coalescing, unite into one mass, and thus destroy all motion.

SPLINTS.

THE STRICT DEFINITION of this disease is " an exostosis from the lower part of the small metacarpal bone, connecting it by bony union with the large metacarpal bone," but among horsemen, any bony growth from the cannon bone is considered a splint, and the latter is almost as common as the former. The regular splint rarely attacks the outer small metacarpal bone alone, but sometimes in very bad cases both are implicated in the disease. It is difficult to give a valid reason for this greater frequency of splint on the inside than on the out, but it is commonly said that the inner splint bone receives more of the weight of the body than the outer one, and that it is more under the centre of gravity, but as it is merely suspended from the carpus, and is not supported from below (in any way, mediately or directly), this can produce no injurious effect upon it. The fact is so, however, whatever may be the cause.

The symptoms of splint are generally a greater or less degree of lameness during its formation, but sometimes it may go on to attain a large size without any such result, especially if its growth is slow, and the horse is not severely worked. It is commonly remarked that a splint is of no consequence unless its situation is such as to interfere with the back sinews, or suspensory ligament, and although it is quite true, as has been asserted by learned veterinarians, that the splint is far removed from the former, and seldom interferes with the latter, yet it is almost always directly connected with the attachments of the sheath of the tendon, and this being stretched every time the leg is extended will occasion the pain which is expressed by the limp in the action. The size of the morbid growth has no relation with the amount, or even with the existence of lameness, for a very small splint will often be far more productive of this symptom than a very large one. In examining a leg it is often only after careful manipulation in the flexed condition that a small bony tumor (of the size perhaps only of a garden pea) can be detected, but when once the finger presses upon it, the horse will almost invariably be found to flinch, and usually it will be thrown out just where the sheath of the tendon is attached. Here there is no union between the small and large metacarpal bones, and the injury is confined to the inflammation produced in the sheath, which will generally go off after proper treatment and rest. These small bony growths are not very uncommonly met with in the hind legs, but they are not recognised there as splints. No constitutional symptoms are met with in these cases, and they must be ascertained by the local symptoms alone. Unless the splint is in the way of the action of the other foot, and the skin on its surface is bruised by repeated blows, there is seldom any swelling of the soft parts, but when this occurs, the skin and cellular membrane become puffed and hot, and extreme lameness is the result, temporarily aggravated by every blow.

The treatment of a splint will depend upon the state in which it exists, and upon the purpose to which the horse possessing it is destined. If no lameness exists, and the blemish is not objected to, it is far better not to meddle with it, for in the course of a few years it will disappear by absorption as a matter of course. Moreover it often happens that in attempting to remove a splint by some irritating application, extensive inflammation is set up in the fibrous strictures attached to it, and lameness, which was not previously in existence, is thenceforth a most troublesome attendant. If, however, the horse is for sale, in which case the existence of a splint would be regarded with suspicion, or if lameness has shown itself, it will be necessary to adopt measures likely to effect the absorption of the morbid growth, and these are chiefly two:—1st, Sub-cutaneous scarification, or without, a seton, or the seton alone; and 2d. Counter-irritation by means of some form of blister. If the soft parts covering the splint are much inflamed, the horse should have his corn taken away, and a dose of physic given him, during which a wet bandage should be kept constantly applied, and indeed, in any case of splint severe enough to require operation, the cooling remedies mentioned above should be adopted beforehand. The operation is performed with a probe-pointed narrow knife, shaped like a scimetar, with the cutting edge on the convex side. A small opening is made in the skin about an inch below the splint, and just large enough to admit the knife, which is then introduced and pushed upwards with its flat side towards the skin, till it reaches the tumor, when the convex edge is turned towards this, and several extensive scarifications are made in the periosteum covering it, after which the knife is withdrawn and a fine seton-needle is introduced in its place, and passed upwards until it reaches above the splint, when it is pushed through, and the tape drawn out, and properly secured with a bandage. Of course the horse must be cast and properly secured before resorting to the knife. In the course of ten days or a fortnight, the tape may be withdrawn, and the splint will almost invariably disappear. Sometimes the seton is tried without the scarification, but it is not nearly so successful, and is nearly as troublesome an operation. In most cases both of these operations are unnecessary, and the application of the following blister (which has a tendency to produce absorption, independently of its counter irritative powers) will have the desired effect.

Take of Biniodide of Mercury . . . . . 1 drachm
Lard . . . . 1 ounce. Mix,

and after cutting the hair short, rub a little into the skin covering the splint, every night, until a free watery discharge is produced from the surface. To facilitate this the leg should be fomented with *very* hot water every morning and afternoon, and this should be continued for several days after the ointment has been discontinued. The horse will not gnaw the skin after this application, and it is a very useful one for general purposes, when counter-irritation is required to produce absorption. If, after a week's interval, the splint does not appear much reduced in size, the ointment should be re-applied, and repeated at similar intervals till the swelling is removed. When the bony growth is very extensive, neither scarification nor counter-irritation will be of much service, and the leg must be fired, and afterwards repeatedly blistered, but even with the best and most energetic treatment, the part will seldom become sufficiently sound to stand anything but slow work.

RINGBONE AND SIDEBONE.

RINGBONE AND SIDEBONE both consist in the throwing out of bony matter about the joints of the os coronæ; the former name being given to the disease when it attacks that between it and the os suffraginis, and the latter when the seat is the parts around its union with the os pedis or coffin bone. Very often and especially in heavy cart or dray horses, ringbone and sidebone co-exist in the same leg, where the three bones are completely anchylosed, and in which, during life, the only action was in the fetlock joint. The disease attacks the hind leg as well as the fore; but it is more common in the latter than in the former.

The *symptoms* are a greater or less enlargement of the leg, of a hard and unyielding nature, either immediately above the coronet, as in sidebone, or a little higher, as in ringbone. In the latter case, if thoroughly established, it surrounds the joint, whence the name of ringbone; but in the early stages it appears at certain points from which it spreads all round. Sidebone is seldom so extensive, and usually attacks the postero-lateral parts of the os coronæ, where the swelling is defined, and, except in very hairy-legged or gummy-heeled horses, can easily be felt. In the early stages the action is not impeded, but there is more or less soreness or lameness. After much bone is thrown out, the joints are either completely fixed or their movements are extremely limited.

The *treatment* in the early stage is precisely similar to that for splint; but the operation of scarifying the periosteum requires great care and some knowledge of the anatomy of these joints, or the knife will pierce the capsular ligament, and increase the evil it was intended to relieve. A seton without the scarification will often be of service, and for sidebone, firing in the early stage will be serviceable, though it is objectionable on account of the blemish it leaves behind. The biniodide of mercury ointment already described is most useful in slight cases, but in severe ones it will rather tend to aggravate the growth, and when anchylosis has taken place, nothing but time and patience for the subsidence of the inflammation will avail. When this has taken place, and the joint is fixed, a high-heeled shoe will enable the horse to work, with some awkwardness it is true, and the addition of a leather sole, will to some extent take off the jar, which occurs in a greatly increased ratio when the elastic action of the pastern joints is destroyed.

OSSIFICATION OF THE LATERAL CARTILAGES.

THIS IS COMMONLY KNOWN as ossification of the cartilages, or false ringbone, no other cartilages being subject to ossification, and these being therefore known *par excellence* as *the* cartilages. In heavy cart-horses it often co-exists with ringbone and sidebone, especially the latter; but it also attacks well-bred carriage-horses, and high-actioned hacks, which are comparatively free from those diseases.

The *symptoms* are more or less enlargement of the back of the coronet, and heel, the part feeling unnaturally hard and irregular or lumpy. If recent, there is generally increased heat on careful examination with the hand; but in old standing cases there is nothing of the kind to be detected. Lameness is not always present, but if the horse is rattled over hard ground, he will be more likely to show the effects on the next day, by going short and sore, than if he were free from this disease.

The *treatment* should be confined to recent cases, for in old standing ones, unless lameness shows itself, it is better to avoid any interference. A seton, with rest, has sometimes proved very efficacious, even in confirmed ossification, and repeated dressings with the biniodide of mercury ointment, will, in those cases where the inflammation does not run very high, afford the best chance of causing the absorption of some of the bone, for a complete cure is never effected. When there is much heat in the part, bleeding from the foot may be adopted, and afterwards, the application of cloths dipped in cold water, with the addition of a glass of tincture of arnica to quart of water. In confirmed cases, where the parts have become callous, a leather sole to the shoe will take off the vibration, and should be used during the summer season. Scarification of the skin covering the enlargement with a lancet, encouraging the bleeding by warm water, and followed by the use of cold water as soon as the bleeding has ceased, will sometimes do wonders in recent cases. The scarification should be repeated at intervals of five or six days, taking care to avoid injury to the coronary substance near the hoofs, which is sometimes followed by troublesome sores.

BONE SPAVIN

THIS DISEASE, so frequently the cause of lameness in those horses which use their hocks severely (as for example race-horses, hunters, carriage-horses, and more particularly cart-horses), consists in exostosis from the adjacent external surfaces of the tarsal bones, always showing itself at the inner side of the hock joint, on the scaphoid and cuneiform bones, and extending to the head of the internal small metatarsal bone. As in the case of splint, the occurrence of exostosis on the internal rather than on the external side of the hock has been accounted for by the supposition that increased weight is thrown upon the internal small metatarsal bone, from the turning up of the outer heel of the shoe, which is the common practice of smiths. It appears to me, however, that the contrary is the case, and that though more stress is laid upon the foot on that side, there is less weight on the inner side of the hock, which has a tendency to spring open in that direction. This will cause a strain upon the ligaments connecting the tarsal bones, and nature coming to their aid throws out bone, which ultimately substitutes anchylosis for ligamentous union between these bones. In all the actions of the hind leg, from the natural shape of the hock, and more especially in those horses which are naturally "cow-hocked," there is a tendency to yield inwards rather than in the opposite direction. The consequence is that there is more strain upon the ligamentous fibres which connect the scaphoid with the two cuneiform and the internal metatarsal, than upon those uniting the cuboid with the os calcis and external metatarsal bone. Hence, although exostosis does sometimes show itself in other parts of the tarsal bones, it here, as in the fore leg, is almost always confined to what is called the "spavin place," namely, the contiguous surfaces of the scaphoid, cuneiform, and internal metatarsal bones. In very bad cases the articular cartilage becomes involved, and there is not only an external casing of new bone, but the internal surfaces absolutely coalesce or anchylose.

THE SYMPTOMS of spavin are a *hard* substance showing itself beyond the proper level of the hock joint. There may or may not be lameness, but if bone is thrown out the disease is established. In recent cases whenever the horse is worked he will *after rest* limp in his action, but the lameness soon goes off, and does not show itself again until the part has been suffered to become stiff by a rest of an hour or two. The lameness is very remarkable, and differs greatly from that shown in any other disease. The leg is drawn up with a quick catch, and yet there is a dragging of the limb, indicating not only pain in the joint, but a want of action in it. In the early stages the latter is not clearly developed, but afterwards it is so well marked that a spavin may be pronounced to exist without an examination of the joint. Where lameness is not established, great care should be exercised in pronouncing on the existence of spavin, for some hocks are naturally formed with prominent heads of the internal metatarsal bones, and the inexperienced eye and hand are very apt to mistake these for exostosis. In such cases, by comparing the two hocks it will generally be seen that they are both exactly alike, while in spavin, although both joints may be the seat of mischief, yet they will seldom manifest the disease to the same extent.

The treatment should be directed to the abatement of the inflammation which gives rise to the pain, and also to promote absorption of the new growth. Veterinary surgeons are very apt to assert that the disease cannot be cured, and that a spavined horse will always remain the subject of it, and therefore unsound. But practically it is known that many a hock which has been the seat of undoubted spavin loses all external enlargement, and no lameness is shown in it, although tried most severely through a series of years. Still on dissection after death, the ligaments will not show their natural white and glistening structure, and the tarsal bones will be to a certain extent united by anchylosis. In very bad cases there will be also caries of the articulatory surfaces, and with it inflammation of the synovial membranes, which may and often does exist without the caries. Now as these are much more formidable diseases than exostosis, and far more difficult either to cure or palliate, it follows that although certain remedies will be generally successful with genuine bone spavin (exostosis), yet they will fail when the above complication exists. The treatment must therefore be adapted to the exact nature and extent of the disease. Prior to the adoption of any plan the joint should be rested, the outer heel of the shoe should be lowered, the corn should be taken away, and the system cooled by appropriate treatment. After these precautions are taken, the next thing is to decide upon the remedies which will be suited to the case. They consist in—1. Blisters, which have a tendency to cause absorption; 2. Firing; 3. Setons, with or without subcutaneous scarification; 4. Division of the nerve. If there is simply a slight exostosis, with little lameness, and no evidence of the joint being implicated, the biniodide of mercury may be applied as described at page 300. Repeated dressings will be necessary, and the joint must have at least two months' absolute rest, the horse being placed in a loose box. This remedy is often successful, but it will fail utterly where the exostosis is extensive, or there is caries, or even severe inflammation of the synovial membrane. Arsenic, sulphuric acid, and other caustic applications, have been counted as infallible cures; but while they are just as certain to produce a blemish as firing, the extent to which the inflammation and sloughing, caused by them, go is far more completely beyond our control. Arsenic has been known to destroy the joint, by producing a slough of the synovial membrane, and it is said that the sulphuric acid, which, however, is often very successful, has had a similar unfortunate result; but of its being followed by serious blemishes there is abundant proof. Firing is the safest, and, therefore, the usual plan adopted for spavin, and on the first intimation of the disease it is often adopted without any necessity for having recourse to so disfiguring a process. Its chief advantage is, that while it is a certain means of establishing a strong counter-irritation, it has no tendency to cause any increase of inflammation in the structures beneath the skin, and therefore the good it does is unalloyed by any counterbalancing evil. It is now the fashion to deny its use, and horsemasters are often tempted to try some substitute for it in the hope of escaping a blemish; but too often they are compelled to submit to it at last, and probably after the disease has been aggravated by some "unfailing" remedy. If there is a strong desire expressed to avoid a blemish, the veterinary surgeon is perfectly warranted in doing all in his power to effect a cure without the use of the irons; but the mere fashion of the day should not induce him to decry a plan which has for so many years been proved to be successful. In human surgery the same course has been adopted, and for the last thirty or forty years the actual cautery has been voted "barbarous" in this country. Now, however, a counter current is setting in, and it is the general opinion of the first hospital surgeons of the day that, in certain diseases of the joints, no remedy is nearly so efficacious. All sorts of attempts are made to render the use of the hot iron less repugnant to the senses; but in the case of the horse it is only necessary to measure its comparative utility and the amount of pain which it gives. The former has been already considered, and as to the latter, if the irons are properly heated, I much doubt whether their action is not less painful than that of any other counter-irritant. Setons, perhaps, give less pain if skilfully inserted, and they are admirable remedies, having nearly the same beneficial effects as firing, and leaving a far slighter blemish. They should be passed beneath a considerable track of the skin, covering the "spavin place," and the tape requires to be smeared with blistering cerate to produce sufficient irritation. Their use by themselves is often sufficient, but when preceded by subcutaneous scarification they seem to act even more certainly than firing.

The method of operation is similar to that described for splints, but it requires more knowledge of the anatomy of the parts to avoid doing mischief by cutting into one of the joints. There is always afterwards considerable effusion into the subcutaneous cellular membrane, demanding two or three months for its removal; but as the spavined horse requires that interval of rest, this is of little or no consequence. When the disease has gone so far that no method of treatment will remove it, the nerve above the hock may be divided, which will enable the horse to work without pain for a time, but the disease goes on the faster, and the benefit derived is only temporary.

EXOSTOSIS OF THE HUMERUS AND SCAPULA.*

THE HEADS OF THE BONES adjacent to most of the joints of the body are more or less subject to exostosis, though not so frequently as those of the pastern bones and tarsus. Next to these probably comes the shoulder joint, the neighborhood of which is often the seat of this disease. The left scapula and humerus of a horse are often completely anchylosed, and of course there co-exists a proportionate

---

* Shoulder-joint lameness, as it is generally called, is much more frequent than formerly, generally resulting in ulceration of the bone. It is readily seen by standing before the horse, and is at once detected by holding up the sound member from the ground and forcing the animal to stand upon the lame one. This is a more serious affection than simple sprain of the muscles of the shoulder.—EDITOR.

amount of lameness during the progress of the disease, while after the anchylosis takes place the want of action is complete. An examination by the hand of the point of the shoulder would readily detect so large a growth of bone as this; but smaller ones are often thrown out beneath the mass of muscles surrounding the shoulder joint, and consequently beyond the reach of the most accomplished finger. The *treatment* should be on the same principle as for spavin, omitting the subcutaneous scarification, which is not here practicable on account of the nature of the joint. Blisters, and especially with the biniodide of mercury, will be the most likely to succeed, but in most cases the cure will be only partial.

FISTULA OF THE WITHERS.*

WHEN A SADDLE has been allowed to press upon the spinous processes of the dorsal vertebræ, it produces inflammation, which, if neglected, leads to the formation of an abscess. But the situation of the part is such that the matter cannot escape, even if the skin over the points of the bones is perforated, and it has a tendency, by the force of gravity, to burrow down among the muscles which connect the shoulder-blade with the trunk. The consequence is, that there is extensive inflammation, and often lameness of the shoulder, which could readily have been prevented by using proper care before the mischief was done, or removed by the adoption of suitable treatment afterwards before the disease is confirmed.

The *symptoms* in the early stage (that is, before a fistula is established) are merely an enlargement of the ends of the spinous processes, accompanied by heat and tenderness, but these go on until an abscess forms, which may be known to the touch by the fluctuating nature of the sensation which it gives on pressure by the fingers of each hand. As soon as this is made out, an opening should be made as low down as possible on the right side, taking care that it will allow all the matter to run out as fast as it forms. The reason why the right side should be chosen is, that most horses lie down on that side; but if the subject of fistulous withers is in the habit of lying on the left side, the opening should be made there in preference. When an actual fistula has been established, and the matter points before or behind the shoulder-blade, a sufficiently large opening should at once be made, taking care again that there is no pouch below it which will permit any accumulation. It is better to divide even important muscles than to suffer this to exist. In recent cases the establishment of this dependent opening will alone suffice to effect a cure; but in those of long standing, the lining of the fistulous passage

---

* Commonly called in the United States, Thislo.—EDITOR.

or passages has become converted into a substance almost resembling cartilage, and refuses to throw out healthy granulations, so as to lead to adhesion of its walls. Here a stimulus must be applied to their interior, which may be either mechanical, in the shape of a seton tape passed through from end to end and left there, or chemical, by means of injections. The latter are best composed of chloride of zinc diluted with water. One drachm of this should be mixed in a pint of water, and carefully injected into every part of the sinus twice or thrice a week.

POLL EVIL.

POLL EVIL is exactly similar in its nature to fistulous withers, being produced by a blow on the prominent ridge, which is situated on the top of the poll. The blow is generally produced in the stable, by the horse suddenly lifting his head and striking it against a low beam or the lintel of the door. Or it may be caused by frequently straining against the halter rein, and thus producing irritation and inflammation of the part. As the ligamentum colli is attached above, and anterior to, the inflamed part, when matter forms it is confined and gives intense pain; besides which, it is a long time before it opens a passage by natural means. The *symptoms* are a painful swelling on the poll, of a soft nature, accompanied by the sense of fluctuation on examination, just like that described as accompanying fistulous withers. The *treatment* must be precisely similar to that described in the last section; but as the matter when formed lies very close to the spinal cord, some caution must be exercised in adopting stimulating injections, which are apt to produce severe inflammation, likely to extend to these important structures. So also in opening it, the knife should not be carried deeply into the situation of the spinal marrow, which here lies exposed, and is easily divided (as in the operation known by the name of pithing), but it should be used in a slanting manner, again selecting the right side in preference to the left. A seton is here the safest plan for promoting granulation and adhesion, and as the fistulous track is seldom very long, the tape will work its way gradually out, by which time the cure is effected.

CARIES OF THE JAW.

THE UPPER JAW, FROM ITS EXPOSED SITUATION, and the lower from the same cause, and also from the abuse of the bit, are liable to mechanical injury, which ends in caries (ulceration), or sometimes in necrosis (mortification) of the part. Caries of the lower jaw, between the tushes and grinders, is extremely common, owing to the barbarous punishment which is inflicted by the use of long levers to curb bits, together with light curb chains. The bony plate forming the roof of the mouth is also often injured by the pressure of the part when a tight noseband is employed to keep the mouth shut. Either may be known by the existence of a sore of a peculiar character; there is a depression indicating a loss of substance, and in this lies a mass of unhealthy granulation (proud flesh), *which is not attached to the surrounding surface, being only fixed to the bottom of the cavity*, or perhaps partially on one side. A watery and offensive discharge goes on constantly, but this is lost in the saliva, and very often the only circumstance that draws attention to the disease is the constant bleeding from the mouth, on the slightest contact of the bit. When this occurs, the mouth being full of *pink* froth, it should be carefully examined, and the state of things here described will generally be found to exist. The *treatment* should consist in the adoption of a bit pressing upon another part of the mouth, changing the curb for a snaffle. The wound should be kept open by the use of caustic (lunar) daily, which should be pushed deeply into it for couple of seconds, and will destroy the unhealthy granulations. By continuing these measures, taking care not to do more with the caustic than necessary to keep down the fungous growth, a cure can always be effected in course of time, without the aid of the trephine or chisel to cut away the diseased bone.

OSTEO SARCOMA.*

THE JAWS are occasionally attacked by a malignant growth from their cellular structure of a substance partaking of the nature both of cartilage and bone. It increases sometimes to an enormous size, and forms a large irregular tumor, which interferes terribly with their functions, often growing so as to prevent the closure of the teeth. The *symptoms* are entirely local, and when a large, unwieldy, and irregularly hard swelling on either of the jaws is met with, it may safely be set down as belonging to this class of disease. No *treatment* is of any avail except excision, which can rarely be carried through without rendering the horse unserviceable for his ordinary duties.

FRACTURES.

BONES are not unfrequently broken in the horse; but as the accident generally occurs either during the violent exertion of the muscles of the limb, or from great external force, it follows that in most cases the injury to the soft parts is so great as to forbid the hope of a perfect reparation. When, for instance, a canna or pastern bone gives way during the shock sustained in coming down

---

* *Osteo Sarcoma* is very frequent in the western and south-western States, and is known by the name of "BIG HEAD" (*Osteo Porosis*), arising from the deposition of too much bony matter. Treatment is unsatisfactory, as the disease is gradual and progressive in its character, stopping mastication; and death from starvation is the result.—EDITOR.

on hard ground from a leap, either at the moment of the fracture
or before the horse can be stopped, the upper end pierces the skin,
and also tears or bruises the tendons which alone connect it to the
part below. In surgical language, the fracture is a compound one;
and from the great tendency to contraction of the muscles, the
difficulty of bringing the disunited ends into apposition (or setting
them) is immense. Moreover, the horse is very unmanageable
when an attempt is made to confine him, and the means which are
adopted to keep the fracture set must therefore be very complete
as compared with those which will serve for the restoration of the
human being who has sustained a similar accident. Hence, unless
the animal is wanted for stud purposes alone, or unless the fracture
is a simple one, with little displacement, it will seldom be worth
the attempt to procure the union of a broken bone in the horse.
Many cases are on record in which after a fracture of a canna or
pastern bone a complete cure has been effected, but they must be
considered as exceptional, and not as affording as much encouragement.

THE SYMPTOMS OF SIMPLE FRACTURE are a greater or less
degree of deformity of the limb, swelling, pain on motion, and a
peculiar grating or jarring which is felt rather than heard, and
which has received the name of "crepitus." The last symptom
can only be made out when the broken ends of the bone can be
brought together; but when this is impossible, the alteration of
form is in itself sufficient to lead to a detection of the nature of
the accident. In fractures of the head and spine there is no
crepitus felt, and the effect upon the brain and spinal cord of
pressure will be often the sole means of coming to a correct
diagnosis. Fractures of the pelvis are very difficult to make out,
unless the ala of the ilium is broken off, which is a common accident, for here the unnatural flatness of the hip, showing itself
without any great difficulty of moving the hind leg of that side,
plainly marks that there is no dislocation, and that the case can
only be one of fracture. It is always the result of a blow, either
when the horse is cast in a stall or in passing through a narrow
door-way, or from a similar cause; and there will therefore be some
swelling of the soft parts which will interfere with the examination
at the time, but as nothing can be done to restore the broken
portion to its place, and as there is no doubt about the diagnosis
from dislocation, this is of little consequence. Fractures of the
ribs cannot be readily detected; but as they almost always follow
a kick on the part, and as they do not require any treatment
unless their broken ends press upon the important viscera of the
thorax or abdomen, it will be well to wait for the symptoms which
are caused by this mechanical irritation before resorting to bandages, &c. When a fracture occurs in any of the bones of the

extremities, which are concealed by a large mass of muscle, the total inability to use the limb, and the loose way in which it is connected to the body, so as to allow it to be moved in any direction, indicate the general nature of the case without difficulty, though a careful examination must be made by a skilful surgeon before the exact particulars relating to it can be ascertained.

The treatment will depend upon the bone which is broken, and whether the fracture is simple or compound. In most cases of the latter description none will avail, and the horse had better be destroyed; but if the owner is averse to this, it will be on the whole the best surgery, though apparently not very scientific, to encase the parts with adhesive plasters and tow, and then treat it as a simple fracture.

IF THE BONES OF THE SKULL are fractured, unless there are symptoms of pressure on the brain, it is advisable to leave all to nature, simply keeping the patient quiet and low, and if in a high state of plethora, bleeding and physicking.

A BROKEN LOWER JAW is by no means uncommon as the result of a kick. The best treatment is to set the fracture, and then mould some gutta percha to it, which may be confined behind by strips round the forehead and poll, and before by a padded strap passed through the mouth between the nippers and tushes, and beneath the tongue. The horse must be fed upon mashes and steamed food.

IN FRACTURES OF THE SPINE AND PELVIS nothing can be done beyond rest and lowering, if necessary, by bleeding and physic.

BROKEN RIBS, when they cause inflammation of the lungs or liver by their sharp ends pressing upon these organs, may be treated by buckling two or three ordinary rollers abreast of one another tightly round the chest, so as to prevent the natural dilatation of the thorax, which takes place in inspiration, and which keeps up the irritation by constantly moving the ends of the ribs. The general means necessary to adopt to relieve the internal mischief will depend upon its extent.

WHEN EITHER THE SCAPULA, HUMERUS, OR FEMUR is broken, all that can be done is to sling the horse, and by bandages endeavor to bring the limb into as natural a position as possible, and keep it there. There must of necessity be great displacement of the ends of the bones, and these cannot by any means be brought into apposition; but the sides in contact with one another, as they override, will unite in course of time, and this is all that can be achieved by the utmost efforts of the veterinary surgeon.

FRACTURES of the lower part of the tibia, of the radius, of the canna bones and the pasterns, if simple, must be treated by adjusting the ends (which is the chief difficulty, and will often require strong extension to be employed), and then adapting to the sides of the bones splints of wood or gutta percha. If, by the aid of assistants, the parts can be brought into a good position, these may be carefully adjusted to maintain it, and may be kept in place by tapes or straps fastened moderately tightly around them. It is useless, however, to attempt a minute description of the means to be employed, which can hardly be understood without a demonstration. Many horses have recovered a fair use of the limb by the application of splints, without slinging, as they will take care to avoid resting on that foot in consequence of the pain it gives; but under the care of an accomplished veterinary surgeon, slings will afford the best chance of recovery.

CHAPTER XX.

INJURY AND DISEASES OF THE JOINTS, MUSCLES, AND TENDONS.

Diseases of Muscle, Tendon, and Ligament—Of Cartilage and Synovial Membrane—Inflamed Tendinous Sheaths—Inflamed Bursæ Mucosæ—Strains—Those of the Back and Loins—Of the Shoulder—Of the Knee—Of the Fetlock—Of the Coffin Joint—Of the Suspensory Ligaments—Of the Back-Sinews—Breaking Down—Strains of the Hip-Joint, Stifle, and Hock—Curb—Dislocation—Wounds of Joints.

DISEASES OF MUSCLE, TENDON, AND LIGAMENT.

MUSCLE is subject to simple atrophy, with or without fatty degeneration. The disease shows itself by a wasting away of the part, accompanied by a flabby feel to the touch. It should be *treated* by friction, gentle but regular work, and steel given internally, one drachm of the sulphate of iron powdered being mixed with the corn twice a day.

RHEUMATIC INFLAMMATION of a muscle or muscles is one of the most common of all the diseases to which the horse is subject. Most frequently it attacks the muscles of the shoulder, or of the loins, sometimes both those parts being involved at the same time. When *acute* it receives the name of *a chill*, and is generally brought on by exposing the horse to a draught of air after work, or by immersing him in cold water up to his belly, with a view either to refresh him, or when the groom is lazy, to save him the trouble of cleaning. *The symptoms* are lameness or inability to use the part, the horse, when forced to do so, giving expressions of severe pain. If the shoulder is affected, the foot is not put to the ground, and when the leg is moved backwards and forwards by the hand, great pain is evidently experienced. In severe cases there is fever with accelerated pulse (70 to 80), accompanied often by profuse sweating, and heaving at the flanks, the legs remaining warm. After a short time the part swells, and is excessively tender. The *treatment* should be by a copious bleeding, if the horse is of a moderately strong constitution; indeed, in severe cases it should be carried on till the pulse is greatly reduced, and repeated the next day, if it returns to its original hardness and fulness. The bowels should be acted on as soon as it is safe to do so, and if the dung is very hard, backraking and clysters should be used, to accelerate the action of the medicine. The best aperient is castor oil, of which a pint may be given with an ounce of sweet spirits of nitre. When this has acted, if the kidneys are not doing their duty, a quarter of an ounce of nitre and a drachm of camphor may be made into a ball and given twice a day.

CHRONIC RHEUMATISM of the muscles is similar in its nature to the acute form, but, as its name implies, it is more lasting, and of less severity. It often flies from one part to another, attacking the ligaments and tendons, as well as the muscular fibres. It is seldom much under control, and attention should be paid rather to improve the general health than to subdue the local affection.

SMALL TUMORS, of about the size of a pea, often form upon the tendons, especially the "back sinews" of the fore legs. They may or may not occasion lameness, but they are always to be regarded with suspicion. As long as they remain indolent, they are better left alone; but when they produce inflammation and pain, the best remedy is the biniodide of mercury ointment, described at page 300.

DISEASES OF CARTILAGE AND SYNOVIAL MEMBRANE.

CARTILAGE is subject chiefly to ulceration. When this occurs, its cells become enlarged and crowded with corpuscles, which burst and discharge their contents; the intercellular structure at the same time splits into bands, which, together with the corpuscles, form a fibro-nucleated membrane on the face of the cartilage. In old horses, the ulcerated cartilage covering the tibial surface of the astragalus is sometimes converted into a soft fibrous substance, which ultimately assumes the appearance of hard and dense bone, commonly known as "porcellaneous or ivory deposit." It is accompanied by no symptoms of inflammation; the sole evidence of disease, during life, being a stiffness of the joint, and a peculiar grating or crackling noise during all attempts at movement. When caries of the head of a bone has caused a loss of substance, the cartilage dies, and is gradually broken down by decomposition; but this cannot be said to be a disease of the cartilage itself. With the exception of navicular disease (which will be included under the diseases of the foot), ulceration of cartilage is not very common in the horse.

ACUTE INFLAMMATION OF THE SYNOVIAL MEMBRANE is seldom met with; but a chronic state, inducing an excessive secretion of synovia, is extremely common. The most usual situation is at the hock, where the swelling has received the name of bag-spavin and thoroughpin; but they also occur at the fetlock and knee joints; in the former case being sometimes confounded with windgalls, which are inflamed bursæ mucosæ.

BOG-SPAVIN is very apt to attack young horses, when they are over-worked, before being fully seasoned; but it may occur at all ages. It shows itself at the inner side of the joint, because here the ligaments are wider apart, and there is more room for distension. Its seat is the capsule between the tibia and astragalus, which is here unprotected by any strong fibrous covering, and readily yields to the gradual pressure of the secretion from its internal surface.

THOROUGHPIN may be either an increased secretion of the synovial capsule, between the astragalus and os calcis, or between the scaphoid and cuneiform bones, or of the bursa mucosa lying between the tendo Achillis and the tendo perforatus. In the first of these cases, it often coexists with bog-spavin, and the synovia may be made to fluctuate from one bag to the other, the only line of demarcation being the astragalo-calcanean ligament.

Both bog-spavin and thoroughpin may exist, or either separately, without occasioning lameness; but where they are just established, there is generally some small degree of active inflammation, which causes a slight lameness on first going out of the stable, but soon disappearing.

The treatment should be by pressure, kept up for a long time, by means of a carefully-adjusted truss, alternated with cold affusion, and the use afterwards of tincture of arnica, diluted with water, as a wash. Subcutaneous scarification has succeeded in some few cases in causing the secretion to cease; but it has so often produced extensive inflammation of the joint, that the operation is by no means to be recommended. Blistering with biniodide of mercury has also occasionally answered; but no plan is so successful, on the whole, as pressure, alternating with cold affusion.

DELICATE YOUNG FOALS are subject to a rheumatic inflammation of their synovial membranes, specially displayed in the knees and hocks, and apparently caused by exposure to cold. It seldom goes on to produce disorganization of the cartilages, but the capsular ligaments are distended with thin yellow synovia, causing considerable stiffness. The cellular tissue around the joints also becomes œdematous, and the legs fill all the way down to the feet. It is commonly known among breeders as the "joint evil," and though in itself it is not dangerous, yet it marks the existence of constitutional weakness which is likely to occasion some more fatal malady. The *treatment* should consist in attending to the general health by strengthening the mare, which is best done by giving her a drachm of the sulphate of iron in her corn twice a day. The joints of the foal should be rubbed with equal parts of soap liniment and spirit of turpentine, and it should be assisted to stand for the purpose of sucking at regular short intervals if unable to help itself. In aggravated cases, however, the foal is not likely to recover its general strength, and it may be better to destroy it, but so long as it can stand and feeds well hopes may be entertained of the joints recovering.

INFLAMED TENDINOUS SHEATHS.

EVERY PRACTICAL HORSEMAN is aware that the sheaths in which the back sinews and other tendons are lodged are liable to inflammation and thickening, without the tendon itself being involved. By passing the hand down the leg, an irregular network may be felt surrounding the tendons, which move up and down without disturbing it; and the surrounding cellular membrane is also thickened, and becomes hard and unyielding. There may be considerable heat about the part, but often it is quite cool; and the disease may continue for months without any great lameness, and with nothing to draw attention to it (excepting a slight stiffness on leaving the stable) but the sensation communicated to the hand. At length, an unusually severe day's work sets up active inflammation, the leg rapidly fills, and there is so much lameness as to cause the horse to be thrown by.—The *treatment* in the early stage, should be the use of bandages, constantly kept wet with arnica and water, and nothing but walking exercise. After the thickening is fully established, no remedy short of blistering, or a charge, will be of the slightest avail, with a rest of two or three months.

INFLAMED BURSÆ MUCOSÆ.

THESE SYNOVIAL BAGS are liable to inflammation, either from hard work, as in windgalls and thoroughpin, or from blows, as in capped hock and elbow. The latter are said by some veterinarians to be serous abcesses; but there is no doubt that in all horses a subcutaneous bursa exists on the cap of the elbow and hock; and these become inflamed and filled with a very thin synovia, when they are bruised. They never extend beyond a certain size, and have no tendency to burst; nor are they inclined to a healthy termination of their own accord, but go on in the same condition from year to year.

WINDGALLS, OR PUFFS, are the most usual forms of these enlargements, and may be observed in the legs (hind as well as fore) of nearly every hard-worked horse, after a time. Great care in the management of the legs by bandaging will sometimes keep them off, and some horses have naturally no tendency to form them; but in most cases, on examining the legs, just above the fetlock joints, of horses at work, a little oval bag may be felt on each side, between the back-sinew and the bone. If recent, it is soft and puffy; but if the work is hard, and the windgall is of long standing, it will be as tense as a drum. The synovial bag has no communication with the fetlock joint; but there is another sac in front of the joint, and beneath the tendons of the extensors, which is often enlarged, though not so much so as the seat of the true windgall, and which is generally, though not always, continuous with the synovial capsule of the joint.—The *treatment* consists in pressure by means of bandages, and the application of cold lotions, if the legs are hot and inflamed. Blistering and rest will remove them entirely; but no sooner is the horse put to work again, than they return as badly as ever. There is no radical cure but subcutaneous puncture and scarification, and this will produce too much adhesion to be advantageously applied.

THE FORM OF THOROUGHPIN in which the bursa mucosa between the tendo Achillis and the tendo perforatus is inflamed and filled with synovia, has been alluded to at page 313, and its *treatment* is there described.

CAPPED HOCK is often the result of a bruise of the superficial bursa, which is situated on the point of the hock, immediately beneath the skin. It indicates either that the possessor has kicked in the stable or in harness; but it is more frequently caused in the former way than in the latter. The swelling is sometimes slight, being then just sufficient to show the point slightly enlarged, and to give a soft, puffy sensation to the fingers, where there ought to be nothing but bone felt beneath the skin. The bursa always rolls freely on the bone, and when large, it can be laid hold of and shaken like a bladder of water.—The *treatment* should be directed to abate any slight inflammation that may exist, if the case is established; but in recent ones, it is doubly necessary to apply cold lotions, which, however, there is some difficulty in doing, owing to the prominent nature of the part. A piece of stout calico or fine canvas may, however, be shaped into a cap, carefully fitting the point of the hock; and this being tied by several pieces of tape in front of the leg, will allow not only of the application of cold lotions, but of pressure also. By this plan, continued for some weeks, considerable enlargements have been removed, but they are very apt to return on the slightest bruise. Setons through the bursa, and injections into its cavity of stimulating applications, have often been tried; but they generally do more harm than good, and nothing can be relied on but the conjoint use of pressure and cold applications. The best lotion is the following:—

Take of Tincture of Arnica	3 ozs.
Muriate of Ammonia	2 "
Methylated Spirit of Wine	4 "
Water	3 pints. Mix.

CAPPED ELBOW is precisely similar in its nature to capped hock, and must be treated in the same way. It is also known by the name of capulet.

OF STRAINS.

THE FIBRES OF MUSCLES, LIGAMENTS, AND TENDONS, AND THE FASCIA covering them, are all liable to be overstretched, and more or less mechanically injured. This is called a strain, the *symptoms* of which are similar to the inflammation of the part occurring ideopathically. They are heat, swelling, and pain on pressure or movement, shown by flinching in the one case, and lameness in the other. In some cases there is considerable effusion of blood or serum, the former occurring chiefly in the muscles, and the latter among the torn fibres of the tendons or ligaments. The *symptoms* and *treatment* will depend upon the part injured, which will be found described under the following heads; but in most cases an embrocation composed of equal parts of laudanum, olive oil, spirit of turpentine, and hartshorn, will be beneficial if applied after the first active inflammation has subsided.

STRAIN OF THE BACK AND LOINS.

WHEN A YOUNG HORSE has been hunted or ridden with hounds over any kind of fence, he is very apt to over-exert himself in his awkward attempts to clear the obstacle, and next day he will often show a stiffness of the loins and back, which is seated in the large muscles connecting the pelvis with the thorax. He is said to have "ricked his back," in the language of the stable, and if the mischief is confined to the muscles alone, he may generally be permanently cured, though he will be more liable to a return than an animal which has never suffered from any accident of the kind. If, however, the spinal cord is injured, either from fracture of the vertebræ, or from effusion of blood or serum pressing upon it, the case is different, and a perfect cure is seldom obtained. It is, however, very difficult to form a correct diagnosis between the one case and the other, and the treatment may generally be conducted with the hope that the more important organ is uninjured. When there is complete palsy of the hind extremities, so that the horse can neither feel nor use them in the slightest degree, the case is hopeless. For the management of the strain of the loins, a full bleeding should be adopted, as i generally happens that the horse is plethoric and full of corn. Then apply a double fold of thick flannel or serge, dipped in warm water, to the whole surface of the loins, cover this over with a layer of indiarubber sheeting, and let it remain on, taking care to renew the water if it has become dry. It generally produces a copious sweating from the part, followed by a slight irritation of the skin, both of which afford relief. In three or four days the flannel may be removed, and the embrocation alluded to above rubbed in two or three times a day, which will generally relieve the muscles so much that at the end of a week or ten days the horse is able to move quietly about in a loose box, and the cure may be left to time, aided by a charge on the back.

STRAIN OF THE SHOULDER.

SHOULDER STRAIN was formerly very often chosen as the seat of lameness in the fore extremity, solely because the case is so obscure that it is beyond the knowledge of the unskilful examiner. Nevertheless, it is by no means so uncommon as is supposed by some writers, and perhaps it may be asserted that it is now more frequently passed over when it really exists, than the reverse. It generally is seated in the serratus magnus, or pectoralis transversus muscles, but it may also occur in the triceps, or, indeed, in almost any of the muscles around the shoulder joint. The *symptoms* are very peculiar, and cannot well be mistaken by a careful observer who has once seen a case of shoulder lameness. In all other kinds (except the knee), the limb is freely moved while in the air, and no pain is expressed until the foot is about to touch the ground; but here the lameness is greatest while the knee is being protruded, and the limb is slung forward sideways, in a circular manner, which gives an expression of great imbecility. It also occasions great pain when the foot is lifted and drawn forward by the hand, just as in rheumatism of the part (already described at page 312). When the serratus magnus has been strained by a fall from a drop leap, or the pectoralis transversus by a slip, causing the legs to be widely separated, there is often great obscurity in the case; but the history of the accident will generally assist in forming a correct diagnosis. The *treatment* in the early stage will consist in bleeding from the plate vein, to the extent of five or six quarts of blood, followed by fomentations with hot water, if there is much heat and swelling, and giving a dose of physic as soon as the bowels will bear it. When the heat has disappeared, or at once, if there is none, apply the embrocation described at page 315; and if this does not produce relief, add to it one quarter of its bulk of tincture of cantharides.

STRAINS OF THE KNEE.

THE KNEE, unlike its analogue in the human subject (the wrist),

27 *

is seldom strained in the horse, in consequence of the strong ligaments which bind the bones of the carpus together. Still it sometimes happens that the internal lateral ligaments are overstretched, or, in calf-kneed horses, the posterior common ligaments, or that connecting the scaphoid with the pisiform bone, or probably all these will suffer from over-extension. The accident may be recognised by the heat and swelling of the part affected, as well as by the pain given on using the joint. The anterior ligaments are seldom strained, but are liable to injury from blows received in various ways. The *treatment* should be conducted on the same principles as those of strains in the shoulder. Cold applications will seldom do anything but harm in the early stage; but after hot fomentations have relieved the active mischief, by encouraging the effusion of serum into the surrounding cellular membrane, the former may be used with advantage. When the heat and other signs of active inflammation have disappeared, the biniodide of mercury ointment may be rubbed in, avoiding the back of the joint.

STRAIN OF THE FETLOCK.

THIS ACCIDENT shows itself at once, in consequence of the superficial nature of the joint, by swelling, heat, soreness to the touch, and lameness. It may be very slight or very severe, but in the latter case it is generally complicated by strain of the back sinews, or suspensory ligament. The *treatment* will be precisely on the same plan as for strain of the knee. When the anterior ligaments of the fetlock joint are strained and inflamed, as so often happens with race-horses, the condition is known as "shin sore."

STRAIN OF THE COFFIN JOINT.

DISSECTION PROVES that this joint is sometimes the seat of strain; but it is almost impossible to ascertain its existence with certainty during life. The diagnosis is, however, not of much consequence, as the *treatment* will be the same, whether the coffin joint, or the navicular joint is the seat of the mischief. In any case, if severe, bleeding from the toe should be had recourse to, followed by cold applications around the coronet, by means of a strip of flannel or felt, tied loosely around the pastern, and kept constantly wet. When the heat has subsided the coronet should be blistered.

STRAIN OF THE SUSPENSORY LIGAMENTS.

THE SUSPENSORY LIGAMENT not being elastic like the back sinews (which, though not in themselves extensible, are the prolongations of muscles which have that property), is very liable to strains, especially in the hunter, and to a less degree in the race-horse. The accident is readily made out, for there is local swelling and tenderness, and in the well-bred horse, which is alone likely to meet with a strain of this kind, the leg is rarely sufficiently gummy to prevent the finger from making out the condition of the ligaments and tendons. There is no giving away of the joints as in "break-down," but on the contrary the leg is flexed, and if the case is a bad one, the toe only is allowed to touch the ground. In ordinary cases, however, there is merely slight swelling of the suspensory ligament in a limited spot usually near its bifurcation, or sometimes in one division only close above the sesamoid bone to which it is attached. The horse can stand readily on that leg, but on being trotted he limps a good deal. Sometimes, however, there is a swelling of the feet without lameness, but in this case the enlargement is generally due to an effusion of serum into the cellular covering of the ligament, and not to an actual strain of its fibres.—The *treatment* will depend greatly upon the extent of the mischief; if there is no great injury done, and the enlargement is chiefly from effusion of serum, rest and cold applications by means of bandages or otherwise will in the course of two or three months effect a cure. Generally, however, the case will last six or eight months before the ligament recovers its tone; and in a valuable horse no attempt should be made to work him before that time. Where the swelling is small, as it generally is, bandages have no power over it, as the projection of the flexor tendons keeps the pressure off the injured part. Here, dipping the leg in a bucket of water every hour will be of far more service than a bandage, and the sudden shock of the cold water will be doubly efficacious. After all heat has disappeared the biniodide of mercury may be used as a blister two or three times, and then the horse may either be turned out, or put into a loose box for three or four months, after which walking exercise will complete the cure.

STRAIN OF THE BACK SINEWS.

IN THIS ACCIDENT the position of the leg is the same as in strain of the suspensory ligament, and there is no giving way of the joints. The flexor tendons are enlarged, hot, and tender, and there is great lameness, the horse having the power to flex the joints below the knee, but resolutely objecting to extend them, by bearing what little weight is unavoidable upon his toe. The case is often confounded with a "break-down," but it may readily be distinguished by the fact that in the latter the joints give way on putting the weight upon them, whilst in mere strains they do not, and the tendency is to the opposite extreme. Frequently after a bad strain of the flexor tendons, the fetlock is "over shot," or beyond the upright, in consequence of the continued flexion of the joint, to prevent pressure upon the injured fibres, and in the management this result should be carefully guarded against. The injury is generally confined to the sheath of the tendons, which in most cases gradually puts on an inflammatory condition for some time before actual lameness is observed. In bad cases, however, the ligamentous fibres which are given off by the posterior carpal ligament to the flexor tendons are ruptured, greatly increasing the amount of inflammation and subsequent loss of strength. In any case the tendon feels spongy, and slightly enlarged, and there is more or less soreness on pressure and on being trotted, but in the latter case exercise removes the tenderness, and very often temporarily causes an absorption of the effused fluid, which is again deposited during rest. This state of things goes on for a time, the groom doing all in his power to alleviate it by wet bandages, &c., but at last a severe race or gallop brings on an extra amount of inflammation, with or without actual strain of the fibres of the tendon, and then there can be no doubt about the propriety of rest and severe treatment. It often happens that both legs are slightly affected, but one being more tender than the other, the horse attempts to save it by changing legs, the consequence of which is that the comparatively sound tendons are strained, and he returns to his stable with both legs in a bad state, but with one of them requiring immediate attention.—The *treatment* should be by local bleeding (from the arm, thigh, or toe), followed at first by warm fomentations, and in a few days by cold lotions. A high-heeled shoe (called a patten) should be put on the foot, so as to allow the horse to rest part of the weight upon the heel without distressing the tendon, and this will have a tendency to prevent him from over shooting at the fetlock joint, which he will otherwise be very apt to do from constantly balancing his leg on the toe. After three or four days the hot fomentations will have done what is wanted, and a cold lotion may be applied by means of a loose linen bandage. The best is composed as follows:—

  Take of Muriate of Ammonia . . . . . . 2 oz.
     Vinegar . . . . ¼ pint.
     Methylated Spirit of Wine . . . . ¼ pint.
     Water . . . . 2 quarts. Mix.

With this the bandage should be kept constantly wet, the application being continued for a fortnight at least, during which time the patient must be kept cool, by lowering his food, and giving him a dose of physic. At the end of three weeks or a month from the accident, the leg must be either blistered or fired, the choice depending upon the extent of injury, and the desire to avoid a blemish if such a feeling exists. The former is the more efficacious plan no doubt, but blistering will frequently suffice in mild cases. If, however, the tendons at the end of a month continue greatly enlarged, a cure can hardly be expected without the use of the "irons."

BREAKING DOWN.

GREAT CONFUSION exists among trainers as to the exact nature of this accident, which is considered by the veterinary surgeon to consist in an actual rupture of the suspensory ligament either above or below the sesamoid bones, which, in fact, merely separate this apparatus of suspension into two portions, just as the patella intervenes between the rectus femoris and the tibia. Whichever part of the suspensory apparatus is gone (whether the superior or inferior sesamoidal ligament is immaterial), the fetlock and pastern joints lose their whole inelastic support; and the flexor tendons, together with their ligamentous fibres which they receive from the carpus, giving way, as they must do, to allow of the accident taking place, the toe is turned up, and the fetlock joint bears upon the ground. This is a complete "break down;" but there are many cases in which the destruction of the ligamentous fibres is not complete, and the joint, though much lowered, does not actually touch the ground. These are still called breaks down, and must be regarded as such, and as quite distinct from strains of the flexor tendons. The accident generally occurs in a tired horse, when the flexor muscles do not continue to support the ligaments, from which circumstance it so often happens in the last few strides of a race. *The symptoms* are a partial or entire giving way of the fetlock joint downwards, so that the back of it either touches the ground, or nearly so, when the weight is thrown upon it. Usually, however, after the horse is pulled up, he hops on three legs, and refuses altogether to put that which is broken down to the ground. In a very few minutes the leg "fills" at the seat of the accident, and becomes hot and very tender to the touch. There can, therefore, be no doubt as to the nature of the mischief, and the confusion to which allusion has been made is one of names rather than of facts. *Treatment* can only be directed to a partial recovery from this accident, for a horse broken down in the sense in which the term is here used can only be used for stud purposes or at slow farm work. A patten shoe should at once be put on after bleeding at the toe to a copious extent, and then fomentations followed by cold lotions should be applied, as directed in the last section. As there must necessarily be a deformity of the leg, there can be no objection on that score to firing, and when the severe inflammation following the accident has subsided this operation should be thoroughly performed, so as to afford relief not only by the counter irritation which is set up, and which lasts only for a time, but by the rigid and unyielding case which it leaves behind for a series of years.

x

STRAINS OF THE HIP JOINT, STIFLE, AND HOCK.

THE HIP JOINT, OR ROUND BONE, is liable to be strained by the hind feet slipping and being stretched apart, or by blows against the side of the stall, when cast, which are not sufficient to dislocate the femur, but strain its ligaments severely. The consequence is an inflammation of the joint, which is evidenced by a dropping of one hip in going, the weight being thrown more upon the sound side than upon the other. This is especially remarkable on first starting, the lameness soon going off in work, but returning after rest. The case, however, is a rare one, and its description need not, therefore, occupy much of our space. When it does happen, it is very apt to lead to a wasting of the deep muscles of the haunch, which nothing but compulsory work will restore to a healthy condition. The only *treatment* necessary in the early stage of strain of the hip joint is rest and cooling diet, &c.; but, after six weeks or two months, a gradual return to work is indispensable to effect a cure.

STRAINS OF THE STIFLE, independently of blows, are rare; but the latter often are inflicted upon this joint in hunting, leaving little evidence externally, so that it is almost always doubtful whether the injury is the result of a blow or strain. The *symptoms* are a swelling and tenderness of the joint, which can be ascertained by a careful examination; and on trotting the horse, there is manifested a difficulty or stiffness in drawing forward the hind leg under the belly. The *treatment* must be by bleeding and physicking in the early stage, together with hot fomentations to the part, continued every hour until the heat subsides. After a few days, if the joint is still painful, a large blister should be applied, or, what is still better, a seton should be inserted in the skin adjacent.

THE HOCK ITSELF is liable to strain, independently of the peculiar accident known as "curb." When it occurs, there is some heat of the part, with more or less lameness, and neither spavin, thoroughpin, nor curb to account for them. The injury is seldom severe, and may be relieved by fomentations for a day or two, followed by cold lotions, as presented at page 320, for strain of the back sinews.

CURB.

THE LOWER PART OF THE POSTERIOR SURFACE of the os calcis is firmly united to the cuboid and external metatarsal bone by two strong ligamentous bands, called the calcaneo-cuboid and calcaneo-metatarsal ligaments. The centre of these ligaments is about seven or eight inches below the point of the hock, and when a soft but elastic swelling suddenly makes its appearance there, it may with certainty be asserted that a "curb" has been thrown out. The accident occurs somewhat suddenly; but the swelling and inflammation do not always show themselves until after a night's rest, when the part is generally enlarged, hot, and tender. The precise extent of the strain is of little consequence; for whatever its nature, the treatment should be sufficiently active to reduce the ligaments to their healthy condition. Some horses have naturally the head of the external small metatarsal bone unusually large, and the-hock so formed that there is an angle between the large metatarsal bone and the tarsus, leaving a prominence, which, however, is hard and bony, and not soft and elastic, as is the case with curb. Such hocks are generally inclined to throw out curbs; but there are many exceptions, and some of the most suspicious-looking joints have been known to stand sound for years. Curbs are seldom thrown out by very old horses, and usually occur between the commencement of breaking-in and the seventh or eighth year, though they are not unfrequently met with in the younger colt, being occasioned by his gambols over hilly ground. The *treatment* should at first be studiously confined to a reduction of the inflammation; any attempt to procure absorption till this is effected being injurious in the extreme. If there is much heat in the part, blood may be taken from the thigh vein, the corn should be removed, and a dose of physic given as soon as practicable. The curb should then be kept wet (by means of a bandage lightly applied) with the lotion recommended at page 316 for capped hocks, and this should be continued until the inflammation is entirely gone. During this treatment, in bad cases, a patten shoe should be kept on, so as to keep the hock as straight as possible, and thus take the strain off the ligaments which are affected. After the part has become cool, it may be reduced in size, by causing absorption to be set up; which is best effected by the application of mercury and iodine (both of which possess that power), in such a shape as to cause a blister of the skin. The biniodide of mercury has this double advantage, and there is no application known to surgery which will act equally well in effecting the absorption of a curb. It should be applied in the mode recommended at page 300, and again rubbed on at an interval of about a week, for three or four times in succession, when it will generally be found that the absorption of the unnatural swelling is effected; but the ligaments remain as weak as before, and nothing but exercise (not too severe, or it will inflame them again) will strengthen them sufficiently to prevent a return. Friction with the hand, aided by a slightly stimulating oil (such as neat's-foot and turpentine mixed, or neat's-foot and oil of origanum, or, in fact, any stimulating essential oil), will tend to strengthen the ligaments, by exciting their vessels to throw out additional fibres; and in course of time a curb may be considered to be sufficiently restored to render it tolerably safe to use the horse again in the same way which originally produced it.

DISLOCATION.

BY DISLOCATION is meant the forcible removal of the end of a bone from the articulating surface which it naturally occupies. In the horse, from the strength of his ligaments, the accident is not common; those that do occur being chiefly in the hip joint, and in that between the patella and the end of the femur.

DISLOCATION OF THE HIP JOINT is known by the rigidity of the hind leg, which cannot be moved in any direction, and is carried by the horse when he is compelled to attempt to alter his position. There is a flatness of the haunch below the hip, but the crest of the ilium is still there, and by this the accident may be diagnosed from fracture of that part. *No treatment* is of the slightest avail, as the part cannot be reduced, and the horse is useless except for stud purposes. The accident is not very common.

DISLOCATION OF THE PATELLA sometimes becomes habitual, occurring repeatedly in the same horse, apparently from a spasmodic contraction of the external vastus muscle, which draws the patella outwards, and out of the trochlea formed for it in the lower head of the femur. When the cramp goes off, the patella drops into its place again as soon as the horse moves, and no treatment is required. Occasionally, however, the dislocation is more complete, and nothing but manual dexterity will replace the bone in its proper situation. Great pain and uneasiness are expressed, and the operator must encircle the haunch with his arms and lay hold of the patella with both hands, while an assistant drags forward the toe, and thus relaxes the muscles which are inserted in it. By forcibly driving the patella into its place it may be lifted over the ridge which it has passed, and a snap announces the reduction.

WOUNDS OF JOINTS.

THE KNEE is the joint most frequently suffering from wound, being liable to be cut by a fall upon it, if the ground is rough; and if the accident takes place when the horse is going at a rapid pace, the skin, ligaments, and tendons may be worn through by friction against the plain surface of a smooth turnpike road. Whether the joint itself is injured, or only the skin, the accident is called a "broken knee," and for convenience sake it will be well to consider both under the present head.

WHEN A BROKEN KNEE consists merely in an abrasion of the skin, the attention of the groom is solely directed to the restoration of the hair, which will grow again as well as ever, if the bulbs or roots are not injured. These are situated in the internal layer of the true skin, and therefore, whenever there is a smooth red surface displayed, without any difference in the texture of its parts, a confident hope may be expressed that there will be no blemish. If the skin is penetrated, either the glistening surface of the tendons or ligaments is apparent, or there is a soft layer of cellular membrane, generally containing a fatty cell or two in the middle of the wound of the skin. Even here, by proper treatment, the injury may be repaired so fully, that the space uncovered by hair cannot be recognised by the ordinary observer, and not by any one without bending the knee and looking very carefully at it. *The best treatment* is to foment the knee well with warm water, so as to remove every particle of grit or dirt; go on with this every hour during the first day, and at night apply a bran poultice to the knee, which should be left on till the next morning. Then cleanse the wound, and apply a little spermaceti ointment, or lard without salt, and with this keep the wound pliant until it heals, which if slight it will in a few days. If the skin is pierced there will generally be a growth *above it* of red flabby granulations, which should be carefully kept down to its own level (not beneath it), by the daily use of blue stone, or if necessary of nitrate of silver. As soon as the wound is perfectly healed, if the horse can be spared, the whole *front* of the knee and skin should be dressed with James' blister, which will bring off the hair of the adjacent parts, and also encourage the growth of that injured by the fall. In about three weeks or a month from its application, the leg will pass muster, for there will be no difference in the color of the old and new hair as there would have been without the blister, and the new will also have come on more quickly and perfectly than it otherwise would.

WHEN THE JOINT ITSELF is opened the case is much more serious, and there is a risk not only of a serious blemish, which can seldom be avoided, but of a permanent stiffness of the leg, the mischief sometimes being sufficient to lead to constitutional fever, and the local inflammation going on to the destruction of the joint by anchylosis. *The treatment* should be directed to cleanse and then close the joint, the former object being carried out by a careful ablution with warm water, continued until there is no doubt of all the dirt and grit having been removed. Then, if there is only a very small opening in the capsular ligament, it may be closed by a careful and light touch of a pointed iron heated to a red heat. Generally, however, it is better to apply some dry carded cotton to the wound, and a bandage over this, leaving all on for four or five days, when it may be removed and reapplied. The horse should be bled largely and physicked, taking care to prevent all chance of his lying down by racking him up.

He will seldom attempt to do this, on account of the pain occasioned in bending the knee, but some animals will disregard this when tired, and will go down somehow. When the cotton is reapplied, if there are granulations above the level of the skin, they must be kept down as recommended in the last paragraph, and the subsequent treatment by blister may be exactly the same. By these means a very extensive wound of the knee may be often speedily cured, and the blemish will be comparatively trifling.

THE KNEE IS SOMETIMES punctured by a thorn in hunting, causing great pain and lameness. If it can be felt externally, it is well to cut down upon it and remove it; but groping in the dark with the knife among important tendons in front of the knee is not on any account to be attempted. The knee should be well fomented, five or six times a day, until the swelling, if there is any, subsides, and, in process of time, the thorn will either show its base, or it will gradually free itself from its attachments and lie beneath the skin, from which position it may be safely extracted with the knife.

CHAPTER XXI.

DISEASES OF THE THORACIC ORGANS AND THEIR APPENDAGES.

General Remarks—Catarrh—Influenza or Distemper—Bronchitis —Chronic Cough—Laryngitis—Roaring, Whistling, Etc.— Pneumonia and Congestion of the Lungs—Pleurisy—Pleurodynia—Phthisis—Broken Wind—Thick Wind—Spasm of the Diaphragm—Diseases of the Heart—Diseases of the Blood Vessels in the Chest and Nose.

GENERAL REMARKS.

THE IMPORTANCE OF SOUNDNESS in the respiratory apparatus is so fully recognised, that in common *parlance* it is put before the organs of locomotion, a popular expression being "sound, wind and limb." It is true that good wind is useless without legs; but the diseases of the latter are known to be more under control than those of the chest, and hence it is, perhaps, that the wind is so carefully scrutinized by all purchasers of horses. There is, also, much greater difficulty in ascertaining the condition of the lungs and their appendages, and the ordinary observer can only judge of them by an absolute trial; while the state of the legs may be seen and felt, and that of the feet can be tolerably well ascertained by a very short run upon hard ground. So, also, with the acute diseases of these parts; while the legs and feet manifest the slightest inflammation going on in them by swelling and heat, the air-passages may be undergoing slow but sure destruction, without giving out any sign that can be detected by any one but the practised veterinarian. In most of the diseases of the chest there is disturbance of the breathing, even during a state of rest; but in some of them, as in roaring, for instance, no such evidence is afforded, and the disease can only be detected by an examination during, or immediately after, a severe gallop.

CATARRH, OR COLD.

CATARRH may be considered under two points of view; either as an inflammation of the mucous membrane of the nasal cavities, accompanied by slight general fever; or as an ephemeral fever of three or four days duration, complicated with this condition of the nose. The latter is, perhaps, the more scientific definition, but for common purposes it is more convenient to consider it as mainly consisting in the most prominent symptom. There is invariably some degree of feverishness, sometimes very considerable, at others so slight as to be easily passed over. Usually the pulse is accelerated to about forty or fifty, the appetite is impaired, and there is often sore throat, with more or less cough. On examining the interior of the nostrils, they are more red than natural, at first dry and swollen, then bedewed with a watery discharge which soon becomes yellow, thick, and, in bad cases, purulent. The eyes are generally involved, their conjunctival coat being injected with blood, and often some slight weeping takes place, but there is always an expression of sleepiness or dulness, partly owing to the local condition of the organ, and partly to the general impairment of the health. The disease is caused in most instances by a chill, either in the stable or out, but sometimes, even in the mildest form, it appears to be epidemic. *The treatment* will greatly depend upon the severity of the seizure; usually, a bran-mash containing from six drachms to one ounce of powdered nitre in it, at night, for two or three consecutive periods, will suffice, together with the abstraction of corn, and, if the bowels are confined, a mild dose of physic should be given. In more severe cases, when there is cough and considerable feverishness, a ball composed of the following ingredients may be given every night:—

> Take of Nitrate of Potass . . . . 2 drachms.
> Tartarized Antimony . . . . 1 drachm.
> Powdered Digitalis . . . . ½ drachm.
> Camphor . . . . 1½ drachm.
> Linseed meal and boiling water enough to make into a ball.

If the throat is sore, an embrocation of equal parts of oil, turpentine, tincture of cantharides, and hartshorn, may be rubbed in night and morning.

Should the disease extend to the bronchial tubes, or substance of the lungs, the treatment for bronchitis or pneumonia must be adopted.

The stable should be kept cool, taking care to make up for the difference in temperature by putting on an extra rug; water should be allowed *ad libitum*, and no corn should be given.

Sometimes the discharge becomes chronic, and it is then known by the name *ozena*.

INFLUENZA, OR DISTEMPER.*

THIS MAY BE CONSIDERED TO BE an epidemic catarrh, but the symptoms are generally more severe and leave greater prostration of strength behind them. They also require more careful treatment, which must be specially adapted to the attack, for remedies which will arrest the disease in one year will totally fail the next time that the epidemic prevails. The fever of late years has had a tendency to put on the typhoid type, and bleeding, which formerly was often beneficial, is now completely forbidden. The *symptoms* are at first similar to those already described as pertaining to common catarrh, but after a few days the accompanying fever is more severe than usual, and does not abate at the customary period. The appetite is altogether lost, and the appearance of the patient is characteristic of severe disease rather than of a trifling cold. It is, however, chiefly from the fact that a number of horses are seized with similar symptoms, either at the same time or rapidly following one another, that the disease is recognised. It usually prevails in the spring of the year, or in a wet and unhealthy autumn. Sometimes almost every case runs on to pneumonia, at others the bronchial mucous membrane alone is attacked; but in all there is extreme debility in proportion to the apparent nature of the disease. The ordinary appearances exhibited in recent epidemics have been as follows:—The first thing observed is a general slight shivering, accompanied by a staring coat. The pulse is weak, and slightly accelerated, but not to any great extent; the mouth feels hot; the eyes and the nostrils are red; the belly is tucked up; there is no appetite; cough, to a varying extent, begins to show itself; and there is generally a heaving of the flanks. The legs and feet are not cold as in pneumonia, but beyond this they afford no positive signs. The cellular membrane around the eyes, and of the legs, generally swells about the second day, and often the head and limbs become quite shapeless from this cause. In the early stage the bowels are often relaxed, but afterwards they are as frequently confined. Sore throat is a very common complication, but it is not by any means an invariable attendant on influenza. It is, however,

---

* CHOKING DISTEMPER—so called—will be found treated of under the name of *Typhoid Fever* in note to chapter on fevers.—EDITOR.

somewhat difficult to ascertain its existence, as in any case there is no appetite for food. *The treatment* should be conducted on the principle of husbanding the strength, and, unless urgent symptoms of inflammation show themselves, the less that is done the better. If the trachea or larynx is involved only slightly, counter irritation, by means of a liquid blister, must be tried, without resorting to strong internal medicines; but if serious mischief ensues, the case must, to a certain extent, be treated as it would be when coming on without the complication of influenza, always taking care to avoid bleeding, and merely acting on the bowels by gentle aperients, and on the skin and kidneys by the mildest diaphoretic and diuretic. The following is the ordinary plan of treatment adopted:

> Take of Spirit of Nitric Ether . . . . 1 ounce.
> Laudanum . . . . 4 drachms.
> Nitrate of Potass . . . . 3 drachms.
> Water . . . . 1 pint.
> Mix, and give as a drench night and morning.

By constantly offering to the horse thin gruel (taking care that it does not become sour), and no plain water, sufficient nourishment may be given, as his thirst will induce him to drink.

During the stage of convalescence the greatest care must be taken. At first, as soon as the cough has somewhat subsided, a mild stomachic ball will be desirable, such as

> Take of Extract of Gentian . . . . 6 drachms.
> Powdered Ginger . . . . 2 drachms. Mix.

Afterwards, if the case goes on favorably, and the appetite returns, the restoration may be left to nature, giving the horse by degrees his usual allowance of corn, and adding to his morning and evening feed one drachm of sulphate of iron in fine powder. It must not be attempted to give this until the appetite is pretty keen, or the horse will be disgusted, and will probably refuse his corn altogether.

Should typhoid symptoms be clearly established, the case must be treated according to the directions hereafter laid down for typhus fever.

BRONCHITIS.

BRONCHITIS is an inflammation of the mucous membrane lining the bronchi, and almost invariably extending to these parts through the trachea, from the larynx and nasal passages, which are primarily affected as in ordinary cold. The membrane in the early stage becomes filled with blood, and as a consequence the diameter of the tubes is diminished, attended by some difficulty and increased rapidity of breathing. After a time a frothy mucus is poured out from it, and this still further interferes with respiration, and necessitates a constant cough to get rid of it. *These symptoms* are always present, but they will vary greatly in intensity, and in the rapidity with which they progress, from which circumstances bronchitis is said to be *acute or chronic*, as the case may be. *In the acute form* there are also several variations, and veterinary writers are in the habit of again subdividing it into acute and sub-acute, but the two leading divisions are sufficient for all practical purposes. It begins with the usual premonitory appearances of a severe cold, accompanied by a staring coat, and entire loss of appetite. The breathing is somewhat quicker than natural, and the pulse is raised to sixty or seventy. The legs remain of the usual temperature, and there is a hard dry cough, the lining membrane of the nostrils being intensely red, and in severe cases dry and swollen. On auscultation there is a dry rattling sound, very different from the crepitation of pneumonia, and as soon as mucus is secreted, succeeded by gurgling, and soap-bubble sounds, easily distinguished when once heard. If the attack goes on favorably, the cough becomes loose, and there is a free discharge of mucus, both from the lungs, as evidenced from the nature of the cough, and from the nostrils, as shown by the running from them. On the other hand, the prognosis is unfavorable when the breathing is very laborious, with the legs extended, and the cough constant and ineffectual in affording relief. Should no relief be afforded, death takes place a week or ten days after the onset of the disease, from suffocation. *The treatment* should depend greatly upon the urgency of the inflammation, which only an experienced eye can judge of. If slight, nitre and tartar emetic internally, and a blister (to one or both sides, according to the extent of bronchi involved), will suffice, but in very severe cases blood must be taken at the onset, or it will be impossible to control the inflammation. Bleeding should be avoided if it is judged prudent to do so, for of late years the type of diseases has changed so much in the horse, that he is found to bear loss of blood badly. Nevertheless, it is not wise to lay down the rule that it is never desirable. The bowels must be acted on by the ordinary physic ball, resorting to raking and clysters, if the time cannot be afforded for the usual laxative preparation. For the special control of the morbid state of the membrane the following ball will be found advantageous:—

   Take of Digitalis . . . . ½ drachm.
      Calomel . . . . ½ drachm.
      Tartar Emetic . . . . 60 to 80 grains.
      Nitre . . . . 2 drachms.
   Mix with treacle, and give twice a day.

Should the disease continue after the blister is healed, a large seton may be put in one or both sides with advantage.

CHRONIC BRONCHITIS seldom exists except as a sequel to the acute form, and after adopting the balls recommended for that state, it may be treated by attention to the general health, a seton in the side, and the exhibition of an expectorant ball twice a day, composed of the following materials:—

> Take of Gum Ammoniacum . . . . ½ ounce.
> Powdered Squill . . . . 1 drachm.
> Castile Soap . . . . 2 drachms.
> Mix and make into a ball.

CHRONIC COUGH.

BY THIS TERM is understood a cough that comes on without any fever or evidences of the horse having taken cold. It differs in this respect from chronic bronchitis, which generally supervenes upon the acute form, and is always attended in the early stage by feverishness. It appears probable that chronic cough is dependent upon an unnatural stimulus to the mucous membrane, for it almost always makes its appearance when much corn is given without due preparation, and ceases on a return to green food. It is, therefore, very commonly termed a stomach cough. The *symptoms* are all summed up in the presence of a dry cough, which is seldom manifested while in the stable, but comes on whenever the breathing is hastened by any pace beyond a walk. Two or three coughs are then given, and the horse perhaps is able to go on with his work, but after resting for a few minutes, and again starting, it comes on again, and annoys the rider or driver by its tantalizing promise of disappearance followed by disappointment. Very often this kind of cough is caused by the irritation of worms, but any kind of disorder of the digestive organs appears to have the power of producing it. *The usual treatment* for chronic bronchitis seems here to be quite powerless, and the only plan of proceeding likely to be attended with success, is to look for the cause of the irritation, and remove it. Sometimes this will be found in a hot stable, the horse having previously been accustomed to a cool one. Here the alteration of the temperature by ten or fifteen degrees will in a few days effect a cure, and nothing else is required. Again, it may be that the corn has been overdone, in which case a gentle dose of physic, followed by a diminished allowance of corn, and a bran-mash twice a week, will be successful. If the stomach is much disordered, green food will be the best stimulus to a healthy condition, or in its absence a few warm cordial balls may be tried. The existence of worms should be ascertained in doubtful cases, and if they are present, the proper remedies must be given for their removal. Linseed oil and spirit of turpentine, which are both excellent worm remedies, are highly recommended in chronic cough, and whether or not their good effect is due to their antagonism to worms, they may be regarded as specially useful.

A very successful combination is the following mixture:—

Take of Spirit of Turpentine	2 ounces.
Mucilage of Acacia	6 ounces.
Gum Ammoniacum	½ ounce.
Laudanum	4 ounces.
Water	2 quarts.

Mix, and give half-a-pint as a drench every night: the bottle must be well shaken before pouring out the dose.

LARYNGITIS, ROARING, WHISTLING, &c.

ONE OF THE MOST COMMON diseases among well-bred horses of the present day, is the existence of some mechanical impediment to the passage of the air into the lungs, causing the animal to "make a noise." The exact nature of the sound has little or no practical bearing on the cause that produces it; that is to say, it cannot be predicated that roaring is produced by laryngitis; nor that whistling is the result of a palsy of some particular muscle, but undoubtedly it may safely be asserted that all lesions of the larynx, by which the shape and area of its opening (rima glottidis) are altered and diminished, are sure to have a prejudicial effect upon the wind, and either to produce roaring, whistling, wheezing, or trumpeting, but which would result it might be difficult to say, although the precise condition of the larynx were known, which it cannot be during life. Until recently veterinary surgeons were puzzled by often finding on examination of a roarer's larynx after death no visible organic change in the opening, and many were led to imagine that this part could not be the seat of the disease. On a careful dissection, however, it is found that a muscle or muscles whose office it is to dilate the larynx is wasted and flabby (crico-arytenoideus lateralis and thyro-arytenoideus). The other muscles are perhaps equally atrophied, but as their office is to close the opening, their defects are not equally injurious, and at all events are not shown by producing an unnatural noise. The cause of this wasting is to be looked for in pressure upon the nerve which supplies these muscles, and which passes through an opening in the posterior ala of the thyroid cartilage, so that whatever causes a displacement of that part will mechanically affect the nerve. For these several reasons it will be necessary to examine first of all into the several kinds of inflammation, &c., to which the larynx is subject, and then to investigate as far as we may, the nature, mode of detection, and treatment of the several conditions known to horsemen by the names of roaring, whistling, &c., which are only symptoms of one or other of the diseases to which allusion will presently be made.

BY ACUTE LARYNGITIS is meant a more than ordinary inflammation of the larynx, and not that slightly morbid condition in which the mucous membrane of that organ is always involved in "the passage of a cold into the chest." In the latter state the ear

CHRONIC LARYNGITIS.

detects no unusual sound, and indeed there is plenty of room for the air to pass. But in true laryngitis, on placing the ear near the throat, a harsh rasping sound is heard, which is sufficient at once to show the nature and urgency of the symptoms. The mucous membrane is swollen, and tinged with blood; the rima glottidis is almost closed, and the air in passing through it produces the sound above described, which, however, is sometimes replaced by a stridulous or hissing one. In conjunction with this well-marked symptom there is always a hoarse cough of a peculiar character, and some considerable fever, with frequent respiration, and a hard, wiry pulse of seventy to eighty. The *treatment* must be of the most active kind, for not only is life threatened, but even if a fatal result does not take place, there is great danger of permanent organic mischief to the delicate apparatus of the larynx, generally from the effusion of lymph into the submucous cellular membrane. A full bleeding should at once be practised, and repeated at the end of twelve hours if there is no relief afforded and the pulse still continues hard. The hair should be cut off the throat, and the tincture of cantharides brushed on in a pure state until a blister arises, when the part may be constantly well fomented, to encourage the discharge. Large doses of tartar emetic, calomel, and digitalis, must also be given, but their amount and frequency should be left to an experienced veterinarian, the preliminary bleeding and blistering being done in his absence to save time. It is a case in which medicine must be pushed as far as can be done with safety, and this cannot well be left to any one who is not well acquainted with its effects, and with the powers of the animal economy. Gruel is the only food allowed during the acute stage, and there is seldom time to have recourse to aperient physic until the urgent symptoms are abated, when an ordinary dose may be given. During convalescence the greatest care must be taken to prevent a relapse, by avoiding all excitement either by stimulating food or fast exercise.

CHRONIC LARYNGITIS may occur as the result of the acute form above described, or it may come on gradually, without any violent inflammation preceding it. In either case *the symptoms* are similar in their nature to those met with in the acute form, but less in degree. The noise made is not nearly so harsh, and can often hardly be heard on the most careful examination. The peculiar harsh, grating cough is, however, always present, and by it the nature of the case may generally be easily made out. The disease often accompanies strangles, although in nine cases out of ten it is overlooked by the careless attendant. Very commonly, however, it makes its ravages in so insidious a manner that no suspicion is felt of its presence, until the horse begins to make a noise, though he must in all probability have shown by the cough peculiar to the complaint, that it has been working its way for some weeks at least. Such cases chiefly occur in the training stable, and are due, according to my belief, to the enormous quantity of oats which it is now the fashion to give to colts from the earliest period of their lives, increased to seven and eight feeds a day during the second year. Continued spirit-drinking has precisely the same effect upon the human being, and the harsh stridulous cough of the confirmed drunkard marks the existence of ulceration of the larynx, in the only way which he will allow it to be displayed, for he is not, like the horse, made to exert his powers of running, whether his wind is good or bad. There is, of course, a considerable difference between the two diseases, but there is sufficient analogy between them to explain why the stimulus of over-corning should affect the larynx in preference to any other part. It would be difficult to show the connection between the two in any other way, beyond the simple fact that roaring has become general in an exact proportion to the prevalence of the present fashion of feeding. The advocates of the plan will say that though the two have come in together, yet it is merely a coincidence, and not a consequence the one of the other; but if it can be shown that in man a similar cause produces a similar effect, the argument is strengthened to such a degree as to be almost unanswerable. But whatever may be the cause there can be no doubt that the *treatment* is most troublesome, and often baffles the skill of the most accomplished veterinarian. Blistering is not so useful as counter-irritation by a seton, which must be inserted in the loose skin beneath the jaw, as close as possible to the larynx. This alone will do much towards the cure, but no pains must be spared to assist its action by a cooling regimen, consisting of bran mashes, and if in the spring or summer, green food, or in the winter, carrots. Corn must be entirely forbidden, and the kidneys should be encouraged to act freely by two or three drachms of nitre given in the mash twice a day. When the case is very intractable, the nitrate of silver may be applied to the part itself by means of a sponge fastened to a piece of flexible cane or whalebone. The mouth should then be kept open with the ordinary balling iron, and the sponge rapidly passed to the situation of the top of the larynx, and held there for a second, and then withdrawn. I have succeeded in curing two obstinate cases of chronic laryngitis by this plan, but some little risk is incurred, as in one of them imminent symptoms of suffocation presented themselves, but soon went off. I should not, therefore, recommend the application excepting in cases where all other means have failed, and in which there is reason to believe that the patient is likely to become a permanent roarer or whistler. The nitrate of silver has great power in producing resolution of inflammation in mucous surfaces, and in this disease little or nothing can be effected by general measures. The solution should be from ten to fifteen grains in the ounce of distilled water.

ROARING is the bugbear of the purchaser at the hammer, and not without good reason. The most experienced veterinarian or dealer will often fail to ascertain its existence, in spite of all the artifices he may call into play. Not the slightest sound is heard during a state of quiescence, or even when the horse is trotted or galloped for the short distance which "the ride" will afford. The blow on the side given with due artistic effect elicits no grunt, and yet the animal is a confirmed roarer, and not worth a shilling perhaps for the purpose to which he is intended to be devoted. On the other hand, many a sound horse is condemned as a roarer for giving out the obnoxious grunt; and though there is no doubt that this sign may be relied on in a great many cases, yet it cannot be accepted as either negatively or positively a certain proof. The only real trial is the noiseless gallop on turf or plough, when the ear can detect the slightest sound, and can distinguish its exact nature, and the precise spot from which it proceeds. Many a horse will, when he is excited, make a harsh noise in his breathing, accompanied by a kind of "gluck," proceeding from a spasmodic flapping of the velum palati; but on galloping him all this goes off, and he may probably exhibit excellent wind. Such cases I have many times known, and they would be condemned as unsound by those who have had little experience, or are content with a careless and inefficient trial. Stallions are particularly prone to make this kind of noise, and it is extremely difficult to ascertain their soundness in this respect by any means which can be safely resorted to. The causes of roaring are of three kinds: 1st, Inflammation, which has left a thickening or ulceration of the mucous membrane, or a fungous growth from it; 2d, Paralysis of the muscles; and 3d, An alteration of the shape of the cartilages of the larynx, produced by tight reining.

In roaring produced by an ulcerated or thickened condition of the mucous membrane, or by a fungous growth, the sound elicited is always the same in proportion to the rapidity of respiration. None of the ordinary expedients by which the breath is introduced in a modified stream (such as a full meal, or pressure on the nostrils or windpipe), will be of much avail, and the horse roars sturdily whenever his pace is sufficiently accelerated. If a horse so affected can be made to grunt by the blow on the side, the sound will always indicate the disease, for it will be harsh and rough, and not the natural grunt of the animal. It is usually supposed that no *treatment* can be of the slightest avail here; but I believe that sometimes the continued application of nitrate of silver, as recommended at page 334, would be followed by a certain amount of amelioration, the extent of which it is impossible to guess at without a trial. In any case, when the animal is rendered almost worthless by disease, it is fair to try experiments which are neither expensive nor cruel; and from the effect of the remedy in those cases in which it has been used, I am led to expect that it may prove beneficial in those of longer standing. Setons, blisters, and embrocations are all useless, as has been proved in numberless cases; and beyond the palliation which can be afforded by employing the horse only at such a pace as his state will allow, nothing else can be suggested. In some cases the roarer will be able to do ordinary harness work, which, however, in hot weather, will try him severely; in others he may be so slightly affected as to be fit to hunt in a country where, from its nature, the pace is not very severe; but by confirmed roarers the slow work of the cart is all that can be performed without cruelty.

Where paralysis of the muscles that open the rima glottidis is the seat of the roaring, no plan has yet been suggested which is of the slightest avail. In the first place, it is extremely difficult, and indeed almost impossible, to diagnose the affection, and I know of no means by which paralysis can be ascertained to exist during life. Hence, although it is barely possible that by the use of strychnine the nerve might be stimulated into a restoration of its functions, yet as the case cannot be ascertained, it is scarcely wise to give this powerful drug in the hope that it may by chance hit the right nail on the head. This paralytic condition seems chiefly to attack carriage horses, and probably arises from the pressure made by the over-curved larynx upon the laryngeal nerve as it passes through the opening in the thyroid cartilage. Many veterinary writers have looked to the recurrent branch of the par vagum to explain the loss of power, but I believe it is rather to the laryngeal nerve that the mischief is due. It must be remembered that carriage-horses are not only reined up for hours while doing their daily work out of doors, but they are also often placed in the same position, or even a more constrained one, by the coachman in the stable, in order to improve their necks. One horse of his pair perhaps has naturally a head better set on than the other, and he wishes to make nature bend to his wishes by compelling the other to do that which the shape of his jaw forbids without a sacrifice. The mouthing tackle is put on in the stable with this view, and the poor horse is "kept on the bit" for three or four hours early in the morning, during which time his larynx is pressed between his narrow jaws into a most unnatural shape. The consequence is either that the nerve is pressed upon, and the muscles to which it is supplied are paralyzed, as in the condition which we are now considering, or the cartilages are permanently disfigured, which is the subject of the next paragraph. When the paralysis is established, I believe no means but the internal use o strychnine are at all likely to be beneficial.

An alteration in the shape of the cartilages, so as to perm anently change their form, is, I believe, the least common of all the causes of roaring. Pressure for a very long time will be required to effect this, and far more than suffices to paralyze the nerve. Cases, however, are recorded, and the parts have been preserved, so that there can be no doubt of their occasional occurrence. No *treatment* can be of the slightest service.

Although roaring, in all its varieties, may be said to be generally incurable, yet it may be greatly palliated by general attention to the state of the lungs and stomach, by proper food, and by the use, while the horse is at work, of a special contrivance, of a most ingenious nature, published by Mr. Reeve, of Camberwell, in the *Veterinarian* for 1858, but said to have been in use for many years among the London omnibus and cab men. At all events, Mr. Reeve deserves the credit of having laid the matter before the profession, and of explaining the true principle upon which it acts. He says, in his paper on the subject: "I thought it possible to so modify the atmospheric supply to the lungs, that, during exercise, the volume of air, when it arrived at the glottis, should not exceed that which passed through its opening when the horse was tranquil, and which (from the fact of the sound being absent) does not at that time produce roaring. A strap was accordingly made to pass around the nose of the horse, just over the region of the false nostrils, and buckle beneath the lower jaw. To the inner surface of this strap, and immediately over the false nostril on each side, was fixed a body resembling in shape the half of a hen's egg, cut longitudinally. When applied, these bodies pressed upon the triangular spaces formed by the apex of the nasal bones and upper jaw, thus closing the false nostrils, and partly diminishing the channel of the true ones. The result was highly gratifying; for the patient, which previously could not travel without stopping every minute to take breath, now travelled, to all appearance, without inconvenience or noise. At first, the strap seemed slightly to annoy the horse; and whenever it became displaced, the roaring would again commence. A slight modification, however, overcame every difficulty: the strap, instead of being buckled around and under the jaw, was fastened on each side of the bit; and, to prevent its descent, another was carried from its centre, and fastened to the front of the harness-bridle." Mr. Reeve asserts that the effect was all he could have wished, and that the horse on which he tried the plan, "which previously had been entirely useless, now performs his work in a heavy brougham, and gives great satisfaction. The roaring is stopped, and, with the usual speed, there appears no impediment to respiration."

He concludes: "I have paid particular attention to this case, and am inclined to think, that when by the compression we have neutralized the action of the false nostrils, the object is effected without the necessity of further narrowing the nasal passage."

Few people would care to drive a roarer, if they could help it, even with the aid of the nasal compress; but if necessity compels such a proceeding, it is well to know how the poor animal may be used with least annoyance to himself and his master.

HIGHBLOWING is a perfectly healthy and natural habit, and cannot be confounded with roaring by any experienced horseman. It is solely confined to the nostrils; and the noise is not produced in the slightest degree during inspiration, but solely during the expulsion of the air, which is more forcible and rapid than usual, and accompanied by a vibratory movement of the nostrils, which is the seat of the noise. Roaring, on the contrary, continues during inspiration, as well as expiration; and by this simple test the two may readily be distinguished. Most highblowers have particularly good wind, of which the celebrated Eclipse is an example; for there is no doubt that he was addicted to the habit.

WHISTLING (AND PIPING, which is very similar to it), are produced by the same causes as roaring, in an exaggerated condition. Thus, a roarer often becomes a whistler as the rima glottidis is more and more closed by disease; on the other hand, the whistler is never converted into a roarer. The noise made is seldom a decidedly shrill whistle, but it has more resemblance to that sound than to roaring, and the name may well be retained as descriptive of it. Whistlers are always in such a state of confirmed disease, that treatment is out of the question—indeed, they can only be put to the very slowest kind of work.

WHEEZING is indicative of a contracted condition of the bronchial tubes, which is sometimes of a spasmodic nature, and at others is only brought on during occasional attacks after exposure to cold. The *treatment* should be that recommended for chronic bronchitis, which is the nature of the disease producing these symptoms.

TRUMPETING is not very well defined by veterinary writers, and I confess that I have never heard any horse make a noise which could be compared to the trumpet, or to the note of the elephant so called.

THE QUESTION RELATING TO THE HEREDITARY NATURE of roaring is one which demands the most careful examination before a reliable answer can be given to it. It would be necessary to select at random a number of roaring sires and dams, and compare their stock with that of an equal proportion of sound animals, which would be a Herculean task, beyond the power of any private individual. Nothing short of this could possibly settle the dispute;

but, as far as opinion goes, it may be assumed that there are strong authorities against the hereditary nature of the diseases which produce roaring. That it is often the result of ordinary inflammation, which in itself can scarcely be considered hereditary, is plain enough; and that it is also produced by mismanagement in tight reining is also admitted, which latter kind can scarcely be supposed to be handed down from sire to son; but that it is safer, when practicable, to avoid parents with any disease whatever, is patent to all.

PNEUMONIA AND CONGESTION OF THE LUNGS.*

THE THEORETICAL DEFINITION OF PNEUMONIA is that it consists of inflammation of the parenchyma of the lungs, independently both of the mucous lining to the air passages, and of the serous covering of the whole mass. The mucous membrane ceases abruptly at the terminations of the bronchial subdivisions, and consequently the air-cells are not lined with a continuation from it. Hence there is an extensive cellulo-fibrous area, which may be the subject of inflammation, without implicating the mucous surface. Until within the last fifteen or twenty years, it was commonly supposed that the air-cells were all lined by mucous membrane, and that the parenchyma was confined to an almost infinitesimally thin structure, filling up its interstices; but the microscope has revealed the true structure of the lungs, and has shown that there is a well-founded distinction between bronchitis and pneumonia, upon the ground of anatomy, as well as observation. Still, it cannot be denied that the one seldom exists to any great extent, or for any long period, without involving the adjacent tissue; and broncho-pneumonia, as well as pleuro-pneumonia, are as common as the pure disease.

PNEUMONIA, OR PERIPNEUMONY, must be examined, with a view, first, to its intensity, whether *acute* or *sub-acute;* and secondly, as to its effects, which may be of little consequence, or they may be so serious as to completely destroy the subsequent usefulness of the patient. It is not, therefore, alone necessary to provide against death by the treatment adopted, but due care must also be taken that the tissue of the lungs is not disorganized by a deposition of lymph, or of matter, so as to lead, in the one case, to a consolidation of the air-cells, and, in the other, to the formation

---

* All diseases of the chest and lungs, among farmers and others, are classed under the general head of Lung Fever. Whether the lungs be inflamed or congested, tincture of aconite is the surest remedy, and is in fact the most successful sedative in all diseases of the chest or lungs. Give 20 drops every four hours, until four or five doses have been given, allowing plenty of cold water and pure air. This last (pure air) is very important, and should not be overlooked.—EDITOR.

of a large abcess, and consequent destruction of substance. The former is a very common sequel of pneumonia; and probably there are few attacks of it without being followed by a greater or less degree of hepatization, by which term the deposit of lymph is known, from its causing the lungs to assume the texture of liver ($\H{\eta}\pi\alpha\rho$). In very severe cases, gangrene of the lungs is induced; but as death almost always speedily follows this condition, it is not necessary to consider it, excepting as bearing upon the fatal result.

The *cause* of pneumonia may be over-exertion, as in the hunting-field, especially in an unprepared horse; or it may come on as a primary disease after exposure to cold; or it may follow upon bronchitis when neglected and allowed to run on without check. In the two first cases it appears to be produced by the great congestion of blood which takes place in the fine network of vessels of which the lungs are in great part composed. The blood in the one case is collected by the increased necessity for its aeration with a failing circulation, as in over-exhaustion, or in the other it is forced inwards upon the vital organs by the chill which the skin has received. The capillaries are then roused to act beyond their strength, and an inflammatory condition is established as a reparatory effort of nature, which may possibly stop short as soon as the object is accomplished, but more frequently goes on beyond this, and an attack of pneumonia sets in with more or less intensity, according to circumstances. For these reasons, when the lungs are evidently congested, no pains should be spared to relieve them by causing the skin to act. before the aid of nature is invoked, since it can never be certain that she will stop short at the proper point.

CONGESTION OF THE LUNGS is too often neglected and allowed to go on to inflammation. Veterinary surgeons, indeed, are seldom called in before this stage has run its course and inflammation is established. It is true that every hunting man endeavors to ascertain all the particulars relating to it, because he is constantly in fear of having to treat it, and he would gladly benefit by the advice and experience of those more competent to treat it than himself. But the great mass of horsemasters are wholly ignorant of its action, and I shall therefore endeavor to lay down instructions which may be beneficial to those who are so unlucky as to have a horse with congested lungs, either caused by over-exertion or by a chill, or by a combination of the two, as most frequently happens.

When a fat "dealer's horse," that is, one made up for sale and not for use, is ridden in a sharp burst across country, his lungs are most unfortunately tried, for he is not only loaded with blood containing an excess of stimulating materials (or in a state of plethora, as it is called), but his heart and blood-vessels are not prepared by previous exercise to carry on the circulation when unusual demands upon them are made. The consequence is that, as soon as he has gone half a dozen miles, he not only tires, but, if pressed, his gallant spirit carries him on until the blood collects and stagnates in his lungs, from a defect in the circulating apparatus, and he becomes absolutely choked from a want of that decarbonization which is necessary to his very existence. Air is taken freely into his lungs, but the circulation almost ceases in them, and in spite of his hurried breathing, as shown by his panting sides, he is almost as completely suffocated as if a cord was tied round his neck. On examining his eyes and nostrils they are seen to be turgid and *purple*, the vessels being filled with carbonized blood, while the heart beats rapidly but feebly, and the countenance is expressive of anxiety and distress. In this state many a horseman finds his steed every winter, and a pretty dilemma he is in. The question of *treatment* is a serious one, even to the most experienced in such matters, but one thing is quite clear, that the more urgent the case the more danger there is in having recourse to the lancet. Bleeding to the extent of a few pounds will sometimes relieve a trifling case of exhaustion, but in a really severe one it will take away the only chance which remains. The best plan is to give the animal plenty of air, turn his head to the wind, and if any kind of fermented liquor can be obtained, give him a little at once. Neat spirits are apt to cause increased distress from spasm of the larynx, but it is even better to risk this than to let the exhaustion continue. If, therefore, the horse is incapable of walking to the nearest farm-house or inn, the better plan is to leave him with a light covering on him of some kind, and at once proceed to procure a quart of ale or wine, or spirits and water, whichever can be obtained the most easily. One or other of these, slightly warmed and spiced, if possible, should be poured down his throat, which can readily be done, as he has no power to resist, and then in a few minutes he may generally be induced to move quietly on towards the nearest stable. Here he must remain all night if the attack is a bad one, or if he recovers soon he may be walked quietly home. When he reaches his stable he may be treated according to the directions given at page 188, and in the evening or the next morning early, if the pulse rises and is hard and jerking, he may be bled with advantage, but rarely should this be done for some hours after the first attack. Congestion is essentially produced by debility, and although an abstraction of blood relieves the vessels of a part of their load, it increases their weakness in a still greater degree, and they are less able to do their work, diminished though it may be, than they were before. Hundreds of over-worked horses have been killed by the abuse of the lancet in the hunting-field, but the principle on which their treatment should be conducted is better understood now than formerly.

WHEN CONGESTION shows itself as the result of a chill, the following *symptoms* are displayed:—First and foremost there is rapid and laborious breathing, the horse standing with his legs wide apart, his head thrust straight forward, and his flanks heaving. The skin is generally dry, but if there is any sweat it is a cold one. The legs are icy cold, and also the ears. The whites of the eyes and lining of the nostrils are of a purplish hue, but not very deep in colour The pulse is slightly accelerated (from forty to fifty), but not hard and incompressible; and lastly, the attack is of recent duration. These signs, however, are not to be fully relied on as marking congestion rather than inflammation, without having recourse to an examination of the lungs by means of the ear. Placing it against the side of the chest, in inflammation there would be certain marked sounds, presently to be described, whilst in the state we are now considering they are wholly absent, and all that is heard is the usual respiratory murmur slightly increased in intensity. It is of the utmost importance to make out exactly the nature of the case, for the *treatment* should be very different in congestion and inflammation. If in the former condition the blood can only be drawn into the skin, relief is at once afforded and all danger is at an end; but in the latter, though some slight advantage would be gained, the progress of the disease would not be materially checked. To produce this determination of blood to the skin without loss of time, is sometimes very difficult; but by the application of hot water and blankets it may generally be accomplished. Two men, supplied with a tub of very hot water and plenty of clothing, should be rapid in their movements, and proceed as follows:—Have an assistant ready to strip the patient when ordered, then, dipping a blanket in the water, it is taken out and partially wrung, leaving as much water in its meshes as it can hold without dropping; as soon as it is cool enough for the human hand to bear its pressure it should be gently, but quickly, laid upon the horse's back, and the rug, which has just come off, while still warm, placed over it, with two or three more over all, the number depending upon the temperature of the air. Another smaller rug may in the same way be wetted and applied to the neck, covering it with two or three hoods, but taking care to avoid pressure upon the windpipe. The legs also should be wrapped in flannel bandages, made as hot as possible before the fire, but dry. In the course of half an hour, if the skin of the parts uncovered does not become warm, and show evidences of sweating coming on, another rug must be dipped in the same way, and substituted quickly for the first.

Usually, however, the desired effect is produced within twenty minutes, and then great care and some little tact are required to manage the operation. If the sweating is allowed to go on beyond a certain point exhaustion is produced, attended by almost as much danger as inflammation; while on the other hand, in attempting to moderate the action of the skin, risk is incurred of a chill, and thus upsetting all the benefit which might otherwise have been derived. But by throwing open the doors to the external air, which may freely be admitted as soon as the skin acts, and by reducing the number of additional rugs, the amount of sweat given off may be kept within due bounds, and in the course of two or three hours the previously wetted rug or blanket may be removed, and a dry, warm one substituted for it, but the assistants must be quick and handy in effecting the change. Many a case of inflammation of the lungs, kidneys, or bowels might be stopped *in limine* by the adoption of this plan; but the misfortune is that it requires all the skill and tact of the veterinary surgeon, first of all to diagnose the case, and afterwards to manage its treatment. Still, if a master will undertake the superintendence of the operation himself, and is accustomed to disease, there is little risk of failure.

THE SYMPTOMS OF ACUTE PNEUMONIA are a quick and distressed respiration, averaging about sixty inspirations in the minute. Pulse quick (from seventy to eighty-five); hard, often small, but always compressible. Nostrils distended, and the lining membrane red (except in the last stage, when suffocation is imminent). Cough short, and evidently giving pain, which occasions it to be checked as much as possible. Legs and ears generally cold, often icy. Feet wide apart; evidently with an instinctive desire to dilate the chest as much as possible. On putting the ear to the chest, if the attack is very recent, there will be merely a greatly increased respiratory murmur; but when fully developed there may be heard a crepitant rattling, which is compared to the crackling of a dried bladder; but I confess that I could never make out the similarity between the two sounds. In the later stages, this is succeeded by an absence of all sound, owing to the consolidation of the lungs, or by mucous rattles depending upon the secretion of mucus. On tapping the exterior of the chest with the ends of the fingers (percussion), the sound given out is dull in proportion to the extent of mischief, the effect of pneumonia being to convert the spongy texture of the lungs into a solid substance like liver. The *treatment* will greatly depend upon the stage of the disease, the age and constitution of the horse, and the nature of the prevailing epidemic, if there is one. In modern days bl eding is very badly borne, either by man or horse, nevertheless few cases of genuine pneumonia will be saved without it. Sufficient blood must be taken to make a decided impression on the circulation, without which the inflammation will not be mastered. The quantity necessary for this cannot be fixed, because the effect will vary so materially, that the abstraction of three or four quarts of blood in one case will do more than double or treble that quantity in another. A large orifice must be made in the vein, and it must not be closed until the lining membrane of the nose or the white of the eye is seen to have become considerably paler. It may possibly even then be necessary to repeat the operation six hours afterwards, or next day, according to the symptoms. The rule should be followed of taking enough but not a drop too much, for blood removed from the circulation takes a long time to replace. With regard to medicine, tartar emetic is the only drug which seems to have much influence over pneumonia, and it must be given every six hours in drachm doses, with from half a drachm to a drachm of powdered digitalis, or white hellebore, to keep down the pulse, and two or three drachms of nitre, to increase the action of the kidneys. Unless the bowels are confined no aperient should be given, and if necessary only the mildest dose should be used. The diet should consist of bran mashes, gruel, and a little hay, or green food if the season of the year allows. A cool airy stable and warm clothing are indispensable in this disease. When the first violence of the attack has subsided, a large blister on the side of the chest will afford great relief, and when it ceases to act, if the disease is not entirely cured a second may be put on the other side.

SUB-ACUTE PNEUMONIA differs in no respect from the acute form, excepting in degree, and the symptoms and treatment will vary only in proportion.

THE TERMINATIONS of pneumonia may be death, or resolution (by which is to be understood a disappearance of the symptoms without leaving any mischief behind), or hepatization, or abcess. The last-named sequel may be very serious in extent, but if an opening is made by nature for the discharge of its contents into the bronchial tubes the horse may recover, and his wind may be sufficiently good for any purposes but the racecourse or the hunting field. Hepatization is always attended with thick wind, but in other respects the health may be good, and the horse may be suited to ordinary work. In process of time some of the lymph is absorbed, and a considerable improvement takes place, but it never entirely disappears, and a horse which has once suffered from pneumonia attended by hepatization remains permanently unsound.

PLEURISY.*

THIS DISEASE is characterized by a very peculiar respiration, the expirations being much longer than the inspirations, owing to the pain which is given by the action of the muscles necessary for the latter, while the former, if the chest is allowed quietly to fall, is almost painless. Nevertheless, the breathing is quicker on the whole than natural, being from forty to fifty per minute. The pulse is quick, small, and incompressible. Nostrils and eyes of a natural color, and the former are not dilated. The countenance is anxious, and the legs are rather drawn together than extended, as in bronchitis and pneumonia, and they are not colder than usual. There is a short hurried cough, with great restlessness, and the sides are always painful on pressure; but this symptom by itself is not to be relied on, as it is present in pleurodynia, which will be presently described.

The treatment should consist of copious bleeding, followed by a mild purgative, and the same ball as recommended for pneumonia, with the addition of half a drachm of calomel. Blisters are not desirable to be applied to the sides of the thorax, as there is so little space between the two surfaces of the pleura and the skin that they are apt to do harm by immediately irritating the former, rather than to act beneficially by counter-irritation of the skin. A large rowel, may, however, be placed in the breast with advantage.

HYDROTHORAX, or water in the cavity of the chest, is one of the sequels of chronic pleurisy, the serum thrown out being the means by which a serous membrane relieves itself. It can be detected by the entire absence of respiratory murmur, and by the dullness on percussion. No *treatment* is of any avail but tapping, which may be readily and safely performed (if the diagnosis is correct) by passing a trocar between the eighth and ninth ribs, near their cartilages. If, however, an error has been committed, the lung is wounded, and death will probably ensue.

PLEURODYNIA.

BETWEEN THIS DISEASE AND THE LAST there is some similarity in the symptoms; but in their nature, and in the treatment required, they are widely separated. It is, therefore, necessary that they should not be confounded, for in the one case bloodletting and other active measures may be unnecessarily adopted, and in the other a fatal result will most probably occur for want

---

* In all diseases the product of which is exudation, or the outpouring of water, bleeding, purging, and other devitalizing agents should be religiously abstained from. Blisters in this disease may be of some service but should be used only when inflammation has subsided. Aconite, pure air, and cold water is the most successful way of curing pleurisy.—EDITOR.

of them. In pleuritis there is a quick pulse, with general constitutional disturbance, which will serve to distinguish it from pleurodynia, besides which, it is rarely that we meet with the former without some other affection of the lungs co-existing. When, therefore, a horse is evidently suffering from acute pain in the walls of the thorax, unaccompanied by cough, hurried breathing, quick pulse, or fever, it may safely be diagnosed that the nature of the attack is a rheumatism of the intercostal muscles (pleurodynia), and not pleurisy. In *treating* it, bleeding and tartar emetic must be carefully avoided, and hot mustard and vinegar rubbed into the sides will be the most likely remedy to afford relief.

PHTHISIS.

WHEN A HORSE HAS LONG BEEN SUBJECT TO A CHRONIC COUGH, and, without losing appetite, wastes away rapidly, it may be assumed that he is a victim to phthisis, and especially if he is narrow-chested and has long shown signs of short wind. On examining the chest by the ear, it will be found to give out sounds of various kinds, depending upon the exact state of the lungs; but in most cases there will be great dulness on percussion, owing to the deposit of tubercles, in which the disease consists. In a confirmed case no *treatment* will avail, and the poor animal had better be destroyed. When the attack is slight, the progress of the disease may be stayed by counteracting inflammation in the ordinary way, avoiding loss of blood when possible. Hæmorrhage, from the breaking down of the substance of the lung, by which a large blood-vessel is opened, is a common result of phthisis, and will be alluded to under the head of diseases of the vessels of the lungs, at the end of this chapter.

BROKEN WIND.

A BROKEN-WINDED HORSE can be detected at once by any horseman possessed of experience, from the peculiar and forcible double expiration. Inspiration is performed as usual, then comes a rapid but not violent act of expiration, followed by a forcible repetition of the same, in which all the muscles of respiration, auxiliary and ordinary, are called into play. This is, of course, most marked when the horse has been gallopped, but even when he is at rest the double expiration is manifest at almost any ordinary distance from the observer. The disease almost (if not quite) invariably consists in emphysema, or entrance of the air into unnatural cells, which is retained there, as the urine is in the bladder, from the valvular nature of the openings, and cannot be entirely expelled, nor in the slightest degree, without calling into play all the muscles of the chest. The presence of unchanged air is a constant source of irritation to the lungs, and although sufficient may be expired easily enough to carry on their functions while the body is at rest, yet instinctively there is a desire to get rid of the surplus, and hence the two acts of respiration. Immediately after this second act the muscles relax, and the flank falls in, and this it is which catches the eye in so remarkable a manner. On examination after death, the lungs are found to remain enlarged, and do not collapse as in the healthy condition. They are distended with air; and this is especially the case when the emphysema is of the kind called interlobular, in which the air has escaped into the cellular membrane. In the most common kind, however, the cells are broken down, several being united together, while the enlargement pressing upon the tube which has opened into them diminishes its capacity, and prevents the ready escape of air. This is the vesicular emphysema of pathologists. The former is generally suddenly produced by a severe gallop after a full meal, while the latter is a slow growth and often occurs at grass, as a consequence of neglected chronic cough, the constant muscular efforts appearing gradually to dilate the cells.

The treatment can only be palliative, as there is no recognised cure for the disease, though M. Hew, of Chaumont, has lately published a report of ten cases in which treatment by arsenic given with green food or straw, and in some cases bleeding, was perfectly successful. The arsenic was given to the extent of fifteen grains daily, and at the end of a fortnight the symptoms of broken wind were completely removed; but as the horses were not subsequently watched, it is impossible to say whether the cure was permanent. It is known, however, that one of them relapsed after three months, but speedily yielded to a repetition of the treatment. It may certainly be worth while to try the experiment of the effect of arsenic where a broken-winded horse is valuable in other respects. The medicine is not expensive, and the length of time necessary for the treatment is not very great. Broken-winded horses should be carefully dieted, and even then confined to slow work. The food should be in small compass, consisting chiefly of wheat-straw chaff, with a proper quantity of oats, and beans may be added if the animal is not very young. The water should never be given within an hour of going out of the stable, but it is better to leave a constant supply, when too much will never be taken. Carrots are peculiarly suited to this disease, and a diet of bran mixed with carrots, sliced, has sometimes been known to relieve a broken-winded horse most materially.

THICK WIND.

THICK WIND is the horseman's term for any defective respiration, unaccompanied by a noise, or by the signs of emphysema just alluded to. It usually follows pneumonia, but it may arise from chronic bronchitis, occasioning a thickening of the mucous membrane lining the bronchial tubes, and thus lessening their diameter, or it may accompany phthisis when the deposit of tubercles is extensive. No *treatment* will be of any service except such as will aid the play of the lungs mechanically, by avoiding overloading the stomach, as mentioned in the last section.

SPASM OF THE DIAPHRAGM.

SOME HORSES, when at all distressed by the severity of their gallops, communicate to the rider a most unpleasant sensation, as if some internal part was giving a sudden blow or flap. This is not only a sensation, but a reality, for the diaphragm being naturally weak, or overstrained at some previous period, acts spasmodically in drawing in the air. If the horse thus affected is ridden onwards afterwards, he will be placed in danger of suffocation and death, either from rupture of the diaphragm, or from its cessation to act, or from its permanently contracting and refusing to give way during expiration. There is no cure for the weakness which tends to produce the spasm, and all that can be done is to avoid using the horse affected with it at any very fast pace, and over a distance of ground. Urgent *symptoms* may be relieved by a cordial-drench, such as the following:—

Take of Laudanum	6 drachms.
Ether	1½ ounce.
Aromatic Spirit of Ammonia	3 drachms.
Tincture of Ginger	3 drachms.
Ale	1 pint. Mix.

Or if there is any difficulty in giving a drench, a ball may be made up and given—

Take of Carbonate of Ammonia	1 drachm.
Camphor	½ drachm.
Powdered Ginger	1 drachm.
Linseed meal and boiling water sufficient to make into a ball.	

Either of the above may be repeated at the end of three hours, if relief is not afforded. Increased strength may be given to the diaphragm by regular slow work, and the daily mixture of a drachm of powdered sulphate of iron with the feed of corn.

DISEASES OF THE HEART.

THE HORSE is subject to inflammation of the substance of the heart (carditis) of a rheumatic nature, and of the fibro-serous covering (pericarditis), but the symptoms are so obscure that no one but the professional veterinarian will be likely to make them out. Dropsy of the heart is a common disease in worn-out horses, and hypertrophy, as well as fatty degeneration, are often met with among well-conditioned animals.

DISEASES OF THE BLOOD-VESSELS OF THE CHEST AND NOSE.

THE HORSE IS VERY SUBJECT TO HÆMORRHAGE from the nose, coming on during violent exertion, and many a race has been lost from this cause. Fat over-fed horses are the most likely to suffer from hemorrhage; but most people are aware of the risk incurred in over-riding or driving them, and for this reason they are not so often subject to this accident (for such it is rather than a disease) as they otherwise would be. It is unnecessary to describe its *symptoms*, as the gush of blood renders it but too apparent, and the only point necessary to inquire into is, whether the lungs or the nasal cavities are the seat of the rupture of the vessel. In the former case the blood comes from both nostrils, and is frothy; while in the latter it generally proceeds from one only, and is perfectly fluid. The *treatment* should consist in cooling the horse down by a dose of physic and a somewhat lower diet; but if the bleeding is very persistent, and returns again and again, a saturated solution of alum in water may be syringed up the nostril daily, or, if this fails, an infusion of matico may be tried, which is far more likely to succeed. It is made by pouring half a pint of boiling water on a drachm of matico-leaves, and letting it stand till cool, when it should be strained, and is fit for use.

HÆMORRHAGE FROM THE LUNGS is a far more serious affair, and its control requires active remedies if they are to be of any service. It may arise from the existence of an abscess in the lung of a phthisical nature, which implicates some considerable vessel; or it may be caused by the bursting of an aneurism, which is a dilatation of a large artery, and generally occurs near the heart. The *treatment* can seldom do more than prolong the life of the patient for a short time, and it is scarcely worth while to enter upon it. Bleeding from the jugular vein will arrest the internal hæmorrhage, and must often be resorted to in the first instance, and there are internal medicines which will assist it, such as digitalis and matico; but, as before remarked, this only postpones the fatal termination.

CHAPTER XXII.

DISEASES OF THE ABDOMINAL VISCERA AND THEIR APPENDAGES.

General remarks—Diseases of the Mouth and Throat—Gastritis—Stomach Staggers—Dyspepsia — Bots—Inflammation of the Bowels—Colic—Diarrhœa and Dysentery—Strangulation and Rupture—Calculi in the Bowels—Worms—Disease of the Liver—of the Kidneys—of the Bladder—of the Organs of Generation.

GENERAL REMARKS.

THOUGH NOT OFTEN PRODUCING what in horse-dealing is considered unsoundness, yet diseases of the abdominal viscera constantly lead to death, and frequently to such a debilitated state of the body, that the sufferer is rendered useless. Fortunately for the purchaser, they almost always give external evidence of their presence, for there is not only emaciation, but also a staring coat and a flabby state of the muscles, which is quite the reverse of the wiry feel communicated to the hand in those instances where the horse is "poor" from over-work in proportion to his food. In the latter case, time and good living only are required to restore the natural plumpness; but in the former, the wasting will either go on until death puts an end to the poor diseased animal, or he will remain in a debilitated and wasted condition, utterly unfit for hard work.

DISEASES OF THE MOUTH AND THROAT.

SEVERAL PARTS ABOUT THE MOUTH are liable to inflammation, which would be of little consequence in itself, but that it interferes with the feeding, and this for the time starves the horse, and renders him unfit for his work, causing him to "quid" or return his food into the manger without swallowing it. Such are lampas, vives or enlarged glands, barbs or paps, gigs, bladders, and flaps,—all which are names given to the enlargements of the salivary ducts,—and carious teeth, or inflammation of their fangs. Besides these, the horse is also subject to sore throat, and strangles, which are accompanied by constitutional disturbance, and not only occasion "quidding," if there is any slight appetite, but they are also generally accompanied by a loss of that function.

SORE THROAT.—When the throat inflames, as is evidenced by fulness and hardness of this part, and there is difficulty of swallowing, the skin covering it should immediately be severely sweated, or the larynx will be involved and irreparable injury done The tincture of cantharides diluted with an equal part of spirit of tur-

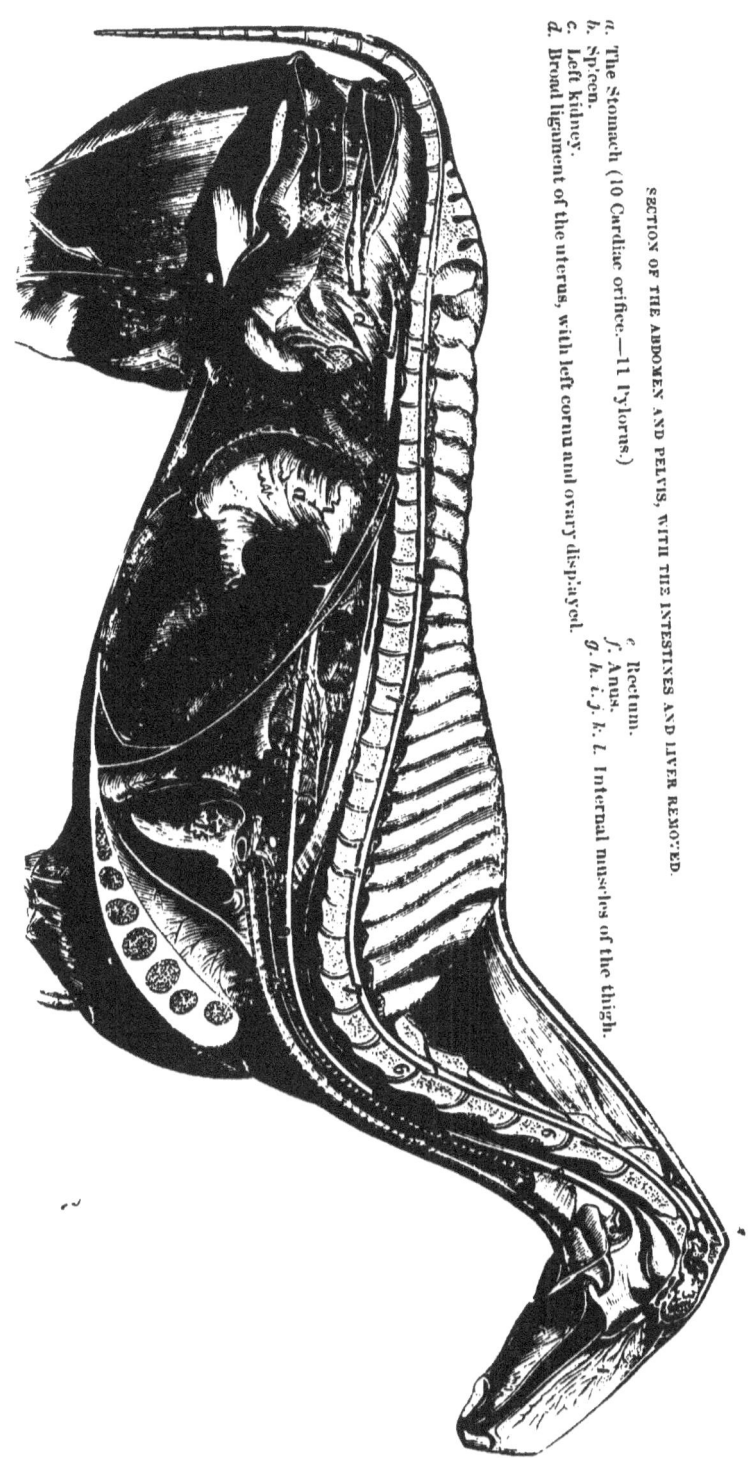

SECTION OF THE ABDOMEN AND PELVIS, WITH THE INTESTINES AND LIVER REMOVED.

a. The Stomach (10 Cardiac orifice.—11 Pylorus.)
b. Spleen.
c. Left kidney.
d. Broad ligament of the uterus, with left cornu and ovary displayed.
e. Rectum.
f. Anus.
g. h. i. j. k. l. Internal muscles of the thigh.

pentine and a little oil, may be rubbed in with a piece of sponge, until it produces irritation of the skin, which in a few hours will be followed by a discharge from the part. Six or eight drachms of nitre may also be dissolved in the water which the horse drinks, with some difficulty, but still, as he is thirsty, he will take it. Sometimes eating gives less pain than drinking, and then the nitre may be given with a bran mash instead of the water.

STRANGLES.—Between the third and fifth year of the colt's life he is generally seized with an acute swelling of the soft parts between the branches of the lower jaw, accompanied by more or less sore throat, cough and feverishness. These go on increasing for some days, and then an abscess shows itself, and finally bursts. The salivary glands are often involved, but the matter forms in the cellular membrane external to them. The *treatment* should be addressed to the control of constitutional symptoms by the mildest measures, such as bran mashes with nitre in them, abstraction of corn, hay tea, &c. At the same time the swelling should be poulticed for one night, or thoroughly fomented two or three times, and then blistered with the tincture of cantharides. As soon as the matter can plainly be felt, it may be let out with a lancet; but it is very doubtful whether it is not the best plan to permit the abscess to break. The bowels should be gently moved, by giving a pint, or somewhat less, according to age, of castor oil; and afterwards two or three drachms of nitre, with half a drachm of tartar emetic, may be mixed with the mash twice a day, on which food alone the colt should be fed, in addition to gruel, and a little grass or clover if these are to be had, or if not, a few steamed carrots. The disease has a tendency to get well naturally, but if it is not kept within moderate bounds it is very apt to lay the foundation of roaring or whistling. Any chronic swelling which is left behind, may be removed by rubbing in a weak ointment of biniodide of mercury (one scruple or half drachm to the ounce; see page 300).

LAMPAS is an active inflammation of the ridges, or "bars," in the hoof of the mouth, generally occurring in the young horse while he is shedding his teeth, or putting up the tushes. Sometimes, however, it comes on, independently of this cause, from over-feeding with corn after a run at grass. The mucous membrane of the roof of the mouth swells so much that it projects below the level of the nippers, and is so tender that all hard and dry food is refused. The *treatment* is extremely simple, consisting in the scarification of the part with a sharp knife or lancet, after which the swelling generally subsides, and is gone in a day or two; but should it obstinately continue, as will sometimes happen, a stick of lunar caustic must be gently rubbed over the part every day until a cure is completed. This is far better than the red-hot iron, which was formerly so constantly used, with good effect it is true, and not accompanied by any cruelty, as the mucous membrane is nearly insensible, but the caustic is more rapid and effectual in stimulating the vessels to a healthy action, and on that score should be preferred. If the lampas is owing to the cutting of a grinder, relief will be afforded by a crucial incision across the protruding gum.

BARBS, PAPS, &c.—The swelling at the mouth of the ducts may generally be relieved by a dose of physic and green food, but should it continue, a piece of lunar caustic may be held for a moment against the opening of the duct every second day, and after two or three applications the thickening will certainly disappear.

WHERE VIVES, or chronically enlarged submaxillary glands, are met with, the application of the ointment of biniodide of mercury, according to the directions given at page 300, will almost certainly cause their reduction to a natural state.

GASTRITIS.

GASTRITIS (acute inflammation of the stomach) is extremely rare in the horse as an idiopathic disease; but it sometimes occurs from eating vegetable poisons as food, or from the wilful introduction of arsenic into this organ, or, lastly, from licking off corrosive external applications, which have been used for mange. The *symptoms* from poisoning will a good deal depend upon the article which has been taken, but in almost all cases in which vegetable poisons have been swallowed, there is a strange sort of drowsiness, so that the horse does not lie down and go to sleep, but props himself against a wall or tree with his head hanging almost to the ground. As the drowsiness increases he often falls down in his attempt to rest himself more completely, and when on the ground his breathing is loud and hard, and his sleep is so unnaturally sound that he can scarcely be roused from it. At length convulsions occur and death soon takes place. This is the ordinary course of poisoning with yew, which is sometimes picked up with the grass after the clippings have dried, for in its fresh state the taste is too bitter for the palate, and the horse rejects the mouthful of grass in which it is involved. May-weed and water parsley will also produce nearly similar symptoms. The *treatment* in each case should be by rousing the horse mechanically, and at the same time giving him six or eight drachms of aromatic spirit of ammonia, in a pint or two of good ale, with a little ginger in it. This may be repeated every two hours, and the horse should be perpetually walked about until the narcotic symptoms are completely gone off, when a sound sleep will restore him to his natural state.

ARSENIC, when given in large doses, with an intention to destroy life, produces intense pain and thirst;—the former, evidenced by an eager gaze at the flanks, pawing of the ground, or rolling; and sometimes by each of these in succession. The saliva is secreted in increased quantities, and flows from the mouth, as the throat is generally too sore to allow of its being swallowed. The breath soon becomes hot and fetid, and purging then comes on of a bloody mucus, which soon carries off the patient by exhaustion, if death does not take place from the immediate effects of the poison on the stomach and brain. *Treatment* is seldom of any avail, the most likely remedies being large bleedings, blisters to the sides of the chest, and plenty of thin gruel to sheathe the inflamed surface of the mucous membrane, which is deprived of its epithelial scales.

CORROSIVE SUBLIMATE* is sometimes employed as a wash in mange, or to destroy lice, when it may be licked off, and will occasion nearly the same symptoms as arsenic. The *treatment* consists in a similar use of thin starch or gruel; or, if the poison has recently been given wilfully, of large quantities of white of egg.

STOMACH STAGGERS.

THE EXACT NATURE of this disease has never been clearly made out, and it is now so rare, that there is little chance of its being satisfactorily explained. The symptoms would chiefly lead one to suppose the brain to be implicated; but there is so close a sympathy between that organ and the stomach, that we can easily account in that way for the cerebral manifestations. A theory has been propounded, that it is seated in the par vagum, or pneumogastric nerve; and as all the parts with which that nerve is connected are affected, there is some ground for the hypothesis; but it is not supported by the demonstration of anatomy, simply, perhaps, because of the difficulty in the way of prosecuting the pathology of the nerves. The first onset of the disease is marked by great heaviness of the eyes, soon going on to drowsiness; the head dropping into the manger, even while feeding is in progress. It generally makes its appearance after a long fast; and it is supposed by some writers to be owing to the demands made by the stomach on the brain, when in an exhausted condition for want of its usual supplies. This theory is supported by the fact that, in the present day, when every horsemaster knows the danger of working his horses without feeding them at intervals of five, or at most six hours, the stomach staggers are almost unknown. Even when the disease shows itself at grass, it is almost always mani-

---

* First.—Give one-half of an ounce of iodide of potassium to convert the mercury into an iodide of the metal, which is harmless comparatively to corrosive sublimate. Then give the white of egg, &c., spoken of in the text.—EDITOR.

fested directly after the horse is first turned out, when he gorges himself with the much-coveted food, which has long been withheld, and his brain is affected in a manner similar to that which follows a long fast from every kind of food. In a short time, if the affection of the brain is not relieved, that organ becomes still more severely implicated, and convulsions or paralysis put an end to the attack. During the course of the disease, the breathing is affected, and there is generally an almost total cessation of the secretions of bile and urine, which may either be the cause or the effect of the condition of the brain. With this state of uncertainty as to the essence of the disease, it is somewhat empirical to lay down any rules for its *treatment;* and, as I before remarked, it is now so rare, that they are scarcely necessary. If care be taken to feed the horse properly, he will never suffer from stomach staggers in the stable; and at grass, the attack is seldom observed until he is beyond the reach of any remedies. Still, it may be as well to observe, that the usual plan of proceeding has been to take away blood, so as to relieve the brain, and to stimulate the stomach to get rid of its load, by the use of warm aperients, such as the following:—

Take of Barbadoes Aloes . . . . . . 4 to 6 drachms.
Tincture of Ginger . . . . . . 3 drachms.
Dissolve the aloes in a pint of hot water, then add the tincture, and when nearly cool give as a drench.*

DYSPEPSIA.

EVERY DOMESTIC ANIMAL suffers in health if he is constantly fed on the same articles, and man himself, perhaps, more than they do. Partridges are relished by him early in September, but *toujours perdrix* would disgust the most inveterate lover of that article of food. Dogs are too often made to suffer from being fed on the same meal, flavored with similar flesh or broth, from one month to another. It is well known that cattle and sheep must change their pasture, or they soon lose condition; and yet horses are expected to go on eating oats and hay for years together without injury to health; and at the same time they are often exposed to the close air of a confined stable, and to an irregular amount of exercise. We cannot, therefore, wonder that the master is often told that some one or other of his horses is "a little off his feed;" nor should we be surprised that the constant repetition of the panacea for this, "a dose of physic," should at length permanently establish the condition which at first it would always alleviate. It is a source of wonder that the appetite continues so good as it

---

* In addition to the treatment, I would recommend that from 15 to 20 drops of the tincture of aconite root be given to control the heart's action, and thereby the circulation of the blood.—EDITOR.

does, in the majority of horses, which are kept in the stable on the same kind of food, always from July to May, and often through the other months also. The use of a few small bundles of vetches, lucerne, or clover in the spring, is supposed to be quite sufficient to restore tone· to the stomach, and undoubtedly they are better than no change at all; but at other seasons of the year something may be done towards the prevention of dyspepsia, by varying the quality of the hay, and by the use of a few carrots once or twice a week. In many stables, one rick of hay is made to serve throughout the whole or a great part of the year, which is a very bad plan, as a change in this important article of food is as much required as a change of pasture when the animal is at grass. When attention is paid to this circumstance, the appetite will seldom fail in horses of a good constitution, if they are regularly worked; but without it, resort must occasionally be had to a dose of physic. It is from a neglect of this precaution that so many horses take to eat their litter, in preference to their hay; for if the same animal was placed in a straw-yard, without hay, for a month, and then allowed access to both, there would be little doubt that he would prefer the latter. Some horses are naturally so voracious, that they are always obliged to be supplied with less than they desire, and they seldom suffer from loss of appetite; but delicate feeders require the greatest care in their management. When the stomach suffers in this way, it is always desirable to try what a complete change of food will do before resorting to medicine; and, if it can be obtained, green food of some kind should be chosen, or if not, carrots, or even steamed potatoes. In place of hay, sound wheat or barley straw may be cut into chaff, and mixed with the carrots and corn; and to this a little malt-dust may be added, once or twice a week, so as to alter the flavor. By continually changing the food in this way, the most dyspeptic stomach may often be restored to its proper tone, without doing harm with one hand while the other is doing good, as is too often the case with medicine. The use of the fashionable "horse-feeds" of the present day will serve the same purpose; and if the slight changes I have mentioned do not answer, Thorley's or Henri's food may be tried with great probability of success.

BOTS.

THE LARVÆ of the *œstrus equi*, a species of gadfly, are often found in large numbers, attached by a pair of hooks with which they are provided, to the cardiac extremity of the stomach; they are very rarely met with in the true digestive portion of this organ, but sometimes in the duodenum or jejunum in small numbers. A group of these larvæ, which are popularly called bots, are represented on the next page, but sometimes nearly all the cardiac extremity of the stomach is occupied with them, the interstices being occupied by little projections which are caused by those that have let go their hold, and have been expelled with the food. Several of these papillæ are shown on the engraving, which delineates also the appearance of the bots themselves, so that no one can fail to recognise them when he sees them. This is important, for it often

FIG. 18.—GROUP OF BOTS ATTACHED TO THE STOMACH.

happens that a meddlesome groom when he sees them expelled from or hanging to the verge of the anus, as they often do for a short time, thinks it necessary to use strong medicine; whereas in the first place he does no good, for none is known which will kill the larva without danger to the horse, and in the second, if he will only have a little patience, every bot will come away in the natural course of things, and until the horse is turned out to grass, during the season when the œstrus deposits its eggs, he will never have another in his stomach.

THE ŒSTRUS EQUI comes out from the pupa state in the middle and latter part of summer, varying according to the season, and the female soon finds the proper nidus for her eggs in the hair of the nearest horse turned out to grass. She manages to glue them to the sides of the hair so firmly that no ordinary friction will get rid of them, and her instinct teaches her to select those parts within reach of the horse's tongue, such as the hair of the fore legs and sides. Here they remain until the heat of the sun hatches them, when, being no larger in diameter than a small pin, each larva is licked off and carried down the gullet to the stomach, to the thick epithelium of which it soon attaches itself by its hooks. Here it remains until the next spring, having attained the size which is represented in the engraving during the course of the first two months of its life, and then it fulfils its allotted career, by letting go and being carried out with the dung. On reaching the outer air it soon assumes the chrysalis condition, and in three or four weeks bursts its covering to become the perfect insect.

FROM THIS HISTORY it will be evident that no preventive measures will keep off the attacks of the fly when the horse is at grass, and, indeed, in those districts where they abound, they will deposit their ova in the hair of the stabled horse if he is allowed to stand still for a few minutes. The eggs are, however, easily recognised in any horse but a chestnut, to which color they closely assimilate, and as they are never deposited in large numbers on the stabled horse they may readily be removed by the groom. Unlike other parasites, they seem to do little or no harm, on account of the insensible nature of the part of the stomach to which they are attached, and, moreover, their presence is seldom discovered until the season of their migration, when interference is uncalled for. On all accounts, therefore, it is unnecessary to enter into the question, whether it is possible to expel them; and even if by chance one comes away prematurely it will be wise to avoid interfering by attempting to cause the expulsion of those left behind.

INFLAMMATION OF THE BOWELS.
(*Peritonitis and Enteritis.*)

A REFERENCE to the cut of the abdomen and its contents, opposite page 278, will explain that there are two divisions of the abdominal serous sac, one of which lines the walls of the cavity, and the other covers the viscera which lie in it. In human medicine, when the former is inflamed, the disease is termed *peritonitis*, and when the latter is the subject of inflammatory action it is called *enteritis*. But though in theory this distinction is made, in practice it is found that the one seldom exists without the other being developed to a greater or less extent. Veterinary writers have generally taken the nomenclature adopted in human anatomy and pathology, but in regard to the inflammations of the bowels they define peritonitis as inflammation of the peritoneal or serous coat, and enteritis as inflammation of the muscular coat. My own belief is, that during life it is impossible by any known symptoms to distinguish the exact *locale* of any inflammation of the bowels but that of their mucous lining, which will presently be described, and that wherever the actual serous covering of the bowels is involved the muscular fibres beneath it will be implicated, but that the serious and fatal symptoms manifested in such cases are not dependent upon the latter, but are due entirely to the lesions of the serous coat. I have examined numberless fatal cases of supposed enteritis, and have uniformly found signs of inflammation of the serous investment, sometimes implicating the muscular fibres beneath, and often extending to the peritoneal lining of the walls of the abdomen, but I have never yet seen marks of inflammation in the muscular tissue without their serous covering being affected to a much greater extent. I believe therefore that the distinction is erroneously founded, and that, theoretically, the same definition should be made of the two diseases as is in use by human pathologists, though practically this is of little importance. There is no well made out inflammation of muscular tissue (except that of the heart) in which the symptoms are so urgent and so rapidly followed by a fatal issue as in the latter stages of the disease described by Mr. Percivall under the head *enteritis*, as follows:—" The next stage borders on delirium. The eye acquires a wild, haggard, and unnatural stare—the pupil dilates—his heedless and dreadful throes render approach to him quite perilous, he is an object not only of compassion but of apprehension, and seems fast hurrying to his end—when all at once, in the midst of agonizing torments he stands quiet, as though every pain had left him and he were going to recover. His breathing becomes tranquillized—his pulse sunk beyond all perception—his body bedewed with a cold clammy sweat—he is in a tremor from head to foot, and about the legs and ears has even a dead-like feel. The mouth feels deadly chill—the lips drop pendulous, and the eye seems unconscious of objects. In fine, death, not recovery, is at hand. Mortification has seized the inflamed bowel—pain can no longer be felt in that which a few minutes ago was the seat of most exquisite suffering. He again becomes convulsed, and in a few more struggles less violent than the former he expires." Analogy would lead any careful pathologist to suppose that such symptoms as these are due to some lesion of a serous and not a muscular tissue, and, as I before remarked, I have satisfied myself that such is really the case. I have seen lymph, pus, and serum effused in some cases of enteritis, and mortification extending to a large surface of the peritoneal coat in others, but I have never examined a single case without one or the other of these morbid results. It may be said that so long as the symptoms are correctly described their exact seat is of no consequence; but in this instance it is probable that the ordinary definition of enteritis as an inflammation of the muscular coat may lead to a timid practice in its treatment, which would be attended with the worst results. I have no fault to find with the usual descriptions of the two diseases, or with their ordinary treatment, but I protest against the definition which is given of them.

AN EXAMINATION OF THE CAUSE of inflammation of the bowels is the only means by which the one form can be distinguished from the other. If it has been brought about from exposure to cold, or from over-stimulating medicines given for colic, the probability is that the serous covering of the intestines themselves is chiefly involved; while if it has followed castration it may generally be concluded that the peritoneal lining of the abdominal muscles has taken on inflammatory action by an immediate extension from the serous lining of the inguinal canal, which is continuous with it. In each case, however, the symptoms are as nearly as may be the same, and without knowing the previous history I believe no one could distinguish the one disease from the other—nor should the treatment vary in any respect.

THE SYMPTOMS of peritoneal inflammation vary in intensity, and in the rapidity of their development, but they usually show themselves in the following order:—At first there is simple loss of appetite, dulness of eye, and a general uneasiness, which are soon followed by a slight rigor or shivering. The pulse becomes rapid, but small and wiry, and the horse becomes very restless, pawing his litter, and looking back at his sides in a wistful and anxious manner. In the next stage all these signs are aggravated; the hind legs are used to strike at but not touch the belly; and the horse lies down, rolls on his back and struggles violently. The pulse becomes quicker and harder, but is still small. The belly is acutely tender and hard to the touch, the bowels are costive, and the horse is constantly turning round, moaning, and regarding his flanks with the most anxious expression of countenance. Next comes on the stage so graphically described by Mr. Percivall in the passage which I have quoted, the whole duration of the attack being from twelve to forty-eight hours in acute cases, and extending to three or four days in those which are denominated subacute.

In the treatment of this disease, as in all those implicating serous membrane, blood must be taken largely, and in a full stream, the quantity usually required to make a suitable impression being from six to nine quarts. The belly should be fomented with very hot water, by two men holding against it a doubled blanket, dipped in that fluid, which should be constantly changed, to keep up the temperature. The bowels should be back-raked, and the following drench should be given every six hours till it operates, which should be hastened by injections of warm water.

    Take of Linseed oil . . . . 1 pint.
    Laudanum . . . . 2 ounces.

If the first bleeding does not give relief in six or eight hours, it must be repeated to the extent of three or four quarts, and at the same time some liquid blister may be rubbed into the skin of the abdomen, continuing the fomentations, at short intervals, under that part, which will hasten its operation. The *diet* should be confined to thin gruel or bran mashes, and no hay should be allowed until the severity of the attack has abated.*

To DISTINGUISH this disease from colic is of the highest importance, and for this purpose it will be necessary to describe the symptoms of the latter disease, so as to compare the two together.

COLIC.

IN THIS DISEASE there is spasm of the muscular coat of the intestines, generally confined to the cæcum and colon. Various names have been given to its different forms, such as the fret, the gripes, spasmodic colic, flatulent colic, &c., but they all display the above feature, and are only modifications of it, depending upon the cause which has produced it. In spasmodic colic, the bowels are not unnaturally distended, but in flatulent colic their distension by gas brings on the spasm, the muscular fibres being stretched to so great an extent as to cause them to contract irregularly and with a morbid action. Sometimes, when the bowels are very costive, irritation is established as an effort of nature to procure the dislodgment of the impacted fæcal matters, and thus a third cause of the disease is discovered. The exact nature and cause are always to be ascertained from the history of the case, and its symptoms, and as the treatment will especially be conducted with a view to a removal of the cause, they are of the highest importance. *The symptoms* in all cases of colic, by which it may be distinguished from the last-described disease, are as follows: In both acute pain is manifested by stamping, looking at the flanks, and rolling; but in enteritis the pain is constant, while in colic, there are intervals of rest, when the horse seems quite easy, and often begins to feed. In both the poor animal strikes at his belly; but in the former he takes great care not to touch the skin, while in the latter (colic) he will often bring the blood by his desperate efforts to get rid of his annoyance. In enteritis the belly is hot and exquisitely tender to the touch, but in colic it is not unnaturally warm, and gradual pressure with a broad surface, such as the whole hand, always is readily borne, and generally affords relief. The pulse also is little affected in colic; and, lastly, the attack is very much more sudden than in peritoneal inflammation.

SUCH ARE THE GENERAL SIGNS by which a case of colic may be distinguished from inflammation of the bowels, but beyond this it is necessary to investigate whether it is pure spasmodic colic, or produced by flatulence, or by an obstruction in the bowels.

---

* Do not bleed, but substitute for it 20 drops of the tincture of aconite root every 3 hours till 4 to 5 doses are given, and allow pure air with plenty of cold water to drink.—EDITOR.

IN SPASMODIC COLIC all the above symptoms are displayed, without any great distension of the abdomen; and if the history of the case is gone into, it will be found that after coming in heated the horse has been allowed to drink cold water, or has been exposed in an exhausted state to a draught of air.

IN FLATULENT COLIC the abdomen is enormously distended; the attack is not so sudden, and the pain is not so intense, being rather to be considered, in the average of cases, as a high degree of uneasiness, occasionally amounting to a sharp pang, than giving the idea of agony. In aggravated attacks, the distension is so enormous as to leave no doubt of the nature of the exciting cause. Here also the spasms are often brought on by drinking cold water while the horse is in a heated and exhausted state.

WHERE THERE IS A STOPPAGE IN THE BOWELS to cause the spasm, on questioning the groom, it will be found that the dung for some days has been hard and in small lumps, with occasional patches of mucus upon it. In other respects there is little to distinguish this variety from the last.

The treatment must in all cases be conducted on a totally different plan to that necessary when inflammation is present. Bleeding will be of no avail, at all events in the early stages, and before the disease has gone on, as it sometimes will, into an inflammatory condition. On the other hand, stimulating drugs, which would be fatal in enteritis, will here generally succeed in causing a return of healthy muscular action. The disease is indeed similar in its essential features to cramp in the muscles of the human leg or arm, the only difference being that it does not as speedily disappear, because it is impossible to get at the muscular coat of the intestines, and apply the stimulus of friction.

AS SOON AS A CASE IS CLEARLY MADE OUT TO BE OF A SPASMODIC NATURE, one or other of the following drenches should be given, the choice being made in proportion to the intensity of the symptoms:—

1. Sulphuric Ether . . . . 1 ounce.
   Laudanum . . . . 2 ounces.
   Compound decoction of Aloes . . . . . . 5 ounces.
   Mix and give every half hour until relief is afforded.

2. Spirit of Turpentine . . . . 4 ounces.
   Linseed Oil . . . . 12 ounces.
   Laudanum . . . . 1½ ounce.
   Mix and give every hour till the pain ceases.

3. Aromatic Spirit of Ammonia . . . . . . 1½ ounce.
   Laudanum . . . . 2 ounces.
   Tincture of Ginger . . . . 1½ ounce.
   Hot Ale . . . . 1 quart.
   Mix and give every hour.

Hot water should also be applied to the abdomen, as described under the head of Enteritis, and if an enema pump is at hand, large quantities of water, at a temperature of 100° Fahrenheit, should be injected *per anum*, until in fact the bowel will hold no more without a dangerous amount of force.

IN FLATULENT COLIC the same remedies may be employed, but the turpentine mixture is here especially beneficial. The use of warm water injections will often bring away large volumes of wind, which at once affords relief, and the attack is cured. Sometimes, however, the distension goes on increasing, and the only chance of recovery consists in a puncture of the cæcum, as it lies high in the right flank, where, according to French veterinary writers, it may often be opened when greatly distended, without dividing the serous covering. The operation, however, should only be performed by an experienced hand, as it is one of great danger, and a knowledge of the anatomy of the parts concerned is required to select the most available situation.

THE TREATMENT OF IMPACTION must be completely *a posteriori*, for all anterior proceedings with aperient medicines will only aggravate the spasms. Injection of gallons of warm water, or of gruel containing a quart of castor oil and half a pint of spirit of turpentine, will sometimes succeed in producing a passage, and at the same time the spasm may be relieved by the exhibition at the mouth of one ounce of laudanum and the same quantity of sulphuric ether. If there is any tenderness of the abdomen, or the pulse has a tendency to quicken, it will be better to resort to bleeding, which alone will sometimes cause the peristaltic action to be restored in a healthy manner. The case, however, requires great patience and judgment, and as no great good can often be effected, it is highly necessary to avoid doing harm, which can hardly be avoided if the remedies employed are not at once successful.

WHEN THE URGENT SYMPTOMS of colic in any of its forms are relieved, great care must be exercised that a relapse does not take place from the use of improper food. The water should be carefully chilled, and a warm bran mash should be given, containing in it half a feed of bruised oats. Nothing but these at moderate intervals, in the shape of food or drink, should be allowed for a day or two, and then the horse may gradually return to his customary treatment, avoiding, of course, everything which may appear to have contributed to the development of colic.

DIARRHŒA AND DYSENTERY.

A DISTINCTION is attempted to be made between these two diseases,—the former name being confined to an inflammation of the mucous membrane of the small intestines, while the latter is said to reside in the large. It is very difficult, however, if not impossible, to distinguish the one from the other by the symptoms during life, and in ordinary practice they may be considered as one disease, the treatment depending in great measure on the exciting cause. This in most cases is to be found in the use of too violent "physic," or in not resting the horse after it has begun to act until some hours after it has completely "set." Sometimes it depends on the cells of the colon having long been loaded with fæces, which causes, at length, their mucous lining to inflame, the consequent secretion having a tendency to loosen them and procure their dismissal, either by solution or by the forcible contraction of the muscular coat. This last disease is known by the name of "molten grease" to old-fashioned farriers, the clear mucus which envelopes the lumps of fæces being supposed to be derived from the internal fat that is generally plentifully developed in the highly fed horses that are especially subject to the attack. For practical purposes, therefore, we may consider the different forms under the head of superpurgation, diarrhœa, and dysentery, meaning by the last name that condition which is brought about by and attended with a discharge of lumps of hard fæcal matter enveloped in mucus.

SUPERPURGATION is sometimes so severe as to place a delicate horse in great danger. When the action of the bowels has gone on for three or four days consecutively, and there is no disposition to "set," the eyes become staring and glassy, the pulse is feeble, and the heart flutters in the most distressing manner; the mouth has a peculiarly offensive smell, the tongue being pale and covered with a white fur having a brown centre. The abdomen is generally tucked tightly up, but in the later stages large volumes of gas are evolved, and it becomes tumid.

The treatment should consist in the exhibition of rice, boiled till quite soft, and if not taken voluntarily, it should be given as a drench, mixed into a thin liquid form with warm water. If the case is severe, one or two ounces of laudanum may be added to a quart of rice milk, and given every time the bowels act with violence. Or a thin gruel may be made with wheat meal, and the laudanum be mixed with that instead of the rice. A perseverance in these remedies will almost invariably produce the desired effect, if they have not been deferred until the horse is very much exhausted, when a pint of port wine may be substituted for the laudanum with advantage.

IN DIARRHŒA resulting from cold, or over-exertion, the treatment should be exactly like that prescribed for superpurgation, but it will sometimes be necessary to give chalk in addition to the remedies there alluded to. The rice or flour-milk may be administered as food, and the following drench given by itself every time there is a discharge of liquid fæces :—

> Take of Powdered Opium . . . . . . 1 drachm.
> Tincture of Catechu . . . . . ½ ounce.
> Chalk Mixture . . . . . . 1 pint.
> Mix and give as a drench.

During the action of these remedies the body must be kept warm by proper clothing, and the legs should be encased in flannel bandages, previously made hot at the fire, and renewed as they become cold.

IN DYSENTERY (or molten grease) it is often necessary to take a little blood away, if there is evidence of great inflammation in the amount of mucus surrounding the fæces, and when aperient medicine does not at once put a stop to the cause of irritation by bringing the lumps away from the cells of the colon. Back-raking, and injections of two ounces of laudanum and a pint of castor oil with gruel, should be adopted in the first instance, but they will seldom be fully efficient without the aid of linseed oil given by the mouth. A pint of this, with half a pint of *good* castor oil, will generally produce a copious discharge of lumps, and then the irritation ceases without requiring any further interference.

Whenever there is diarrhœa or dysentery present to any extent, rice-water should be the sole drink.

STRANGULATION AND RUPTURE.

MECHANICAL VIOLENCE is done to the stomach and bowels in various ways, but in every case the symptoms will be those of severe inflammation of the serous coat, speedily followed by death, if not relieved when relief is possible. Sometimes the stomach is ruptured from over-distension—at others the small intestines have been known to share the same fate, but the majority of cases are due to strangulation of a particular portion of the bowels, by being tied or pressed upon by some surrounding band. This may happen either from a loop of bowel being forced through an opening in the mesentery or mesocolon, or from a band of organized lymph, the result of previous inflammation—or from one portion of the bowels forcing itself into another, like the inverted finger of a glove, and the included portion being firmly contracted upon by the exterior bowel, so as to produce dangerous pressure (intussusception), or, lastly, from a portion or knuckle of intestine forcing its way through an opening in the walls of the abdomen, and then called hernia or rupture, which being pressed upon by the edges of the opening becomes strangulated, and if not relieved inflames, and then mortifies. None of these cases are amenable to treatment (and indeed they cannot often be discovered with certainty during life, the symptoms resembling those of enteritis), except strangulated hernia, which should be reduced either by the pressure of the hands, or by the aid of an operation with the knife— which will be described under the chapter which treats of the several operations. Whenever inflammation of the bowels is attended with obstinate constipation, the walls of the abdomen should be carefully examined, and especially the inguinal canal, scrotum, and navel, at which points in most cases the hernia makes its appearance. A swelling at any other part may, however, contain a knuckle of intestine, which has found its way through the abdominal parietes in consequence of a natural opening existing there, or of one having been made by some accidental puncture with a spike of wood or iron. The swelling is generally round, or nearly so, and gives a drum-like sound on being tapped with the fingers. It feels hard to the touch in consequence of the contents being constricted, but it gives no sensation of solidity, and may be generally detected by these signs. None but an educated hand can, however, be relied on to distinguish a ventral hernia from any other tumor. When it occurs at the scrotum or navel the case is clear enough.

CALCULI IN THE BOWELS.

A STOPPAGE IN THE BOWELS sometimes obstinately persists, in spite of all kinds of remedies, and, death taking place, it is found on examination that a large calculus has blocked up the area of the canal. Sometimes one of these calculi is found in the stomach, but this is extremely rare. On making a section they are found to consist of concentric layers of bran, chaff, and other hard particles of the food, mixed generally with some small proportion of earthy matter, and arranged around some foreign body, such as a piece of stone from the corn, or the head of a nail. Treatment is out of the question, as it is impossible to discover the calculus during life, and even if it could be ascertained to exist, no remedy is known for it. Those who are curious about the composition of these calculi, will be pleased with the following letter by Mr. Buckland, surgeon to the 1st Life Guards, in reply to an inquiry made in *The Field* as to the composition of a calculus found in a horse belonging to a correspondent:—

"Mr. C. Pemberton Carter having, in his interesting letter, requested me to throw some light upon this subject, I have great pleasure in giving what little information I am able to afford, with apologies for delay, as Aldershot camp is by no means a favorable spot for scientific investigations or literary pursuits. As regards the actual composition of calculi such as he has sent, we learn from the catalogue of the museum of the Royal College of Surgeons that they are composed for the most part of the phosphate of magnesia and ammonia, with small quantities of phosphate of lime. They also contain an animal and extractive matter, to which the brown color of the calculus is owing. They also contain muriates of soda, and various alkaline salts derived from the intestinal juices. The animal matter resembles that of all other concretions, and separates in concentric laminæ when the calculus is dissolved in an acid. In more impure varieties, grains of sand, portions of hay, straw, &c., are frequently found imbedded in the calculus, and there is one specimen in the museum which contains an entire layer of vegetable hairs. Mr. Carter remarks that 'his impression is that the calculus is made up of bran' (chemically speaking). He is not far wrong, for we read in the College catalogue, ' Most authorities agree that these calculi are formed from phosphate of magnesia, *contained in wheat, oats, hay,* &c., and this opinion derives confirmation from the circumstance that they occur most frequently in *millers' and brewers'* horses, which are fed upon grains, bran, and substances known to contain a much larger proportion of magnesian salts than other vegetable matters.' Mr. Carter has detected minute portions of wheat, oats, and hay in the calculus, which therefore may be said to consist of two substances, viz., the vegetable and the mineral. So much, then, for the composition of the calculus; now for its mechanical structure. Most decidedly it may be compared to an onion, layer being packed over layer, so as in section to present a ringed appearance. We may also liken it to other objects. It has lately struck me to examine the structure of a common cricket-ball, which combines hardness, lightness, and elasticity in such an admirable way. Upon making a section, I found the cricket-ball to be composed of layers, one over the other, round a central nucleus. The layers are composed of leather, alternated with a vegetable fibre, the nucleus being a bit of cork. The calculus in the horse is formed in a similar way. The nucleus in Mr. Carter's specimen is a bit of flint; in a capital instance I have in my own collection, of a common shot, about No. 5 size, which has been crushed by the horse's teeth, and subsequently swallowed; in another instance, of a chair nail of brass; in another of a single oat-seed; in another of a minute bit of cinder, and so on, as it seems to be absolutely necessary that these calculi should have a commencement—a starting-point. Where is the school-boy who can make a gigantic snowball without beginning with a small lump of snow or a stone, as a nucleus upon which he builds all the rest?

" Mr. Carter seems to wonder at the weight of the specimen, 5 lbs.; this is by no means a large size; in the museum of the Royal College of Surgeons we have a very fine collection of calculi, the largest, taken from the intestines of a horse, weighs no less than 17 lbs., and is about the size and shape of an ordinary skittle-ball. In the case where this is contained he will see many other specimens, cut in sections to show the nuclei; he will observe that calculi also form in the intestines of the camel and of the elephant, and even in the wild horse, for there is a good specimen from the intestines of a Japanese wild horse. Stones, not true calculi, are sometimes found in animals, which have been actually swallowed by them, and have not been chemically formed in this walking laboratory. There is a case containing several pebbles—thirty in number—found in the stomach of a cow at Barton-under-Needwood, Burton-on-Trent. These stones belong to the geological formation of the neighborhood; it is curious to see how they have been acted on by the action of the stomach, for they are highly glazed and polished. I have seen specimens of gravel pebbles which I took from the gizzard of an ostrich, which are as highly polished as an agate marble. The bird swallowed the stones to assist its digestion; the cow out of a morbid appetite. I know of a somewhat similar instance that lately happened: A young lady was taken ill, and died of very strange symptoms; it was subsequently ascertained that the stomach was quite filled with human hair, which had moulded itself into the shape of the interior of that organ. The poor girl had naturally very long and beautiful hair, and she had an unfortunate habit of catching the loose hairs with her lips and swallowing them; in time they felted together, became a solid mass, and killed her—a warning to other young ladies which should not be neglected. In the lower animals we frequently find rolled balls of hair from the creatures licking themselves. I have seen one at Bristol from a lioness; it is formed of hairs licked with her rough tongue from her cubs. Curious concretions are found in goats, &c., called 'bezoar' stones; they were formerly supposed to have medicinal virtues: of this at another time. F. T. BUCKLAND."

WORMS.

INTESTINAL WORMS in the horse are chiefly of two species, both belonging to the genus *ascaris*. Bots, as inhabiting the stomach, have already been described with that organ; and, moreover, they should never be confounded with what are called properly and scientifically, "worms." Of these, the larger species resembles the common earthworm in all respects but color, which is a pinkish white. It inhabits the small intestines, though it is sometimes, but very rarely, found in the stomach. The *symptoms* are a rough, staring, hollow coat—a craving appetite—more or less emaciation—the passage of mucus with the fæces, and very often a small portion of this remains outside the anus, and dries there. That part generally itches, and in the attempt to rub it the tail is denuded of hair; but this may arise from vermin in it, or from mere irritation of the anus from other causes. When these several symptoms are combined, it may with some degree of certainty be supposed that there are worms in the intestines, but before proceeding to dislodge them, it is always the wisest plan to obtain proof positive of their existence, by giving an ordinary dose of physic, when, on watching the evacuations, one or more worms may generally be discovered if they are present. When the case is clearly made out the plan of *treatment* is as follows:—

> Take of Tartar Emetic* . . . . 1 drachm.
> Powdered Ginger . . . . ½ drachm.
> Linseed Meal sufficient to make into a ball with boiling water.

One should be given every morning for a week, then a dose of physic; linseed oil being the most proper. Let the stomach rest a week; give another course of balls and dose of physic, after which let the horse have a drachm of sulphate of iron (powdered) twice a day with his feed of corn.

There is no medicine which is so effectual for removing worms in the horse as tartar emetic, and none which is so entirely innocuous to the stomach. Calomel and spirit of turpentine were formerly in use as vermifuges, but they are both dangerous drugs; the former, if given for any length of time, causing great derangement of the stomach and liver; and the latter often producing considerable inflammation after a single dose, if sufficiently large to cause the expulsion of the worms. Linseed oil given in half-pint doses every morning is also an excellent vermifuge, but not equal to the tartar emetic. If this quantity does not relax the bowels it may be increased until they are rendered slightly more loose than usual, but avoiding anything like purgation.

The smaller species of intestinal worm chiefly inhabits the rectum, but is occasionally found in the colon and cæcum. It produces great irritation and uneasiness, but has not the same prejudicial effect on the health as the larger parasite. It is about one to two inches in length, and somewhat smaller in diameter than a crow quill. These worms are commonly distinguished as *ascarides*, but both this species and the round worm belong to the genus *ascaris*. The term *thread worm* is more correctly applied, as they are not unlike sections of stout thread or cotton. The only *symptom* by which their presence can be made out is the rubbing of the tail, when if, on examination, no vermin or eruption is found in the dock, it may be presumed that worms exist in the rectum. The *remedy* for these worms is by the injection every morning for a week of a pint of linseed oil, containing two drachms of spirit of turpentine. This will either kill or bring away the worms, with the exception of a few which are driven by it higher up into the

---

* Omit the Tartar Emetic, and substitute 2 drachms of powdered Sulphate of Iron.—EDITOR.

colon, but by waiting a week or ten days (during which time they will have re-entered the rectum) and then repeating the process, they may generally be entirely expelled. The sulphate of iron must be given here, as before described.

DISEASES OF THE LIVER.

THE LIVER OF THE HORSE is less liable to disease than that of any other domestic animal, and the symptoms of its occurrence are so obscure that it is seldom until a post-mortem examination that a discovery is made of its existence. This unerring guide, however, informs us that the liver is sometimes unnaturally enlarged and hard, at others softened, and in others again the subject of cancerous deposits. It is also attacked by inflammation, of which the *symptoms* are feverishness; rapid pulse, not hard and generally fuller than usual; appetite bad; restlessness, and the patient often looking round to his right side with an anxious expression, not indicative of severe pain. Slight tenderness of the right side; but this not easily made out satisfactorily. Bowels generally confined, but there is sometimes diarrhœa. Very frequently the whites of the eyes show a tinge of yellow, but anything like jaundice is unknown. The *treatment* must consist in the use of calomel and opium, with mild purging, thus:—

Take of Calomel,
 Powdered Opium, of each one drachm.
 Linseed Meal and boiling water enough to make into a ball, which should be given night and morning. Every other day a pint of Linseed Oil should be administered.

The *diet* should if possible be confined to green food, which will do more good than medicine; indeed, in fine weather, a run at grass during the day should be preferred to all other remedies, taking care to shelter the horse at night in an airy loose-box.

DISEASES OF THE KIDNEYS.

THESE ORGANS are particularly prone to disease, and are subject to inflammation; to diabetes, or profuse staling; to hæmaturia, or a discharge of blood, and to torpidity, or inaction.

INFLAMMATION OF THE KIDNEYS (*nephritis*) is generally produced by an exposure of the loins to wet and cold, as in carriage-horses standing about in the rain during the winter season. Sometimes it follows violent muscular exertion, and is then said to be caused by a strain in the back, but in these cases there is probably an exposure to cold in a state of exhaustion, or by the rupture of a branch of the renal artery or vein, as the inflammation of one organ can scarcely be produced by the strain of another. The *symptoms* are a constant desire to void the urine, which is of a very dark color—often almost black. Great pain, as evidenced by the expression of countenance and by groans, as well as by frequent wistful looks at the loins. On pressing these parts there is some tenderness, but not excessive, as in rheumatism. The pulse is quick, hard, and full. The attitude of the hind quarters is peculiar, the horse standing in a straddling position with his back arched, and refusing to move without absolute compulsion. It is sometimes difficult to distinguish nephritis from inflammation of the neck of the bladder, but by attending to the state of the urine, which is dark brown or black in the former case, and nearly of a natural color in the latter, the one may be diagnosed from the other. To make matters still more clear, the oiled hand may be passed into the rectum, when in nephritis the bladder will be found contracted and empty (the urine being so pungent as to irritate that organ), while in inflammation or spasm of its neck, it will be distended, often to a large size. The *treatment* to be adopted must be active, as the disease runs a very rapid course, and speedily ends in death if neglected. A large quantity of blood must at once be taken. The skin must be acted on energetically, so as to draw the blood to its surface, and if a Turkish bath (see page 215) is at hand, it will be highly beneficial. If not, the application of hot water, as recommended at page 342, may be tried, and in many cases it has acted like a charm. Failing the means for carrying out either of these remedies, the loins should be rubbed with an embrocation consisting of olive oil, liquid ammoniæ and laudanum in equal parts, but cantharides and turpentine must be carefully avoided, as likely to be absorbed, when they would add fuel to the fire. A fresh sheepskin should be warmed with hot (not boiling) water, and applied over the back, and the liniment should be rubbed in profusely every hour, restoring the skin to its place immediately afterwards. Mustard is sometimes used instead of ammonia, and as it is always at hand, it may form a good substitute, but it is not nearly so powerful an irritant to the skin as the latter, especially when evaporation is prevented by the sheepskin, or by a piece of any waterproof article. A mild aperient may be given, linseed oil being the best form, but if the bowels continue obstinate, and it is necessary to repeat it, eight or ten drops of croton oil may be added to a pint of the oil, great care being taken to assist its action by raking and injection, the latter being also useful as a fomentation to the kidneys. The *diet* should consist of scalded linseed and bran mashes, no water being allowed without containing sufficient linseed tea to make it slightly glutinous, but not so much so as to nauseate the patient. If the symptoms are not greatly abated in six or eight hours, the bleeding must be repeated, for upon this remedy the chief dependence must be placed. A mild and soothing drench, composed of half an ounce of carbonate of soda, dissolved in six ounces of linseed tea, may be given every six hours, but little reliance can be placed upon it. The inflammation either abates after the bleeding, or the horse dies in a very few hours.

DIABETES of late years has been much more frequent than was formerly the case, and especially among race-horses and hunters, probably owing to the enormous quantities of corn which they are allowed in the present day. But whatever may be the cause, the *symptoms* are clear enough, the horse constantly staling and passing large quantities of urine each time. *The treatment* should be conducted on the principle that the cause should if possible be ascertained and removed. Mowburnt hay will often bring on diabetes, and new oats have a similar tendency in delicate horses. In any case it is wise to make a total change in the food as far as it can possibly be done. Green meat will often check it at once, and a bran-mash containing a few carrots has a similar chance of doing good. With these alterations in the *quality* of the food attention should also be paid to the *quantity* of the corn, which should be reduced if more than a peck a day has been given, and beans should be substituted for a part of the oats. Half a drachm of the sulphate of iron (powdered) should be mixed with each feed (that is, four times a day), and the horse should be well clothed and his legs warmly bandaged in a cool and airy (but not cold and draughty) loose box. By attention to these directions the attack may generally be subdued in a few days, but there is always a great tendency to its return. Should it persist in spite of the adoption of the measures already recommended, the following ball may be tried:—

Take of Gallic Acid . . . . ½ drachm.
Opium . . . . 1 drachm.
Treacle and Linseed Meal enough to make into a ball, which should be given twice a day.

HÆMATUREA, like diabetes, is easily recognised by the presence of blood in greater or less quantities passed with the urine. It is not, however, of the bright red color natural to pure blood, but it is more or less dingy, and sometimes of a smoky-brown color, as occurs in inflammation. Bloody urine, however, may often be passed without any sign of that condition, and therefore unaccompanied by pain, or any other urgent symptom. The causes are exceedingly various. Sometimes a parasitic worm (*Strongylus gigas*) has been discovered, after death from hæmaturea, in the kidney, and was apparently the cause of the mischief. At others, this organ has been found disorganized by cancer or melanosis—and again a sharp calculus has been known to bring on considerable bleeding, and this last cause is by no means unfrequent. The *symptoms* are the existence of bloody urine unaccompanied by pain or irritation, marking the absence of nephritis. As to *treatment*, little can be done in severe cases, and mild ones only require rest, a dose of physic, and perhaps the abstraction of three or four quarts of blood. Green food should be given, and the diet should be attended to as for diabetes. If the urine is scanty, yet evidently there is no inflammation, two or three drachms of nitre may be given with the mash at night, but this remedy should be employed with great caution.

INACTION OF THE KIDNEYS is so common in every stable that the groom seldom thinks it necessary even to inform his master of its occurrence. An ounce of nitre is mixed and given with a bran-mash as a matter of course, and sometimes more violent diuretics are resorted to, such as powdered resin and turpentine. Very often the kidneys are only inactive because the horse has not been regularly watered, and in those stables where an unlimited supply is allowed this condition is comparatively rare. There is no harm in resorting to nitre occasionally, but if it is often found necessary to employ this drug, the health is sure to suffer, and an alteration in the diet should be tried in preference. At all events, if it is given, the horse should be allowed to drink as much and as often as he likes, without which the stimulus to the kidneys will be doubly prejudicial, from being in too concentrated a form.

DISEASES OF THE BLADDER.

THE BLADDER is subject to inflammation of its coats or neck—to spasm—and to the formation of calculi.

INFLAMMATION OF THE BLADDER (cystitis) is not very common excepting when it is produced by irritants of a mechanical or chemical nature. Thus, when the kidneys secrete a highly irritating urine, the bladder suffers in its passage, and we have the two organs inflamed at the same time. Again, when cantharides have been given with a view to stimulate exhausted nature, or when they are absorbed from the surface of the skin, as sometimes happens in blistering, the bladder is liable to become inflamed. The *symptoms* are—a quick pulse—pain in the hind-quarter, evinced by the looks of the animal in that direction—and constant straining to pass the urine, which is thick and mixed with mucus, or in aggravated cases with purulent matter. The *treatment* to be adopted if the case is severe will consist in venesection, back-raking, and purgation with linseed or castor oil, avoiding aloes, which have a tendency to irritate the bladder. Linseed tea should be given as the sole drink, and scalded linseed mixed with a bran-mash as food. The following ball may also be given, and repeated if necessary:—

Take of Powdered Opium . . . . 1 drachm.
Tartar emetic . . . . 1½ drachm.
To be made up into a ball with Linseed Meal and boiling water, and given every six hours.

RETENTION OF URINE may be due either to inflammation of the neck of the bladder, occasioning a spasmodic closure of that part, or there may be spasm unattended by inflammation and solely due to the irritation of some .offending substance, such as a calculus, or a small dose of cantharides. The *treatment* in either case must be directed to the spasmodic constriction, which is generally under the control of large doses of opium and camphor, that is, from one drachm to two drachms of each, repeated every five or six hours. If the symptoms are urgent, bleeding may also be resorted to, and when the bladder is felt to be greatly distended, no time should be lost in evacuating it by means of the catheter, which operation, however, should only be intrusted to a regular practitioner accustomed to its use.

CALCULI IN THE BLADDER are formed of several earthy salts, and present various forms and appearances, which may be comprised under four divisions. 1st. The mulberry calculus, so named from its resemblance to a mulberry, possessing generally a nucleus. 2d. A very soft kind resembling fuller's earth in appearance, and being chiefly composed of phosphate of lime and mucus. 3d. Calculi of a white or yellowish color, rough externally and easily friable. And 4th. Those which are composed of regular layers, and which are harder than the second and third varieties.

The mulberry calculus, from its extremely rough surface, occasions more irritation than other forms, but during life it is impossible to ascertain the exact chemical nature of the calculus which may be ascertained to exist. These calculi sometimes attain an immense size, weighing several pounds. The *symptoms* are a difficulty of voiding the urine, which generally comes away in jerks after great straining and groaning. The horse remains with his legs extended for some time afterwards, and evidently indicates that he feels as if his bladder was not relieved. Often there is muco-purulent matter mixed with the urine, which is rendered thick and glutinous thereby, but this only happens in cases of long standing. The *treatment* must be either palliative or curative. If the former, it should consist in the adoption of the means employed for subduing irritation and inflammation of the bladder which have been already described. The *cure* can only be effected by removing the stone. This requires the performance of a difficult and dangerous operation (lithotomy), the details of which can be only useful to the professed veterinary surgeon. and I shall therefore omit them here.

DISEASES OF THE ORGANS OF GENERATION.

BALANITIS, or inflammation of the glans penis ($\beta \acute{a} \lambda a \nu o \varsigma$, glans), is very common in the horse, being brought on by the decomposition of the natural secretions, when they have been allowed to collect for any length of time. At first there is merely a slight discharge of pus, but in process of time foul sores break out, and very often fungous growths spring from them, which block up the passage through the opening of the sheath, and cause considerable swelling and inconvenience. These are quite distinct from warts, which occur in this part just as they do in other situations. The *treatment* requires some skill and experience, because mild remedies are of no use, and severe ones are not unattended with danger. The parts must first of all be well cleansed by syringing, or if the end of the penis can be laid hold of, by washing with a sponge. The following wash may then be applied. and it should be repeated every day :—

>   Take of solution of Chloride of Zinc . . . . . . 2 drachms.
>   Water . . . . 1 pint. Mix.

If the morbid growths are very extensive, nothing but amputation of the penis or the use of corrosive sublimate will remove them. Severe hæmorrhage sometimes follows both of these measures, but it seldom goes on to a dangerous extent. Still it is scarcely advisable for any one but a professional man to undertake the operation.

IN THE MARE THE VAGINA is sometimes inflamed, attended with a copious yellow discharge. An injection of the wash mentioned in the last paragraph will generally soon set the matter right. At first it should be used only of half the strength, gradually increasing it, until the full quantity of chloride of zinc is employed.

INVERSION OF THE UTERUS sometimes follows parturition, but it is very rare in the mare. The uterus should be at once replaced, using as little force as possible, and taking care before the hand is withdrawn, that it really is turned back again from its inverted position.

NYMPHOMANIA occurs sometimes in mares at the time of being "in use," and goes on to such an extent as to render them absolutely regardless of pain, for the time being, though not to make them lose their consciousness. They will kick and squeal till they become white with sweat, and no restraint will prevent them from trying to continue their violent attempts to destroy everything behind them. These symptoms are especially developed in the presence of other animals of the same species, whether mares or geldings; but the near proximity of an entire horse will be still worse. If placed in a loose box, without any restraint whatever, they generally become more calm, and when the state is developed, such a plan should always be adopted. It is chiefly among highly-fed and lightly-worked mares that the disease is manifested; and a dose of physic with starvation in a loose box, away from any other horse, will very soon put an end to it in almost every instance.

CHAPTER XXIII.

DISEASES OF THE NERVOUS SYSTEM.

Phrenitis, or Mad Staggers—Epilepsy and Convulsions—Megrims —Rabies, Hydrophobia, or Madness—Tetanus, or Lock-jaw— Apoplexy and Paralysis—String Halt—Coup de Soleil, or Sun stroke.

PHRENITIS, OR MAD STAGGERS.

PHRENITIS seldom occurs, except in over-fed and lightly-worked horses, nor among them is it by any means a common disease. The early *symptoms* are generally those of an ordinary cold; there is heaviness of the eyes, with a redness of the conjunctiva, and want of appetite. After a day or two occupied by these premonitory signs, which will seldom serve to put even the most experienced observer on his guard, the horse becomes suddenly delirious, attempting to bite and strike every one who comes near him, regardless of the ordinary influences of love and fear. He plunges in his stall, attempts to get free from his halter rein, and very often succeeds in doing so, when he will stop at nothing to gain still further liberty. If unchecked he soon dashes himself to pieces, and death puts an end to his struggles. The only *treatment* which is of the slightest use is bleeding till the horse absolutely falls, or till he becomes quite quiet and tractable, if the case is only a mild one. Immediately afterwards a large dose of tartar emetic (two or three drachms) should be given, followed in an hour or two by a strong physic ball; or, if the case is a very bad one, by a drench, containing half a pint of castor oil and six or eight drops of croton oil. Clysters and back-raking will of course be required, to obviate the risk of hard accumulations in the bowels, but where there is great violence, they cannot always be employed and the case must take its chance in these respects. The *diet* should be confined to a few mouthfuls of hay or grass, with a plentiful supply of water.*

EPILEPSY AND CONVULSIONS.

THESE DISEASES, or symptoms of disease, are not often met with in the adult, but in the foal they sometimes occur, and are not unattended with danger. The young thing will perhaps gallop after its dam round and round its paddock, and then all at once stop,

---

* No treatment, however well directed, will be of any use. The better way will be to shoot the horse at once, before he has a chance of destroying the stable and other property within his reach.—EDITOR.

stagger, and fall to the ground, where it lies, struggling with more or less violence, for a few minutes or longer, and then raises its head, stares about it, gets up, and is apparently as well as ever. It is generally in the hot days of summer that these attacks occur, and it appears highly probable that the direct rays of the sun playing on the head have something to do with it. Death seldom takes place during the first attack, but sometimes after two or three repetitions the convulsions go on increasing, and the foal becomes comatose and dies. A mild dose of linseed oil is the only *remedy* which can safely be resorted to, and as it is supposed that worms will sometimes produce these convulsive attacks, it is on that account to be selected. Epilepsy is so very rarely met with in the adult and of its causes and treatment so little is known, that I shall not trouble my readers with any account of them.*

MEGRIMS.

THIS TERM is used to conceal our ignorance of the exact nature of several disordered conditions of the brain and heart. In fact, any kind of fit, not attended with convulsions, and only lasting a short time, is called by this name. The cause may be a fatty condition of the heart, by which sudden faintness and sometimes death are produced, or it may consist in congestion of the vessels of the brain, arising from over work on a hot day, or from the pressure of the collar, or from disease of the valves of the heart. Attacks reputed to be megrims have been traced to each of these causes, and as in every case, the horse, while apparently in good health, staggers and falls, and after lying still for a minutes (during which there is seldom an opportunity of examining the state of the circulation) rises as well as before, there is no chance of distinguishing the one from the other. The most usual *symptoms* are the following:—The horse is perhaps trotting along, when all at once he begins shaking his head as if the bridle chafed his ears, which are drawn back close to the poll. The driver gets down to examine these facts, and observes the eyelids quivering, and the nostrils affected with a trembling kind of spasm. Sometimes the rest will allow of the attack going off, but most frequently, the head is drawn to one side, the legs of that half of the body seem to be paralyzed, and the horse making a segment of a circle goes down, lies a few minutes on the ground, and then rises as if nothing had happened beyond a light sweating, and disturbance of the respiration. *Treatment* can be of little avail, however, unless a correct diagnosis is made, for remedies which would be suited to congestion would be prejudicial to a diseased heart. If the attack has happened while

---

* Cerebro-spinal meningitis of some New York writers, will be found treated of in our note on chapter on "Fevers," article "Typhoid Fever"— the so-called choking distemper.—EDITOR.

in harness, the collar should always be carefully inspected, and if at all tight it should be replaced by a deeper one. A diseased state of the valves of the heart ought to be discoverable by auscultation, but it requires a practised ear to do this, and the directions for ascertaining its presence are beyond the scope of this book. The only plan which can safely be adopted, is to take the subject of megrims quietly home to his stable, and carefully examine into the condition of all his functions with a view to improve the action of any organ which appears to be out of order, whatever it may be. If all seems to be going on well—if the appetite is good, and the heart acts with regularity and with due force, while the brain seems clear, and the eye is not either dull or suffused with blood—nothing should be attempted, but the horse being subject to a second attack, as proved by manifold experience, should be put to work in which no great danger can be apprehended from them. He is not safe in any kind of carriage, for it can never be known where the fall will take place; and as a saddle-horse he is still more objectionable, and should therefore be put to some commercial purpose, in executing which, if he falls, the only injury he can effect is to property, and not to human life.

RABIES, HYDROPHOBIA OR MADNESS.

ONE REASON ONLY can be given for describing this disease, which is wholly beyond the reach of art; but as the horse attacked by it is most dangerous, the sooner he is destroyed the better; and for this reason, every person who is likely to have any control over him, should be aware of the symptoms. As far as is known at present, Rabies is not idiopathically developed in the horse, but must follow the bite of a rabid individual belonging to one or other of the genera *canis* and *felis*. The dog, being constantly about our stables, is the usual cause of the development of the disease, and it may supervene upon the absorption of the salivary virus without any malicious bite, as has happened according to more than one carefully recorded case. The lips of the horse are liable to be ulcerated from the action of the bit, and there is reason to believe that in the early stages of rabies these parts have been licked by a dog, the saliva has been absorbed, and the inoculation has taken place just as it would do from any other wound. It is difficult to prove that this is the true explanation of those cases where no bite has been known to have occurred, but as the mouth has in each instance been shown to have been abraded, there is some reason for accepting it as such. To proceed, however, to the *symptoms*, Mr. Youatt, who has had great opportunities for examining rabies, both in the dog and horse, describes the earliest as consisting in "a spasmodic movement of the upper lip, particularly of the angles of the lip. Close following on this, or contemporaneous with it, are the depressed and anxious countenance, and inquiring gaze, suddenly, however, lighted up, and becoming fierce and menacing from some unknown cause, or at the approach of a stranger. From time to time different parts of the frame, the eyes, the jaws, particular limbs, will be convulsed. The eye will occasionally wander after some imaginary object, and the horse will snap again and again at that which has no real existence. Then will come the irrepressible desire to bite the attendants or the animals within its reach. To this will succeed the demolition of the rack, the manger, and the whole furniture of the stable, accompanied by the peculiar dread of water, which has already been described. Towards the close of the disease there is generally paralysis, usually confined to the loins and the hinder extremities, or involving those organs which derive their nervous influence from this portion of the spinal cord; hence the distressing tenesmus which is occasionally seen." How paralysis can produce tenesmus is not very clear, but of the very general existence of this symptom there can be no doubt. The dread of water, as well as of draughts of cold air, is also clearly made out to exist in this disease (as in human rabies), and the term hydrophobia will serve to distinguish it better than in the dog, where it is as clearly absent. Whenever, therefore, these symptoms follow upon the bite of a dog, unless the latter is unquestionably in good health, rabies may be suspected, and the bare suspicion ought always to lead to the use of the bullet, which is the safest way of killing a violent horse. There is only one disease (*phrenitis*) with which it can be confounded, and in that the absence of all consciousness and, in milder cases, of fear, so that no moral control whatever can be exercised, marks its nature, and clearly distinguishes it from rabies, the victim to which is conscious to the last, and though savage and violent in the extreme, is aware of the power of man, and to some extent under his influence.

TETANUS—LOCK-JAW.

TETANUS, one form of which is known as lock-jaw, has its seat apparently in the nervous system, but, like many other diseases of the same class, the traces it leaves behind are extremely uncertain, and are displayed more on the secondary organs, through which it is manifested, than on those which we believe to be at the root of the mischief. Thus the muscles, which have been long kept in a state of spasm, show the marks of this condition in their softened and apparently rotten condition. They in fact have had no interval of rest, during which nutrition could go on, and have lost much of the peculiarity of structure which enables them to contract. The stomach often shows marks of inflammation, but as all sorts of violent remedies are employed, this may be due to them rather than to idiopathic disease. The lungs also are generally congested, but here, like the state of the muscles, it may be a secondary effect of the long-continued exertions of the latter, which nothing but the absence of all important lesions of the brain and spinal cord would induce the pathologist to pay the slightest attention to.

TETANUS may be either idiopathic or symptomatic, but the former condition is somewhat rare. It almost always follows some operation, or a severe injury in which a nerve has been implicated, the most frequent causes being the piercing of the sole by a nail, or a prick in shoeing, or the operations of docking, nicking, castration, &c.

THE SYMPTOMS are a permanent rigidity of certain voluntary muscles, and especially of the lower jaw (whence the popular name, lock-jaw). The mouth is kept rigidly shut, the masseter muscles feeling as hard as a deal board. One or both sides of the neck are rigid, in the former case the head being turned to one side, and in the latter stretched out as if carved in marble. The nostrils are dilated; the eyes retracted, with the haws thrust forward over them; the ears erect and stiff, and the countenance as if horror-struck. At first the extremities are seldom involved, but as the disease progresses their control is first lost, and then they become rigid, like the neck and head. The patient is scarcely able to stand, and plants his feet widely apart to prop himself up, while at last the tail also becomes a fixture. The pulse varies a good deal, in some cases being quick, small, and hard, and in others slow and labored. The bowels are generally costive, and the urine scanty; but this last symptom is not so well marked as the state of the bowels alluded to. The *treatment* should be of a two-fold nature, partly palliative and partly curative. Since the introduction into use of chloroform we have possessed a drug which invariably enables us to remove the spasm for a time, and if it does nothing more, it gives room for other remedies to act and relieve the patient from the horrible tortures which are occasioned by the spasm, while it also allows the muscular and nervous powers to be recruited. When, therefore, a case of tetanus occurs in a horse of any value, an apparatus for applying chloroform (described under the chapter on Operations) should be procured, and the animal at once placed under its influence. This done, the whole length of the spine should be blistered with tincture of cantharides, and an active aperient should be given, consisting, if practicable, of a pint of castor oil, and six or eight drops of croton oil. This may be pumped down the throat by the usual syringe and tube, if the front teeth can be separated; but if this cannot be done, some solid cathartic must be selected, though there is often as much difficulty in forcing a ball down as in passing an elastic tube. Failing in either of these, two drachms of calomel, and the same quantity of tartar emetic should be slightly damped, and placed in the mouth as far back as possible, in the hope that they may be gradually swallowed; the bowels should be raked, and copious injections of castor oil and turpentine, mixed with several quarts of gruel, should be thrown up. If these remedies fail, nature must be left to her own resources, and they will sometimes be found equal to the task, for many cases have recovered after having been given up as beyond the reach of our art. Opium, henbane, digitalis, hellebore, and a host of other drugs have been tried, sometimes with, and sometimes without success, and perhaps it is worth while, after the bowels have been well relieved, to give a full dose of one or other of these powerful remedies, such as two drachms of solid opium; but I confess that I think little reliance is to be placed on them, and I prefer the adoption of chloroform every six hours, continued for about two or three hours and gradually withdrawn, leaving the cure to the action of the blister and purgatives.*

APOPLEXY AND PARALYSIS.

USUALLY these are only different degrees of the same disease, but there are exceptions in which the latter is produced by some chronic affection of the spinal cord or brain. As a rule both depend upon pressure made on the brain by an overloaded state of the vessels, commonly known as congestion, or by extravasation of blood, in which it escapes from them.

APOPLEXY, known among writers of the old school as sleepy staggers, is not often met with in the present day, owing to the improvement in the management of our stables, and specially to their better ventilation. It is marked by great sleepiness, from which the horse can be with difficulty roused, soon going on to absolute unconsciousness, attended by a slow snoring respiration, and speedily followed by death. The only *treatment* likely to be successful is copious bleeding, purgation, and blisters to the head and neck.

PARALYSIS is marked by a loss of power over the muscles of a part, and may be confined to one limb or organ or extend to more. It is a *symptom* of pressure on, or disorganization of, some part of the nervous system, and must be considered as such, and not as a disease of the affected muscles. Thus it requires a knowledge of anatomy to trace it to its seat, without which its treatment would be conducted on false principles. By far the most common form of paralysis is hemiplegia, or paralysis of the muscles of the hinder extremities and loins, generally arising from an injury to the spine.

---

* The greatest success met with in curing lock-jaw is by the administration of 30 drops of dilute prussic acid, of the U. S. Pharmacopœia, night and morning, keeping the horse in a quiet place. In violent cases the chloroform spoken of in the text will be of advantage.—EDITOR.

Sometimes the body of a vertebra is broken, and the parts being separated, their edges press upon the spinal cord and produce the disease. At others the vessels within the canal have received a shock, and the serous membrane secretes (or allows to ooze out) a bloody fluid which presses upon the cord, and produces the same effect but in a more gradual manner. In India, a disease known there as Kumree causes paralysis of the hinder extremities, and is due to inflammation of the membranes, which secrete a bloody serum. In this country, however, paraplegia is very rare excepting as the result of accident.

WHEN A HORSE FALLS in hunting, and never moves his hind legs afterwards, but lies with his fore legs in the position to get up, groaning and expressing great pain and distress, it may be concluded that he has fractured or dislocated his spine and that the case is hopeless. Sometimes, however, after lying for a few seconds, he slowly and with difficulty rises and is led to a stable, but after two or three hours lies down and cannot be got up again. Here there will be some difficulty in ascertaining whether the mischief is confined to a strain of the muscles or is situated within the vertebral canal. If the former is the case the pain is extreme, and generally there will be some quivering or slight spasm of one or more of the muscles of the hinder extremity, which feel naturally firm, while in paralysis they feel soft and are as quiet as they would be after death. By attention to these signs the two cases may be distinguished, but when the case is made out to be true paralysis the *treatment* is not likely (even if successful in preserving life) to bring about a useful restoration to healthy action. In valuable horses an attempt may be made by bleeding, physicking and blistering, to produce an absorption of the effused serum or blood, but the recovered animal is seldom worth the outlay, and too often as soon as he is put to any kind of work is subject to a relapse.* The most humane and certainly the most economical plan is to put him out of his misery at once by a pistol ball or knife, but if it is determined to try what can be done towards effecting a cure, no better means can be adopted than those I have alluded to.

STRING HALT.

THIS IS A PECULIAR SNATCHING UP of the hind leg, and is supposed to depend upon some obscure disease of the sciatic nerve. It however is very doubtful whether this explanation is well founded, and there is evidence that in some cases the hock itself has been affected. The extensor pedis seems to be the muscle most severely implicated, though not the only one which is thrown

---

* Use instead, 30 drops of the tincture of nux vomica three times daily, turn the horse from side to side twice in the day to prevent scalding of the skin, and rub well over the loins.—EDITOR.

into spasmodic action. No *treatment* is of the slightest avail. Horses with string halt are able to do any kind of work, but it is considered to be a form of unsoundness.*

[SUNSTROKE—COUP DE SOLEIL.

THIS DISEASE of late years has become of so frequent occurrence, that although not mentioned by previous veterinary writers, it demands a notice from us. The chief symptoms are exhaustion and stupidity, the animal usually falling to the ground and being unable to go further.

To PREVENT IT, allow the horse at short intervals a few mouthfuls of water, and fasten a wet sponge over the forehead. The sun-shades now used by extensive owners of horses, will go very far in lessening the occurrence of this affection.

The following *treatment*, when attended to at once, in the majority of cases will prove effectual.

First. Remove the horse from the harness to a cool shady place. *Second.* Give two ounces of sulphuric ether; 20 drops of the tincture of aconite root and a bottle of ale or porter as a drench to sustain the vital powers, and to act as a powerful stimulant in equalizing the circulation throughout the body; whilst, *Thirdly.* Chopped ice is to be placed in a coarse towel, cloth or bag, and laid between the ears and over the forehead, secured in any way the ingenuity of the person in charge may suggest. If the legs be cold, bandages will be of advantage. Do not put the horse to work again until he is completely restored. Dumbness is the usual result of sun-stroke—a species of coma—for which there is no cure. Horses so affected are of little use in warm weather, but are useful in winter.—EDITOR.]

---

* This affection is generally observed in well-bred horses of a highly nervous temperament, and is noticed when the horse is about starting; much difficulty being experienced before the animal gets fairly down to his work. Once under way the peculiarity entirely disappears, but returns when another start is to be made. It rarely, if ever, disqualifies the animal for any kind of work, except where he is liable to be *suddenly* called upon for any unusual exercise of power or speed.

The Editor, in his previous work on the "Diseases in the American Stable, Field, and Farm Yard," says: "The causes are twofold. *First.* The loss of nervous influence, whereby the extensor-pedis muscle is deprived of its power. *Second.* The peculiar anatomical articulation and general structure of the hock-joint of the horse are such, that when the leg of a *dead* horse is stripped of its muscles the ligaments are not disturbed at all; and if the leg, above and below the hock, be caught hold of by the hands, and the leg straightened out, the moment the hands are taken from it, will *spring* into a bent position on the instant, thus imitating string halt, as near as can be. Thus the balance of power is not equal; the articulary ligaments of the hock-joint are stronger than the muscles of the thigh. Hence, the moment the horse lifts his foot from the ground the leg is instantaneously *snatched* up by the power of the ligaments."—EDITOR.

CHAPTER XXIV.

DISEASES AND INJURIES OF CERTAIN SPECIAL ORGANS.

Diseases of the Ear—Inflammation of the Eye—Cataract—Amaurosis — Buck-eye — Surfeit — Hidebound —Mange—Lice—Mallenders and Sallenders—Warbles, Sitfasts and Harness-Galls— Grubs—Bites and Stings of Insects—Swelled Legs—Chapped Heels— Grease and Scratches —Warts —Corns — Sandcrack — False `Quarter—Quittor—Thrush—Canker—Laminitis—Seedy Toe—Contraction of the Foot—Navicular Disease—Accidents to the Legs and Feet.

DISEASES OF THE EAR.

DEAFNESS is sometimes met with in the horse, but I know of no symptoms by which its precise nature can be made out; and without ascertaining the seat of the disease, it is useless to attempt to treat it.

SOMETIMES FROM A BLOW on the external ear inflammation is set up, and an abscess forms; but all that is necessary is to open it, so that the matter can readily flow out as fast as it forms, without which precaution it will not readily heal.

INFLAMMATION OF THE EYE.

THIS IMPORTANT ORGAN is subject to three forms of inflammation, to opacity of the lens, and to paralysis of the nerve, called amaurosis.

SIMPLE INFLAMMATION is the most common of all the diseases to which the horse's eye is subject, and it precedes most of the others. It is always the result of any injury of this part, or of cold; and it shows itself if there is a tendency to inflammation of this organ, whenever the horse is in a state of plethora. The *symptoms* are an intolerance of light, so that the eye is kept half closed, by which it looks smaller than the other; a gummy secretion glues the lids together at the angles; the eyelids are slightly swollen, showing a distended state of their veins; and there is more or less watering or overflowing of tears. When the lids are separated, their internal surface looks more red than natural, and the white of the eye is covered with a net-work of fine red vessels. After the second day the transparent cornea loses its clearness, and becomes muddy, sometimes over the whole surface, and at others in specks. If the disease is allowed to go on unchecked, the cornea is involved, and the lining membrane of the aqueous humor follows; a secretion of pus takes place into the chamber, or the cornea ulcerates, and the contents of the eye escape. The *treatment* should be a copious bleeding from the jugular vein, followed by a ball, such as—

> Take of Common Physic Ball . . . . . . 2 drachms.
> Tartar Emetic . . . . 1 drachm.
> Mix and give every six hours.

This not only acts on the intestines, but it keeps up a constant nausea, and so tends to lower the action of the heart. The eye should be bathed with warm water frequently; and, if the mischief be severe, a seton should at once be put into the skin covering the upper jaw, about two inches below the eye. On the next day, if "the white" still looks red, the bleeding must be repeated; and, if the bowels are much moved, the tartar emetic may be continued without the aloes, while if they are obstinate, the dose of the latter may be increased. When the acute symptoms have somewhat diminished, a camel's-hair brush may be dipped in wine of opium, and the eye gently touched with it daily, which will generally complete the cure. The *diet* must be low, corn being forbidden entirely, and the stable should be kept very cool and airy.*

PURULENT OPHTHALMIA is confined to the conjunctiva, and it may be recognised by the profuse discharge of purulent fluid which takes place. The eyelids are much swollen, and the white of the eye is covered with a puffy red membrane, which rises up above the level of the cornea, sometimes in fungoid excrescences. This form of inflammation is generally epidemic, and sometimes runs through a stable without a single exception. The *treatment* should be, at first, similar to that recommended for simple inflammation; but when it reaches the chronic stage, a more powerful stimulus is required to restore the vessels to a healthy condition. A wash composed as follows, must therefore be applied :—

> Take of Nitrate of Silver . . . . 6 grs.
> Distilled Water . . . . 1 oz.
> Mix, and drop a little into the eye from a quill daily.

IRITIS, or inflammation of the iris, generally known as *specific ophthalmia*, is the most formidable of all the diseases to which the eye is subject, and, if not checked, rapidly disorganizes it; while it also, even when running an unusually favorable course, is very apt to produce opacity of the lens or its capsule (cataract). This pest of the stable is, undoubtedly, often brought on by over stimulation, first of the whole body, through the food, and secondly, of the eyes themselves, through the foul emanations from the accu-

---

* The treatment recommended in the text is certainly, to say the least, injudicious, heroic, and unsound. Apply cold water cloths to the eye for a day or two, then use, rain-water 4 ounces, nitrate of silver 12 grains, and apply twice daily with camel's hair pencil or brush. Allow green or soft feed.—EDITOR.

mulated urine and dung. But these would produce no su th effect in a horse, unless he were predisposed to ophthalmia; and we find that cattle and sheep are often fed to an enormous degree of obesity, in far closer and worse ventilated stalls, without any prejudicial effect upon their eyes. It may, then, be assumed, that these organs in a horse have a tendency to put on inflammation; but though these words are true they explain nothing of the real cause, and only serve to conceal our ignorance of it. There is another question bearing upon this subject, which is of the highest importance. Is the stock of blind horses more liable to blindness than that of sound ones? This has been discussed so often, that it is scarcely possible to throw any fresh light upon it, chiefly because it is so difficult to rely upon the facts adduced *pro* and *con*. Blindness is often the result of accident, and such cases are believed to be exceptional, and not at all likely to hand down the disease; but, on the contrary, I am inclined to believe that many of them show a marked tendency to its development; for an accident never destroys both eyes, and when one follows the other, it is a pretty sure sign that there is a tendency to ophthalmia. On the whole, it may, I think, be assumed, that the tendency to specific ophthalmia is handed down from generation to generation, and, consequently, that the offspring of a horse who has gone blind from that cause is peculiarly prone to it. Its *symptoms* appear very rapidly, the eye having been quite right over night, looks contracted and almost closed next morning, and on inspecting it closely " the white" looks of a *deep* red, the cornea looks muddy, and the colored part of the eye (the iris) has lost its bright color, and often shows one or two white specks upon it (these must not be confounded with specks on the cornea). As the disease advances, the intolerance of light is very great, the cornea and iris become gradually more muddy, and either lymph is thrown out on the latter in the shape of white patches, or pus is secreted and fills the chamber of the aqueous humor, in part or wholly. If the *treatment* is sufficiently energetic, these signs abate, the pus or lymph is absorbed, and the eye recovers its transparency; but there are generally some traces left behind. Bleeding (either from the jugular or the angular veins of the face), moderate purging, and a seton, are the remedies best calculated to effect this object, conjoined with an airy stable and a light diet. Unfortunately, however, iritis is almost sure to return on the restoration of the usual food, and exposure to the elements; and hence it is of the utmost consequence in purchasing a horse to examine his eyes for the marks left behind by it. If the case is hopeless, it becomes a question whether or not it will be wise to put an end to the inflammation by destroying the affected eye, for it is well known that if it goes on for any length of time the other, sound eye, becomes affected. The only difficulty consists in feeling assured that there is really no chance of recovery; for when once the eye is finally condemned, the sooner it is opened and its contents evacuated, the sooner will the horse return to his work, and the more chance has the other eye of escaping. The operation is very simple, and merely requires a sharp-pointed knife to be passed into the anterior chamber from one edge of the cornea, and driven back till it cuts into the lens, when it is to be brought out on the other side of the cornea, and the whole of the humors will escape on making pressure upon the upper eyelid.

IN INJURIES of the eye, fomentation with warm water should be carried on for half an hour, and then omitted for three or four hours; after which it may be repeated again and again, at similar intervals. Great care should be taken to remove any extraneous bodies, such as particles of dust, &c.

CATARACT, or opacity of the lens, is very commonly the result of iritis, its capsule having been coated with a layer of white lymph, deposited by the inflamed vessels; but it also sometimes makes its appearance without being preceded by any of the signs of inflammation. In the former case, the early symptoms are those of iritis; but in the latter, the opacity often goes on increasing, without the owner of the horse, or his groom, having his attention drawn to the eyes, until he finds that he is nearly blind. This progress is generally marked by the development of an unusual timidity; the previously-bold animal is alarmed at objects advancing on the road, and covered carts and wagons, of which he formerly took no notice, occasion him to shy in the most timid manner. On examining his eyes carefully, instead of the beautifully clear pupil, with the reflection of tapetum lucidum shining through it, there is seen either a mass of dull white, generally more opaque in the centre, or an appearance of mottled, semi-transparent soap, or, lastly, one or two distinct white spots, not quite circular, but with irregular edges. In confirmed cataract, the white pupil can been seen at any distance; but in the very early stage, only a practised eye can detect the opacity, which, however, is so manifest to him that he wonders it is not visible to every one else. The reason of this difficulty of detecting the alteration of structure seems to be, that inexperienced examiners look at the eye in such a manner that they are confused by the reflection on it of their own faces, hiding all beneath. If, however, they will turn their heads a little more on one side, this will disappear, and they cannot fail to perceive the disease. When cataract is clearly proved to exist, all idea of *treatment* may be abandoned, as nothing but an operation can procure a removal of the opacity; and that would leave the horse in a more useless condition than before, since he could see nothing clearly, and would only be subject to continual alarms. In the human being, the operation is performed with great success, because the lens which is sacrificed can be replaced externally by means of convex glasses; but in the horse, nothing of the kind can be done. Hence, it is useless to dream of effecting any improvement in this disease; and if both eyes are the subject of cataract, the horse is incurably blind. But supposing there is a cataract in one eye only, is the other sure to go blind, or may a reasonable hope be entertained of its remaining sound? Here the history of the disease must be examined before any opinion can be formed. If the opacity followed an accident, there is no reason for concluding that the other eye will become diseased; but if it came on idiopathically, either preceded by inflammation or otherwise, there is great risk of a repetition in the sound eye. Nevertheless, instances are common enough of one eye going blind from cataract, while the other remains sound to the end of life; and those are still more frequent in which the one sound eye continues so for six or seven years.

AMAUROSIS.

THIS IS A PALSY of the nervous expansion called the retina, produced by some disease, either functional or organic, of the optic nerve, which is generally beyond the reach of our senses, in examining it after death. The *symptoms* are a full dilatation of the pupil, so that the iris is shrunk to a thin band around it, and is so insensible to the stimulus of light, in confirmed cases, that, even when the eye is exposed to the direct rays of the sun, it does not contract. In the early stages, this insensibility is only partial; and though there is such complete blindness that the horse cannot distinguish the nature of surrounding objects, yet the pupil contracts slightly, and the inexperienced examiner might pass the eye as a sound one. The unnaturally large pupil, however, should always create suspicion; and when, on closing the lids and re-opening them in a strong light, there is little or no variation in its size, the nature of the disease is at once made apparent. The *treatment* of amaurosis must depend upon the extent to which it has gone, and its duration. If recent, bleeding and a seton in close proximity to the diseased organ will be the most likely to restore it. Sometimes the disease depends upon a disordered condition of the stomach, and then a run at grass will be the most likely means to restore both the affected organs to a sound state. Generally, however, an amaurotic eye in the horse may be considered as a hopeless case.

BUCK EYE.

A BUCK EYE is, strictly, rather a congenital malformation than a disease; but practically, in reference to the utility of the animal, it matters little. It depends upon an excess of convexity in the cornea, by which the focus of the eye is shortened too much, the image being thus rendered indistinct as it falls on the retina. No *treatment* can be of the slightest use.

SURFEIT.

An eruption of the skin, which shows itself in the form of numerous small scabs, matting the hair, and chiefly met with on the loins and quarters, is known by this name. Doubtless, it has been supposed to arise from an excess of food, causing indigestion; but it often comes on in horses which, apparently, are quite free from that disorder. The most common cause appears to be, sweating the horse when he is in a gross or plethoric condition, and then exposing him to a chill. Colts are very subject to surfeit while being broken, as are horses fresh from grass during the summer, when they are usually over-fat, and require great care in reducing this plethoric condition. The usual course of the eruption is for the scabs to dry and gradually loosen, when the hair of the part is slightly thinned by being pulled out in dressing, a fresh crop of pustules forming, and, to the casual observer, keeping up the appearance of a permanent state of the original scabs. Surfeit is not confined to gross horses, as it sometimes makes its appearance in those which are low in condition, exhibiting the same appearance to the eye; but, on examination, the secretion from the skin will be found to be thinner, and of a more purulent nature. The *treatment* must greatly depend upon the state of the general health. If the horse is very gross, it may be desirable to take a little blood away; but this will seldom be necessary, and never is desirable. Physic seems to do little immediate good; and, indeed, it is very doubtful whether any treatment is of much service, excepting such as will gradually bring the horse into working condition. The disease, in most cases, has its origin in obstruction of the sebaceous and perspiratory pores; and until these are restored to their proper functions, by gradually exercising them, little good can be done. Unfortunately, the very means which will accomplish this object are apt to increase the disease for a time; but still this must be put up with, as a matter in which no choice can be made. Regular exercise and grooming must be fully attended to, using the whisp only in dressing the skin, when the eruption shows itself, and carefully avoiding the brush and currycomb. By acting on the kidneys, more good will be done than by purging physic, which seems to be of little or no service in any case but when the stomach is greatly out of order. An ounce of nitre may be given with a mash twice a week, or the following balls may be administered:—

> Take of Nitre,
> Sulphur, of each . . . . 3 drachms.
> Sulphuret of Antimony . . . . . 2 drachms.
> Linseed Meal and Water enough to form two balls.

HIDEBOUND.

THIS IS ESSENTIALLY a disorder of the skin produced by sympathy with the stomach. It rarely occurs in any horse but one sadly out of health from a deficiency either in the quantity or quality of the food. Sometimes it comes on in the latter stages of consumption or dysentery, without any previous mismanagement; but in the vast majority of cases the cause may be laid to the food. The skin of a horse in health feels supple, and on his sides it may readily be gathered up by the hand into a large fold, but in hidebound it is as if it were glued to the ribs, and were also too tight for the carcase which it invests. The name, indeed, is expressive of this state, and the disease can scarcely be mistaken when once seen, or rather felt. Coincident with this condition of the skin, there is also, generally, either a distended state of the abdomen from flatulence, or a contracted and "tucked up" appearance from diarrhœa. The *treatment* should be addressed to the digestive organs, the state of which must be carefully examined, and if possible rectified. A pint of linseed, scalded, and mixed with a bran mash every night, or scalded malt given in equal quantities with the corn; or in the spring time, vetches, clover, or lucerne, will do more than any medicine; but when there is a deficient appetite, or the bowels or stomach, or either of them, are evidently much weakened and disordered, a stomachic ball once or twice a week will do good. The remedies appropriate to these several conditions will be found under their respective heads at pages 354, and 363, 364.

MANGE.

MANGE corresponds with the itch of the human subject in being produced by a parasitic insect, which is an acarus, but of a different species to that of man, and of a much larger size, so as to be readily visible to the naked eye. It is generally produced by contact with horses previously affected with the same disease, but it appears highly probable that a poor, half-starved animal, allowed to accumulate all kinds of dirt on his skin, will develop the parasite, though how this is done is not clearly made out. The whole subject of parasites is wrapped in mystery, which modern researches appear likely to fathom, but hitherto little progress has been made except in the history of the metamorphoses of the tape-worm, from the analogy of which some idea may be formed of the probable modes of production of other parasites. When caused by contagion, as certainly happens in the vast majority of cases, the first *symptoms* noticed will be an excessive itching of the skin, which is soon followed by a bareness of the hair in patches, partly caused by constant friction. The disease usually shows itself on the side of the neck, just at the edges of the mane, and on the insides of the quarters near the root of the tail. From these parts the eruption extends along the back and down the sides, seldom involving the extremities excepting in very confirmed cases. After a time the hair almost entirely falls off, leaving the skin at first bare and smooth, with a few small red pimples scattered over it, each of which contains an acarus, and these are connected by furrows, along which the acari have worked their way to their present habitation. In process of time the pimples increase in number and size, and from them a matter exudes which hardens into a scab, beneath which, on examination, several acari may readily be seen, moving their legs like mites in a cheese, to which they are closely allied. At first the mangy horse may keep his health, but after a time the constant irritation makes him feverish; he loses flesh, and becomes a most miserable object; but such cases of neglect are happily rare in the present day. The *treatment* must be addressed to the destruction of the life of the acarus, which, as in the human subject, is rapidly destroyed by sulphur, turpentine, arsenic, hellebore, and corrosive sublimate. Some of these drugs are, however, objectionable, from being poisonous to the horse, as well as to the parasite which preys upon him, and they are, therefore, not to be employed without great and urgent necessity, in consequence of the failure of milder remedies.* The following recipes may be relied on as perfectly efficacious, the former being sufficient in mild cases, and the latter being strong enough in any.

1. Take of Common Sulphur . . . . . 6 oz.
    Sperm or Train Oil . . . . 1 pint.
    Spirit of Turpentine . . . . 3 oz.
   Mix and rub well into the skin with a flannel, or in preference with a painter's brush.

2. Take of Compound Sulphur Ointment . . 8 oz.
    Train or Sperm Oil . . . . . 1 pint.
    Spirit of Turpentine . . . . . 3 oz.
    Mix and use as above.

One or other of the above dressings should be well rubbed in every third day for at least three or four weeks in bad cases, and two in trifling ones, when the inflammation resulting from the

---

* Take a floor cloth, damp the face of it with soap and water, dip it in fine sea sand and give the mangy parts a good scrubbing to expose the acari, wash off dry, and apply hepar sulph. one ounce, cold water two pints. Sulphurous acid gas is a certain remedy for this and other skin diseases, and is used as follows:—Place one ounce of roll sulphur on hot coals in a chafer and place it where the horse is. Close all the doors and windows but the one the animal is to stand opposite to. Continue the fumigation for an hour or so.—EDITOR.

acari and also from the application may be allowed to subside in the hope that all the parasites are killed, in which case the eruption disappears, but the hair does not always come on again as thickly as ever. All the stable fittings around the stall or box in which the horse has been standing should be thoroughly washed over with a solution of corrosive sublimate, made as follows:—

  Take of Corrosive Sublimate . . . . . 1 oz.
  Methylated Spirit of Wine . . . 6 oz.
  Water . . . . 1 gallon.

Dissolve the sublimate in the spirit by rubbing in a mortar, then mix with the water, and use with a brush, stirring it up continually to prevent its settling.

The clothing should be destroyed, as it is scarcely possible to cleanse it completely from the parasites; but if it is determined to risk a return of the disease, it should be thoroughly washed, and when dry, saturated with spirit of turpentine.

When the health has suffered from the irritation of mange, a few tonic balls may be required, but generally the removal of the cause will be sufficient.

LICE.

IN FORMER DAYS LICE were not uncommon in the horse, but they are now comparatively rare. Still they are occasionally met with, and their presence is readily ascertained, being of a considerable size, and easily seen with the naked eye. They may be destroyed by rubbing into the roots of the hair white precipitate, in powder, taking care to avoid sweating the horse or wetting his skin for some days afterwards.

MALLENDERS AND SALLENDERS.

THESE ERUPTIONS are both of the same nature, differing only in the locality where they are displayed. The former shows itself in the flexure at the back of the knee, and the latter at the bend of the hock. The *symptoms* are shown in the appearance of a foul scurf mixed with a few thin scabs, the skin underneath being stiff and unyielding. They are generally brought on by washing the legs and leaving them undried. The *treatment* required is merely the application of the following ointment, which should be well rubbed in every night:—

  Take of Cerate of Superacetate of Lead . 2 oz.
  Creosote . . . . 10 drops. Mix.

If the skin continues to be very hard and stiff, a little glycerine should be brushed on two or three times a week.

WARBLES, SITFASTS, AND HARNESS GALLS.

WHEN THE SADDLE HAS GALLED the skin beneath it, the inflammation resulting is called a "warble," and if this is neglected, so as to cause a troublesome sore, the term. "sitfast" is applied. The effect produced is similar to a harness gall, and there is not the slightest necessity for inventing names to distinguish each stage of cruelty in the rider, for if attention is paid to the warble no sitfast will ever make its appearance. Prevention is better than cure, and it may almost always be effected by the adoption of the plan of always keeping the saddle on (after loosing the girths) for a quarter of an hour or twenty minutes. Sometimes, however, in spite of this precaution, the skin of the back swells, and when a heavy man has been riding for six or eight hours on a horse unaccustomed to his weight, the cuticle will perhaps peel off, bringing the hair with it. When the swelling is considerable it should be well fomented for an hour, and then bathed with a lotion composed of one drachm of tincture of arnica in half a pint of water. The saddle should never be re-applied until the skin is quite cool and free from all inflammation, even if considerable inconvenience is thereby suffered. The same treatment will also apply to harness galls. Oiling the inside of the collar will often prevent the shoulder from suffering excoriation.

GRUBS.

THE LARVA OF SOME BEETLE, but of what species I do not know, is occasionally met with in the horse, causing a small lump, about the size of a raisin, and usually on the back. This obstinately continues for months, if its nature is not understood, in spite of all ordinary applications. At last a white larva or grub, with a black head, and very similar in everything but size to the maggot found in the nut, makes its appearance, and either escapes to fall on the ground and become a chrysalis, or else it is squeezed out by the groom, which is easily done as soon as the head is visible. When discovered previously, an opening may be made with the point of a penknife, and then the larva may be gradually squeezed out, avoiding too much haste in the operation, which will only retard the process.

BITES AND STINGS OF INSECTS.

HORSES ARE LIABLE TO BE STUNG by hornets, wasps, and bees. If there are only one or two stings made, no interference is necessary; but sometimes a larger number of poisonous punctures have been effected, and then the best *treatment* is the application of spirit of turpentine and laudanum in equal proportions.

THE BITES OF THE GADFLY are so troublesome in their effects that it is sometimes desirable to prevent them if possible. This is effected by making a strong infusion of the green bark of the elder and washing the flanks, &c., with it before going out.

SWELLED LEGS.

THE SKIN OF THE LEGS AND THE CELLULAR MEMBRANE beneath it are liable to two kinds of swelling, one of which is of an inflammatory character, while the other is solely due to a deposit of serum (œdema), owing to the non-performance of their office by the kidneys. Both kinds are much more frequent in the hind legs than the fore, but especially the former.

INFLAMMATORY SWELLED LEG, sometimes called *weed*, is generally accompanied by a certain amount of feverishness, and comes on suddenly, almost always showing itself on the inside of the hind leg, which is hot and extremely tender. It is not a very common disease, and merely requires the ordinary low *treatment*, by purging physic, and, if necessary, bleeding. Should it continue for more than two or three days after these are tried, an ounce of nitre may be given every night in a bran mash.

ORDINARY SWELLING OF THE LEGS, OR ŒDEMA, occurs in every degree, from a slight "filling," to which many horses are always subject, whether they work or stand in the stable, to an enlargement extending up to the stifles and elbows, sometimes rendering the legs almost as round and as hard as mill-posts. When horses are first brought in from grass their legs almost always fill more or less, and until they are regularly seasoned to their work there is seldom that clean condition of the suspensory ligaments and back sinews which one likes to see even before the daily exercise is given. The œdema appears to depend partly upon a deficient action of the kidneys, but chiefly on the vessels of the legs not acting sufficiently without constant walking exercise, such as is natural to the horse when at liberty, and which he takes at grass. Half an hour's walking will generally produce absorption completely, so that a daily remedy is forthcoming; but as a rule, whenever there is this tendency to "filling" of the legs, the cellular membrane is not the only tissue in fault, but the tendons and joints are also liable to inflammation. The *treatment* will greatly depend on the exact cause. If the swelling is only due to the change from grass to the confinement of a warm stable, time alone is wanted, taking care not to overwork the horse in the mean time. Bandages will always assist in keeping down the swelling; but they should not be used without necessity, as when once the horse becomes accustomed to them his legs can hardly be kept fine without their aid. If weakness is the cause, a drachm of sulphate of iron given in the corn twice a day will often strengthen the system, and with it the legs. Diuretics may be adopted as an occasional aid to the kidneys, but they should be of the mildest kind, such as nitre, or they will do more harm, by weakening the body generally, than good by their stimulus to the kidneys. Indeed, they are often the sole cause of the legs filling, for some grooms use them so continually, whether they are wanted or not, that the kidneys become diseased and refuse to act, which is a sure forerunner of œdema. Where swelling of the legs is confirmed, bandages must be regularly applied as recommended at page 196.

CHAPPED HEELS.

WHEN A HORSE SUFFERS FROM ŒDEMA of the legs, he is particularly prone to an eruption of a watery nature in the cleft between the heels and behind the lesser pastern. Those also whose legs are washed and not dried are still more prone to it, especially if the hair is white. The skin cracks, and, in bad cases, is so inflamed and swollen that the leg cannot be bent without great pain, and often there is a bleeding from the cracks, caused by the action of the limb, but only to a sufficient extent to show that blood has escaped. The *treatment* must be local as well as general if the eruption is not entirely due to mismanagement. In any case, the part should be dressed with cerate of acetate of lead, a little of which should be rubbed in every night. Next morning some glycerine should be brushed on an hour at least before the exercise, and renewed before the daily work is commenced. This will prevent all risk of the skin cracking, while the ointment will act beneficially on the vessels of the part. In addition to these applications, the general health should be attended to if in fault, and tonics or diuretics should be given, as the case may require.

GREASE.

[Commonly called "Scratches" in the United States.]

THE ERUPTION KNOWN AS GREASE is sometimes only an aggravated form of chapped heels, and is often preceded by them. At others the appearance of the disease is ushered in by constitutional symptoms, such as feverishness, œdema of the limbs and hidebound. The first local *symptom* is a slight swelling of the skin of the heels and adjacent parts, which soon cracks, and from the fissures there exudes an offensive discharge which looks greasy, but is really watery, being of a serous nature. It inflames every part that it touches, and has a tendency to cause a spread of the eruption in all directions, but chiefly downwards. The legs go on swelling to a frightful extent, and are thereby rendered so stiff and sore that great lameness is produced. If this stage is neglected the whole surface ulcerates, and a fungous growth makes its appearance, chiefly from the original cracks. The discharge becomes purulent and has a most foul smell, and the leg can with difficulty be bent at all. *Finally*, the fungous excrescences cover the whole of the diseased skin, being of a bright red color, and slightly resembling grapes in form, from which circumstances this stage has been

GREASE, OR SCRATCHES.

called "the grapes." It is now very rare to meet with grease in any of its forms except in the cart-stable, where the hairy legs of its inmates render them peculiarly prone to its attacks, from the time required to dry them when wet. They are so difficult to clean without water that the carters may well be excused for using it, but if they do they ought carefully to dry the legs afterwards. The *treatment* when grease is established must be founded upon the same principle as in chapped heels. The skin must be kept supple, and at the same time stimulated to a healthy action. For the former purpose glycerine is most valuable, being far more efficacious than any greasy dressing, such as we were obliged to employ before the discovery of this substance. In all the stages of grease, this latter agent may be employed, and as it is readily soluble in water it can be washed off and renewed as often as it may be desired. The discharge is so foul and irritating that it ought to be thoroughly removed at least once in twenty-four hours, and one of the chief advantages of the use of glycerine is that it so greatly assists this cleansing process from its solubility in water. In addition to this emollient plan, some stimulus must be selected, and none answers so well (in all stages but the very earliest) as chloride of zinc. When, therefore, the heels are in that state that it is almost doubtful whether the disease is the mere chap or absolute grease, the treatment recommended for the former may be tried, but should this fail, the groom should at once proceed to cut the hair of the skin which is diseased as short as possible. Then let him take some soap and warm water and gently wash the parts with a sponge till the skin is perfectly clean and free from scab or scurf, taking care to remove every particle of soap by well rinsing it. Next dry the leg, and then with a small paint-brush rub gently into the inflamed parts enough of the following lotion to damp them, but not to wet them thoroughly :—

    Take of Chloride of Zinc . . . . 30 grs.
    Water . . . . 1 pint. Mix.

A quarter of an hour afterwards apply a little glycerine over the whole, and keep the parts sufficiently supple with it. If there is much discharge the cleansing may be repeated night and morning, followed by the chloride of zinc, but in most cases once a day will be sufficiently often. If the ulcerated or inflamed skin does not put on a healthy appearance in a few days, the lotion may be increased in strength, using forty, fifty, or sixty grains to the pint, as required; but the remedy will be found to be almost a specific, except for the grapy form, if properly proportioned in strength. When the fungoid growths are very extensive, nothing but their removal, either by the knife or by the actual or potential cautery, will suffice. The least painful plan is to slice them off to a level with the skin and then just touch the bleeding surface with a hot iron, which will have the double good effect of stopping the bleeding and inducing a healthy action. The glycerine may then be applied, and next day the leg may be treated in the same way as for ordinary grease described above. When the disease is of long standing, local applications may cure it for a time, but either it will return, or there will be some other organ attacked, unless the unhealthy state of the blood is attended to. It must be remembered that during the existence of grease this vital fluid is called upon to supply the materials for the secretion which is constantly going on. Now if on the cessation of the demand for them the blood still goes on obtaining its supplies from the digestive organs, it becomes overloaded, a state of plethora is established, which Nature attempts to relieve in some one or other of her established modes by setting up disease. To avoid such a result arsenic may be given internally, for this medicine has a special power in counteracting this tendency. How it acts has never yet been made out, but that it does exert such a power is thoroughly ascertained, and if the doses are not too large it is unattended by any injurious effect. Indeed for a time it seems to act as as a tonic. The arsenic should be given in solution and *with the food*, so as to procure its absorption into the blood without weakening the stomach. A wine-glassful of liquor arsenicalis (1½ oz.) should be poured over the corn twice a day, and continued for a couple of months, when it may be discontinued with a fair hope of its having had the desired effect. Should the skin, however, look inflamed, a second course of it may be given, and it will be found that if it is given with the corn it will not be followed by any injurious consequences.*

WARTS.

WARTS are, generally, only to be considered as eyesores; for, unless they appear on the penis, they are not injurious to health; nor do they interfere with work unless they happen to appear on the shoulders beneath the collar in a harness horse, which is very rare indeed. They are, doubtless, very unsightly, and, for this reason, it is often desired to remove them, which may be done by first picking off the rough outer surface, so as to make them bleed, and then rubbing in, with a stiff brush, some yellow orpiment, wetted with a little water. This will cause considerable inflammation, and in a few days the wart will drop off, leaving a healthy sore, which soon heals. Sometimes the whole wart does not come away on the first application, in which case a second must be made. When the glans penis is completely covered with warts,

---

* The best treatment for scratches will be found to be carbolic acid one part, cold water forty parts, applied from one to three times daily.—EDITOR.

the best plan is to amputate it, as it requires the greatest caution and tact to remove them by arsenic or any other caustic without destroying, also, as much of the penis as is taken away by the knife.

CORNS.

THESE TROUBLESOME results of bad shoeing, or subsequent neglect of the feet, make their appearance in the sole of the foot, in the angle formed between the crust and the bar (see fig. 20 (E), Chap. XXVI.). Where the foot is properly prepared for the shoe, and the smith seats the heel of the crust and the bar on a level surface, no corn will make its appearance in a healthy foot; but if a corn has previously existed, or if the shoe is allowed to press upon the sole at E (see fig. 20, Chap. XXVI.), the delicate blood-vessels of the sensible sole are ruptured, and, instead of secreting a sound horn, capable of bearing the slight strain upon it which is required, a fungoid growth is formed. presenting a reddish appearance, and exquisitely sensitive. This morbid substance does not at all resemble the hard corn of the human subject, which is a thickened secretion of cuticle, but it bears some comparison with the soft corns that form so often between the toes, and give so much trouble in their removal. It is, in fact, a new growth of a semi-fungoid character, partly made up of granulations and partly of horny matter, the two being closely united. The corn may arise from improper pressure made on this part of the sensible sole, either directly from the shoe, or indirectly by pressing a thin brittle crust inwards upon it. Generally, however, it is met with at the inner heel, from the shoe being overgrown by that part of the foot when kept on too long. The outer nails do not allow it to work in the contrary direction, and if there is a clip on the outer quarter this is rendered still more improbable. If, therefore, shoeing is properly managed, corns may always be prevented, and we shall see in the directions for shoeing, at Chap. XXVI., how this is to be managed. At present I have to consider how they are to be relieved or cured when they are already established.

THE ORDINARY MODE OF TREATING CORNS is simply to cut them out, leaving the bar and heel of the crust full, and thus taking all pressure off them. This enables the horse to do his work for about ten days, but then the shoe must be removed, and the paring-out repeated, a process which weakens the already weak crust by making additional nail-holes in it. The shoe at the same time is generally "sprung," that is, it is so bent or filed that the heel does not fully bear upon it; but this does not last many hours, and is of little real utility. The plan answers well enough for the purposes of fraudulent sellers, as the horse runs sound for about ten days; and when he fails, and on taking off his shoe he is discovered to have a corn, it is impossible to prove that it existed at the time of sale by any evidence but that of the smith who shod him previously to it. Excepting, therefore, in very slight and recent cases, in which it will sometimes be followed by success, this plan of treatment is only palliative, and what is worse, it tends to increase the weakness of the foot and consequent tendency to the disease.

FOR THE CURATIVE PLAN we must do something more than merely take the pressure off the sole; the bar and heel of the crust must also be relieved, and the sensible sole must be stimulated, by a proper application, to secrete healthy horn, as well as by pressure on the frog. If the horse is to be rested, this can be done easily enough by taking off his shoes, but he may be kept at work by putting on a bar-shoe, and cutting down the bar and crust, so as to throw all the pressure off them upon the frog. A double purpose is effected in this way. First, the sensible sole is relieved of the constant pressure which the crust bears upon it laterally; and, secondly, the jar on the frog, communicated through the shoe, from the ground, induces a healthy action in the foot, and the sole has a greater tendency to secrete healthy horn. There is no doubt in my mind that all horses would work much better, and keep their feet in much sounder condition, if their frogs could be brought into use, without being guarded as they are by the ordinary shoe. This part is intended by nature to take upon itself great pressure; and if it has not its natural stimulus it becomes weak itself, and, moreover, it does not stimulate the surrounding parts to a healthy action, as it ought to do. The bar-shoe is inconvenient for many purposes, and, therefore, it is not generally applied; but as a curative agent these objections are to be dispensed with, and then it will be found to be extremely valuable, not only in relieving the diseased part (the corn) but in giving a healthy action to its seat, the sole. The smith should, therefore, pare down the crust at the heel, so that when the bar-shoe is applied it will allow a penny-piece to be insinuated between the two surfaces. With this the horse does his work comfortably on the road; and in process of time, that is, in two or three months, the heel grows up, and takes its own share of pressure, or a part of it, becoming gradually accustomed to the amount which it will have to bear when the bar-shoe is discontinued. In the mean time a little of the following lotion may be applied daily to the situation of the corn by means of a feather.

  Take of Chloride of Zinc . . . . 1 drachm.
    Water . . . . 6 oz.
    Glycerine . . . . 2 oz. Mix.

In every case, the bar-shoe must be continued until the heel of the crust and the bar grow down strongly; and then a common shoe may be applied.

SANDCRACK.

IN THE ANATOMICAL DESCRIPTION OF THE FOOT, at page 291, it will be seen that the crust is composed of fibres, running parallel to each other in a direction from the coronet to the ground surface. These fibres are glued together firmly in a sound and strong hoof; but, in a weak one, it sometimes happens that the gelatinous matter is not in sufficient quantity, and then the fibres separate, and leave a crack of greater or less extent, according to circumstances. This, called a sandcrack, happens at the thinnest part, which is the inner quarter in the fore foot, and the toe in the hind. *To cure it*, the foot must be rested, or at least that part of it where the crack occurs, which in the fore foot may be effected by the use of a bar-shoe, throwing the pressure entirely on the frog, as recommended in the last section on corns, and taking care that the crust behind the crack is not in contact with the shoe. By adopting this plan, I have succeeded in curing sand-cracks during moderate work; but if it happens in the hind foot, complete rest must be given, as the toe cannot be relieved by any possible contrivance. The next thing to be done is to open the crack slightly, so that any grit getting into it shall not cause its further expansion; and in doing this, if there is any little cellular cavity, it should be exposed. If the crack extends to the coronet, which it rarely does, nothing can be done until it has grown out for at least half an inch from that part, when the point of a hot iron may be applied to the angle of the crack for a second, so as to keep out water, which has the effect of causing the fibres to split by the capillary attraction which is exercised. The burn should be very slight, and should not be carried deeply into the substance of the horn. A fine nail should then be driven from below through the crust, the shoe being removed; and when brought out at the usual place, should be left projecting. The shoe should be put on, and the innermost nail also left projecting. These two should then be firmly bound together by fine wire, so as to bring the edges of the crack together; and the foot should be left in this state for at least a month or five weeks, when the shoe may be taken off, and the operation repeated. This is far better than binding wire or twine round the whole foot, as it acts more completely on the crack, without confining the growth of the remainder of the foot. Of course, after the wire is twisted on, the nails must be clenched, and there will be a greater projection than usual; but this is of no importance whatever. In cracks of the hind foot the nails in each quarter will keep the two sides from separating, but the horse cannot be worked.

FALSE QUARTER.

WHEN, FROM AN ACCIDENT, the coronary substance is permanently injured, it ceases to secrete sound horn, and a stripe of the crust, defective in strength, runs all the way down from the coronet to the plantar edge. This generally happens at the inner quarter, and is owing to the horse treading on his coronet; but it may also occur on the outside, either from the tread of another horse, or from some kind of external violence. The result is similar to that of a sandcrack; there is no strength in the affected heel, and lameness is produced. The *treatment* is very much the same as for sandcrack. In the first place, the pressure must be taken off the quarter, and a bar-shoe applied, so as to convey the weight on the frog, as described under the head of Sandcrack. The heel of the affected quarter should be lowered, and thus further injury will be prevented. The next thing to be done is to stimulate the coronet to a healthy action by blistering it, which must be done two or three times, taking care that the blister is not of too violent a nature, and that the skin heals before a second is applied. By these means, a cure may sometimes be effected; but it takes a considerable time, and until the quarter is reproduced in full strength, or nearly so, the bar-shoe should be continued. By its use, any horse with a sound frog can travel very well on the road, even if the quarter is entirely and permanently separated from the toe by inefficient horn; and without it, the chance of a cure is not to be reckoned on.

QUITTOR.

BY THIS TERM IS UNDERSTOOD a chronic abscess of the foot, the matter always forming sinuses, from the difficulty which nature has to overcome in finding a way for it to reach the surface. Generally, the mischief is occasioned by an overreach, or a bruise of the sole, or by the inflammation resulting from a neglected thrush, or, lastly, from a nail-prick. From any of these causes, inflammation of the delicate investment of the coffin-bone is set up, pus is secreted, and, in working its way to the surface, it burrows between the horn and the bone, and forms one or more sinuses, or pipes, as these fistulous tubes are called by the farrier. A quittor is recognised by the eye and nose detecting an opening in the horn, from which a foul discharge proceeds; and on introducing a probe, it will generally pass freely in two or three directions, sometimes giving a grating sensation to the finger, showing that the bone is denuded, and most probably carious. There is generally a considerable increase of temperature in the foot, and always more or less lameness, with, in most cases, swelling of the bulbous heels and coronet. On examining the sole carefully, some part will either show a difference of color from the adjacent horn, or there will be a yielding on pressure, owing to its being undermined. The *treatment* must be conducted on the same principle as for fistulous sores. In the first place, a dependent opening must be formed, so that no matter shall be confined, but it shall be allowed to come away as fast as it forms. This can only be done by probing; and if the original opening is in the coronet, the probe must be passed down as low as possible, and then the sole should be pared away till the end can be reached. In tolerably recent quittors, this plan alone will allow the sinus to heal; but in old ones, the internal surface has become callous, and no granulations are thrown out. Here an injection should be thrown in every day with a syringe, a saturated solution of sulphate of zinc being that generally recommended; but I have found the chloride answer still better, using one drachm of the salt to a pint of water at first, and going on up to two drachms. By injecting this daily, and introducing a piece of lint, wetted with it, into the superior opening, leaving the lower one free, I have cured many bad quittors, even when there was evidence of caries of the coffin-joint. The disease requires a careful adjustment of the remedies to its extent and nature, and a theoretical description of it is of little use.

THRUSH.

ANY OFFENSIVE DISCHARGE FROM THE FROG is called by this name, although the cause and treatment may be as different as possible. It varies greatly in the fore and hind feet; and, indeed, it must never be forgotten that, in every case, the cause which has produced the discharge must be clearly made out before any plan of *treatment* can be carried out with any prospect of success. Sometimes thrush is merely the result of the decomposition of the horny frog, from the foot being constantly kept wet with urine, which is most common in the hind foot. Here the surface becomes soft, and is gradually dissolved; while the cleft, from its retaining the moisture, is increased in size. This state is often brought on by the too frequent use of cowdung-stopping in horses with soft frogs; and, instead of doing good by his treatment of the foot, the groom is really destroying it by encouraging the decomposition of the healthy defence which Nature has given to it. For this kind of thrush, very little treatment is required, if the cause which produced it is withdrawn. Still it is not always easy to keep the frog dry, and stop the decomposition, without the application of some astringent; and if the mere use of dry litter, and the application of tar ointment, do not seem to harden the frog at once, it may be touched with a wash composed of ten grains of bluestone to the ounce of water. This will soon dry it; or, if it fails by any chance, the chloride of zinc may be used in the same way, by dissolving five grains in an ounce of water.

THE SECOND KIND OF THRUSH is that in which from a gross habit of body there is a simple inflammation of the sensible frog, and instead of sound horn being secreted, a spongy substance is deposited, which breaks away in places, and the frog looks ragged and uneven, with a greasy surface, smells very foul, and *feels* hot to the touch. Here the *treatment* must be general as well as local. A dose of physic should be given, the food should be of a less stimulating quality, and care should be taken that regular exercise is allowed every day. The stable should be kept cool, and of course attention should be paid to cleanliness both of the foot and the litter. As to local remedies, they must not be of the stimulating kind, which will suit the thrush from decomposition, or that presently to be described. The foot should be placed in a bran poultice, and kept in it for some days, till the united action of the local and general treatment have reduced the inflammation. After a few days it will be well to dress the frog with tar ointment, or the poultice will do more harm than good, by causing the decomposition of its horny covering, and indeed it is seldom that this wet application should be employed for more than a week. After this time has elapsed, all the good to be derived from it has been accomplished, and the subsequent treatment may generally be effected by attention to the health, and dressing the frog with tar ointment. Sometimes it may be necessary to employ a slight stimulus, and then the solution of chloride of zinc will be found to be the best.

THE THIRD KIND OF THRUSH occurs in contracted feet, and is due to the same cause, namely, chronic inflammation of the sensible frog, produced by overwork, aided in many cases by neglect in shoeing. There is a tendency to the secretion of unsound horn over the whole foot, sometimes too thick and hard, and at others of a cellular structure, without sufficient strength to bear the pressure of the road. The horny frog generally looks shrunken and withered; and in its cleft there is a foul discharge, on wiping which out a soft spongy matter may be seen at the bottom, which is the sensible frog itself, but in a diseased condition. In bad cases, the sides of the horny frog have separated, and even the toe is sometimes deficient of its covering; but generally the horn has only disappeared in patches, and there are ragged portions remaining. The disease here is of too chronic a nature to be easily cured, and if there is much disorganization of the laminæ it will be almost impossible to effect a perfect cure. The first thing to be done is to clear away all the ragged portions of horn, so as to be able to reach the sensible frog. Some tow is then to be smeared with the following ointment:—

  Take of Ointment of Nitrate of Mercury . . . . . 1 drachm.
     Zinc Ointment . . . . 1 oz.
     Creosote . . . . 4 drops. Mix.

and pressed into the cleft of the frog, where it can best be retained by a bar-shoe lightly tacked on, and in this case taking its bearing on the heels and not on the frog. Sometimes a wash answers better than a greasy application, and then a strong solution of the chloride of zinc may be employed, about six grains to the ounce of water. Tow dipped in this may be applied in the same way as with the ointment, and either one or the other should be re-applied every day. As the new horn grows, it must be kept supple by tar ointment, and until it is fully developed the bar-shoe should be kept on, applying some degree of pressure by means of the tow, which should be stuffed in so as to compress the frog, beginning with very light pressure, and, as the horn increases in substance, augmenting it in proportion. By attention to these directions a thrush of this kind may be cured, if the foot is not damaged throughout, and even the frog may be restored to a comparative state of health.

CANKER.

CANKER is generally an extension of the third form of thrush, the ulceration spreading to the sensible sole, and afterwards to the coffin-bone itself. At first the ulcerated surface is concealed by the old horn, but gradually this breaks away, and then the extent of the mischief may be seen. A part or the whole of the sole and the frog may be in a state of ulceration, generally depending upon the time during which the disease has been in existence, and the care which has been taken of it, or the reverse. The only *treatment* to be adopted is the careful removal of every loose piece of horn, so as to expose the unsound surface to the action of remedies, and at the same time to avoid poisoning it by the decomposing horn, which has a most irritating effect. The sulphate of copper, and chloride of zinc, are the best applications, and they must be used in full strength. These cases, however, require an experienced eye to enable the prescriber to judge of the proper amount of caustic required; and beyond suggesting the kind of remedy required, no good can be done by written prescriptions. If it is impossible to obtain the advice of a veterinarian, it will be better to begin by using a mild caustic, and then increase the strength as it is found to be wanted. Pitch ointment forms the best greasy application to the adjacent sound surfaces to protect them from the irritation of the discharge.

LAMINITIS.

(*Founder or Fever of the Feet.*)

THE TERM LAMINITIS is now familiar with every one at all accustomed to horses, though it has not long been introduced into the vocabulary of the professional man. The disease, however, has been recognised for many years under the terms "founder" and "fever of the feet." It consists in an inflammation (which may be acute or chronic) of the parts between the crust or wall and the pedal bone, including the laminæ, whence the name by which it is now distinguished. These parts are supplied with a profusion of blood-vessels (see page 294), and when inflammation is set up in them, the progress which it makes is rapid, and the constitutional disturbance is unusually great, owing probably to the want of space for the swelling which accompanies all inflammations, and especially of vascular substances. The *causes* are either, 1st. Localization of fever, whence the name "fever in the feet." 2d. The mechanical irritation of hard roads upon feet not accustomed to them; and 3d. Long confinement in a standing position on board ship. When it is recollected that in our system of shoeing, the laminæ are made to support the whole weight of the body in consequence of the shoe being in contact with the crust only, it can only occasion surprise that this disease is not more frequent. Nature framed the horse's foot so that an elastic pad should interpose between its back parts and the ground, intending that the edge of the crust should take its share, but not *all* of the weight. The laminæ are therefore called upon to do far more than their structure is designed for, and when there is the slightest weakness or tendency to inflammation, they are sure to suffer. Acute laminitis is not very often met with, because horsemen are aware of the risks they run, and take their measures accordingly; but the chronic form is common enough, and hundreds of horses are more or less lame from this cause. Too often it is not suspected until irreparable mischief is done, the elasticity of the laminæ being destroyed, and the foot having assumed a shape which utterly unfits it for bearing the pressure of the shoe upon hard roads. When the disease has been going on for a long time, the elastic substances between the laminæ and the pedal bone, as well as the fine horny lamellæ between them and the crust, lose the property of extension, and the horn of the crust is secreted by nature of a more spongy character, and much thicker in substance, than in health. On making a section of such a foot, the arrangement of parts will be such as is here delineated in fig. 19, in which 1 is the os suffraginis, 2, the os coronæ, and 3, the pedal bone, with its anterior surface separated from that of the crust (7) by a wide space occupied by spongy matter. Here the toe of the pedal bone projects into the sole and renders it convex, instead of being concave, and corresponding with the lower surface of the pedal bone.

The laminæ and elastic substances between them and their contiguous structures no longer suspend the pedal bone to the crust, but the weight falls partly upon the sole by means of the toe of the pedal bone, and partly on the frog, which descends so low that in spite of the thickness of the shoe it touches the ground.

LAMINITIS.

This descent of the frog is a very marked feature in laminitis, and whenever it is apparent that disease may be suspected.

But to produce such a marked alteration of form as is here delineated and described takes a long time, and even then it is only in a few cases that the disease reaches to this stage. It will, therefore, be necessary to trace its progress from the commencement, and the effects which are exhibited as it goes on.

When acute laminitis sets in, there is a considerable amount of fever, indicated by a rapid pulse, usually full and hard, and hurried respiration. There is a general look of restlessness from pain, the horse stamping gently with his feet, and constantly

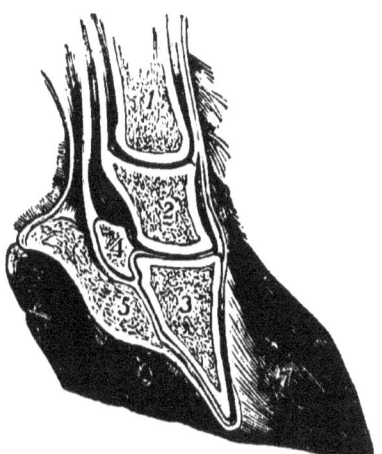

FIG. 19.—SECTION OF THE FOOT IN CONFIRMED LAMINITIS.
1. Os suffraginis.
2. Os coronæ.
3. Pedal bone.
4. Navicular bone.
5. Frog.
6. Sole.
7. Wall or crust greatly thickened.

lying down and then getting up again. When, as usually happens, the fore feet only are affected, the hind feet are brought under the body to bear as much weight as possible, and the fore feet are so carried forwards that the heels support the legs rather than the toes. On examining the feet, there is great reluctance to allow one to be picked up, on account of the necessity which is thrown upon the other of taking the whole weight of the fore quarter. The coronet and hoof feel very hot, and, when wetted, may be seen to steam very perceptibly. If this state of things is not speedily stopped, the laminæ cease to secrete horn, and the connection between them and the hoof ceases, causing the latter to separate, and the sensible parts to be exposed, covered with a thin scaly horn. This has happened in many cases which have afterwards secreted new hoofs; but the horn is not so strong and useful as before, and a horse with such feet is not fit for hard work on the road. If proper treatment is adopted, the inflammation either subsides entirely, leaving no mischief behind it, or there is a chronic inflammation left which induces the alterations of structure which have been alluded to. The *treatment* should be by first removing the shoes, and then, after paring down the sole so as to allow of the expansion of the sensible parts, a large quantity of blood is taken from the toe, making sure that a vessel of sufficient size is opened to produce a strong shock on the heart and arteries, as well as to relieve the local affection. If the blood does not flow freely, the foot may be placed in a pail of warm water, but when the operation is properly performed there is never any difficulty in obtaining any quantity of blood which may be required. Next tack the shoes on lightly again, and then give a smart dose of physic, or else, what is perhaps a better plan, give the following:—

Take of Barbadoes Aloes
   Tartar Emetic, of each . . . . 1 drachm.
   Powdered Digitalis . . . . $\frac{1}{2}$ drachm.
Syrup enough to form a ball,

which should be given every six hours, until the bowels act, when the other materials may be continued without the aloes. The feet should be kept constantly wet and cool by tying a piece of felt or flannel around each pastern, and allowing it to fall over the hoof, when it is to be continually wetted. If the inflammation is not abated next day, the bleeding may be repeated, and it will be well also to act on the kidneys by adding two or three drachms of nitre to the tartar emetic and digitalis.

CHRONIC LAMINITIS is generally first shown by a slight soreness or lameness, generally appearing in both fore feet, and, therefore, being often overlooked by casual observers. In coming in from work the coronets feel warmer than natural; but this goes off during the night, and, for a time, no great fears are entertained of the feet recovering their former condition, the blame being, perhaps, laid upon the shoe. In a month or two, however, the smith (who has, perhaps, been ordered to take off the shoes two or three times, by which the injury is increased) finds that his nails do not hold, and the quarters break away; while the action of the horse becomes more shambling every day, and he cannot make a sound trot on any hard road, *especially with a weight on his back.* In many cases a horse with chronic laminitis can run in hand sound enough for an ordinary observer; but when the extra weight of a rider is placed on him the feet cannot bear the pain, and the gait is shambling in the extreme. Such animals have a strong propensity to save their toes, and prefer (if their shoulders will allow it) bringing their heels to the ground first, so that, although their action is excessively low and shambling, they seldom fall. An experienced horseman at once detects this peculiar style of going, and condemns its possessor for laminitis. Indeed, it may be assumed as a rule, that wherever the heel is put carefully down upon the ground *with low action*, the foot is the subject of laminitis to some extent. When the heel is naturally brought to the ground first, the knee is well bent, and the foot is raised high in the air; but in process of time work tells on it, the laminæ become inflamed, and then the action is reduced in height, and the feet are moved in the manner peculiar to foundered horses, including those which before they were foundered perhaps exhibited " toe action," or, at all events, a level fall of the foot. This state of disease ought to be well studied, and compared with the remarks on sound action at page 82 *et seq.*, which it will serve to illustrate and explain. The foot itself is changed in form, and the toe and sole have more or less altered their relations, as explained already. Sometimes there is a large space or cavity between the outer surface and the inner, shown at 7, fig. 19, page 405. This hollow in the crust is more or less cellular, and the disease is called a "seedy toe," but for what reason I am at a loss to know. The sole, moreover, is always either flatter than natural or absolutely convex, and its horn is brittle and spongy, constituting what is termed the "pumiced foot." The frog is generally large and spongy; and on placing a straight-edge across the shoe, from heel to heel, it is found to touch that part, or nearly so, indicating that the relations between it and the crust, as well as the sole, are altogether changed from a natural state. The laminæ are no longer slings for the foot, but the whole pressure is taken by the parts lying beneath the pedal or coffin bone and the navicular bone. Such being the *symptoms*, the next thing is to consider what can be done. If the disease is of long standing, little hope can be given of a perfect recovery. The shape of the external parts may be partially restored, but the internal delicate structures no longer have the power of performing their offices; and the elastic action of the horse suffering from the effects of laminitis can seldom be restored on hard ground. After proper treatment, he may, and generally does, go on turf well; but either on hard ground or on plough (on the latter of which, though soft enough for the laminæ, the sole has to bear considerable pressure) he is dreadfully sore and lame. This is shown after all inflammation has ceased, the foot being as cool as possible, and sometimes exhibiting very slight evidences of previous mischief.

In *treating* such cases, if there is no heat or other sign of inflammation, bleeding and similar lowering measures will be of no avail. They may be required soon enough, it is true, for a foundered foot is always in danger of inflammation when battered; but until symptoms of this kind of mischief are exhibited it is better to avoid all depletory measures. At the same time, everything which will tend to keep off increased action should be avoided; the horse should be fed on the least heating food which will serve the purpose for which he is intended, and his stable should be kept as cool as possible. Beans ought never to be allowed to the possessor of feet with the slightest suspicion of founder; and no more oats should be used than are necessary for the condition required. For horses at slow work, bran mashes and nitre, with small doses occasionally of physic, will serve to keep down the tendency to inflammation, and by their use, joined to cold applications *after work* (they are of no use at other times), and a cool stable, the horse may be enabled to do moderately fast work. If the frog is not very prominent, a leather sole, put on in the usual way, will save the jar, and in some measure supply the place of the natural elastic tissue, destroyed in this disease. Usually, however, it only adds to the mischief by increasing the pressure on the frog, and then the leather must be introduced between the foot and the shoe, but cut to the same shape as the latter, so as not at all to bear on the frog. Many horses with slight traces of laminitis can work for years with leather applied in this way, and it may be said to be the most useful mode of treating this disease when exhibited in a mild form. Sometimes by throwing a horse by for six months, taking off his shoes, and blistering his coronets two or three times, a great deal of good may be done, but he must be put to stand on tan or sawdust during the whole time, and never allowed to go on hard ground, even for half a mile at a walking pace. By this plan, and by very careful and gradual increase of exercise at the end of that time, I have succeeded in restoring an elastic condition of the foot; but I have never known one so patched up bear hard work, and I should never advise the risk incurred by submitting him to it. Hunting and racing, or, indeed, any kind of work on soft ground, will do no harm; but battering on the roads, especially without leather, applied as above described, is sure to bring back the inflammation.

THE SEEDY TOE.

THIS TERM is so generally employed among horsemen, that though the state which it describes is one of the ordinary consequences of laminitis, I prefer to give it a distinct section. I have already described its nature in the preceding page, and have only now to allude to its *treatment*. This may generally be so conducted as to restore the shape of the foot, if the inflammation has not lowered the toe of the pedal bone, as shown at fig. 1; for if this has taken place, although it is perhaps possible to get rid of the cavities in the horn, the relative positions of the bony parts cannot be changed. When, however, as is often the case, a moderately small hollow has been formed between the layers of the wall, and the foot retains a tolerably healthy shape, by cutting away all the external horny walls, exposing the parts in contact with the laminæ, and resting the horse in a loose box, the secreting surface will form a new wall, without any spongy texture, in the course of three or four months, if the coronary band is constantly stimulated by external applications. To effect this, the horse should be put to stand on red deal sawdust, without shoes; and his coronets, after being gently stimulated by a mild liquid blister, should be kept dressed with tar ointment, which should also be applied to the exterior of the horn. It is seldom, however, that a foot which has been thus treated is sufficiently sound to bear hard work.

CONTRACTION OF THE FOOT.

This reputed disease has been long the bugbear of the horse-master; but it is now discovered to be a complete mistake. Some of the most contracted feet in point of width are particularly free from all risk of disease, and on the other hand many open ones are as liable to it. The donkey, whose heels are shaped exactly like those of the contracted horse's foot, is so seldom lame, that few can recall having seen one in that condition, and, therefore, reasoning from analogy, one would be led to doubt that this shape renders the horse prone to lameness. At the same time it is quite true that in the disease which will next be investigated, the frog withers and contracts, and the heels are thereby drawn in; but here the contraction is a consequence and not a cause of disease, and certainly cannot be considered as a disease in itself. Bad shoeing will do much to cause either laminitis or navicular disease, and it will certainly produce corns and inverted heels, but it will not waste the frog, or induce that condition of the foot where the sole is arched so high that the frog does not touch the ground when the shoe is off. Such a state of things can only be brought on either by thrush or navicular disease, and is never the result of the mechanical mismanagement of the foot, to which what used to be called contraction was generally attributed. All sorts of plans have been suggested for expanding the heels and for allowing them to expand; but the real truth is that so long as the frog is sound and the parts above it, allowing the proper amount of pressure to be communicated to the sole, bars and heel of the crust, these latter divisions of the foot have no room to contract, and of a certainty they never do.

NAVICULAR DISEASE.

This formidable disease, called also the navicular *joint lameness*, and *naviculararthritis*, is the chief danger to be apprehended from a good-looking strong foot, just as the open flat one is prone to laminitis, and is rarely subject to disease in the navicular joint. The reason of this immunity on the one hand, and the contrary on the other, is this. The open foot, with a large spongy frog, exposes the navicular bone and the parts in contact with it to constant pressure in the stable, so that these parts are always prepared for work. On the other hand, the concave sole and well-formed frog are raised from the ground by our unfortunate mode of shoeing, and when the whole foot is exposed to injury from battering, and in addition the tendon which plays over the navicular bone presses it against the os coronæ, the unprepared state in which this part is allowed to remain is sure to produce inflammation, if the work is carried far enough. Thus in each case the weak part suffers, but occasionally, though very rarely, the foot with an arched sole contracts laminitis, and the flat one is attacked by navicular disease; the exceptions, however, are so few that they may be thrown out of the calculation, and from the shape of the foot alone it may almost invariably be pronounced, when a horse is known to be subject to chronic lameness, whether its seat is in the laminæ or in the navicular joint.

WHEN A FOOT IS EXAMINED AFTER DEATH which is known to have been the subject of navicular disease, the parts implicated are invariably either the navicular bone, or the soft parts in contact with it, or often all together. Most frequently on dividing the tendon of the flexor perforans and turning it down so as to expose the back of the joint between the navicular and coronal bones, that part will be greatly thickened and inflamed, the tendon being often adherent to it. In the healthy condition there ought to be no adhesion of the fibres of the tendon to any part of the navicular bone but its postero-inferior edge, to which the tendon is fixed by some few fibres, the bulk passing on to be inserted in the os pedis. The posterior face of the navicular bone should be beautifully smooth, and lined by synovial membrane which forms a lubricating sac for it to play upon, and thus take off the friction between the tendon and the bone. Such is nature's provision against mischief in this delicate part of the machinery of the foot, which she keeps in order by the constant supply of synovia or joint oil. But when the sac is not stimulated to a healthy action by the pressure of the frog below it in doors and out, synovia is no longer secreted in proper quantity, and as soon as the horse is put to hard work inflammation takes place for want of it. The result is some one of the consequences of inflamed joints. Either ulceration takes place in the postero-inferior surface, where the tendon glides over it, sometimes ending in caries of the bone itself; or adhesion takes place without ulceration of the tendon with the surface of the bone, or there are small exostoses thrown out, or lastly there is simple inflammation without either adhesion or ulceration, and in this stage the disease is amenable to treatment without leaving any trace behind.

The symptoms of navicular disease are the same, whether the mischief has extended to ulceration or not; but the history will guide us in ascertaining how far it has gone. Of course they vary in degree, for there may be only a slight extent of ulceration, or a high degree of simple inflammation; but in the former case the lameness will not be so marked as in the latter, though the prospect of recovery will be much less. There is always more or less lameness; but, in consequence of its affecting both feet, it is not so marked to the careless observer as in some much more trivial cases where only one is diseased. The distinguishing sign, though not absolutely infallible, is the pointing of the toe, and a peculiar rounding forward of the fetlock joint, so as to relieve the navicular bone of any weight. In laminitis, the object of the sufferer is to relieve all pressure as much as possible, by bringing the hind legs under the body, and by bearing the weight of the fore quarter on the heels. Here, the reverse of the latter attitude is observed—the heels are not allowed to take any pressure, and the toes alone are placed at all firmly on the ground. This is marked in the stable by the pointing of the toe (in each foot alternately, if both are diseased, but in the one only, if they are not both affected). Out of doors, the toes dig into the ground, the heel never being brought firmly down, and frequent stumbles mark the difference between this species of lameness and laminitis. The subject of navicular disease generally walks sound; but the moment he is trotted, he goes as if his legs were tied together, his stride being shortened in a remarkable manner, but without exhibiting the peculiar fumbling gait of the foundered animal. As in his case, soft ground suits him, and he has no fear of plough, because his sole is hard and unyielding. Many tolerably confirmed cases of navicular disease may, therefore, be hunted, except when the ground is hard, supposing, of course, that they are kept off the road; but no plan of management will enable them to bear the jars incidental to harness-work or hacking. When one foot only is the subject of navicular disease, it often happens that it is smaller altogether than the other; but it is somewhat difficult to say whether this is a cause or a consequence of inflammation. One thing is quite clear, that many horses are met with, still perfectly free from lameness, in which there is a difference of size in their fore feet; but whether or no these are afterwards invariably the subjects of navicular disease, it is almost impossible to ascertain. It is, however, the general opinion, founded on experience, that when this variation exists, navicular disease is extremely likely to attack the smaller foot, if it is not already there; and for this reason, horses with such feet are generally avoided by the intending purchaser.

The treatment of navicular disease, as before remarked, is only successful in the early stage, before either ulceration or adhesion has taken place. If a horse with strong concave soles suddenly becomes lame, points his toe, and shows other signs that his navicular bone is inflamed, he should be treated in the usual way suited to inflammation, and at the same time liberty should be given to the vascular tissues to expand, by reducing the substance of the horn. Bleeding at the toe has the double good effect of abstracting blood, and at the same time weakening the sole, so as to allow of the expansion which is desired. The operation should, therefore, at once be performed; at the same time, the whole sole may be reduced in thickness, and the heels lowered in proportion. The foot should then (after the shoe is tacked on) be placed in a cold bran poultice, which will soften the horn; and the system should be reduced by the exhibition of the medicines recommended under Laminitis, at page 406. Next day, if the pulse continues high, more blood may be taken; but, in ordinary cases, it is better at once to insert a seton in the frog (see OPERATIONS, Chap. XXV.), and trust to this for relieving the chronic inflammation remaining, by its counter-irritation. But when the disease itself is mastered, there is still a good deal to be done to prevent the injurious effects which are so apt to follow. The horse contracts a habit of stepping on his toes, to prevent hurting his navicular structures; and hence the frog is not used, the heels of the crust and the bars are not strained, and there being no stimulus to the soft parts which secrete them, they waste and contract in size. If the human hand is allowed to lie idle, the palm and the insides of the fingers are covered with a delicate cuticle, which affords so poor a protection to the cutis, that, on using it with any kind of hard work, it actually separates, and leaves an exposed surface, which speedily inflames. But by gradually exposing the same hand to pressure, a thickened and tougher cuticle is secreted; and this will bear any moderate amount of pressure or friction without injury. Nevertheless, even the hand so prepared must be continually stimulated by work, or the skin returns to its original delicate state, and is then exposed to the same risk of injury as before. So it is with the horse's foot, even in a state of health; but this is far more marked after an attack of disease. The tendency then is to produce the natural horny growths of a smaller substance than before; and if the secreting surfaces are not stimulated by pressure, they become doubly idle, and the frog, as well as the adjacent parts beneath the navicular bone, shows a wasted and shrivelled appearance. To avoid the risk of these ill consequences, the horse should be placed, for two or three hours daily, on a bed of wet clay, which will allow the shoe to sink into it, but will yet be tenacious enough to make firm and steady pressure on the frog, while its low temperature will keep down inflammation. No plan is of so much service in producing what is called expansion of the heels and growth of the frog as this; not, as is commonly supposed, from the clay mechanically pressing the heels out, but from the stimulus of its pressure causing the soft parts to secrete more horn, and of a sounder quality than before.

SHOULD THESE REMEDIES FAIL in restoring the foot affected with navicular disease to a healthy state, recourse can only be had to the operation of neurotomy, which is perfectly efficacious in removing the lameness; and if there is no ulceration, and merely an adhesion of the tendon to the bone, it will, by causing the horse to step more on his heels. effect an absolute improvement in the shape of the foot, and hence it has sometimes been considered to have produced a cure. Where, however, there is caries of the bone, or even ulceration of the synovial membrane, the disease progresses even faster than before the operation, and in process of time the joint becomes mechanically unfit to perform its duties.

ACCIDENTS TO THE LEGS AND FEET.

THESE PARTS ARE SUBJECT to a variety of accidents, trifling perhaps in the cause which produces them, but serious in their effects, from the lameness which ensues. The chief of these are ordinary cutting, speedy cutting, and pricks of the foot either from putting the sole down upon a nail or a piece of glass, or driving a nail improperly in shoeing. Bruises and over-reaches also come under this head.

ORDINARY CUTTING may occur either before or behind, the latter being the more common. It is often met with in poor horses, where the flesh is so reduced in substance that the legs are brought nearer together than in a proper condition. Here all that is required is patience, till the legs are restored to their proper relative position, taking care in the mean time that there is no permanent injury done. Usually the inside of one or both feet strikes the the fetlock joint of the other leg in passing it, but sometimes the blow is given higher up, and it may occur anywhere on the cannon bone except just below the knee, when it is called "speedy cutting," which will be separately considered. Sometimes this blow on the side of the cannon bone is either the cause or the effect of a splint, the blow of the foot having a tendency to produce exostosis (See SPLINTS, page 298). But if a splint is thrown out on a part of the cannon bone which comes in the way of the natural action, the horse whose foot previously passed clear of that part of the other leg will hit it, and not only give pain, but cause a considerable access of inflammation in the previous enlargement. In the *treatment*, therefore, of cutting, it is necessary to prevent the habit being continued from the swelling produced either by a splint or by previous blows. A horse perhaps, either from weakness or bad shoeing, hits his leg and produces considerable swelling and soreness. Here, unless the swelling is reduced or protected, there is no chance of preventing the cutting, because there is a projection of the swollen soft parts right in the way of the other foot. No alteration of the shoeing, and no increase of strength or flesh, will be of service until the inflammation is reduced, and the sore, if any exists, is healed, and this can only be done either by rest or by protecting the leg with a boot. The latter is the better plan, and wherever a horse cuts, it is, in my opinion, advisable to let him wear a boot for some weeks, until the skin is quite sound again and reduced to its proper thickness. A piece of an old rug folded round the leg so as slightly to overlap, and then tied with a tape and turned down over the fetlock joint, is quite sufficient to serve this temporary purpose, and being soft it is well calculated to protect a swollen joint; but if it is worn for any length of time, the pressure of the tape and the friction of the grit from the road wear away the hair, and cause an unsightly appearance, which is sometimes permanent. If, therefore, the cutting is not rectified completely in the course of a month or six weeks, a leather or india rubber boot should be nicely adapted to the joint and buckled round it, the flat surface of the strap not having so injurious an effect as the tape of the cloth boot. When the cutting takes place above the joint, a pad must be adapted to its inside, and fastened round the cannon bone by two or three buckles, according to the height at which the injury takes place.

SUCH IS THE BEST MODE of guarding against the injury done by cutting, but we must also consider how it can be entirely prevented. In the first place it should be carefully ascertained by what part of the foot or shoe the blow is given. Most commonly it will be found, by chalking the inside of the foot, that a small patch is rubbed clear of chalk, about half an inch above the middle of the quarter, and corresponding with the hindermost nail hole, especially when four inside nails are used. When this is the hitting point, if great care is taken to avoid driving in a nail there, the tendency to cut can never be increased as it often is by a raised clench, and at the same time the rasp may safely be used to reduce the thickness of the hoof at least the eighth of an inch, or often much more. The crust is usually here about three-eighths of an inch thick, and very often it is so sound that it will bear to be rasped down till there is only one-eighth left, *provided it has not to bear the pressure of a nail near it*, and that the reduction is not carried up too near to the coronet. In the hind foot the quarter is fully half an inch thick, and it therefore will bear reduction better even than the fore foot. Sometimes the blow is given by the shoe itself, which is fixed on so as to overlap the crust, and then the remedy is simple enough, for this ought never to occur, and can easily be prevented by any smith. But supposing, in spite of these precautions, the cutting still continues after the horse is restored to his natural strength and flesh, can anything be done by shoeing? In most cases this question may be answered in the affirmative, by the use of what is called a feather-edged shoe. By its aid the heels are both raised, not the inner one only (which is entirely useless and even prejudicial, for then the ground surface of the shoe is not a true plane), but both heels, the inner one being narrow, and having no nail holes beyond the two near the toe, so that there is no danger of the web projecting; nor is there any nail hole required, with the fear of a clench rising, or of the crust being weakened so as to prevent its being thinned to a proper degree. By thus raising the heels (in the hind foot especially), the fetlock is less bent, and as in horses that cut there is almost always a tendency in their fetlock joints to bend inwards as well as backwards, this diminution of the angle will not only straighten the leg in a forward direction, but will also increase the distance between the joints, which is the object to be desired. In the fore foot the obliquity in this direction is not so frequent, and then the high heel will be of no use; indeed, it is only when the toes are much turned out that this plan of shoeing the fore foot is ever successful. When cutting occurs before, unless there is this turn out, it is better to put the shoes on in a perfectly level manner, and trust to the reduction of the thickness of the quarter, and the absence of the third nail. If, with these precautions, the horse, when in good condition, still strikes his fore legs, it will be better to put up with the constant use of a boot. Generally, however, if the inflammation is first subdued, and the foot is shod in a perfectly true and level manner, taking care to rasp away the particular part which strikes the other leg, it will be found that the cutting is avoided.

SPEEDY CUTTING is more dangerous than ordinary cutting, because the pain given by the blow is generally more severe, and is often so great that the horse falls as if he were shot. On examining the leg of a confirmed speedy cutter there is always apparent a small scab or bruise on the inside of the cannon bone, immediately below the knee; but in slight cases rest may have been used to allow the skin to heal, and then no mark may possibly be left. A careful examination will, however, generally detect a small bare place, partially concealed by the growth of the adjacent hair. In bad cases the periosteum is swollen, and there is a considerable enlargement of the surface of the bone. In the *management* of slight cases of this kind of cutting, the action should be examined while the hoof is covered with chalk, and the latter should be treated in the same way as already described. If, however, this fails, as it generally does in this form of cutting, there is no remedy but to put on a regular speedy-cut boot, in which there is a pad buckled on the inside of the leg, and reaching from the knee to the fetlock. It must be of this length, because otherwise it cannot be kept in its place, as the leg allows it to slip down until it reaches the larger circumference presented by the joint. Where there is pain and swelling caused by the contusion, it must be treated in the ordinary way, by the application of cold water and tincture of arnica, a wine-glassful of the latter in two quarts of water.

PRICKS IN SHOEING occur from the want of skill in the smith

who drives the nail too near the laminæ, and sometimes even absolutely wounds them. It may be that the nail in its passage upwards is not within an eighth of an inch of these delicate parts, and the horse may not have flinched during the driving of it, but when he is put to work the nail opposes a hard unyielding line to the soft parts, inflammation is established, and possibly even matter is formed which may end in quittor. When, on the day after shoeing, a horse which was previously sound, goes lame, and the foot is hot to the touch, it may generally be assumed that a nail or nails have been driven too near to the quick, unless there is evidence of laminitis from other causes. On tapping the crust with a hammer, the horse will flinch at some particular spot, and there is the nail which is in fault. Sometimes there is little inflammation as yet set up, but the pressure of the nail is sufficient to cause lameness, and in either case the shoe should be taken off. Then, if there is reason to suppose that matter has formed, the opening from which the nail came out should be enlarged, and the matter allowed to escape. If, however, the foot has been merely "bound," it may be either left to nature, with a shoe lightly tacked on, and a wet "swab" round the coronet, or it may be placed in a bran poultice, which is the safest plan.

WHEN A NAIL IS PICKED UP ON THE ROAD, the prognosis will depend upon the part which it has penetrated. If it has entered deeply into the toe of the frog, the probability is that the navicular joint has been wounded, or probably the tendon of the flexor at its insertion into the pedal bone, either of which are very serious accidents. If the wound is further back, there is less risk of permanent injury, as the bulbous heels or cushion of the frog will bear a considerable amount of injury without permanent mischief. In any case the *treatment* should consist in cutting away the horn round the opening, so as to allow of a free escape of matter if it forms. At the same time inflammation should be kept under by cold "swabs" to the coronet, or by putting the whole foot into a bran poultice.

OVER-REACHES, when slight, may be treated by the application of friar's balsam, or tincture of arnica in full strength, which will have a tendency to dry them up and prevent suppuration. If, however, the heel is very much bruised, a poultice must be applied, but even then a little tincture of arnica should be sprinkled on it. When the bruise is so severe that a slough or core comes away, the wound may be dressed with a piece of lint, dipped in a solution of nitrate of silver, eight grains to the ounce of distilled water, and over this a bran poultice. In most cases, however, it is better to foment the part well and then apply the tincture of arnica neat.

A BRUISE on a thin sole will sometimes cause matter to form, in which case the horn must be cut away, and the case treated as for quittor. Before matter forms, the horn should be reduced, and the foot should be placed in a cold bran poultice.

CHAPTER XXV.

CONSTITUTIONAL DISEASES.

Fevers—Anasarca—Glanders—Farcy.

FEVERS.

THE HORSE is very rarely subject to fever as a disease of itself, independently of inflammation, under which head I have already described catarrhal fever, both of the simple kind and when epidemic, and known as influenza. Indeed, all the important inflammations of the body are attended with fever; but in them the local affections are evidently more serious than the general disturbance of the system, which we call by the name of fever. By many veterinarians it is doubted whether fever ever shows itself in the horse without inflammation; but occasionally it may be observed under the form of simple fever, presenting all the symptoms which accompany ordinary inflammation, but without any such complication, and more rarely of the typhoid form, which now sometimes attends influenza and other epidemics.

SIMPLE FEVER shows itself by dulness and reluctance to move, a staring coat, and cold legs and feet, with increased warmth of the body. The pulse is quick, soft, and variable—breathing a little accelerated, but not much—appetite entirely lost—bowels confined, and urine scanty. These symptoms continue for two or three days, and then either go on into the typhoid form, or they are complicated by inflammation in some organ of the body. The *treatment* merely consists in giving a mild dose of physic, followed by a febrifuge drink, such as the following:—

Take of Spirit of Nitrous Ether . . . . 1 oz.
        Nitre . . . . 3 to 5 drachms.
        Tincture of Ginger . . . . 2 drachms.
        Camphor Mixture . . . . 6 oz.
                      Mix, and give twice a day.*

TYPHOID FEVER sometimes appears as an epidemic, occurring either as a sequel to influenza, or in its pure form, without any

---

* Nothing in the veterinary Materia Medica will cure fever so certainly and successfully as aconite; and for this purpose give 10 to 15 drops of the tincture of the root two to three times in the twenty-four hours, and allow plenty of pure air and cold water.—EDITOR.

complication. The latter condition is, however, extremely rare. In its early stage, it can scarcely be recognised or distinguished from simple fever; but in the course of two or three days the strength is so much reduced, the breath is so fetid, and the mouth is loaded with such a black discharge from the tongue and gums, that the nature of the disease is clearly manifested. The pulse is very low, the languor increases, and there is often more or less delirium. The course of the disease is extremely rapid, and in five or six days a strong horse will sink beneath its powers, refusing food, and dying without any attempt to rally. The *treatment* should be of the most generous kind, as soon as the bowels have been gently moved, which should be effected, if possible, by injection. Then give a ball two or three times a day, composed thus:—

Take of Carbonate of Ammonia . . . . ½ to 1 drachm.
Powdered Ginger . . . . 1 drachm.
Powdered Yellow Bark . . . . 3 drachms.
Syrup enough to make into a ball.

This should be washed down with a quart of ale caudle, and hay tea should be allowed as the drink *ad libitum*; or, if there is diarrhœa, rice-water may be used in the same way. Few cases, however, will recover, in spite of every exertion and careful treatment on the part of the attendant.*

---

* As will be perceived by the text, typhoid fever is of rare occurrence in Great Britain; and when it does occur, it is mostly as a sequel to influenza and other debilitating diseases. Indeed, this may with truth be said of all countries where the land is dry by nature, or made so by drainage and cultivation.

Until of late years, no mention is made in the books on hippopathology, of "*typhosus*" as one of the ailments of the equine species. Typhoid fever among horses in different parts of this country is of yearly occurrence, and is known by several and distinct names—depending upon the chief symptom observed. Thus, in Kentucky, and the South West, it is called "*black tongue*," because that organ, as in man under similar circumstances, varies in color from a deep purple to black. It is known in New York as *cerebro-spinal-meningitis*, because it is thought by M. Liautard, to present symptoms similar to those when man is the subject. In Delaware it is named "*choking distemper*." In the West it is "*putrid fever*," so called from the fetid smell emanating from the diseased animal.

Isaiah Michener, Esq., of Bucks county, Pennsylvania, in a lecture delivered before the class of the Philadelphia Veterinary College, calls it "*paralysis of the par-vagum*," on account of the loss of power to swallow. The multiplicity of names given to the disease can do no possible harm, whilst, at the same time, they serve to point out to us the chief symptoms, so that they may be grouped together and as a whole, under the head of typhosus or typhoid fever.

The symptoms differ with the intensity of the attack, but at first they are very obscure and likely to be overlooked, a general debility being the most noticeable; and in a day or two a difficulty in swallowing will be ob-

ANASARCA.

ANASARCA, OR MOOR-ILL, occurs chiefly among horses turned out in marshes or low commons, and may readily be known by the general swelling of the body, increasing by gravitation in the legs during the standing posture, but showing itself chiefly in the lower side of the body in the early morning, when the horse has been lying down all night. The disease is now rare, but it occasionally appears under the circumstances above described. The *treatment* must be by acting on the kidneys, the following being a useful recipe for the purpose:—

Take of Nitre	4 drachms.
Powdered Resin	3 drachms.
Ginger	1 drachm.
Spirit of Nitrous Ether	1½ oz.
Warm Water	2 pints.

Mix and give as a drench every night.

---

served. Soon the horse staggers and is unable to walk, and in the majority of cases, lies or falls down unable to rise again.

There are other symptoms presented in this affection which might be described, but are unnecessary, as they are common alike to other debilitating diseases, such as the quickened and wiry pulse, heaviness of the head, fetid breath, shortened breathing, and wasting of the muscles of the body. The animal dies in from three to ten days, though sometimes lasting as long as two weeks, a loathsome sight, with nothing but skin and ligament covering the bones.

No disease of the horse can, after the third day, or when the animal is unable to stand, be mistaken for typhoid fever, if it be not *paralysis*, which occurs only in single and separate cases, whereas, in typhoid fever it is almost always epizootic (epidemic), attacking every horse on the place and even neighborhood.

The causes of typhoid fever in the horse do not differ from those that give rise to *typhus* in man, namely, miasma arising from level land, decaying vegetable matter, and stagnant water.

On many splendid country seats overlooking our noble rivers and bays along the eastern coast, the stables are often, for the sake of convenience, located near the river banks, with sometimes pools of stagnant water in the immediate vicinity. This is a fruitful source of this disease, especially during an unusually rainy season. In treating it, it is especially important that the horse be removed from the neighborhood of the miasma to a dry location: thus the cause will cease, and a cure is more likely to be effected.

Give the following in a drench, morning, noon, and night:

Cold Water	1 pint.
Powdered Carbonate of Ammonia	½ oz.
Capsicum	1 drachm.
Powdered Pimento Berries	½ oz.
Tincture Nux Vomica	20 drops.

If the horse is unable to stand, give him a good bed and turn him from one side to the other twice daily, to prevent sores on the body; and if unable to swallow, drench him with cold water and meal several times daily—adding thirty drops of commercial sulphuric acid to the drench.—EDITOR.

GLANDERS.

This frightful constitutional disease appears to consist in the generation of some poisonous matter in the blood, which nature attempts to throw off by establishing a discharge in the nostrils. It is perfectly incurable, and therefore it is only necessary to study its *symptoms*, with a view to distinguish it from ozena, with which alone it is liable to be confounded. Its chronic character and insidious onset will serve to distinguish it from catarrh and strangles.*

At its commencement, it seems to be confined to the internal lining of the nostrils, which is not reddened, as in chronic catarrh (ozena), but presents a leaden or purple colour, sometimes of a deep shade, but at first generally very light and pale. This is accompanied by a thin acrid discharge, transparent, and without odor. Generally, one nostril only is affected, which in this country is more frequently the left, and in France the right; but why this should be so has never yet been even conjectured with any appearance of probability. This state of things usually only lasts for a few weeks, but it may go on for an indefinite time, and is recognised as the first stage; during which the health does not suffer, and the horse can, and often does, go on with his ordinary work. It may be distinguished from ozena by the purple color of the lining membrane, and by the transparency and freedom from smell of the discharge.

In the second stage, the discharge increases in quantity, and though still watery and transparent, it is slightly sticky, indicating the presence of mucus. The lymphatic glands below the jaw en-

---

* To produce putrid disease amongst horses is an easy matter, for, by neglect of the ordinary laws of health, it will soon show itself in Glanders or Farcy. The blood of horses in badly-ventilated stables soon acquires toxical properties, from effete matter or miasma exhaled from and inhaled by the lungs, or even in some cases by direct inoculation. This poison, when introduced, acts as a ferment, so that the development of a peculiar train of symptoms quickly follows by the operation of the principle of *catalysis* (resolving matter into new compounds). This is the character of glanders, a malignant disease, infectious and contagious. This specific blood-poison is produced by placing horses and mules in conditions that depress their vital powers, as badly-ventilated stables, poor food, overwork, exhaustion from debilitating disease, &c.

Many cases of glanders, since the discovery of an anti-ferment, have been cured, and few cases of farcy die from it. *Treatment.*—Half-ounce doses of the sulphite of soda three times daily, five grains powdered Spanish fly once in the day, and allow good, generous diet. The soda checks the fermentation, and the Spanish fly acts as a tonic, and at the same time removes effete matter from the system. When the lungs in glanders are diseased, which is known when the horse has a cough, the case then is more like consumption, and cannot be cured. It is then called *equinia glandulosa*, or glanders with tubercles of the lungs.—Editor.

large, *and become adherent to the bone,* feeling hard to the touch, and almost like exostosis. Here the permanent character of the discharge and the adherence of the glands to the bone are the diagnostic signs from ozena.

IN THE THIRD STAGE, the discharge increases rapidly, and becomes yellow and opaque—in fact, it is pure pus. If the nose is carefully examined, its lining membrane will be seen to present one or more sores, with depressed centres and ragged edges, and surrounded by small varicose vessels leading to them from all directions. In proportion to the extent of the local mischief, constitutional disturbance is displayed. The appetite fails—the horse loses flesh and spirits—the coat is turned the wrong way—the skin is hidebound, and the legs fill slightly during the day, but go down at night—the nose is, at last, frightfully ulcerated, the sores spreading to the larynx—ulcers break out on the body—and the horse finally dies, worn to a skeleton.

When the diagnosis of the disease is confirmed, as it is undoubtedly highly contagious, both to other horses and to man himself, the patient ought to be destroyed. By the use of green food, his life may be prolonged for a time, and a certain amount of work may be got out of him; but the risk of contagion is too great to be incurred, and no man who regards his own welfare, and that of his neighbors, should keep a glandered horse.

FARCY.

THIS DISEASE appears to depend upon the development of the same poison as in glanders; but the attempt at elimination is made in the skin, instead of the mucous membrane lining the nose. A horse inoculated with glanders may exhibit farcy, and *vice versâ;* so that the essence of the disease is the same, but its seat is a different tissue.

FARCY usually shows itself first by one or two small hard knots in the skin, called "farcy buds." These soon soften, and contain a small quantity of pus; but as this is rapidly absorbed, the lymphatics which convey it into the circulation inflame; and at a short distance another bud is formed, and then another, and another. These buds are usually met with in the thin skin covering the inside of the thighs and arms, or the neck and lips. They vary from the size of a shilling to that of a half-crown; and as they increase in numbers, the skin becomes œdematous. In process of time, the general system suffers, as in glanders, and the horse dies, a miserable, worn-out object. No *treatment* can be relied on to cure the disease; and as it is equally contagious with glanders, every farcied horse ought at once to be destroyed. The hard nature of the buds, and the thickened lymphatics extending like cords between, clearly make known the nature of the disease.

36

CHAPTER XXVI.

SHOEING.*

The art of shoeing appears to have been unknown to the ancients, although the need of it was greatly felt, especially in the rough campaigning and long marches constantly recurring in those warlike times. In several campaigns the cavalry was rendered worthless and was disbanded on account of the bad condition of their horses' feet, and the animals themselves were relieved from duty until their hoofs were restored. The value of a horse depended more upon the soundness and strength of his hoof than upon any other qualification, and various methods of rendering it harder and more serviceable were proposed by Xenophon and other early writers. But while acknowledging the importance of a sound, vigorous hoof, and striving to harden and preserve it, it does not seem to have occurred to them to protect it by fastening to it by nails, a band or shoe of iron, although Beckman states that horse shoes and nails have been found in the graves of some German and Vandal tribes of unknown antiquity in the northern part of Germany. To William the Conqueror tradition ascribes the introduction of the practice of shoeing into England, whence it has remained until the present time.

When the delicacy of organization of the foot of the horse is considered, its extreme sensitiveness and wonderful adaptability for the purpose of locomotion, the enormous wear and tear incident upon constant use in the service of man, its liability to abuse and injury, and the consequent suffering of the dumb animal and pecuniary loss to the owner, it is surprising that there has been so little real improvement in the art. While the past half century has been so fruitful of results in almost every other branch of industry, it has witnessed few or none in this. This is due in great measure to the indifference of the artisan to whom the care of the horse's foot is committted, who, ignorant of the nature and structure of the living member before him, so recklessly handles and mutilates it, in much the same manner as his ancestors years before him.

The feet of most of the horses of the present day, and especially those used for drafty purposes and heavy work in our large cities, are in bad condition, and more subjects are brought to the knack-

---

* This article was prepared at our request, by a gentleman who has given the subject much time, and patient investigation.—EDITOR.

er's yard from this cause than all others combined. A healthy, vigorous foot is the exception even among horses used for lighter work. Brittle, shelly hoofs, ridged and dished, indicating internal derangement, withered frogs with the centre arch or stay entirely absorbed, high heels bound up by hard, unyielding crust, all these deformities and many others are chargeable in some degree to bad shoeing. Sometimes injuries are attributed to the blacksmith that are due to accident or brutality of the driver, but in as far as our system of shoeing interferes with the natural functions of the foot, it will induce disease.

The question then presents itself, Why not teach the mechanic the design of the structure, to the repair of which his lifetime is devoted? You may command him to treat your horse as you direct, but you must convince his judgment, if you expect obedience at all times; as well dictate to a physician what medicines he shall give your child at some stages of disease, and depend on him at others; he will treat the case in his own way, or not at all; the head, heart and hand must accord to make perfect work.

Our public schools have been a great power in the advancement of the mechanical arts; much of the labor-saving machinery now building up great wealth in the country, is the fruit of the philosophical truths there disseminated, and the improved social condition of the laboring classes is due to their influence. We have schools of science, and colleges for the instruction of students in the treatment and cure of horses, yet we expect those whose daily business is to perform important surgical operations upon a delicately organized member, to be reasonably successful, without having learned the alphabet of their profession. There are among them, individuals, intelligent and ingenious, who would be glad of an opportunity of testing the validity of their practice by an appeal to the condition of the hidden springs, levers, pulleys, cushions, and powers comprising the mechanism of the feet and legs explained by those who have made such their lifelong study. Many of these have, by long experience, discovered for themselves a fair system of shoeing, and are successful in the treatment and prevention of injury, but, ignorant of physiology, are unable to transmit their knowledge to others with sufficient reason to establish its truth.

To such fully educated to their profession, we must look for improvement in the art, and we hope that the day is not far distant when America may be able to boast of her veterinary colleges and schools for farriers, as of her other institutions of learning.

A small proportion of the pecuniary loss annually sustained in our large cities alone, would support such an institution, the good results of which would be incalculable. But while all thinking men admit the benefits which must result from its establishment, it is too customary to regard the idea as visionary and impracticable, and maintain that the craft would not avail themselves of its advantages.

At first, doubtless, only the most intelligent would do so, but these, applying the theoretical knowledge received there to the commonest details and every-day experience of the smithy, would convince the most unreasoning that labor, when directed by skill and judgment, is more saving of money, strength, and material, than when unenlightened and unreasoning; and soon public opinion would force their more ignorant brethren to follow their example. A great painter was once asked how he mixed his colors. "With brains, sir," was the apt reply. When this is the rule and not the exception, we may indeed look for decided improvement in the art, the dumb animal be relieved of much suffering, and the community from unnecessary loss.

Veterinarians may propose theories, but lack the practical experience and opportunity of observation which the workmen alone can have, while the number of the latter who have combined scientific education with a thorough knowledge of the details of their profession, has been too small to stamp any decided character upon it.

With but very few exceptions the entire literature of shoeing is European, and to these writers the American public is indebted for all knowledge outside of that which an inquiring mind will gather from individual observation.

If horse owners would resort to the books for physiological facts, study their own horses, and use their own judgment, they would in most cases discover the best style of shoeing for their particular use.

Countries and sections differ greatly in the fashion of horse-shoes, and the manner of fitting them to the foot, but the general principles are the same.

We do not pretend to advocate any particular form of shoe, nail, or system of shoeing as an ultimatum of success, but wish to draw the attention of horse owners to the importance of the subject, that they may judge for themselves, the practice best suited to their own animals, and may arrive at a more accurate conception and a better appreciation of the hazard of a sole dependence on the general ignorance of blacksmiths.

A careful study of the construction of the foot, as explained in this work, will show the necessity of great caution and intelligence in its treatment; more than is usually displayed by our mechanics. This will be better understood by a reference to the member itself by dissection, which is practicable to most farmers, as they may frequently obtain specimens in their vicinity, and are possessed of the facilities for examination.

Sever the foot at the upper joint of the pastern bone, trace the veins, arteries and tendons, as suggested by the description; note the principal resistant parts affected by locomotion, the position of the coronary bone and its inclination within the hoof (not as frequently engraved entirely without or above it, and vertical when at rest), the navicular bone and joint, the tendons and sheath, with the action of each, the elastic property of the fatty heels, the tough, springy frog, its shape and position, the structure of the coffin bone, sole, crust and bars, and their mutual relations. Let the examination be careful, and guided by reflection, with due regard to each particular hoof, fore and hind, near and off, and condition of health. Form no hasty conclusions from partial investigations, and study for practical benefit, not for a show of wisdom. A wooden vice, butcher's saw, chisel, knives and nippers, are about all the instruments necessary, and after becoming acquainted with the natural tone of the crust, the operation may be facilitated by the use of warm water to soften the horn.

If this has excited an interest in the subject, let the student experiment with the shoeing of his own horses, young and old; having the entire control and supervision of their working, driving, stabling, pasturing and shoeing, he must learn something, if but his own ignorance. If resident of a country of light sandy soil, and the nature of the work will allow, the hind feet, if not all, might be left unshod to illustrate natural development; we have seen such with hard glossy hoofs, that could travel over turnpike roads with a light load, without breaking the crust or flinching on the frog.

The detail of horse-shoeing has been subjected to such adverse teachings by different authors (many of whom have but repeated palpable errors of their predecessors without attempt at originality), that it would be impossible to produce positive rules that will not meet with opposition, but the indications of disease, may be related without assigning their particular cause, of which there is much difference of opinion and uncertainty.

The conditions of a good, sound foot as apparent, are a smooth, glossy, resilient crust, almost circular were it continued around at the bars, but fuller on the outside quarter, which difference is seldom seen on a foot that has been shod a dozen times; a concave sole not too dry and hard; a full frog elastic throughout, with its centre or frog stay complete; heels sufficiently low and free from crust to bear their share of the springiness of action, and full and well developed to allow freedom to the bones and tendons in their movements. In horses the general rule is that dark hoofs are harder than light ones. The internal organization is in conformity with the external, the healthy state has been already described under the heads of bones, muscles, &c. In disease, we find within a concave, furrowed crust, the elastic process or bed of the same

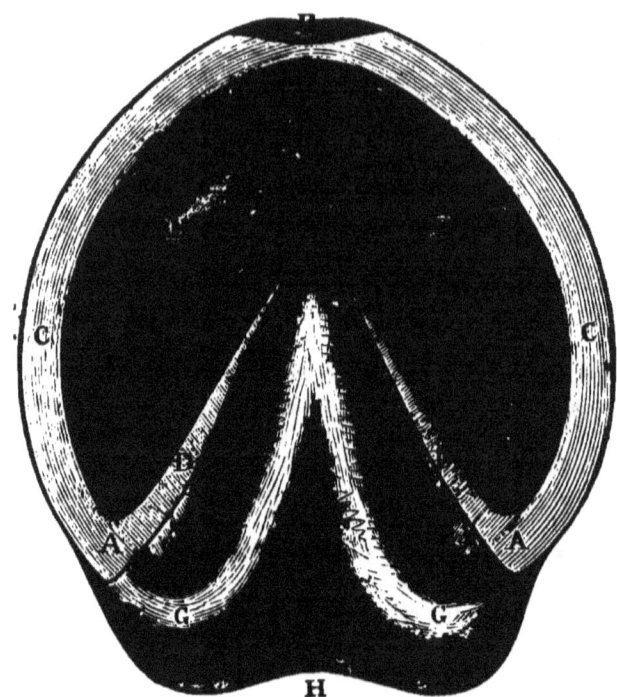

Fig. 20.—A SOUND FORE FOOT PREPARED FOR THE SHOE.

A. The heel of the crust.
B. The toe.
C C. The quarters of the crust.
D D. The bars as they should be left with frog between them.
E E. The angles between the heels and bars where corns appear.
F F. The concave surface.
G G. The bulbous heels.
H. Cleft.

form, and a dished coffin bone; under a convex sole a coffin bone turned up in front by absorption and flattened like the hoof, spongy and deficient in bony matter, the sensible sole diminished and the horny sole increased in substance; in long-standing cases of contracted heels, the interior organizations are alike reduced. Whichever may be the primary change, internal or external, or whether either be a result of bad shoeing, no satisfactory solution has yet been given. Veterinarians wrangle over their favorite theories, charge one another with causing the diseases they profess to prevent, and are so completely antagonistic in their doctrines, that the public cannot be confident of truth, in implicit reliance upon the assertions of any.

In comparing the horse's foot with the human, we must be careful not to fall into error; their relations to the body are the same, but to understand the comparative structures, we must imagine ourselves upon all fours, resting upon the finger and toe nails, our wrist and heel corresponding to the knee and hock-joints of the horse, though the bones are of different relative lengths and shape. The crust of the hoof is secreted in much the same manner as our nails, and growing downwards, or towards the extremities, slides over a laminated and highly sensitive bed, which, when injured, produces intense pain, on account of the unyielding nature of the crust, and the swelling consequent to inflammation. We may then realize the suffering produced by the prick of a horse-shoe nail, under a horn so much thicker than our finger or toe nails.

As qualifications of resistance, and ease to superincumbent structures, we have, of the human foot, the main arch of the soles (which must be taken together to establish their completeness), and the transverse arch of the ball of the foot, displayed when the toes are brought to the ground. Of the horse there is the arch of the sole, and those formed by the heels and frog. The sole and coffin bone of the mule are more concave than those of the horse.

As propellers and levers, we find the same action from heel to toe, as the body moves forward in progression. The horse having two sets of levers, one for the fore part of the body and one for the hind, all working in connection, must make exactly the same length of step with each foot to avoid interference. From this fact, we account for a frequent cause of forging and stumbling. Both horse and man accustom the motion of the body to the length of step; if we then attempt to walk in a pair of shoes so much shorter than usual, as to cramp the toes and shorten the foot, we will be unable to carry the body as far with each motion from heel to toe, to correspond with our ordinary forward spring of the body; the tendency, therefore (until we learn better), is to a short, quick, stumbling gait. Now, take a horse whose hoofs have been slowly growing in length for a month, every motion of his body trained to accord, pull off his shoes, which will be found (owing to the forward growth of the hoof) farther from the heels than when first applied, pare away the crust down to the sole, cut out a big notch at the toe for a clip, set the new shoe back within the front of the foot (more on the fore feet, as they are supposed to grow faster), then rasp off the outer part of the toe back to the shoes, and clench the nails as tight as possible. This is a common mode of shoeing; his shoes are too small for him; he swings into a trot with the usual body motion, but the feet, all shortened, fail their part, while the fore feet, diminished more than the hind, are not thrown out quite as far, and the horse, unaccustomed to the change, dwells too long on them to escape a blow from behind. Weariness and laziness will also cause forging, by a tardy movement in front, and stumbling, by a failure to raise the toe sufficiently to avoid scrubbing the ground when thrown forward.

It is too common, especially in cities, among draught-horses, to use up the lower part of the crust too fast for its growth If the human finger-nail be pierced with a fine needle in the manner of a horse-shoe nail driven through the crust of a hoof, it will be observed that the hole will remain, until the growth of the nail has carried it beyond the flesh; that is, the fibres of horn once separated will never unite. Horses used for heavy work are shod with heavy shoes, thick toe and quarter clips, high calks and steel toes, and either because of the severe strain on the stones, the weight of the shoes and nails, the leverage of calks and toes, waste of crust to accommodate clips, or of all combined, they require shoeing about once in three weeks, and frequently oftener. At each shoeing, a little more crust and sole is taken off of the ground surface, a few more holes made (or nails driven into old ones, enlarging the aperture by working about and bending under the clenching iron). The surface of the crust is again rasped, diminishing the thickness, new furrows made to accommodate the clenches, and the horn burned and softened by a hot shoe each time. The blacksmith will insist that all these operations are necessary, but the fact is, he is using up material too fast, and we leave it to horse owners to judge by experiment, how these operations may be modified. The French method of bringing the points of the nails out low down on the surface of the hoof, appears rational, as it destroys the vitality of the crust to a less degree than our custom, and leaves a greater proportion of sound foot to bear the shocks.

Our practice has been, after removing the old shoes (with care not to enlarge the old holes by dragging crooked nails through them), to pare off the crust and bars well down to the outer edge of the sole, without taking a shaving from the sole, frog, or inside of the bars. If the crust has not been broken by wear, this leaves the foot as near its natural shape as possible, and a shoe must be made to fit it. For roadsters, a narrow, light shoe is fitted to the crust in length and width, then made perfectly level, without twist or pritchell burs at the nail holes, and while sufficiently hot, slightly touched to the crust, to mark any inequalities that may have been left after paring. Six nails are used, three on each side, dividing the space from about an inch from the centre of the toe, to the centre of the quarters. The nail holes are set well back from the outside edge, and made straight through the iron; the nails are

SHOEING.

small, smoothed off with the hammer, and slightly bevelled on one side of the point; the position of the holes in the shoe brings the nails out low down on the surface of the crust, but care must be taken to start them in the centre of the holes, that the foot may not be cramped or forced out of its natural shape. The projecting nail points are filed close to the hoof, that they may be broken off without twisting the nail, or enlarging the hole in the crust; the nails are then driven up, and the clenches turned over and hammered down.

No rasp has been used, no crust wasted by mutilation for clips, and but little injury by nail holes; if the nails be of good iron, they are sufficient in number, and the light clenches on a sound foot, will hold the shoe perfectly tight, and will not cause abrasion of the legs in travelling.

The foot presents what we might call a beautiful fit, the tender part of the frog is protected by the thickness of the shoe, while as it is renewed from within, the outside will be worn off by friction, and nature will keep it exactly low enough to obtain its necessary exercise; moreover, by driving the nails straight through the middle of the hole in the shoe, the foot will be free from that disagreeable, cramped feeling, we have imagined a horse to experience, when the nails are started at either side of the hole in the iron, forcing the more yielding fibres of horn to its centre.

There have been many forms of shoes recommended by different authors, but few of which are used in this country. The French shoe has a convex ground surface, and the foot is fashioned to it, by leaving the quarters full, and the crust sloped off towards the toe and heels. Why the bearing should be taken off the heels we cannot imagine, and forcing the quarters to bear an undue amount of concussion would apparently induce quarter crack, but having had no experience with this shoe we may be wrong in our conclusions.

Another fashion imitates an old shoe worn off at the toe, which is certainly an advantage to roadsters, as it would be to us, if we could buy new shoes to fit our feet exactly like the old ones. Some writers advocate nailing the shoe only upon the outside quarter, or with but two nails on the inside, toward the toe, with the idea of allowing unimpeded expansion of the crust when the foot strikes the ground. Inasmuch as nails injure the crust, the practice of using as few as possible is wise, but we have been unable to discover any expansion of the anterior half of the ground surface in hoofs that have never been shod. A careful examination will convince any one that there is no mechanical necessity for such spreading, and from the nature of the organization of the foot, it is simply impossible; all the spring needful to the front of the crust is gained by the elasticity of its fibres. The line of bearing of the lower part of the fore leg, is directed behind the centre of the foot, and the yielding points of the framework are the pastern, coronary and navicular joints; as the upper part of the coronary bone works backward and downward, it, with the action of the tendon, slightly spreads the heels laterally, and the whole crust partakes of the movement, diminishing in effect towards the toe; were the foot completely inelastic, the motion might be detected at the quarters, but the whole of a healthy foot is of a yielding nature; the fatty heels, in particular, may be compressed like cork, while the frog resembles a piece of india-rubber, and there is a spring in every fibre of the crust. These conditions so far distribute motion, that there is practically none in the ground surface of the crust forward of the centre.

From the fact of this style of shoe allowing free expansion, its advocates proclaim it a preventive of contracted heels (which, unfortunately, is so prevalent among shod horses); but if, as we suppose, there be no spreading of the front part of the crust by pressure, a shoe nailed only at, and forward of the quarters, will not interfere with any natural movement of the heels.

This disease (contracted heels), which has been described on page 409, appears to be an absorption or waste of a portion of the frog and fatty heels, accompanied by an undue secretion of crust at the posterior part of the foot, encroaching upon the province of the softer tissue of the heels.

Many reasons have been assigned for this disturbance of the natural nutrition of the different parts, all or none of which may be correct, for no theory has yet been so clearly demonstrated and proven, as to leave the causes and nature of the disease beyond a doubt, but we have never known any tendency to contraction, in horses that have been shod in such manner as to allow the frog a fair amount of exercise, indicated by its position.

An india-rubber shoe intended to be used as a cushion between the iron and the foot, has been designed, patented and tried, within the last two or three years, but we believe has failed to give general satisfaction. The rubber mashes out in a short time by concussion, and leaves a loose shoe. Good sole leather is much more durable.

Until recently, the whole process of making the shoe was performed by hand, but now in the United States, the greater bulk is made by machinery, and at one immense establishment.

The manufactory of Messrs. Burden & Sons, at Troy, New York state, with its six forging machines, turns out six shoes per second, and in four years made twenty-five thousand tons; or calculating one and a half pounds to the shoe, thirty-seven million shoes. These shoes are of the very best iron, warranted to bend double cold, and to wear as long as any made by hand; the iron used in their manufacture bearing a tensile strain of seventy-eight thousand pounds to the square inch.

The power of the factory is gained by a large stream of water, with a head of seventy-two feet, acting on an overshot wheel sixty feet in diameter, with buckets twenty-two feet long and six feet four inches deep, the whole wheel weighing over three hundred tons. Connected with the establishment is a horse-shoe museum, comprising many hundred specimens of shoes of all ages and all countries, collected together at much expense with a view to improvement upon the old types. There are now three different patterns manufactured, and they will furnish any other pattern desired, if ordered in sufficient quantities. The cost of the shoe to the blacksmith, is about a cent and a half per pound above the price of the iron.

Independent of the immense curtailment of expense, the advantage of machinery directed by one master mind over the old system, or rather want of system of individual effort and incongruous labor, is great; and it should be the aim of the manufacturer, as self-interest will dictate, to study and experiment to attain the most desirable pattern, in width of web, seating, fullering, position of nail holes, and quality of iron, and the mechanics will necessarily adopt his improvements.

In short, it should be an aim in shoeing a horse, as in man, to make a fit as neat and easy, and of as light material as would be adapted to its use, and experience has proven, that heavy shoes with high calks and toes, are not necessary for successful hauling over our city cobble stones, or hard roadways.

In this article we have given no positive directions for shoeing, judging the art in its present state too imperfect to satisfy this progressive age, but have sought rather to stimulate inquiry and experiment, that may lead to improvement in the system.

CHAPTER XXVII.
OPERATIONS.

Administration of Chloroform—Methods of confining the Horse—Bleeding—Firing—Setons and Rowels—Blistering—Castration—Docking and Nicking—Unnerving—Reduction of Hernia—Administration of Physic—Clysters—Back-Raking.

ADMINISTRATION OF CHLOROFORM.

THE USE OF CHLOROFORM to procure insensibility to pain is a great aid to the operator on the horse, who without it acts under great difficulties, owing to the nervous twitch which the poor animal gives at each touch of the knife. Under chloroform, however, he lies as if dead; and as long as its effects continue, the most elaborate dissection may be conducted with comparative ease. There is some little danger of overdoing this powerful agent, but the risk is not so great as is generally supposed, and with ordinary care it is more than one thousand to one that no injurious effects are produced.

THE BEST AND MOST SIMPLE APPARATUS for the purpose of administering chloroform is a common wire muzzle, to the upper edge of which a strip of leather six inches deep is stitched, and so arranged that it may be buckled round the upper part of the jaws. This insures that all the air inspired shall pass through the wires, and by covering them with a cap of very loose flannel, in which a few holes are cut to facilitate respiration, the muzzle may be made ready for use. The horse is first cast, after which the above apparatus is put on and buckled round the jaw, when on sprinkling the chloroform over the cap of flannel, it may be applied or removed in an instant, and the amount of anæsthesia regulated accordingly. Without some guard such as the wire affords, the chloroform runs over the nostrils and lips, and blisters them to a serious extent; but when it is used, such an accident can only occur from over-saturating the flannel. The necessary quantity of this powerful agent must be employed; but when once it is found that a prick of a pin or other pointed instrument is borne without shrinking, the flannel may be withdrawn, and the operation quickly commenced, taking care to have an assistant ready to put it on again if the horse shows signs of returning sensibility to pain. Six or eight ounces of chloroform must be provided, as the quantity required is rather uncertain, the average dose being about three or four ounces.

IF CASTING is objected to, either from the absence of hobbles, or from fear of injury to the horse, a soft bed of straw should be provided, and a strong halter must be put over the muzzle with two cords, one of which should be held by a man on each side. These will serve to guide the horse in falling; but it is extremely difficult to make sure of his going down where he is wanted to lie; and there is also considerable time lost in securing him after he is down, which the safety of the operator imperatively requires. The effect of the chloroform must therefore be kept up for a much longer time than if it is given after the horse is cast and secured.

METHODS OF CONFINING THE HORSE.

THERE ARE VARIOUS PLANS adopted by veterinary surgeons to bind the horse's limbs, so that he cannot injure himself or them when undergoing an operation. Even when chloroform is employed, some coercion of this kind must generally be adopted, as directed in the last section; for if it is given in the standing position, the horse is very apt to injure himself in falling, which is often accompanied by powerful convulsive motions, and moreover he cannot with certainty be placed in a suitable position. The plan adopted by Mr. Rarey is seldom suitable, because it can only be employed on subjects previously taught to go down without resistance, for the severe struggle which the untaught horse makes before he submits is calculated to produce injurious constitutional disturbance, and, moreover, it would sadly increase any of the various diseases of the limbs for which operations are so often performed. Sometimes, however, it might advantageously be introduced into veterinary surgery, as for instance in castration, when the colt will not suffer his hind legs to be touched, but even then it will be necessary to throw him two or three times, or he will be in such a state of arterial excitement that inflammation will be likely to follow. The usual methods of confinement are: 1st. The hobbles. 2d. The side line. 3d. The trevis, or break. 4th. The twitch and barnacles.

HOBBLES consist of four broad padded leather straps, provided with strong buckles, and long enough to encircle the pasterns. To each of these an iron ring is stitched, and to one of them a strong soft rope, six yards in length, is securely attached. Provided with four, or, if possible, five assistants, the operator buckles the hobble with the rope attached to the near fore leg, and the remaining three to the other legs. Then passing the rope through their rings, and through the first also, it is held by three assistants, the nearest of whom stands about a yard from the horse, so as to pull upwards as well as away from him; a fourth assistant holds him by the head to keep him quiet, and to be ready to fall on it as soon as he is down, and the fifth stands at his quarters, ready to push him over on his off side. This place is sometimes occupied by the operator himself when he is short of hands. Casting should never be attempted on any hard surface, a thick bed of straw being necessary to prevent injury from the heavy fall which takes place. The hind legs should be brought as far forward as possible before beginning to pull the rope, and when the men do this they should do it "with a will," but without jerking, so as to take the horse off his guard, when he will resist much less stoutly than if he is allowed more time. As soon as the legs are drawn up together, the man at the quarters is quite safe from injury, and he may lean forcibly against that part, and force the horse over to the off side, upon which he falls: the assistant at the head keeping that part down, no further struggling takes place, and he is secured by passing the end of the rope under the hobble rings between the fore and hind legs, and securing it with a hitch. Something more, however, is necessary to be done before any of the usual operations can be performed, as all of the legs are at liberty to a certain extent and the scrotum cannot be reached in safety. The following further precautions must therefore be taken, varying according to the part to be operated on.

FOR CASTRATION the horse should be cast on his near side, with a web halter in the usual place of a collar. The rope of the halter is then passed through the ring of the hobble on the off hind leg, and using it as a pulley the foot is drawn forcibly forward beyond the arm and firmly secured to the webbing round the neck, and bringing it back again it may be passed round the thigh above the hock (which should be guarded from friction by a soft cloth or leather), and again secured to the webbing. By these precautions the scrotum is completely exposed, and the hind legs cannot be stirred beyond the slight spasmodic twitch which extends to the whole body.

TO PERFORM ANY OPERATION ON THE FORE LEG, it must be taken out of its hobble, and drawn forward upon the straw by a webbing attached to its pastern, where it must be held by an assistant, the horse having little or no power over it in this position.

THE HIND LEG IS SECURED in the same way as for castration, unless the fetlock is to be fired, when webbing must be applied to the thigh above the hock only. With most horses, however, firing can be performed without casting, by buckling up the fore leg, or by having it held by a competent assistant.

WHEN THE HORSE is to be released, the hobbles are quietly unbuckled in succession, beginning with the undermost hind leg.

SEVERAL IMPROVED HOBBLES have been invented, but they are suited rather for the veterinary surgeon than for the ordinary horsemaster, who will only require them for castration and minor operations.

THE SIDE LINE is sometimes used for securing one hind leg thus:—the long rope and single hobble only are required, the latter being buckled to the hind pastern, which is to be secured. The rope is then passed over the withers and brought back round the bosom and shoulder of the same side as the leg to which it is secured, and then passed inside the first part of the rope. By pulling at the end of this cord the hind leg is drawn up to the shoulder, and secured there with a hitch, but the plan is not nearly so safe as casting.

THE TREVIS OR BREAK consists of four strong posts driven into the ground, at the corners of a space six feet long by three feet wide. They are strongly braced together by wooden stays, three feet six inches from the ground on three sides, the fourth being left open for the horse to enter, after which this also is made good by a padded bar passed through stout iron rings fixed at three feet from the ground to the uprights. By means of this framework, to which sundry rings are bolted, the body of the horse is first securely confined by two broad bands under the belly and two above the shoulders and croup. Thus he can neither rear nor kick to any extent sufficient to free himself, and all that is necessary is to lay hold of any limb selected for operation, and confine it to one of the uprights, or to some other convenient point. This is the best plan to be adopted for firing and other operations on the legs, and if the belly-bands are wide, strong, and secure, chloroform may be administered in it, without the horse going down.

THE TWITCH is a short stick of strong ash, about the size of a mopstick, with a hole pierced near the end, through which is passed a piece of strong but small cord, and tied in a loop large enough to admit the open hand freely. This is passed over the upper lip close to the nostrils, and then, by twisting the stick, compression is made to a painful extent, which will keep horses quiet for any slight operation. Sometimes it is placed on the ear in preference, but in either case the effect is dependent on the pain produced.

BARNACLES consist in the application of pressure by means of the handles of a pair of pincers enclosing the muzzle, and held firmly by an assistant. They are, however, not so useful as the twitch.

BLEEDING.

IN THE EARLY PART OF THE PRESENT CENTURY bleeding was resorted to on every appearance of the slightest inflammation, and often without the slightest necessity. Many horses were regularly bled " every spring and fall," to prevent mischief, as was supposed; but at last it always happened to every horse which lived long enough, that the more frequently blood was taken the more the operation was required, and when it was absolutely wanted to lower the heart's action, such a quantity of blood must be taken that the system was reduced to a dangerous degree. Stallions were constantly submitted to this treatment, and mares as long as they were worked, so that in course of time it has happened to the horse, as it has also to man himself, that the horrible abuse of the lancet for two or three consecutive generations has completely changed the type of the diseases to which they are both subject. Inflammation does not now follow the same course that it used to do, but is of a much milder type, and the attendant fever is inclined to assume a typhoid character, if lowering measures are pushed to any great extent. An attempt has been made to account for this change in human diseases by the alteration in the habits of the present generation, which are certainly more temperate than those of the previous one; but in the case of the horse the reverse holds good, for he is now stimulated by more corn than ever. The only point, as far as I can make out, in which the horse and his master have been similarly maltreated, is in the abuse of the lancet, which undoubtedly may account for the change in the type of their diseases to which I have alluded, and it is, therefore, reasonable to refer it to this cause. But though this powerful agent has been thus abused, we must not be deterred from having recourse to it when severe inflammation occurs in the horse. Sometimes there is no time to wait for the effects of a slower remedy, even if there is one which will be sufficiently powerful to control the heart's action. The only sensible plan in such case is to choose the lesser of the two evils, and to save life, or the integrity of the organ attacked, as the case may be, by abstracting blood, always remembering that this is to be avoided as long as it is safe to do so, but that when it is decided on, a sufficient quantity must be taken to produce a sensible effect, without which there is no attendant good to counterbalance the evil.

BLEEDING is either performed in the jugular vein, when the whole system is to be affected; or when a part of the body only is inflamed, it may be desirable to abstract blood locally, as for instance from the toe or from the plate vein, in inflammation of the foot, and in ophthalmia from the vein which lies on the face just below the eye.

THE INSTRUMENTS USED are either the lancet or the fleam, the former being the safer of the two, but requiring some practice to manage it properly. In bleeding from the jugular vein a string is sometimes tied round the neck below the part to be opened, which is four or five inches below the fork in the vein in the upper part of the neck. The skilled operator, however, makes pressure with his left hand answer the purpose of causing the vein to rise, and during this state either uses the lancet with his right or the fleam with the aid afforded by the blow of a short stick, called a "blood stick." When the blood begins to flow, the edge of the bucket which catches it is pressed against the same part, and as long as this is continued a full stream will run until faintness occurs. After sufficient blood has been taken, the two lips of the wound are raised between the fingers, and a *small* common pin passed through both, when the point is cut off and some tow is twisted round, by which the edges are kept together and the pin is retained in position. In a couple of days the pin may be withdrawn without disturbing the tow, and the wound will heal with little or no deformity. Sometimes the blood continues to flow beneath the skin after it is pinned, and a swelling takes place in consequence, which is called ecchymosis. When this happens, cold water should be freely applied and the head kept up by racking to the manger.

THE QUANTITY OF BLOOD necessary to be taken will vary according to circumstances, and can scarcely be fixed from the appearance of the blood drawn, but a repetition of the operation may be decided on if the clot of the blood, after standing, is very concave at the top (cupped), or if it is very yellow (buffed), and especially if both these signs are present. In inflammation of a severe character less than six quarts of blood will seldom lower the pulse sufficiently to be of much service, and sometimes seven or eight quarts even must be taken from a large plethoric animal.

INFLAMMATION OF THE VEIN will sometimes supervene upon bleeding, the *symptoms* being a slight swelling appearing in the evening, or the next day, with a little oozing from the wound. These are soon followed by a hard cord-like enlargement of the vein, which feels hot to the touch, and the parts at the angle of the jaw swell considerably. The consequence generally is that the vein is obliterated, occasioning some disturbance to the circulation, especially when the head is held down, as it is at grass. The *treatment* consists in cold applications as long as there is heat, the lotion recommended at page 316 being generally useful. When the heat has subsided, and the vein remains enlarged, the biniodide of mercury will procure the absorption of the new deposit, by rubbing it in as recommended at page 300.*

FIRING.

THE PURPOSE for which the heated iron is employed is twofold; first, to produce immediate counter-irritation, by which the previous inflammation is reduced; and secondly, to cause the formation of a tight compress over the part, which lasts for some months. It is the fashion to deny the existence of the latter effect of this operation; but every practical man must be aware that it follows

---

* Bleeding in veterinary practice is by no means so general as formerly, the substitution of pure air, cold water and aconite, except in diseases of the head, proving very satisfactory.—EDITOR.

upon firing to a greater or less extent, according to circumstances but always lasting for a few months, until the skin stretches to its previous condition. The blemish which it leaves, and the pain which it occasions, both during and after the application of the irons, should cause it to be avoided when any equally useful substitute can be employed; but, unfortunately, there are many cases where it stands without a rival, as being at once the safest and the most efficient remedy which can be adopted. Blisters and setons can be made to cause the same amount of counter-irritation; but the inflammation accompanying the former often extends beneath the skin, and increases the mischief it was intended to relieve; while the latter has no effect whatever in producing pressure upon the parts beneath. The pain of firing can be relieved entirely at the time of the operation by chloroform; but the subsequent smarting is quite as bad, and this is beyond the reach of any anæsthetic. Independently, however, of the interests of the master, it is also to the advantage of the horse to get thoroughly cured; for if he is not, he will either work on in misery, or he will be consigned to the knacker's yard; and, therefore, the adoption of the most efficacious plan of treatment, even if somewhat the most painful, is the best for both.

FIRING MAY BE PERFORMED STANDING, by the use of the side line for the hind leg, or by fixing up one fore leg when the other is to be operated on. There is, however, nothing like the break or trevis, where more than a slight extent of surface is to be lined. The firing-iron should have a smooth edge, about the thickness of a worn shilling; and it should be heated to the point when it shows a dull red in the dark. When the disease for which the irons are used is slight, the skin should not be penetrated; but in bad cases, where the mischief is great, and particularly when it is wanted to have a good permanent bandage, the cauterization must be deeper; but this requires some practical knowledge to decide. The hair of the part should be cut very closely with the scissors, or shaved; then, having secured the leg, the iron is to be steadily but rapidly passed in parallel lines over the skin, making just the proper pressure which is required to burn to the requisite depth. A light brown mark should be left, which shows that the proper effect has been produced; and the color should be uniform, unless it is desired to penetrate deeper at certain parts, which is sometimes practised with advantage. The lines are sometimes made in a slanting direction round the leg, and at others straight up and down; but it is useless to describe the details of this operation, which *can* only be learned by watching its performance by another hand. Badly done firing is always an eyesore; but when the lines are evenly drawn, and they have healed without any sloughs, caused by irregular or excessive pressure, they show that a master-hand has been at work, and that the poor beast has been treated scientifically. In very severe diseases, a blister is sometimes applied over the part, immediately after the firing; but this can seldom be required, and as it aggravates the pain tenfold, it should be avoided, if possible. On the following day, a little neat's-foot oil should be gently rubbed, or brushed with a feather, over the leg; and this should be repeated daily, until the swelling which comes on has nearly subsided. Less than three months' rest should never be allowed for the operation to have its full effect, as, if the horse is put to work before that time has elapsed, the disease will almost certainly return. Indeed, it is far better to allow double this time, especially if the horse is wanted for fast work.

SETONS AND ROWELS.

SETONS are pieces of tape or lamp cotton, passed through and beneath the skin, leaving the two ends hanging out, either tied together or with a knot upon each. The latter is the safer plan, as the loop is always liable to be caught on a hook or other projecting body. The needle with which the passage is effected has a spear point, slightly turned up, and an eye at the other end (see fig. 22), through which the tape or cotton is threaded. The

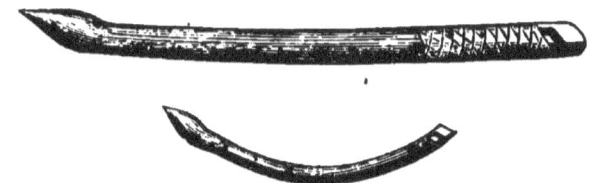

FIG. 22.—SETON NEEDLES ONE QUARTER SIZE.

ordinary one is about nine or ten inches long, and by its means a tape or piece of lamp cotton, smeared with blister cerate, may be passed through a long track of the cellular membrane, by pinching up the skin into a fold, and piercing this close to the body with the needle, which is then to be carried straight through. On drawing the tape out of the eye, it must be tied in a large knot at each end, which will prevent its slipping out. In three or four days, a profuse discharge will come on, and it must ke kept up, if necessary, by repeated applications of blister cerate, or digestive ointment, as may be necessary. The ends should be sponged occasionally, to remove the accumulated matter.

A SMALLER CURVED NEEDLE, about five or six inches long (see lower figure, 22) is used for introducing a seton into the frog, or beneath the eye. For the former operation, a twitch is first applied, and the foot is then buckled up to the arm, as described at page 167. The needle then, armed with the tape, greased with blister cerate, and a little oil to lubricate the surface, is thrust in at the heel and out at the cleft of the frog, taking care not to go deep enough to wound the tendon as it passes over the navicular bone. The needle is then forcibly drawn through, and the tape knotted, as already described. The openings must be kept clean by sponging daily; and in three or four weeks the tape will have nearly worked its way out, when it may be withdrawn.

ROWELS are now seldom employed, being very unmanageable plans for causing counter-irritation. An incision, about an inch long, is made in the skin, selecting a part where it is loosely attached, and into this a blunt instrument, called a "cornet," is pushed, and worked about in all directions, until the skin is separated from the subjacent parts for a circle with a diameter of from two to three inches. Into this a piece of thick leather of that diameter, with a hole in the middle, is inserted, previously having smeared it with blister cerate; and the part is then left to nature. In a few days, a discharge of matter comes on, which must be washed off occasionally; and in the course of time, the leather, if allowed, would find its way out by ulceration. Before, however, this takes place, it is generally removed.

BLISTERING.

WHEN IT IS DECIDED TO BLISTER any part, the hair should be cut off as closely as possible; the ointment is then rubbed in with the hand for ten minutes, leaving a good quantity smeared on the surface. If the legs are to be blistered, the heels should be protected by lard. Considerable itching is caused after the first two or three days, and many horses, if allowed, gnaw the part to such an extent as to cause a serious blemish. It is therefore necessary to keep the head away, which is done by putting a "cradle" on the neck. The irritation of loose straw is very aggravating, and the stall or box should either be bedded with tan, or sawdust, or with used litter, so damp as to lie smoothly. It is generally the practice to put the blistered horse on a bare floor; but he will often do great harm to his legs and feet (which are of course unsound, or they would not be treated in this way), by constantly stamping from the pain occasioned while the blister is beginning to rise. When the legs are stiff and sore from the swelling, he stands still enough, but at first there is nothing of this kind to keep him quiet. James's blister, which is very mild, and useful for trifling diseases of the legs, or for bringing on the hair after "broken knee," can generally be used without a cradle; but even with it, horses will sometimes gnaw themselves, and it is better not to run any risk. At the end of a week, some neat's-foot oil should be applied every morning, with a feather or soft brush, to keep the scabs as supple as possible. The various formulas for blisters will be given in the list of materia medica.

CASTRATION.

FOR REMOVING THE TESTICLES several methods of operation have been proposed; but hitherto none has been tried which is so successful as the old plan, in which the division of the cord is performed by a heated iron with a sharp edge. In human surgery the spermatic artery is tied, and all danger of hemorrhage is over, because the small amount of bleeding which takes place from the artery of the cord is of no consequence, as it cannot enter the cavity of the peritoneum. In the horse, on the other hand, the inguinal canal communicates with that cavity, and if the ligature is used, there is a double danger of inflammation—first, from effused blood, and secondly, from the irritation of the ends of the ligature. This plan, therefore, is now generally abandoned, though some few practitioners still adhere to it, and the choice rests between two methods of removal by cautery, namely, the actual and potential,—the former giving more pain at the moment when the heated iron is applied, but the latter being really far more severe, as the caustic is a long time in effecting a complete death of the nerve and other sensitive parts. Torsion of the vessels has been also tried, but it is often followed by hæmorrhage, and, moreover, the pain which is caused during the twisting of the artery is apparently quite as great as is given by the heated iron. We are all inclined to fancy that fire occasions more agony than it really does, but those who have in their own persons been unfortunately able to compare the effects of the two kinds of cautery, have uniformly admitted that the actual is less severe than the potential, if the two are used so as to produce the same amount of cauterization.

THE BEST PERIOD FOR PERFORMING THE OPERATION on the foal is just before weaning, provided the weather is mild. If, however, his neck is very light. and the withers low, its postponement till the following spring will give a better chance for the development of these parts. The cold of winter and heat of summer are both prejudicial, and the months of April, May, September, or October should always be selected.

NO PREPARATION IS REQUIRED in the "sucker," but after weaning the system always requires cooling by a dose of physic and light food before castration can safely be performed. Horses which have been in training, or other kind of work attended with high feeding, require at least three weeks' or a month's rest and lowering, by removing corn, mashing, &c., together with a couple of doses of physic, before they are fit to be castrated.

FOR THE ORDINARY METHOD OF OPERATING, a pair of clams should be provided, lined at the surfaces where the compression is made, with thick layers of vulcanized india-rubber. This ma terial gives a very firm hold without bruising the cord, and causing thereby inflammation. A large scalpel and a couple of irons will complete the list of instruments, over and above the apparatus necessary for casting the horse (see Casting, page 433). The horse being properly secured according to the directions there given, and a twitch being put on the lip in case he should struggle much, the

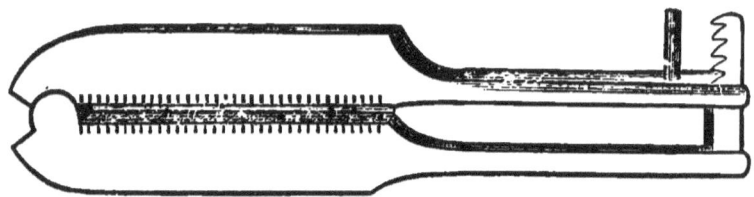

FIG. 23.—CLAMS LINED WITH VULCANIZED INDIA-RUBBER.

operator, kneeling on the left side, grasps the testicle so as to make the skin of the scrotum covering it quite tense. A longitudinal incision, about three inches long, is then made down to the testicle, which, if care has been taken that there is no rupture, may be rapidly done—a wound of its surface not being of the slightest consequence, and giving far less pain than the slow niggling dissection of its coverings, which is sometimes practised to avoid it. The testicle can now be cleared of its coverings, and the hand laying hold of it gently, the operator raises it from its bed, and slips the clams on each side the cord, at once making the proper pressure with them, which should be sufficient to prevent all risk of the part enclosed slipping from between its jaws. Great care should be taken that the whole of the testicle, including the epididimis, is external to the clams; and as soon as this is satisfactorily ascertained, the cord may be divided with the ordinary firing-iron at a red heat. To make sure that no hæmorrhage shall occur, some operators sear the artery separately with a pointed iron; but if the division is slowly made with the heated iron, and avoiding any drag upon the cord, no such accident will be at all likely to follow, though very rarely it will happen in spite of every care. The clams may now be removed, and the other testicle treated in the same way; after which the hobbles are cautiously removed, and the patient is placed in a roomy loose box, where he can take sufficient exercise to insure the gravitation of the discharge, but no more.

THE FRENCH PLAN, by means of caustic, requires two pieces of wood, each about six inches long and an inch square, with a notch or neck at each end, to hold the twine by which they are tied together, and a groove in the two opposite surfaces, to hold the caustic. This is composed of one part of corrosive sublimate and four of flour, made into a paste with water, and it is introduced while moist into the grooves, which it should completely fill. The horse is then secured as before, the cord is exposed, the pieces of wood are adjusted on each side, and firmly held together with pincers by an assistant, while the operator binds their ends together with waxed string. The testicle may now be removed with the knife, if the string has been tied sufficiently tight; but unless the operator has had some experience, it is safer to let it remain on till it comes away by the ulceration of the cord. This is *the uncovered operation*, the *covered one* being performed with the same instruments, as follows. The scrotum is grasped, and opened, taking care to avoid wounding the tunica vaginalis reflexa, or *outer* serous investment, but cutting down to it through the skin, dartos muscle, and cellular membrane. These are to be carefully dissected back, until the cord can be isolated without wounding its serous investment (tunica vaginalis), which is so thin that it is easy to ascertain with certainty the nature of its contents by examination with the fingers. If there is no hernia, the caustic can at once be applied to its outside in the same way as before; and if there is, it must be pushed back into the cavity of the abdomen, by a little careful manipulation.

SOME VETERINARY SURGEONS operate in a similar way to one or other of the two last described plans, with the omission of the caustic, which they maintain is wholly unnecessary, for there *must* be sufficient pressure to cause a sloughing of the cord There is certainly some truth in this argument, but if the pressure has not been sufficient to cause the sloughs, the caustic will assure that essential process, and thus it renders the operation safer, though it somewhat increases the subsequent local inflammation. The plan without caustic is almost precisely the same, as far as safety is concerned, as that formerly adopted by country farriers, called "twitching," in which two pieces of wood were applied on each side the base of the scrotum, and tied firmly at each end. The pain, however, occasioned by the pressure on so large a surface of skin is intense, and the operation is on that account indefensible, besides which it is not nearly so successful as either the ordinary English or French operations.

[The accompanying engraving represents the Ecraseur introduced to his students by the Editor some eight years since. Its use obviates the necessity

FIG. 24.

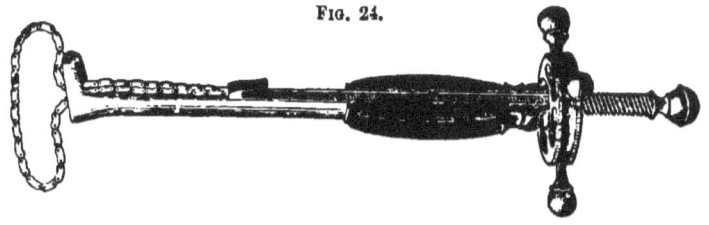

of any previous preparation, so that a horse of twenty years is operated upon with as much safety as a colt of as many months; the pain caused by it lasts but a few minutes, while under the old system of clams and red hot irons, it often continued from twelve to twenty-four hours. It is now very extensively, and in some parts of the country exclusively, used, giving perfect satisfaction alike to the operator and owner of the horse.—EDITOR.]

DOCKING AND NICKING.

THESE OPERATIONS ON THE TAIL are subject to the fashion of the day, the former being used for the purpose of shortening its length, which is inconvenient to the rider or driver in dirty weather, and the latter for altering its carriage, when this is too low for the taste of the owner. Nicking, is, however, very seldom practised in the present day, and never to the extent which was the fashion fifty years ago.

DOCKING is very rapidly performed by the aid of the docking-knife, which is made on the principle of the guillotine. As the tail is removed at one sudden and forcible chop, the horse need not be confined in any way beyond fixing up his fore leg, unless he

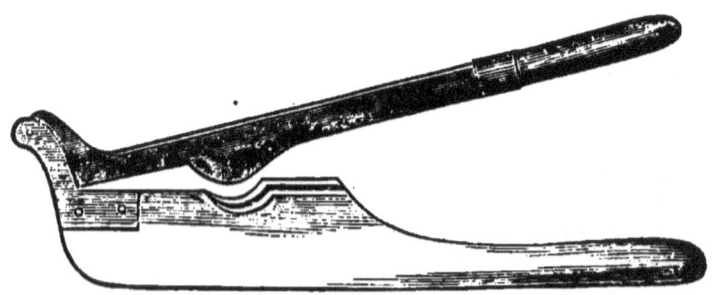

Fig. 25—DOCKING-KNIFE.

is a very violent animal, when he must be placed in the break (see page 435). The exact length of the dock to be left being fixed upon, the hair is cut off close below, and the remainder tied back to the root of the tail. The situation of the joint, which may be ascertained from its greater prominence, is then marked, by carefully removing the hair with the scissors, and then laying it in the rounded groove of the wooden frame in which the knife plays, so that the edge of the latter shall exactly correspond with the part to be cut, the handles are suddenly and forcibly brought together, and the end is removed at one blow. A pointed iron should have been previously heated, and then raising the tail to a level with the back, the arteries are first seared, which a very slight touch will effect, and then the point is pushed into the sheath of the tendons lying at the top of the stump, so as to cause them to adhere in that position, and effect a handsome carriage of the tail.

Lastly, a little resin is melted over the end of the stump with the iron now pretty nearly cooled, and the operation is concluded by untying the hair.

NICKING was formerly carried to such an extent that the poor horse *could not* lower his tail, but was always obliged to carry it over his back. Several deep cross-cuts were made in the underside after being docked, and then a cord was fastened to the hair, and being carried over a pulley attached to the ceiling, the tail was kept drawn up over the back by a weight at its end. The horse could lie down by raising the weight, but by no possible means could he lower his tail, and in course of time the wounds healed by granulation filling up their spaces, and the nicking was completed. When a horse now carries his dock too low, a subcutaneous incision of the flexor tendons is made, which is generally sufficient, but if not the pulley is adopted for a few days. Sometimes the tail is carried on one side, and then a similar operation by subcutaneous division of the tendons on the side to which the tail is carried will have the desired effect, always taking care in each case to keep the knife clear of a joint.

UNNERVING.

THE NERVES distributed to the foot are sometimes divided for navicular disease, as they lie on each side of the bone above the fetlock joint. No one, however, should attempt this operation without having previously seen it performed, as it requires considerable dexterity for its due execution. I have described such operations as may be wanted in the parts of the country where a veterinary surgeon cannot always be reached, but unnerving is but seldom required, and I shall therefore omit any detailed account of it.

REDUCTION OF HERNIA.

HERNIA is sometimes strangulated; that is to say, the protruding portion of bowel is confined in its situation by such pressure on its neck as to cause danger of mortification. Under such circumstances, if it is found to be impossible to return the bowel by careful manipulation, an operation must be performed. This consists in carefully dissecting through the coverings of the bowel, and when it is exposed, a long and narrow guarded knife (*Bistouri caché*) is passed by the side of the intestine through the opening into the abdomen, and then making the blade prominent it is withdrawn, and the fibres causing the pressure are divided. This usually allows of the bowel being passed back again into the abdomen, when the operation is completed by bringing the parts together with one or two stitches.

WHEN HERNIA OCCURS IN THE COLT either at the navel or scrotum, it is often desired to effect a cure by returning the bowel and causing the opening to close by adhesive inflammation. If the colt is uncut, the performance of the covered operation on the French plan (see page 443) will generally succeed, great care being of course necessary to return the intestine before the clams are applied. In umbilical hernia a similar plan has been tried, but the adhesion is too superficial to be of much use; and the only successful method is the passage of one or two skewers through the opposite edges of the opening, and then winding some waxed twine round them, with a moderate degree of force. This should not be sufficient to cause mortification, or the opening will only be increased in size, and the bowel will protrude without any covering of skin; but it should be just sufficient to cause adhesive inflammation; experience in such matters alone enabling the operator to hit upon the right amount.

IN ALL OPERATIONS FOR HERNIA chloroform is of great assistance, as it prevents the risk of a protrusion of the bowel while the knife is being used, which will otherwise sometimes happen during the struggles of the horse.

THE ADMINISTRATION OF PHYSIC.

MEDICINE may be given to the horse either in the solid form as a ball, or liquid, and then called a drench, or as a dry powder, when in small compass and with little taste, mixed with the corn or mash. Sometimes also a small quantity of a tasteless liquid, such as liquor arsenicalis, may be given with the food.

IN GIVING A BALL, place a halter on the head with a knot, so that the jaws may be widely opened. Then turn the horse round in the stall and back him up to the manger, lay hold of the tongue and draw it out of the mouth, grasp it with the left hand, which must also hold the halter-cord so short that the strain is partly taken off the tongue, and then holding the ball in the right hand with the fingers enclosing it like a cone, and, the arm bare, it should be rapidly carried to the back of the mouth and deposited there, holding the head up till it is seen to pass down the gullet. Cautious grooms use a balling iron, which gags the mouth and protects the arm, but a handy man will have less difficulty in introducing his hand than in inserting the gag, unless the horse is a determined biter, when it may be absolutely necessary. In that case the gag is insinuated with as much ease as a bit in a flat direction, and the handle being suddenly depressed, the mouth gapes and the teeth cannot be brought together. Then holding its handle together with the halter in the left hand, the right easily introduces the ball into the pharynx.

IN GIVING A DRENCH, two persons are necessary, the operator standing at the right shoulder, while the assistant is ready to steady the head and aid him on the left. The operator raises the head with his left hand beneath the jaw, and with his right he forces the lip of the horn into the side of the mouth, and, raising the small end, pours the contents in. If the horse is violent, a twitch must be placed on the nose, and held by the assistant. The horn must not be passed far into the mouth, or any unnecessary violence used, for fear of producing a cough; in which case, the hand must be instantly lowered. A neglect of this precaution will probably cause some of the liquid to pass into the larynx.

CLYSTERS

ARE MOST VALUABLE AGENTS, if properly administered. The best syringe for the purpose is Read's, by which any quantity may be thrown up; and in colic, some gallons of warm water are sometimes required to produce the desired effect. For an ordinary opening clyster, a handful or two of common salt may be dissolved in five or six quarts of warm water.

BACK-RAKING

Is EFFECTED by passing the greased hand and arm into the rectum, and withdrawing any hardened fæces which may have accumulated there. When the quantity of these is great, the hand must be passed several times, until it cannot reach any more. Whenever physic is given to an unprepared horse, as is sometimes necessary in severe disease, this precaution should never be neglected. Mr. Gamgee, of Edinburgh, is of opinion that this operation is more safely and easily performed by the aid of instruments, supporting his views by the assertion that the introduction of the hand gives unnecessary pain. On one or two occasions I have certainly seen a shoulder of mutton at the end of a human arm, and this would perhaps cause some little difficulty; but no hand of average size is nearly so large as the mass of dung usually passed; and those who are *not above doing a dirty job when duty requires it*, well know by experience that the hand and arm may be passed to the shoulder without giving any pain whatsoever. Instruments are useful when they cannot be dispensed with, but they are always liable to cause laceration.

CHAPTER XXVIII.

THE PRINCIPAL MEDICINES, AND THE DOSES IN WHICH THEY CAN SAFELY BE ADMINISTERED:—

Alteratives—Anodynes—Antiseptics—Anti-Zumins—Aperients—Astringents—Blisters—Caustics, or Cauteries—Clysters—Detergents—Diuretics—Embrocations, or Liniments—Febrifuges—Injections—Lotions, or Washes—Physic Balls and Drenches—Stimulants—Stomachics—Tonics—Traumatics—Vermifuges, or Worm Medicines.

(The Formulæ enclosed in [ ] are by the American Editor.)

ALTERATIVES.

THIS TERM IS NOT VERY SCIENTIFIC, but it is in very general use, and easily explains its own meaning, though the *modus operandi* of the drugs employed to carry it out is not so clear. The object is to replace unhealthy action by a healthy one, without resorting to any of the distinctly-defined remedies, such as tonics, stomachics, &c. As a general rule, this class of remedies produce their effect by acting slowly but steadily on the depuratory organs, as the liver, kidneys, and skin. The following may be found useful:—

1. IN DISORDERED STATES OF THE SKIN—
    - Emetic Tartar . . . . . 5 ounces.
    - Powdered Ginger . . . . 3 ounces.
    - Opium . . . . . . 1 ounce.

    Syrup enough to form 16 balls: one to be given every night.

2. SIMPLY COOLING—
    - Barbadoes Aloes . . . . 1 ounce.
    - Castile Soap . . . . . 1½ ounce.
    - Ginger . . . . . . ½ ounce.

    Syrup enough to form 6 balls: one to be given every morning. Or,

3.
    - Barbadoes Aloes . . . . 1½ drachm.
    - Emetic Tartar . . . . . 2 drachms.
    - Castile Soap . . . . . 2 drachms. Mix.

4. ALTERATIVE BALL FOR GENERAL USE—
    - Black Sulphuret of Antimony . 2 to 4 drachms.
    - Sulphur . . . . . 2 drachms.
    - Nitre . . . . . . 2 drachms.

    Linseed meal and water enough to form a ball.

APERIENTS—ANODYNES. 449

5. For Generally Defective Secretions—
   Flowers of Sulphur . . . . 6 ounces.
   Emetic Tartar . . . . . 5 to 8 drachms.
   Corrosive Sublimate . . . . 10 grains.
Linseed meal mixed with hot water, enough to form 6 balls, one of which may be given two or three times a week.

6. In Debility of Stomach—
   Calomel . . . . . . 1 scruple.
   Aloes . . . . . . 1 drachm.
   Cascarilla Bark,}
   Gentian Root, of each in powder . 1 drachm.
   Ginger,
   Castile Soap . . . . . 3 drachms.
Syrup enough to make a ball, which may be given twice a week, or every other night.

ANODYNES,

Sometimes called Narcotics, when taken into the stomach, pass at once into the blood, and there act in a special manner on the nervous centres. At first they exalt the nervous force; but they soon depress it, the second stage coming on the sooner according to the increase of the dose. They are given either to soothe the general nervous system, or to stop diarrhœa; or sometimes to relieve spasm, as in colic or tetanus. Opium is the chief anodyne used in veterinary medicine, and it may be employed in very large doses:—

1. Anodyne Drench for Colic—
   Linseed Oil . . . . . 1 pint.
   Oil of Turpentine . . . . 1 to 2 ounces.
   Laudanum . . . . . 1 to 2 ounces.
Mix, and give every hour till relief is afforded.

2. Anodyne Ball for Colic (only useful in mild cases)—
   Powdered Opium . . . . $\frac{1}{2}$ to 2 drachms.
   Castile Soap . . . . . 2 drachms.
   Camphor . . . . . . 2 drachms.
   Ginger . . . . . . $1\frac{1}{2}$ drachm.
Make into a ball with Liquorice powder and Treacle, and give every hour while the pain lasts. It should be kept in a bottle or bladder.

3. Anodyne Ball (ordinary)—
   Opium . . . . . . $\frac{1}{2}$ to 1 drachm.
   Castile Soap . . . . . 2 to 4 drachms.
   Ginger . . . . . . 1 to 2 drachms.
   Powdered Aniseed . . . . $\frac{1}{2}$ to 1 ounce.
   Oil of Caraway Seeds . . . $\frac{1}{2}$ drachm.
Syrup enough to form a ball, to be dissolved in half a pint of warm ale, and given as a drench.

4. Anodyne Drench in Superpurgation, or Ordinary Diarrhœa.
   Gum Arabic . . . . . 2 ounces.
   Boiling Water . . . . . 1 pint.

2 F

Dissolve, and then add—
  Oil of Peppermint . . . . 25 drops.
  Laudanum . . . . . ½ to 1 ounce.
Mix, and give night and morning, if necessary.

5. In Chronic Diarrhœa—
  Powdered Chalk and Gum Arabic, each 1 ounce.
  Laudanum . . . . . ½ ounce.
  Peppermint Water . . . . 10 ounces.
Mix, and give night and morning.

6. In Colic—
  Spirit of Turpentine . . . 3½ ounces.
  Laudanum . . . . . 1½ ounce.
  Barbadoes Aloes . . . . 1 ounce.
Powder the Aloes, and dissolve in warm water; then add the other ingredients, and give as a drench.

7. Clyster in Colic—
  Spirit of Turpentine . . . 6 ounces.
  Aloes . . . . . 2 drachms.
Dissolve in 3 quarts of warm water, and stir the turpentine well into it.

8. Antispasmodic Drench—
  Gin . . . . . . 4 to 6 ounces.
  Tincture of Capsicum . . . 2 drachms.
  Laudanum . . . . . 3 drachms.
  Warm Water . . . . . 1½ pint.
Mix, and give as a drench, *when there is no inflammation*.

[ANTISEPTICS.

Antiseptics are those medicines which prevent and destroy putrescence in sores and ulcers.

1. Carbolic Acid* . . . . 1 drachm.
  Oil, Glycerine, or Water . . . 2 ounces.

---

* This substance, a product of gas tar, was formerly known to the scientific world as Phenile or Phenic Acid, but is now generally known as Carbolic Acid. Its smell resembles that of Creosote, which is Carbolic Acid and a fixed oil, and is very offensive to most persons. Its form is that of an acid solution though sometimes sold in crystals. Its great importance is due to its property of coagulating the albumen of the animal tissue, and hence its value in sores, wounds, and ulcers. It may be applied with safety to all parts of the body or legs, and is invaluable for destroying lice, wood ticks, and all forms of parasite life, and by merely washing or moistening those parts of the legs and body of horses, cattle, and sheep, and chosen by the bot, horse or other flies to deposit their eggs, their hatching or even deposit may be prevented.

As a disinfectant in stables and buildings affected with fevers and all kinds of distempers, it was found extremely serviceable in England, in checking the ravages of the Rinderpest by washing the floors and stalls; and adding a tablespoonful of the solution of the acid to a bucketful of water, in whitewashing the walls and ceilings.—Editor.

2.	Chloride of Zinc	.	.	.	. 10 grains.
	Water	.	.	.	. 2 ounces.
3.	Sulphate of Soda	.	.	.	. 1 ounce.
	Water	.	.	.	. 1 pint.
4.	Charcoal or Brewers' Yeast.]				

[ANTI-ZUMINS.

A CLASS OF MEDICINES which are now deemed indispensable in meeting certain pathological conditions—fermentation of the blood, as exhibited in glanders, farcy, &c.

1.	Sulphate of Soda	.	.	.	. 3 drachms.
	Spanish Fly	.	.	.	. 5 grains.

To be given once daily.

2.	Carbolic Acid	.	.	.	. 20 grains or drops.
	Sulphate of Iron, in powder		.	.	. 2 drachms.
	Gentian Root, in powder	.	.	.	. 3 drachms.

Give one powder daily.

3. Inhalation of Sulphurous Acid Gas, by placing the animal in a house by himself, and generating the gas, by placing 1 ounce of Roll Sulphur on top of a brazier filled with burning coal, and allowing the horse to breathe the gas from twenty minutes to half an hour, two or three times in the week.]

APERIENTS.

(Physic Balls and Drenches.)

APERIENTS, or purges, are those medicines which quicken or increase the evacuations from the bowels, varying, however, a good deal in their mode of operation. Some act merely by exciting the muscular coat of the bowels to contract; others cause an immense watery discharge, which, as it were, washes out the bowels; whilst a third set combine the action of the two. The various purges also act upon different parts of the canal, some stimulating the small intestines, whilst others pass through them without affecting them, and only act upon the large bowels; and others, again, act upon the whole canal. There is a third point of difference in purges, depending upon their influencing the liver in addition, which mercurial purgatives certainly do, as well as rhubarb and some others, and which effect is partly due to their absorption into the circulation, so that they may be made to act, by injecting into the veins, as strongly as by actual swallowing, and their subsequent passage into the bowels. Purgatives are likewise classed, according to the *degree* of their effect, into laxatives acting mildly, and drastic purges, or cathartics, acting very severely.

1. **Ordinary Physic Balls—**
   - Barbadoes Aloes . . . . . 3 to 8 drachms.
   - Hard Soap . . . . . . 4 drachms.
   - Ginger . . . . 1 drachm.

   Dissolve in as small a quantity of boiling water as will suffice; then slowly evaporate to the proper consistence, by which means griping is avoided.

2. **A Warmer Physic Ball—**
   - Barbadoes Aloes . . . . . 3 to 8 drachms.
   - Carbonate of Soda . . . . ½ drachm.
   - Aromatic Powder . . . . 1 drachm.
   - Oil of Caraway . . . . . 12 drops.

   Dissolve as above, and then add the oil.

3. **Gently Laxative Ball—**
   - Barbadoes Aloes . . . . . 3 to 5 drachms.
   - Rhubarb Powder . . . . 1 to 2 drachms.
   - Ginger . . . . 2 drachms.
   - Oil of Caraway . . . . . 15 drops.

   Mix, and form into a ball, as in No. 1.

4. **Stomachic Laxative Balls, for Washy Horses—**
   - Barbadoes Aloes . . . . . 3 drachms.
   - Rhubarb . . . . 2 drachms.
   - Ginger . . . . 1 drachm.
   - Cascarilla Powder . . . . 1 drachm.
   - Oil of Caraway . . . . . 15 drops.
   - Carbonate of Soda . . . . 1½ drachm.

   Dissolve the Aloes as in No. 1, and then add the other ingredients.

5. **Purging Balls, with Calomel—**
   - Barbadoes Aloes . . . . . 3 to 6 drachms.
   - Calomel . . . . ½ to 1 drachm.
   - Rhubarb . . . . 1 to 2 drachms.
   - Ginger . . . . ½ to 1 drachm.
   - Castile Soap . . . . . . 2 drachms.

   Mix as in No. 1.

6. **Laxative Drench—**
   - Barbadoes Aloes . . . . . 3 to 4 drachms.
   - Canella Alba . . . . . . 1 to 2 drachms.
   - Salt of Tartar . . . . . 1 drachm.
   - Mint Water . . . . . . 8 ounces. Mix.

7. **Another Laxative Drench—**
   - Castor Oil . . . . . . 3 to 6 ounces.
   - Barbadoes Aloes . . . . . 3 to 5 drachms.
   - Carbonate of Soda . . . . 2 drachms.
   - Mint Water . . . . . . 8 ounces.

   Mix, by dissolving the Aloes in the Mint Water by the aid of heat, and then adding the other ingredients.

8. **A Mild Opening Drench—**
   - Castor Oil . . . . . . 4 ounces.
   - Epsom Salts . . . . . . 3 to 5 ounces.
   - Gruel . . . . 2 pints. Mix.

9. **A very Mild Laxative—**
   - Castor Oil . . . . . . 4 ounces.
   - Linseed Oil . . . . . . 4 ounces.
   - Warm Water or Gruel . . . 1 pint. Mix.

APERIENTS—ASTRINGENTS. 453

10. USED IN THE STAGGERS—
  Barbadoes Aloes . . . . 4 to 6 drachms
  Common Salt . . . . . 6 ounces.
  Flour of Mustard . . . . 1 ounce.
  Water . . . . . . 2 pints. Mix.
11. A GENTLY COOLING DRENCH IN SLIGHT ATTACKS OF COLD—
  Epsom Salts . . . . . 6 to 8 ounces.
  Whey . . . . . . 2 pints. Mix.
12. PURGATIVE CLYSTER—
  Common Salt . . . . . 4 to 8 ounces.
  Warm Water . . . . . 8 to 16 pints.

ASTRINGENTS.

(For Diarrhœa and Dysentery.)

ASTRINGENTS appear to produce contraction on all living animal tissues with which they come in contact, whether in the interior or on the exterior of the body; and whether immediately applied or by absorption into the circulation. But great doubt exists as to the exact mode in which they act; and, as in many other cases, we are obliged to content ourselves with their effects, and to prescribe them empirically. They are divided into astringents administered by the mouth, and those applied locally to external ulcerated or wounded surfaces.

1. FOR BLOODY URINE—
  Powdered Catechu . . . . ½ ounce.
  Alum . . . . . . ½ ounce.
  Cascarilla Bark in powder . . 1 to 2 drachms.
Liquorice Powder and Treacle enough to form a ball, to be given twice a day.
2. FOR DIABETES—
  Opium . . . . . . ½ drachm.
  Ginger powdered . . . . 2 drachms.
  Oak Bark powdered . . . . 1 ounce.
  Alum, as much as the tea will dissolve.
  Chamomile Tea . . . . 1 pint.
Mix for a drench.
3. EXTERNAL ASTRINGENT POWDERS FOR ULCERATED SURFACES—
  Powdered Alum . . . . 4 ounces.
  Armenian Bole . . . . 1 ounce.
4. White Vitriol . . . . . 4 ounces.
  Oxide of Zinc . . . . . 1 ounce. Mix.
5. ASTRINGENT LOTION—
  Goulard Extract . . . . 2 to 3 drachms.
  Water . . . . . . ½ pint.
6. Sulphate of Copper . . . 1 to 2 drachms.
  Water . . . . . . ½ pint. Mix.

7. ASTRINGENT OINTMENT FOR SORE HEELS—
  Acetate of Lead . . . . . 1 drachm.
  Lard . . . . 1 ounce. Mix.

8. ANOTHER FOR THE SAME—
  Nitrate of Silver powdered . . ½ drachm.
  Goulard Extract . . . . 1 drachm.
  Lard . . . . . . 1 ounce.
Mix, and use a very small portion every night.

BLISTERS.

BLISTERS are applications which inflame the skin, and produce a secretion of serum between the cutis and cuticle, by which the latter is raised in the form of small bladders; but in consequence of the presence of the hair, these are very imperfectly seen in the horse. They consist of two kinds—one, used for the sake of counter-irritation, by which the original disease is lessened, in consequence of the establishment of this irritation at a short distance from it; the other, commonly called "sweating" in veterinary surgery, by which a discharge is obtained from the vessels of the part itself, which are in that way relieved and unloaded. There is also a subsequent process of absorption in consequence of the peculiar stimulus applied.

1. MILD BLISTER OINTMENT (COUNTER-IRRITANT)—
  Hog's Lard . . . . . 4 ounces.
  Venice Turpentine . . . . 1 ounce.
  Powdered Cantharides . . . 6 drachms.
Mix, and spread.

2. STRONGER BLISTER OINTMENT (COUNTER-IRRITANT)—
  Spirit of Turpentine . . . . 1 ounce.
  Sulphuric Acid, by measure . . 2 drachms.
Mix carefully in an open place, and add—
  Hog's Lard . . . . . 4 ounces.
  Powdered Cantharides . . . 1 ounce.
Mix, and spread.

3. VERY STRONG BLISTER (COUNTER-IRRITANT)—
  Strong Mercurial Ointment . . 4 ounces.
  Oil of Origanum . . . . ½ ounce.
  Finely-powdered Euphorbium . . 3 drachms.
  Powdered Cantharides . . . ½ ounce.
Mix, and spread.

4. RAPIDLY ACTING BLISTER (COUNTER-IRRITANT)—
  Best Flour of Mustard . . . 8 ounces.
Made into a paste with water; then add—
  Oil of Turpentine . . . . 2 ounces.
  Strong Liquor of Ammonia . . 1 ounce.
This is to be well rubbed into the chest, belly, or back, in cases of acute inflammation.

5. SWEATING BLISTER—
 - Strong Mercurial Ointment . . 2 ounces.
 - Oil of Origanum . . . . 2 drachms.
 - Corrosive Sublimate . . . 2 drachms.
 - Cantharides powdered . . . 3 drachms.

Mix, and rub in with the hand.

6. STRONG SWEATING BLISTER, FOR SPLINTS, RING-BONES, SPAVINS, &c.—
 - Biniodide of Mercury . . . 1 to 1½ drachm.
 - Lard . . . . . . 1 ounce.

To be well rubbed into the legs, after cutting the hair short; and followed by the daily use of Arnica, in the shape of a wash, as follows, which is to be painted on with a brush:—
 - Tincture of Arnica . . . . 1 ounce.
 - Water . . . . . . 12 to 15 ounces.

Mix.

7. LIQUID SWEATING BLISTERS—
 - Cantharides . . . . . 1 ounce.
 - Spirit of Turpentine . . . 2 ounces.
 - Methylated Spirit of Wine . . 1 pint.

Mix, and digest for a fortnight; then strain.

8.
 - Powdered Cantharides . . . 1 ounce.
 - Commercial Pyroligneous Acid . 1 pint.

Mix, and digest for a fortnight; then strain.

CAUSTICS, OR CAUTERIES.

(To destroy Proud Flesh in Wounds.)

CAUSTICS are substances which burn away the living tissues of the body, by the decomposition of their elements. They are of two kinds, viz.: First, the actual cautery, consisting in the application of the burning iron, and called firing; and, secondly, the potential cautery, by means of the powers of mineral caustics, such as potassa fusa, lunar caustic, corrosive sublimate, &c.

FIRING is described in the chapter on Operations, at page 438.

The following are the ordinary chemical applications used as potential cauteries:—

1. FUSED POTASS, difficult to manage, because it runs about in all directions, and little used in veterinary medicine.
2. LUNAR CAUSTIC, or Nitrate of Silver, very valuable to the veterinary surgeon, and constantly used to apply to profuse granulations.
3. SULPHATE OF COPPER, almost equally useful, but not so strong as Lunar Caustic. It may be well rubbed into all high granulations, as in broken knees, and similar growths.
4. CORROSIVE SUBLIMATE in powder, which acts most energetically upon warty growths, but should be used with great care and discretion. It may safely be applied to small surfaces, but not without a regular practitioner to large ones. It should be washed off

after remaining on a few minutes. For the mode of applying it in castration, see page 442.

5. YELLOW ORPIMENT is not so strong as Corrosive Sublimate, and may be used with more freedom. It will generally remove warty growths, by picking off their heads and rubbing it in.

6. MURIATE OF ANTIMONY, called Butter of Antimony; a strong but rather unmanageable caustic, and used either by itself or mixed with more or less water.

7. CHLORIDE OF ZINC is a most powerful caustic. It may be used in old sinuses in solution—7 drachms in a pint of water.

MILDER CAUSTICS :—

8. Verdigris, either in powder or mixed with Lard as an ointment, in the proportion of 1 to 3.
9. Red Precipitate, ditto, ditto.
10. Burnt Alum, used dry.
11. Powdered White Sugar.

MILD LIQUID CAUSTICS :—

12. Solution of Nitrate of Silver 5 to 15 grains to the ounce of distilled water.
13. Solution of Blue Vitriol, of about double the above strength.
14. Chloride of Zinc, 1 to 3 grains to the ounce of water.

CLYSTERS, OR INJECTIONS.

CLYSTERS are intended either to relieve obstruction or spasm of the bowels, and are of great service when properly applied. They may be made of warm water or gruel, of which some quarts will be required in colic. They should be thrown up with the proper syringe, provided with valves and a flexible tube.

ANODYNE CLYSTER IN DIARRHŒA—
    Starch, made as for washing . . 1 quart.
    Powdered Opium . . . . 2 drachms.
The Opium is to be boiled in water, and added to the Starch.

[DETERGENTS

ARE THOSE AGENTS which possess the property of cleansing ulcers, wounds, and sores, inducing in them a healthy action.

1. Solution of the Sulphate of Zinc.
2. Sulphate of Copper . . . . 1 ounce.
  Water . . . . . . 1 pint.
3. Acid Nitrate of Mercury of the drug-shops.
4. Carbolic Acid . . . . . 1 drachm.
  Water . . . . . . 2 ounces.]

DIURETICS.

(To increase the Flow of Urine.)

DIURETICS are medicines which promote the secretion and discharge of urine, the effect being produced in a different manner by different medicines; some acting directly upon the kidneys by sympathy with the stomach, while others are taken up by the blood-vessels, and in their elimination from the blood cause an extra secretion of the urine. In either case their effect is to diminish the watery part of the blood, and thus promote the absorption of fluid effused into any of the cavities, or into the cellular membrane in the various forms of dropsy.

1. STIMULATING DIURETIC BALL—
    - Powdered Resin . . . . . 3 drachms.
    - Sal Prunelle . . . . . 3 drachms.
    - Castile Soap . . . . . 3 drachms.
    - Oil of Juniper . . . . . 1 drachm. Mix.

2. A MORE COOLING DIURETIC BALL—
    - Powdered Nitre . . . . $\frac{1}{2}$ to 1 ounce.
    - Camphor . . . . . 1 drachm.
    - Juniper berries . . . . . 1 drachm.
    - Soap . . . . . 3 drachms.

    Mix, adding linseed meal enough to form a ball.

3. DIURETIC POWDER FOR A MASH—
    - Nitre . . . . . $\frac{1}{2}$ to $\frac{3}{4}$ ounce.
    - Resin . . . . . $\frac{1}{2}$ to $\frac{3}{4}$ ounce. Mix.

4. ANOTHER MORE ACTIVE POWDER—
    - Nitre . . . . . 6 drachms.
    - Camphor . . . . . $1\frac{1}{2}$ drachm. Mix.

EMBROCATIONS, OR LINIMENTS.

EMBROCATIONS, OR LINIMENTS, are stimulating or sedative external applications, intended to reduce the pain and inflammation of internal parts when rubbed into the skin with the hand.

1. MUSTARD EMBROCATION—
    - Best Flour of Mustard . . . 6 ounces.
    - Liquor of Ammonia . . . . $1\frac{1}{2}$ ounce.
    - Oil of Turpentine . . . . $1\frac{1}{2}$ ounce.

    Mix with sufficient water to form a thin paste.

2. STIMULATING EMBROCATION—
    - Camphor . . . . . $\frac{1}{2}$ ounce.
    - Oil of Turpentine . . . . $1\frac{1}{2}$ ounce.
    - Spirit of Wine . . . . . $1\frac{1}{2}$ ounce. Mix.

3. SWEATING EMBROCATION FOR WINDGALLS, &c.—
    Strong Mercurial Ointment . . 2 ounces.
    Camphor . . . . . . ½ ounce.
    Oil of Rosemary . . . . 2 drachms.
    Oil of Turpentine . . . 1 ounce. Mix.
4. ANOTHER, BUT STRONGER—
    Strong Mercurial Ointment . . 2 ounces.
    Oil of Bay . . . . . 1 ounce.
    Oil of Origanum . . . . ½ ounce.
    Powdered Cantharides . . . ½ ounce. Mix.
5. A MOST ACTIVE SWEATING EMBROCATION—
    Biniodide of Mercury . . . ½ to 1 drachm.
    Powdered Arnica Leaves . . . 1 drachm.
    Soap Liniment . . . . . 2 ounces. Mix.

FEBRIFUGES

(Fever Balls and Powders),

GENERALLY CALLED fever medicines, are given to allay the arterial and nervous excitements which accompany febrile action. They do this partly by their agency on the heart and arteries through the nervous system, and partly by increasing the secretions of the skin and kidneys.

1. FEVER BALL—
    Nitre . . . . . . 4 drachms.
    Camphor . . . . . . 1½ drachm.
    Calomel and Opium, of each . 1 scruple.
    Linseed meal and water enough to form a ball. Or,
2. Emetic Tartar . . . . . 1½ to 2 drachms.
    Compound Powder of Tragacanth . 2 drachms.
    Linseed meal as above. Or,
3. Nitre . . . . . . 3 drachms.
    Camphor . . . . . . 2 drachms.
    Mix as above.
4. COOLING POWDER FOR MASH—
    Nitre . . . . . . 6 drs. to 1 ounce.
    May be given in a bran mash.
5. COOLING DRENCH—
    Nitre . . . . . . 1 ounce.
    Sweet Spirit of Nitre . . . 2 ounces.
    Tincture of Digitalis . . . 2 drachms.
    Whey . . . . . . 1 pint.
6. [Tincture of Aconite Root . . . 15 drops.
    Extract of Belladona . . . 2 drachms.
    To be repeated, if necessary, three times daily.]

INJECTIONS. (See CLYSTERS.)

LOTIONS, OR WASHES

Consist in liquids applied to the external parts, either to cool them or to produce a healthy action in the vessels.

1. Cooling Solution for External Inflammation—
    - Goulard Extract . . . . . 1 ounce.
    - Vinegar . . . . . . 2 ounces.
    - Spirits of Wine, or Gin . . . 3 ounces.
    - Water . . . . . . 1½ pint.

    Mix, and apply with a calico bandage.

2. Another, useful for Inflamed Legs, or for Galled Shoulders or Back—
    - Sal Ammoniac . . . . . 1 ounce.
    - Vinegar . . . . . . 4 ounces.
    - Spirits of Wine . . . . 2 ounces.
    - Tincture of Arnica . . . . 2 drachms.
    - Water . . . . . . ½ pint. Mix.

3. Lotion for Foul Ulcers—
    - Sulphate of Copper . . . . 1 ounce.
    - Nitric Acid . . . . . ½ ounce.
    - Water . . . . . . 8 to 12 ounces.

    Mix.

4. Lotion for the Eyes—
    - Sulphate of Zinc . . . . 20 to 25 grains.
    - Water . . . . . . 6 ounces. Mix.

5. Very Strong One, and only to be dropped in—
    - Nitrate of Silver . . . . 5 to 8 grains.
    - Distilled Water . . . . 1 ounce.

    Mix, and use with a camel-hair brush.

PHYSIC BALLS AND DRENCHES. (See Aperients.)

STIMULANTS.

By this term is understood those substances which excite the action of the whole nervous and vascular systems. Almost all medicines are stimulants to some part or other, as, for instance, aperients, which stimulate the lining of the bowels, but to the general system are lowering. On the other hand, stimulants, so called *par excellence*, excite and raise the action of the brain and heart.

- Old Ale . . . . . . 1 quart.
- Carbonate of Ammonia . . . ½ to 2 drachms.
- Tincture of Ginger . . . . 4 drachms.

Mix, and give as a drench.

STOMACHICS.

STOMACHICS are medicines given to improve the tone of the stomach when impaired by bad management or disease.

1. STOMACH BALL—
   - Powdered Gentian . . . . ½ ounce.
   - Powdered Ginger . . . . 1½ drachm.
   - Carbonate of Soda . . . . 1 drachm.

   Treacle to form a ball. Or,

2.
   - Cascarilla, powdered . . . 1 ounce.
   - Myrrh . . . . . . 1½ drachm.
   - Castile Soap . . . . . 1 drachm.

   Mix, with syrup or treacle, into a ball. Or,

3.
   - Powdered Colombo . . . . ½ to 1 ounce.
   - Powdered Cassia . . . . 1 drachm.
   - Powdered Rhubarb . . . . 2 drachms.

   Mix as in No. 2.

TONICS

AUGMENT the vigor of the whole body permanently, while stimulants only act for a short time. They are chiefly useful after low fever.

1. TONIC BALL—
   - Sulphate of Iron . . . . ½ ounce.
   - Extract of Camomile . . . 1 ounce.

   Mix, and form into a ball. Or,

2.
   - Arsenic . . . . . . 10 grains.
   - Ginger . . . . . . 1 drachm.
   - Powdered Aniseed . . . . 1 ounce.
   - Compound Powder of Tragacanth . 2 drachms.

   Syrup enough to form a ball. It is a very powerful tonic.

[TRAUMATICS

ARE THOSE MEDICINES which excite the healing process in wounds, ulcers, or sores.

1.
   - Carbolic Acid . . . . . 1 drachm.
   - Water . . . . . . 2 ounces.

2. Tincture Aloes and Myrrh.

3.
   - Chloride of Zinc . . . . 5 grains.
   - Water . . . . . ¼ ounce.

4. Yeast and Charcoal.]

VERMIFUGES, OR WORM MEDICINES.

Their action is partly by producing a disagreeable or fatal impression on the worm itself, and partly by irritating the mucous lining of the bowels, and thus causing them to expel their contents. Failing the remedy recommended at page 368, the following may be useful:—

1. Worm Ball (recommended by Mr. Gamgee)—
  Asafœtida . . . . . 2 drachms.
  Calomel . . . . . . 1½ drachm.
  Powdered Savin . . . . 1½ drachm.
  Oil of Male Fern . . . . 30 drops.
  Treacle enough to make a ball, which should be given at night, and followed by a purge next morning.
2. Mild Drench for Worms—
  Linseed Oil . . . . . 1 pint.
  Spirit of Turpentine . . . . 2 drachms.
  Mix, and give every morning.
3.   [Tincture Nux Vomica . . . 15 drops.
  Give three times daily for two or three days.]

CHAPTER XXIX.

LIST OF IMPORTED HORSES.

In order to show how largely the Americans are indebted to English blood, I here insert the following list of horses imported by them from England, with the date of foaling of each, for which I am indebted to Mr. Herbert:—*

  Abjer, 1817, by Old Truffle—Briseis by Beninborough.
  Actæon, 1837, by Comus or Blacklock—Panthea.
  Admiral, 1799, by Florizel—Spectator mare.
  Admiral Nelson, 1795, by John Bull—Olivia.
  Ainderby, 1832, by Velociped—Kate.
  Alderman, 1778, by Pot8os—Lady Bolingbroke.
  Alexander, by Alexander, son of Eclipse; dam's pedigree unknown.
  Alexander, 1791, by Champion—Countess.
  All-Fours, 1772, by All-Fours—Blank mare.
  Ambassador, by Emilius—Trapes by Tramp.
  Americus, 1755, by Babraham—Creeping Molly.
  Amurath, 1832, by Langar—Armida.
  Apparition, 1827, by Spectre—Young Cranberry.
  Archduke, 1796, by Sir Peter Teazle—Horatia, by Eclipse.
  Archer, 1760, by Faggergill—Eclipse mare.
  Archibald, 1801, by Walnut—Bay Javelin.
  Arrakooker, 1789, by Drone—Camilla.

---

* From his last and crowning work, "The Horse and Horsemanship of the United States and British Provinces of North America," by kind permission of the publishers, Messrs. W. A. Townsend & Adams.—Editor.

Autocrat, 1822, by Grand Duke—Olivetta.
Bachelor, 1753, by Blaze—Smiling Tom mare.
Barefoot, 1820, by Tramp—Rosamond.
Baronet, 1782, by Vertumnus—Penultima.
Bay Richmond, 1769, by Feather—Matron.
Bedford, 1792, by Dungannon—Fairy.
Belshazzar, 1830, by Blacklock—Manuella.
Bergamot, 1788, Highflyer—Orange Girl.
Berner's Comus, 1827, by Comus—Rotterdam.
Black Prince, 1760, by Babraham—Riot.
Blossom, 1795, by Bordeaux—Highflyer mare.
Boaster, 1795, by Dungannon—Justice mare.
Bolton, 1752, by Shark—Partner mare.
Brilliant, 1691, by Phenomenon—Faith.
Brian O'Lynn, 1756, by Aston—Le Sang mare.
Brutus, 1748, by Regulus—Miss Layton.
Buffcoat, 1742, by Godolphin Arab—Silverlocks.
Buzzard, 1787, by Woodpecker—Misfortune.
Camel, 1822, by Whalebone—Selim mare.
Cannon, 1789, by Dungannon—Miss Spindleshanks.
Cardinal Puff, 1803, by Cardinal—Luna.
Celer, 1774, by Old Janus—Brandon.
Centinel, 1758, by Blank—Naylor, by Cade.
Cetus, 1827, by Whalebone—Lamia.
Chance, 1787, by Lurcher—Recovery.
Chariot, 1789, by Highflyer—Potosi, by Eclipse.
Chateau Margaux, 1822, by Whalebone—Wasp.
Citizen, 1785, by Pacolet—Princess.
Claret, 1850, by Chateau Margaux—Partisan mare.
Clifden, 1797, by Alfred—Florizel mare.
Clifton, 1797, by Abbé Thullè—Eustatia, by Highflyer.
Clockfast, 1774, by Gimcrack—Miss Ingram.
Clown, 1785, by Bordeaux—Eclipse mare.
Cœur de Lion, 1789, by Highflyer—Dido.
Commodore, 1820, by Caleb Quot'em—Mary Brown.
Consol, 1828, by Lottery—Cerberus mare.
Consternation, 1841, by Confederate—Curiosity.
Contract, 1823, by Catton—Helen.
Cormorant, 1787, by Woodpecker—Nettletop.
Coronet, 1828, by Catton—Paynator mare.
Crab, 1736, by Crab—Councillor mare.
Crawler, 1792, by Highflyer—Harriet.
Creeper, 1786, by Tandem—Crawler's dam.
Cub, 1739, by Old Fox—Warlock Galloway.
Cynthius, 1799, by Acacia—Yarico.
Dancingmaster, 1787, by Woodpecker—Madcap.
Dare Devil, 1787, by Magnet—Hebe.
David, 1756, by Gower Stallion—Fox Cub mare.
De Bash, 1792, by King Fergus—Highflyer mare.
Denizen, 1836, by Actæon—Design.
Derby, 1831, by Peter Lely—Urganda.
Diomed, 1777, by Florizel—Spectator mare.
Dion, 1795, by Spadille—Faith.
Doncaster, 1834, by Longwaist—Muley mare.
Don John, 1835, by Tramp or Waverley—Sharpset's dam.
Don Quixote, 1784, by Eclipse—Grecian Princess.

LIST OF IMPORTED HORSES. 403

Dormouse, 1753, by Dormouse—Diana, by Whitefoot.
Dragon, 1787, by Woodpecker—Juno.
Driver, 1784, by Driver—Dorimont mare.
Drone, 1778, by Herod—Lily.
Druid, 1790, by Pot8os—Maid of the Oaks.
Dungannon, 1793, by Dungannon—Miss Spindleshanks.
Eagle, 1796, by Volunteer—Highflyer mare.
Eastham, 1818, by Sir Oliver—Cowslip.
Eclipse, 1778, by Eclipse—Phœbe.
Emancipation, 1827, by Whisker—Ardrossan mare.
Emilius Colt, 1836, by Bourbon—Fleur de Lis.
Emu, 1832, by Picton—Cuirass.
Englishman, 1812, by Eagle—Pot8os mare.
Envoy, 1827, by Comus—Aline.
Escape, 1798, by Precipitate—Woodpecker mare.
Espersykes, 1837, by Belshazzar—Capsicum mare.
Eugenius, 1770, by Chrysolite—Mixbury.
Expedition, 1795, by Pegasus—Active.
Express, 1785, by Postmaster—Syphon mare,
Exton, 1785, by Highflyer—Io.
Fairfax Roan, 1764, by Adolphus—Tartar mare.
Fearnought, 1755, by Regulus—Silvertail.
Fallower, 1761, by Blank—Partner mare.
Fellow, 1755, by Cade—Goliah mare.
Felt, 1826, Langar—Steam.
Figaro, 1731, by Figaro—Catton mare.
Figure, 1747, by Standard—Beaufort Arabian mare.
Firebrand, 1802, by Braggart—Fanny.
Firetail, 1795, by Phenomenon—Columbine.
Flatterer, 1830, by Muley—Clare.
Flexible, 1822, by Whalebone—Themis.
Flimnap, 1765, by South—Cygnet mare.
Florizel, by Florizel—Alfred mare.
Fop, 1832, by Stumps—Fitzjames mare.
Frederick, 1810, by Selim—Englishman's dam.
Friar, 1759, by South—Sister to Lowther Babraham, by Babraham.
Fylde, 1824, by Antonio—Fadladinada.
Gabriel, 1790, by Dorimont—Highflyer mare.
Genius, 1753, by Babraham—Aura.
Gift, 1768, by Cadormus—Old Cub mare.
Glencoe, 1831, by Sultan—Trampoline, by Tramp.
Gouty, 1796, by Sir Peter Teazle—Tandem mare.
Granby, 1759, by Blank—Old Crab mare.
Grecian, 1821 (Brother to Alasco), by Clavalino—Pioneer mare.
Grey Highlander, 1787, by Bordeaux—Teetotum mare.
Greyhound, 1796, by Sweetbriar—Miss Green, by Highflyer.
Hambleton, 1791, by Dungannon—Snap mare.
Hamilton, 1793, by son of Highflyer—Eclipse mare.
Hector, 1745, by Lath—Childers mare.
Hedgeford, 1826, by Filho-da-Puta—Miss Craigie.
Hark Forward, 1840 (brother to Harkaway), by Economist—Naboclish mare.
Hibiscus, 1834, by Sultan—Duchess of York.
Highflyer, 1782, by Highflyer—Angelica.
Honest John, 1794, by Sir Peter Teazle—Magnet.
Hugh Lupus, 1836, by Priam—Her Highness.

Humphrey Clinker, 1822, by Comus—Clinkerina.
Invalid, 1822, by Whisker—Hamilton mare.
Jack Andrews, 1794, by Joe Andrews—Highflyer mare.
Jack the Bachelor, 1753, by Blaze—Gallant mare.
James, 1746, by Old James—Little Hartley mare.
John Bull, 1799, by Fortitude—Xantippe.
John Bull, 1833, by Chateau Margaux—Woful mare.
Jolly Roger, 1741, by Roundhead—Partner mare.
Jonah, 1795, by Escape—Lavender mare.
Jordan, 1833, by Langar—Matilda.
Julius Cæsar, 1757, by Young Cade—Snip mare.
Juniper, 1782, by Babraham—Aura.
Junius, 1752, by Starling Crab—Monkey mare.
Justice, 1782, by Justice—Curiosity.
Justice, 1759, by Blank—Aura, by Stamford Turk.
King William, 1777, by Herod—Madcap.
King William, 1781, by Florizel—Milliner.
Knowsley, 1795, by Sir Peter Teazle—Cupella, by Herod.
Kouli Khan, 1772, by The Vernon Arab—Rosemary.
Lancelot, 1837, by Camel.
Langar colt, by Langar—Malvina.
Langford, 1853, by Starch—Peri.
Lapdog, 1823, by Whalebone—Canopus mare.
Lath, 1763, by Shepherd's Crab—Lath mare.
Leopard, by Liverpool—Sneaker, by Camel.
Leviathan, 1823, by Muley—Windle mare.
Lofty, 1753, by Godolphin Arab—Croft's Partner mare.
Ludford, 1832, by Wamba—Idalia.
Lurcher, 1832, by Greyleg—Harpalice, by Gohanna.
Luzborough, 1820, by Williamson's Luzborough—Dick Andrews mare.
Lycurgus, 1767, by Blank—Snip mare.
Magic, 1794, by Volunteer—Marcella.
Magnum Bonum, 1774, by Matchem—Snip mare.
Manfred, 1796, by Woodpecker—Mercury mare.
Mark Antony, 1767, by Spectator—Rachel.
Margrave, 1829, by Muley—Election.
Marmion, by Whiskey—Young Noisette.
Marplot, by Highflyer—Omar mare.
Master Robert, 1793, by Star—Young Marske mare.
Matchem, 1773, by Matchem—Lady.
Matchless, 1754, by Godolphin Arab—Soreheels.
Medley, 1776, by Gimcrack—Arminda, by Snap.
Mendoza, 1778, by Javelin—Pomona.
Merman, 1835, by Whalebone—Orville mare.
Merryfield, 1808, by Cockfighter—Star mare.
Messenger, 1778, by Mambrino—Turf mare.
Meux, 1816, by Chorus—Diana.
Mexican, 1775, by Snap—Matchem mare.
Moloch, by Muley Moloch—Sister to Puss.
Monarch, 1834, by Priam—Delpini mare.
Monkey, 1825, by Lonsdale Bay Arab—Curwen's Bay Barb mare.
Mordecai, 1833, by Lottery—Miss Thomasina.
Moro, by Starling—Brown Slipby.
Morven, 1836, by Rowton—Nanine, by Selim.
Moscow, 1746, by Cullen Arab—Croft's Starling mare.
Mousetrap, by Careless—Regulus mare.

LIST OF IMPORTED HORSES. 465

Mufti, 1783, by Fitz Herod—Infant mare.
Nicholas, 1833, by St. Nicholas—Moss Rose.
Non Plus, 1824, by Catton—Miss Garforth, by Walton.
North Star, 1768, by Matchem—Lass of the Mill.
Northumberland, by Old Bustard—Old Crab mare.
Onus, 1835, by Camel—The Etching, by Rubens.
Oroonoko, 1745. by Old Crab—Miss Slamerkin.
Oscar, 1795, by Saltram—Highflyer mare.
Othello, 1743, by Crab—Miss Slamerkin.
Pam, 1757, by Regulus—Cade mare.
Pantaloon, 1778, by Herod—Nutcracker.
Partner, 1760, by Partner—Camilla.
Partner, by Duke of Hamilton's Figure—Old Figure mare.
Passenger, 1836, by Langar—My Lady.
Passaic, 1836, by Reveller—Rachel.
Paul, 1807, by Saltram—Purity, by Matchem.
Phenomenon, 1780, by Herod—Phrenzy.
Pharaoh, 1753, by Moses—Godolphin mare.
Phil Brown, by Glaucus—Bustle.
Phœnix, 1798, by Old Dragon—Portia.
Pilgrim, 1762, by Samson—Regulus mare.
Play or Pay, 1791, by Ulysses—Herod mare.
Plenipo, 1837, by Plenipo—Polly Hopkins.
Portland, 1834, by Recovery—Caifacaratodaddera.
Post Captain, 1835, by The Colonel—Posthuma.
Precipitate, 1787, by Mercury—Herod mare.
Priam, 1827, by Emilius—Cressida.
Priam, 1834, by Priam—Soothsayer mare.
Prince, 1773, by Herod—Helen, by Blank.
Prince Ferdinand, by Herod—Matchem mare.
Punch, by Herod—Marske mare.
Regulus, 1747, by Regulus—Partner mare.
Restless, 1788, by Phenomenon—Duchess.
Reveller colt, 1836, by Reveller—Rachel.
Rutland, 1810, by Stamford—Worthy mare.
Riddlesworth, 1828, by Emilius—Filagree.
Roan colt, 1802, by Sir Peter Teazle—Mercury mare.
Robin Redbreast, 1796, by Sir Peter Teazle—Wren.
Roman, 1815, by Camillus—Leon Forte.
Rotherham, 1838, by Grey Conqueror—Camilla mare.
Rosalio, 1836, by Vanish—Rose Leaf.
Rowton, 1826, by Oiseau—Katherina.
Rowton colt, 1836, by Nanine—Nannie.
Royalist, 1790, by Saltram—Herod mare.
Ruby, 1836, by Emilius—Eliza.
St. George, 1789, by Highflyer—Sister to Soldier.
St. Giles, 1829, by Tramp—Arcot Lass.
St. Patrick Colt, 1835, by St. Patrick—Maria, by Whisker.
St. Paul, 1791, by Saltram—Purity, by Matchem.
Saltram, 1780, by Eclipse—Virago.
Scout, 1836, by St. Nicholas—Blacklock mare.
Scythian, 1851, by Orlando—Scythia.
Selim, 1780, by Bajazet—Miss Thigh.
Scrab, 1821, by Phantom—Jessie.
Shadow, 1759, by Babraham—Bolton Starling mare.
Shakspeare, 1823, by Smolensko—Charming Molly.

Shamrock, 1827, by St. Patrick—Fairy.
Shark, 1771, by Marske—Snap mare.
Shock, by Stork—Partner mare.
Shock, 1729, by Jig—Snake mare.
Silver, 1789, by Mercury—Herod mare.
Silver Eye, by Cullen Arab—Curwen's Bay Barb.
Sir Harry, 1794, by Sir Peter Teazle—Matron.
Sir Peter Teazle, 1802, by Sir Peter Teazle—Mercury mare.
Sir Robert, 1833, by Bobadil—Fidalma, by Waxy Pope.
Skylark, 1826, by Waxy Pope—Skylark.
Slender, 1779, by King Herod—Rachel.
Slim, 1768, by Wildman's Babraham—Babraham mare.
Sloven, 1756, by Cub—Bolton Starling mare.
Slouch, 1745, by Cade—Little Hartley mare.
Sorrow, 1836, by Defence—Tears.
Sour Crout, 1786, by Highflyer—Jewel.
Sovereign, 1836, by Emilius—Fleur de Lis.
Spadille, 1784, by Highflyer—Flora.
Spark, by Honeycomb Punch—Miss Colville.
Speculator, 1795, by Dragon—Herod mare.
Spread Eagle, 1792, by Volunteer—Highflyer mare.
Stafford, 1833, by Memnon—Sarsaparilla.
Star, 1786, by Highflyer—Snap mare.
Starling, 1800, by Sir Peter Teazle—Magnet mare.
Stirling, 1797, by Volunteer—Harriet.
Stirling, 1762, by the Bellsize Arabian—Simpson's Snake mare.
Strap, 1800, by Beninborough—Highflyer mare.
Stratford, 1834, by Shakspeare—Pheasant.
Swiss, 1821, by Whisker—Shuttle mare.
Tarquin, 1720, by Hampton Court Arab—Leedes mare.
Telegraph, 1795, by Guildford—Fame.
Tickle Toby, 1786, by Alfred—Cælia, by Herod.
Tom Crib, by Gladiator—Jemima.
Tom Jones, 1745, by Partner—True Blue mare.
Tranby, 1826, by Blacklock—Orville mare.
True Blue, 1797, by Walnut—King Fergus mare.
Truffle, 1825, by Truffle—Helen.
Trustee, 1829, by Catton—Emma.
Tup, 1756, by Javelin—Flavia.
Valentine, 1823, by Magistrate—Miss Forester.
Valparaiso, 1831, by Velocipede—Juliana.
Vampire, 1757, by Regulus—Steady mare.
Vanish, 1834, by Vanish—Elephant's dam.
Victor, 1838, by Defence—Vivid.
Volney, 1833, by Velocipede—Voltaire's dam.
Volunteer, by Volunteer—Whipcord mare.
Whale, 1830, by Whalebone—Rectory.
Whip, 1794, by Saltram—Herod mare.
Wildair, 1753, by Cade—Steady mare.
William the Fourth, 1795, by Blacklock—Juniper mare.
Wonder, 1786, by Florizel—Saccharissa.
Wonder, 1794, by Phenomenon—Brown Fanny.
Wrangler, 1794, by Diomed—Fleacatcher.
Yorkshire, 1834, by St. Nicholas—Miss Rose.
Zinganee, 1825, by Tramp—Folly.
Zinganee colt, 1840, by Zinganee—Miss Andrews.

Photographed from Life by GLOVER.

Copyright Secured.

ESSAY

ON THE

AMERICAN TROTTING HORSE.

BY

ELLWOOD HARVEY, M.D.

THE
AMERICAN TROTTING HORSE.

The trotting gait has been brought to such a degree of excellence in this country, and the breeding, training, and driving of trotting horses claims so large a share of attention, both in town and country, that a book on horses would be incomplete if it did not treat more fully of these subjects than any foreign work could be expected to do.

This Essay is therefore intended to give some account of the history of American trotting and of trotters of distinction, together with a few suggestions on breeding and training of this class of horses.

Though trotting has been greatly cultivated here, and enters more largely into the business and pleasure of Americans than of any other people, it would be an error to suppose that no attention has been given to it in any other country, or that the matching of trotters in races had its origin here. The trot is a natural gait to the horse, as it is to many other quadrupeds, and wherever horses are driven in harness their trotting is likely to be improved. A horseback rider finds the gallop and the canter easier to him, and horses are chiefly trained to those gaits in countries where light vehicles and good roads are unknown; as in Asia, Africa, the eastern part of Europe, and all of America except the United States and Canada.

Trotting, as a sport, began in England as early as 1791, in which year we find an account of a brown mare, eighteen years old, that trotted on the Essex road 16 miles in 58 minutes. On the 13th of October, 1799, a trotting match was decided on Sunbury Common, England, between Mr. Dixon's brown gelding and Mr. Bishop's gray gelding, each carrying 168 pounds, which was won in 27m. 10s. The distance is not stated, but the time shows that it was a trial of endurance as well as speed. Nearly all of the English trotting matches of that early period were of great distance. A Mr. Stevens drove a pair of his own horses tandem, in 1796, from

Windsor to Hampton Court, 16 miles, in less than an hour; and the celebrated English trotter, Archer, carried 210 lbs. 16 miles in 55 minutes. At about this period a variety of roadsters called Norfolk trotters came into notice in England, and still maintain a good reputation there, though none of them have ever attained a speed that would be considered very fast here. No other European country has produced trotters worthy of notice.

Trotting as a public amusement began somewhat later in this country. Porter's *Spirit of the Times*, of December 20, 1856, states: "The first time ever a horse trotted in public for a stake was in 1818, and that was a match against time for $1000. The match was proposed at a jockey-club dinner, where trotting had come under discussion, and the bet was that no horse could be produced that could trot a mile in 3 minutes. It was accepted by Maj. Wm. Jones, of Long Island, and Col. Bond, of Maryland, but the odds on time were immense. The horse named at the post was Boston Blue, who won cleverly, and gained great renown. He subsequently was purchased by Thomas Cooper, the tragedian, who drove him on several occasions between New York and Philadelphia, thereby enabling him to perform his engagements in either city on alternate nights." This performance was more then twenty years later than the first public trotting in England, where the sport was then receiving some encouragement; and Boston Blue was taken to that country, where he trotted 8 miles in 28m. 55s., winning a hundred sovereigns. He also trotted several shorter races, making about 3m. time. He was a rat-tailed, iron-gray gelding, 16 hands high, and nothing is known of his pedigree.

Trotting received very little attention here until after 1820, when the descendants of Messenger attracted notice by their speed, spirit, and endurance; chiefly about Philadelphia and New York.

In 1825 the New York Trotting Club was organized, and established a trotting course on Long Island.

In 1828 the Hunting Park Association was established in Philadelphia—"for the encouragement of the breed of fine horses, especially that most valuable one known as the trotter." Its course, known as the Hunting Park, was located about four miles north of the city.

Before the era marked by the organization of these two associations, three minutes was about the shortest time in which any horse here or in England had trotted a mile. In imitation of the four-mile running heats then and now common, the first trials of trotting speed were usually for three miles or more; and effort was not then directed to the development of the greatest degree of speed for a single mile. For several years, two and three-mile heats were trotted at about the rate of 2m. 40s. to the mile, and this is about the average speed of to-day, estimating from the reports of trotting races in the *Spirit of the Times*, though we now have many that can go the mile in less than 2m. 30s., a few that can make 2m. 24s., and two or three that have trotted in less than 2m. 20s. Among the early celebrities were Screwdriver, Betsy Baker, Topgallant, Whalebone, Shakspeare, Paul Pry, Trouble, and Sir Peter; all grand-colts of Messenger, except the first named, and he was a great-grand-colt. As many of the most distinguished trotters of the present day claim the same lineage, and as the influence of this great progenitor on the trotting stock of the country was immensely greater than that of all others together, a history of Messenger and his descendants would be a pretty full history of the eminent trotting horses of the world.

Messenger was an English thorough-bred, foaled in 1780, and imported, as were many other English thorough-breds, on account of his value as a running horse, and for the improvement of thorough-breds in this country. He had run successfully in several races, and at five years old won the King's Plate. It was three years after this performance, 1788, that he was imported into New York by Mr. Benger. The first two seasons after his arrival he was kept at Neshaminy Bridge, near Bristol, in Bucks county, Pa. Mr. Henry Astor then purchased him, and kept him on Long Island for two years. About this time Mr. C. W. Van Rantz purchased an interest in him, and for the remainder of his life he was kept in various parts of the state of New York, with the exception of one year at Cooper's Point, in New Jersey, opposite Philadelphia. He died January 28, 1808.

Messenger was a gray, 15 hands 3 inches high, and stoutly built. His form was not strictly in conformity with the popular notions of perfection, being upright in the shoulders and low on the withers, with a short, straight neck and a large, bony head. His loins and hind quarters were powerfully muscular, his windpipe and nostrils of unusual size, his hocks and knees very large, and below them limbs of medium size, but flat and clean; and whether at rest or in motion, his position and carriage always perfect and striking. It is said that during the voyage to this country the three other horses that accompanied him became so reduced in flesh and strength that when the vessel landed at New York they had to be helped and supported down the gang-plank; but when it came Messenger's turn to land, he, with a loud neigh, charged down the gang-plank, with a colored groom on each side holding him back, and dashed off up the street at a stiff trot, carrying the grooms along in spite of their efforts to stop him.

Though his name has been made illustrious chiefly by the performances of his trotting descendants, he was also the sire of some of the best running horses of his day. The most famous on the turf of his immediate thorough-bred descendants were Potomac,

Fair Rachel, Miller's Damsel (dam of American Eclipse), Bright Phœbus, Hambletonian, Sir Solomon, and Sir Harry. The celebrated four-mile racer, Ariel, had Messenger in her pedigree four times in five generations.

In his day trotting was not much in fashion, as we have shown, and nothing is known of the trotting speed of this great fountainhead of trotters, nor were any of his sons or daughters ever trained to that gait. It was the second generation of his descendants, the grand-colts of Messenger, and mostly those produced by a cross with the common stock of the country, that attracted attention by their trotting speed. This fact is easily explained. The thoroughbreds of his get were trained to running, and were not used as road horses, or some of them would probably have surpassed any of his half-bred descendants in trotting. But even his own half-bred colts made no mark as trotters, though some of them became celebrated as the sires of trotters. This is somewhat remarkable; but we should bear in mind that public attention had not then been given to that gait, good roads and light vehicles were not so common, and the next generation being more numerous, the probabilities were greater that this remarkable quality of the family should not remain undiscovered.

The sons of Messenger to which nearly all the fast trotters of the present day trace their pedigree were Plato, Engineer, Commander, Why-Not, Mount Holly, Mambrino, and Hambletonian.

Mambrino, named after the sire of Messenger, was thoroughbred, a bright bay, 16 hands high, long bodied, and, like his sire, upright in the shoulders. He was not only a large, but also a coarse horse, badly string-halted; a disease that seldom impairs a horse's usefulness, though it was hereditary in this case, and many of his descendants had it. He had a free, rapid, swinging walk, a slashing trot, and running speed of the first order. He was the sire of Betsy Baker, one of the first eminent American trotters; of Abdallah, from whom are descended many of the fastest, including the get of Rysdyk's Hambletonian, who was sired by Abdallah, and of Mambrino Paymaster, from whom are descended Mambrino Chief and all his get, including Lady Thorn, Mambrino Pilot, Bay Chief, &c. This son of Messenger stands undoubtedly at the head of the family as a progenitor of trotters.

Next in celebrity is Hambletonian, also thorough-bred. He was a dark bay, 15 hands 1 inch, beautifully moulded, and without a single weak point. He was the sire of Topgallant, Whalebone, Sir Peter, Trouble, and Shakspeare; all ranked among the best of the early American trotters.

Abdallah was a grandson of Messenger, and deserves especial mention in this connection because so many trotters of celebrity are descended through him. He was foaled in 1826, the property of Mr. John Treadwell, of Jamaica, L. I. His sire was Mambrino, and his dam a daughter of Messenger, called Amazonia. Thus Abdallah was closely inbred. He was a bay, and inherited much of the plainness of his sire; but also inherited the trotting quality of Messenger in great degree. He was trained at four years old, and was considered the fastest young horse of his day. In the spring of 1840 he was sold to Mr. John W. Hunt, of Lexington, Ky.; but, on account of the great value of his stock, he was bought back the next year, at a high price, and died in 1852. Beside being a progenitor, through his son, Rysdyk's Hambletonian, of that numerous and highly-distinguished family of trotters of which Dexter, George Wilkes, and Mountain Boy are the most eminent representatives, he is equally remarkable for the number of mares of his get from whom very fast trotters have been bred. To say that a horse is "out of an Abdallah mare," is pedigree enough on that side with most horsemen.

Of the other sons of Messenger it is not necessary to speak at length, though we find many horses of the present day descended from them, and inheriting the Messenger characteristics. When the pedigree of any fast trotter can be traced far enough, it rarely happens that Messenger is not found in it. Many horses that show good trotting speed, and are considered by their breeders and owners to be nothing but common stock, are found to be descended from Messenger, when intelligent investigation reveals their pedigrees.

Another imported horse that added something to the trotting quality of our stock was Bellfounder, a stallion foaled about 1817 and brought from England to Boston in 1823 by Mr. James Boot. He was a bay of fine form, size, and action; and these characteristics were transmitted to his colts with great uniformity. Many of them were very good and stylish carriage horses, with considerable speed, but only those infused with Messenger blood were very fast. Nothing is known of his pedigree, though his appearance indicated that he was nearly thoroughbred. It was said that he had trotted in England 2 miles in 6m. when three years old and 10 miles in 30m. at four years old. It was also asserted that he had trotted 17½ miles in an hour; but these statements, not being very well authenticated, are deemed apocryphal by the best horsemen of this day. One of his colts, of the same name, stood several years in Delaware county, Pa., and left a numerous family of handsome, lively trotters, nearly all of which became lame in the fore feet, and some even to the fifth generation. His advent to that locality was a loss of many thousands of dollars to breeders. The name of Bellfounder, there, is about synonymous with worthlessness, and will long remain in disrepute; though this particular son of the imported horse probably inherited his constitutional tendency to lameness from his dam, as the Bellfounders elsewhere are not charged with the same defect. Many distinguished trotters are in part descended from some of the many thorough-breds that have been imported from England at various times, and, indeed, our most celebrated horses have a strong infusion of that blood, derived from other sources than Messenger. Conceding the value of good thorough-bred crosses in giving spirit and endurance to trotting horses, and admitting that Diomed, Whip, Trustee, Glencoe, Margrave, and other imported thorough-breds have eminent trotters among their descendants, it may be safe to say that all of them together would not have produced a family of trotters without a cross from Messenger; and equally safe to assert that the fame of Messenger would have been no less if any one of the others had never been foaled. The imported Arabian, Grand Bashaw, had the luck to have his name perpetuated in a family of good trotters that originated in Bucks county, Pa., but the trotting quality all came from Messenger, who stood in that county two years. The first of the Bashaws that manifested any trotting quality was Young Bashaw, a son of the Arabian; and he was the only one of the whole get (if we may coin a word) that was thus endowed. The explanation is found in the fact that Young Bashaw's dam was a granddaughter of Messenger.

Of American horses not descended from Messenger that have contributed to establish the reputation of our trotters, the number is not large nor the influence very considerable. Sir Henry, the famous competitor of American Eclipse, and Duroc, both thoroughbreds, and both descended from imported Diomed, seem to have transmitted some trotting quality to their descendants, but it is very doubtful that either, or both, would have established a family of trotters. Seely's American Star, quite famous as the sire of modern trotters, combines the blood of both, being sired by American Star, a son of Duroc, and out of Sally Slouch by Sir Henry; but his grand-dam was by Messenger. American Eclipse, the progenitor of many good trotters, had also the blood of Duroc, his sire; but as his dam, Miller's Damsel, was by Messenger, the Duroc part of the pedigree is seldom thought of. Americus, who beat Lady Suffolk on the Hunting Park Course in a five-mile match to wagons in the remarkable time of 13m. 54s. and 13m. 58½s., was by Red Jacket, a son of Duroc, and not known to have inherited his trotting from any other source.

Canada has added something to our trotting stock. In Lower Canada, where the earliest settlers were French, and brought with them a breed of horses now known in France as Normans, they have a breed of hardy, spirited, compactly built horses, descended from the larger French horse, inheriting much of his form and general appearance, but greatly diminished in size. These Canadian horses are often called Cannucks, and by some are known as French horses, a designation likely to lead to misapprehension. They are of all colors, with thick, long manes, heavy tails, and hairy legs. Their heads are generally very good in size and form, faces dished, indicating gamy dispositions; necks well arched, often heavy in the crest but carried well up; backs short, rumps steep, particularly in those that pace; bodies round and roomy, the ribs sometimes projecting from the backbone nearly horizontally, giving a peculiar, flat appearance to the back. Their legs are generally good, but somewhat inclined to spring in the knees; feet often narrow and mulish, but very durable. In trotting they are usually short, quick steppers with very high knee action, and are spirited, trappy harness horses, and long-lived. These horses are often said to be degenerated from their Norman ancestry by reason of the coldness of the climate, the long winters and scanty fare. There have been numerous importations from France to this country of the choicest specimens of Norman horses, and an impartial comparison shows that the Canadian has gained in spirit and speed more than enough to compensate for all he has lost in size.

The best of the Canadians that ever came to the States was, probably, Pilot, a black pacing and trotting horse whose descendants inherited trotting speed. He was often distinguished as Old Pacer Pilot. Wallace's American Stud Book says of him: "Foaled about 1826. Nothing is known of his pedigree. He was called a Canadian horse, and both trotted and paced; at the latter gait, it is said, he went in 2m. 26s. with 165lbs. on his back. He was bought about 1832 by Major O. Dubois, from a Yankee peddler in New Orleans, for $1000. He was afterwards sold to D. Heinsohn of Louisville, Ky., and was kept in that vicinity until he died about 1855. His stock were very stout and fast." As nothing is known of his pedigree, and as he was in all appearance a genuine Cannuck, it is likely that he did not owe anything to Messenger. One of his get, Alexander's Pilot, Jr., out of Nancy Pope by Havoc, was the sire of many fast trotters, the fastest of which was John Morgan, out of a mare by Medoc and he by American Eclipse. The dam of Mambrino Pilot was also by Pilot, Jr., and, like John Morgan, was of Messenger descent on the dam's side. Though the best of the descendants of Old Pilot are part Messenger, there is none of that blood in Pilot, Jr., and it must be confessed that Old Pilot sired some very good horses that took the trotting all from himself.

Another horse of Canadian origin, though not a Cannuck, deserves notice in this connection. Royal George, called Warrior before he came to the States, the sire of the fast stallion Toronto Chief, and several other good trotters, was a native of Canada and probably out of a Cannuck mare, but his sire was Black Warrior, and he by an imported English horse.

Some very good colts have been bred out of Cannucks by good trotting stallions. Thus the celebrated sons of Rysdyk's Hambletonian, Bruno and the Brother of Bruno, and their full sister Brunette, are out of a Canadian mare. At three years old Bruno made the astonishing time of 2m. 39s. in harness. At four years old, 2m. 30s. and 2m. 34s. At six years old he trotted to the pole with Brunette, seven years old, on the Fashion Course in 2m. 35½s.

Gift, a chestnut gelding by Mambrino Pilot, was out of a small pacing Cannuck. At four years old he received five forfeits, and challenged, through the Spirit of the Times, any colt of the same age to trot in harness or to wagon for $1000, without being accepted. Though these colts are out of Canadian mares, it must be considered that the mares themselves were not very fast, and that Rysdyk's Hambletonian and Mambrino Pilot are the best two trotting foal getters in the world. The bay stallion St. Lawrence, the sire of several fast trotters, was a Canadian, and one of the best of his breed. He died at Kalamazoo in 1858. There is one other horse deserving especial notice as a progenitor of trotters, in whose veins no blood of Messenger can be found, though his pedigree is too obscure to warrant the assertion that none existed there. Black Hawk, often called Vermont Black Hawk to distinguish him from the equally celebrated Long Island Black Hawk, and also called Hill's Black Hawk, was of Morgan stock on his sire's side; being a son of Sherman, one of the best sons of Justin Morgan, the founder of the Morgan family. The dam of Black Hawk was raised in New Brunswick, and nothing is known of her pedigree. Black Hawk was foaled in 1833 at Greenland, N. H. At four years old he was sold to Lowell, Mass., where he was used as a carriage horse for seven years. He then became the property of David Hill, of Bridport, Vt., where he acquired great fame; begetting more high priced colts than any other horse of his day. He had remarkable power in propagating his own characteristics, and his stock were uniformly stylish, spirited harness horses, many of them fast and some of them among the fastest. Another history of his pedigree mades him the son of a Canadian named Paddy; and still another declares him a veritable native of Canada, though not a pure Cannuck. The story, as it was given the writer by Mr. Lucien Béchard, a Canadian horse dealer, is as follows: An old Canadian Frenchman engaged in smuggling tobacco from the States, bought there and took home with him a brown mare with foal. In due time she had a bay colt, that at two years old begot Black Hawk out of a little gray mare not over 14 hands high. The fortunate possessor of the black colt was a widow who lived by the Chambly river in the Montreal district. At four years old he was sold to John Harris for $200, and at six years old was sold again to Van Loiseu, a dealer, for $400. Van Loiseu taught him many tricks, at learning which he showed great aptitude, and sold him in New York to a Bostonian for $600. From Boston he got to Lowell, &c. This story is probably all true of some horse, but the identity is not established. Black Hawk's colts were never gray, as many of them would have been if his dam was that color, but many of them were chestnuts with white feet and faces, which was the color of Sherman and of Sherman's dam. This fact pretty clearly shows that neither the "Paddy" story nor the Canadian pedigree are correct, but that Black Hawk was truly a Morgan. He was a little under 15 hands, and weighed about 1000lbs. In 1842 he won $1000 by trotting five miles over the Cambridge Park Course in 16m. In 1843 he won a race of two-mile heats with ease in 5m. 43s. and 5m. 48s., and several times trotted single miles in 2m. 42s. He was the sire of Ethan Allen, Black Ralph, Lancet, Belle of Saratoga, Black Hawk Maid, Flying Cloud, and many others of good repute for speed. His colts were in great demand, particularly in the West and South, where hundreds were sold at very high prices. As many of his sons were, and still are, kept as stallions, his descendants are very numerous; and he undoubtedly has done much to improve the stock of American horses. But, notwithstanding these facts, the reputation of the family appears to be diminishing. Of fifty-two trotting stallions advertised in the Spirit of the Times in 1868, only three are descendants of Vermont Black Hawk, and all of these are also part Messenger.

Every one of the fifty-two is descended from Messenger, and those most distinguished as sires of trotters have each several crosses of Messenger blood in their pedigree. These are very remarkable facts, and, taken in connection with the whole history of trotters, prove that we not only owe to Messenger the origin of American trotting horses, but also that the continuance of that particular quality, down to the present day, in increasing force, is due to the perpetuation of his stock, and to breeding together his descendants so as to combine the greatest quantity of Messenger blood in one animal. The value of his descendants depends, undoubtedly, in great degree, upon the quality of the horses crossed with the Messenger blood; and those other horses, both native and foreign, whether thorough-breds, Cannucks, or of mixed blood, that may justly claim a share in establishing the fame of American trotters, have done very little more than cross well with the Messengers. It is, probably, no exaggeration to say that all of them together would have failed to establish a family of trotters in the country if Messenger the Great had not been imported. The trotting quality runs out of all of them in a few generations if not crossed with the Messenger blood. They are but the tributary streams to the great river of which Messenger was the source. The immense influence of this one horse has a universal recognition in the common expression: "A full-blooded Messenger," than which nothing can be more absurd. There was never but one full-blooded Messenger, and he died sixty years ago. Another expression often used in pedigrees is: "Out of a Messenger mare." This may not be so absurd as the other, for the mare may be well endued with Messenger blood and quality, and almost entitled to the distinction; but in strict meaning none were Messenger mares except those of his own begetting. The Messengers are not a breed, as Cannucks and Mustangs and thorough-breds are, but only a family; and we have not arrived yet to the perpetuation of the family names of horses in the male line, as is common among people of civilized countries.

Pacing is not considered a good harness gait, but some of our fastest road and sporting horses have been pacers, and they are frequently matched with trotters in races. Many horses both trot and pace, and of those that have both gaits, some go faster in one and some in the other. To teach a trotter to pace is somewhat difficult unless the horse naturally inclines to it, but it may be done sometimes by riding with a severe curb-bit and spurs. Of course it requires good horsemanship, as well as means and appliances, to urge the movement desired, and to restrain the animal from the steps he is most accustomed to take. When the saddle was more in use than now, pacing was a favorite gait with many riders, but unless the horse can occasionally change his way of going into a canter, it becomes very tiresome on a long journey. Though the rider may not be jolted from the saddle so much as by a trotter, the wabbling twists his back first one way and then the other most fatiguingly.

Pacing and cantering are pleasant gaits for ladies' hackneys, and are well enough adapted to short journeys. In harness the pacer is not graceful. There is a gait, somewhat between a pace and a trot, and called a single-footed pace, that does pretty well in harness, but very few horses have it. For taking weight in harness, or on muddy or rough roads, the trot is greatly preferable.

To teach a pacer to trot, various expedients are resorted to. Fence-rails are put down about as far apart as a trotter steps in a jog. The pacer is ridden over them and finds it difficult to lift his feet over them in that gait, and adopts the trot. When a horse has become very tired by long pacing he will sometimes ease his weary muscles by a change of action into a trot; and this he is more likely to do if the roads are muddy. From such a beginning a skilful driver may make the trotting permanent.

Some very good and fast trotters were first pacers and were taught the better way of going, and some of them after they had acquired speed in their natural gait.

Pelham was first a very fast pacer, and afterward became a distinguished trotter. In 1849 he was the first to win a heat in harness in 2m. 28s. Cayuga Chief was a pacer in a livery stable, in Worcester, Mass., and a favorite ladies' hackney. One day he struck a trot, and soon became distinguished. In 1844 he trotted to a wagon with 220lbs. in 2m. 36½s. The black gelding Pilot, probably a son of the old pacer of the same name, was first a fast pacer. He surprised his owner by striking a trot, and improved so rapidly that in a short time he trotted in 2m. 28½s. Tip, and Dart, and Sontag were all pacers that afterward trotted fast. Old Pacer Pilot went fast in both gaits, and so did his grandson, Tom Wonder, the sire of the famous twenty-mile trotter, John Stewart.

Though there are objections to pacing as a road gait, in harness, some of the fastest have been pacers; and though it is generally believed that a pacer soon tires, there are performances on record that prove them capable of keeping in the best of trotting company for any distance. In 1843, Sir Walter Scott paced on Beacon Course eighteen miles in less than an hour without a break or halt. In the same year, Oneida Chief paced against the best trotters of that time—Lady Suffolk, Confidence, and Dutchman—and won more races than he lost, making 2m. 28½s., the best time then on record. In the following year, Tippecanoe paced at New Orleans in 2m. 36s., carrying a very heavy rider; and Unknown paced on Beacon Course in 2m. 23s., a performance that had never then been equalled by trotter or pacer. Old Pacer Pilot paced in 2m. 26s. with 165lbs. on his back. In 1850, Roanoke paced under saddle in 2m. 21½s. He was a roan gelding, and nothing is known of his pedigree. In 1854, Pocahontas paced three heats in a race at New Orleans in 2.20, 2.25, and 2.20. But in the next year she brought the figures down to something less than has ever been equalled by any trotter but Dexter, and not surpassed by him. In a race with Hero, the pacer, in a wagon that weighed with the driver 265lbs., Pocahontas paced the first mile in 2.17. This was never beaten but once, and not until 1868, when Billy Boyce paced at Buffalo faster than any other horse has ever trotted or paced. In a race with Rolla Golddust, a trotter, mile heats, 3 in 5, to saddle, Boyce paced the second mile in 2.15¼, and the third in 2.14¼, pacing the last half of the second mile in 1.5¼, and the first half of the third mile in 1.6.

Many pacers belong to trotting families, and some trotters seem to take their speed from a pacing ancestor, though this is not common. Oneida Chief was half brother of Flora Temple's sire. Woodpecker, the trotter, and James K. Polk, the pacer, both took their speed from the same dam. Hero, the pacer, and competitor of Pocahontas in her wonderful performance, was begotten by Harris's Hambletonian, the sire of the trotters True John, Green Mountain Maid, John Anderson, and Sontag, a mare that was at first a natural pacer and afterward trotted very fast. Saltram, the sire of Highland Maid, was a pacer, and his dam, Roxana, was also a pacer. Highland Maid paced naturally, but was taught to trot, and went very fast. At six years old she trotted against Flora Temple, and lost the race by getting tired, being young, and going into a pace, which was her natural and easiest gait. She won the first heat in 2.29, the second in 2.27, but was distanced in the third. Highland Lass, a daughter of Highland Maid, was a fast trotter, and died in 1865. Her daughter, Highland Ash, by Ashland, is also a trotter, and in 1868 won the Spirit of the Times Stake for three-year olds, over four thousand dollars, in 2.48. Flatbush Maid, one of Mr. Robt. Bonner's pair that trotted to a road wagon in 2.26, was begotten by a chestnut pacing horse that also trotted. Pocahontas is nearly thorough-bred, and was begotten by Cadmus, a son of American Eclipse. She, therefore, takes her wonderful pacing speed from Messenger, the sire of Miller's Damsel, who was the dam of American Eclipse. Her daughter, Pocahontas, Jr., by Ethan Allen, is a trotter and very fast.

Billy Boyce, a bay gelding, and very bloodlike in his' appearance, is by Corbeau, a horse owned near Harodsburg, Ky., and the sire of several trotters. Corbeau was by a Canadian, not known as a begetter of trotters; but his dam was by Frank, a thorough-bred, by Sir Charles, his granddam by Sir Archy; which gives Corbeau two lines of descent from imported Diomed, and probably gives him also his trotting quality.

Boyce has a cross of the Messenger, through American Eclipse, the sire of his granddam, and this gives him another cross of Diomed, through Duroc, the sire of American Eclipse. He is, therefore, of kindred blood with Lady Thorn, Dexter, Mambrino Pilot, Kemble Jackson, Independent, John Morgan, Peerless, and others of celebrity; that is, they all combine in their pedigrees the blood of Messenger and Diomed.

These facts, a few of the many that could be cited, show the close relationship between pacers and trotters. They derive their speed from the same sources; trotters beget pacers, and pacers beget trotters; many go fast in one gait, and, after being taught the other, go equally fast in that; so that they may properly enough be classed together, and designated by the common title of American Trotters.

Though trotters are derived from so few sources as to be nearly all related to all the others, there are certain families that claim especial notice.

At present the most celebrated are the Hambletonians. The founder of this family is Rysdyk's Hambletonian, owned in Chester, N. Y., and having more Messenger blood than any other stallion living. See pedigree, Table I. He was foaled in 1849, and is still (in 1869) standing at $500 to insure. He is the sire of Dexter, George Wilkes, Bruno, Brunette, and many others of celebrity. Mountain Boy, owned by Commodore Vanderbilt, was begotten by Major Winfield, a son of Hambletonian.

The Abdallahs are an older family, and not less distinguished. Abdallah's pedigree and history are mentioned on pages 472 and 473.

The Vermont Black Hawks were once very popular, and for a few years their fame quite eclipsed all other families. On page 476 may be found a more extended account of them.

The Bashaws are a very excellent family of trotters, but nearly obliterated now by admixture with others. They are a branch of the Messenger family that took their name from an imported Arabian, but not the trotting quality. The first of the family was Young Bashaw, a son of the Arabian; and his best colt was Andrew Jackson, the first stallion that ever trotted in a public match. From him are descended many sub-families—the Clays, the Patchens, &c. In the pedigree of Green's Bashaw, Table III., may be seen the pedigree of Andrew Jackson, and why he was the best son of Young Bashaw. Charlotte Temple, a very fast mare that was taken to France, her full brother, the stallion Saladin, and Black Bashaw, another stallion, were all begotten by Young Bashaw, and the two last named were both progenitors of many good trotters. Comet, Whiskey, Lantern, Belle of Baltimore, and Lightning, were all by Black Bashaw. One of Andrew Jackson's best colts was the stallion Long Island Black Hawk, often confounded with Vermont Black Hawk, the Morgan Horse. They should be carefully distinguished. Long Island Black Hawk had Messenger blood by four lines of descent (see pedigree of Green's Bashaw, Table III.), and his descendants inherit the trotting in large degree. Vermont Black Hawk begot many good horses, but the speed seems to run out in a few generations. He had no Messenger in him.

George M. Patchen was descended from Long Island Black Hawk through Henry Clay and Cassius M. Clay, with a cross of Imported Diomed and another of Imported Trustee. See pedigree, Table VI. Patchen had speed and bottom worthy of such a good pedigree, but his descendants have not met the expectations of breeders. They are coarse in form, and subject to curbs and ringbones. Lucy, the best of his get, was out of a May Day mare, and thus got another cross of the Diomed from Sir Henry, the sire of May Day.

Long Island Black Hawk's best son as a stock horse was Henry Clay, out of Surry, a mare of great speed from Canada. Henry Clay begot trotters, and died in 1867, aged 30 years. His son, Cassius M. Clay, out of a fast mare of unknown pedigree, was the sire of Patchen, and the ancestor of a numerous progeny of trotters. He may be considered the founder of a family of Clays, including C. M. Clay, Jr., Harry Clay (believed by many to be the sire of Dexter), Amos's C. M. Clay, the sire of American Girl, that trotted in 2m. 40s. at 4 years old, and 2m. 32½s. at 5 years old; Clay Pilot, Kentucky Clay, Cora, Nonpareil, and others.

A very good and handsome family are the Morrills, a branch of the Morgans; Morrill being a descendant of Justin Morgan, with two crosses of Diomed and four of Messenger to account for the trotting. His best colt was Young Morrill, owned by Samuel Perkins, Cambridge, Mass., now about 20 years old, and sire of Draco, Fearnought, Danville Boy, Mountain Maid, Hiram Woodruff, and many others that are among the best of road horses. He is more of a Morgan than his sire (see pedigree, Table V.), having two lines of descent from Justin Morgan on his dam's side.

The Morgans are not distinguished as fast trotters, though many of them, like the Canadians, from whom they are in part descended, are good and smart road horses; and when crossed with Messenger, as Ethan Allen, Flying Cloud, Morrill, Lone Star, &c., they are among the best.

Another family of very excellent reputation are the American Stars. The founder of the family was foaled in 1837, and died in 1861, the property of Jonas Seely, Orange county, N. Y. He had some Messenger blood, but more of Diomed through Duroc in one line and Sir Henry in another. See his pedigree in the pedigree of Dexter, Table VII. The dam of Dexter was by American Star, as were a good many fast trotters, the best of which is Peerless, a gray mare, foaled in 1853, and owned by Robert Bonner, of New York. Hiram Woodruff said she was the fastest animal that he or any other man ever drove to a wagon, and that he drove her a quarter in 30s. and a mile in 2m. 23⅛s. Her dam was full of Messenger blood. American Star was a rat-tailed horse, and some of his colts are rather deficient in hair on their tails; but they are fast and very gamey.

Green's Bashaw, foaled in 1855, and owned in Muscatine, Iowa, has some superior colts, among them Kirkwood and Bashaw, Jr., both fast; and this, together with his remarkable pedigree (Table III.), justifies the expectation that he will become the head of a distinguished family. On his sire's side he has the Messenger blood through four channels, and on his dam's side the same pedigree as Rysdyk's Hambletonian with an additional cross of Webber's Tom Thumb, a fast horse that looked like a Canadian and begot trotters.

Golddust, a chestnut, foaled about 1855, and owned by L. L Dorsey, Lexington, Ky., has begotten quite a numerous family of trotters considering his age. He is a very bloodlike horse, a fast walker and a fast trotter. He takes his speed from his sire, Vermont Morgan, whose dam was by Cock-of-the-Rock, he by Duroc, a son of Diomed. Cock-of-the-Rock's dam was Romp, a full sister to Miller's Damsel, by Messenger. On his dam's side he has some Arabian and thorough-bred blood that shows in the style and form of his colts. See Table IV.

The Pilots, another Kentucky family, are descended from the Old Pacer Pilot, and are best represented by one of his sons, Alexander's Pilot, Jr., and his descendants. Pilot, Jr., owned by R. A. Alexander, Lexington, Ky., is a black, and was foaled about 1845. His dam was Nancy Pope, by Havoc, a grandson of Diomed, and thus he takes the trotting from both sides, and in excellent combination. (See pedigree, in the pedigree of Mambrino Pilot, Table II.) He is the sire of John Morgan, Jim Rockey, Tackey, Pilot Temple, Dixie, Tattler, and many more. John Morgan was the closest competitor of Flora Temple in her best days, and every way one of the best trotters in the country. His dam was by Medoc, a son of American Eclipse, and he thus had another cross of Diomed, and one of Messenger. Tackey has trotted in 2m. 28s.; Pilot Temple, out of the dam of Flora Temple, trotted in 1868 in 2m. 31s.; Jim Rockey trotted in 1859 in 2m. 32s.; and Tattler, 5 years old, trotted in 1868 in 2m. 26s., a performance that probably has never been equalled by any horse of the same age. The famous twenty-miler, John Stewart, is a descendant of Old Pilot, through Tom Wonder and Tom Crowder—the last, a son of the old pacer.

A modern family, that rivals the Hambletonians, is composed of the descendants of Mambrino Chief—a horse that was bred in the East, and taken to Kentucky by James B. Clay in 1854, where he died in 1861. His sire was Mambrino Paymaster, by Mambrino, the best son of Messenger in the trotting line. (See pedigrees of Lady Thorn and Mambrino Pilot, Tables IV. and IX.) His fast progeny is very numerous and very famous, and includes Lady Thorn, Bay Chief, Mambrino Pilot, Ericsson, Mambrino Patchen, Brignoli, Kentucky Chief, Ashland, &c.

Lady Thorn stands first among all trotters now in public, and second only to Dexter and Flora Temple. Her pedigree and her performances are in perfect accord; the speed and bottom both represented by three lines of descent from Messenger, and three from Diomed; herself almost thorough-bred.

Bay Chief, unfortunately shot by guerrillas, trotted half a mile when 4 years old in 1m. 8s., a performance rarely equalled at any age. Ericsson trotted at 4 years old in 2m. 30½s., to a wagon, and is now at the head of the large breeding stud of K. C. Barker, Detroit, Mich. Brignoli, at 5 years old, trotted two-mile heats in harness in 5m. 20½s., 5m. 18½s , and 5m. 17½s. Mambrino Patchen is a full brother of Lady Thorn, and wretchedly misnamed, being related to Patchen only in a remote degree, though both inheriting largely the Messenger blood.

The most distinguished son of Mambrino Chief, is Mambrino Pilot, owned by C. P. Relf, of Norristown, Pa.; and, though foaled so lately as 1859, is already distinguished as a sire of trotters. He is a brown of large size and pony built, faultless in form and action, with an air of majesty in every attitude. At 6 years old, with very short preparation, he trotted against time in 2m. 27s. He inherits the blood of Messenger through three channels, and of Diomed through two, with a cross of Old Pilot, through his best son, Pilot, Jr.

Considering that his oldest colts are but 5 years old, and that when those now old enough to show speed were begotten, he had not made his reputation, and did not receive the best of trotting mares, the number and speed of his fast colts is truly astonishing.

Gift, ch. g., received five forfeits at 4 years old, and challenged through the "Spirit of the Times" any colt of the same age, to trot in harness for $1000 a side, without being accepted. Bellringer, b. s., trotted in 2m. 40s. before he was 4 years old. Gift and Bellringer both belong to Mr. Relf. Cranston, owned by Amasa Sprague, R. I., at 3 years old, trotted the second mile in a two-mile heat in 2m. 40½s. Vosburgh, ch. s., the property of A. & T. H. Carpenter, of Lyons, Iowa, when just 3 years old, trotted several times in 2m. 40s., and challenged any other horse in the world of the same age, to trot for any amount, at 4 years old, in September 1869. Charles S. Dole, of Chicago, Ill., has a chestnut mare in his breeding stud, by Mambrino Pilot, that in the management of Dr. Kerr, of Lexington, Ky., trotted in 3m. at 2 years old. Eschol, Detective, Etta, Agitator, and Mambrino Messenger are other fast colts of the same family.

Horsemen have been looking among the coming stallions for a successor to the renowned Rysdyk's Hambletonian, whose age must soon end his usefulness; and if the colts of Mambrino Pilot keep the early promise, and improve with maturity, as his remarkable pedigree and performances seem to justify us in expecting, then is a successor of even greater merit already indicated.

There are many good trotting foal getters in the country not named in these allusions to the families of trotters. To mention half of them individually would be beyond the scope and limits of this Essay, but most of them belong to some of the families named. The object is not so much to instruct the reader in facts as in principles. There is a very prevalent opinion that trotters are chance horses, and that there is no certainty in breeding for them. So prevalent was this opinion a few years ago, that then trotters *were* chance horses, no well directed effort was made to produce the desired result, by applying the same principles of breeding that had been so long acknowledged in the breeding of thorough-breds for running races. But when trotting became more popular as a public amusement, when the value of good trotting horses for road driving became more fully appreciated, and when the increased demand ran the prices of even good roadsters into the thousands, enlightened breeders began to apply to the breeding of trotters the laws of hereditary descent, that had been discovered in the breeding of other animals, and with the usual result.

Now there are numerous large breeding establishments in Kentucky, New York, Iowa, New Jersey, Pennsylvania, Ohio, Illinois, Michigan, and perhaps some other states, in which especial attention is given to breeding trotters. Beside these breeding studs, where much care and judgment are used in the matter, there are thousands of farmers and others who in breeding horses, always have in their minds the possibility of drawing a capital prize in the shape of a fast trotter; but who have never had an opportunity to be well informed in regard to the best method of accomplishing that desirable result.

These farmers and others who only rear one or two colts a year, each, are in the aggregate the great horse breeders of the country; and it is to them chiefly that the facts and arguments of this essay are addressed.

A very slight examination of the pedigrees of distinguished trotters, will show their relationship to each other in so many cases, that no one can doubt the derivation of their trotting speed from a common ancestry. A few tabulated pedigrees are given at the end of this essay, to facilitate the examination of them, and to more fully impress on the minds of breeders the importance of breeding their mares to stallions of good families, if they would reasonably expect success. A horse may trot fast enough to make a public reputation, and never beget fast colts, because he does not himself inherit the quality strongly from his ancestors; for it may be that the quality comes down to him through a single line of descent, and perhaps that has been broken by one or more generations that showed no speed. In such a case, the horse would be said to have "bred back" to a speedy ancestor, and though he might beget fast colts with fast mares, the probabilities of their being fast from common mares would be very small. John Henry, a chestnut stallion, bred in Salem county, New Jersey, trotted well, and begot many colts; but the best of them all, Bob Johnson, was nothing remarkable.

John Henry had not the trotting quality by a long and continuous line of hereditary descent, and hence the disappointment of breeders, who depended on his speed alone to give the trotting to his colts. Similar cases are quite common.

If a mare that cannot trot better than four minutes was by a horse of good speed and good pedigree, such as Mambrino Chief, or American Star, the probabilities of her breeding a fast colt by some other good horse, as by Hambletonian, would be much greater than if she had no trotting ancestor in her pedigree. Such a mare, though not fast herself, might produce a fast colt from a common horse; or if she did not herself produce anything smart, some of her descendants in the next generation might show speed. This is called breeding back, or atavism, and all breeders are familiar with it.

In choosing a stallion to breed from for speed, the first thing to be considered is his pedigree. Many breeders will differ from that opinion, but it is not hastily expressed. The longer the lines of trotting descent in his pedigree, and the more numerous they are, the greater will be the probability that his colts will inherit the desired quality.

Next to pedigree should be considered the speed, bottom, health, size, style, color, &c. If the pedigree is good and the horse sound, he will beget fast colts, though he may not himself be fast; but if he has the speed, too, so much the better. Many diseases are hereditary, and the stallion should be sound; it is poor policy to breed from a horse with contracted feet, spavin, ringbone, sprung knees, or weak eyes.

In breeding for speed, it should be remembered that size is important if the colt turns out fast, and still more if he does not. If he is large enough for taking a carriage with two persons over common roads at a lively gait, the breeding was not a failure, though he may not be very fast. The style and color are matters of taste, about which each breeder will make his own choice. It is generally admitted that a good horse is always the right color, but he might sometimes be equally good and a better color. If the mare has any particular defect, a horse should be chosen that will correct it in the progeny.

Much speculation has been indulged in concerning the relative influence of the sire and dam on the offspring. By some it has been asserted that if either parent is more vigorous than the other by reason of youth, health, or better care, the offspring will most resemble that parent. This theory is not sustained by facts. In crossing the horse and the ass, some facts of interest are elicited. The mule takes size from its dam, the mare; but takes its outward form and its voice from the sire, the ass. The ears are long, the tail and mane are scantily furnished with hair, and the feet are narrow. But if the female ass is bred to a horse, the produce, called a hinny, is quite unlike the mule. It inherits its organization by the same law, and has the small size of its dam, the female ass, with ears, feet, mane, tail, and voice like its sire, the horse.

Now these statements, though correct in a general sense, need some qualification. The ears of the mule are not as long as its sire's in proportion to the body, the feet are not as narrow, the tail and mane are not so scantily supplied with hair. In all the points of greatest resemblance to the ass, there is still some resemblance to the other parent, the mare. In other words, the mule does not take any part of its conformation from either parent alone; but every part is like both parents in some degree. The same remarks apply to the hinny. Its mane, tail, ears, and feet are more like a horse's than a mule's are, but not exactly like a horse's. In every part of its body it has some resemblance to the ass, its dam. The point established is this:—That the mule and the hinny both take their outward form and appearance from their respective sires more than from their dams; but neither of them is exactly like either parent in any respect.

These facts are constant when the two species are bred together, and the produce is a hybrid; and we might infer that some certainty was attainable in the same direction when animals of the same species are bred together, as in breeding horses. That is, we might expect the colt to always inherit its ears, mane, tail, and feet more from the horse than from the mare. The rule may apply to some extent, but it is not to be relied on with anything like the certainty that is observed in breeding the horse and ass together. Rat-tailed stallions beget rat-tailed colts, and hoof-bound mares have colts inheriting the same tendency to disease of the feet.

Every part of every offspring partakes of the quality of both parents in some degree; and in the present state of our knowledge, we can neither control nor foresee the amount of any particular quality that the offspring will inherit from either parent.

In a family of children, one may be tall like the father and have black hair like the mother; another may be short like the mother with light hair like the father; and a third may have stature and complexion that partake more evenly of the qualities of both parents. If three more children are to be born to the same parents, no physiologist can predict their stature nor the color of their hair. If parents are much alike in all respects, the children will be much alike; but the children of the same family will be much diversified in appearance and character if their parents are much different from each other in these respects. If parents are alike in any particular, though different in all other respects, their children will all inherit that quality strongly which comes from both parents, and will transmit it to the next generation with greater certainty than if they had inherited it from only one parent. Of course these rules may all have exceptions; atavism, or breeding back, may modify the results.

If one parent belongs to a particular breed, as a cow to the Devonshires, and is bred with another of no particular breed, the offspring will resemble the full-bred parent more than the other of common stock, because the form, color, &c., of the full-bred parent have become fixed by a long line of ancestry in which all the ancestors had the same qualities. It does not follow that the full-bred parent gives more than half of the quality to the offspring, but only that the other half may resemble some of the ancestors of common stock that were quite unlike the low-bred parent. Thus, if a Devonshire cow were bred to a common bull of a white color, more of the calves would be red than white, because all the ancestors on the cow's side were red, and a part of them on the bull's side were probably of the same color. As many as bred back to the Devonshire side for color would be red; those that bred back to the common side for color might be black, or brindle, or any other color. It is simply a case in which atavism has an influence, as it always has in all breeding. There is no law by which a high-bred parent transmits more than half of the organism of the offspring; the low-bred parent has an equal influence in the matter; but there is more probability that the progeny will resemble the high-bred parent than the common one. If by atavism it resembles any ancestor on the well-bred side, it resembles the parent on the same side, for they are all much alike; but if it breeds back to the low-bred side, there has been so much diversity in the ancestors on that side that nothing is certain.

In breeding for trotters, these principles must always be considered. We have no breed of trotters that can be called thorough-bred or full-blooded trotters, in the same sense as we speak of the thorough-bred race horse, or of the thorough-bred Durham or Devonshire cattle; but we have families of trotters, in which the trotting quality has been transmitted for several generations, and in several lines of descent; and, in breeding, the best practice will be that which most nearly conforms to the principles here stated. The more trotting quality in the family, the greater the probability of its being transmitted to the descendants.

In choosing a mare to breed from, the same rules are applicable as in choosing a stallion. If a breeder chance to have a mare of good speed and good pedigree, he may expect more from her than from a common mare if both are put to the same horse. It is somewhat the fashion to select thorough-bred mares to breed to trotting stallions, that the spirit and endurance of the thorough-bred may be combined in the colts with the trotting action; and trotting mares are put to thorough-bred stallions with the same object in view. The practice is good, and will improve the breed of trotters in the long run; but for immediate results, more trotting speed may be expected when trotting mares are bred to trotting stallions. It should not be disregarded that we already have trotting families quite equal to thorough-breds in spirit and bottom; and though these may have been inherited from a thoroughbred ancestry, that is not a reason why we should breed again to thorough-breds and risk the loss of the trotting quality. The famous trotter Flora Temple was frequently put to Mambrino

FLORA TEMPLE.

Pilot without success, but she became with foal by a two-year old. Old mares will often breed to a colt when they will not to a matured horse. The colt selected on this occasion was Rysdyk, by Rysdyk's Hambletonian, out of a thorough-bred mare by Lexington. Now, this dam of Rysdyk had no trotting quality, and he is just as likely to inherit running speed from his dam as trotting speed from his sire. Or he may take the trotting action from his sire and have that action made good by the Lexington side of his pedigree—Lexington being the sire of more winners in running races than any other horse in America. But the probability is strong that Rysdyk will not be very speedy, though he will probably have good bottom, and still stronger that his colts out of Flora will not equal their celebrated dam.

Flora Temple's pedigree is not very well known, but this much appears to be reliable : Her sire was One-Eyed Kentucky Hunter, he by Kentucky Hunter, the sire of the famous pacer Oneida Chief. Her dam, Madam Temple, was by a spotted horse called an Arabian, though he probably was not. That her trotting was inherited from her sire's side is quite certain, and her dam also may have added something, as she afterward produced a very good trotter, Pilot Temple, but he was by a very good horse, Alexander's Pilot, Jr. Though Flora Temple has enough in her pedigree, so far as known, to account for her trotting, the probability of speed in her colts by Rysdyk is not very great. It is a pity she would not breed to Mambrino Pilot, that any deficiency in her own pedigree might have been made up by his extraordinary good breeding. The portrait of Flora Temple and her colt, facing the title page, is from a photograph, and gives a very good idea of them as they appear in their winter coats.

The effect on offspring of breeding blood relations together, called breeding in-and-in, is a matter that has received much attention from breeders and physiologists; and these two classes of observers have arrived at somewhat different conclusions about it; the physiologists condemning the practice among human beings, the breeders approving of it among domestic stock. As the same laws govern all nature, this difference of opinion must grow out of an imperfect knowledge of the law, and might be reconciled by a more comprehensive view of the facts relating to the subject.

When blood-relations intermarry, the children are often imperfect, being idiotic, or blind, or scrofulous; or if they escape these and a host of other ills that in-bred flesh is heir to, they are seldom so healthy and strong in mind and body as their parents were.

This is too well known to admit of a doubt, though, happily, the evil consequences of such intermarriages are not always noticeable in such unpleasant forms. On the other hand, many good horses have been the result of close in-and-in breeding. By referring to the pedigree of Rysdyk's Hambletonian, Table I., it will be seen that Abdallah was by Mambrino, out of his half-sister; Hambletonian was by Messenger, out of one of his own daughters; and One-Eye was by in-bred Hambletonian, out of his half-sister. Then comes one out-cross with Bellfounder, and again the offspring of that cross, the Charles Kent Mare, is bred to in-bred Abdallah of the same stock. The result was a stallion that has for several years stood at the head of the list of trotting foal getters.

How are these two classes of facts to be reconciled? The theory that gregarious animals—animals that, like horses, cattle, and sheep, go naturally in herds—are an exception to the rule that in-breeding is attended by debility in the offspring, is not very satisfactory. It cannot be true, as has been asserted, that in a wild state one stallion would keep his own herd of mares and all of his own female progeny to himself for several years, and that hence breeding with his own offspring would be in accordance with Nature's plan. In a wild state there would be as many males as females; his herd of mares would be but one or two; half of his offspring would be males; they would each contend for and obtain some sexual opportunities; the fillies of one sire would naturally be squandered everywhere among other herds before they were old enough to breed; and all the conditions would favor continual out-crossing rather than in-breeding. Pigs are gregarious, and in-breeding spoils the breed of them in one generation. No matter how near the hog-breeder has brought his stock to perfection, one single in-breeding spoils all. In chickens, if in-breeding is continued for several years, the first noticeable result is their increased productiveness of eggs. The stock becomes smaller and more delicate with each successive in-breeding; and all weakly animals are more prolific than stronger ones, hence the increased number of eggs. When the conditions of life depress and retard the development of plants or animals, they become more prolific because their offspring will come into being under circumstances unfavorable to the continuance of their existence, and Nature equalizes the chances by producing more of them. It is in accordance with this law that fat animals and idle animals are not sure to breed; that families living luxuriously for a few generations have very few children, while those that "live from hand to mouth" are proverbially fruitful—"A fool for luck, and a poor man for children." The chickens are more prolific for a few generations, but continue the in-breeding, and they become so very weakly and small that the experiment will end in a good out-cross. If it were continued longer in the same direction, the result would probably be the extinction of the stock.

Hambletonian, Plato, and Abdallah, the in-bred descendants of Messenger, were remarkable for giving the trotting quality to their descendants. Taking Messenger as a single source of the trotting quality, and supposing there was not another horse in the country above mediocrity in that respect, we might expect some of his fillies to inherit his trotting in great degree. To perpetuate that particular quality in her offspring, it would be better to breed her to her sire than to any horse of another stock, though her offspring might lose something in stamina by the in-breeding. It might be still better to breed her to any son of Messenger that also, equally with herself, inherited the trotting quality. In either case, her colts would take the trotting from two directions, and would consequently transmit it with more certainty to their descendants than if they inherited it from only one side. The trotting quality was a peculiarity of Messenger, and by in-breeding it was perpetuated; so would any other peculiarity have been— any imperfection. If Messenger had been lop-eared, that quality could have been perpetuated in the same way; but as breeders would not choose his lop-eared colts to breed from, and would choose his perfect colts, the desirable qualities of the stock could be, and would be, perpetuated, and the defects would become extinguished from his family.

The purpose of in-breeding the Messenger family was not, at first, to produce trotters; but the result followed without regard to the intention. Whatever loss of stamina accompanied the practice was remedied by out-crossing, and the trotting was still preserved by careful selection.

Taking this view of the subject, we see how the perpetuation of any particular quality may be effected by in-breeding, and how, also, the evils of the practice may be to a great extent avoided. It should be borne in mind that Messenger was remarkably free from defects, and had so much strength of constitution that his descendants from good mares might be in-bred and still give good constitutions to their offspring. It was because of this excellence that the in-breeding was practised. Not for the purpose of reproducing in the progeny any particular quality, but with a desire to get as much as possible of the general characteristics of a horse recognised as greatly superior to all others in the same vicinity. The same reasons that induced to the practice made it physiologically safe.

Now let us suppose that another equally good trotting family had existed at the same time and place, and that instead of breeding Messenger's descendants together closely they had been crossed with the other family. The result would have been equal speed, with equal power of transmitting it to offspring, and better constitutions. There came to this country another thorough-bred, that was foaled in England one year before Messenger, and died here, one year before Messenger died. His name was Diomed, and a reference to the tabulated pedigrees will show how much many of our best trotters are indebted to him for their speed. He was not brought to this country until he was twenty-two years old, and was kept in Virginia, while Messenger was in the North. Diomed's colts were nearly all thorough-breds, and used for running, not trotting. Trotting did not become so highly valued in the South, and how much trotting quality the immediate descendants of Diomed possessed was not known. The best results have followed breeding the two families together after several generations of descent; and there is no reason to doubt that if Diomed had come with Messenger to this country, and had stood somewhere near Philadelphia or New York, instead of coming seventeen years later, and standing in Virginia, the two families would have been inter-bred sooner. Two good results would have attended: first, all the advantage of breeding trotters with trotters without the disadvantage of in-breeding; and, second, the interbreeding of two good trotting families before the trotting quality was diluted by other crosses not possessing it. American Eclipse, who gave so much trotting quality to his descendants, combined both bloods. See pedigree of Mambrino Pilot, Table II. Eclipse was known only as a running horse, and was one of the very best thorough-breds ever foaled in America. He was equally distinguished on the turf and in the stud. Post Boy, a distinguished race-horse that lived to a great age, had many trotting descendants. He, too, combined the blood of Messenger and Diomed. See pedigree of Young Morrill, Table V. All the trotting of Morrill on his sire's side was inherited from Post Boy. Another thorough-bred of the same descent was Cock-of-the-Rock. He too was a race-horse that begot trotters. Golddust inherits all of his trotting from him. See Table IV. These and other similar cases that might be adduced, show that the produce of a cross between two trotting families has equal power of transmitting its peculiar qualities to offspring that the produce of in-breeding has.

In breeding two trotting families together, if one has any defect the other may correct it, as it is improbable that both will have the same defect; but by in-breeding any defect of the family will be pretty surely perpetuated, as the colt will inherit it from both sides. Now that we have trotters enough to allow of a free selection without breeding near relations together, there are no reasons why the practice should be continued, and many why it should not be.

The opinion is quite prevalent among breeders, that every horse a mare is bred to modifies, not only his own get, but all the colts she may afterwards have by any other horses. Without denying the facts set forth in the body of this book by Stonehenge, of a mare that had colts by a horse, and that they resembled the quagga she was first bred to, I am prepared to assert that no such effects are commonly noticed when mares are bred to different stallions. I have looked for such results in various species of animals—the human included—and could never detect the slightest resemblance in the offspring of one sire to any other sire the dam had previously borne offspring to. Practically, the theory is of no value whatever. Another notion, about equally common, is, that a mare that has bred a mule will not breed to a horse. It is equally unfounded. Mares are often bred to horses after having been bred to an ass, and nobody ever sees a foal by a horse from such a mare look like a mule. I have known several instances of white women having mulatto children, and afterwards having children by white men; and in no instance was the influence of the negro perceptible on the child of the Caucasian father. If any man has a good mare that has produced a colt from a scrub stallion, he need not hesitate, on that account, to breed her to a good horse, if he has an opportunity.

Breeders often desire that a colt shall be a male, or a female; but that is always left to chance for the best of reasons. It is probably possible, however, to discover the laws governing the production of sex, and also possible to so control their action as to attain the desired result. Some chance experiments in breeding dogs, so long ago as 1845, induced me to a more careful investigation of the subject. I discovered, that if a slut were kept until near the last of her heat, before a dog was admitted to her, the pups would be chiefly males; but if she were at large, with all the dogs of the neighborhood, from the beginning of the heat, they would be mostly females. Further experiments, and on other species of animals, were prevented by removal to a city; but having called public attention to the matter, in lectures on physiology in several states, others have pursued the investigation with very satisfactory results. Dog-breeders make practical application of the discovery in hundreds of instances, and a few dairy-men have found it applicable to cows. The theory is, that if the female is long in heat before conception, it implies a scarcity of males, and Nature supplies the deficiency by producing them. I also noticed that if a cock had many hens, the chicks would be mostly males. This I had but one opportunity of observing. The single observation, however, is in conformity with the same law. Applying the law to horses, it would follow that, other things being equal, the more mares he served in one season, the more of his colts would be males. The action of the law would be modified by the time of the mare's heat when put to him, and by the circumstance that his sire, his grandsire, and so on, for many generations, had been used to serving many mares in one season—so that the power to do so without forcing the action of the law would have become hereditary. If the mare were served in the beginning of her heat, we might expect a mare foal; and if in the last part of the erotic season we might, by the same rule, expect a horse foal. Of course, the conditions mentioned as affecting the stallion might modify the result. If a mare were put to a horse in the last part of her heat, and if the horse had quite recently served one or more other mares, the conditions would be favorable on both sides to the production of a male offspring. If the case were reversed—if she were in the first part of her season of excitement, and he had not served a mare for a considerable time, the conditions would favor the begetting of a female.

Many horsemen attempt to discern the speed of a horse in his form, and in his way of going. Various signs are relied on, by those who know less than they think they do, but there is but one sign, and it is infallible; it is that the horse goes fast when tried. A shoulder that slants well backward to the withers is considered a good point in any horse—but Messenger had upright shoulders, and so have some very good trotters of to-day. A long back, with an open flank between the hip and ribs, is thought to allow of a long stride, and some good trotters have that conformation; but many others have short backs, and are ribbed close up to the hips. Of these two forms, the last is the best, as it indicates that the animal will keep in good condition on less food. Flat-sided horses have trotted fast, but not because they were flat-sided. War Eagle had that conformation, and though he trotted in the best of company, he was not an all-day horse. I drove him a year in a country practice before he trotted in public, and did not consider the narrow chest and small abdomen any advantage. A steep rump is a sign that a horse paces; but with the same form he may be a trotter; and in either case it has no relation to speed. The hind legs may be more crooked or more straight than usual, and the fore legs may be a little sprung forward, or a little set back, like a calf's; the pasterns may be thick or slender, upright or oblique; but none of these forms indicate speed, nor the absence of it. Many fast horses are short in the rump—that is, from the croup, or highest point, to the root of the tail. This is pretty common among trotters; but some that are not fast have the same shape.

In the way of going, there is as much difference with as little significance. Some lift their fore-feet very high, with a great deal of knee action; others go fast, with a low, long stride. There is a way of reaching out with the fore-feet, that seems utterly incompatible with speed. It is a long, pitching step, such as is seen in horses trotting slowly and loftily in a field when startled. To go fast, the fore-feet should be struck at the ground, as if they were pulling the horse along, whether the stride be long or short.

If a horse stands with the toes of his fore-feet turned in, he will paddle in trotting; that is, he will swing his feet out right and left from a straight line; and the foot that is most turned in at the toe in standing will be most swung around like a paddle in a mush-pot, in trotting. The movement is unsightly and objectionable, but not absolutely incompatible with speed. If the toes are turned out in standing, they will be turned in in trotting, and may strike the opposite knee. This is so common in fast trotters, as to have received the appellation of speedy-cut. It should not be inferred, that cutting the knee is any sign of speed. It only happens, that a horse with this defect in his way of going, hits his knee when he goes fast enough to get his foot up that high. It is a serious objection, but many more fast horses have that action than the opposite one of paddling.

Nearly every good trotter goes with his hind-feet wide apart, when he goes fast. There are some exceptions to this rule, but they are not numerous. Some horses have a short stride, and as they generally show plenty of knee-action, and step fast, they appear to go very fast, and so they do sometimes. The Cannucks, from Canada, generally go in that way; and all of such steppers are usually spirited and pleasant road horses, being free-goers. Long-striders are sometimes rather heavy in a jog-trot; but they get over the ground faster than they appear to, and on the road will often pass short-steppers that appear to be going as fast, or faster. Many of the best are long-striders, and, other things being equal, the probabilities are greater of a horse going fast in a long stride than in a short one.

Hiram Woodruff, in his admirable work on "The Trotting Horse of America," expresses the opinion that short-steppers are better weight-pullers at speed, and gives reasons—speculative reasons—for the opinion: but his own instances do not sustain the rule, unless we accept the logic, that as exceptions prove the rule, the more exceptions the stronger the proof. The truth appears to be, that the ability to pull weight does not depend much on the stride. The strongest movers are stout, muscular horses, broad behind, with the knees and hocks let well down; that is, with short cannon bones.

A horse may be lazy, and yet trot fast when called on; or he may be very spirited, always willing to do his best, and not be able to trot in four minutes. A very strong horse, that can trot off with a loaded market-wagon behind him at a good gait, and keep it up for miles, may not be a fast trotter at any weight. Or a horse may have most excellent bottom—may take two men in a wagon over common roads sixty miles in a day, and repeat it every day in the week; or he may be good for ten miles an hour under the same circumstances, and not be able to trot a single mile in four minutes.

Speed, then, does not depend entirely on the form, nor on the way of going, nor on the strength, nor on the spirit of a horse. The value of a fast trotter may depend greatly upon these qualities, but not his speed. Any form, and any style of going, may do, if he can step *fast* enough; and the power to step fast does not depend on form, spirit, strength, nor stamina—though all of these do modify the manifestation of that power upon which speed does depend.

Let us now consider the essential element of speed at any gait, whether it be running, pacing, or trotting. All the movement is effected by the contraction of those masses of lean meat called muscles. The muscles of voluntary motion are each attached to two bones by its two extremities, and the bones being attached to each other by a movable joint, when the muscle contracts one or both of the bones must move; and, of course the rapidity of the movement depends on the rapidity of the contraction. An animal wills the movement of a limb; that will, which originates in the brain, is transmitted through nerves to the muscles; they contract and the limb moves. It would seem, then, that if a horse desired to go fast, and his muscles were large enough and his joints supple, he must needs do so whenever he tries; for if the muscles obey the will, and the will is that they shall contract quickly, the whole thing would be accomplished. Speed would then depend on the size of the muscles, and the willingness of the horse to contract them rapidly. But the facts are clearly against such a theory; for all have noticed that a highly spirited horse that is very strong to pull a load, may not be able to go fast in any gait.

The truth is, that all power to move, lies not in the brain which is the seat of the will, nor in the muscles which are the place of the movement, but between the two, in the spinal cord, which is the centre of the nervous system, and the generator of the power. The spinal cord lies in the back bone, filling the canal or hole that extends through its whole length, and giving off nerves from every part of it that go to all parts of the body. It is connected to the brain, and appears like a prolongation of it from the cavity of the skull along the cavity of the spine; but the rational view of the spinal cord, and the one that is sustained by comparative anatomy, is that which considers it the centre of the nervous system; the brain being an extension of it in one direction, and the nerves an extension of it in another direction, the whole constituting the nervous system.

The brain is the seat of all mental manifestations—of thought, memory, love, fear, emulation, courage, &c. The disposition and character depend upon the brain, but it is not necessary to animal life. The nerves extend to every part of the body; some of them convey sensations to the brain, as of heat, or cold, or pain; others of them go to the muscles, and convey to them the power that is generated in the spinal cord by which they contract. The *will* to move is conceived in the brain, and goes to the spinal cord, which then generates the *power* to move. The power, which for convenience of language we will call nerve force, is sent through the nerves and expended in the muscles, effecting their contraction and a consequent movement of the bones to which they are attached. The brain may be compared to a telegraph operator, the spinal cord to his galvanic battery, and the nerves to the wires. A chicken with its head off kicks and flutters with strength enough to fly over a barn, or to run around it. The spinal cord generates the power for a short time, and would do so longer but for the loss of blood; but the brain, that gives intelligent direction to the power, is not there. The battery is sending its electricity along the wires without the control of the operator.

If enough of the nerve force is sent to the muscles to move the body a mile in six minutes, it is six minutes in being generated. If the same amount of nerve force can be generated and sent to the muscles in three minutes, we might suppose that the body would be moved the same distance in three minutes; and herein would appear to lie all the difference of speed. But the *amount* of force generated by the nervous centre, and expended by the muscles, in a given time, does not exactly explain the difference of speed. One horse may expend as much nerve force in pulling a load a quarter of a mile in three minutes, as another does in trotting a whole mile in the same time, and yet not be able to trot a mile in four minutes. The speed depends on the ability of the spinal cord to generate and send to the different sets of muscles concerned in locomotion, the required amounts of nerve force in a quick succession of discharges; and on the capability of the nerves to transmit it to the muscles in large quantity in a short time. The difference between trotting fast and drawing a heavy load, is not in the amount of force used, but in the manner of using it. In one case, the nerve force is sent to a muscle during the whole time of taking a slow step with a heavy load; and in the other, it is all expended in an instant, causing the muscle to contract quickly, and thereby projecting the horse rapidly forward—the acquired momentum continuing after the muscle ceases to contract. It is like driving a nail by a succession of blows, that could not be moved by the same aggregate amount of pressure diffused and continued over the whole time of driving.

The essential quality of speed, at any gait, is therefore a certain organization of the nervous system, and this is the one thing needful in every case. This is what we breed for when we breed for speed; this is the quality that has been transmitted through so many generations from Messenger, Diomed, Pilot, Bellfounder, and other progenitors of American trotters. A descendant of Messenger might have neither his form, size, nor way of going, but if he had a similar organization of the nervous system, he would have speed. We cannot detect this peculiarity of organization by any outward sign; we can know of it only by its manifestations. We know that it is hereditary, and we also know that it may be associated with any form. We therefore must respect the pedigrees of the horses and mares we breed from; and the more of the trotting quality we find in their pedigrees, the more reason we will have for expecting a fast colt. Form, size, style, and action are all important matters in the constitution of any horse, and particularly important in trotters, because they are kept for use and for pleasure-driving as well as for racing; but the speed is not a result of any combination of these qualities. The right kind of a nervous system will accomplish more if the form and action are good than if they are bad; and all the necessary conditions of speed may exist in a horse, and yet he may be valueless because of an incurably bad temper, or because he inherits a strong tendency to some disqualifying disease. These matters every breeder will use his own judgment on. If a mare is good in all respects except speed, and is bred to a horse of speed, but of bad organization in other respects, the colt may have all the good qualities of the dam and the speed of the sire; or may have the bad qualities of the sire and the want of speed of the dam. It is impossible to foresee in what proportion the two parents will transmit their respective qualities to the offspring; so that the safest rule in breeding, is to have as much of all the qualities we breed for in both parents as is possible. The speed should be in both families to make its inheritance certain; but if it is strongly inherited by one side, we may reasonably expect all of the progeny to go faster than the parent that is not speedy. Thus a slow mare bred to a good trotting-foal getter, will always produce faster colts than she would if bred to a slow stallion like herself.

The condition of parents at the time of conception has a powerful influence on the progeny—whether it be mental or physical condition. Offspring inherit both the congenital and the acquired qualities of parents, as is well exemplified in the familiar case of dogs taught to hunt birds, and when they are found, to stand and wait for a man to shoot them, instead of rushing on to catch them as the instinctive impulse would prompt. The standing is an acquired quality, the effect of teaching, and yet it is transmitted by hereditary descent as certainly as any other quality. A well-bred setter or pointer pup will stand stanchly at a game bird, when only four months old, without any teaching. The effect on offspring of the transient condition of parents, may be seen in every family. No two children of the same parents are alike, unless they be twins. The reason is plain; the parents change from year to year, and the children inherit the changed conditions. The father may have a lawsuit, and a child may inherit the contentiousness and obstinacy engendered by it; he may afterwards be engaged in active business enterprises, and transmit energy and a clear intellect to another child; a third may be idiotic, because his father was enervated by a debauch. Many causes of change will occur to each parent in the year or two that elapses between the births of children, and these changes in the parents modify the constitutions of the children. Twins may be much alike, because there is no time for change, commonly, between the times of their conception; though they may differ by resembling different parents, or by an interval between the times of conception, or even by being the children of different fathers.

It is not essential to the transmission of acquired qualities, that they shall have been long acquired; a few days of strength or of debility, even perhaps a single hour of difference in the parent, may make a life-long difference to the child. A mental impression, however short, if only strong enough, may be transmitted. Well-authenticated cases have been related to me, one of a full-bred Durham calf that resembled neither parent, but a brindle ox that strongly impressed the minds of both parents at the time of conception; and another of a litter of pigs of the white variety, common in Chester and Delaware counties, and famous everywhere, that were part of them black, because a black sow from Maryland was conspicuously present at the time of conception. Several cases have come within my own knowledge, of mares that produced foals colored and marked like some stable or field companion, and entirely unlike both parents in that respect.

It is a popular belief that impressions made on the mind of the mother during pregnancy, may be transmitted to the offspring; but that cannot be true, because there is no connection by nerves between the mother and child; and a mental impression could not be conveyed by the blood. All of such supposed cases were probably instances in which the impression was made on the mind of the mother before conception—became a part of herself—and was then transmitted to her offspring by the same law that any other quality of a parent is transmitted. This accounts, probably, for the well-authenticated case, before alluded to, of colts resembling a quagga that was not their sire. The mare had a distinct recollection of the strange beast associated in her mind, with the sexual intercourse she had first with him; and subsequent occasions of a similar kind with horses recalled the mental impression, and it was transmitted, being, and having been for years, a part of her mental constitution.

It follows, that in breeding for trotting horses, we should not be unmindful of the temporary condition of the sire and dam. Mares are generally worked, and are nearly always in very good condition for breeding. With stallions, it is usually quite different. They are kept, as if their use was procreating colts for beef, rather than speed, spirit, and endurance. They are overfed and underworked; they are fat and feeble; their muscles and ligaments are not strengthened by exercise; their blood is not purified by the increased secretions that accompany a quickened circulation of blood; their courage and endurance are not developed by a long journey occasionally; their emulation is not stimulated by racing; and consequently these qualities, all so desirable in the offspring, are not transmitted in the intensity and power they might be if a more rational plan were pursued. The health and longevity of the stallion are endangered by these debilitating causes, and the best horse might lose reputation as a good trotting-foal getter in a few years of the enervating management too common everywhere. It is supposed by many, that a horse that serves many mares has demand enough upon his strength without working. The truth is, he needs plenty of well-regulated exercise to keep his strength up, and his health good, that he may safely and profitably meet the great demand upon his vitality.

It is becoming quite common to test the speed of trotting colts at three, at two, and even at one year old; and with proper care, it may be done safely. The trial should be made after a little preparation, by gradually increased exercise, and the distance should be short. Curiosity being gratified by a few trials, should be also satisfied, for colts cannot stand much speeding without danger of injury.

To teach a young horse to trot well requires judgment and care. He is to be improved by practice, there is no other way; and he should be made to like it, not fear it. He should make his best effort, willingly, eagerly, and doing so repeatedly, he cannot fail to improve. Kindness and gentleness are always necessary in the management of horses, and especially so in the taming and teaching of young horses. No horse should be put to a high rate of speed until he is first warmed up and breathing freely, and then he should be rested a little by a slow gait, but not allowed to cool off before he is called on to do his best.

The young horse does not always know just what is wanted of him, and it is therefore a good plan to trot him on the same piece of level road always, and when he comes to it he will expect to trot. He should never be made tired of it, but always stopped while he is still anxious to go. The training is as much a mental as a physical discipline; it must be both. Some horses need the stimulation of the voice or whip; others will require only to be held to their work. The dull one should be stimulated by emulation—another horse should be trotted or galloped alongside of him; and whether the accompanying horse should be kept just even with him, or a little before or behind, must be ascertained by trial. An intelligent horse becomes discouraged by being beaten in a race, and either breaks into a run to catch up, or quits making any strong effort. Young horses being more impulsive and less under the influence of training and experience, feel the mortification of defeat more than older ones. Some colts are so anxious to beat, that it is impossible to keep them trotting with a competitor of equal or greater speed, but if put in double harness they understand that they cannot get ahead of the other by running, and will do their very best trotting honestly. All animals, except men, have more intelligence than they get credit for; and a great many failures in the management of horses come from men's over-estimate of themselves, and their failure to appreciate and properly regard the intelligence of the other animal.

The ground should be smooth, and level, or a little descending. If rough it throws him out of his step; and if ascending he may get to hopping, or hipping, as it is sometimes called—that is, he does not trot square, but goes in a half gallop with his hind legs, as an easier way of taking the weight along, while he trots with his fore legs. Taking too much weight, or being pushed beyond his speed, may make him do it; and the remedies are, avoidance of the causes, and driving at a moderate speed until the habit is forgotten. The common notion that a horse can better trot up hill than down, is too absurd to merit serious refutation. Whether the hill be steep or otherwise, long or short, the horse can trot down it, either under saddle or in harness, easier than he can trot up it.

A high speed for a short distance does not injure even quite young horses, but keeping them at it until the ligaments that bind the bones together at the joints are overtaxed, and feel sore the next day, is the way to stiffen the joints, to cause knuckling of the hind fetlock joints, and springing of the knees. No horse should be so tired by a day's work that a night's rest will not make him fresh again, and this is especially true of young horses. If a horse is worked moderately at first, and a little more is exacted of him in each succeeding day, but without violation of the rule just stated, his powers will gradually increase to meet the increased demand; but if that rule is violated for days in succession, the horse's powers daily diminish, and the experiment will end in injury to his health and spirit.

In trotting young horses the greatest difficulty is in keeping them squarely at their work. They will try to go as fast as they can, and they know that they can run faster than they can trot. The colt that can naturally trot very fast will have less desire to run, and being necessarily descended from trotting ancestors, he will naturally be more disposed to do his best going in that way. If possible, he should never be driven "off his feet," but should be made to understand that he has but one way of going, and that is trotting.

Inexperienced drivers are never satisfied with their horse's trotting until they have driven them out of their gait, and then they are more dissatisfied than before. Rude snatching and sawing of the mouth by the bit make matters worse—but the man who always makes his horse break up, always punishes the horse for doing it; and particularly is this true when some other horse is out-footing his. He then imagines that his horse is not doing as much as he could, if he were disposed to; the whip is brought into passionate use, and the bit is cruelly made an instrument of torture to counteract the effect of the whip. This kind of driving teaches a young horse that trotting is to always end in a break, and the break in a painful and alarming punishment. These unskilful, ungentlemanly drivers find a remedy for the horse's too much willingness in fatiguing him by a long drive at speed, after which the poor creature may stick to his trot from sheer exhaustion. A more skilful driver would get all the speed the horse was capable of while he was fresh and strong, and without injury to his health or disposition. A high-strung young horse may need to have the wire-edge taken off sometimes before he will go steadily; and it should be done by a long jog-trot, with a few short brushes of speed occasionally, which will work off his exuberance of spirits without injury.

No trotter attains his greatest speed before maturity; and the best of them continue to improve up to fifteen and eighteen years of age. To do this a horse must have a good constitution; one that will carry him to a great age without disease, and will stand the hard work necessary to develop his powers. Breeding from such horses will therefore improve the stock of the country—not only in speed, but also in stamina. The cultivation of thoroughbreds, for running races, has been of immense benefit to the road stock of the country, by improving its speed and stamina, and by giving it better form and style. The American trotter gets more of his peculiar excellence from the thorough-breds, than from all other sources. But a thorough-bred of acknowledged excellence as the sire of racers, might be utterly worthless to improve the road stock. Lexington, the sire of more winners than any other horse now in this country, is blind; his sire, Boston, was blind; and many of the Lexington colts go blind at an early age. In 1868 two of his get were foaled blind. Yet the best thoroughbred mares are bred to him, because the progeny will probably keep good sight until five years old, before which age nearly all the racing is done. If he were a trotting stallion breeders would not use him, because his colts would go blind before they had attained their greatest usefulness.

We may, therefore, reasonably expect the breeding of trotting horses to improve the road stock of the country, even far more than was done by the thorough-breds. A thorough-bred that fails as a racer, may be only a middling kind of a horse for any other use; but the trotting horse that may not be among the fastest on the course, may, and probably will be, a very superior road horse.

The following table shows the best performances from the beginning of trotting as a public amusement in this country in 1818, to 1868, in which year a larger number of very fast horses trotted in public than in any former period. The driving of horses long distances at speed, is a practice that cannot be too strongly reprobated. Four horses have trotted twenty miles within an hour, and several others have tried it and failed. Black Joke, that trotted fifty miles in less than four hours, was severely injured by it. The Orange County horse, that trotted a hundred miles in less than nine hours, died the same day. Such cruelties bring discredit on trotting races, and should not be countenanced. Ordinary racing is not cruel—albeit, many good people who never saw a race think differently; and though these performances at long distances are introduced to show the utmost capacity of horses, it is "devoutly to be wished," that there may never be any more to record.

ONE MILE.

Year.	Name of Horse.	Place of Performance.	Style of Going.	Time.
1818	Boston Blue,	Boston,	Harness,	3m. 0s.
1824	Albany Pony,	Long Island,	Saddle,	2m. 40s.
1834	Edwin Forrest,	Long Island,	Saddle,	2m. 31½s.
1839	Dutchman,	Beacon Course,	Saddle,	2m. 28s.
1847	Highland Maid,	Long Island,	Harness,	2m. 27s.
1849	Lady Suffolk,	Cambridge,	Saddle,	2m. 26s.
1855	Pocahontas (pacer),	Long Island,	Wagon,	2m. 17s.
1858	Ethan Allen,	Long Island,	Wagon,	2m. 28s.
1859	Flora Temple,	Kalamazoo,	Harness,	2m. 19¾s.
1859	Flora Temple,	Long Island,	Wagon,	2m. 25s.
1863	Peerless,	Long Island,	Wagon,	2m. 23¼s.
1865	Dexter,	Long Island,	Saddle,	2m. 18¼s.
1866	Dexter,	Buffalo,	Saddle,	2m. 18s.
1867	Dexter,	Buffalo,	Harness,	2m. 17¼s.
1868	Lady Thorn,	Boston,	Harness,	2m. 20½s.
1868	Mountain Boy,	Boston,	Harness,	2m. 20¾s.
1868	Bashaw, Jr.	Clinton, Iowa,	Harness,	2m. 21s.
1868	Geo. Palmer,	Boston,	Harness,	2m. 21⅛s.
1868	Geo. Wilkes,	Cranston, R. I.,	Harness,	2m. 22s.
1868	Lucy,	Cranston, R. I.,	Harness,	2m. 22½s.
1868	Goldsmith Maid,	Boston,	Harness,	2m. 23s.
1868	Fearnought,	Buffalo,	Harness,	2m. 23½s.
1868	Rhode Island,	Fashion Course,	Harness,	2m. 23½s.
1868	Draco Prince,	Cranston, R. I.,	Harness,	2m. 24¼s.
1868	American Girl,	Buffalo,	Harness,	2m. 24½s.
1868	Myron Perry,	Cranston, R. I.,	Harness,	2m. 25½s.
1868	Tattler (5 yrs.),	Louisville,	Harness,	2m. 26s.
1868	Billy Boyce (pacer),	Buffalo,	Saddle,	2m. 14¼s.
1868	Lamplighter (pacer),	Detroit,	Harness,	2m. 24¾s.
1868	Rolla Golddust,	Island Park, N.Y.	Harness,	2m. 21s.

Two Miles.

Year.	Name of Horse.	Place of Performance.	Style of Going.	Time.
1831	Top Gallant, . . .	Philadelphia,	Saddle,	5m. 19¾s.
1847	Lady Suffolk, . . .	Long Island,	Saddle,	5m. 3s.
1852	Tacony, ...	Long Island,	Saddle,	5m. 2s.
1858	Lady Franklin, . .	Long Island,	Wagon,	5m. 11s.
1859	Flora Temple, . . .	Long Island,	Harness,	4m. 50½s.
1865	Dexter, ...	Long Island,	Wagon,	4m. 56¼s.
1867	Dexter, ...	Long Island,	Harness,	4m. 51s.

Three Miles.

Year.	Name of Horse.	Place of Performance.	Style of Going.	Time.
1827	Screwdriver, . . .	Philadelphia,	Saddle,	8m. 2s.
1832	Columbus, ...	Long Island,	Saddle,	8m. 0s.
1839	Dutchman, ...	Beacon Course,	Saddle,	7m. 32½s.
1841	Lady Suffolk, . . .	Philadelphia,	Saddle,	7m. 40¼s.
1853	Pet, ...	Long Island,	Wagon,	8m. 1s.
1864	Stonewall Jackson, .	Long Island,	Harness,	7m. 39s.

One Mile in Double Harness.

1856	Lantern and Whalebone, ...	2m. 42s.
1861	Ethan Allen and running mate, ...	2m. 19¾s.
1862	Lady Palmer and Flatbush Maid (private trial), . . .	2m. 26s.
1867	Bruno and Brunette, ...	2m. 25¼s.
1867	Ethan Allen and running mate, ...	2m. 15s.

Two Miles in Double Harness.

1842	Lady Suffolk and Rifle, ...	5m. 19s.
1862	Lady Palmer and Flatbush Maid, ...	5m. 1¼s.

Twenty Miles.

Year.	Name of Horse.	Place of Performance.	Style of Going.	Time.
1848	Trustee, ...	Union Course,	Harness,	59m. 35½s.
1855	Lady Fulton, . .	Centreville Course,	Harness,	59m. 55s.
1865	Capt. McGowan,	Boston,	Harness,	58m. 25s.
1868	John Stewart, . . .	Fashion Course,	Harness,	58m. 30s.
1868	John Stewart, . . .	Boston,	Wagon,	59m. 23s.

Fifty Miles.

1842	Black Joke,	3h. 57m.

One Hundred Miles.

1840	Kate,	9h. 45m.
1842	Fanny Murray,	9h. 41m. 26s.
1845	Fanny Jenks,	9h. 38m. 34s.
1853	Orange County Horse,	8h. 55m. 53s.

If these few pages, written hastily in hours snatched from a laborious profession, and from sleep, should inspire the reader with a higher respect for and more tender sympathy with man's most useful and willing servant, they have not been written in vain.

CHESTER, PA., February 1869.

TABLE I.

RYSDYK'S HAMBLETONIAN
- Abdallah
  - Mambrino
    - Messenger.
    - Dam by Imp. Sourcrout.
  - Amazonia
    - Messenger.
    - Dam unknown.
- Charles Kent Mare
  - Imp. Bellfounder.
  - One Eye
    - Hambletonian
      - Messenger.
      - Dam
        - Messenger.
        - Dam unknown.
    - Silver Tail
      - Messenger.
      - Dam unknown.

The dotted lines show the trotting descent.

(507)

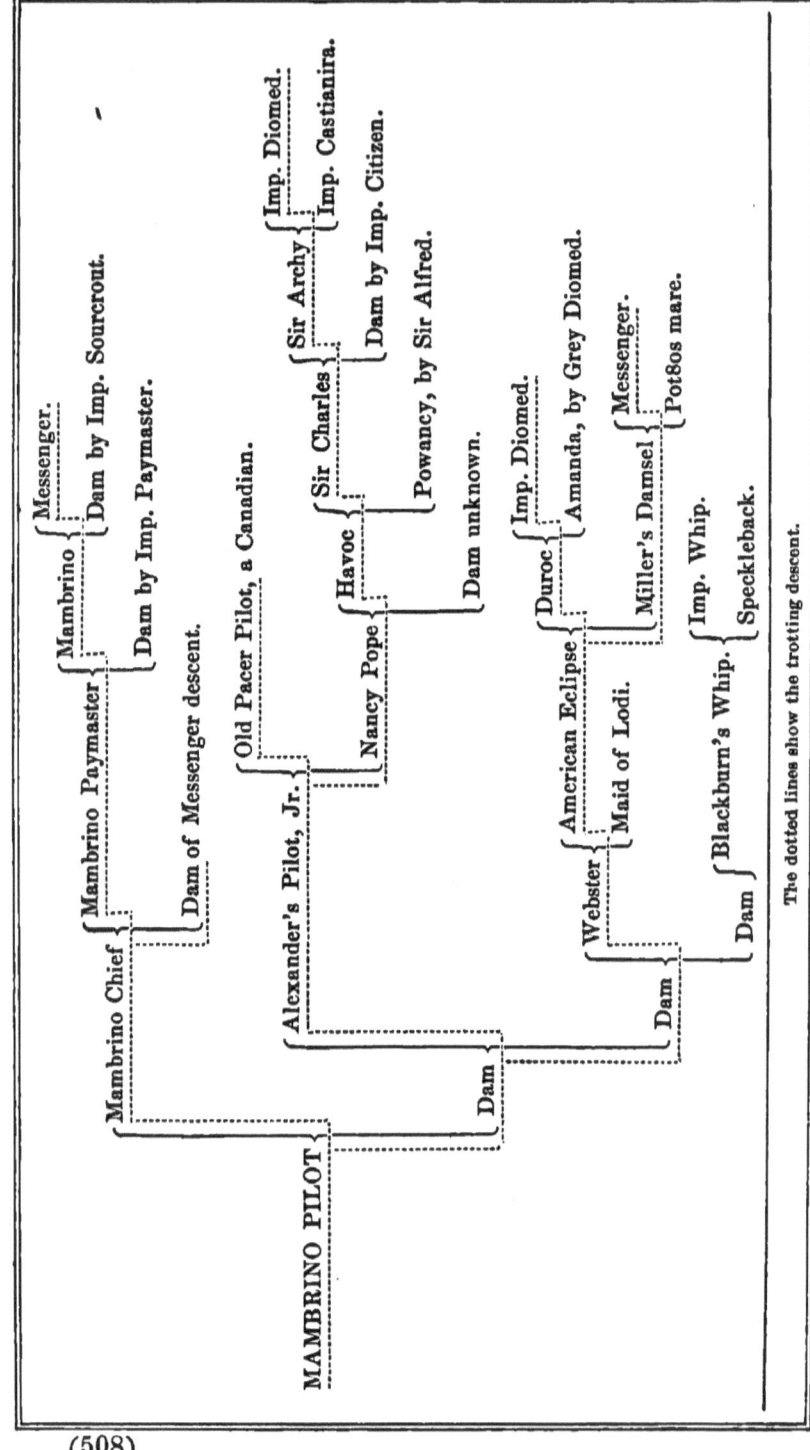

TABLE III.

GREEN'S BASHAW
- Vernol's Black Hawk
  - L. I. Black Hawk
    - And. Jackson
      - Young Bashaw
        - Imp. Arabian, Grand Bashaw.
        - Pearl
          - First Consul.
          - Fancy, by Messenger.
      - Dam
        - Why Not
          - Messenger.
          - Dam unknown.
        - Dam by Messenger.
    - Sally Miller, a very fast mare
      - Mambrino
        - Messenger.
        - Dam by Sourcrout.
  - Dam
    - Kentucky Whip.
    - Dam a fast trotter, by thorough-bred Shakspeare.
- Belle
  - Webber's Tom Thumb, the sire of trotters, Pedigree unknown.
  - Charles Kent Mare
    - Imp. Bellfounder.
    - One Eye
      - Hambletonian
        - Messenger.
        - Dam by Messenger.
      - Silvertail, by Messenger.

The dotted lines show the trotting descent.

Table IV.

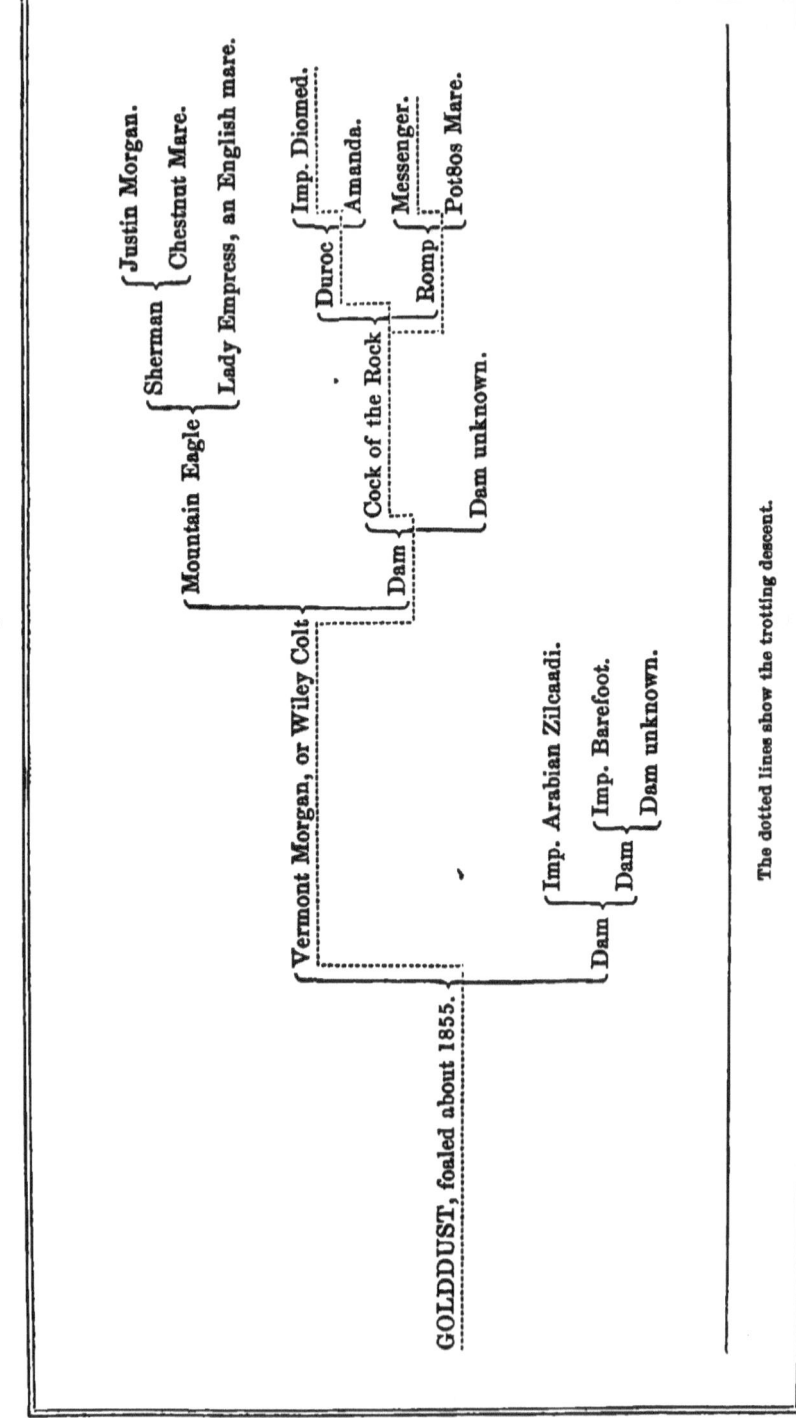

GOLDDUST, foaled about 1855.
- Vermont Morgan, or Wiley Colt
  - Mountain Eagle
    - Sherman
      - Justin Morgan.
      - Chestnut Mare.
    - Lady Empress, an English mare.
  - Dam
    - Cock of the Rock
      - Duroc
        - Imp. Diomed.
        - Amanda.
      - Romp
        - Messenger.
        - Pot8os Mare.
    - Dam unknown.
- Dam
  - Imp. Arabian Zilcaadi.
  - Dam
    - Imp. Barefoot.
    - Dam unknown.

The dotted lines show the trotting descent.

TABLE V.

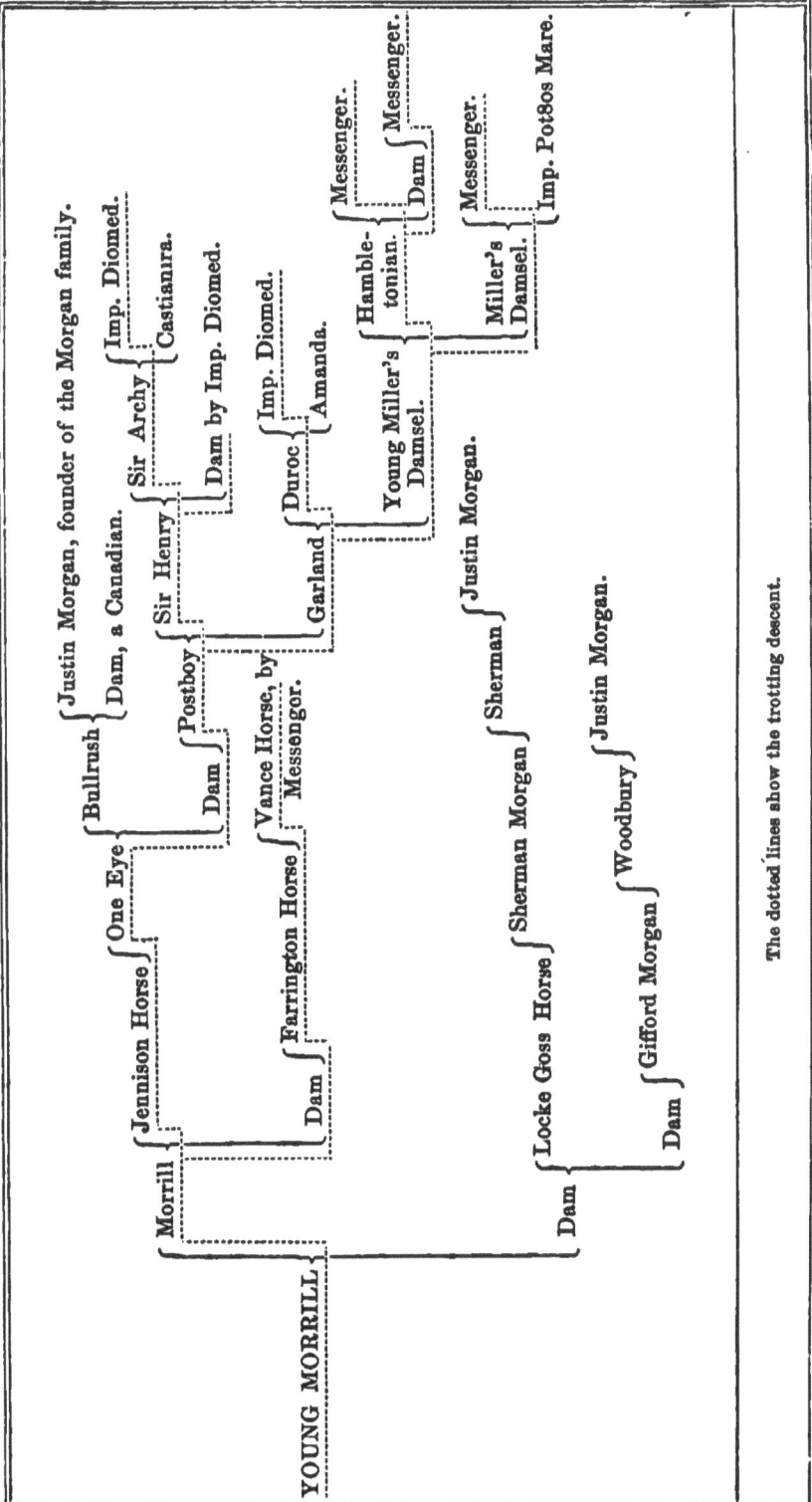

The dotted lines show the trotting descent.

(511)

TABLE VI.

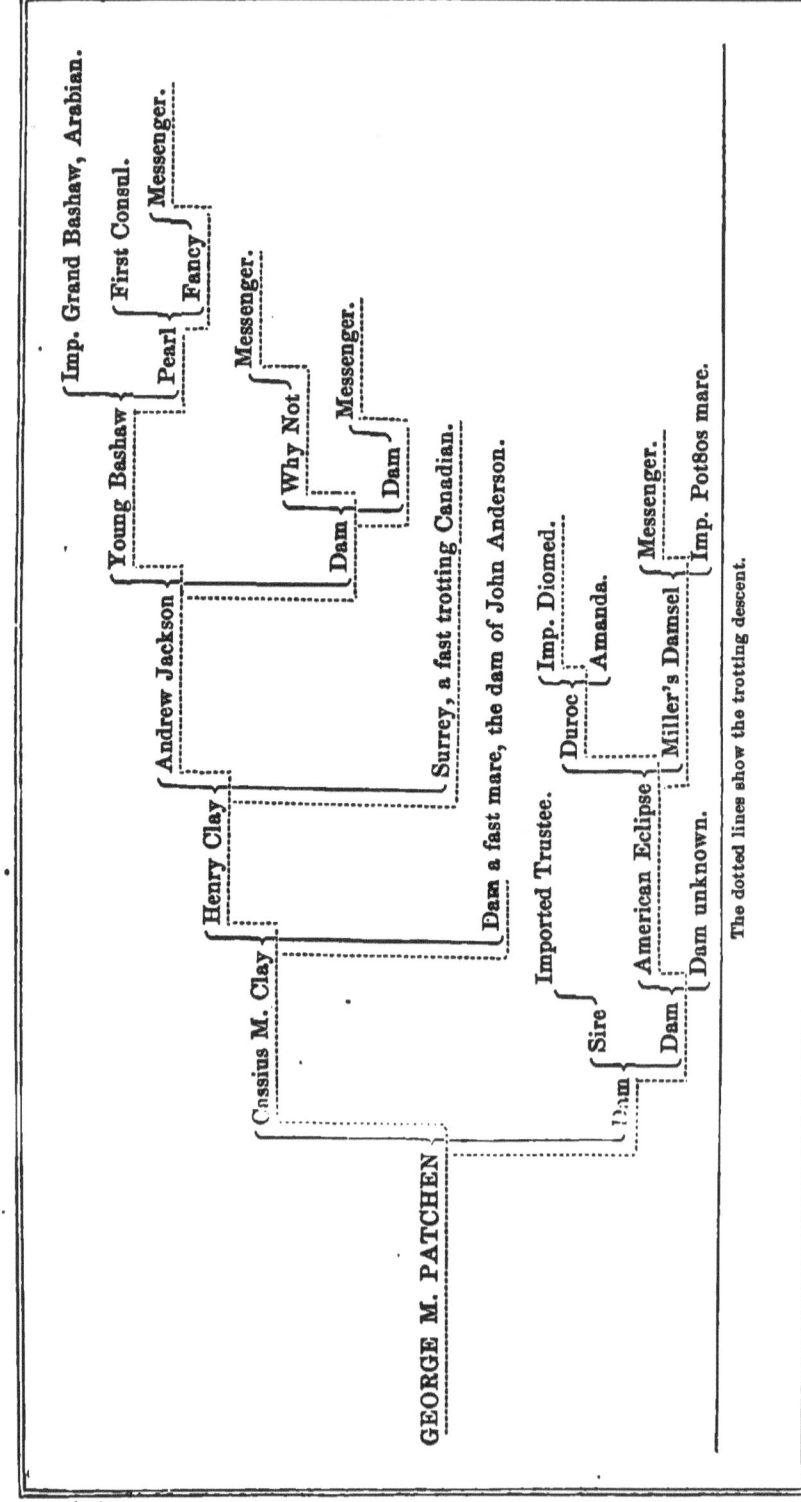

The dotted lines show the trotting descent.

Table VII.

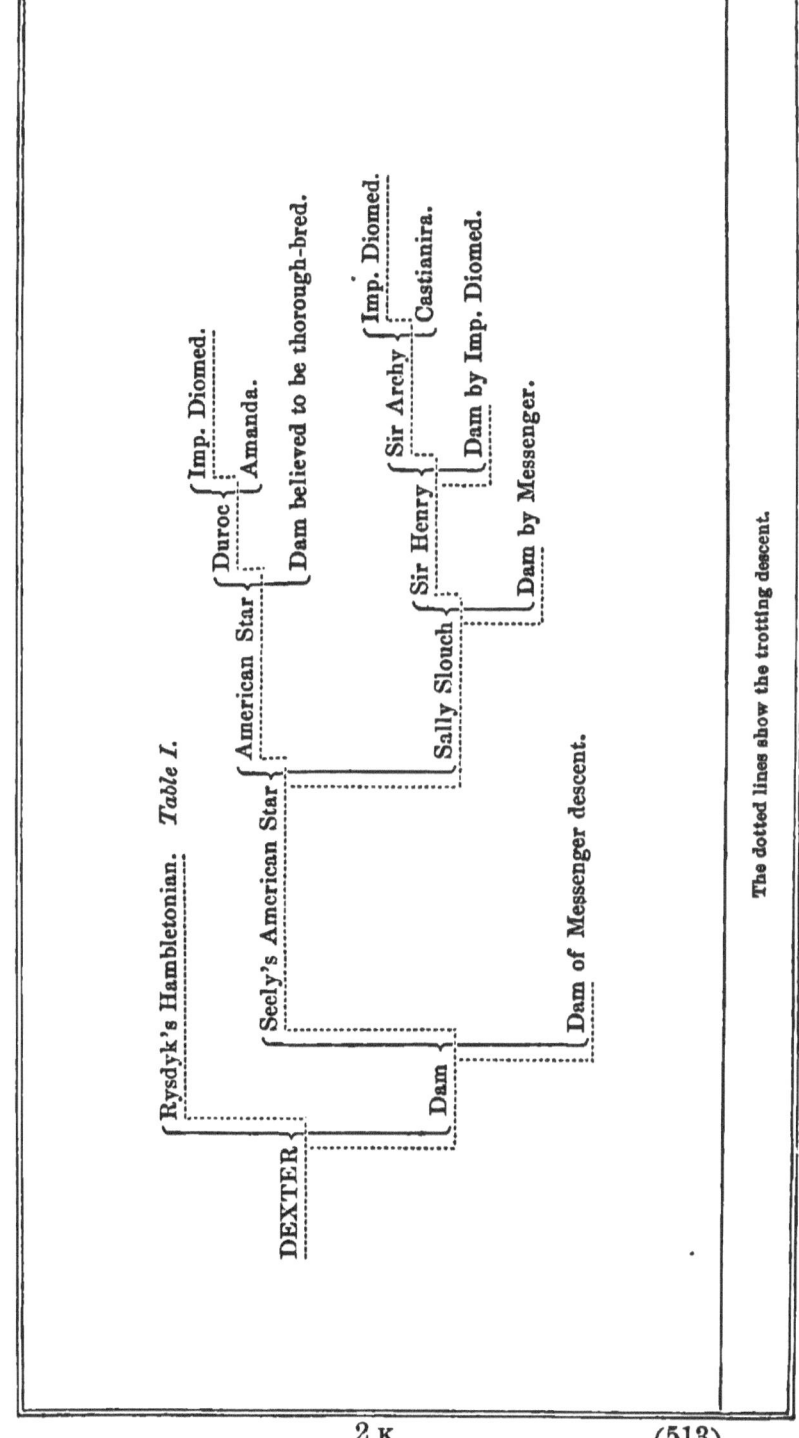

The dotted lines show the trotting descent.

Table VIII.

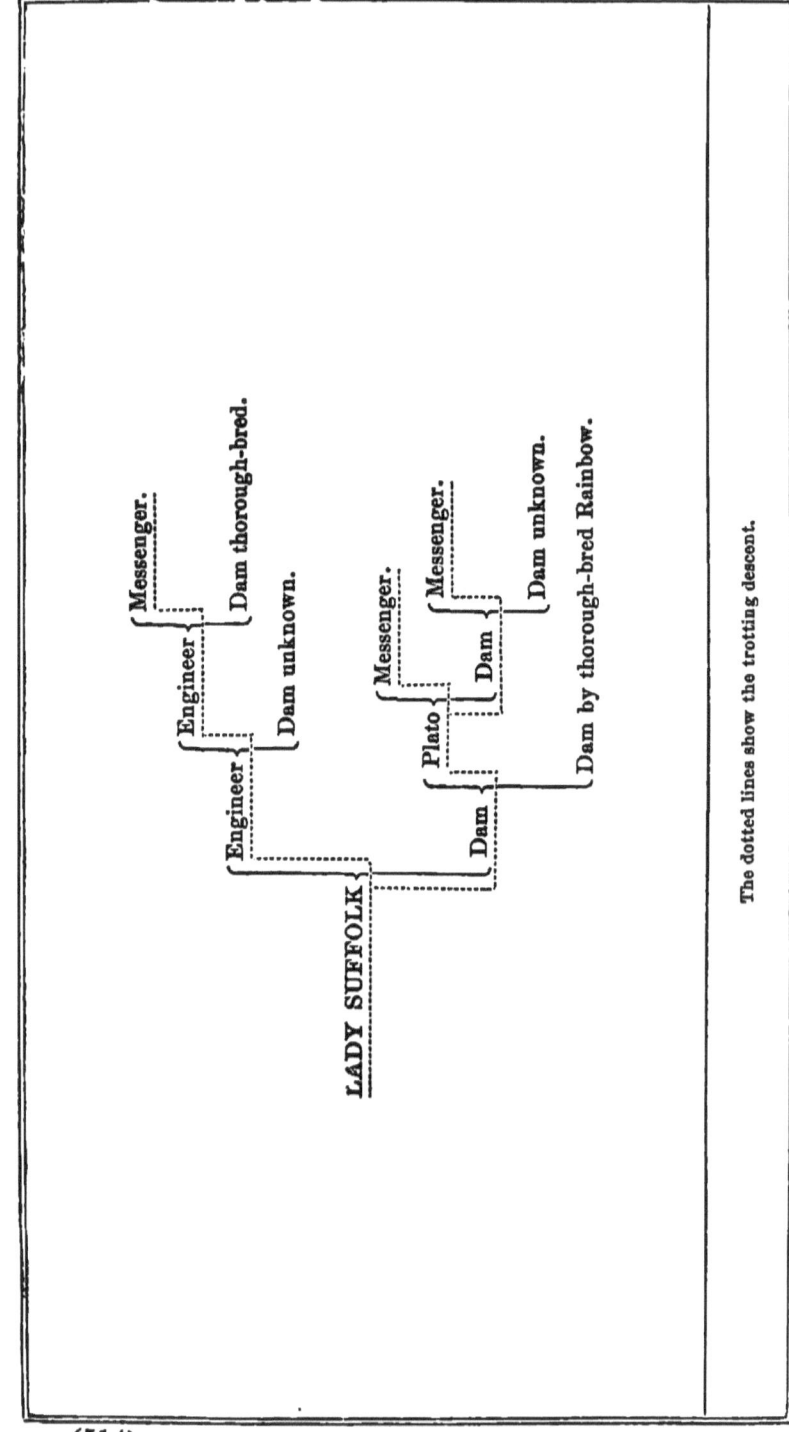

The dotted lines show the trotting descent.

TABLE IX.

LADY THORN
- Mambrino Chief
  - Mambrino Paymaster
    - Mambrino
      - Messenger.
      - Dam by Imp. Sourcrout.
    - Dam by Imp. Paymaster.
  - Dam of Messenger descent.
- Dam
  - Gano
    - American Eclipse
      - Duroc
        - Imp. Diomed.
        - Amanda, by Grey Diomed.
      - Miller's Damsel
        - Messenger.
        - Imp. Pot8os mare.
    - Betsy Richards
      - Sir Archy
        - Imp. Diomed.
        - Imp. Castianira, by Rockingham.
      - Dam by Rattle.
  - Dam
    - Potomac
      - Imp. Diomed.
      - Fairy, by Pegasus.
    - Dam unknown.

The dotted lines show the trotting descent.

(515)

TABLE X.

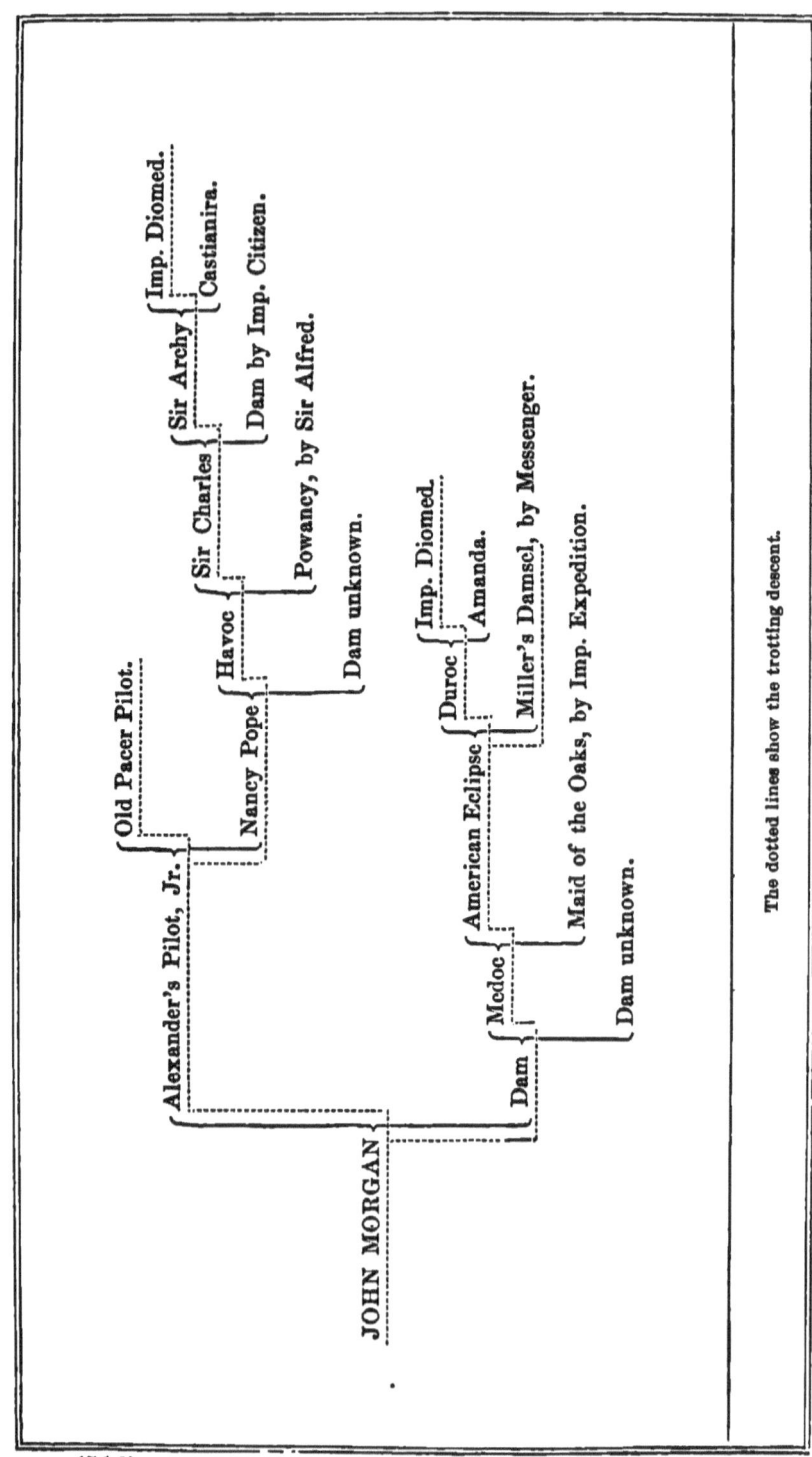

The dotted lines show the trotting descent.

TABLE XI.

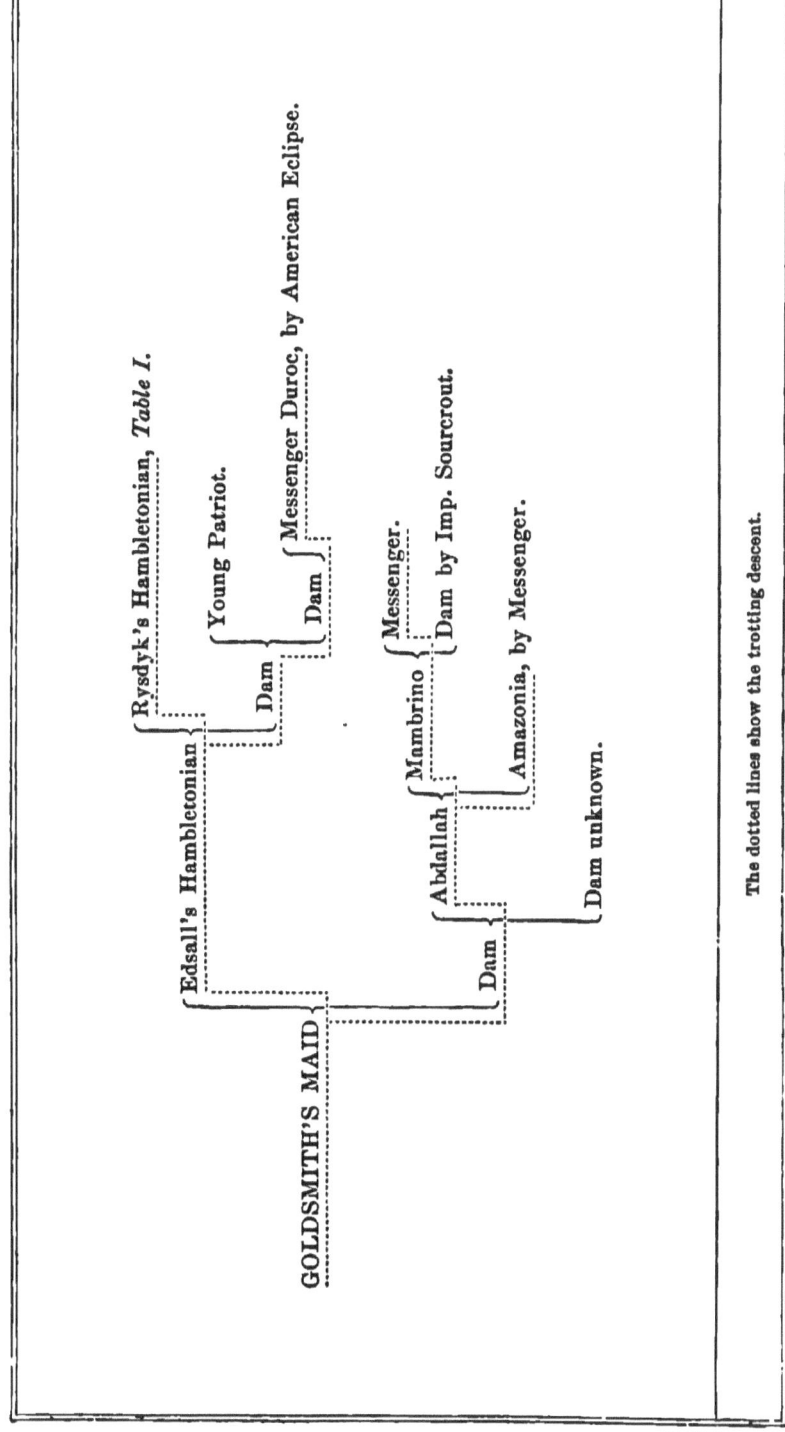

The dotted lines show the trotting descent.

(517)

TABLE XII.

KEMBLE JACKSON
- And. Jackson
  - Young Bashaw
    - Imp. Arabian, Grand Bashaw.
    - Pearl
      - First Consul.
      - Fancy, by Messenger.
  - Dam
    - Why Not, by Messenger.
    - Dam by Messenger.
- Fanny Kemble
  - Sir Archy
    - Imp. Diomed.
    - Castianira.
  - Maria
    - Gallatin
      - Imp. Bedford.
      - Imp. Mambrino, by English Mambrino, the sire of Messenger.

The dotted lines show the trotting descent.

(518)

TABLE XIII.

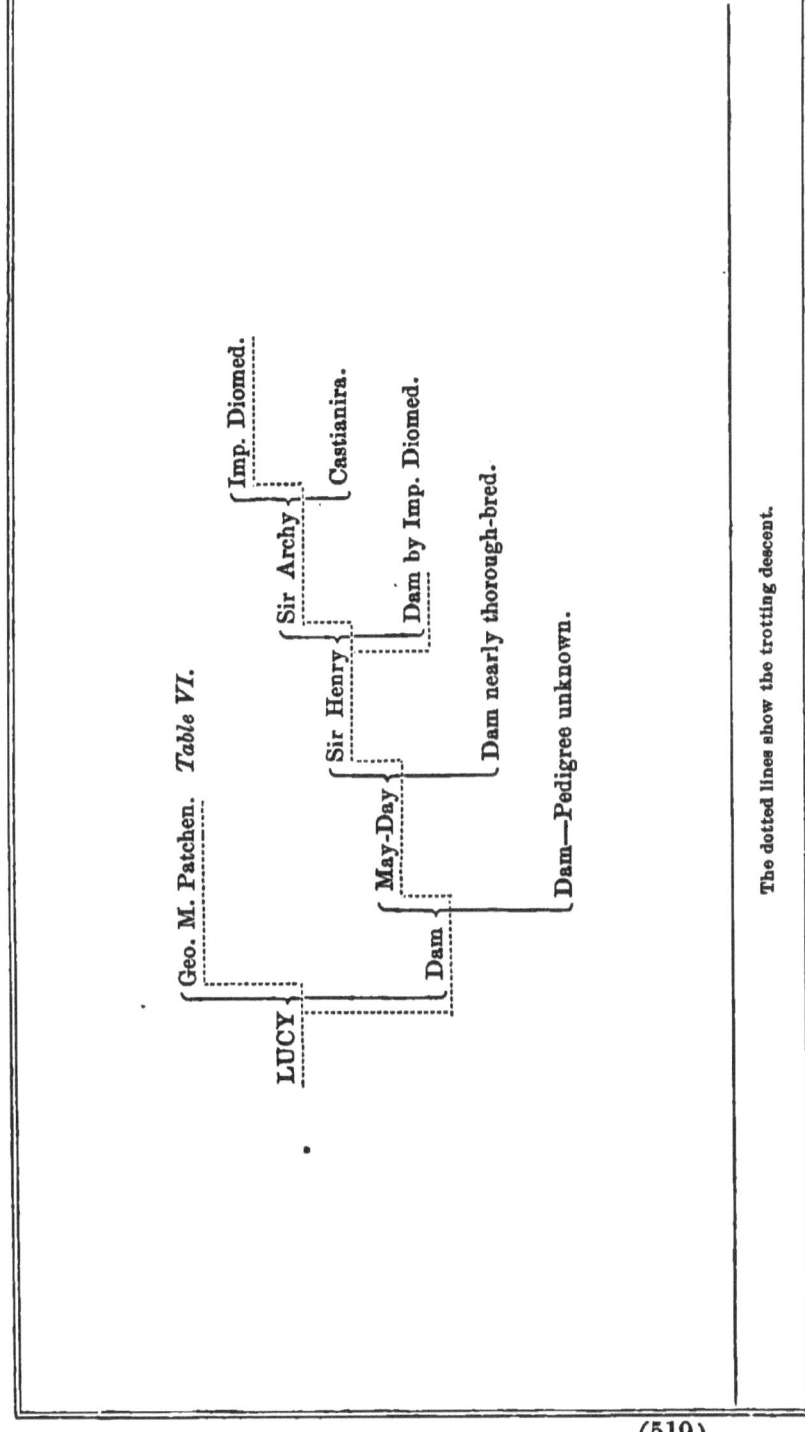

Table VI.

The dotted lines show the trotting descent.

Table XIV.

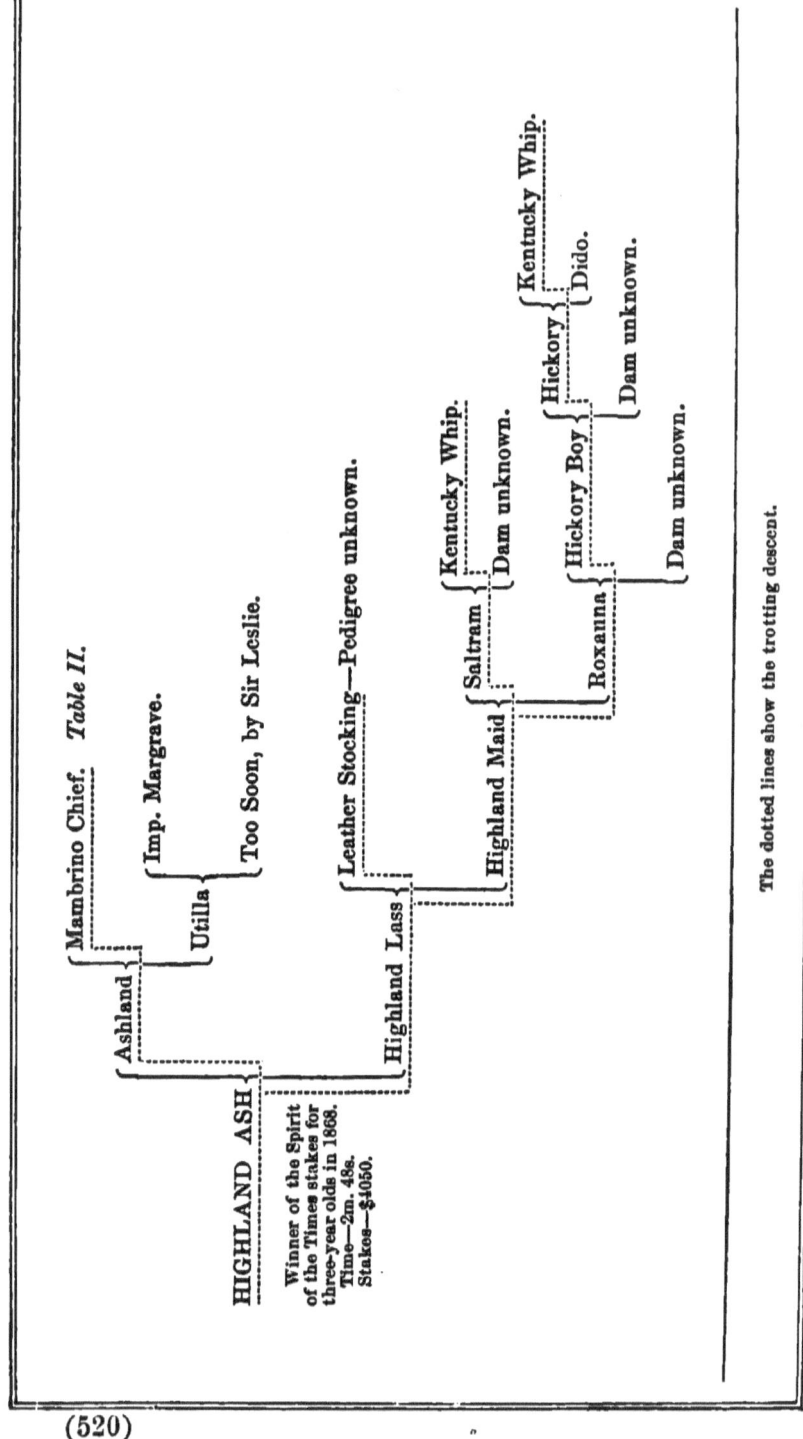

HIGHLAND ASH

Winner of the Spirit of the Times stakes for three-year olds in 1868. Time—2m. 48s. Stakes—$4050.

- Ashland
  - Mambrino Chief. *Table II.*
  - Utilla
    - Imp. Margrave.
    - Too Soon, by Sir Leslie.
- Highland Lass
  - Leather Stocking—Pedigree unknown.
  - Highland Maid
    - Saltram
      - Kentucky Whip.
      - Dam unknown.
    - Roxanna
      - Hickory Boy
        - Hickory
          - Kentucky Whip.
          - Dido.
        - Dam unknown.
      - Dam unknown.

The dotted lines show the trotting descent.

(520)

TABLE XV.

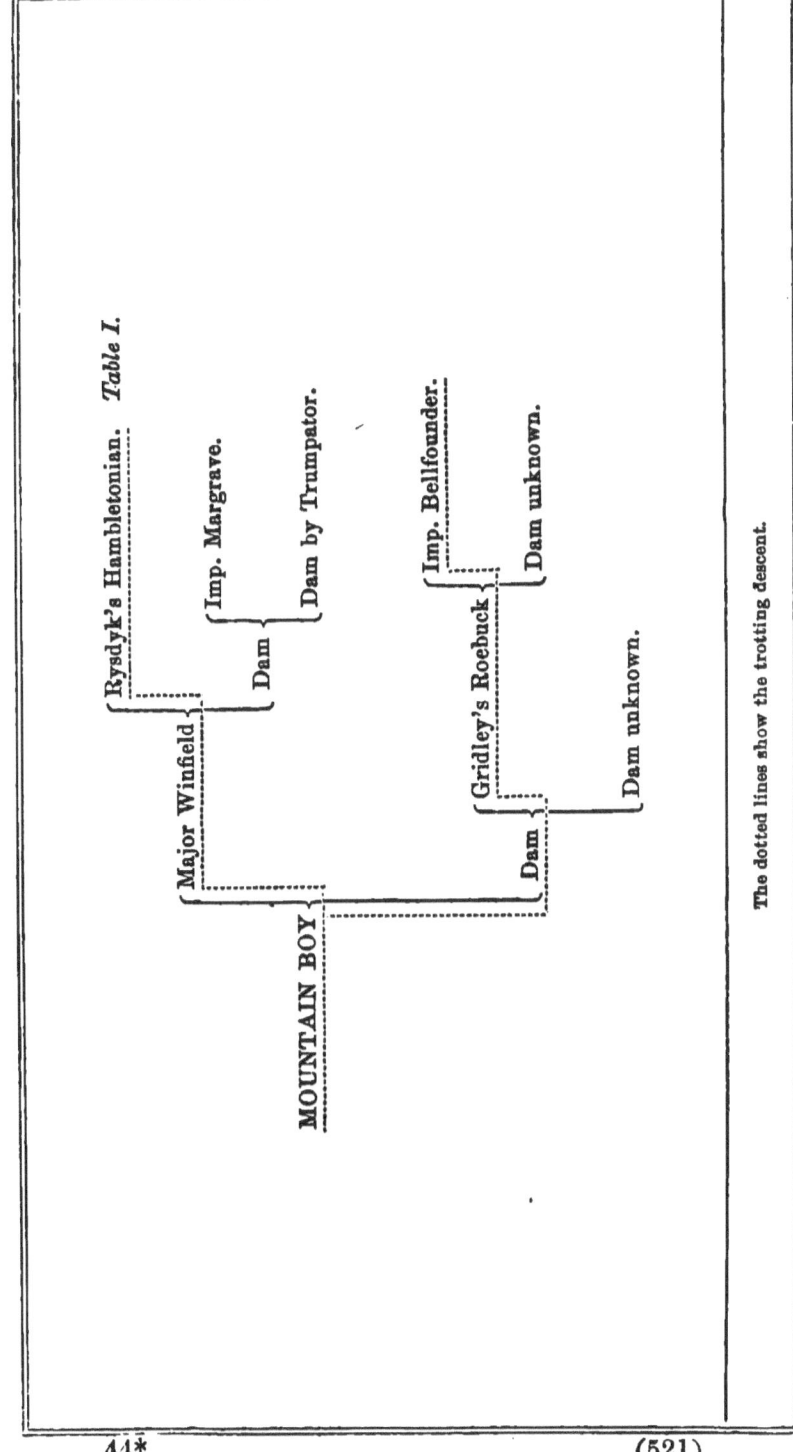

MOUNTAIN BOY
- Major Winfield
  - Rysdyk's Hambletonian. *Table I.*
  - Dam
    - Imp. Margrave.
    - Dam by Trumpator.
- Dam
  - Gridley's Roebuck
    - Imp. Bellfounder.
    - Dam unknown.
  - Dam unknown.

The dotted lines show the trotting descent.

(521)

TABLE XVI.

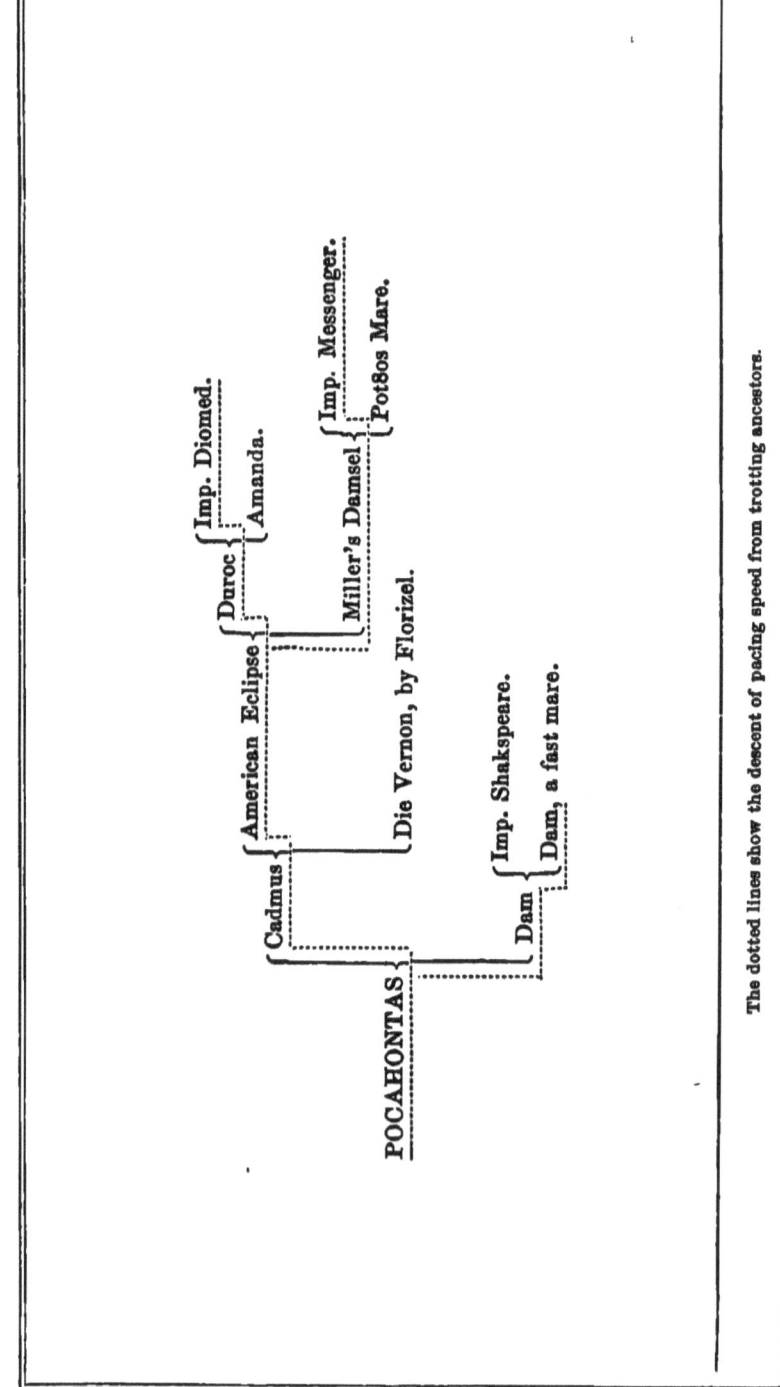

The dotted lines show the descent of pacing speed from trotting ancestors.

Table XVII.

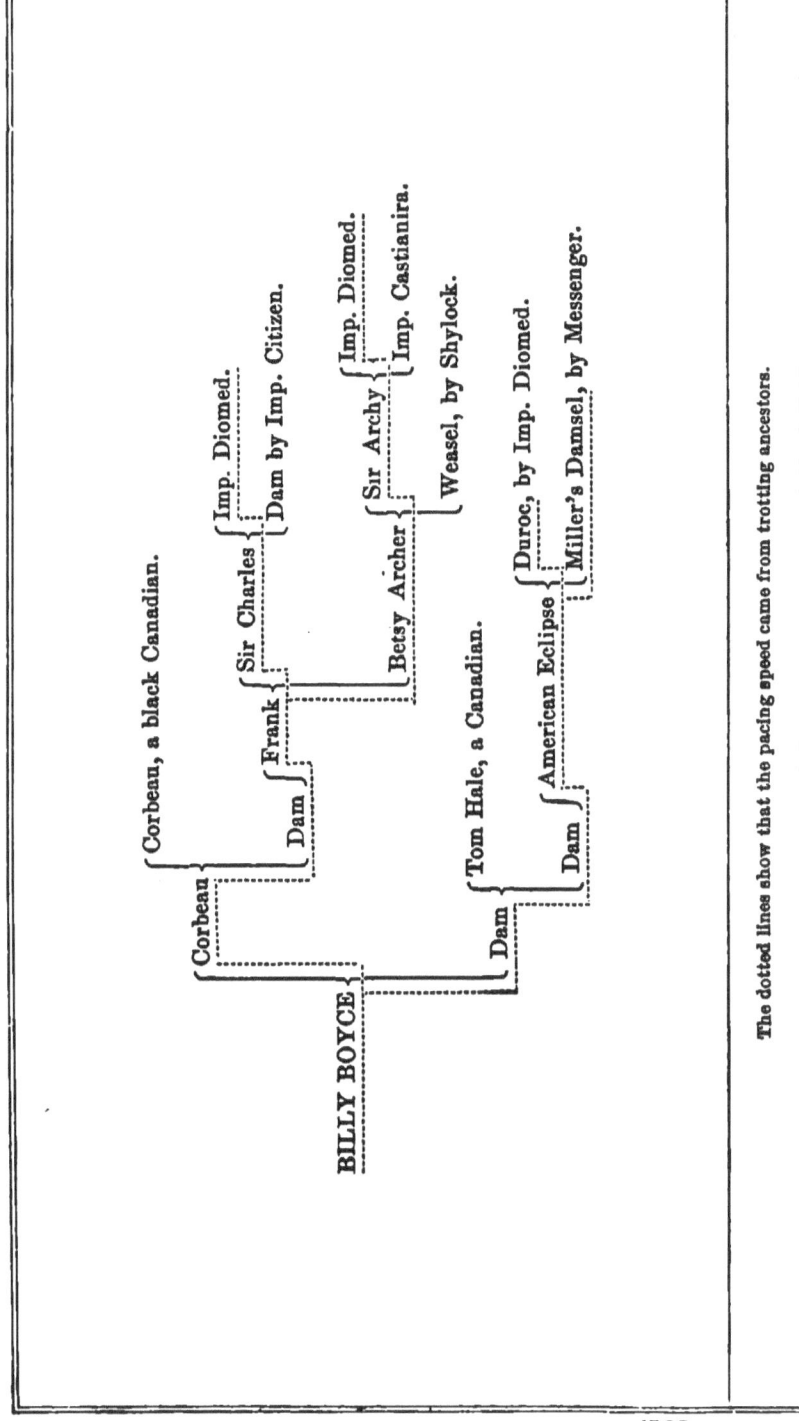

The dotted lines show that the pacing speed came from trotting ancestors.

INDEX.

ABDALLAH, history of, 472; as a stallion, 473; inbred, 490, 491.
Abd el Kader, on the Arab horse, 40; on the influence of the sire and dam respectively in breeding, 110.
Abdomen, boundaries of the, 278; contents of the, 279.
Abdominal viscera, diseases of the, 350.
Abyssinia, the horses of, 32.
Accidents to the legs and feet, 413.
Action, locomotive, of the various parts, 76.
Administration of chloroform, 432; of physic, 446.
Africa, South, the horses of, 32.
Age, shown by the dental system, 258; average, 28; best to breed from, 109.
Ali Bey, his description of the modern Arab, 33.
Alice Carneal, 55.
Alice Hawthorne (English thoroughbred), 58.
Alimentary canal, absorption of fluid from, 280.
Alteratives, action of, 448; recipes for, 448.
Amaurosis, nature of, 387; symptoms of, 387; treatment of, 387.
Amble, description of the, 95.
America, South, the horses of, 45.
American Eagle (trotter), 49.
American Eclipse (thorough-bred), pedigree of, 474; influence of upon trotting stock, 474, 493.
American Star (Seeley's), description of, 482; pedigree of, 482; as a stallion, 482.
American thorough-bred, the, 52; stoutness of the, 54.
American trotter, the, 50; essay on the, 467 et seq.
Americus (trotter), 474.
Anasarca, symptoms and treatment of, 419.
Anchylosis, nature of, 298.
Ancient methods of using the horse, 17.
Andrew Jackson (trotter), by Young Bashaw, as a stallion, 481.
Anodynes, action of, 449; recipes for, 449.
Antiquity, the Arab of, 16.
Antiseptics, 450; recipes for, 450.
Anti-Zumins, 451; recipes for, 451.
Aperients, action of, 451; recipes for, 452.
Apoplexy, nature of, 380; treatment of, 380.
Apparatus for breaking to harness, 152.
Arab horse, the, color of, 37; disposition of, 36; food of, 36; of antiquity, 16; the modern, 33; size of, 35; speed of, 37; Abd el Kader's description of the modern, 40; Ali Bey's description of the modern, 33; Capt. Shakspear's description of the modern, 37; the mare, 40.
Archer (an English trotter), 470.
Ariel (thorough-bred), 472.
Arsenic, the effects of, 352; treatment of the effects of, 353.
Arteries of the foot, the, 295; of the

INDEX.

foot, view of, injected, 294; of the frog and sole, view of, injected, 295.
Asiatic horses, the, 42.
Astringents, action of, 453; recipes for, 453.
Atavism, principles of, 486.
Atmospheric air, changes produced in by respiration, 277.
Attitude assumed in standing, 78.
Australian horse, the, 44.
Average age, 28.

BACK and loins, symptoms of strains in, 316; treatment of strain in, 317.
Back-raking, mode of performing, 447.
Back-sinews, strain of the, 319; symptoms of, 319; treatment of, 320.
Bail, the, hanging, 168; gangway, 170.
Balanitis, symptoms of, 373; treatment of, 374.
Bandages, use and application of, 196.
Barb, the, 30.
Barbs, treatment of, 352.
Barnacles, 435.
Bashaw (Grand) imported Arabian stallion, influence of upon trotting stock, 474.
Bashaw (Green's), as a stallion, 482; pedigree of, 482, 509.
Bashaw (Young), 474; as a stallion, 481.
Bath, the Turkish, 213; ground plan of, 214.
Baucher's method of horse-breaking, 145.
Bay Chief, by Mambrino Chief, 483.
Bellfounder (imp.), description of, 473; history of, 473; influence of upon trotting stock, 473; reputation as a stallion, 473.
Bellringer, by Mambrino Pilot, 484.
Bengal, the horses of, 43.
Berenger, his description of the Barb, 30.
Big-head, nature and symptoms of, 308.
Billy Boyce (pacer), 479; pedigree of, 480, 523; performances of, 504.
Birmah, the horses of, 44.
Bishoping, 264.
Bit used for horse-breaking, 143.
Bites of insects, treatment of, 392.
Biting, remedy for the vice, 206.

Black Hawk (Hill's, also called Vermont), 49, 476, 477; influence upon trotting stock, 476; as a stallion, 477.
Black Hawk (Long Island), 481; as a stallion, 482.
Blacking, recipes for harness, 230.
Bladder, anatomy of the, 284; calculi in, 373; diseases of, 372; inflammation of, 372.
Bleeding, 435; instruments used in, 436; quantity of blood taken in, 437; inflammation of the vein, when performed, 437.
Blindness, caused by various diseases, 385.
Blink Bonny (an English thoroughbred), external formation of, 62.
Blistering, 440.
Blisters, action of, 454; recipes for, 454.
Blood, the, 273; circulation of the, 274; purity of in the thorough-bred, 60; spavin, (see Bog Spavin).
Blood-vessels of the chest and nose, diseases of the, 349.
Bog spavin, nature of, 313; symptoms of, 313; treatment of, 313.
Bone, diseases of, 297; office of, 249; structure of, 248; fracture of the canna, 310; strain of the round, 322.
Bone-spavin, nature of, 302; symptoms of, 303; treatment of, 303.
Bones, number of, composing the skeleton, 252.
Bornou, the horses of, 32.
Boston, pedigree of, 103; stoutness of, 53.
Boston Blue (trotter), 470, 504.
Bots, 355; group of, attached to the stomach, 356.
Bowels, calculi in the, 365; nature of inflammation of the, 357; symptoms of inflammation of the, 359; treatment of inflammation of the, 359.
Break, or trevis, the, 435.
Breaking, Rarey's principles and practice, 128; Rarey's apparatus, 130; for the saddle, ordinary method, 141; Baucher's method, 145; superiority of the ordinary method, 151; to harness, 151.
Breaking down, 321; symptoms of, 321; treatment of, 321.

INDEX. 527

Breathing, essence of, 277; physiology of, 277.
Breed of race-horses, object of encouraging the, 58.
Breeding, atavism, or breeding back, 486; best age for, 109; causes of a hit in, 106; choice of sire and dam in, 113, 486; condition of parent at time of conception, 499; in-and-in, 103, 490; importance of health and soundness in, 107, 486; influence of the sire and dam respectively, 110, 486; out crossing, 104; principles of, 99, 487 *et seq.*; kind of horse most profitable for, 116; theory of generation, 99, 494.
Breeding-back, 486.
Bright Phoebus (thorough-bred), 472.
Brignoli (trotter), by Mambrino Chief, 484.
British horse, the original, 17.
Broken knee, treatment of, 324.
Broken wind, nature of, 346; symptoms of, 346; treatment of, 347.
Bronchitis, nature of, 329; symptoms of, 329; treatment of, 330; treatment of chronic, 330.
Brood mare, the, 117; after treatment of the foal, 127; early treatment of the foal, 125; general management of, 122; hovel for, 119; paddock for, 118; time of sending to the horse, 123; treatment of the, when in foal, 123; treatment of the, after foaling, 125; weaning of the foal, 127.
Bruce, his description of the horse of Dongola, 32.
Brunette (trotter), 476, 505.
Bruno (trotter), 476.
Buck eye, nature of, 387.
Burden's horse shoe manufactory, description of, 430.
Bursæ mucosæ, anatomy of, 271; inflammation in, 314.
Butterfly (English thorough-bred), 61.

CALCULI, in the bowels, nature of, 365; urinary, 373; symptoms of urinary, 373; treatment of urinary, 373.
Canadian horse, the, 47, 475, 476; portrait of, 47; influence of upon trotting stock, 476.

Canker, nature of, 403; treatment of, 403.
Canna bone, fractures of, 310.
Cannucks (see Canadian horse), 475.
Canter, the, 89; mode of starting into a, 238.
Capped elbow, treatment of, 316; hock, cause of, 315; treatment of, 315.
Capulet (see Capped Elbow).
Carbolic acid, description of, 450.
Caries, nature of, 298; of the jaw, symptoms of, 307; treatment of, 308.
Cart-horse, the Vermont, 55.
Cartilage, 266; diseases of, 312; structure and composition of, 267; ulceration of, 312.
Cartilages, ossification of the lateral, 301; symptoms of, 301; treatment of, 302.
Cassius M. Clay (trotter), reputation of as a stallion, 481, 482.
Casting, method of, 432; for operations upon the fore leg, 434; for castration, 434.
Castration, 441; method of casting for, 434; operation for, 441.
Cataract, nature and causes of, 386.
Catarrh, nature of, 327; treatment of, 327.
Catchpit, section of, 163.
Caustics, action of, 455; recipes for, 455.
Cauteries (see Caustics).
Cayuga Chief, (trotter), 479.
Cerebro-spinal meningitis, nature of, 328, 376, 418; symptoms of, 418; treatment of, 419.
Chaban, an Arabian stallion, portrait of, 35.
Chanticleer (English thorough-bred), 75.
Chapped Heels, symptoms of, 394; treatment of, 394.
Chest, diseases of the blood-vessels of, 349; water on the, 345.
Choking, distemper (see Cerebro-spinal meningitis).
Chillaby, an Arab horse, 36.
China, the horse of, 44.
Chloroform, apparatus for administering, 432; mode of administration, 432.
Chronic cough, 331; symptoms of, 331; treatment, 331.

Chyle, the, 280.
Circulation, plan of the, 275.
Clipping, 189.
Clothes, tearing off the, 204; remedy for, 205.
Clubs, trotting, establishment of, 470.
Clysters, mode of administering, 447; action of, 456; recipe for, 456.
Coach-house, 174.
Coat of the thorough-bred, 75.
Coffin-joint, strains of the, 318.
Cold, nature of, 327; treatment of, 327.
Colic, nature of, 360; symptoms of, 360; flatulent, signs of, 361; from stoppage, symptoms of, 361; signs of spasmodic, 361; treatment of, 361; treatment of flatulent, 362; treatment of impaction, 362; treatment required after, 362; remedies for, 452.
Color, of the Arab horse, 37; of the thorough-bred, 75.
Colt, breaking of the, 128.
Commander, by Messenger, influence of upon trotting stock, 472.
Conestoga draught-horse, the, 55; portrait of, 56.
Confining the horse, methods of, 433.
Congestion of the lungs, nature and cause of, 339; symptoms of, 341; treatment of, 342.
Constitutional diseases, 417.
Consumption (phthisis), symptoms of, 346; treatment of, 346.
Contraction of the foot, 409; of the heels, 430.
Convulsions, symptoms of, 375; treatment of, 376.
Corbeau (trotter), character of as a stallion, 480; pedigree of, 480.
Cord, spinal, the source of power of moving, 497.
Corns, nature of, 397; treatment of, 397.
Coronary frog-band, the, 293.
Coronary substance, anatomy of the, 293.
Corrosive sublimate, treatment of effects of, 353.
Cough, nature of chronic, 331; symptoms of chronic, 331; treatment of chronic, 331.
Counter-irritants, 454.
Coup de soleil, treatment of, 382.

Crab (imp.), 53.
Cranston (trotter), by Mambrino Pilot, 484.
Crib-biting, 202; bar-muzzle for, 203.
Cruiser, 36, 128, 131; in the power of his master, 133; with the leg-strap and surcingle on, 132.
Crust of the foot, anatomy of the, 292.
Curb, nature of, 322; treatment of, 323.
Cushion of the frog, 293.
Cuts, stable management of simple, 222; contused, 222.
Cutting, ordinary, 413; description of speedy, 415; prevention of, 415; treatment of ordinary, 413; treatment of speedy, 415.
Cystitis, symptoms of, 372; treatment of, 372.

DAILY exercise, 200.
Dart (trotter), 479.
Deafness, 383.
Depuration, its office in the animal economy, 281.
Detergents, 456; recipes for, 456.
Dexter (trotter), performances of, 50, 504, 505; pedigree of, 473, 480-2, 513.
Dgelfe, a breed of Arab horse, 33.
Diabetes, symptoms of, 371; treatment of, 371; remedies for, 453.
Diaphragm, symptoms of spasm of, 348; treatment of spasm of, 348.
Diarrhœa, nature of, 362; treatment of, 363; medicines for chronic, 450; clyster for, 459; remedies for, 452, 456.
Digestion, physiology of, 280.
Diomed (imp.), 474, 492; influence of upon trotting stock, 474.
Dishing, in the trot, 88.
Dislocation, nature of, 324; of the hip joint, 324; of the patella, 324.
Distemper, nature of, 328; treatment of, 329; choking, 376, 418.
Diuretics, action of, 457; recipes for, 457.
Docking, operation for, 444.
Dongola, the horses of, 32.
Door for loose box, 161.
Doors of stables, materials for, 161.
Drainage of stables, 163.
Draught-horse, the Conestoga, 55; portrait of, 56.

INDEX.

Dressing of horses before work, 183; after work, 186.
Duct, the thoracic, 280.
Ducts, the lacrymal, 289.
Duroc (thorough-bred) 474, 483.
Dysentery, nature of 362; treatment of, 362; remedies for, 453.
Dyspepsia, nature of, 354; symptoms of, 354; treatment of, 355.

Ear, anatomy of the, 289; diseases of, 383; scratching the, remedy for, 204.
Early maturity of the thorough-bred, 57.
East, the horses of the, 30.
Eclipse (American thorough-bred), influence upon trotting stock, 474.
Eclipse (English thorough-bred), description of, 27; Percival's description of, 28.
Ecraseur, the, 443.
Egyptian horse, the ancient, 16; the modern, 32.
Elbow-joint, treatment of capped, 316.
Embrocations, action of, 457; recipes for, 457.
Engineer, by Messenger, 472.
Enteritis, nature of, 357; symptoms of, 358.
Epilepsy, symptoms of, 375; treatment of, 376.
Ericsson (trotter), by Mambrino Chief, 483, 484.
Eruptions of the skin, 388 *et seq.*
Essentials in the thorough-bred, 60.
Ethan Allen (trotter), 49, 482, 505
Excretion, physiology of, 281.
Exercise, daily, 200.
Exhaustion, after work, treatment of, 221.
Exostosis, nature of, 297; of the humerus and scapula, treatment of, 305.
External form as indicated by points, 19; formation of the thorough-bred, 61.
Extremities, anatomy of the anterior, 254; of the hind, 253; considered as organs of support, 255; of locomotion, 256.
Eye, anatomy of the, 287; appendages of, 289; simple inflammation of, 383; symptoms of simple inflammation of, 287; treatment of simple inflammation of, 384; treatment of purulent ophthalmia, 384; irites, 384; injuries of, 386; treatment of injuries, 386; cataract, 386; amaurosis, 387; buckeye, 387; wash for the, 459.

Face, anatomy of the, 254.
Fair Rachel (thorough-bred), 472.
False quarter, nature of, 399; treatment of, 400.
Farcy, symptoms of, 421; treatment of, 421; remedies for, 451.
Fearnought (imp.), 53.
Febrifuges, action of, 458; recipes for, 458.
Feeding, theory and practice of, 177.
Feeling, 290.
Feet, accidents to the, 413; management of, 197; dryness of the, 198.
Femur, treatment of fracture of the, 310.
Fetlock, remarks on the strain of the, 318; treatment of the strain of the, 318.
Fevers, remarks on, 417; symptoms of simple, 417; symptoms of typhoid, 417; treatment of simple, 417; treatment of typhoid, 418.
Fever balls and powders, 458.
Fibre, muscular, 270.
Fibrous tissue, nature of, 268; chemical composition of, 269.
Firing, method of performing, 438; remarks on, 437.
Fisherman (English thorough-bred), portrait of, 62.
Fistula of the withers, nature of, 306; symptoms of, 306; treatment of, 306.
Flatbush Maid (trotter), 480.
Flatulent colic, symptoms of, 361; treatment of, 362.
Flora Temple (trotter), 50, 489, 490, 504, 505; portrait of, 489.
Flying gallop, the, 92.
Foal, the, 125; after treatment of the, 127; early treatment of the, 125; weaning of the, 127.
Foals, rheumatic inflammation peculiar

to, 313; treatment of rheumatic inflammation of, 314.
Foot, anatomy of the, 290; lateral cartilages of, 296; section of, 291; the parts entering into the composition of, 290; view of the under surface of, 292; with the hoof removed, view of the, 292; contraction of the, 409, 430; the hoof, 292; the arteries of, 295; founder of the, 403; conditions of a good sound, 425.
Fore-quarters, relative proportions of the, 21.
Formation, external, of the horse, 61.
Founder of the foot, 403.
Fractures, remarks on, 308; simple, 309; treatment of simple, 310; of the femur, 310; treatment of, 310; of the humerus, 310; treatment of, 310; of the canna bones, 310; treatment of, 310; of the lower jaw, 310; treatment of, 310; of the pelvis, 310; treatment of, 310; of the pasterns, 310; treatment of, 310; of the bones of the skull, 310; treatment of, 310; of the radius, 310; treatment of, 310; of the ribs, 310; treatment of, 310; of the scapula, 310; treatment of, 310; of the spine, 310; treatment of, 310; of the tibia, 310; treatment of, 310.
Frog, anatomy of the, 293.

Gad-fly, bites of the, 392; treatment for, 392.
Gallop, the flying, 92; variation on length of stride of, 95; correct view of the 94; received interpretation of the, 91; the hand, 90; the extended, 91; method of starting to the, 239.
Galls, treatment of harness, 391; remedy for, 459.
Gangway, bail for stable, 170.
Gastritis, rarity of, 352; symptoms of, 352; treatment of, 352.
General characteristics of the horse, 18.
Generation, anatomy of the female organs of, 286; anatomy of the male organs of, 285; theory of, 99, 494.
Generative organs, diseases of the, 373.
George M. Patchen (trotter), reputation of as a stallion 481; pedigree of, 512.
George Palmer (trotter, 504.
George Wilkes (trotter), 473, 481, 504.
Gift (trotter), 474, 484.
Gland, the kidneys, 284; the liver, 283; the pancreas, 284.
Glands, structure of the, 280.
Glanders, symptoms of, 420; treatment of, 421; remedies for, 451.
Glencoe (imp.), 474.
Godolphin Arabian, history of, 31.
Golddust (trotter), 483; pedigree of, 493, 510.
Goldsmith's Maid (trotter), 504; pedigree of, 517.
Granary, construction of, 160.
Grand Bashaw (imp.), influence of upon trotting stock, 474
Grass, turning out to, 225.
Grease (Scratches), symptoms of, 394; treatment of, 395.
Green's Bashaw, reputation as a stallion, 482, 483; pedigree of, 509.
Greek horse, the ancient, 14.
Grooming, after work, 184; before work, 186.
Grubs, removal of, 392.

Habits in a wild or free state, 18; out-door bad, 243; remedies for bad, 202.
Hacks, preparation of for work, 220.
Hæmaturia, causes of, 371; symptoms of, 371; treatment of, 371.
Hæmorrhage, from the lungs, treatment of, 349; from the nose, treatment of, 349.
Halters used for breaking colts, 142.
Hambletonian (Harris'), 480.
Hambletonian (Rysdyk's), thoroughbred, 490; character of as a stallion, 481; closely in-bred, 490; pedigree of, 507.
Hambletonian (thorough-bred), by Messenger, 472; influence of upon trotting stock, 472.
Hand-gallop, the, 90.
Harness, blacking, recipes for, 230; breaking to, 151; care of, 229; direction for cleaning, 229; fittings for, 173; room in stables, 173; galls, 391

Havoc (thorough-bred), 483.
Hay, chamber, 159.
Head, bones of the, 254; relative proportions of the, 19.
Health, importance of in sire and dam, 107, 486; upland grass useful in restoring, 226.
Heart, diseases of the, 348.
Heels, symptoms of chapped, 394; treatment of chapped, 394; treatment of contracted, 430; remedies for sore, 454.
Height of the thorough-bred, 75.
Henry Clay (trotter), by Long Island Black Hawk, 481, 482; character of as a stallion, 482.
Hepatization of the lungs, 340.
Herbert's description of wild horse of America, 46.
Hernia, reduction of, 445.
Hero (pacer), 479, 480.
Hidebound, nature of, 389; symptoms of, 389; treatment of, 389.
Highblowing, nature of, 338.
Highland Ash (trotter), 480; pedigree, 520.
Highland Lass (trotter), 480.
Highland Maid (trotter), 480, 504.
Hill's Black Hawk, 476; character of as a stallion, 476; pedigree, 476.
Hind quarters, points of the, 25.
Hip-joint, dislocation of the, 324; strain of the, 322.
Hiram Woodruff (trotter), 482.
"Hit," causes of a, 106.
Hobbles, description of, and method of using, 433.
Hobgobblin, 31.
Hock, cause of capped, 315; treatment of capped, 315; treatment of strain of the, 322.
Hock-joint, strain of the, 322.
Hogging the mane, 194.
Hoof, anatomy of the, 291; development of by secretion, 293; view of the, 292.
Horsemanship, Baucher's method of, 150.
Hounds, riding to, 240.
Hovel, the, for the brood mare, 119.
Hughes, Mr., tames the Arabian stallion Chillaby 36.
Humerus, and scapula, exostosis of,
305; and scapula, treatment of exostosis of, 305; treatment of fracture of, 310.
Hunter, final preparation of the, 219; preparation of the, 206; treatment of blows on the legs of the, 221; treatment of exhaustion of the, 221; treatment of overreach of the, 222; treatment of thorns in the legs of the, 221.
Hunting Park Association, established, 470.
Hydrophobia, nature of, 377; symptoms of, 377; treatment of, 378.
Hydrothorax, a sequel of pleurisy, 345; treatment of, 345.

IN-AND-IN breeding, 103, 490 *et seq.*
Incisor teeth, section of, 257.
Independent, (trotter), 480.
India, horses of, 43.
Indian pony, the, 46.
Indigestion (dyspepsia), causes of, 354; treatment of, 354.
Inflamed bursæ mucosæ, 314; of tenderous sheath, 314.
Inflammation of the bones, 298; of bursæ mucosæ, 314; of the bladder, 372; of the bowels, 357; of the brain, 375; of the bronchi, 329; of the eye, 383; of the kidneys, 369; of the laryngitis, 332; of the lungs, 339; of the pleura, 345; of the stomach, 352; of the vein after bleeding, 437; rheumatic, 311; wash for external, 459.
Influenza, nature of, 328; symptoms of, 328; treatment of, 328; typhoid, symptoms in, 329.
Injections (see Clysters).
Insects, treatment of bites and stings of, 392.
Intersusception, nature and symptoms of, 364.
Intestines, anatomy of the, 282; large, 283; small, 282.
Inversion of the uterus, 374.
Iritis, cause of, 384; symptoms of, 385; treatment of, 385.
Iron fitting for stalls and loose boxes, 172.

INDEX.

James K. Polk (pacer), 479.
Java, the horse of, 44.
Jaw, caries of, 307; symptoms of caries of, 308; treatment of, 308; fracture of the bones of, 310; osteo sarcoma of, 308.
Jenny Cameron (imp.), 53.
Jim Rockey (trotter), 483.
Jog-trot, the, 236.
John Anderson (trotter), 480.
John Henry, failure as a stallion, 485.
John Morgan (trotter), 480, 483; pedigree of, 475, 483, 516.
John Stewart (trotter), 479, 483, 505.
Joint, strain of the coffin, 318; treatment of strain of the coffin, 318; strains of the hip, 322; treatment of, 322; dislocation of the hip, treatment of, 324.
Joints, remarks on the, 266; wounds of, 324.
Jolly Roger (imp.), 53.
Jugular vein, when obliterated, renders the horse unfit to be turned out, 227.
Jumping, 96.
Justin Morgan, 476, 482.

Kailhan, a breed of Arab horses, 34.
Kate (trotter), 506.
Kemble Jackson (trotter), pedigree of, 480, 518.
Kentucky, by Lexington, (thorough-bred), 55.
Kentucky Chief (trotter), 483.
Kentucky Clay (trotter), 482.
Kicking, out of doors, prevention of, 245; in the stable, 203, 206.
Kidneys, diseases of the, 369; inflammation of the, 369; inaction of, 372; situation of the, 284.
Knee-joint, remarks on the strain of the, 317; symptoms of strain of the, 318; treatment of punctured, 326; treatment of strain of the, 318; broken, 324; wounds of the, 324.
Kochlani, a breed of Arab horses, tradition of the, 34.

Lacrymal apparatus, anatomy of, 289.
Lacteals, the, 280.
Lady Franklin (trotter), 504, 505.
Lady Fulton (trotter), 505.
Lady Palmer and Flatbush Maid (trotters), 505.
Lady Suffolk (trotter), 474, 479, 504, 505; pedigree of, 514.
Lady Thorn (trotter), 472, 480, 483, 504; pedigree of, 515.
Lameness, shoulder joint, 305.
Laminæ, anatomy of the, 294.
Laminitis, nature of, 403; section of a foot in confirmed, 405; symptoms of, 405; treatment of acute, 405; treatment of chronic, 409.
Lamp for singeing, 193.
Lampas, symptoms of, 351; treatment of, 351.
Lamplighter (pacer), 504.
Lantern (trotter), 481; performance with Whalebone, 405.
Laryngitis, nature of, 322; symptoms of acute, 332; symptoms of chronic, 333; treatment of acute, 333; treatment of chronic, 334.
Lateral cartilages, ossification of, 301; symptoms of ossification of, 301; treatment of ossification of, 302.
Lath (thorough-bred), 31.
Leaping, 96.
Lecompte (thorough-bred), stoutness of, 55.
Legs, accidents to, 413; inflammatory swelled, 393; ordinary swelled, 393; lotion for inflamed, 459.
Lexington (thorough-bred), shape of, 54; stoutness of, 53; as a getter of trotters, 489.
Libyan horse, the ancient, 17.
Lice, destruction of, 391.
Ligaments, 268; diseases of, 311; strains of the suspensory, 318.
Lighting of stables, 165.
Lightning (trotter), 481.
Limbs, as agents of locomotion, 256; as means of support, 255.
Liniments, action of, 457; recipes for, 457.
List of English stallions imported into America, 461.
Litter, remedy for eating the, 205.
Liver, anatomy and function of the, 283; disease of the, 369; symptoms of disease of the, 369; treatment of disease of the, 369.

INDEX. 533

Lock-jaw, nature of, 378; symptoms of, 377; treatment of, 378.
Loins, strains of the, 316; treatment of strains of the, 316.
Lone Star (trotter), 482.
Long Island Black Hawk, 481; reputation as a stallion, 481, 482.
Loose boxes, remarks on, 157.
Lotions, action of, 459; recipes for, 459.
Lower jaw, treatment of fractures of the, 310.
Lucy (trotter), 481, 504; pedigree of, 481, 519.
Lungs, remarks on congestion of the, 340; symptoms of congestion of the, 340; treatment of congestion of the, 341; inflammation of (pneumonia), 339; treatment of hæmorrhage from the, 349.
Lying down at work, 245.

MADNESS, nature of, 377; symptoms of, 377; treatment of, 378.
Mad staggers, nature of, 375; symptoms of, 375; treatment of, 375.
Mahomet, the traditional founder of the Kochlani, 34.
Major Winfield, by Rysdyk's Hambletonian, 481.
Malcom, Sir John, his description of the Persian horse, 41.
Mallenders, symptoms of, 391; treatment of, 391.
Mambrino (thorough-bred), description of, 472; influence upon trotting stock, 472, 483.
Mambrino Chief, 472, 483; character as a stallion, 483; pedigree of, 483.
Mambrino Messenger (trotter), 484.
Mambrino Patchen, by Mambrino Chief, 483, 484.
Mambrino Paymaster, by Mambrino, 472, 483.
Mambrino Pilot, description of, 484; pedigree of, 472, 480, 483, 484, 508; character as a stallion, 484.
Mane, of the race horse, the, 76; hogging the, 194.
Manege, paces of the, 96.
Mange, insect, 389; nature of, 389; symptoms of, 389; treatment of, 390.

Mangers for stables, 170; material for, 171.
Mare, management of the brood, 122; after treatment of the foal of, 127; choosing the, for breeding, 489; early treatment of the foal of, 125; hovel for, 119; paddock for, 118; time of sending to the horse, 123; treatment of after foaling, 125; treatment of when in foal, 123; weaning of the foal of, 127; the Arab, 40.
Margrave (imp.), 474.
Marrow, the, 250.
Match, trotting, first on record in England, 469; first on record in America, 470.
Maturity of the horse, 28.
Medicines, list of the principal, and recipes for, 448; alteratives, 448; anodynes, 449; antiseptics, 450; anti-zumins, 451; aperients, 451; astringents, 453; blisters, 454; caustics, 455; clysters, 456; detergents, 456; diuretics, 457; embrocations, 457; febrifuges, 458; lotions, 459; stimulants, 459; stomachics, 460; tonics, 460; traumatics, 460; vermifuges, 461.
Mefki, a breed of Arab horse, 33.
Megrims, nature of, 376; symptoms of, 376; treatment of, 376.
Membrane, synovial, acute inflammation of the, 313; rheumatic inflammation of, 313; treatment of rheumatic inflammation of the, 313.
Meningitis, cerebro-spinal, nature of, 376, 418; symptoms of, 418; treatment of, 419.
Mental development, 29.
Messenger (imp), description of, 471; influence upon trotting stock, 471, 472, 477; character as a stallion, 471; his progeny in-bred, 492.
Methods of using the horse, ancient, 17.
Middlepiece of the horse, proportions of, 23.
Miller's Damsel (thorough-bred), 474, 483.
Miss Colville (imp.), 53.
Mode of progression in horses, 78.
Modern Arab, the, 33; Ali Bey's description of, 33; size, 35; docility of, 36; food of, 36; color of, 37; speed

45*

of, 37; Capt. Shakspear's description of, 37; the mare, 40.
Molten grease, treatment of, 364.
Monkey (imp.), 53.
Moor-ill, symptoms of, 419; treatment of, 419.
Moorish horse, the, 17.
Morgan horse the, 48, 482; Linsley's description of the, 48.
Morrill, pedigree of, 482.
Morrill (Young), influence upon trotting stock, 482; pedigree of, 482, 493, 511.
Moulting, periodical, 29.
Mountain Boy (trotter), 473, 481; pedigree of, 521.
Mountain Maid (trotter), 482.
Mount Holly, by Messenger, 472.
Mounting, directions for, 230; Rarey's directions for, 232; Richardson's directions for, 230.
Mouth, the three-year old, 259; the six-year old, 263; the five-year old, 261; the four-year old, 260; the three-year old, 259; the two-year old, 259; the eight-year old, 263; of the very old horse, 264; diseases of the, 350.
Mucosæ, Bursæ, anatomy of, 271; inflamed, 314.
Muscles, anatomy of, 270; diseases of the, 311; appearance of to the naked eye, 270; chronic rheumatism of, 312; identical in composition with the fibrine of the blood, 270; mode of describing, 271; physiology of, 269; diseases of, 311; rheumatic inflammation of, 311.
Mustang, horse the, 46.
Myron Perry (trotter), 504.

Nancy Pope, by Havoc, 483.
Narraganset Pacer, the, 52.
Navicular disease, nature and cause of, 409, 412; symptoms of, 410; treatment of, 411.
Neck, relative proportions of the, 21.
Nejdi, a breed of Arab horse, 33.
Nephritis, cause of, 369; symptoms of, 369; treatment of, 370.
Nerves, the, 286.
Nervous system, diseases of the, 375.
Neurotomy, for navicular disease, 412.

New York trotting club organized, 470.
Nicking, operation for, 444.
Nonpareil, by Cassius M. Clay, 482.
Norfolk trotter, the, 89, 470.
North America, wild horse of, 46.
Nose, the, 287; diseases of the blood-vessels of the, 349; hæmorrhage from the blood-vessels of the, 349.
Numidian horse, the, 17.
Nymphomania, nature and symptoms of, 374; treatment of, 374.

Object of encouraging the breed of race-horses, 58.
Œstrus equi, history of the, 356.
Oneida Chief (pacer), 479.
Operations, 432; administration of chloroform, 432; methods of confining the horse, 433; bleeding, 435; firing, 437; setons and rowels, 439; blistering, 440; castrating, 441; nicking and docking, 444; unnerving, 445; reduction of hernia, 445; administration of physic, 446; clysters, 447; back-raking, 447.
Ophthalmia, symptoms of purulent, 384; treatment of purulent, 484.
Orange county horse, the, 504, 506.
Organs, classification of the various, 248.
Original British horse, the, 17.
Ossification of lateral cartilages, 301; symptoms of, 301; treatment of, 301.
Osteo sarcoma of the jaw, nature and symptoms of, 308.
Out-crossing in breeding, 104, 491.
Over-reaches, stable management of, 222; treatment of, 416.
Ozena, nature of, 328.

Pacer, the Narraganset, 52.
Pacers, 479; belonging to trotting families, 480; to teach to trot, 478; performances of, 479.
Paces, natural and acquired, 76; modes of starting to the various, 235.
Pacing, nature of, 96; close relationship to trotting, 479.
Paddock, the, for brood mares, 118.
Pancreas, anatomy of the, 284.
Paps, treatment of, 352.

INDEX.

Paralysis, nature of, 380; from injury of the spine, 380; symptoms of, 381; treatment of, 381; of the par-vagum, 418.
Par-vagum, paralysis of the, (see Typhosus).
Pastern, fractures of the, 310.
Pasturing, 225.
Patella, dislocation of the, 324.
Paul Pry (trotter), 471.
Pedigrees, importance of in breeding, 486; tables of, 507–523.
Peerless (trotter), 480, 482, 504.
Pelham (trotter), 479.
Pelvic arch, anatomy of the, 255.
Pelvis, the, boundaries of, 284; fractures of, 310.
Performances of American trotters, tables of, 504 et seq.
Perichondrium in the cartilage, 267.
Periodical moulting, 29.
Periosteum, the, 250.
Peritonitis, nature of, 357; symptoms of, 359; treatment of, 359; to distinguish from colic, 360.
Persian horse, the, 41.
Pet (trotter), 505.
Phrenitis, nature of, 375; symptoms of, 375; treatment of, 375.
Phthisis, symptoms of, 346; treatment of, 346.
Physic, circumstances which modify the dose of, 217; cooling powers of 218; effects of. in getting rid of injurious food, 217; injurious effects of, 219; mode of administering, 446; superseded by the Turkish bath as a mode of reducing flesh, 218.
Physic balls and drenches, 459.
Physiology, of the blood, 273; of digestion, 280; of muscle, 269; of respiration, 277; of secretions, 281.
Pilot (bl. g.), 479.
Pilot (Canadian), 475; influence of upon trotting stock, 475.
Pilot, Jr. (Alexander's), 479, 483; influence of upon trotting stock, 475.
Pilot, Old (pacer), 479.
Pilot Temple, 483.
Piping, nature of, 338.
Plato (thorough-bred), influence upon trotting stock, 472, 491.
Pleura, anatomy of the, 272.

Pleurisy, symptoms of, 345; treatment of, 345.
Pleurodynia, nature of, 345; treatment of, 346.
Plunging, treatment of, 245.
Pneumonia, cause of, 340; definition of, 239; sub-acute, 344; hepatization in, 344; symptoms of acute, 343; termination of, 344; treatment of acute, 343.
Pocahontas, Jr. (trotter), 480.
Pocahontas (pacer), performances of, 96, 470, 480; pedigree of, 480, 522; progeny of, 480.
Points of the trotter, 495; of the horse, 20; proportions of the various, 26.
Poll-evil, nature of, 307; symptoms of, 307; treatment of, 307.
Porter, Sir Robert Ker, his description of the Persian horse, 41.
Post Boy (thorough-bred), influence upon trotting stock, 493; pedigree of, 493.
Potomac (thorough-bred), 471.
Preparation, final, of the hunter, 219; of the hunter, 206; for work, 206; of hacks for work, 220.
Pricks, from a nail picked up on the road, 416; in shoeing, 416; treatment of in shoeing, 416; treatment of from a nail picked up on the road, 416.
Prioress (thorough-bred), her staying qualities, 54.
Progression, mode of, 78.
Proportions of the various points, 26.
Proud-flesh, in wounds, medicines for destroying, 455.
Puffs, treatment of, 315.
Purges (See Aperients).
Purity of blood in the thorough-bred, 60.
Purulent opthalmia, symptoms of, 384; treatment of, 384.
Putrescence in sores and ulcers, medicines for, 450.
Putrid fever (See Typhosus).

Quarter, points of the fore, 21; points of the hind, 25; nature of false, 399; treatment of false, 400.
Queen Mab (imp.), 53.
Quittor, nature of, 400; treatment of, 400.

Rabies, nature and symptoms of, 377.
Race-horse, croup of the, 65; back of the 65; back ribs of the, 70; belly of the 70; bone of the leg of the, 73; coat of the, 75; color of the, 75; external formation of the, 61; flank of the, 70; fore-arm, or arm of the, 73; head of the, 71; height of the, 75; hind quarter or the, 74; knee of the, 73; loins of the, 65; mane of the, 76; neck of the, 70; object of encouraging the breed of, 70; purity of blood in the, 60; shoulder blade of the, 72; tail of the, 76.
Racing or hunting stable, ground plan of, 175.
Racking, 95.
Racks for stables, 170; material for, 171.
Radius, fracture of the, 310.
Rarey's apparatus for breaking horses, 130; halter or bridle for colts, 142; method of training, 128; reflections on plans of, 137.
Rearing, management of, 244.
Red Jacket, influence of as a stallion, 474.
Reduction of hernia, 445.
Reins, management of, 233.
Relationship of pacers to trotters, 480.
Relative influence of sire and dam, 110, 486.
Relative proportions of the fore-quarters, 21; of the head, 19; of the horse, 19; of the neck, 21.
Respiration, effect of on atmospheric air, 277; physiology of, 277.
Retention of urine, treatment of, 373.
Rheumatic inflammation, 311; peculiar to foals, 313.
Rheumatism, symptoms of acute, 311; treatment of acute, 312; symptoms of chronic, 312.
Rhode Island (trotter), 504.
Ribs, treatment of fractured, 310.
Riding, 230; to hounds, 240; to hounds, rules adopted in, 240; to hounds, directions for, 241; modes of starting the horse in the various paces, 235; mounting and dismounting, 230; management of the reins in, 233; necessity of good hands in, 238; the seat in, 232; starting into a gallop, 239; starting into a trot in, 236; starting into a walk in, 235.
Ring bone, 300; nature of, 300; symptoms of, 301; treatment of, 301; remedy for, 455.
Roanoke (pacer), 479.
Roaring, nature and causes of, 335; produced by alteration in the shape of the cartilages, 337; produced by thickening of the mucous membrane, 335; produced by paralysis of the muscles of the larynx, 336; remarks on, 335; plan for stopping the noise made in, 335.
Rolla Golddust (trotter), 479.
Roman horse, the, 16.
Romp (thorough-bred), 479.
Round worms, 367.
Rowels, 439.
Roxana (thorough-bred, English), 31.
Royal George, 475; pedigree of, 475.
Running, the pace, 96.
Running away, management of, 245.
Rupture of the bowels, 364.
Rysdyk's Hambletonian, pedigree of, 472, 473, 481, 507; closely inbred, 490.

SABI, a breed of Arab horse, 33.
Saddlery, care of, 227.
Saladin (trotter), 481.
Sallenders, symptoms of, 391; treatment of, 391.
Salt, as food, 180.
Saltram (pacer), 480.
Sand-crack, nature of, 399; treatment of, 399.
Sarcoma, Osteo, 308.
Saunterer (an English thorough-bred), 64; portrait of, 64.
Scapula, exostosis of, 305; fractures of the, 310; strains of the, 310.
Scratches (Grease), 394; nature and treatment of, 395.
Scratching the ear, management of 204.
Screwdriver, (trotter), 471, 505.
Scripture, the horse of, 13.
Seat in riding, directions for, 232.
Seclaoni, a breed of Arab horses, 33.
Secretion, physiology of, 281; medicines for defective, 449.
Seedy toe, nature and treatment of, 408.

Seeley's American Star, pedigree of, 474, 482; character as a stallion, 482.
Selima (imp.), 53.
Sensation, nerves of, supplied to the lips, 290.
Servants' rooms in stables, 174.
Setons, insertion of, 439.
Seton needles, description of, 439; view of, 439.
Shakspeare (trotter), 471, 472.
Shakspear, Capt., his description of the Arab horse, 37.
Shaving, 193.
Sheaths, inflamed tendinous, nature and treatment of, 314.
Sherman, by Justin Morgan, 476.
Shoe, clenches for the, 200; losing the, 200; removal of the, 199; view of a sound fore foot prepared for the, 426.
Shoeing, 422 et seq.; pricks in, 415.
Shoulder, oblique, 22; remarks on strain of, 317; symptoms of strain of, 317; treatment for strain of, 317; upright, lotion for galled, 22; galled, 317.
Shouldering, the habit of, 245.
Shoulder-joint lameness, nature and treatment of, 305.
Shying, management of, 243.
Siam, the horses of, 44.
Sidebone, nature of, 300; symptoms of, 301; treatment of, 301.
Side line, description and use of, 434.
Sight, the organ of, 287.
Sinews, strains of the back, 319.
Singeing, 192; lamp for, 193.
Sire and dam, relative influence of, 486; condition of in breeding, 500.
Sir Harry (thorough-bred), by Messenger, 472.
Sir Henry (thorough-bred), influence of upon trotting stock, 474, 481.
Sir Peter (trotter), 471, 472.
Sir Solomon, by Messenger (thoroughbred), 472.
Sir Tatton Sykes (English thoroughbred), 63, 75.
Sir Walter Scott (pacer), 479.
Sitfasts, treatment of, 391.
Size, importance of in the stallion, 486; of the trotting horse, 495.
Skeleton, the, 250; number of bones composing the, 252; the artificial, 251.

Skin, the organ of touch, 290; medicines for disordered state of the, 448.
Skull, treatment of fractures of, 310.
Sleepy staggers (See Apoplexy), 380.
Smell, anatomy of the organ of, 287.
Soiling, 223.
Sole, anatomy of the, 293; treatment of bruises of, 416.
Sontag (trotter), 479, 480.
Sore-throat, treatment of, 350; treatment of catarrhal, 327.
Sovereign (imp.), 103.
Soundness, importance of, in sire and dam, 107, 486.
South American horse, the, 45.
Spark (imp.), 53.
Spasm of the diaphragm, symptoms of, 348; treatment of, 348.
Spasmodic colic, treatment for, 361.
Spavin, nature of bog, 313; nature of bone, 302; symptoms of bone, 303; treatment of bog, 313; treatment of bone, 303; remedy for, 455.
Speed of the Arab horse, 37; importance of, in the stallion, 486; of the trotter, 495.
Spinal column, bones composing the, 252; general anatomy of the, 252.
Spinal cord, the source of the power to move, 497.
Spine, injury of the, causing paralysis, 380; fractures of the, 310.
Spleen, anatomy and function of the, 283.
Splints, definition of, 298; symptoms of, 298; treatment of, 299; remedy for, 455.
St. Lawrence, influence of upon trotting stock, 476; character as a stallion, 476.
Stable management, 177; vices and bad habits, 202.
Stables, aspect of, 156; doors of, 161; drainage of, 163; coach house of, 174; chaff or grain shoots in, 160; floors of, materials for, 161; enamelled tiles for, 172; fittings, 168; foundations of, 157; gangway bail for, 170; granary of, 160; ground plans of, 174; harness room, for, 173; hay-chamber of, 159; lighting of, 165; mangers for, 170; material for mangers of, 170; necessity for

airing new, 176; number of stalls in, 157; plan of for three or four horses, 176; proper temperature of, 200; racks for, 170; servants' rooms of, 174; situation of, 155; stalls and loose boxes of, 157; the travis, 169; ventilation of, 165; ventilating windows in, 162; walls, lining of, 173; water pipes for, 165; water supply of, 165; windows for, 162.
Stafford, tamed by Rarey, 128, 130, 131.
Staggers, mad, nature and symptoms of, 375; mad, treatment of, 375; sleepy, 380; stomach, nature, and symptoms of, 353; stomach, treatment of, 354; remedy for, 453.
Stallion, choosing a, for breeding purposes, 486; importance of a good pedigree in, 486; of soundness in, 486; of size of, 486; of color of, 486.
Stallions, list of, imported into America, 461.
Stalls, 157; iron fittings for, 172.
Standing, attitude assumed in, 78.
Strangulation of the bowels, nature and symptoms of, 364.
Starting the horse in his various paces, modes of, 235.
Stench traps, 164.
Stifle joint, symptoms of strain of the, 322; treatment of strain of the, 322.
Stimulants, action of, 459; recipes for, 459.
Stings of insects, treatment of, 392.
Stomach, anatomy of the, 282; medicines for debility of, 449; small, 29; staggers, 353.
Stomachics, action of, 460; recipes for, 460.
Stonewall Jackson (trotter), 505.
Strains, nature of, 316; of the back sinews, symptoms of, 319; of the back sinews, remarks on, 319; of the back sinews, treatment of, 320; of the back and loins, nature and symptoms, 316; of the back and loins, treatment of, 316; of the coffin-joint, remarks on, 318; of the coffin-joint, treatment of, 318; of the hock, symptoms of, 322; of the hock, treatment of, 322; of the fetlock, remarks on, 318; of the fetlock, treatment of the, 318; of the hip-joint, symptoms of, 322; of the hip-joint, treatment of, 322; of the knee, symptoms of, 317; of the knee, treatment of, 315; of the shoulder, symptoms of, 317; of the shoulder, treatment of, 317; of the stifle-joint, symptoms of, 322; of the stifle-joint, treatment of, 322; of the suspensory ligaments, symptoms of, 318; of the suspensory ligaments, treatment of, 319.
Strangles, symptoms of, 351; treatment of, 351.
Stride, in trotting, essential elements of the, 495.
String halt, nature and causes of, 381.
Structure of bone, 248.
Stumbling, management of, 246.
Summering, 222.
Sunstroke, nature of, 382; treatment of, 382.
Superpurgation, symptoms of, 363; treatment of, 363; remedy for, 449.
Surfeit, nature and symptoms of, 388; treatment of, 388.
Surplice (English thorough-bred), 75.
Suspensory ligaments, strain of the, symptoms of, 318; strain of the, treatment of, 319.
Sweat, mode of giving the ordinary, 210.
Sweating, object of, 208; the ordinary, 210.
Swelled legs, inflammatory, treatment of, 393; ordinary, nature and symptoms of, 393; ordinary, treatment of, 393.
Synovial membrane, nature and treatment of acute inflammation of, 313; nature and treatment of rheumatic inflammation of, 313; diseases of, 312.

TACKEY (pacer), 483.
Tacony (trotter), 505.
Tail, anatomy of the, 255; of the thorough-bred race horse, 76.
Tartary, the horses of, 43.
Tattler (trotter), 483, 504.
Teeth, after nine years, 264; at nine years, 264; at about the eighth year, 263; at the end of the first year, 258; bishoping of, 264; composition of,

257; development of the, 257; during the second year, 259; during the third year, 259; horseman's nomenclature of, 258; irregularities in the growth of, 265; lower nippers and tushes at five years, 262; mouth at three years, 260; mouth at four years, 260; mouth at five years, 261; of the very old horse, 264; shedding of, between four and a-half and five years, 261; the six year old mouth, 263; view of the mouth at four and a-half years, 260; view of the upper nippers and tushes at five years, 261; upper nippers in the eight year old horse, 263; formula of, 257; section of incisor or nipper, 257; molar or grinder, 258; milk incisors, 258; canine teeth, or tushes, 258.

Tendinous sheaths, inflammation of, 314; treatment of inflamed, 314.

Tendon, 268; disease of the, 311; in muscle, 269; treatment of small tumors on the, 312.

Tetanus, nature of, 378; symptoms of, 379; treatment of, 379.

Thick wind, nature of, 347.

Thisclo (see Fistula of the Withers).

Thoracic, arch, anatomy of the, 254; organs, diseases of the, 326.

Thorax, boundaries of, 273; contents of, 272; plan of the, 272.

Thormanby (English thorough-bred), 58.

Thorns in the leg of the hunter, treatment of, 221.

Thorough-bred, the, 57; essentials in the, 60; external formation of, 61; general history of the American, 52; stoutness of the American, 54.

Thoroughpin, nature and symptoms of, 313; treatment of, 313; treatment of when in the bursa, 315.

Thread worms, 368.

Throat, treatment of sore, 350.

Thrush, varieties of, 401; treatment of, 402.

Tibia, fractures of the, 310.

Tiles, enamelled for stables, 172.

Tip (trotter), 479.

Tippecanoe (pacer), 479.

Tissue, fibrous, 268; white, 268; yellow, 268; red, 268; chemical composition of, 269.

Toe, treatment of seedy, 408.

Tom Chowder, 483.

Tom Thumb (Webber's), influence upon trotting stock, 482.

Tom Wonder, 483.

Tongue, black (See Typhosus).

Tonics, action of, 460; recipes for, 460.

Toorkistan, the horses of, 42.

Topgallant (trotter), 471, 472, 505.

Touch, anatomy of the organ of, 290; sense of, necessary to the appreciation of form, 290.

Training colts to trot, 501.

Training horses, Rarey's method, 128.

Traumatics, action of, 460; recipes for, 460.

Traveller (imp.), 53.

Travis, the, of stables, 168.

Trevis, the, or break, 435.

Trimming, 193.

Trot, the, 86; action in the true, 88; starting into a, 236; the jog, 87; the flying, 87; dishing, in the, 88; teaching the colt to, 501.

Trotter, the American, 50, 467 et seq.; the Norfolk, 89, 470; early American, 471; influence of imported thorough-breds, 471; influence of Canadian stallions, 474; trotting families, 481; breeding of the, 485; principles of breeding of, 485 et seq.; points of a, 495; elements of speed in, 497; training, 501 et seq.; performances of, 504 et seq.

Trotting, origination of, in England as a public amusement, 469; origination of, in America as a public amusement, 470; first match on record, 470; establishment of trotting clubs, 470; influence of imported thorough-breds upon the trotting stock of America, 471; relationship to pacing, 480; principles of breeding and training, 485.

Trouble (trotter), 471, 472.

Trumpeting, nature of, 338.

Trustee (imp.), 474, 505.

True Briton, the founder of the Morgan stock, 48.

True John (trotter), 480.

Tumors, treatment of small, on the tendons, 312.

Turkish bath, description of the, 213 plan of a, 214.

Turkish horse, the, 42.
Turning out to grass, 225.
Twitch, the, 435.
Typhoid fever (See Typhosus).
Typhosus, nature and symptoms of, 418; treatment of, 419.

Ulcers, lotions for foul, 459.
Umpire (thoroughbred), 54.
Unknown (pacer), 479.
Unnerving, remarks on, 445.
Unsoundness of the feet and legs, marshes useful in, 225.
Urine, bloody, nature and symptoms of, 371; bloody, treatment of, 372; retention of, causes of, 373; retention of, treatment for, 373; bloody, medicines for, 453; medicines to increase the flow of, 457.
Uterus, inversion of the, 374.

Vagina, inflammation of the, 374; treatment for inflammation of the, 374.
Vein, inflammation of, after bleeding, 437.
Venous blood, action of air on, 277.
Ventilating shaft, 167; windows, 162.
Ventilation of stables, 166.
Vermifuges, action of, 461; recipes for, 461.
Vermont Black Hawk (also called Hill's), 476, 477; influence upon trotting stock, 476; character as a stallion, 477, 481.
Vermont cart horse, the, 55.
Vertebræ, anatomy of the, 253.
Vices, out door, 243; treatment of, 243; shying, 243; rearing, 244; kicking, 245; lying down, 245; plunging, 245; running away, 245; stumbling, 246; cutting, 246; stable, remedies for, 202.
Viscera, abdominal, diseases of the, 350.
Vives, treatment of, 352.
Vosburgh, by Mambrino Pilot, 484.

WALK, action in the, 82; exceptional mode of starting for the, 82; mode of starting the horse into a, 235; of horses, the, 78; received interpretation of the, 81; starting for the, 80; order of sequence of the feet in the, 79.
Walking, rate of, 86.
Warbles, treatment of, 391.

War Eagle (trotter), conformation of, 495.
Warts, removal of, 396.
Washes, action of, 459; recipes for, 459.
Water in the chest (Hydrothorax), nature and treatment of, 345.
Water pipes for stables, 165.
Water, remarks on, 180; proper quantity of, 181; proper temperature of, 182; quality of, 182.
Weaving, remedy for, 205.
Webber's Tom Thumb (trotter), influence upon trotting stock, 482.
Weight, distribution of, 76.
Western hemisphere, horses of the, 45.
Whalebone (trotter), 471, 472.
Wheezing, nature of, 338.
Whip (imp.), 474.
Whistling, nature of, 338.
Why Not, by Messenger, 472.
Wild Dayrell (English thorough-bred), 75.
Wild horse of America, Herbert's account of the, 46.
Wild Tartar horse, the, 43.
Wilkes' Old Hautboy Mare (imp.), 53.
Wind, broken, nature and symptoms of, 346; broken, treatment of, 347; thick, nature of, 347.
Windows for stables, 162.
Wind-galls, nature and treatment of, 314; remedy for, 458.
Withers, fistula of the, nature of, 306; fistula of the, symptoms of, 306; fistula of the, treatment of, 306.
Woodpecker (trotter), 479.
Work, preparation for, 206; treatment of, after, 220.
Worms, intestinal, 367; symptoms of intestinal, 367; treatment of intestinal, 368.
Worm medicines, action of, 461; recipes, 461.
Wounds, medicines to destroy proud flesh in, 455; of joints, treatment of, 324.

Xenophon, his directions for purchasing a horse, 14.

Young Bashaw, 474; character of, as a stallion, 481.
Young Morrill (trotter), pedigree of,

www.ingramcontent.com/pod-product-compliance
Lightning Source LLC
Chambersburg PA
CBHW031941290426
44108CB00011B/636